Matrose
The Story of Reinhold Scholz

Matrose: The Story of Reinhold Scholz
© 2014 Jeanette O'Callaghan. All rights reserved.

Originally published in the United States in 2014

No part of this work may be reproduced without written permission from the publisher, except brief quotations for review purposes.

Cover design by Jeanette O'Callaghan.
Cover photo by Reinhold Scholz.
Interior photographs courtesy of 7seasvessels.com, WikiCommons, and Reinhold Scholz.

ISBN: 978-0-692-25732-6

Matrose
The Story of Reinhold Scholz

As Told By Jeanette O'Callaghan

A Note from Reinhold Scholz:

I've lived most of my life in a time when right was right and wrong was wrong. Life was harder when I was younger, and simpler. I walked into this country with twenty one dollars in my pocket and a dream, the American Dream. I worked hard, saved my money, and made a life for myself.

When I used to tell stories of my childhood and my Merchant Marine days, people always told me I should write a book. There was never the time for that. Life went on and I worked to survive, had a wife, children, and home to take care of. I got older and had some time on my hands. Then I ran into someone who listened to these stories and told me 'I can help you write this book'.

Things have changed a lot since I came here. I don't know why I'm still here, on this Earth, when so many people I love have gone on to a better place. I can only think it must be for some reason. Maybe this book might be one of them. It has taken more than two years but here it is. It is just fine if this work is read only by my family, it is for them. My daughter tells me how proud she is of me and that stops me in my tracks. If other people want to read it, that is great. I always lived my life as an adventure and I want people to read about it.

Reinhold Scholz
April 8, 2014

A Note from the Author:

I would like to thank Miguel Sehested Zambras, Webmaster of 7seasvessels.com for his help in locating pictures of Reinhold's ships as well as with answering my questions regarding the life and duties of a sailor. It was invaluable. Thank you also to my husband, Terry, for the support and encouragement.

Table of Contents:

Title Page
Note From Reinhold
Note from Author

Chapter 1	15	Where The Beautiful People Are
Chapter 2	25	What Happened To Those Skies?
Chapter 3	29	The Stick She Always Had With Her
Chapter 4	33	Sleep In The Bunker
Chapter 5	36	A Small Army Constructing Something
Chapter 6	39	Why Would Soldiers Be Here?
Chapter 7	44	Heinilaken
Chapter 8	48	That Isn't A Very Strong Fence
Chapter 9	54	Why Didn't You Go To School?
Chapter 10	60	They Are Only Children
Chapter 11	65	*Schluesselblume*
Chapter 12	72	Brown Shirt, Black Short Pants, A Scarf Tie
Chapter 13	79	Malente
Chapter 14	83	War Comes
Chapter 15	90	But The War Was Over
Chapter 16	98	How?
Chapter 17	106	A Dog For A Cat
Chapter 18	109	Hamburg
Chapter 19	116	A Farm Boy, Huh?
Chapter 20	120	Captain Hermann And The *Eos*
Chapter 21	127	The New Deck Boy
Chapter 22	134	Get Up, Boy
Chapter 23	140	Terror and Humiliation
Chapter 24	147	Lessons
Chapter 25	151	Enough!
Chapter 26	159	Ninety Kilos
Chapter 27	165	Unlock The Gate
Chapter 28	171	Reeperbahn

Chapter 29	176	Don't Ever Change
Chapter 30	182	Why Did I Come Back Here?
Chapter 31	188	Experience
Chapter 32	194	*Stina*
Chapter 33	204	Shore Life
Chapter 34	208	The Lifestyle Of A Sailor
Chapter 35	227	Partners in Crime
Chapter 36	236	"Vacation"
Chapter 37	243	*Fona*
Chapter 38	252	Ever Consider Being A Diver?
Chapter 39	266	Together Again
Chapter 40	277	Jensen
Chapter 41	282	Message In A Bottle
Chapter 42	289	An Eerie Feeling
Chapter 43	295	North Karelia
Chapter 44	301	Eva
Chapter 45	306	Is It Broken?
Chapter 46	314	On The Bum
Chapter 47	318	Introductions
Chapter 48	323	Life On The *Midgard*
Chapter 49	335	Anya
Chapter 50	342	Rostok
Chapter 51	347	Watchman!
Chapter 52	351	Biarritz
Chapter 53	356	Pasaia
Chapter 54	360	Viana do Castelo
Chapter 55	365	A Very Bad Thing
Chapter 56	368	Like A Canned Herring
Chapter 57	373	Portugal
Chapter 58	379	Shore Leave
Chapter 59	391	Return
Chapter 60	395	Those Girls
Chapter 61	400	Straits of Gibraltar

Chapter 62	406	The Soviets?
Chapter 63	415	Are Those Sheep?
Chapter 64	419	Back To Salvage
Chapter 65	425	*Christoffer Oldendorff*
Chapter 66	434	Hot and Dry
Chapter 67	443	He Left You?
Chapter 68	447	Strangers In A Strange Land
Chapter 69	459	Games
Chapter 70	465	India
Chapter 71	474	Disgusted
Chapter 72	481	We Have So Much
Chapter 73	489	The Long Trip Home
Chapter 74	494	Welcome Home, Scholz
Chapter 75	500	I Miss The Sea
Chapter 76	502	*Windar*
Chapter 77	515	On The Bum, Again
Chapter 78	518	A Fateful Letter
Chapter 79	521	*Leipzig*
Chapter 80	532	Panama Canal
Chapter 81	536	*Schellfisch*
Chapter 82	541	The Natives
Chapter 83	549	Lima
Chapter 84	554	Opportunity
Chapter 85	558	Valparaiso
Chapter 86	563	Asleep At The Helm
Chapter 87	571	Punishment
Chapter 88	578	New York City
Chapter 89	587	Where America Keeps Its Navy
Chapter 90	594	The Dirtiest Port
Chapter 91	605	Going To Get A Ship
Chapter 92	612	A Very Logical Decision
Epilogue	618	

Chapter One: Havana, 1956: Where The Beautiful People Are

Reinhold blinked open his eyes.
Holy Jees, why is it so bright? He thought, slowly focusing on a white ceiling.
Without moving his head, he looked around the room. Everything was white; there wasn't even a picture on the wall, just bright white in the morning sunlight. He was lying on a bed in the corner of this room, his legs tangled in white sheets. Across the room from where he lay, through the curtainless window, he could see blue sky and hear birds chirping. He thought he heard the rhythmic sounds of breathing coming from his left. Turning his head slightly toward the noise, he looked to see who was making it.
Oh, crap! He thought to himself, *That is the darkest girl I have ever seen! Who the hell is this? Where am I? Am I Shanghaied?*
He jumped out of bed, his head swimming briefly, and started yanking on his clothes. He had to get back to his ship. He didn't want to think about the girl or how he had gotten to this room. He didn't have time to think about her. The sun was high in the sky and he knew he was late. His mind was throbbing, with just one word passing the hazy barrier of the growing hangover. Late. Late. Late. Then the girl woke up. She purred something in Spanish.
What had she said? Panic seized Reinhold. No longer caring about his state of dress, he gathered up the rest of his clothes and took off out the door and down a flight of stairs. He heard the girl scream and the sound of running feet coming after him. He hit the cobblestone street sprinting, headed for the port. The girl screamed something at him. He just kept running.
People on the street paused to watch the half-naked blond man streak past. The vendors were already out selling their wares. Reinhold almost ran headlong into a fruit wagon as he turned a sharp corner. Swerving nimbly, he avoided the wagon, but knocked down the man piloting it. He didn't stop. All he could focus on was the fact that he was late getting back to his ship and that meant he was in a world of trouble.
What happened last night? All he remembered was drinking *Cuba Libres* with his buddies and now, here he was, running through

the narrow streets of Old Havana being chased by what he could only assume was a lady of the night. She tried to keep up with him, she even managed to avoid the fruit wagon, but Reinhold was just too quick. He lost her right before he entered the port, streaking past the security booth manned by a sleeping guard. Without slowing down, he headed straight for the cargo ship *Brandenburg* docked not far away.

He breathed a slight sigh of relief as he mounted the gangway but it was short-lived relief. The First Mate met him at the top of the incline. Without saying a word, the officer swung and punched Reinhold in his chin sending him stumbling backward into the rail of the ship still clutching his clothing.

"You are not quite an hour late so I won't dock you this time, but next time, I'll dock you double. You will report for watch the next ten days, starting tomorrow. You'll be reporting out of your desire to assist this ship however you can, not for the overtime. Now, get to work!" The First Mate barked as he turned on his heel, stalking off, leaving Reinhold to regain his footing and his breath. He cursed his luck for coming aboard while the First Mate was on deck.

Now I have to stand watch like a Leichtmatrose[1], *he thought. And not even get paid for it!*

Rubbing his jaw as he walked to his bunk to get dressed for the day's work, Reinhold had to chuckle to himself at the ridiculousness of the situation in which he had found himself. He looked toward the shore and saw the palm trees swaying in the warm tropical breeze against a cloudless azure sky. It was such a beautiful place. So beautiful that he momentarily forgot the throbbing in his chin and the pounding in his head.

What the hell happened last night, he wondered. *Why did Max and Heine leave me? Just wait until I get my hands on them! When did I go upstairs with that girl? How did I get a girl? And a black girl! That was my first one that color! I don't speak Spanish. Heine must have done it for me. Or maybe not.*

Grinning, he reminded himself that some things transcend words. In the two dozen countries he had visited, he never had a problem with getting a girl, regardless of the language barrier.

Well, there was a time, he reminded himself. *But everyone has trouble getting girls when they are fifteen years old.*

---

[1] *Leichtmatrose* is a German term for an Ordinary Seaman

He had definitely always paid the ladies of the night for their services, in one way or another. He felt a twinge of guilt about running off the way he did but he wasn't even sure that he slept with her. He didn't remember it and he was sure he would have remembered sleeping with a girl that dark. Did he have to pay for something he didn't remember? Unconsciously, the sailor reached into the front pocket of his shirt, one of the only pieces of clothing he had managed to get on before fleeing the white room. His guilt melted away instantly. His money was gone.

They're all the same, no matter where you go, Reinhold said to himself, shaking his head at human nature.

Reinhold pushed the thoughts out of his head. He didn't have the time, or mental capacity, to ponder the nature of humans at the moment. He had to get himself together and get to work. Sloppiness on a six thousand ton cargo ship could lead to pain and death. He had experienced this before. Just four years earlier he himself had a brush with death while countless times over his almost ten years at sea he had seen daydreaming or drunken sailors do stupid things that led to bad conclusions. An involuntary shutter ran through him as a flood of memories flashed through his pained skull. He couldn't take any chances that some horrid trick of thoughtlessness or stupidity would happen on his trip.

I am almost done with these ships, he thought.

This was his last voyage as a deckhand, a boatswain, a cobblescot, or any of the other titles he held in the last nine years. The next time Reinhold left Hamburg on a ship it would be as a passenger on the first ship that suited his needs. He hoped it would be a Hapag vessel.

He had always known he was going to leave Germany. Even when he was a child, existing in Schleswig- Holstein, he knew. It became all too clear when he was sixteen years old that he didn't belong in his home country.

Home, he thought. *Such a strange concept. It should be the easiest place to find. It should be right in front of your face, you'd think.*

Reinhold realized now that he had never truly considered his home to be home. The place never welcomed him unconditionally, the way read in countless books home should. And what of this imposed home and its incessant warring? Wars were pointless, expensive, and destructive. There was always talk of more wars. What did they accomplished for regular everyday people besides confusing the local populations with fluctuating borders and starving them out of house and home? Germany was in ruins in many places still today at the end of 1956, a full decade after the end of that stupid *arschloch*[2] trying to conquer the world.

Reinhold also recognized now that the compulsion to find a better place, a real home, was what led him to the high seas under the guise of needing better employment. There had to be somewhere he could settle and establish himself, some place away from Germany and Europe. He knew that this made him no different from millions of other Europeans, millions of other people. There was always talk on the seas about good places to jump ship and disappear, or jump ship and get caught. Reinhold traveled to many of them, never really feeling that he had found his place. On several occasions, he considered settling but it was never anywhere that really, truly made sense to him.

Reinhold shook himself out of his ponderings. He had made his decision, cast the seed to the wind, and took a step toward finding a home. He would see it through because it made sense. Now, it was time to get to work, pounding head and all. He could only hope that his bastard crewmates felt as bad as he did this morning, worse even.

It would serve them right for leaving me behind, he snorted to his empty bunk.

Later that evening, Reinhold berated his friends over dinner.

"Why did you leave me?" he demanded. "I woke up with the darkest girl I have ever seen in the whitest place I have ever been! How did I end up with a black girl?"

Max laughed at his friend. "You really don't remember, do you?"

"No! Tell me!"

"She came round, trying to get you interested, said she had never had a real Aryan before." Max told him.

Reinhold snorted, wondering where such language came from in Cuba.

"You weren't having it, kept pushing her away," Heine cut in. "There was a Spanish girl you were interested in but she was with someone else."

---

[2] *Arschloch* is a German term which translates roughly to 'asshole' in English.

Reinhold remembered that. The Spanish girl was at the table next to theirs with some other guy, an officer from an American ship. He was feeding her drinks and money, tucking coins into her cleavage or the waistband of her skirt. The black girl was planted at their table. Heine had gotten her attention if memory served, but she liked Reinhold more, apparently.

"It just made her want you more, Scholz." Max laughed again. "She finally got you by telling you that she going to be the best lay you'd ever had. She told you that black women had special *pflaume*[3]."

"That would do it, I guess," Reinhold conceded. "That doesn't explain why you left me."

"You disappeared!" Heine said. "You went off, saying you'd be back in fifteen minutes and we never saw you again."

"We looked," Max added. "We even tried to ask but the guy behind the bar didn't like that at all. He told us to get lost."

"We didn't think anything was going to happen to you, Reinhold," Heine said. 'The worst we expected was you'd come back with no clothes or money."

Max laughed again. "Boy, were we way off on that!"

Reinhold had to join them having a good laugh at his expense. His arrival back at the ship was probably quite entertaining.

After sorting out the events of the night before, the sailors planned a trip to the Tropicana. The *Brandenburg* was leaving Havana the next morning and they wanted to spend as much time exploring as possible before the ship's rigorous schedule kept them onboard. Reinhold was particularly interested in having fun given his ten day watch punishment. They heard the night club was the best of the best, the place to be. One sailor in Hamburg told Reinhold that everywhere else in the Caribbean was uncivilized and poor.

"Not a lot to do there, in the Caribbean" the guy told him. "It's a poor place full of shanties and thieves, unless you stay at one of the resorts they're building, which you won't be. Go to the Tropicana and don't go anywhere else, except the beach. There's lots to do at the Tropicana."

The prospect was very exciting, even more exciting than the first time he went to the Reeperbahn. But, as Reinhold understood it, the Tropicana and the Reeperbahn were two different creatures. The Reeperbahn is a cross section of the German population, every type of

---

[3] *Pflaume* is a German slang term for a lady's womanly parts

person from paupers to princes walked along that narrow cobblestone street in Hamburg. The Tropicana is the elite, the wealthy, the dignified, and the elegant.

"It is where the beautiful people are," the sailor in Hamburg told him.

The sailors were looking forward to having a good time in the company of the well dressed and beautiful. Aristocratic bums, Reinhold called sailors. They like to be around those that have even though they are have-nots. They got their tuxedos on, piled into a taxi at the port, and headed to the outskirts of Havana to the world-renowned nightclub.

Reinhold watched Havana whiz by through the window of the taxi. The sun was setting in a spectacular display of pink and red. The white washed facades caught the light and amplified it to almost blinding brilliance. He thought it was a beautiful city. The architecture and narrow streets reminded him of Spain and Portugal but with more color. Everywhere there were murals of blues, greens, and oranges decorating buildings painted yellow and robin egg blue. The capital building was especially impressive with its domed roof and columned portico.

As they left the old town behind the streets widened and the houses became larger, surrounded by wrought iron fences and gates. The street leading to the Tropicana was the widest and was lined with tall, swaying palm trees. The three sailors pulled up in front of the very grand façade of the nightclub. A valet in a crisp white tuxedo came out of the shadows to open the door of their taxi. Assuming very dignified posture the men sauntered into the building, their aristocratic bum masks firmly in place.

Inside, the club was huge! First, they encountered the gaming salons positioned just off the main foyer. After these came the main hall of the cabaret and what they learned were called the *Arcos de Cristal*, alternating vaults of masonry and glass that made it appear in some spots that the building didn't have any walls, like it was an enormous greenhouse with tables and a bandstand instead of flowers. There were even tall palm trees growing in the building that broke through the roof. The cabaret spilled out of this greenhouse into a lush, tropical garden complete with fountains, Classical statues, and covered walkways. It gave the impression of a modern day Eden.

The entertainment exceeded the men's expectations. Since they were lucky enough to be there on a Saturday, there were three shows for their enjoyment: a modern dance number that incorporated some jazzy swing moves, a Spanish show complete with flamenco dancers and castanets, and a high-energy Cuban number. The dancers and showgirls were gorgeous. They stood out amongst the crowd in their provocative and colorful ensembles. The costumes were unforgettable with sequins, rhinestones, and metallic beads flashing amongst feathers of all colors, sizes, and textures. They fit the dancers like gloves, reveling every delicious curve.

Reinhold and his mates wasted no time getting into the spirit of the Tropicana. They found a spot at one of the nine bars where they could see the dance floor and the tables of festive, well-groomed club goers. Reinhold had no interest in the gambling areas. He learned in France that casinos were bad places. This gambling salon was overflowing with loud, swarthy looking Americans wearing tuxedos that probably cost more than a car in Germany. They were escorting women wearing fur and dripping in diamonds and gold. Their sailor's intuition told them to avoid those types.

They arrived at a good spot on the bar just in time to watch one of the stages rise up from below the dance floor. It was time for the Spanish show, a dramatic and alluring flamenco number. There were easily two dozen, probably more, pairs of dancers on the stage and scattered around the dance floor. They were mesmerizing and exciting to watch, altering so exquisitely from intricate control to wild, uninhibited jubilation, letting the sounds of the guitars and the castanets guide their movements. Their rhythmic stomping was thunderous. The audience let out tension breaking cries of "Ole!" during a particularly long and intense set of footwork. Just when the crowd could barely stand another minute of the spectacle, it broke off with a roaring crash of feet, hands, voices, and guitars, leaving the dancers breathless and the watchers cheering.

The number had proved infectious for Reinhold. He wanted to dance. He glanced around the room for possible partners. So many of the tables contained mixed company, gentlemen with ladies. This could be a dicey situation. He didn't want to end his evening before it really began by asking the wrong lady to dance. His gaze settled on one table in particular that looked promising.

Not far from where they were standing at the bar was a table with a mother and her three daughters. They were beautiful Cuban girls close to Reinhold's age with glowing brown skin, raven colored hair, and dark brown eyes.

After a couple of *Cuba Libres* and a brief discussion with Heine about how to say "Can I have this dance?" in Spanish, Reinhold found the courage to ask one of them to dance with him. The band struck up a lively waltz and he could no longer resist the impulse to whirl a girl around a proper dance floor. His chosen daughter agreed to dance with him, with the consent of her mother.

He was a good dancer, guiding his partner around the floor with grace and precision. It was part of his education as a child in Germany when the bombs drove them underground. It didn't hurt that Reinhold had something that many people lacked: rhythm. He also had manners and managed to make it through the whole waltz without touching any sensitive spots on his partner. The band shifted their attention to a quick foxtrot for the next number. Wordlessly, the couple decided they would stay on the floor for this dance. They also danced the rumba number that followed. After the third dance, Reinhold returned the young lady to her table, bowing slightly and politely to her mother before he turned to take his leave.

Before he could leave the table she stopped him, saying something in beautifully metered Spanish. Reinhold did not understand what she meant and gestured to his friends for help. They were still leaning on the bar, grinning at their waltzing, fox-trotting friend in sheer amusement at his debonair demeanor. They strolled slowly over to the table to help their linguistically challenged shipmate. Introductions were quickly made in halting Spanish and broken German. She gestured for all of them to join her and her daughters at their table. Graciously, the men accepted.

Reinhold didn't spend much time at the table once the introductions and pleasantries were finished. He spent the rest of the evening dancing with the three lovely daughters. There were more waltzes, foxtrots, mambos, and rumbas as well as cha-chas, salsas, and tangos. The huge house band even played a polka. He didn't know how long he had been dancing when the music stopped. People left the floor to return to their tables while the dance floor again rose up to become the stage. It was time for the Cubana show. Reinhold took this opportunity to reconnect with his friends.

"They think we are interns." Heine said, a sly smile on his lips. He was the only one of the sailors who could speak a bit of Spanish.

"Interns?"

"Yeah, the youngest daughter asked if we were interns at the hospital. It sounded good, so I said yes. I sure wasn't going to tell her we're sailors."

The action on stage had grown so loud that all Reinhold could do was smile at his friend, shaking his head in bemused acknowledgement. It was definitely true that doctors and nurses working in hospitals had far better reputations than sailors working for Hapag.

Heine nudged Reinhold out of his thoughts. With a slight, barely perceptible inclination of his head, he directed Reinhold's attention to the mother of the lovely young ladies. She was staring at the three men like a child at a birthday cake. For an instant her dark eyes met his blue eyes and she beamed a wide smile at him. Reinhold found it immensely amusing.

The Cubana show came to an end. The crowd erupted into applause and cheers. The men looked at each other, silently agreeing that they should end their night at the Tropicana. The gleam Reinhold had seen in the mother's eyes earlier had become a full blown drool by the time the men made their excuses to leave. Laying a hand on Heine's sleeve, she said something, smiling innocently. Her daughters giggled in the background. Heine replied and a short conversation followed. Reinhold had no idea what she said but he saw Heine smile a smile of humble assent. The mother handed Heine a matchbook, smiling more brightly than ever. Bowing to kiss the hands of the young ladies, the three sailors took their leave.

"What was that all about?" Reinhold asked as they made their way toward the door.

"She wants us to come to tea tomorrow."

Max snorted. "Of course she does. She is trying to marry off those daughters of hers. I have never seen a woman smile so much!"

The others nodded in agreement, chuckling at the predicament of the widowed woman with three daughters to marry off.

"They are beautiful girls. They'll find husbands. They just might not be doctors!" Reinhold said, renewing the chuckling

While they waited for their taxi to pull around to the front of the building, the sailors decided that it was too late and they were too well dressed for additional, less elegant, entertainment. Instead, they returned to the *Brandenburg*. During the cab ride back to the port, the sailors laughed about their night as 'interns'.

Chapter 2: What Happened To Those Skis?

Brandenburg
Photograph courtesy of 7seasvessels.com

The *Brandenburg* left Havana early the next morning. The twenty seven hundred ton cargo ship was scheduled to pick up and drop off cargo at nine islands in the Caribbean before returning to Hamburg. It was going to be a busy trip with a lot of sailing and a shortage of shore leaves. That meant not a lot of excitement for the crew, but a whole lot of work. The ship was entering the Windward Passage when Reinhold took his place near the aft castle to stand the first of his punishment watches. It was a warm, humid day and he had lost his shirt several hours before during cast off, standing in the brilliant sunlight clad only in his dungarees. He was watching the crystal blue of the sea slip past, noting that he could make out the shapes of reefs and large fish beneath the surface of the water. It reminded him vaguely of the Red Sea but the Caribbean had a different feel to it: tropical where the Red Sea was desert.

He enjoyed every minute of the warm weather knowing that it was colder than hell in Germany. He was as tan as he had ever been in his entire life, even when he was a child working on a farm. The sun shone in Europe, of course, but not with the intensity or frequency as the tropics. Then there were the northern winters; long, cold, dark winters when the winds howled, freezing precipitation fell, lakes and streams iced over, and sometimes the easiest way to get around on land was to use skis.

Leaning shirtless against the warm rail of the ship in the warm tropical sun, Reinhold found himself thinking about skis. His earliest clearly defined, and decidedly happiest, memory of his childhood was of skis. His father was drafted into the German army in 1939. The government didn't care that the man was the only caregiver to his children since their mother passed away three years earlier. The *Braunenpatie*[4] gave him a choice: he could marry again or he could go to the army wifeless. If he didn't marry, the *Braunenpatie* would sell his house and put his children in a home. Not wanting either of those situations, he married a widower ten years his senior, a women he barely knew a month, before going off to boot camp and to war. He left Reinhold and his two sisters to survive with a woman who had no maternal instinct. The next two years were a hazy blur of verbal assaults, nightly beatings, and an empty, rumbling stomach.

When he was seven, Reinhold's father came home from the war on leave. He remembered quite clearly seeing his father riding down the hill near their home on a borrowed bicycle, a knapsack on his back. The soldier, also named Reinhold, was in Norway, training in alpine warfare. He brought a new pair of skis for his son and some dolls for his daughters. That was the greatest thing that had happened to young Reinhold. New skis! Professionally made skis with spring bindings, not the home hewn wooden boards with straps of leather he was accustomed to using. Reinhold had the best skis in the whole town and the other children were so jealous! He could still see those skis in his mind, the natural blonde color of the wood burnished to a high shine and the red enamel racing stripe that ran from tip to tail. He remembered boyishly wishing that northern Germany had more snow and mountains so he could really see what the skis could do.

Reinhold's thoughts turned from the prized skis to the man that had carried them from Norway as a gift. For two weeks, his father was home on leave. It seemed like the only two weeks he was around during the boy's entire childhood, not that Reinhold saw his father much during his leave either. The boy had to work and go to school. He was up before dawn every morning, headed to Walter Muuss's farm to tend animals before going to school for a few hours. After school, it was back to the farm. By the time he arrived home in the

---

[4] *Braunenpatie* translates to Brown Party. When Reinhold was young, the adults around him referred to "Nazis" as the Brown Party.

evening after milking the cows, his father was gone, off to the dancehall or Küster's guesthouse to drink and socialize.

Reinhold's older sister Lisa thought that their father left home to go drinking to get away from their stepmother, Olga. The couple fought incessantly. She was a wicked woman, selfish and mean. Reinhold recognized now, but hadn't as a child, that their marriage was a business contract. It served a purpose to both of them, but the fulfillment of those purposes didn't lead to an amiable relationship.

Reinhold could still hear the two of them bickering about the radio. Ratekau, their small, isolated town, received only two stations, the BBC and the state run German station. The German station wasn't good for gathering news about the outside world. All they played was sternly voiced people talking about Germany's need to defend their ancient culture against inferior races, and the music of Richard Wagner. His father liked to listen to the BBC. He believed they told him the truth about how the war was going and about what was going on in the world abroad. He sat in the small, sparsely furnished living room listening intently to the staticy voice coming over the radio waves, staring through the lace curtain covering the window into the forest across the street.

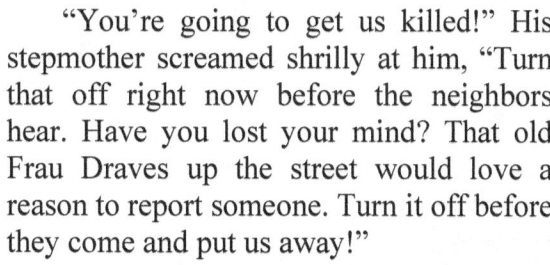

"You're going to get us killed!" His stepmother screamed shrilly at him, "Turn that off right now before the neighbors hear. Have you lost your mind? That old Frau Draves up the street would love a reason to report someone. Turn it off before they come and put us away!"

"Just a few more minutes. I haven't heard anything about the Western Front yet." His father responded.

The older Reinhold didn't doubt that the ever present and officious 'they' would come arrest the family for treason. He was just more willing to take chances than his wife. Reinhold, the soldier, told his family that twice he was caught broadcasting the BBC over the PA system in his training camp. He seemed quite proud of his antics, even though they could have landed him in prison with a charge of treason and sentenced to death.

"They are going to take us away because of your obstinacy!" Olga spit at him before launching on another tirade about the prying eyes and ears of the neighbors, about the tenseness in the streets because of the disappearances of people who had openly spoke against the *Braunenpatie*. "We have true *Braunenpatie* on this street who would not hesitate to turn us in if it meant a loaf of bread for them!"

The soldier ignored her. A few days later, Reinhold's father left to return to war.

What happened to those skis? The sailor thought to himself.

He had a vague recollection of an accident. He hit a tree fleeing from a group of bored older boys in his town. They wanted to pass the time by doling out a beating. The impact proved too much for one of his precious skis, breaking off the tip. After that, it just kept getting stuck in the snow. Several weeks later his sister Isolde convinced him it was time to throw away the broken skis.

"You've gotten three good years out of them. They are almost too small for you now anyway. We could use the extra fuel for the fire. The resin on those skis will burn slow and hot, too."

He had so few possessions that he was reluctant to part with them but logic had won out and into the fire they had gone. He watched them burn, smelling the acidic scent of the burning resin, warming his hands against the heat, thinking he would never have anything so fine again.

Reinhold's thoughts turned to his sister Isolde. She always looked out for him when they were kids. When they were late getting home to start dinner or when something went missing or something got broken, she would say, "Let me go in first and deal with Mama." She always took the beating, the punishment, before him. It seemed to him now, as it had back then, that their stepmother was harder on her than on him. Now that he thought about it, Lisa also seemed to have a harder time with their stepmother than Reinhold. This led him to conclude that his stepmother wasn't fond of other women, or other people's children, so they had suffered doubly.

Chapter 3: The Stick She Always Had With Her

The memories of his stepmother and her treatment of them as children brought a strange feeling to Reinhold. It was a weird, unpleasant soup of apprehension, disdain, pity, and indifference. These were all feelings he tried to avoid but once they surfaced, he had to deal with them, let them run their course.

The sailor paced a few steps back and forth on the iron deck, clenching and unclenching his fists several times, trying to work through each emotion.

The apprehension was an old hat for him. It was rooted in her violence, her malice. She was quick like a snake with a slap or an insult and he always approached her like he would a snake, a poisonous one. She loved nothing more than a moment of pleasure had at the expense of her husband's children.

The disdain was rooted in dislike and a lack of respect. He never liked the woman. She only gave him reasons to dislike her. She also never gave him a reason to respect her. Her position of authority didn't count, in his opinion.

The pity was a bit harder to work out. It was a new emotion for him; one that he hadn't known existed until recently. It came with maturity and experience. She was cruel and self-serving but he thought maybe, sometimes, he judged her too harshly. She had a hard life, same as him, same as everyone. She never intended to be a mother, or a motherly figure, to someone else's children. She never intended for her first husband to die, leaving her to fend for herself.

Indifference pulled the emotional train into its final station because, in all honesty, he just didn't give a crap about her anymore. He had moved on, made a new life for himself but still she lingered on in his subconscious, forever a part of his childhood, like a scar.

One thing Reinhold knew for sure, that he wouldn't begrudge her, was that she had done him a huge favor when she taught him how to play chess, not that he knew it at the time.

"Herr Klausen says you don't pay attention in school. You fidget too much, your mind is always elsewhere. You are not concentrating." She had said to him one night in early winter when he was seven years old.

He made no reply. The boy had learned that it was better not to say anything when she spoke unless she asked a direct question.

Instead of smacking him, as he expected, she had simply sighed and left him sitting at the table in their small, cramped kitchen staring at the front of the old wood stove, savoring his nightly slice of bread.

Reinhold dropped his shoulders in relief, and then stuck his tongue out at where she had been standing in childish rebellion. This drew a burst of giggling from Isolde and a snicker from Lisa. Isolde was sitting across the table from him knitting a new pair of socks and Lisa was mending what was once one of Reinhold's shirts but had been reduced to what more closely resembled a rag by years of use.

He hoped his stepmother was retiring to her room for the night or at least for a couple of hours. He had plans to go into the forest to knock down a tree with his friends but they had to wait until it was safe. This meant well after dark when most of the little town was asleep. Getting caught taking trees out of the forest carried a heavy penalty that the family couldn't afford to pay. The neighbors told him that the inability to pay the fine resulted in prison time, even for children. It was a risk he had to take. They were running low on wood for the fire. Reinhold figured if he got a good sized tree tonight he and Isolde could spend the next two days chopping it up. That would provide them with fuel for a couple of weeks.

Reinhold was disappointed when Olga reappeared holding a wooden box. She seated herself at the head of the table, slid open the side panel of the box, and started to remove small, carved figures of light and dark color. In a matter of minutes, she had set the wooden pieces up on either side of a light and dark checkerboard field that comprised the top of the box. Reinhold thought they looked like mini wooden armies facing each other for battle.

"This is a game called Chess. Have you ever heard of it?" She asked him. He shook his head in response. "It would be good for you to learn it. It might help your problems at school. It requires a great deal of concentration."

For the next two hours, she taught the boy the game of Chess. She explained the pieces, how they could move, and their weaknesses and strengths. Reinhold resented every minute of it but he had to pay attention. If he drifted away for a second, she would pick up the stick she seemed to always have with her and hit him with it. Isolde and Lisa watched silently, keeping their hands busy with their tasks, winching when the stick made contact with Reinhold's arm.

He didn't like this game. It had too many rules. He didn't like the condescending tone in his stepmother's voice. He didn't like being so close to her for so long. It unnerved him. He definitely didn't like her smacking his arm with that damn stick.

When the tap at the window next to the door came, Olga jumped in fright. Reinhold turned toward the noise. Just visible in the corner pane was Willie Pingel's small, round face. It quickly disappeared when he realized Reinhold's stepmother was in the kitchen. The stepmother looked hard at Reinhold, searching the boy's unreadable face, and then her gaze fell on Lisa and Isolde. Neither of them looked up from their tasks. It was too late for a social call. Something was going on that could end badly. Olga, Reinhold knew, was weighing the consequences.

Finally, whatever debate she had been having in her head found its resolution. She announced she was tired and they were done for the night. She had probably figured out what the plan was for this evening. It was not the first time he had gone out at night to get wood and it wouldn't be the last. She was too shrewd to try to stop him. Just as quickly as she had laid the game out, she packed it back up in its wooden box, leaving the children to their own devices.

A few minutes later, Reinhold slipped out the front door into the cold night, leaving his sisters sitting at the table. He, Willie, and Egon met across the street, at the tree line, where they could easily hide in the shadows to decide which direction to head. They had just come to the decision to go south to a stand of smaller fir trees set far enough in the forest that they wouldn't be heard or seen but close enough that they wouldn't have to trek too far with the heavy load when Isolde emerged from the shadows.

"Did I scare you?" She giggled at the alarmed faces of the boys before announcing, "I am coming with you."

The boys didn't try to stop her. They were hoping to get at least two trees that night. Another helping hand was always welcome, especially one that wouldn't rat them out later.

Reinhold was dead tired and frozen to the bone when they returned home. The wooden clogs on his feet were soaked and he thought one of his toes had frostbite. They had felled the two trees, disbranched them, and chopped them into log sections small enough to carry. It took the four children several nervous trips to stow in the barn in the backyard what amounted to almost an entire fir tree.

Tomorrow, the task of chopping and splitting it into firewood would begin.

He didn't want to think about that right now though. That was for tomorrow. Quickly, he undressed in the kitchen, draping his clothes over the back of one of the chairs at the table. As he made his way up the steep steps to the attic where he slept he hoped silently that the snow that was falling lightly outside wouldn't blow through the gaps in the roof shingles.

Chapter 4: Sleep In The Bunker

It was just a few weeks later, not long after his eighth birthday, that the air raid sirens went off. Without thinking, Reinhold got out of his warm, down filled bed and made his way down the steep steps to the kitchen. Isolde and Lisa were waiting for him. Once he had his ragged clothes on and had slipped his feet into a pair of wooden clogs stuffed with straw, Lisa took his hand and pulled him out the door. They ran around to the back of the house, past the rabbit hutches, the small barn, and the chicken coop, through the small plot of the now dead vegetable garden, and further still out into the field that separated the backyards of the residents of Blüchereiche from those of the residents of Bäderstaße. The sirens were still wailing when, two hundred and fifty feet from their house, they threw themselves onto the straw covered benches that lined the walls of the bunker that Reinhold and the other neighborhood children had built the previous autumn. A few minutes later, their stepmother and her daschund joined them.

The night was cold, so very cold, and tense, so very tense. Once the siren quieted the slightest noise seemed to carry for miles. They could hear their neighborhood waking up, people calling to friends and loved ones, everybody headed to their respective bunkers, desperate to get away from any source of light that might attract the attention of a pilot. The full moon in the cloudless sky made it possible to look out from their hiding place and see people running through long, narrow back yards into the field, clutching children and belongings.

Judging by the position of the moon, Reinhold figured it was close to midnight, probably a little bit before. He had the feeling that there was something different about tonight's air raid warning. In the past few months, the sirens went off and they headed for cover but never more than one plane was sighted. Rarely did that one plane drop any bombs. If it did, the bomb landed in the countryside without harming anything or anyone.

But tonight, Reinhold thought, *has a sinister feel to it.*

He didn't say anything to his sisters about his thoughts. Instead, he sat, huddled in the doorway of the bunker, watching a search light's erratic movements across the cloudless sky, listening to the sounds of the approaching planes getting steadily louder.

A single distant whistling noise pierced the night. Then all hell broke loose. Bombs fell with terrific frequency. The sounds of the explosions were masked by the sounds of more explosions only to be drowned out by the droning of plane engines as they swept overhead. Every few seconds there was a burst of distant machine gun fire, every minute the whoosh and whistle of a missile being launched. The sky to the south took on an eerie red hue that grew brighter as the fires creating it found fresh material to consume. Crisscrossing the red glow were the beams of the powerful searchlights looking for the planes. The four people watching from the doorway of the bunker looked at each other in mute and horrified awareness that, just 6 miles south of them, Lübeck was under attack.

The first violent attack subsided almost as quickly as it began. The droning of the planes became more and more distant. With the sounds of war gone for the moment, the red glow to the south took on a surreal nature. It pulsed with smoke and heat, getting brighter, and then fading.

At first, when the bombing stopped and the planes left, there were no sounds, just cold winter night silence. Then, slowly, humanity stirred in the field outside their bunker. Reinhold could hear children crying, women weeping, and men exchanging information. He strained to hear what his neighbors Paul Easberger and Max Draves were saying. They speculated that it was the British carrying out the raid. They didn't think it was over yet. Reinhold's own sense of foreboding led him to agree with the men.

"We should just stay here tonight, sleep in the bunker." Lisa said. "It's a good thing you built this bunker, Reinhold."

Reinhold looked around at his bunker. He admitted to himself that it was a good thing he dug it out. It took him and the neighborhood boys several weeks, but they did it. It was about five feet tall, six feet wide, and fifteen feet long with sloping walls, like an upside down trapezoid. It took five days, working by the light of the moon, just to fell and disbranch the small pine trees that made the roof and lined the walls. It was another night to drag them out of the forest across Blüchereiche and into the field behind the houses. Once in position, another five days had been spent cutting and arranging the sections of sod that served as a waterproof roof. The finishing touch was the straw that was scattered on the ground and on the benches. The straw made a comfortable surface for sleeping, as his stepmother proved by promptly curling up on her side on the floor and falling asleep, after cursing the British, the Germans, men in general, and God for their collective stupidity.

The second wave of the attack started just a few minutes later. The sirens went off again. The planes came. The spotlights lit up the sky, trying to capture one of the iron birds in its beam so the machine guns could take it out. The bombs fell. The machine guns popped. It was during this wave that they heard a plane whine like they hadn't heard before. It streaked right over top of the bunker. Reinhold watched it disappear over the tree line to the northeast. He was sure it was going to crash. He made a mental note to see if he could find the wreckage later.

The third wave of the attack awoke Reinhold from an uneasy slumber. He stuck his head out of the bunker to confirm what he already knew: Lübeck was being bombed again. The fires were still sending pulsing red light into the sky. Looking up, he sought the moon. Judging that it was about 2:00 in the morning, he went back to sleep, too tired to care if a random plane dropped a bomb in the wrong place.

Chapter 5: A Small Army Constructing Something

The next morning Lübeck was still burning, spewing black smoke into the frosty, cloudless March sky. There was a strong smell of fire on the breeze.

"Do you think there is anything left?" Isolde asked.

"Reinhold!" Reinhold turned toward the sound of his name to see Willie and Egon running toward him.

"Did you see that plane go down?" Egon asked with the kind of excitement only a little boy could have about such an event.

"Yeah, it disappeared over there." Reinhold responded, pointing to the spot above the trees to the east.

"Let's go see if we can find it." Willie suggested.

Without further conversation, the boys took off for the forest. Reinhold heard Lisa yell after him that it was laundry day and she needed help getting the water but he didn't care. Isolde could help her with the water today. The boys crossed Blüchereiche, plunging into the forest at a run, laughing and teasing each other about their bravery, or lack thereof, the night before. Two hundred feet into the forest, they crossed the train tracks. Once across the tracks, the boys slowed down, walking cautiously down a hill toward the swamp they called Kuhlsee. It was a tricky place, always changing, shifting, even in the winter. One had to move quickly and be very careful where they placed their feet or they could end up sinking into the murky water, sucked down into its bottomless depths. Lucky for them, today the swamp seemed frozen solid.

Once on the other side, before reentering the forest, the boys stopped to consider their next direction. Before they could decide, their attention was drawn by the sounds of hammering and voices shouting. Instinctively, they crouched down, making themselves as small as possible, listening. Egon motioned that the sound was coming from their left, almost directly north of where they were stopped. Staying low and moving quickly from tree to tree, they made their way toward the noise. The trees in this part of the forest were old and had substantial girth so the boys could easily use them as cover. They hadn't gone too far, maybe a hundred feet, when the cause of the noise became apparent. Another fifty feet ahead of them, a small army was constructing something.

Several dozen men in *Braunenpatie* uniforms were building three new structures. They were wooden, single floor, and stood parallel to each other but at an angle to the road to Sereetz just beyond. One was positioned a bit further from the other two, a rough driveway occupied this wider space. It looked to the boys that these buildings were almost finished but what were they? They watched as a big brownish green army truck laden with building materials pull off the road, maneuvering around the construction site until it was positioned near the two buildings that were closer together. Men approached the truck and began unloading the supplies, taking them into the building in the middle, to the right of the truck, through some door the boys couldn't see. Reinhold thought he saw a stove, not a stove like the one he had at home, but bigger and still shiny with newness.

"Pssst!"

Reinhold turned toward the noise and saw Willie motioning that they should go around the construction site to the north to continue their search for the downed plane. Noiselessly, they made their way around and out of sight of the soldiers.

The boys searched the frozen fields and forests north and east of the road to Sereetz but had no luck finding the plane. They mused that such a large, heavy object would have left a path of destruction behind it as it crashed but they found nothing. When they were standing on the banks of the Hemmelsdorfer See[5] near the town of Offendorf, two miles from their street in Ratekau, they decided to call off their search for the day.

"Maybe it went into the lake." Willie offered.

Reinhold and Egon were not convinced.

"We should look further north next time." Egon suggested.

Willie and Reinhold nodded their agreement.

Staring at the semi-frozen surface of the lake, Reinhold wished he had something to turn into a fishing hook and some line. He could catch supper. A bit wistfully he wished he had a cow's head. He could throw it in the water today and come back in a few weeks to collect the head and the eels that it would catch. He ended up leaving the shore of the lake with his friends empty handed and knowing instinctively that, no matter how hard they looked, that they would

---

[5] *See* is the German word for lake

never find that plane. His interest had moved to the new buildings in the forest.

The thought of fish made Reinhold's stomach rumble with hunger. The last thing he had eaten was a slice of bread and a mug of milk the night before. He hoped that Lisa had managed to find something for dinner after washing the laundry. Usually on Sunday, they slaughtered a chicken but the scrawny birds wandering about the backyard were not ready for eating yet. He felt guilty about taking off on her when she needed help and decided that he couldn't go home empty handed.

"Where do you think we can get some food?" Willie asked.

It was as if he had read Reinhold's mind. The boys considered the question for a minute, running down the list of farmers in town, comparing notes about the state of their winter stores.

"Let's try Zepoline's place. He should be out at his *Braunenpatie* meeting by the time we get there." Reinhold suggested. "He still had a good amount of potatoes the last time I was there."

The boys agreed. Tonight's supper, would be liberated from the stores of Herr Zepoline.

Chapter 6: Why Would Soldiers Be Here?

As Reinhold remembered, it wasn't long before he knew what the purpose was for those buildings in the forest. Spring arrived and the world was coming back to life after the long, cold winter. Birds returned to northern Germany after wintering in warmer climates. The air was filled with their songs and calls. The trees were filling out with new leaves turning the landscape from brown and grey to the fresh color of new greens. Reinhold was out in the forest one morning with Isolde gathering the first of the dandelions and looking for where the birds were nesting when their explorations brought them around the Kuhlsee close to the construction site. The sounds of voices made them take cover but curiosity made them move closer.

"What is that?" Isolde had asked as they crouched behind the trunk of a particularly large oak tree.

The site had changed dramatically since Reinhold had last seen it. An eight foot tall chain link fence now marked a perimeter around the buildings. It stretched into the forest at least a hundred feet, almost to the northern boundary of the Kuhlsee. Inside the enclosure, the trees had been stripped of low hanging branches and the trunks were wrapped with razor wire. Several military looking trucks and jeeps were parked in a small lot behind the buildings. Soldiers in brown uniforms were everywhere working.

"I don't know." Reinhold finally answered his sister. "I think, it is for soldiers, somewhere for them to live. Let's go over there and get a better view." Reinhold pointed to a spot just north of the enclosure, closer to the road.

"That doesn't make sense. Why would soldiers live here? There is nothing around here. Look!" Isolde pointed down the road to the south.

The largest truck either of them had ever seen was rumbling up the road. It was obviously an army truck. It pulled off the road and stopped in front of the gate that blocked the driveway into the mysterious site. A man in a brown uniform hurried out of the southern building and opened the gate, motioning the truck through. It lumbered into the small parking lot and came to a halt between the two northern buildings.

Men in brown uniforms emerged from the buildings and approached the truck with rifles drawn and aimed at the truck. When the tailgate opened, the children saw the vehicle was loaded with men with a strange look wearing strange clothing. Stranger still was their bound hands. They looked like soldiers, but not like the soldiers who held the guns. The confused children watched while the men were quickly unloaded into one of the buildings. When this was done, the truck lumbered back out on to the road, returning the way it came. The driver had never set a foot outside the cab. The gate was firmly locked behind it. The whole operation took only a few minutes.

"Come on. We promised Lisa we would bring home the dandelions in time for dinner." Isolde pulled on Reinhold's sleeve to get him moving. "Do you have your slingshot with you? Maybe we can get a duck in the Kuhlsee."

Reinhold got up from his crouched position and followed his sister but his mind was still quite interested in the buildings and the soldiers. He wanted to know more about the men that were brought in on the truck. Why were they bound and held at gunpoint? It was obvious to Reinhold that they were soldiers. Also obvious was that they were the "enemy" that he heard so much about at school, the Russians or the British. He remembered the poster tacked to the wall at the front of his classroom: a man's body wearing a British army uniform and sporting a wolf's head. The caption implied that these foreigners were animals that would eat the children of Germany alive, if they had the chance. Those men that got off the truck didn't look like they could eat anyone alive, some of them were lucky they could stand on two legs.

"I bet they are prisoners from the war." He said finally, faintly, his mind still daydreaming about wolves and enemies.

"What would prisoners from the war be doing here?" she asked.

Reinhold didn't have any answer for her but, once again, it was a good question. Why were there prisoners of war in the woods?

Reinhold and Isolde were picking their way across the Kuhlsee, looking for ducks and duck eggs, when a train whistle pierced the early afternoon, sending adrenaline pouring into Reinhold's veins. Without thinking, he kicked off his wooden clogs and took off for the tracks, his bare feet slipping on the cold, wet earth of the swamp. He had to get to the tracks at the right time or he would have to wait until the next train. Next time he doubted that he would be so conveniently placed. He cleared the swamp in a few well-placed steps and bounded up the wooded incline that bordered the wetland to the west.

Thank goodness for this little incline. It was just a small hill but it caused the trains to slow down, to make them labor after crossing miles of easy flatland after leaving Lübeck. This small break in the speed of the locomotive made it possible to grab a hold of a passing bit of metal and climb up into one of the cars. He reached the tracks just as the freight train started up the small rise. Freight, not passenger, was what he was looking for. Freight trains carry coal.

"This one has coal!" Reinhold shouted to his sister.

She let out a cry of joy and started running up the hill. Reinhold shrugged out of his backpack and let it fall to the ground. It contained their dandelion haul for the day but he knew that Isolde would collect it for him.

Carefully, the boy approached the tracks and the moving train. He let the engine overtake his position then jogged alongside against the direction the locomotive was traveling until he saw a handle that looked promising, sturdy and not too high off the ground. Quickly, he jumped and grasped the cold metal handle, let himself go limp, and let the train carry him off his feet for a brief second. That little bit of momentum was all Reinhold needed to swing his small child's body on to the porch of the lead car. He landed heavily on his knees on the metal deck but regained his feet quickly. He scrambled up on to the thin metal railing that enclosed the porch, using the support for the small roof to steady himself. Gathering all his courage and strength, not wasting a single second of precious time to consider his precarious position, Reinhold leaped across the coupling to the coal car, grabbing onto the lip and hanging there for a second before pulling himself up, using arms and feet, to get into the car.

Once in the car, the boy wasted no time and set about to get as much coal off the train as possible. He picked up armloads of the black gold and threw it over the side of the moving car. When another boy, Herman Rehbein, landed next to him, Reinhold nodded to his neighbor but didn't stop throwing coals over the side. Usually, the boys were mortal enemies, locked in a power struggle for control of their gang of kids on Blüchereiche but in the coal car, they were just neighbors.

Reinhold paused in his work to look around. The train was regaining its speed after laboring up the hill and soon it would be leaving the small town of Ratekau. Spotting the old church and judging its distance, Reinhold figured he had time for one more armload of coal. Quickly, he stooped, gathered, and heaved. Then he scrambled up to the edge of the train car, throwing one leg over the side, straddling the metal like a horse, the wind ripping through his blond hair. Glancing back over his shoulder he saw Herman struggling to gather another batch of coal.

"Herman!" Reinhold screamed over the chugging of the engine. His rival looked up at him, questioningly. "*Pass auf!*[6]"

Herman nodded his acknowledgement before throwing his armload of coal over the side. Then he pulled himself up to the edge of the coal car and disappeared over the side. Reinhold swung his other leg so he was sitting on the edge of the car and jumped, landing heavily on one knee on the porch of the lead car. Then carefully, he grabbed the handle and lowered himself so that his feet were running as fast as they could along the ground before he let go. Then he flung himself on the ground, tucked, and rolled to a stop.

It took a few minutes for the boy to catch his breath. He arms tingled from the exertion and his left hip throbbed slightly where it had made contact with the ground. He was pretty sure he had scraped up his right leg and the bottoms of his feet on the gravel that lined the tracks. He was still lying face up in the grass next to the train tracks when Isolde found him. She looked down at him, concerned.

"Did you hurt yourself?" She asked.

"No."

"Get up then. We have to walk all the way back. I hid your backpack and clogs in the woods. We have to go get them."

"Did you get the coal?"

"Yup. We got lots."

She smiled broadly as she pointed to her canvas backpack to show that it was overflowing with the grimy black substance.

"I saw Herman but he must have come alone. There was no one else here this time. There is still some coal left further down the tracks. I only took the big pieces first. We can stuff more in your backpack or come back for it later, after dinner."

Reinhold sat up, groaning slightly with the effort, and looked down the tracks. He saw Herman about a hundred feet away and on

---

[6] *Pass auf* in German translates to 'watch out'.

the opposite side, collecting coal in what looked like an old wheelbarrow.

Where did he get that? And how did he get off the train? Had he just jumped from the coal car? He's going to get killed doing it that way.

Reinhold admired his rival for just a brief minute before scolding himself. As it stood right now, Herman had control of the little gang of boys from Blüchereiche. Sometime in the next couple of days he was going to have to fight Herman to regain his place as ringleader. Reinhold briefly considered jumping the bigger boy now and taking his wheelbarrow. He could carry more coal and dandelions home if he had that wheelbarrow. But, the victory wouldn't count if no one saw it. They would just have to fight again in public to make the leadership transfer official. Taking his mind off Herman, Reinhold realized that Isolde was right, there was no one else near the tracks, trying to steal the boys' hard earned coal. They were lucky this time.

Chapter 7: Heinilaken

"I didn't go back to that camp for the entire summer?"

Reinhold asked the question aloud to himself and the seagulls circling the sun baked *Brandenburg*. He struggled for a second to piece together the events of his eighth summer.

He had to work, of course. That was definitely a deterrent to free time. He went to Walter Muuss' farm to work for food. He wasn't an official employee but, if he came and did some work, the foreman would send him home with some grain or some milk. Reinhold went there for the various harvest seasons that summer and fall; wheat, rye, clover, mustard, potatoes, peas, beans. Reinhold harvested them all.

His work at the farm also paid the rent on the small plot of land that his family rented from the Muuss'. That had been more work for Reinhold, but at least he had his sisters to help him. Between the three of them, they brought in a nice winter supply of potatoes. There had also been beans and greens during the summer.

He remembered that it was that summer that he and his neighbors had started guarding their fields at night. Several of the families on Blüchereiche had their plots close together, about a half a mile north of their street, near the old church. The older folks noticed a few strangers moving through the town and the fields, coming from the east. They said these people were fleeing the war and they were hungry after such a long journey. His neighbors seemed to think there would be more of them coming through Ratekau sooner or later and they wanted to be prepared. They set up a system, taking turns standing watch over their little fields of precious food. Many nights Reinhold slept in the fields with a club as his only weapon, training himself to be alert even when asleep. When he heard a noise, he would spring into action, racing across the fields, screaming threats, and waving his club. It was so dark some nights, that he had a hard time finding his way back to his original position.

Then there was the constant need for firewood. He was always chopping wood. Looking back at his childhood, Reinhold came across many memories that involved him with an axe in his hand. Isolde wasn't spared this task either. When his shoulders couldn't take one more swing, she would take over. They would trade off and on like this for hours, slowly piling up firewood for the stove. Not a single swing of that axe for that wood came from his stepmother but she had certainly enjoyed the warmth. Reinhold the sailor spit in silent disgust off the side of the *Brandenburg*.

As Reinhold recalled, it was in his eighth summer that he and his friend Heinilaken had grown closer than they had been before. They had been classmates for a couple of years and had played together on the playground during their brief recesses in school but Heinilaken lived on the other side of town, near Ruppersdorfer See. He wasn't part of Reinhold's usual gang on Blüchereiche so they didn't see each other that much outside of school. He always felt a bit sorry for the other boy. Reinhold knew, had seen with his own eyes, the torment the other kids doled out to poor Heinilaken. The boy was born with a hair lip and he suffered enormously for it. Reinhold never partook in the antics of his peers, except for the nickname. He was the only boy Reinhold could remember having a nickname. His real name was David, but had earned the nickname because he was always licking his hair lip. The poor soul also spoke with a bit of a lisp, making him an even greater target for the cruel taunting.

That summer, Herr Klausen set Reinhold to work with Heinilaken picking cherries from the tree in the yard of the school. They were Herr Klausen's cherries by authority of his position as schoolmaster but he was too busy to pick them himself. He chose Reinhold because he thought the boy, regardless of his lack of discipline, was a hard working youth.

"I want to hear you whistling out here. If I don't hear you whistling I will assume you are eating the cherries and you will be sorry for that. Do you understand?"

"Yes, Herr Klausen."

The two boys sat in the tree whistling and picking, making faces at each other and occasionally throwing the odd rotten cherry at the other. It took them more than a week of picking several hours a day to complete the task. On the last day of the harvest, Reinhold suggested they go to the beach. The heat of the summer was on and Ratekau had been experiencing an abnormally high percentage of humidity. It was muggy and uncomfortable. The beach was only four miles away and there was still several hours of daylight.

"We can go and stay there tonight." Reinhold suggested. "I'll get my tent."

Heinilaken thought about it for a minute before agreeing. He was in a similar situation as Reinhold at home. He had an evil stepmother and his father was away with the army. Reinhold thought Heinilaken might have had it a bit worse because he was the oldest of several children; there was more pressure on him to pitch in. And his deformity didn't help.

Their trip to the beach near Timmendorfer Strand that day was the first of several that summer. Sometimes it was just the two of them trying to escape the horrors and physical abuse of going home. Sometimes Reinhold's little gang from Blüchereiche would go too. They spent their time at the beach being kids, playing in the waves and cooking fish over a fire. They quickly learned that the fishing boats serving the nearby processing plant did not have the best nets. The fish would fall out of them during unloading. If they got there in time, before all the other hungry villagers, they could get a bunch for dinner. Sometimes, when there was competition for the fish, there would be a brawl over the smallest morsels. Somehow, the boys always ended up with a few.

After filling their bellies, the boys sat around the fire and told stories about the horrible things they heard, mostly about Klaus Störtebeker[7], sea monsters, or the war. They watched the boats in the bay and wondered about where they were going. Well, Reinhold did, anyway. The other boys didn't seem much concerned with strange destinations but there was a universal love of boats, especially the big ones. Often, to the delight of the boys, they were treated to a glimpse of a Navy ship either docking or embarking from Neustadt, a small coastal town on the other side of the bay.

It was at the beach that first night with Heinilaken that the boys devised a prank to play on Herr Klausen. They thought it would be the greatest of all time. Their little slice of Germany was infested with beetles. Every year the authority figures turned a day of education in school into a day of gathering beetles. The children went out into the fields with jugs to collect as many as they could find or their jug could hold. The beetles were exterminated with steam. Reinhold suggested they collect a whole bunch of these beetles and bring them to school. Instead of killing them, they would put them in the ink wells in the desks of their classroom. The flap that covered the

---

[7] Klaus Störtebeker was a 14th century privateer based out of Lübeck. Many tales exist of his life, capture, and death.

well would keep the bugs from escaping and if they took the pots of ink out, there would be room for quite a few of the beetles. When Herr Klausen shouted "*Diktat!*" all the children would open their ink flaps to start writing. Instead of dipping their pens in ink, the bugs would fly out.

There were seventy desks in the room, so the amount of bugs they needed was enormous. It took them all night and most of the early morning to collect the creatures. During their brief recess, Reinhold and Heinilaken set about removing inkpots and filling the wells with beetles. All went according to plan. The room filled with bugs, children went screaming, and Herr Klausen turned bright red before shouting "Reinhold!"

He remembered receiving a severe beating that day. He walked funny and painfully for days afterwards. Heinilaken wasn't spared. He got his own punishment for being an accomplice.

"You are not a stupid person, Reinhold. You are really quite smart, you just need to focus. Your mind is scattered like leaves in the fall." Herr Klausen offered this observation after he doled out the punishment.

That wasn't the worst beating I took that summer, the sailor thought to himself.

His stepmother held that honor. She knocked him out cold with a fire poker. If he remembered correctly, it was partially his fault she had chosen a fire poker as a weapon. He had hidden her usual stick behind a free standing cabinet in the kitchen. When she slipped and fell off the chair she was using to try to reach down behind this cabinet, the fire poker was the first thing she saw, so she grabbed it. It made contact with the boy's head and knocked him out. When he came to later, he was neatly tucked into bed and a very concerned stepmother was hovering about. All of a sudden, for the first and only time in his life, she offered him candy. His mind had been too fuzzy at the time to wonder where she had gotten the candy.

Chapter 8: That Isn't A Very Strong Fence

The following winter, as he remembered it, Reinhold returned to the buildings in the woods. He and his gang from Blüchereiche were out after the first snowfall with their skis exploring the forest, looking for downed trees they could take home with them. After the boys got tired of asking Reinhold if they could use his Norwegian skis, the conversation turned to the buildings and the activities of the mysterious new site.

"I am telling you, there are soldiers there! Russians, I think. Their uniforms are greener than the German ones. They just stand near the fence or sit around the fire." Willie was saying.

They were making their way through the trees toward the camp, skirting the western edge of the Kuhlsee. He had been out this way last week before the snowfall looking for birch nuts when he came across the camp. Now, he claimed, it was full of enemy soldiers. The other children didn't quite believe him, but Reinhold did. He had seen it last spring.

Carefully and quietly, the children approached the camp. The sound of voices drifted across the forest to them, but they didn't understand the language. They took their skis off and hid them in the snow, creeping from tree to tree until they were just a few yards from the perimeter. Willie was right, there were dozens of soldiers standing near the fence, staring out into the forest, or positioned around the fire, sitting on logs, looking dejected.

"What are they doing?" Egon asked.

"Nothing." Reinhold answered. "That's all they can do. They are prisoners."

The full realization of the situation spread across Egon's face. He was actually seeing prisoners collected on the battlefields of the war that was raging somewhere out there. "Oh" was all he could say in return.

"They look hungry. I wonder if they feed them. I heard that prisoners at other camps aren't fed and are forced to work until they die." Abby remarked, peering around the tree as he spoke. The other boys scoffed at him in disbelief.

"Where did you hear such nonsense?" Egon asked.

"No, he is right. I heard that too. The Draves were talking about it with Herr Klausen." Willie came to Abby's defense.

His adopted parents, the Draves, were members of the *Braunenpatie*. Everyone in Ratekau believed the information they grudgingly offered to their Communist neighbors about the war. Nobody ever questioned them. They just accepted the information as fact. Frau Draves was known to turn people in for any infraction she encountered and she didn't like to be questioned. "But, the Draves said that it was a mistake, an accident, that those prisoners were worked to death. They had been 'improperly assigned' to a work gang that was too much for them because they were old. It hasn't happened since, they said."

Willie's explanation of the situation had seemed logical enough to the boys but they still weren't sure about the group of men they were watching move restlessly on the other side of the fence. Some of them had the pinched look that comes with hunger or sickness. More than a few were limping.

"That isn't a very strong fence." Egon observed. "And there are no guards in the towers. Shouldn't there be guards in the towers?"

No one answered. They were watching a newly appeared German guard move through the prisoners. He carried a bucket. He handed what looked like a slice of bread to each of the prisoners. Behind him, another guard pushed a small wheel barrow that carried a steaming pot. The boys watched as each prisoner was handed a tin mug of the steaming liquid. They dipped their slice of bread in it and ate ravenously. It was half an answer to one of their two questions. What was in the mugs? And where did the German soldiers watch from? Someone had to be watching these men.

"Come on. I promised Lisa I would kill the chicken for dinner tonight." Reinhold started back toward where they left their skis.

He was still thinking about the prisoners when he got home. He told Isolde what happened while he ripped the feathers out of the chicken. She was sitting next to him gathering the feathers for stuffing. He felt bad for the Russians. They looked so underfed and despondent.

"You be careful around that camp, Reinhold," was all Lisa said when he brought the subject up to her.

Reinhold couldn't exactly remember what prompted the next couple of months, but by the beginning of the New Year, he and his friends were regular visitors to the prison camp. At first, they ran up to the fence and handed stolen potatoes, turnips, and parsnips through the gaps to the men standing closest. Every day, they picked a farmer to unknowingly contribute to their adventure before going to the camp. It wasn't long before the men were waiting along the fence for the boys to arrive. The men washed the roots with snow before taking them to the fire to roast them.

On a couple of occasions, the guards noticed the boys at the fence, but they did nothing to stop the activities. They actually seemed a bit amused by the antics. Once or twice an officer in charge saw them standing on the other side of the barrier, trying to communicate with the Russians. It was the officers that seemed to care about the antics. They shouted at the boys to go back to their homes and not return to the site. If they returned, one threatened, he would shoot them in the name of the *Führer*. This sent the boys running. But they returned the next day, undeterred by threats.

Then someone, Reinhold wasn't sure who, got the idea to cut a seam in the flimsy chain link fence and actually enter the camp. The boys figured they could sit around the warm fire with the Russians and roast vegetables. After securing a pair of wire cutters from the Easberger's tool shed, the boys once again headed to the camp. They hid their skis in the snow, cut a small seam in the fence and entered the camp. The Russians were surprised at first to see their young friends inside their prison. Then they were very amused.

Almost every day for the rest of the winter, Reinhold and his friends went to visit the camp, bringing food for themselves and the Russian prisoners. They sat on the hard logs positioned around the fire pit with their backs to the forest outside the fence. They didn't speak the same language as the men, but they found ways to communicate with body language and hands. There was one man, an officer as Reinhold figured, who spoke a bit of German. The boys learned that the men had been captured in the east and shipped in tightly packed train cars to a big city, they didn't know which one, and then to the camp in the woods by truck. They didn't even know where in Germany they were until the boys told them.

"*Da*, Lübeck, *da, da*[8]. North.", the officer said, turning to his fellow soldiers.

He said something to them in his native language, something Reinhold didn't catch at all, but it got their attention. They stopped eating and talking with the people around them to listen to what the

---

[8] *Da* in Russian means 'yes'

officer was saying. When the officer was finished speaking, all the men around the fire started nodding in understanding. Reinhold figured that they all knew where they were in Germany, in the north, near Lübeck. This information seemed to make them a bit more cheerful.

As the winter wore on, the boys spent more of their day at the camp. The guards got used to seeing them appear out of the tree line. They didn't try to stop the caper. Reinhold believed that they were just as bored as the prisoners. Looking back, he was sure they were very bored.

It wasn't long after the boys started visiting the camp that the soldiers started visiting the town. They found their way right to Reinhold's own house. He could distinctly remember his stepmother introducing him to his "uncle so and so" and then sending him and Isolde out to chop wood or steal some potatoes while the adults partied in the house. Sometimes they came singly, sometimes there was a few of them. Sometimes they brought his stepmother candy or cookies that she never shared with the children. Reinhold wondered if they recognized him from the camp. If they did, they never said a word.

The officers, on the other hand, caused problems. When they saw the boys along the fence, they threatened to shoot them. One actually fired a shot at them. What would they have done if they caught them inside the camp? Luckily, the boys never found out. The German soldiers began to warn the young visitors when the officers were approaching by whistling. The Russians, in turn, devised a system of hiding the boys under their coats. When they heard the whistle, a Russian man would open one side of his long, heavy military issue jacket. The boy closest would quickly get in as close to the man as possible then the jacket would be closed around them. Just for good measure, all the men would crowd close together so it was difficult to tell when one man ended and the other began. To the patrolling officer, it probably just looked like they were huddled together for warmth.

The sailor on the *Brandenburg* in the Caribbean did a quick count on his fingers, trying to recall what years it was that he and his friends visited the camp. As he figured, it was the winters of 1942-43 and 1943-44. During those two years, the same group of men occupied the rough logs by the fire, the same Russian officer acted as a kind of interpreter between the men and boys, not that he knew that much German. They came to know each other as well as could be expected.

One day, toward the end of that first winter, the boys were getting ready to leave the camp when the Russian officer called Reinhold back to the fire. Without speaking, he pressed something into the boy's hand. Then he turned and walked away, toward the buildings, his shoulders slumped. Reinhold opened his hand and stared with open mouthed disbelief at a gold ring. It was beautiful and, he thought, very old. The gold was subtly lustrous. It was set with a red stone that was scratched but still luminous. He stared at it for a moment, blinking to clear his vision of this impossible gift. There was no way it was real, but every time he opened his eyes, it was there, in his hand where the Russian had placed it. Reinhold could hear his friends calling to him so he shoved the ring deep into the pocket of his pants and left the fire, baffled.

"Why did he give you that?" Isolde asked him when he showed her the ring.

"I don't know."

"You hide that. If Mama sees that, she'll take it from you." Reinhold heeded this advice from Lisa and hid the ring.

It was early in the spring of 1943 that the missiles appeared in the forest. They just appeared one day, out of thin air.

"Whoa! Those are rockets!" Kule said as, once again, the boys cautiously approached something in the forest.

This something was spread out over half a mile in as perfect rows as could be accomplished in the tight spaces between the trees, six by four. It was an eerie sight, missiles with no one around watching them or using them. It was destruction waiting to be directed in the dark and quiet of the misty, early morning forest.

"What are they doing here?" Willie asked, incredulously.

The rockets were stacked in five or six foot pyramids on trailers and covered somewhat haphazardly by army issue canvas. Obviously, they had been dragged there by trucks and unhitched. They were deposited not far from the southern end of the camp. Someone passing on the road to Sereetz would never even know they were there unless they took the time to look carefully.

After looking to make sure they were truly alone, Reinhold lifted the greenish brown canvas covering one of trailers. The rockets were green, a light green though, not dark like the trailer or the canvas. There were maybe a dozen of them in the pyramid formation. They were pointy with white tips at one end and had three fins at the other. Toward the base, there was an almost invisible panel that could be opened. Inside, there were colored buttons and switches. Reinhold flipped open one of these panels and flicked one of the switches. The rocket came to life with a humming noise. Quickly, he flipped it back to off position before the rocket could really come alive and fly away to blow something up.

"They need fuel, I think." Willie said. "Right? Isn't that why they say 'rocket fuel'? They need rocket fuel."

The missiles became a favorite play place for the boys, once they figured out that they were harmless. They must have blown up half the country and conquered many invading forces with those missiles.

The winter of 1944-45 wasn't as much fun as the previous two. The Russians they had grown to know weren't there when they went to visit after the bringing in the harvest in 1944. In their place was a new group. They were brown people with small black eyes. They didn't seem friendly at all. They were actually a bit frightening. The boys tried to give them food the first time they encountered them but it wasn't as readily accepted as with the Russians. These new men snatched the potatoes and parsnips out of the boy's hands like starving, snarly dogs. They didn't go back after that.

Chapter 9: Why Didn't You Go To School?

The blond man on the sun baked ship ran a calloused hand through his hair. Thoughtfully, he removed a Lucky Strike from the pack in his pocket, tapping it twice on the rail before lighting it. The memories of his childhood were swirling around in his head like the smoke that curled around his body. He saw the green fields of Schleswig-Holstein, dotted with cows, covered in a blanket of swaying grain crops. He saw the clumps of tall, leafy trees and hazelnut bushes that divided field from field. He could feel the damp, fertile earth under his bare feet and smell the fresh scent of newly cut greens. He was only nine years old. And his hands were already calloused.

It was early summer. The clover and mustard finally achieved a height sufficient to cut it. The boys that worked for Walter Muuss on his farm were out in the fields swinging away with their sickles. Walter Muuss himself was away at war. In his place was a foreman, an elderly man, of course. There was nothing left but old men, women, and children.

Reinhold sat perched on a horse harnessed to a high-sided wagon. The workers in the field were throwing the newly cut greens into the back of the wagon while others trampled it down. This continued until the wagon was piled high, perilously high. Then it was Reinhold's turn to play his role. He expertly, particularly so for a nine year old boy, guided the horses out of the field on to the rocky, uneven, dirt road. He had to make it the mile back to the barn without the wagon tipping. This meant maneuvering over deep ruts that cut their way across the road while not losing a wheel in the deep ditches that lined the edges. It hadn't been a problem in the last week of the cutting so he didn't anticipate a problem now. The horses seemed to respond well to Reinhold's gentle but firm commands to move right or left.

Farms in Germany were arranged differently than their counterparts in other countries. The farmhouses and barns are within the town limits while the fields surrounded the town in a blanket of green. It took about twenty minutes to travel from the clover fields to the barn at Walter Muuss' place which was in the middle of Ratekau. At the barn, the boy slid down off his mount, giving the animal a few stokes, telling him he did a good job, before limping to the wagon to help pitch the clover into the silo. After a week perched on the back of a horse, Reinhold was one sore little boy.

"Get in there and start stomping it down, Reinhold," the foreman directed him.

Reinhold squeezed his way into the silo through the narrow door and started stomping down the clover. He was joined shortly by the other boys just arriving from the fields. Together, they made a game of the stomping, exaggerating their movements, swinging their arms, like soldiers marching. One of the boys, Walter Muuss' son, also named Walter, fell to the ground and rolled around in the clover, gripping his chest and moaning, pretending he had been shot by an unseen enemy. The laughing drew the attention of the foreman.

"Quit playing around in there!" He barked at them.

The boys snap themselves back to attention still smiling.

"You boys get yourselves down to the cow corral now. It is time for milking."

The boys dutifully filed out of the silo and headed to the far side of the barnyard where the cows were already gathering for their evening milking. Reinhold had learned how to milk a cow two months ago when he was officially "hired for the season" by the foreman. He decided he hated it one month ago. It was boring, repetitive, dirty work. The worst part, in his opinion, was the flicking of the cows tail. The hairy tuft at the end was always all full of mud and crap. When she flicked it just right, it would wrap around his neck, flinging that nasty mixture in his face. *Ekelhaft*[9]*!*

With the last wagon load of greens safely in the silo and the cows milked, the day at the farm came to a close. Reinhold lingered outside the barn trying to decide if he felt like making the long trek back to his own home or if he wanted to sleep in the Muuss' barn. Somewhere off to the right, near the cow corral, he heard sounds of a pursuit, running feet and screaming. Turning toward the noise, Reinhold saw one of the kitchen maids, Emma, running toward him across the dirt and gravel of the barn yard, braids and skirts flying behind her. She was being chased by Erik, a farm hand about twenty years old who most believed was not right in the head. Why else hadn't the army taken him? When she spotted Reinhold, the wild eyed maid started screaming for him to help her. The look of terror on her

---

[9] *Ekelhaft* in German translates roughly to 'gross' or 'disgusting' in English.

face reminded Reinhold of the horses during a thunderstorm. It was in stark contrast to the crazed look of joy on the face of her pursuer.

"He is crazy! Help me!"

She swept past him, trying to make it to the sanctuary of the farm house, just forty feet from where the boy stood.

"Get her!" screamed Erik. "Grab her. Lift up her dress! Lift up her dress!"

Thinking it was some kind of game, Reinhold took off after Emma. He didn't have much chance of catching her. He was only nine years old, his legs were still youthfully short. The she was a teenager, a long legged one. He had only run a short distance after her when Erik raced past him, fueled by lust and mental instability. He caught her just at the other edge of the barnyard, knocking her to the ground and grabbing her skirts in one fell movement. They wrestled for a moment. Erik managed to position Emma on her back with him straddled across her legs, effectively immobilizing her. She shrieked as he yanked up her skirt exposing that she had nothing on underneath. The sight of her nakedness gave the crazy man pause long enough for her to push him off her. He landed on his back in the dust of the barnyard while she took off faster than before, making a beeline across the small patch of grass that qualified as a front yard for the farmhouse. Reinhold watched Erik roll around in the dirt of the barnyard, unable to get up, his arms wrapped around his abdomen, laughing hysterically. The kitchen door slammed in the distance.

Reinhold shook his head in confusion. What happened? How was that fun? He didn't get it. It seemed like a lot of work for nothing. A moment later Herr Muuss' old, weather beaten, witch of a mother appeared out of the farmhouse, a wooden kitchen spoon in her hand, yelling angrily for Erik. The crazy man suddenly found his feet and took off at a sprint down the road away from the farm. The boy decided to take the two mile trek home. He didn't want to be around the farm with the old woman on the war path.

In order to reach his home on Blüchereiche, Reinhold had to walk through the center of town, past the old church and the school. There were always people milling about in the evening. He wondered whom he would run into. There were several he was hoping to avoid. Peering around a corner into the town square, he noted that the streets were relatively empty. Sighing slightly in relief he continued on his way.

His relief was short lived. Around a corner just ahead of him appeared Herr Klausen. The sharp eyes of the man sighted Reinhold immediately.

Verdammt![10] Reinhold thought to himself but, trying to be an obedient young man, he planted his feet in the ground, raised his right arm as they had taught him and said "*Heil*!"

The schoolmaster smacked his hand out of the air. Before the boy could even register the shock, Herr Klausen grabbed the hat off his small head and threw it on the ground.

"Take off your cap when you salute the *Führer*! And you say '*Heil Hitler*' not just '*Heil*'. You must learn respect! Why were you not in school today?"

He didn't wait for an answer. He knew the answer. He saw the jug of milk and small bag of grain the boy carried, his pay for a day's work. How else was he supposed to provide food for his sister and stepmother?

"I certainly hope I will see you tomorrow."

Once again, he didn't wait for an answer. The schoolmaster walked away.

"*Verdammt!*" Reinhold thought to himself again.

Why did he have to take his hat off when he saluted someone he had never met? He almost made it home without getting in trouble. He trudged the rest of the way, getting more tired the closer he got.

"Herr Klausen told me you weren't in school today. Why didn't you go to school?"

His stepmother hadn't even waited for him to close the door to their small kitchen behind him before she questioned him. She saw the jug of milk he carried. Without hesitation, she smacked him in the head and took the milk from him. She poured herself a mug full and left the room.

He seated himself at the kitchen table as close to the wood stove as he could get. The night chill was settling in. He poured himself a mug full of milk. His sister Isolde appeared a few minutes later. She helped herself to the milk and seated herself down next to her brother.

"Lisa is gone." She whispered to him.

Reinhold stared at her not comprehending what she was talking about.

---

[10] *Verdammt* in German translates to 'damn' in English

"Mama sent her away to work for some *Braunenpatie* family in Lübeck."

"Oh" was all he could get out before Olga swept back into the kitchen.

"You children need to learn how to do things for yourself. Lisa isn't going to be here to do it for you anymore."

She deposited a pile of their knit socks that needed darning on the table in front of them along with a sewing kit.

"They aren't going to fix themselves." was all she said before she left the room again.

"She did it on purpose, sending Lisa away." Isolde whispered to him. "Lisa knows what Mama does with those soldiers, the ones that come here during the day."

Reinhold and his sister sat at the table mending socks until they were falling asleep. Like good obedient children, they went to say good night to their stepmother. As always, she was sitting in her chair near the radio, listening for news about the war. Her daschund was sitting in her lap. Each child went to give her a kiss good night on the cheek and was rewarded by a nip on the arm from the dog and the cackle of their stepmother laughing at them. Reinhold stumbled up the steep, rickety stairs to their second floor attic to sleep under the leaky roof.

He wasn't sure what time it was when he woke up on the floor with a strange noise reverberating in his ears. He knew something bad had happened. As quickly as his sleep addled body could move, he hefted the trap door and went downstairs. Isolde was already standing in the kitchen, her mouth hanging open as she looked around. The floor was covered in glass.

"What happened?" Reinhold asked.

"It was a bomb, obviously" his stepmother snapped at him. "It blew out every window in the house!"

"The sirens didn't go off. Where did they drop it?" This time is was Isolde who questioned.

"Who knows? Who cares? The point is that the windows are gone. What are we going to do for windows is a better question."

His stepmother stormed out of the kitchen to go back to bed, leaving the two children to stare at each other.

It took several weeks for Reinhold and Isolde to tape the glass back together and refit it to the window frames. On one his foraging trips across the railroad tracks, Reinhold couldn't help but notice that a new pond had formed in the swamp just north of the Kuhlsee and the road to Sereetz. He wondered if it was a crater from the bomb that blew the windows out of his house and every other house on the eastern side of Ratekau.

Chapter 10: They Are Only Children

The man on the ship flicked the butt of his cigarette into the sea, remembering the next few months. Olga hadn't been kidding. She taught them once how to do various chores. After the initial lesson, she expected them to do it for themselves. Isolde was right in her thoughts that their stepmother sent Lisa away because of the soldiers that came to visit. After Lisa left, their stepmother entertained soldiers and officers every day. Reinhold and Isolde, if they were home, were relegated to the outdoors during these times. They chopped wood, tended the small garden patch, took care of the chickens and rabbits, and did the laundry, listening to the laughter coming from inside the house.

"What do you think they are doing?" Isolde asked one day.

It was a crisp Sunday morning in early fall. She and Reinhold were watching the laundry boil in a big black kettle over the fire they constructed in the yard between the house and the small barn. Lisa had been gone for three months. It was the first time they were attempting to do the laundry properly since she left. They had washed a shirt here or a pair of dungarees there, usually in the nearby stream, but they decided that it was time to do the bedding. Their stepmother even threw hers into the pile when she saw what they were doing. It was an arduous task. The kettle alone weighted as much as Isolde. It took them five trips, each with their yoke and buckets, to the water pump down the street to fill it.

"Don't you worry about what they are doing in that house."

The children turned to see their neighbor, Anna Easberger, waddling her way toward them. She surveyed their laundry project with some satisfaction.

"You children are doing well here. You had enough soap? You know how long you have to let it simmer? This looks like too much for just your drying line. You can hang what is left over on mine."

"Yes, ma'am."

"It is a shame that Lisa had to go away to work and leave you to yourselves here." She shot a disapproving look at the children's house. "How are your ration tickets holding up? Supplies are getting tighter, you know. The drop in the rations last year wasn't enough, apparently. They are really squeezing us. We are all going to starve before this folly is over."

Before the sentence was completely out of her mouth, Anna's face went white. She looked around quickly to make sure no one had overheard her transgression.

"*Heil Hitler!*" She added hastily.

"We don't know." Esoldea answered. "Mama has them. She only gives them to us when we have to go get something."

"Mama?"

Paul Easberger, Anna's husband and the father of her eleven children, was coming to join the little group in Reinhold's backyard. He practically snorted out the word.

"That woman isn't your Mama. Your Mama was a good woman. She wouldn't have left her children to do their own laundry and cook their own meals by themselves. She'd be here still today with another brother or sister if your father wasn't so adamant about not wanting more children." Herr Easberger snorted again. "It wasn't her fault she got pregnant. Some men just can't take responsibility for their actions as well as others." He shook his head sadly.

"Paul, stop, before you say too much. They are only children." Anna warned her husband.

"What happened?" Reinhold asked quickly, before Frau Easberger could scold her husband into silence.

He wanted to know the truth about what happened to his mother. Every day, he wondered how his life would be different if his real mother was there, taking care of them.

"Your real Mama tried to get rid of a baby with a knitting needle, young man." Herr Easberger informed Reinhold rather matter of factly. "She bled to death."

The two children could just stare at the man in shock. Neither one of them knew how to respond. They also weren't sure if they fully understood what he meant and whether or not it was true. Maybe Herr Easberger was just fooling with them. But he wasn't.

Frau Easberger had enough from her husband. She scolded him roundly and shooed him away. As consolation for her husband's insensitive and unprovoked revelation, she stayed and helped get the sheets and blankets out of the kettle and on to the drying lines. Later in the day, she appeared in their kitchen with a delicious plum cake. It must have taken almost half her weekly rations to make it. With eleven children to feed, this was an expensive gift.

"Don't you go thinking about what Herr Easberger said today. God does what he wants and he wanted your mother to return to him in Heaven. That's all that matters now."

Reinhold was unconvinced that God had anything to do with it. Who was this guy anyway? He lives in the sky and has control over everything that happens in the world? Herr Klausen had told them in school that God sent his son, Jesus Christ, to die for the sins of the world. Then he was resurrected three days later and went back to Heaven to be with his father. Who dies and comes back to life? It all sounded like a bunch of *scheiße*[11].

The revelation about their mother and the plum cake from Frau Easberger wasn't the only surprise Reinhold and Isolde had that day. Just before sunset Lisa appeared in their tiny kitchen. She hated the family she worked for and ran away. They were all sure the police would be there in the morning to collect her. The three siblings were sitting by the stove, chatting about Lisa's experiences in Lübeck and eating plum cake when their stepmother came looking for them.

"Ah, good, you're home. You can help Reinhold get some apples. There has got to be some still on the trees at one of the orchards. You got a plum cake, I want an apple cake. Get going."

Lisa and Reinhold left the house against their will. Reinhold saw the wisdom of getting apples but resented being told what to do by his stepmother, especially when it came to stealing from the orchards. It wasn't as easy as it used to be. All the fields were guarded by the farmers and some of them were armed with old army castoff rifles. Reinhold purposely chose an orchard on the southern outskirts of town owned by someone he didn't know. They took the railroad tracks there. Luckily there was an almost full moon out or they would have stumbled their way down the uneven terrain in the dark.

They hadn't even made it off the tracks near the orchard when they heard the guard on duty that night. Lisa became instantly frightened but Reinhold took control of the situation.

"Get down!" he told her.

Just ahead of them, not far from the tracks, there was a hastily erected wooden structure. It was just a small, square building with no windows and just one doorway. There wasn't even a door hanging on the framed doorway. It reminded Reinhold of the shelters in the fields

---

[11] *Scheiße* is German translates to 'shit' in English

for the animals except this was a smaller shelter for humans. They crouched in the shadows, listening.

"He's sleeping." Reinhold finally announced.

"Are you sure? He was talking a minute ago."

"Listen. He is snoring." They both listened for a minute. "He must have been talking in his sleep. We should go now, before he wakes up."

Before Lisa could respond, Reinhold crept away from the building toward the trees, covering the open ground in a kind of duck walk. They went far enough into the orchard to keep from being seen then they filled their back packs with apples. It took only a few minutes. There were lots of apples still on the trees. The shortage of people to harvest them was obvious. They each ate two, savoring the sweet, luscious fruit, before they started back toward the tracks.

They crept past the sleeping guard as quietly as they could. Once on the tracks, they ran a little way to put some distance between themselves and the scene of the crime. They traveled in a kind of guilty silence to their section of the tracks. Reinhold was calming down, happy to be near home, thinking they had gotten away with their petty crime when the air raid sirens went off. They both fled to the cover of the trees on the western side of the tracks, the only true barrier separating them from Blüchereiche and home. They watched silently as people streamed out of their houses, looking up at the moonlit sky, judging whether they had to flee to their backyard bunkers.

"*Verdammt!*" Reinhold cursed to himself. Lisa looked at her little brother, surprised by his very adult response. "Now we are stuck here."

Lisa understood what he meant. If they tried to make it home with their backpacks full of apples, they would be caught. Their neighbors would know they had been stealing. Some wouldn't care, they would turn a blind eye, but there were a couple that would report them. Reinhold wasn't sure what the punishment was but he was pretty sure it would be bad. Lately, people who had been caught stealing had disappeared from the town. No one knew what happened to them. Reinhold was hoping now that it was a false alarm and no planes would show up to put on a show for the people standing outside their homes on Blüchereiche. After a few minutes of no action, they would get bored and cold and go back inside their homes.

"*Verdammt!*" he cursed again when he heard the droning of engines.

Would they ever be free of these infernal raids? It was getting very cold and he was tired. The searchlights went on, trying to track the planes. There were a few bursts of machine gun fire. Somewhere to the north, closer than was comfortable for Reinhold, a bomb landed with a deafening explosion and a tremor. And then they left. A few minutes later, Reinhold and Lisa were back in their small kitchen, peeling apples.

"They are looking for something, a munitions factory." Lisa told her siblings how she had overheard the *Braunenpatie* people talking about it in Lübeck. "That's why the British keep bombing here. They are hoping to hit it but it is underground. They planted trees and grass on the roof so no one could find it." She looked around at the windows in the kitchen. "Is that what happened to the windows?"

All Reinhold and Isolde could do was nod.

Chapter 11: Schluesselblume

Die lichter von Bremerhaven,
Sie leuchten für uns bei nacht.
Die lichter von Bremerhaven,
Sie haben uns gluck gebracht[12].

Reinhold sang in a deep, rich voice as he and Isolde walked through the fields surrounding Ratekau. He wasn't sure where he had heard the song, one of the field hands at the farm probably, but he liked it and wondered when he sang it if he would ever see these *lichter von Bremerhaven*, the lights of Bremerhaven, that bring such luck.

It was a lovely spring day in May. The world was coming to life in shades of green and brown but it was yellow the children were after today. The *schluesselblume*, a short plant with very green leaves that sent up tall flowers, was in bloom. These flowers resembled the shape of a trumpet and were yellow with orange specks on the interior side of the petals. During the spring, there were whole fields of them on the outskirts of Ratekau, like yellow blankets covering the earth. They were very resilient to temperature and fluctuations in rainfall, making them excellent cut flowers. Reinhold got the idea to cut lots of these flowers, bundle them into bouquets, and sell them in Lübeck to the city people.

He figured the whole plan would take three days to execute. He and Isolde would gather the flowers today. They both carried the round wooden baskets they used for harvesting peas and potatoes. The plan was to cram as many flowers as possible into their baskets today before Reinhold went to Walter Muuss' to milk the cows. Tomorrow, they would sort the flowers into bundles and secure them with small pieces of wire that their neighbor, Herr Wagner, had given them. The following day, they would walk to Bad Schwartau and get on the train to Lübeck.

Once in Lübeck, they would position themselves near the train station on a bridge over the Trave River and sell their flowers to people entering the city from the west. Reinhold didn't know how

---

[12] "The lights of Bremerhaven, they light up for us at night. The lights of Bremerhaven, you have brought us good luck."

much money their flowers would make them, but he was hoping it brought in something. The price of goods like soap and cloth was increasing every day and ration tickets were enough to cover their need. They had to resort to the black market for some items. Any money they could make was a bit of a relief.

"We should do different sizes." Isolde suggested on day two of their operation.

They were sitting at the kitchen table, surrounded by yellow flowers in jugs and bowls of water. The blooms were truly beautiful today. A night inside in the warm air of the kitchen had caused the buds to open. It seemed every stem was bursting with yellow flowers.

"Just small ones and large ones." Reinhold answered. "The small ones will be six flowers and the large will be ten."

They spent the next couple of hours plucking stems out of water and tying them with the bits of colored wire, twisting them up tight, but not so tight that the stem was bruised. Once assembled, the bouquets went back into the water to await their trip to Lübeck. Their stepmother took a great deal of interest in the children's project.

"She just wants to see if what we are doing will bring in any money. That's all she cares about. Oh, and those damned soldiers." Reinhold said when Isolde pointed out that she was watching them.

The following day, Reinhold and Isolde left the house just after dawn headed for Bad Schwartau. They decided to take the tracks because it was faster and easier than walking along the road. They made good time even though they were burdened with their baskets of bouquets.

"How much are we charging for the flowers?" Isolde asked as they walked.

Reinhold thought for a minute. "Fifty *pfennig*[13] for the big ones and thirty *pfennig* for the small ones, I think."

By midmorning, Isolde and Reinhold were standing on a short bridge over the Trave River. It was an old bridge, maybe hundreds of years, and was decorated with pitted and scratched stone sculptures of soldiers wearing uniforms that included skirts and swords. Reinhold guessed that they were supposed to be defending the city from enemies. The bridge entered the oldest section of Lübeck right in front of the *Holstentor*, one of the original stone city gates.

---

[13] A *pfennig* is the German equivalent of a cent.

From their position, they could watch the trains pull into the station on the western shore of the Trave and the people disembark. Throngs crossed the bridge onto the island that held the main town of Lübeck. Many were wearing the *Braunenpatie* uniform. Many were country people looking to sell goods and merchandise. One old timer had wooden clogs for sale while another old woman had the first mushrooms of the season. Reinhold noted that he and Isolde were the only ones with flowers.

Few of the people that passed them on the bridge were businessmen wearing tailored suits. These people reminded him of the big man who used to come to Ratekau to sell his wares door to door. He was a nice man with pockets full of candy for the kids. It dawned on Reinhold that he hadn't seen that man in a couple of years. He wondered briefly why he stopped frequenting Ratekau. Then their first customer of the day approached them to look at their flowers.

"How much for the flowers?" Questioned the man in the *Braunenpatie* uniform.

He had a bandage on his right hand and walked with a limp. He had a pretty young woman with blonde hair and a frayed dress at his side, her gloved hand tucked into his elbow.

"They are fifty *pfennig* for the large one and thirty *pfennig* for the small ones." Isolde answered him.

"I want a big one," said the girl, pointing to the larger bouquets.

"You heard the lady, one large bouquet, please."

The soldier made an elaborate and overly dramatic display of handing the flowers to the young lady by bowing in front of her with a flourish. The lady giggled and accepted her gift of yellow flowers graciously. They started to leave when something the woman said caught Reinhold's attention.

"I wish there was a place to buy a purse. Mine is awfully worn out."

Her tone was wistful, accepting of the state of affairs regarding her purse but something about that simple statement got Reinhold thinking.

The thought plagued him all day. They sold out of their bouquets after only a couple of hours and headed for home and still Reinhold's mind churned. How does one make a purse? Could he make a purse? He thought he could but he would have to enlist the help of his neighbor.

"We made fifteen *mark*!" Isolde announced on the train home.

She was very excited by their accomplishment but all Reinhold could think was how much more he could make if he sold purses. How much could he charge for a purse?

"We should do this again before all the *schluesselblume* are gone." Isolde suggested. Reinhold nodded absent mindedly.

Three days later, Reinhold and Isolde were back in Lübeck, standing on the bridge, selling their bouquets of bright yellow flowers. They increased the amount of bouquets they had to sell by half and were looking forward to making more money.

"Mama is just going to take it from us again." Isolde grumbled as they waited for their first customer of the day.

When they arrived home after their previous trip, their stepmother was waiting for them. She figured out what they were up to and demanded 'her share' of the money. By her share, she meant all of it.

"I don't know why you told her how much we made." Isolde scolded Reinhold. "We could have kept some of it."

"I know, I didn't think she was going to take all of it." Reinhold was shocked by their stepmother's greed.

Reinhold shoved his stepmother out of his mind so he could concentrate on the goal at hand. He had decided he was going to try to make purses. His neighbor, Herr Wagner, had suggested Reinhold use the colored wire from the airplane factory.

"Nobody is going to buy anything ugly." Herr Wagner warned him. "You should look at the purses that the women are carrying, use that as a guide for making yours. You won't have the same materials, but wood can be shaped into almost anything and I have a bunch of old plywood you can have."

Reinhold looked around at the women walking by. They all carried some kind of purse with them. Some were bigger than others, some were bright colors, most were black or brown, some were simply carried in the hand, some had a strap that went across the shoulder but they were all the same design. They were rectangular in shape with two sides and a bottom, covered in some material, it varied by purse, and held together at the top by a fastener that could be opened and closed. It was really simple and Reinhold was sure he could make them. He could use the plywood for the sides and cover the whole piece in the colored wire. He was going to need a lot of that colored wire. He wondered how he could make the bottom.

During his purse peeping, Reinhold noticed something else: there were many people carrying satchels, dirty, burlap or canvas satchels that seemed stuffed with things. Looking at the people that carried these bags, the boy noted that they appeared to be out of place and dirty themselves. They wandered without a direction or goal. They milled about on the bridge, stopping to look over the side at the Trave flowing past or sit on the railing. When they spoke, Reinhold didn't understand all of what they said. They weren't speaking his kind of German. Many of them had their hands out as if they were hoping someone was going to give them something. When an older gentleman in a highly decorated *Braunenpatie* uniform stopped to buy a bouquet from them, Reinhold asked him who these people were that seemed so out of place.

"Refugees." He answered with a snort of disgust.

When he saw that Reinhold didn't quite understand what he meant, he elaborated saying, "They are refugees from the east. They are fleeing the fighting, the war. They wouldn't be staying. Once we crush the Soviets, they will all go back where they came from, to the east. *Heil Hitler!*"

Reinhold had no choice but to respond in kind with a halfhearted "*Heil Hitler!*"

"We made twenty six *mark*!" Isolde exclaimed on the train on the way home. "Too bad the *schluesselblume* are almost all gone. We could do it again. Next year we should start earlier."

"I have another idea, one that will make us more money."

He briefly recounted his design idea, using wood to form the body and the colored wire to decorate and hold them together. Isolde listened quietly.

"How much do you think we could sell them for?" She asked when he finished.

"Herr Wagner thinks we could get ten mark for one. He is going to get more wire for us."

Isolde's eyes lit up at the possibility. They chatted happily about their new endeavor for the rest of the brief train ride home.

"How much did you bring home today? Another fifteen *mark*? It looked like you had more flowers this time."

Once again, their stepmother was waiting for them and, once again, Reinhold handed over everything they had made.

"Why did you do that?" Isolde asked him, exasperated.

"I don't know. Maybe if we give her the money, she'll stop hitting us."

"Oh. Well, ok."

The children got started immediately on the purses. Reinhold started by cutting the wood frames, round pieces roughly ten inches in diameter, out of the old plywood. It took a couple of days, a few tries, and some additional help from Herr Wagner but eventually they made a decent looking purse that also functioned properly.

The finished product was circular with tightly woven rope sides. The wood was covered by an attractive and colorful patchwork of green, yellow, red, blue, and white woven airplane wire. The purse was attached to a short shoulder strap of braided wire. The result was actually quite festive and lighthearted. Somehow, it reminded Reinhold of the beach. They knew they were done designing and would be able to sell the finished product to women when their stepmother demanded she have the first one.

Word quickly spread that Reinhold and Isolde were making colorful new purses. All the ladies on their street came by the house to take a look at them. Several placed an order for one. The children took Herr Wagner's advice and sold to the local ladies at five *mark*, which was much more than most could spend on something as frivolous as a handbag.

"Charge the city people more. They can afford it." He told them with a wink.

His wife and daughter got their purses for free in exchange for the wire and the plywood. By the time they were done with the orders, someone watching Reinhold's deft hands would have thought he had been making women's handbags for more than a few days.

"We should get some mushrooms, too, before we go to Lübeck."

Almost month after they began, Reinhold and Isolde were ready to go sell the dozen or so purses they created to the women of Lübeck. Reinhold was a bit nervous. The local women loved their new purses but what if the city women didn't like them? They would have wasted a lot of time and effort and a trip to the city. He wanted to take something else to sell, but the flowers were gone and it was too early for any produce from the fields. The peas wouldn't be ready for another couple of weeks and they didn't fetch high a price at a *pfennig* a pound. Reinhold remembered Lisa telling him that their mother used to go into the forest before dawn to gather mushrooms. Mushrooms were always a big hit. Isolde shrugged her indifference.

"What are these you have here?"

Reinhold and Isolde were back on the bridge over the Trave facing the *Holstentor,* selling their mushrooms and purses. The mushrooms attracted their first customer of the day, an elderly gentleman in an expensive looking suit. He had already paid when the purses caught his attention.

"They are purses, for ladies." Isolde answered him.

"Ah. Yes, very clever. Did you make them yourselves?"

"Yes, sir."

"I think my wife would appreciate one of those. She has been complaining that her purse is wearing and there is nowhere to purchase another. Is that wire you used there? She probably won't like that it is not leather but who has leather nowadays?"

The old man walked away with his mushrooms and purse, lamenting the condition of his shoes and the lack of leather.

The mushrooms went faster than the purses but it wasn't long before all their merchandise was gone. Reinhold's nervousness had been unwarranted.

Chapter 12: Brown Shirt, Black Short Pants, And A Scarf Tie

It was early afternoon when Isolde and Reinhold headed for home. They were thrilled with the money they made, one hundred and thirty *mark*, but Reinhold was not as happy as he should have been. It was Wednesday, which meant that he had to go to his weekly *Hitlerjugend*[14] meeting. He sighed heavily. He hated those damn meetings. He hated getting dressed in the uniform, a brown shirt and black short pants with a scarf tie. He hated marching around the town like a *dummkopf*[15].

It had only been a month since he was force to join the organization. An older boy dressed in a black uniform came to the house and spoke to his stepmother. Reinhold recognized the boy as one of the *arschlocher*[16] he saw around town harassing women and kicking old men in the butt. He brought a package with him that contained a new *Hitlerjugend* uniform for Reinhold. He informed Olga that Reinhold had to wear it to every meeting. She, in turn, told Reinhold that now that he was ten years old, he had to take his place amongst the defenders of the Aryan race. When he asked what an Aryan was, she had told him to shut up and not ask questions. All that mattered was his membership in this group. If he didn't show up for meetings, they would both be arrested.

He dressed in the new uniform and went to his first meeting only by force, his stepmother dragging him there by his shirt, hitting him with her damned stick to whole way. He wasn't the only one who had to be beaten into submission. There were several other boys, some of them Reinhold's close friends, who were red eyed and marked by the hands of their mothers.

Reinhold would never forget his first experience with the *Hitlerjugend*. The commanders, one of whom was the black uniformed teenager that came to Reinhold's house, were young men with bad reputations in Ratekau. These youthful commanders explained, for the benefit of the new members, that they trained in the *Schutzstaffel*[17] and were put in charge of this branch of the

---

[14] *Hitlerjugend* was the organization known today as the Hitler Youth.
[15] *Dummkopf* in German translates to 'fool' in English.
[16] *Arschlocher* is the plural of *arschloch* and translates to 'assholes'.
[17] *Schutzstaffel* in German translates to Protection Squadron or defense corps. It is

Hitlerjugend. They were going to teach the group how to be good soldiers, and therefore, good Germans.

They lined the boy soldiers into rows three across to march. The marching began near the old church and was supposed to continue until they did a circuit of the entire town. This meant there was an hour and a half of marching to be done before they could be released for the night. It wasn't long into their drills that some of the younger boys became fidgety and uncooperative. The ranks became disorganized and the pace slackened to the point that they looked like a wandering group instead of disciplined soldiers. No matter how much they yelled and threatened, the commanders couldn't get the ranks back in line and moving together.

Disgusted and frustrated, the commanders directed the disorganized group to the local police station. The site of the station got the attention of most of the boys. There had been too many disappearances recently, too many whispers of raids on homes. Just the day before someone had been asking what happened to the old postman. Most of the town was afraid of the police, especially boys like Reinhold who stole something from someone almost daily to feed himself.

Once they organized the ranks again in the dusty yard in front of the imposing stone building, the commanders vanished inside. They emerging a few minutes later with a large, dark, well groomed man in a *Braunenpatie* uniform, a cigar clenched between his teeth. He surveyed the haphazard rows of boys silently. Reinhold perceived the air to change, to get colder and his heart started pounding.

"Why are you boys giving your commanders trouble?" The dark man asked. No one answered. "You do understand that it is your duty to participate in this program, to give it all your efforts, in order to keep the Aryan race strong?"

Again, no one answered. Finally, the man directed his question to a small boy in the front row. Reinhold recognized him from school. They were the same age.

"Is there something you feel is more important than your responsibility to your country, your culture?"

The boy went white. He started to shake visibly. Reinhold felt bad for him, being singled out and asked such an unfair question.

---

abbreviated SS.

None of the boys his age gave a rat's ass about this Aryan race they kept hearing about or the *Hitlerjugend*.

"Well?" The large man in the *Braunenpatie* uniform barked at the trembling boy.

"We just want to play." The boy finally answered in a hoarse whisper.

The man lifted his right arm and back handed the boy across the left side of his face. The impact sent him flying backwards to land on his back. Blood trickled from his nose and mouth.

"You can play when you are dead!" The man bellowed. "You are Germans, now act like it!"

The experience left a bad taste in Reinhold's mouth. What did that even mean, acting like Germans? Now, sitting on the train from Lübeck, he felt apprehensive about his *Jugend* meeting that night. There was a bright side though. At least he didn't have to milk the cows. He would also see his friends, Bernard, Kule, and Heinilaken, that he didn't see that often. Tonight, he would suggest to them that they go to the beach to have fun and forget about the *Hitlerjugend*.

The shirtless man on the *Brandenburg* traced a welded seam in the rail with his finger, feeling the imperfections of the joining. The metal was so hot from the sun that he fancied he could embed new patterns in it using just his finger.

Reinhold remembered that night well, that *Hitlerjugend* meeting after selling purses in Lübeck. They marched through the town as they always did, but something was different this time. He noticed there were more people like the ones he had seen in Lübeck, the type the old man called refugees. It had become usual in the past couple of years to see the odd stranger or two passing through town. But, this was more than one or two. There were dozens of men, women, and children loitering in the town center, near the church, and the school. They looked lost and helpless. They were dirty and scrawny with clothing more ripped and tattered than Reinhold's own. Some, their skin drawn and sallow, looked like they were on the verge of falling over dead.

As they marched back into the schoolyard, Reinhold noticed one boy in particular was attracting a lot of attention. He was standing under one of the tall oak trees that separated the schoolyard from the street with a big pack on his back. Herr Klausen was standing not far from the boy, he had his hands held up in front of him palms out.

Reinhold could tell even from across the distance that he was speaking in a low pitch. Men from the town were slowly closing in around the tree from all sides. It looked to Reinhold like they were trying to catch an animal, which seemed odd because the boy was neither very big nor very scary. He was only a bit taller than Reinhold.

"*Entlassung!*", called one of the commanders to his boy soldiers, signaling the end of their meeting. The boys broke rank. A few started to wander over to see what was going on.

"What is that boy doing?" Bernard asked.

"I don't know." Reinhold answered right before it dawned on him what was happening.

As he got closer, Reinhold realized that the boy was carrying another person on his back, stuffed into his backpack. It wasn't a small person, either. It was a fully grown adult. He could see reddish blonde hair spilling in a tangled mess over the shoulder of the boy. The men closing in were trying to coax the frightened boy into taking his backpack off. They were telling him that everything was going to be ok, they weren't trying to hurt him, they wanted to help. Reinhold took a few more steps forward, and then the smell hit him. It was the horrible, rancid, overpowering smell of death and decay.

Oh my God, he thought, *that woman is dead! Why does he have a dead woman?*

He watched as Herr Klausen moved closer to the boy, slowly, right up to his side. The boy just trembled in place, not saying a word, tears running down his grimy face. With the help of several of the men, Herr Klausen removed the boy's backpack. No sooner had they laid it on the ground then the boy collapsed, sobbing and screaming.

Reinhold couldn't make out everything he said but he caught that the woman was the boy's mother and that she had died almost two weeks ago. He didn't want to leave her on the road for the animals to eat. Reinhold tore his eyes from the scene, disgusted. He admired the boy's fortitude but the woman was dead! He wondered what he would have done in the same situation. It didn't take long for him to conclude that he would leave his stepmother to be eaten by wolves.

"I certainly hope you will be in school tomorrow, Reinhold. I haven't seen you for a couple of weeks. And, from what I understand, all of you in the *Jugend* will be leaving us for six weeks in July and August."

Herr Klausen had spotted Reinhold. Leaving the other men to tend to the boy, he approached his student. Still slightly disturbed by the scene, Reinhold simply nodded in response. He was rewarded by a smack in the head by the schoolmaster.

"I am not one of your friends. You answer me with words!"

"Yes, sir. I will be in school tomorrow. We leave for camp at Malente in two weeks." Reinhold answered.

"Good. We are meeting in the cellar now. There have been too many air raid sirens lately. But, not to worry, we will be learning to waltz!"

Herr Klausen loved a reason to play his violin for the children. A wagon pulled into the schoolyard, distracting the schoolmaster's attention. They took away the boy and his dead mother. Reinhold wondered briefly what would happen to the boy.

"Reinhold!" Kule was calling to him. "We are going to the beach. Are you coming?"

Reinhold, Kule, Heinilaken, and Bernard Muuss (no relation to the farmer) went to the beach that night. It wasn't his usual group of kids from Blüchereiche. He only saw Heinilaken and Kule at school or on *Hitlerjugend* nights. Bernard was a different story. He went to private school in Lübeck and wasn't seen around town much, only on *Jugend* nights. Reinhold liked this group for different reasons then he liked his gang from Blüchereiche. These boys were thinkers. The Blüchereiche kids were doers.

The boys took to the fields on their way to the beach to get vegetables for dinner. The peas and cabbage were ripe and ready for eating. They got fish from the boats coming in to the processing plant. But it wasn't as easy as it used to be, not that it was ever truly easy. There were several dozen people hanging around waiting for the nets to drop the crumbs. It was a mob scene when the first few fish hit the ground. People were grabbing and elbowing, but the boys managed to get themselves a small cod. They cooked the fish over a small fire and ate the vegetables raw.

"What do you think we'll do at the *Jugend* camp in Malente?" Kule asked once the meal was done. They were laying on the soft sand, staring at the stars.

"March." Heinilaken snorted in response.

The group laughed. Of course they would be marching.

"I don't know but I hope there is lots of food." Reinhold said wistfully.

"I hope I get to see my father before we go." Bernard said, his voice reflecting his internal concern about his father's whereabouts.

"Where is he?" Reinhold asked, surprised. He had never heard Bernard mention his father before.

"I don't know. He is a sailor. He fixes engines on ships. He could be anywhere."

"He gets paid to do that? To sail around on a ship, fixing engines?" Reinhold was fascinated by the concept.

Everyone he knew worked on a farm or in the town. There wasn't a lot of traveling. Bernard's mention of sailing stirred a memory in his subconscious. He had an uncle, his father's brother, who was a sailor but he hadn't seen him in years and years. He couldn't even remember what the man looked like. There were rumors that he jumped ship in India and never came back.

"Yes, that is his job." Bernard answered. "He has been to a dozen countries. Last time I saw him, he was coming back from America." The boy frowned slightly. "He said it was getting dangerous on the ocean. Lots of ships were getting sunk by the submarines."

"Damn war." Kule said, spitting.

With the exception of Bernard, all of their fathers were enlisted men fighting in the army. None of them had a letter in a long time. Reinhold's stepmother wrote to his father often. Once a week she would send Reinhold and Isolde with a letter down to the post box at the train station. On his way home, Reinhold liked to stop at the postman's house to milk his goat. The postman, as of when he disappeared, hadn't figured out who was stealing his goat's milk. Now that he was gone, so was the goat. He missed that goat, the milk, more specifically.

"Can anyone be a sailor?" Reinhold asked, his mind working.

"Yup. You just have to be picked."

"What do you mean, 'picked'? Picked by what?"

"By a Captain," Bernard elaborated on his point when he saw that Reinhold was still a bit confused. "My father says that the Captain picks his crew. There is a place where you go and apply for a job. Then the Captains come when they need someone and pick you. My father always gets picked." Bernard said with childlike pride.

Reinhold mulled this new information. He had only been farming for a year but knew already that he hated it. He liked the animals, particularly the horses. One of his favorite things to do on a Sunday afternoon was to go to the fields where the horses were resting for the day. He and his friends would ride the swift footed creatures bare back for hours, savoring the feeling of flying with the wind in their hair and pulling at their clothes. He didn't like the mundane aspects, the shoveling dung and hauling water. He hated harvest season. The only relief was joking around with the prisoners from the camp that the farmers hired to help bring in the crops.

Maybe I could be a sailor, he thought. *I could go see new things in faraway places.*

Reinhold fell asleep that night with thoughts of high ocean waves and distant shores playing in his head. He knew that it was impossible for him to leave his sisters and his home. But he allowed himself to dream that night.

Chapter 13: Malente

Two weeks later, Reinhold boarded a train in Lübeck with hundreds of other boys. He was wearing his regulation brown button up shirt, black short pants, and black scarf tie held in place by a shiny brass ring emblazoned with symbols that Reinhold didn't understand. His blonde hair was perfectly combed, there was not a strand out of place, his stepmother wouldn't allow it. He was headed to Malente, a town twenty miles northwest of Lübeck, for a six week training program as part of the *Hitlerjugend*. He and his friends joked the whole way there about what was going to be expected of them but none of them were really sure what to expect. They were a bit anxious about it. Very few of them had been this far from home before.

They knew the train arrived at their destination when it stopped but not because it stopped at a station. It simply stopped in the middle of a field. To the left of the train were green fields that ran to a tree lined lakeshore, about two hundred yards away. There was a unit of brown clad boys drilling half way to the lake. They looked like a miniature army doing maneuvers before a battle. To the right of the train were more green fields and a good sized, very old farmhouse with several large newer barns. A small herd of cows gathered at the fence near the farmyard, their tails swishing in the warm July air. More noticeable than the cows was the crowd of people near the cluster of buildings. The kids from the Lübeck area weren't the only ones attending this training camp.

The boys were ordered to disembark and assemble themselves by their town groups in the field. The train wasted no time in departing, chugging away in puffs of smoke to the west. Reinhold wondered briefly where it was going, what its next stop would be. Maybe he should have stayed on the train. How long would it be before someone noticed his absence? A call to attention by a black uniformed man brought Reinhold back to reality. He quickly explained that they would be sleeping in the barn and bathing in the lake. Reinhold shivered just thinking about it. That water was probably no more than 60 degrees. The first activity on the agenda for their first day, he continued, was marching.

The rest of the days in Malente were filled with marching and weapons training. Reinhold learned how to disassemble and clean a hand gun as well as a rifle. They made the boys practice until they could do it blindfolded. When they weren't cleaning the rifles or shooting them at straw targets, the boys marched endlessly with the weapons leaning against their left shoulder, the butt supported in the palm of their hand. They learned how to engage a hand grenade. The trick was to pull the pin and count to three, then throw it. They practiced with live grenades by throwing them in the lake. The first time the small, sticklike device exploded under water was great fun to the boys. In a matter of minutes the surface of the lake was covered in the fish that had been unfortunate enough to be swimming close by. By the end of the six weeks, there wasn't a fish to be had from that lake.

They also played war games, lots of war games. It seemed to Reinhold that every day he was in the woods, chasing and hiding from boys on the other team, trying to capture their base camp. When someone from the other team got in to close to him, Reinhold was expected to physically overpower them, to do anything to prevent them from getting away to safety. The boys quickly became good wrestlers and hand-to-hand combatants. Two weeks into the six week camp everybody was displaying the marks of these matches, some more than others. Reinhold had a black eye from an elbow to the face he took from a boy twice his size and a slight limp from twisting his ankle when he tripped over an exposed tree root while chasing a member of the rival team.

Internally, every muscle in his body ached from running, jumping, stretching, fighting, and crawling. He was one of the lucky ones. He had been fighting with the other boys in his town for as long as he could remember. There were lots of other boys who had never been in a fight. Reinhold could pick them out in the crowd because they were the most injured, the most beat up looking. They were also the individuals singled out by their commanding officers for ridicule.

At night, there were pranks to be played and to fall victim to, depending on how quick you were to figure things out. Reinhold only had to be woken out of a dead sleep once to have his ass shined with shoe polish to learn that he had to be proactive. The second time the perpetrators came to get him while he slept, he dumped water on them from the rafters of the barn. This scenario was far more amusing to Reinhold then the previous one. To his surprise, and the surprise of his victims, the commanding officer of his unit was quite proud of him.

"Good, Reinhold. That is how you outsmart your enemy. You have to be on your toes. You have to learn from what came before. You have to be quick and smart, like a fox." He was told the morning after the water incident. Then they punished him by sending him to the kitchen to peel potatoes.

And, of course, there were speeches. Once a week, people in black uniforms talked to the boys. It was the same crap they told him in Ratekau. The Germans were the chosen people. Everyone else was inferior. They had to be ready to lay down their lives for the fatherland. Jews were bad, the British were bad, the Americans were bad, everyone was bad and everyone was trying to prevent Germany from reaching its true potential. He was getting tired of this rhetoric. If they survived the war, the black uniformed men said, which was going to rage for as long as it took to win, it was their job as men to go forth and procreate, to increase the German population. But, only pure bred Germans were true Germans. Blah, blah, blah. Reinhold knew for a fact that he was a true German and that his great grandfather had come from Mongolia. These men just spewed *scheiße*.

Reinhold was very happy, and just a bit sad, when he found himself back on the train to go home. He was very conflicted and was not entirely sure why. What else could he do but go home, back to his life with his sisters and his stepmother? As they passed Ratekau, Reinhold wished that he could get off right here in his woods near the missiles and the prison camp. His house was less than one hundred meters from the tracks. He sighed. He would have to make the journey back from Lübeck with the rest of his unit of *Hitlerjugend*. It would be late afternoon by the time he got home.

"We are going to the beach. Are you coming?" Egon asked him as they walked back to Blüchereiche from the schoolyard in Ratekau where they had been dismissed from their *Hitlerjugend* responsibilities. "Everyone is going. It should be lots of fun tonight." He added.

"Sure. I'll go." Reinhold agreed.

He couldn't help but notice that the amount of refugees had increased again since they left for Malente.

That night, he was quite surprised when Abby appeared at the beach with a new boy. Abby was the youngest of the bunch and wasn't required to join the *Hitlerjugend* yet. While the rest of his friends were gone, Abby made friends with a refugee boy named Arnold. Arnold enrolled at their school along with a number of other new children. He said that he and his family had fled the fighting and pillaging to the east. He spoke German, not the same German as the Ratekau kids, but they could understand each other.

That night at the beach with the waves as a backdrop and the firelight flickering across the sand, Arnold held the other boys captive as he recounted stories of his plight. He saw things that none of them could imagine: fires, bombings, raping, murder, and people starving to death in the streets. He and his family were chased out of town after town by residents who couldn't afford to feed any more people. Reinhold listened intently to what Arnold said. He heard the horrible details, but it was the broader stroke that interested him. This boy, this refugee, had seen things, he had traveled and Reinhold was envious of him.

Chapter 14: War Comes

The man on the ship lit another cigarette, rolling it between his thumb and forefinger as he thought. Looking back, it seemed to Reinhold that things got bad for him, for his town, after his trip to Malente. Air raids increased in frequency. Lisa said, on one of her rare visits home, that the enemy was still looking for the munitions factory. They finally gave up on sleeping in their beds and went to sleep every night in the bunker. Coal was more difficult to loot from the passing trains. Everyone in town ran for the tracks when they heard the whistle. Half of the time they arrived to find there was no coal on the train. Food became even more scarce than it had been.

Reinhold never really had a problem stealing what he needed from the farmers around him, but the competition increased tenfold with the influx of refugees. The local creek where Reinhold and his friends had always been able to get a meal became overfished. The price of everything from sugar to butter to soap to flour increased and the amount allowed through the rationing decreased again. Money was becoming worthless. The price for a loaf of bread was somewhere near thirty *mark* and was increasing every day. That was more than the average person made in a month.

One day in February, out of desperation, Reinhold and his friends spooked the horse pulling the bread cart causing the animal to bolt. A little ways up the street, it crashed into another wagon, spilling its precious load. The boys were able to make off with a decent amount of good rye before the bread man arrived on the scene.

The icing on the cake was when his father's parents arrived from the east. They, like all the other refugees, were fleeing the fighting. They walked all the way from Silesia, Poland. It took them weeks, but they made it to the safety of Ratekau. They were grudgingly given the bedroom downstairs by his stepmother. Isolde moved into the attic with Reinhold. She taught him a new game called Doctor, where they took turns taking off their clothes and examining each other. It made him a bit uncomfortable, but Isolde enjoyed it, so he played along.

The one bright spot came when he was nearing his eleventh birthday in March, 1945. He was awarded an apprenticeship with a mason in Bad Schwartau. This was good news! Now he wouldn't have to be a farmer. When he finished school at fourteen, he would enter the mason's union and have the full benefits of an apprenticeship. Reinhold was sure that Herr Klausen had arranged this for him.

A month later, the war was unleashed in his usually quiet corner of Germany. They heard through the gossip mill that it was not going well for the Germans even though the radio still broadcast shiny reports of victory. Less than a month left, they said, but the rumors of an impending surrender circulated with growing certainty. When the German soldiers fled the prison camp, dropping their weapons were they stood and leaving the prisoners unguarded, Reinhold knew it was over.

"We should go to the camp today." Reinhold told Isolde early the day after they heard the soldiers were gone.

"Why? There is not going to be anybody there."

"That's why. Maybe there is some stuff lying around."

Reinhold didn't have to elaborate any further. Isolde knew he wanted to go loot the place.

When they left, the soft pink dawn was brightening the spaces between the treetops. They hadn't crossed the tracks yet when they heard a man yelling, the sound echoed through the crisp morning air. They didn't pause to try to listen to what he was saying. They were running down the incline to the Kuhlsee when the gunshot rang out, Reinhold instinctively hit the ground, pulling his sister down with him.

"What was that?" Isolde asked.

"It was a gunshot; probably a rifle by the sound of it." Reinhold's time in the *Hitlerjugend* had given him an ear for weapons.

"Why was there a gunshot?" Isolde asked, nervous.

"I don't know."

It was the only answer Reinhold could give her. Just a couple of days earlier, stories had begun to be whispered between neighbors about people being killed for their food or clothing or valuables by the prisoners that were released from the camps further west. Many women had been raped and killed, more than several houses had been burned.

"Let's just get out of here quick, just in case."

They picked their way across the Kuhlsee and headed toward the prison camp, ducking from tree to tree. Reinhold's training during the war games was coming in handy. He scanned the forest with his eyes while he listened intently for sounds other than those of nature. After he determined that they were alone, he beckoned to Isolde to follow and they ran to the fence.

They slipped through the seam that Reinhold and his friends made three years before, grateful that no one had found it and welded it back together. The place was deserted. They moved like deer toward the three buildings, slowly, gingerly, alert, and ready to run at the slightest noise. The closer they got to the buildings, they more stuff they encountered scattered on the ground: rifles, jackets, boots, empty tins of meat and milk, and bits of furniture. Reinhold cursed to himself, someone had beaten them here. The camp had already been looted, probably by the prisoners before they left.

If his memory was right, Reinhold saw them bring a huge, shiny new stove into the middle building. That must be where the kitchen was located. He gestured to Isolde that he was headed that way. She nodded and followed after him, obviously not completely comfortable with actually entering the building.

They entered directly into the kitchen. It had been looted, as he expected, but not everything was gone. A lot of the portable canned goods were missing but there were huge tubs of butter and flour as well as dried, salted pork, bags of beans, and loaves of bread hidden on a shelf in the corner near the door.

"Look at all this food!" Reinhold exclaimed as he opened a tub of butter.

He ran his finger along the surface of the creamy yellow substance, scooping up a small mound to sample. He savored the taste for a minute before looking around to see what else he could eat. He quickly consumed half a loaf of bread, three pieces of salted pork, and a can of some kind of meat in brown gravy, washing it all down with a can of condensed milk. Isolde said nothing, she simply stood there in that white tiled kitchen with stainless steel tables and stoves staring wide eyed.

"We have to get as much of it home as we can before more people show up." Reinhold said.

"How? The containers are so big."

Isolde had a point. How were they going to get it home?

"We can bury it near the tracks." He suggested. "Then we can take it from there. No one will think to look for a buried tub of butter." Isolde agreed.

The man on the ship took a long drag from his Lucky Strike. That had been a good day for him. He and Isolde spent the morning dragging twenty five pound tubs of butter and sacks of flour from the kitchen at the camp to a field on the western side of the tracks, not far from where they were crossed by the road to Sereetz. They dug the hole with their hands, not wanting to waste time looking for a shovel. Once their loot was in the ground, they planted a stick on top to mark its location. Reinhold figured they could come back for it after they got their hands on a wheelbarrow.

It was not, as he learned, a good day for one of his neighbors. When they were done with stashing the food, they headed back toward town, cutting across the tracks to Blüchereiche north of their own home. This was where the people with more money, who worked for the state and the town, lived. The place was in a flurry of activity. There were people milling about one house in particular. Men were whispering amongst themselves and shaking their heads, a few women were crying silently into handkerchiefs. An official looking man in a suit was asking questions of a small group of people. Reinhold noted that they were the people who lived in the houses on this part of the street. He had seen them often enough in passing. A flat backed wagon was parked in front of the house. There was something on the back of the wagon wrapped in a white and red sheet. It took Reinhold a minute to process that it was a bloody sheet. What happened here? He thought to himself. He and Isolde stopped walking to observe the scene, looking for someone they knew. Reinhold spotted Herman Rehbein.

"Herman," he called, "What is going on here?"

Herman sauntered over to them. Reinhold had to control his urge to jump the boy. There was no need to fight Herman today. Reinhold currently had control of the Blüchereiche kids. He just wanted to vent his aversion to Herman's persona.

"This guy got shot." Herman stated flatly, yanking a thumb at the wagon.

"Why?" Isolde asked shortly.

She didn't like Herman either. He was always pulling her braids and calling her 'girl'. She particularly hated when he stared at her when they were all swimming in the Kuhlsee. It made her uncomfortable, so she said. Reinhold thought she secretly enjoyed the attention

"They say it looks like he tried to stop someone from stealing his pig. They think it was one of the prisoners they let out of the camp. The pig is gone." Herman summed up for them.

"That's what the gunshot was earlier, maybe." Isolde suggested. "When did he get shot?"

"Earlier this morning." Herman answered. "I heard a gunshot, too." He lowered his voice and added, "They say that a lady was kidnapped on the other side of town, over near Hauptstraße. They found her in the forest, half dead. They also went after Herr Zepoline. They were going to kill him for his cows but his workers stopped them."

"Who was going to kill him?" Isolde asked.

"People from the town here; people who weren't part of the *Braunenpatie*. They went looking for anybody that supported the war. They were going to kill them."

"*Verdammt!*" Reinhold snorted and turned away, toward home.

This is crazy, he thought, *all this violence for no reason.*

When he arrived at his door, he was surprised to see it opened for him by Lisa. She gave him a big hug and a kiss, telling him that he looked well. She actually sounded somewhat surprised, like she expected them to all be half dead. They sat at the kitchen table for a bit, chatting. She told him and Isolde about her eight mile journey home through the woods and the fields.

"I heard they were killing people on the roads. Someone said the Russians were raping women, any women they could get their hands on. So, I took the long way, through the woods. I left this morning and I just got here. It was a really long walk. I left the Frau of the house a note telling her that I didn't have to work for her anymore because the war was over. I packed my stuff and left."

They were just finishing their catching up when there was a knock on the door. It was a member of the *Braunenpatie* party. They were looking for Lisa. The women she worked for in Lübeck said that she had stolen a bunch of stuff before she left for home. They had come to arrest her.

"It is all a bunch of lies! She is just mad because I left her with no one to watch her children." Lisa adamantly defended herself. "And why would I steal cigarettes? I don't even smoke!"

Their stepmother stepped in, resolving the situation and preventing Lisa being shipped off to jail or having to pay restitution.

Later that day, Reinhold and his friends were in the woods playing on the missiles when Abby suggested they go to the camp.

"Come on", he said, "Let's go see if there is anything left."

Reinhold didn't mention that he had already been there. Once again, he found himself ducking from tree to tree as he approached the camp. This time the boys really played it up, giving each other signals and taking turns being the first to advance closer to the perimeter, using all the tactics they learned in the *Hitlerjugend*. Somehow, though, it didn't feel entirely like a game. After the mornings events in town with the pig and the kidnapped women, the boys figured there could be real danger lurking.

Where Reinhold had been focused on food earlier, the boys now got caught up in the weapons. There were rifles and handguns just lying on the ground. Egon was the first to encounter one, a Karabiner standard issue rifle. The boys had become all too familiar with this weapon during their *Jugend* training. Egon quickly checked and confirmed that it was still loaded. Taking aim, he shot at a knot in a tree outside the perimeter of the fence, fifty feet away.

"Whoa! That's not fair! You guys know how to use these!" Abby protested, a Karabiner held awkwardly in his hands. "Teach me!" he demanded.

The boys spent the rest of the afternoon teaching Abby to use a rifle and a handgun. They shot at everything that came across their field of vision: trees, leaves, logs, animals, birds, and random bottles that they placed on tree stumps and shot from as far away as they could. The real fun came when Willie found two boxes of hand grenades in an abandoned army truck. In impromptu trip to

Hemmelsdorfer See was quickly agreed upon but departure was delayed by the whistle of a train.

The boys took off for the tracks, hoping that there was coal on this one. It was the end of April so homes didn't have to be heated so much but before they knew it, winter would be here again. Reinhold's stash in the small barn behind the house was getting disturbingly low even though they used it sparingly this past winter. They, along with the three dozen other desperate people that showed up, were disappointed. This train had no coal. The boys left for the lake, spending a couple of hours tossing hand grenades into the murky depths and happily collecting the fish that rose to the surface.

Chapter 15: But The War Was Over

Reinhold spent the next several days with his friends, throwing grenades into lakes and shooting targets. They arranged a mock battle in a potato field that ended with Kule getting his thumb blown off. He held on to the hand grenade too long while deciding where to throw it.

Afterwards, someone suggested they go to the beach to relax. The weather wasn't warm enough for swimming, but the opportunity to get fish, and get away from disapproving parents with questions about why they were playing with hand grenades, was enough to lure them toward the shore. Fish was the one food source that didn't seem to be diminishing right before their eyes. They took their time getting there, scouring the countryside for edibles, shooting at animals and birds. Egon managed to get a rabbit but it was so small and emaciated after the northern winter that it was barely worth keeping. They were all counting on the fish the ocean would provide. Reinhold had even decided he was going to try fishing in the shallows instead of just waiting for crumbs to fall from the nets.

All their plans were replaced by something they didn't expect in their wildest childhood imaginations. The first thing they noticed, about a mile from the Timmendorfer Strand, was the smell. It drifted toward them on the breeze that flowed off the sea in a perpetual current. Looking skyward, the boys saw black smoke clouds in front of them. Something was burning, but it wasn't wood. It was like nothing Reinhold had smelled before but it reminded him faintly of the smell that lingered after the bombing of Lübeck. As they entered Timmendorfer, they were struck by the quiet that shrouded the village. The smell was stronger now, the smoke clouds blacker billowing higher into the sky. Reinhold couldn't help feeling a bit apprehensive. Something bad was going on. His gut told him so.

"Where is everybody?" Arnold asked.

As the boys advanced toward the beach, the quiet was gradually being replaced by shouting voices and the sounds of metal scraping across rock.

"Sounds they're at the beach." Willie answered him.

There was a new quality to the strange smell. Reinhold was afraid to admit smelled like death.

The boys were unprepared for the scene that they came upon when they reached the top of the dunes that sheltered the town from the ocean. Spread out before them like a scene from a story or an evil fairy tale was a beach littered with dead and bloated bodies, contorted in ways that were unimaginable in someone living. There were men, women, and children. Some were soldiers wearing uniforms, some were wearing what looked like black and white striped suits, some were clad in everyday street clothes, some were so scrawny that they looked like skeletons wearing skin suits. There must have been hundreds, thousands, of them stretching for miles down the beach in both directions.

Moving among them were men wearing cloths over their noses and mouths, leaving only their eyes and foreheads to express their grim determination. They were working in teams of two, carefully picking up one person at a time and moving them to one of the horse drawn sleds that stood at intervals on the sand. One of these sleds, led by a tired and drawn looking woman, slid almost silently past the boys, loaded with people on their way to where more men were lowering the dead into the ground. The woman didn't look up from the sand to glance at the boys.

"Oh my God!" Willie was the first to speak. "What happened here?"

"They're dead." Egon whispered.

"Look out there." Arnold said, pointing toward the sea.

Reinhold hadn't been able to tear his eyes away from the horrific scene on the beach but now he lifted his gaze to the ocean and was met with an even more ghastly site.

In the middle of the bay was a huge capsized ship belching smoke. It was the most bizarre thing Reinhold had ever seen. The bow was shoved sideways into the water, lifting the stern, the huge propeller spinning slowly, uselessly in the wind. The waves made the huge black hull look like it was undulating slowly on the surface of the sea. It gave the impression that the ship was sinking in slow motion but in reality, Reinhold knew, the bay was so shallow at that spot that the huge ocean liner would never sink. Several smaller vessels were shooting streams of water at the ship, trying to stop the fire that still burned somewhere within.

Around the ship from one side of the bay to the other was a gruesome coating of floating corpses. They bobbed along, the waves carrying them toward the shore to rest with the ones that made the journey before them. Reinhold felt his stomach drop to his knees, he was close to being physically ill, but managed to pull himself together.

"I thought the war was over." He croaked out. "Why is this here if the war is over?" No one answered him.

Egon, Willie, Abby, Arnold, and Reinhold stood on the top of the dunes, watching the men in the cloth masks carrying out their morbid task. They stood there for more than an hour, watching. The amount of bodies didn't seem to decrease; it actually increased as the waves brought in the victims the sea was slowly relinquishing. It was all wrong, Reinhold thought to himself. This wasn't supposed to happen here, at this beautiful beach, his place of solitude and freedom. This was stuff they told stories about around the camp fire. It didn't happen for real. His pristine beach would forever be tainted by this tragedy.

"Let's get out of here." He said to his friends.

He couldn't look anymore. It was horrible, gut wrenching. Those people had families that would never hear from them again. They would be placed in the mass grave in Timmendorfer Strand and, doubtless, other places around the bay and that would be it.

But the war was over, he reminded himself, bitterly.

A couple of days later a small detachment of the British Armed Forces came rolling into Ratekau with jeeps packed with soldiers carrying rifles at the ready. The jeeps were followed closely by several rumbling tanks. They experienced no resistance from the population of the small town and proceeded to set up a temporary camp in the town square near the school. Reinhold went to look at these British people and was somewhat surprised to find that they didn't have wolf's heads and claws on their hands and feet.

I knew that was all a bunch of scheiße, he thought to himself.

His thought was confirmed to him when one of the British soldiers gave candy, delicious chocolate, to the children that came to gawk at the drab green and brown tanks piloted by strangers.

"Where do you think he got the chocolate from?" Willie asked as they slowly savored the foreign delectable.

He and Reinhold were sitting on the low wall that surrounded the church, watching several dozen British soldiers carrying out various tasks in their camp. Both boys could hear the other's stomach rumbling as clearly as he could hear his own.

"They must have their own food with them. I wonder where they keep it."

Reinhold looked around the camp. There was no kitchen or any provisions to be seen. He knew they had food because he smelled them cooking over campfires but where were they keeping it?

The British were very careful with their actions in front of "enemies" in "occupied territory", so it took the boys several days of watching to figure out where they kept their provisions. In the meantime, Reinhold saw lots of things they had that he would like to have: tools, tents, clothes, blankets, soap.

"It is on the tanks!"

Willie had gotten to their watching spot before Reinhold. He saw the soldiers take their breakfast out of compartments built into the tops of the tanks.

"The chocolate is on the tanks?" Reinhold asked.

"All the food is on the tanks in that box, there along the side." Willie pointed to one of the tanks to illustrate his point. Reinhold looked where he was pointing and saw the metal boxes on the tank.

Verdammt, he thought to himself. *Getting that chocolate wouldn't be anywhere near easy.*

As his eyes scanned the camp, something else caught his attention. Off to the left side, along the perimeter, near where the soldiers usually parked their Jeeps, there was a tire still on the heavy metal rim. Reflexively, Reinhold's eyes scanned the camp to do a head count. There were only two soldiers visible. One was obviously sleeping under a tree near the tanks. The other was cleaning his weapon near the fire. The rest were out, moving from home to home, searching for weapons. They had been to Reinhold's house just yesterday, starting in the sparsely furnished attic and working their way down to the empty root cellar. They didn't find Reinhold's guns. He was smart enough to stash them in the woods. His stepmother would have beaten him to death if he brought a gun into the house.

"Come with me." He said to Willie as he walked away.

He wanted that tire. He could sell it to Arnold's father, the gypsy.

As they walked along the unmarked but somehow understood perimeter of the camp to where the tire was lying unprotected,

Reinhold could see that the two soldiers were the only ones he had to worry about. There were no others lurking in the shade of the trees or the tanks. These two soldiers were not paying attention. When they got near the tire, Reinhold decided to go for it.

"Grab that tire." He told Willie.

Willie didn't think twice about it, he did what Reinhold told him and grabbed the tire, reaching his fingers under the tread to get it upright. Reinhold did the same. Between the two of them, the heavy tire was upright and rolling away within seconds.

"Keep a lookout," Reinhold hissed at Willie as the bounced the tire through town, "Make sure no one sees us. They'll steal our tire."

The town center was deserted so the boys had nothing to worry about. The residents of Ratekau stopped hanging around in town when the British moved in, even the refugees found better places to be. Most of the residents only left their homes when necessary. Reinhold and Willie rolled the tire down Hauptstraße to an unnamed guesthouse where they knew the black market thrived.

"You stole this from the British?"

The man asking the question was a tall, dark man in his forties with lots of stubble on his lined and tanned face. He was a gypsy, a tradesman in the post war black market where people sold and bought everything from false teeth to automobile parts to slabs of meat. Because of his connections with other gypsies, it hadn't taken him long to set up his illegal business in Ratekau. He was looking from the tire and rim to the two boys with a strange grimace. Reinhold couldn't tell if he was angry or happy.

"Yes, sir, we stole it from the camp in town." Reinhold answered him. He was surprised when the man started laughing.

"You must be good thieves to get a tire away from an army."

The man laughed again, saying something in a rapid foreign language to the equally tall, dark, and grimacing man next to him. They both laughed again. Reinhold was getting uncomfortable. He was suddenly afraid they were going to turn him in or take the tire without paying him. He was just about to say something when the first man spoke again.

"I'll give one hundred and fifty *mark* for the tire and rim. Sound good? It is a good price for a good thief."

Reinhold was dumbfounded by the amount. All he could do in response was nod and hold out his hand for the money.

"If you get anything else from the army, you come see me." The gypsy told him after he had counted out Reinhold's money.

The boy watched as Arnold's father loaded the tire into the back of his recently acquired car. It was one of the only cars in Ratekau. Reinhold couldn't help being a bit envious of Arnold.

The man on the ship in the Caribbean chuckled to himself. It had been an audacious move on his part to steal that tire. He still remembered the look on Willie's face when he handed him seventy-five *mark* for his help. The money and the reaction from the gypsy was all the positive reinforcement Reinhold had needed to try for the ration box on the tank. That morning's heist had taught him that there were not always enough soldiers in the camp. Apparently, when business drew them abroad they left only a couple of men to stand sentry.

For the next several mornings, Reinhold sat on the low wall near the church, waiting for his opportunity but it didn't come as he thought it would. Now, when the soldiers left they appointed more than two people to stay behind, some times as many as five. He couldn't help but think he may have had something to do with this decision. Maybe that tire was more important to them than he had thought.

Food was almost non-existent in Ratekau by the summer of 1945. Even the rationing had broken down. The bread wagon no longer came around to deliver the much needed sustenance. Farmers were guarding their fields more intently than previously. People were so desperate that they were attempting to steal produce that wasn't even ripe yet. Reinhold's desperation led him to try for the ration box even though there were four men in the camp.

"We have to be quick." Reinhold said to Willie and Egon, his partners for this crime.

The soldiers were having their afternoon meal around the fire. Reinhold figured it was the most distracted they were ever going to be. They snuck quietly toward the camp from the east. The tanks were positioned in a semi-circle, starting at the west and arching north to the east. They went to the first tank they encountered. Egon stood lookout as Reinhold got up on the tank and opened the box. He almost shouted with joy when he saw the goodies it contained: chocolate, dried milk, dried meat and vegetables. He quickly started handing it down to Willie, who shoved it into a backpack. They got all the food packed up and Reinhold closed the top to the box, like they were never there. He closed it a bit too hard causing it to make a harsh, loud metal on metal sound. He didn't need Egon's warning to tell him that the soldiers had looked to see what made the noise.

Cursing himself, Reinhold took off after Willie and Egon who were already several steps ahead of him. They ran down Hauptstraße, to Bäderstraße, and hung a left past the cemetery. Over the blood pounding in his ears, Reinhold thought he heard the high pitched droning of an engine. He glanced over his shoulder to see that two of the British were coming after them on motorcycles.

Verdammt! He cursed to himself.

"Faster! They are coming! Get off the street!" he screamed to his friends in front of him.

Willie, in the lead, heard him and turned right, crossing Bäderstraße, with Egon right on his heels. They headed across a long field that ran parallel to the cemetery. Reinhold's legs were moving as fast as he thought they could until he heard a gunshot. When the live round hit the ground just ahead of him and to the right, he found a new burst of speed. He quickly overtook Egon and drew even with Willie.

"Faster! They are shooting!" He screamed at an already terrified Willie as more rounds hit the ground around them. Seconds later, they were at the tracks.

"Left!" Reinhold called.

The other boys followed his lead. They ran north on the rough gravel for about two hundred feet before Reinhold directed them into a stand of trees on their right. This part of the tracks had a hedgerow that ran along the eastern side. The hedgerow marked a drainage ditch. By heading into the trees, Reinhold hoped to lose the motorcycles long enough to make it to where the hedgerow started so they could take shelter in the drainage ditch. As they ran through the trees, the British were riding along the open terrain of the tracks, firing at them. Bullets ricocheted off trees all around them. Finally, they reached the ditch.

"Into the ditch!" Reinhold called.

All three boys disappeared into the three foot deep trench right before another burst of gunfire hit the trees. They huddled there, tucked into small human balls, arms covering their heads. The sounds of the motorcycles became steadily further away and the sounds of gunshots ceased all together. They heard the British shouting to each other. In his adrenaline fueled fear, Reinhold expected any minute to look up and see green clad soldiers standing on the rim of the ditch, aiming rifles at them. They stayed huddled for some time before they felt safe enough to move.

They headed back to Blüchereiche the long way, through the fields, staying a good distance from the tracks on the east side. Once they were standing in Reinhold's kitchen, they opened the backpack to see what they had almost died for. They each ended up with a good bit of dried milk, meat and vegetables, enough for a meal for their families anyway. They also got a tiny portion of coffee and a bar of chocolate each. Reinhold split his candy with Isolde, eating the bar one square at a time over the course of a week. It was the most delicious thing he had ever tasted. The partners in crime decided that it would best for them not to go near the camp again.

Chapter 16: How?

The rest of 1945 brought no relief from food shortages, no increase in opportunities to survive. Reinhold's work at the farm was instrumental in keeping his family from starving. Frau Muuss often sent him home with an extra bit of grain in addition to the milk he earned. Lisa and Isolde went out every day looking for food in the forest: mushrooms, wild birds, game, fish, field greens, nothing was turned away and everything they brought home was eaten. The chickens, rabbits, and pigeons that the family had relied on for years as a source of protein were exhausted. There was no way to renew the supply.

The harvest festival in the fall was a particularly giddy one. Walter Muuss had returned from the war just in time for his farm's harvest party. And what a party it turned out to be! Everyone was celebrating the crops and the life it would ensure but there was also a kind of tension breaking. After the unpleasant events, harsh conditions, and hard work of the summer and autumn, people just wanted to have some fun. Reinhold couldn't remember if he knew the punch was spiked when he had his first cup, he just remembered it being delicious and fruity with chucks of apple floating in it. It was the first time he got drunk. It was also the first time he got very sick from drinking. He slept in the barn that night with the cows periodically waking to empty his stomach.

1946 began with less enthusiasm than 1945. At least at the beginning of 1945 the war still on and the radio was still broadcasting hope and victory. Now, there was no radio. There were no laws. There was no food. There was no moral majority to point out that unscrupulous traders were gouging people for needed goods. In a moment of weakness, Reinhold gave his stepmother the gold ring with the red stone the Russian officer gave him. All she could get for it was two blankets. Lisa and Isolde made these into coats for themselves.

There was no sense of safety. In a small town were no crime had ever happened, people were locking their doors day and night. Streams of prisoners from the camps still came through the town on their way east causing destruction as they went on their own search for food and vengeance. Thousands were turned away from Russian occupied East Germany and were forced to wander the countryside, terrorizing local populations while trying to find a place for themselves. The spring and summer passed with almost daily tales of woe from abroad. Reinhold and his friends had long since taken to arming themselves with the discarded military weapons when they were in the forests and fields but, fortunately, they never saw any danger themselves.

Even in the face of all this misery, things were about to get worse for Reinhold. He was in town selling the cigarettes he rolled from the tobacco he grew in the backyard when Herr Klausen found him.

"Reinhold, I am glad I found you."

Something in Herr Klausen's voice made the hair stand up on the back of Reinhold's neck.

"I have some bad news. Your apprenticeship with Herr Braun has been cancelled. His company has gone out of business. When you leave school, you will need to find something else to do." He paused for a second before adding, "I am sorry this didn't work out."

He gave the stunned boy a sympathetic pat on the shoulder before leaving him.

Reinhold's mind whirled. His apprenticeship was cancelled! The company was gone! What was he going to do? The prospect of spending the rest of his life as a farmer made his heart sink. All he could think of was the cows with their tails flicking crap in his face as he yanked on their utters, filling bucket after bucket with milk. The more he thought about it, the more claustrophobic he became. Suddenly the walls of the buildings were too close, people were too loud. He quickly sold the rest of his cigarettes so he could get out of the town. He wanted to go to the beach and watch the ships, feel his feet sinking into the cool sand, hear the waves crashing against the shore.

He was leaving town by way of Bäderstraße when a car pulled up beside him, rolling along, matching his speed. Glancing up, expecting to find a disapproving adult glaring at him, Reinhold saw his friend Arnold's smiling face.

"Where are you going, Reinhold?" he asked

"The beach."

"Want a ride?"

Reinhold's spirits lifted immediately. He nodded eagerly and Arnold swung open the long, heavy door so he could scramble into the front seat. No sooner had Reinhold settled in his seat then Arnold's father slammed on the gas and took off down the road with two squealing boys. It was exhilarating!

"Let's take this way." Arnold's father said as he turned on to the entrance ramp for the Autobahn.

Twenty minutes later, the car dropped the two boys off at the beach with the driver promising to come back and get them later.

"Let's go climb the ship." Arnold suggested.

The wreck of the capsized ship still haunted Reinhold's beach but since Arnold had first suggested they swim to it and play on it, Reinhold had been able to look at it differently. Instead of seeing a smoking metal mass surrounded by floating bodies, he saw a playground, a good place to sit in the sun and relax, a metal beach in the middle of the bay. Every time they came, it seemed to get closer to the shore.

As a man in his early twenties looking back back at his early teens, Reinhold realized that those trips to the beach saved him. They helped him keep his sanity in an otherwise wretchedly unhappy world. He could have easily ended up like one of the many housewives in Ratekau that gave up and went out to their barns to hang themselves from the rafters. This thought made the man pause.

How many had killed themselves? Was it five, maybe six? He shook his head sadly.

He also realized that it was Arnold, the refugee, and his father, the gypsy, that saved him from a life of farming and obscurity. They had such wonderful tales to tell about their travels from the east.

"Why do you have to be a mason?" Arnold asked the following summer.

1947 came with nothing but desperation and anxiety. The boys' trips to the beach and the woods to get away from the miserable adults became more frequent. They woke up every morning with two goals in mind: to get done all the work that needed doing so they could earn their milk and grain. Secondly, to get out of Ratekau. Reinhold and Arnold adhered to these goals more strictly than others but they never lacked for company at the beach. Reinhold particularly liked when Bernard Muuss came with them. He liked to hear the stories about Bernard's father and his experiences on the ships.

"I don't know. What else can I do? I don't want to be a farmer. It is boring and disgusting." Reinhold answered.

He still had the idea stuck in his head that he could find someone else to apprentice for but it was looking more and more unlikely. There was just nothing going on. No one had any money to do anything. The other day he heard his stepmother say that she would be surprised if they rebuilt Lübeck in her lifetime. In her lifetime! That was an absurdly long time. What if Germany never came back? He had heard the old timers speculating about this very subject. They said that the recovery would be slow and would probably not get far before the next war broke out. The next war! The thought was unbearable to Reinhold. He didn't want to sleep in a hole in the ground ever again.

"Why not be a sailor?" Bernard Muuss asked as he drew patterns with his finger in the grime that had built up on the hull of the dead ship.

Reinhold felt the air sucked out of him, he had a brief vision of himself on the deck of a big ship wearing a wool coat over the sailor suit that his father had sent him a couple of years ago from some foreign country, staring over the railing at the waves that crashed around him. Maybe he would go to India and run into his uncle. He inhaled sharply, almost whistling with the effort.

"How?", was the one word he got out in response to Bernard suggestion.

"You have to get a sailor's book. You can probably get one in Lübeck. I think you have to be fourteen, though. I'll ask my father next time I see him."

True to his word, about a month later on another trip to the beach, Bernard told Reinhold everything he gathered from his father about becoming a sailor. They were laying on the hull of the capsized ship

"You have to go get a seaman's book. You can get one when you turn fourteen, but your father has to sign a paper saying that it is ok for you to go on the ships to work." Bernard informed him.

"What is a seaman's book?"

"It is a book that you give the Captain of the ship you work for. My father said is like a passport, whatever that is. You can't be hired without one."

"Where do I go get a book?" Reinhold asked.

"My father says you can get one in Lübeck."

"That would be the life." Arnold said. "We could sail around, go from country to country, seeing what the world has to offer." He looked at Reinhold. "We should do it. You would never have to milk a cow again, as long as you lived."

Reinhold mulled this new information, saying nothing to his family about it. He was too young right now anyway. He still had seven months until his fourteenth birthday in March. He went about his work and schooling like a robot. He stole food to survive from wherever he could find it. He endured the increasingly violent and hateful attacks from his stepmother. Often, to avoid her, the boy slept in the barn at Walter Muuss'. Cows may not have been his favorite animal, but their company was more enjoyable to him than Olga's. The only thing keeping him from running away from his wretched existence was his friends and his dreams about sailing around the world. Arnold's words played continuously in his subconscious: "You would never have to milk a cow again."

On a cold, windy day in January, 1948, Reinhold was chopping wood in the backyard of his house. Sixteen year old Isolde had just gone inside to warm her hands in front of the fire. Something caught Reinhold attention. He stopped swinging and focused his vision southward on Blüchereiche. Through the yards of other houses, Reinhold watched an under dressed man with a broken bicycle approaching slowly, painfully. He continued watching without moving as the tall, skinny man turned on to the pathway of Reinhold's own house. With surprisingly little emotion, the boy realized it was his father. He had finally come home from the war. He caught the man right before he collapsed of exhaustion and dehydration on the front steps.

Lisa and Isolde experienced and displayed the emotion that Reinhold himself couldn't muster. After the boy helped his weak and emaciated father into the kitchen, the girls fawned over him like he was a child.

He practically was a child, Reinhold thought to himself. *He could barely walk, he could barely speak, and he couldn't lift his arms above his head. How did he even make it home?*

It was amazing to Reinhold what sheer determination could accomplish.

Over the course of the next several weeks, Reinhold the returned soldier told his family about his experiences during and after the war. He was captured in Italy in the winter of 1944. His captors, who he thought were Americas, sent him to a prisoner of war camp in the Caucasus Mountains. It was a swamp, he told him, a nasty, stinking swamp entirely ringed by high, sheer mountains where only the goats could get footing. The jailors didn't even bother to lock them up behind fences and walls because there was nowhere to escape to, nowhere to take refuge. The few who tried were swallowed by the treacherous swamp or shot as they tried to climb to the precipices. Their bodies were hauled back to the camp and hung on poles as a warning to others. Of course, he wasn't fed. But, he said, the worst part was the standing. They would stand for hours on end because there was no place to sit or lay down without getting wet.

"I feel like I have been standing for years." He said to his family as they tucked him in bed.

He remained in that bed for several months before he recovered enough of his strength to go back to work at the fish processing plant. He managed to get Lisa a job as well. Every morning, they set out for the four mile walk to work with Lisa near tears. She hated the factory, the smell of it. Every morning her father reminded her that if she didn't work, she didn't eat. That was the way of the world. When she got another job, she could quit the processing plant. It didn't make a lot of sense to Reinhold because no one in their town could afford to purchase food, no matter what their occupation. A loaf of bread cost ninety *mark*. They were better off foraging. At least that was free.

Two months after the return of his father, six days after his fourteenth birthday, Reinhold slowly approached his father's bedroom. It was the day he told his father he wanted to be a sailor. He had already discussed it with his stepmother. Two days earlier, he had approached her thinking he would be rewarded for his suggestion with a slap in the head and a stream of insults. Instead, she had been very supportive, which was somewhat more unnerving than her smacking him. She agreed that she would go to Lübeck and help him get his sailor's book, if his father would sign the necessary papers. It didn't take the boy long to figure out that she would do anything required to get him out of the house. Next, he had to convince his father.

"No." His father said shortly after Reinhold had explained the situation.

And that was the end of the discussion. Reinhold left the room dejected and angry. Who was this man to tell him what to do? Where had he been his whole life? Now he comes back and thinks he can just step right into the role of being a father? Reinhold snorted in impatience and defiance. He had done very well taking care of himself and the family while that man was gone and he didn't see why he needed his permission now.

The man on the ship squinted into the sun to gaze at the horizon. He could see an island taking shape, a small, mountainous piece of land jutting out of the sea. He wondered if he would have made it here, to where he was, and on the road he had traveled if it wasn't for his stepmother. The thought of giving her credit for anything was abhorrent to him, but they had had a common goal in that instance. He wanted to get out of the town before he got stuck being a farmer for the rest of his life and she wanted him out of the house so she wouldn't have to look at him anymore.

"We'll go to Lübeck tomorrow so be ready in the morning. You are applying for a job, so look presentable. Wear your suit." She had told him one night about a week after his father had flat out rejected his request for a signature on the appropriate piece of paper. Reinhold blinked at her in surprise.

"Why?" he asked, anticipating a smack in the arm with her stick for questioning.

"You want to be a sailor, right? Your father finally saw the wisdom of letting you go. He signed the paper today. So, tomorrow, we can go apply for your book, as you call it."

He was so amazed by this turn of events that he said nothing. The next morning found him up and dressed in his tweed brown, ill-fitting confirmation suit, ready to go before his stepmother was even out of bed.

"You actually went and applied for a seaman's book?" Arnold asked, incredulously.

"Of course. Why wouldn't I? What is there to do around here? Aren't you going to come with me?" Reinhold responded.

"I will." Bernard piped up.

"I will too." Arnold agreed. "You are right, there is nothing to do around here. Sailing sounds like a lot more fun."

"You should go apply soon. The guy at the office said it takes several weeks, sometimes months, to get the paperwork ready and completed."

Reinhold sounded very official as he said this. He felt slightly superior to his friends for having made the effort to get his sailor's book.

"They take your picture." He added.

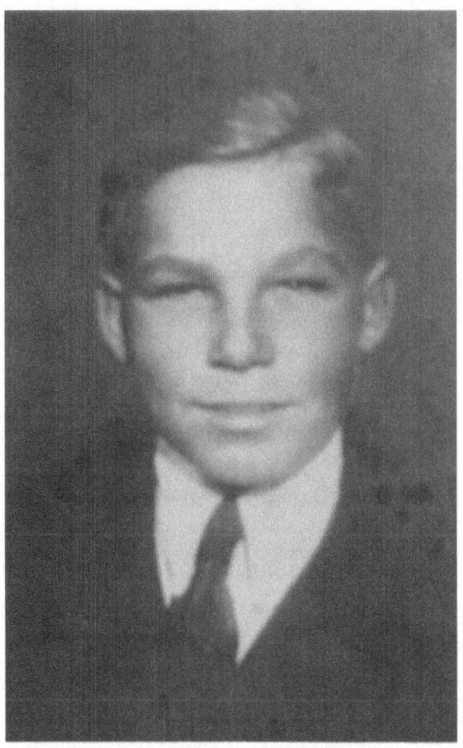

Reinhold at 14 years old
Photograph courtesy of Reinhold Scholz

Chapter 17: A Dog For A Cat

The rest of 1948 passed with little to no change in the situation for Reinhold. He worked on the farm that summer to earn food for the family. He farmed his little plot of land for vegetables. He went fishing and foraging. There was a bright spot in July when his seaman's book arrived. He spent the night lying in bed, thumbing through the empty, ivory colored pages of the vinyl covered book, wondering how many times it would be stamped. He showed his friends triumphantly. He was the first of the three that had applied to get his book.

The continued food storage was taking its toll on people. They had the look of hunger, sunken, glazed eyes and taunt facial features. Even the harvest didn't lighten the mood because it didn't increase the food supply. No one had anything left to barter with for food and farmers were keeping more for themselves than they had in the past, doling it out as they saw fit. Tension was running very high. Reinhold's own father snapped one day in the autumn when his wife's dog stole and ate a precious piece of bread.

"Why does that dog get food when humans can find none for themselves?" He questioned loudly as he stormed out of the house.

He returned a few minutes later, demanding his wife give him the little dog. Olga refused and an intense argument ensued. They fought for a good twenty minutes before the elder Reinhold finally gave up and wrestled the animal from her arms. He stormed out of the house again as she dissolved into tears on the kitchen floor.

Out of curiosity, Reinhold followed his father. He watched the man, clutching the dog securely to his chest, walk down a few houses to the Draves residence. The dog barked twice along the way but seemed to sense that this was just further enraging the man who held him hostage. The man met Max Draves in the backyard and handed over the dog, who promptly tried to bite this new tormentor. Without hesitation and maybe with a bit of revenge in mind, Herr Draves pinned the dog down to a stump used for splitting wood with one hand while with the other he slit the poor beast's throat.

Once the animal was dead, he removed the head, tied the back legs together, and hung the limp carcass from the roof of his wood shed next to what Reinhold quickly realized was, when it was alive, the Draves' fluffy, grey cat. For two days, those two grizzly reminders of how hungry people were hung from that roof. Once they were drained and skinned, Herr Draves gave Reinhold's father the cat while his family kept the dog. Even though Isolde and Lisa cooked it for hours, that cat was still tough when the family sat down on Sunday to eat it.

After that, Reinhold had the claustrophobic feeling again. Only when he was out and about in the countryside did he feel better, freer. His favorite place was still the beach. Even in October and November when the winter winds began to howl and the waves pounded the beach, he found solace there with the sea birds. His friends had gotten their seaman's books so he and Arnold decided to set a date to leave.

"We should leave after the new year." Arnold said, resolutely.

"That only gives us six weeks." Reinhold pointed out, frowning slightly.

"What are we waiting for?" Arnold asked. "We should just go and get it over with. Maybe there is more food on the ships." He frowned. "But, I should wait until after my father's birthday. He'll be forty-five on January 15th."

Reinhold's stomach growled at the mention of food. He hadn't had anything to eat yet that day and it was getting on toward evening. And why was he stalling? What was holding him back? His family didn't need him anymore. His father was home and working again as was Lisa. Isolde also joined them at the fish processing plant. The only one without a job was his stepmother. But, still something gripped him, prevented him from just going.

"Ok," Reinhold agreed. "We will leave two months from today. Where do we go?"

"Duh. Hamburg!" Arnold said. "That is where all the big ships go. There is an office there, like Bernard said. You go to the office and wait for someone to hire you."

Reinhold's heart sank a bit. "That's a long walk, to Hamburg."

"We can take the train, from Lübeck. That's not far away."

Arnold seemed to have an answer for everything that day. They parted ways, agreeing that they would leave for Hamburg in two months, which put them in the middle of January.

The agreed upon morning dawned dark, cold, and blustery. Reinhold was up well before the winter dawn. Sleep had eluded him.

He tossed and turned, wondering if he should stay, if he was making a foolish decision but the prospect of seeing new things outweighed his doubts. The prospect of never milking a cow again outweighed his fears. Finally, giving up on sleep, Reinhold got his clogs, extra socks, and his one other shirt into an old plywood suit case and waited in the kitchen, staring at the strange patterns the low burning fire made in the darkness. Arnold and Bernard were supposed to meet him at his house. If they were going to make the train from Lübeck to Hamburg, they had to leave Ratekau at five o'clock in the morning.

Five o'clock came and went without the other two boys showing up. He didn't ever really think that Bernard was going to go through with leaving but he was surprised by Arnold's absence. He was the one who had talked Reinhold into leaving!

"You have to go now if you are going to make it to Lübeck in time to get your train."

His stepmother pointed out after glancing at the clock in the kitchen. The tone of her voice almost dared him not to leave. She handed him fifteen of the new *Deutsche Mark*, enough to get him to the port in Hamburg. Then, without another word, she went to rejoin her husband in bed. Reinhold felt his resolve strengthen again at her obvious snub accentuated by his father's declination to get out of bed to see him off. Anger flooded his blood, leaving him short of breath and shaking. He would leave, and leave now, just to get away from that infernal bitch and that colossal *arschloch*! He kissed his sisters goodbye and walked out his door in Ratekau on to Blüchereiche, heading south toward Bad Schwartau.

Chapter 18: Hamburg

Reinhold remembered fuming his way to Bad Schwartau, cursing his father and stepmother with every step. How could she be so callous, so unconcerned, and so indifferent? He threw himself into a window seat on the bus. The trip to Lübeck from Bad Schwartau was brief and uneventful. Reinhold would have preferred to take the train, but they weren't running.

In Lübeck, he boarded the train to Hamburg, settling himself into a window seat to watch the countryside flash past. It was grey and brown and dismal in its winter clothing. The ruins of buildings and the sight of bomb craters in the middle of fields along the way added human heartbreak to nature's usual winter depression. The whole scene made him feel more angry, alone, and anxious. He was becoming apprehensive about what he would find in Hamburg. Hopefully, the port was open and functioning.

As the train sped closer to its destination, Reinhold's anxiety grew. The anger that propelled him out the door in Ratekau had dissipated. Butterflies began to flutter madly around his abdomen. Nevertheless, infused into his apprehension was a ribbon of liberation and exhilaration. He had done it, had gotten out of that house, away from that woman and that oppressive future. He was going to go see the world! He wondered what kind of a ship would hire him. What would the people be like? What would the work be like? Where would he go first? Asking himself these questions and coming up with fanciful answers helped him keep his anxiety under control, until the train reached Hamburg.

Reinhold was unprepared for the sight that met his eyes through the window of the train. His stomach tied itself into knots at his first glimpse of the famous city of Hamburg. There was nothing left. There was no city. It was rubble, just rubble. Everywhere he looked, there were destroyed foundations and huge piles of brick and mortar. Pieces of building lay around like a giant had sprinkled them like drops of water. There was not a complete building standing for miles in either direction of the train tracks. Off in the distance, he could see one tower standing, seemingly intact.

People wandered amongst the piles holding shovels and pushing wheelbarrows, dwarfed by the fallen pieces of buildings. Some hopefuls were picking over the remains looking for what, the boy couldn't imagine. What could be left? Nothing had been spared. The devastation went on and on from the outskirts of the city to the heart at the port on the Elbe River where the destruction was truly horrifying. In spite of the efforts to clean it up, there was twisted, melted metal everywhere forming shapes that made no sense to the eye. It was almost impossible for Reinhold to determine the former purpose of much of what he saw. Where once he assumed there must have been buildings, there was nothing, just an open expanse of burnt asphalt and the outlines of structural foundations that had gone up in flames. He was happy, however, to see that there were ships in the harbor and moving along the river.

Reinhold heard that Hamburg was bombed, but Lübeck was bombed also. This was so much worse than Lübeck. The destruction was utter, complete, appalling. How could men do this to their fellow men? How many had died? Were they ever going to rebuild it or at least get rid of the rubble? Where were all these people living? He couldn't help wondering. The bombing was years ago. He always heard that Hamburg was one of the biggest, busiest cities in Germany, possibly the world, but that was not what he saw as the train pulled into the roofless skeleton of a once beautiful train station. Where would he find somewhere to stay in such destruction?

Reinhold disembarked the train at the main station, not far from the river, thinking that he would be lucky if he made it anywhere at all. The streets were clogged by debris with only foot paths making them navigable. Before leaving the station, he paused momentarily to get his bearings. He had no idea where he was going. Looking around, he spied a police officer standing, shivering in the winter wind off the harbor, where the curb should have been.

Odd, he thought to himself as he approached the uniformed man, *that there is a police officer. What is he protecting?*

"Can you help me?" He asked when the officer turned to inspect him, taking in the ragged clothes, the hand hewn wood clogs with straw sticking out of them, and the small beat up plywood suitcase. Without waiting for the man to answer, Reinhold elaborated, "I need someplace to stay. How do I get to the port from here?"

"You can't stay at the port, young man." The officer answered. "There is a youth center in Altona. You can stay there. It's not far from the port."

"Where is Altona?" Reinhold asked.

The officer pointed him down a clogged street, saying that he would go up a hill. At the top he should start looking for a big cement building.

"It's a bunker. Pretty scarred, too. That is the youth center. You can't miss it."

Reinhold huddled into his thin coat and trudged along the narrow path between the piles of fallen buildings toward Altona, suitcase in one hand, the other shoved deep in his pocket. His eyes roved over the features of the city that were still standing. Somehow a red brick church with a domed spire and a huge clock had survived the bombing intact but heavily damaged. People gathered in the small courtyard that surrounded it, mostly women.

As he progressed further into Hamburg, he noticed groups of people clustered here and there, involved in conversation, hands flying in animated gesturing. Packs of ratty, dirty children roved through the rubble. In several spots, there were people lined up outside ramshackle buildings. He contemplated asking why they were standing on line, but thought better of it and kept walking in silence, absorbing the activities around him.

After one of the most uneasy miles of his life, Reinhold came to the big cement building the police officer had told him about. It was more than big, it was massive and ugly. It was just pitted and scarred grey concrete, lacking in windows and any frivolous adornment. It was taller than he had been expecting. His bunker at home was flat in shape and underground while this one was several stories tall. He figured he must be in the right spot because instead of adults loitering outside, there were children. Some were about Reinhold's age, some were younger, and some were older, barely passing for children in post war Germany. Gathering his courage, Reinhold climbed the steps to the bleak building and pushed open the heavy metal door. He was greeted inside by a large woman, sweating despite the cold.

The rest of his first night so far away from home, and alone, was a blur in his memory. He was shown to a big room with an arched ceiling. It was lined with bunks that were built into the interior cement walls. There were six to a stack and probably a hundred in the room, which comprised an entire floor. Reinhold was given a middle bunk, three below and two above. He had to wiggle into the cramped space like he was trying to shimmy under a fence. He imagined that the space was really no bigger than coffins he had seen. He just had the benefit of still possessing a child sized body.

"Supper is at 6:00 so you are just in time tonight. If you miss it, you aren't fed. And it is not free."

The woman waddled away toward the stairs yelling that it was time to eat. A small flood of young adults followed her to the roomy but cheerless dining area on the lower floor. Since he had about a *mark* left from the fifteen his stepmother gave him, Reinhold decided to follow the woman and eat too. The only part of the meal he remembered was potatoes, lots of potatoes.

During dinner, he questioned the other boys about the location of the port. The response to the questions was, in essence, follow the hill down toward the river and you will find the port. When Reinhold asked if anyone knew anything about the sailor's office, no one responded. These city boys were engaged in other employment interests, the construction industry mostly. They were friendly enough, but Reinhold couldn't help feeling a bit out of his element, a bit defensive. These boys had a different way of looking at the world.

The next morning, Reinhold awoke before dawn and headed for the port. He followed the directions he got from the other boys and went downhill, toward the river. He could see the taller ships and the looming metal cranes long before he actually reached the water. Standing on the industrialized, yet weirdly empty and burned, northern bank of the Elbe River, Reinhold surveyed the vast harbor. He had no idea it was so large, so encompassing. In every direction, there were docks and piers with ships of all sizes and makes moored to them. Several larger ships were anchored not far from where he stood. Twisted and blackened metal girders that were once cranes for moving cargo lay half submerged in the water on the opposite bank. There was already a crew of people out with blowtorches, trying to tame to the metal mess.

The boy on the cusp of manhood, who had at times in the past felt so large, never felt so small. He had a momentary sick feeling in his stomach but he scolded himself out of it, remembering what awaited him at home should he fail to find employment. That was if he could even get home. He spent all of his money getting here. He had to find that sailor's office before he lost his nerve and ran back to Ratekau. He willed his feet to move toward what he thought was the main area of the port. Nervously, his hand went into the pocket of his jacket, feeling the vinyl backed books, reassured by the promise of their presence.

Walking along the shore, Reinhold watched the ships moving in and out of the harbor. They were graceful, gliding through the waves, their wakes flowing out behind them, causing the river to lap at the piers and docks. The movements of the ships seemed very peaceful to him, tranquil almost, but there was a flurry of activity on the shore and on the ships still docked. On every deck, there were men working with ropes and metal lines, hauling and lifting and climbing masts. As he walked, he tuned in to their shouted communications but couldn't make out any one line of conversation in particular. Cranes painted bright colors like red and yellow moved huge containers from the shore into cargo holds with little effort but a great amount of metal on metal grinding noise that seemed to carry for miles across the water in the cold morning air, echoing in the distance.

Reinhold took his eyes off the river and the ships to look where he was headed. He had to find the office. Just ahead, positioned on the water's edge, was a long stone building with several domes in the roof and tower at either end. Next to this structure was a smaller stone building with a single dome. As he got closer, he saw that the smaller building was badly scarred, chucks were missing from the stone and the windows were boarded. He also noted that this was the entrance to a tunnel for walking under the river. He wondered briefly if he would have to use that tunnel today. Was the employment office on one of the many islands he saw in the river?

The long building was much grander with smoke blackened domes positioned over large arched doorways that bore the name Bruckes. A large section of it was missing, like a wrecking ball had swung and taken the stone and masonry with it, leaving just a gaping hole right down to the ground. Looking through the doorways, Reinhold saw just the river on the other side. He wondered what was supposed to be there. A large, two dozen or so, group of people were clustered around the arched doorway at the far end of the building. He directed his feet toward them, spying an official looking man in a navy blue jacket complete with gold buttons and matching pants standing off by himself at the head of the group.

"Can you tell me where the sailor's employment office is?" Reinhold asked.

The man looked at him for a second, taking in his bedraggled appearance, before answering. He seemed slightly surprised by the question.

"Just on the other side of this building here there is a white wooden building. It is small, just one room. That is the sailor's office." The man paused, still looking curiously at Reinhold. "You are looking for a job?" Reinhold nodded in response. "Good luck." The man replied, genuinely it seemed, before turning to his group of people to call them to attention.

A small red passenger boat pulled up to the concrete retaining wall, a break in the rail opened, and a wooden plank was thrown out to bridge the gap over the water. Reinhold watched curiously as the people filed out to the boat and walked carefully across the plank into the boat. Once loaded, it moved away slowly, leaving the uniformed man standing on the shore, waiting for the next group of travelers to assist. Reinhold shrugged and turned in the direction of the sailor's office.

Chapter 19: A Farm Boy, Huh?

The building was easy enough to spot. It was very simple, shabby even, after the impressive stone building with the domes and arches. He strode towards the door, facing his future from the outside. All he had to do was walk in, which he did, and was instantly greeted by the hard eyed stares of three dozen other men. They were sitting in metal chairs organized in rows. Quickly, anxiously, Reinhold's eyes swept the room for some kind of person in charge. He found an office at the front of the room, to his right. The old man sitting behind a desk inside the office gestured for Reinhold to come to him.

"You are looking for work?" The man asked in his gravelly voice before Reinhold had a chance to saying anything.

"Yes." He replied.

"You have a book?"

Without answering, Reinhold pulled his black vinyl seaman's book and a smaller passport book from the pocket of his jacket and handed them to the man. He watched as the man opened the book, noting that he was moving strangely. It took a moment for him to realize that this man was missing an arm. The sleeve of his dark grey wool jacket was neatly folded at the elbow, the cuff pinned to the shoulder. He couldn't help but stare. He had never seen someone missing an arm before. If the man noticed Reinhold staring, he ignored it and set about asking a series of questions a few of which were really just confirmations of what was contained in Reinhold's sailor's book.

"You know that this book is your passport to enter foreign countries for the purpose of work and only for the purpose of work?"

The man held up the smaller of the two books that Reinhold had handed him. Reinhold nodded.

"Do not lose this book. There is a special disclaimer in here that allows Germans to enter the United States, France, Britain, and Russian as sailors and only as sailors." The man looked sharply at Reinhold to make sure he understood before continuing.

"You are from Ratekau?" he asked.

Reinhold nodded, "Yes."

"You are fourteen years old?"

Again, Reinhold nodded, "Yes, almost fifteen."

"You applied for your book and passport in Lübeck?"

"Yes."

"What kind of work have you done in the past? What kind of experience do you have?"

Reinhold thought for a moment. "I have worked on a farm, milking cows, and picking vegetables, digging up potatoes. I can cook. I can clean. I can sew. I mean, I can mend my own socks."

Reinhold stopped there, blushing under the intense scrutiny of the one armed man. He felt for a brief moment like the cows on the farm when the farmer looked them over for sickness or injury.

"A farm boy, huh?" The man said gruffly. "We don't get many farm boys here."

He made several notes on a piece of paper in front of him then handed Reinhold back his books.

"Take a seat. You have to wait. The Captains come here and chose their crews based on what they need and your prior experience. Do not be surprised if it takes a few days to get a position, if you get one at all."

Reinhold exited the office and surveying the larger room, looking for a good spot to settle down, noting that it lacked any kind of adornment. Not even a picture hung on the walls. As he walked toward the back of the room he was struck by the diversity, and amount, of the men waiting. Some were young, his own age probably but not nearly as stocky. They stared hostility at him as he crossed the room.

City boys, Reinhold thought to himself with just a hint of disgust.

There were also more than a couple of old timers. These were hard, grizzled looking men that Reinhold quickly decided to avoid. In between these two extremes was a sprinkling of middle aged sailors dressed to work, managing to appear relaxed and anxious at the same time. Reinhold found an empty metal chair and settled into it wait. When the office closed at two o'clock in the afternoon, he wandered back to the youth center to wait for the next day.

Three days later, Reinhold was sitting in the sailor's employment office. Once again, he had risen before dawn and headed to the port to sit in the bland room and wait. The one armed man recognized him, nodding in greeting and acknowledgement. Over the last three days, Captains, all kinds of Captains, had come and gone, hiring men, but they didn't choose him. One, on his second day there, questioned him but had not picked him, hiring one of the old timers instead. No matter how many Captains came and went or how many times the one armed old guy gave someone orders for a ship that came in over the radio, the number of men looking for work didn't decrease. As men were hired and left others took their places. The population of the room held steady at around thirty people. Reinhold would not allow himself to become discouraged by the waiting. He would not go back to Ratekau in defeat.

Reinhold already learned to like, to love, his freedom. Over the last few evenings, he had strolled through the wrecked city of Hamburg, watching and observing everything. He saw the magnificence of the architecture that survived the bombing and the struggle to clear away the rubble. He witnessed the acts of kindness and the deeds of desperation carried out by the residents, both young and old. At the youth center, his pocket knife provided him with free meals. All he had to do was peel potatoes. This was a fine arrangement for him. At least he didn't have to dig the tubers up first. His talks with the other boys, broadened his mental scope, allowing for other points of view. The defensiveness he felt the first night was replaced by a general sense of self-preservation. The other boys also taught him not to trust without justification.

The door to the office opened, a cold draft rushed into the room, rousing Reinhold out of a bored stupor. He glanced up to see a wall of a man entering. This guy was easily one of the biggest men the boy had ever laid his eyes on. Most striking was his lack of a neck. His head sat square on his shoulders. The man crossed ponderously to the little office in the corner, greeting the one armed man with a handshake and a slap on the back. They had a quick exchange that ended in both of them looking in Reinhold's direction.

"Reinhold Scholz!" The one armed man called.

Everybody in the room turned to look at him as he walked down the aisle and into the office. He felt a blush spread up his neck to his forehead. Once inside, he stood there, waiting to be addressed further.

"This is Captain Hermann of the *Eos*. He has a couple of questions for you." The one armed man gestured to the big man.

Reinhold looked at the imposing figure of the Captain, waiting for the questions. He figured that Captain Hermann had to be in his fifties, his face was creased and red with wind burn, where it wasn't covered with a thick, black and grey bread. He was dressed in the same manner as the fishermen Reinhold saw on his many trips to the beach: wool navy blue jacket with the two sets of buttons and a big collar, black dungarees, and black leather boots stained with salt. A black wool hat covered his enormous head.

"Karl tells me you can cook and clean. Is this true? You know how to work?"

Captain Hermann barely moved his lips when he spoke, his words coming out more like an animal growl than anything human.

"Yes, sir. My stepmother taught me how to cook and she made us do our own cleaning, laundry, and sewing." Reinhold answered. "We even did her cleaning." He added, somewhat bitterly.

"You have worked on a farm? Milking cows and harvesting crops?"

Captain Hermann made no attempt to hide that he was assessing Reinhold's physical ability. Once again, the boy felt like a cow being assessed by the farmer.

"Yes, sir."

The Captain Hermann grunted something to the one armed man named Karl.

"You can return to your seat." Karl said.

Reinhold left the room, returning to his seat. A moment later, he was called back to the office.

"I want you to come work on my ship." Captain Hermann said.

Reinhold felt a thrilling rush go through him. A job! A real job on a real ship!

"Yes, sir." He replied, hiding his childish glee.

"You will come with me now."

The huge Captain turned to Karl and shook his hand, slapping him on the back again. It was official; Reinhold was employed by Captain Hermann of the *Eos*. Without another word, he left the office. Reinhold glanced at Karl, who nodded goodbye to him, then followed the Captain out into the blustery, January day.

Chapter 20: Captain Hermann and The Eos

Eos
Photograph courtesy of 7seasvessels.com

I was never so scared, thought the sailor on the ship in the Caribbean with a self-indulgent smile. *I am surprised still today that I went and didn't run home.*

The Captain led the way down the shore to the west. They passed several new sets of piers and the roped off construction site of another. The Captain said nothing as they walked and neither did Reinhold. They came to a stop about half a mile from the sailor's office along a stretch of wrecked dock space. Out in the middle of the river, at the head a large island, was a small, grey ship with three naked masts laying at anchor. The Captain let out an ear piercing whistle.

"That is my ship, the *Eos*, out there. One of my deckhands will come get us." The Captain explained in a clipped growl. He looked hard at Reinhold and asked, "You know how to whistle?"

"Yes."

Reinhold demonstrated his whistling abilities which, after the Captain's, were pretty dismal.

"That is no whistle. You better learn to whistle. If you are here on the shore and can't whistle, then no one will come to get you."

As the Captain finished this first of many lessons, a small, battered, wooden boat floated up to the dock, bumping to a stop against the concrete. It was piloted by a huge, scary man with a dark, bushy, wiry beard and a cloudy left eye.

"Reinhold, this is Dirk, one of my deckhands."

The scary man with the beard nodded at Reinhold, grunting something in the form of a greeting. Reinhold, unsure what to do and greatly unnerved by the look and manner of the man, nodded in return.

The Captain motioned Reinhold into the small boat. The boy climbed down the metal rungs set in the concrete, gingerly stepping into the boat. The Captain followed and off they went. The small boat was propelled through the water by Dirk working a single oar back and forth. Reinhold was surprised, and fascinated, by how fast a single oar could move the boat with three people in it. Before he had time to absorb the mechanics of the single oar technique, the small craft was bumping against the grey iron hull of the *Eos*.

The first thing that struck Reinhold about the *Eos* was its obvious age. This was not a new ship. There were rust stains running down the side, staining the thick paint. Several patches were visible.

The second observation Reinhold made was the ship's height. The deck of the ship didn't sit very far off the water, three to four feet at the most. He could have scrambled over the rail without using the short ladder. It would have been no different than getting into the coal cars back home. But, since it was there and this was his first time on board, he went up the four slick, frozen rungs of the metal ladder and swung his leg over the rail, landing lightly on the worn wooden deck of the ship. Thank goodness he had gotten a decent pair of real shoes before he left home. He couldn't even imagine doing that in wooden clogs.

The third feature of the ship that struck him was the height of the masts. He leaned back to look towards the top and had the sensation that he was falling backwards.

"Forty feet they are, those masts, not including the lightening rod." Captain Hermann informed him, heading toward the back of the ship. "Follow me. I'll show you where you will be working."

They walked between two white wooden buildings with small windows to a small, brown building with small windows on all sides. It was made from the same wood as the deck and had the same salt weathered patina. The large man opened the door and motioned Reinhold inside, closing the door behind him.

"This is the wheelhouse. Do not touch anything in here unless you are instructed too." Captain Hermann looked hard at Reinhold again, this time to make sure he was understood. Inside the building was all kinds of equipment that Reinhold had never seen before. Actually, the only thing he recognized was the wheel with the spiky handles. He knew that was for steering the ship. In the corner, there was a tiny table covered in maps and papers. The Captain led him through this room out the door on the opposite side. They emerged near a door that went into one of the white buildings. The Captain led the way down an incline into the galley.

"This is the galley. You'll be working here, cooking food for the crew. It is your responsibility to make sure the food is served on time and that the galley is cleaned after every meal. The first mate will wake you at five o'clock in the morning. You get the stove going and make the coffee first, then get breakfast made. Then, you clean this place until I can see myself reflected in the metal." Captain Hermann informed him, his gravelly voice echoing slightly off the metal.

Reinhold looked into the galley. It was a short narrow space the size of a larger kitchen table lit by several brass oil sconces. The whole space was the same dull shade of grey as the exterior of the ship with the exception of a few wooden cabinets that sat mounted high on the wall to the right above a small sink and a bench that ran along the left side. The sink was fed by a hand pump bolted to the counter. At the end of the room was a large, black stove much like the one Reinhold had used at home. It was only missing the chipped enamel coating.

"A coal stove." He observed aloud. The Captain nodded at him.

"I'll show you where to get the coal. First, let me show you the rest of your duties." The Captain exited the galley and opened a door to the other white building.

"This is my cabin. You will clean it every day. Sweep, make the bed, dust, whatever you have to do to make it clean. And you will always knock before entering." Again, he looked hard at Reinhold to make sure he was clearly understood.

Reinhold looked around the room. It wasn't very large, ten feet by six feet, with the same grey iron walls. There was a brown couch along the wall to his right and a couple of blue upholstered chairs sat around a wooden desk to his left. In the corner, near the desk, was a coal stove. On the floor was a dark red carpet, worn almost threadbare. Directly across the room from the entrance was a pair of paneled doors. The room was dully lit by the weak winter sun coming in through the small windows.

Without commenting, Capt. Hermann exited to the deck, ignoring the icy gust of wind that threatened to knock Reinhold right off his feet. He followed the big man to a big metal box painted the same grey as everything else. It was positioned under the windows of the wheelhouse. The Captain opened it, cursing under his breath. There was almost no coal in the container.

"This is the coal box. If no one tells me that it is getting low and we run out, then there is no heat and no hot food on this ship until we get to a port."

He slammed the lid loudly, the sound of metal on metal making Reinhold wince. Turning he surveyed the deck. There was a guy greasing what looked like the winch of the middle sail and Dirk was leaning against the rail, waiting to be called to the shore. No one else was in sight.

"The deck and all the fixtures have to be cleaned daily. Every time we go from the sea to fresh water, the ship has to be washed. A fresh coat of paint is applied as soon as the last coat is finished. Follow me." Capt. Hermann ordered, heading toward the bow of the ship.

The deck was comprised of a series of wooden platforms surrounded by walkways. The platforms were elevated about two feet and there were panels built into the wood with hooks set about ten feet apart on alternating sides. Reinhold followed the Captain down the left side walkway. The wood made a hollow sound as they walked. He wondered how they lifted the panels to get the cargo below. They looked heavy. Set in the middle of the platforms was the second of the three masts. The guy, who couldn't be more than sixteen years old, greasing the winch for this mast sneered at him as they walked past, baffling and unnerving Reinhold.

At the front of the ship, Captain Hermann stepped lightly for such a big man up another short ladder. Reaching down, he opened the hatch to reveal a ladder leading below deck, once again gesturing for Reinhold to enter. He scurried down the ladder, stepping to the side at the bottom to let the captain pass while he regained his vision in the dim surroundings. There was only one door. Swinging it open,

Captain Hermann said, "This is where you sleep. Just take whatever bunk is available. The others will be taken by the rest of the crew."

Reinhold looked into the room. It was a small room with a curving quality to it that mimicked the exterior bow. The walls were, of course, the grey metal of the ship's hull. There was no carpet on the grey metal floor nor were there any chairs or couches. There was, however, a strange stale smell that had been absent in the Captain's cabin. He wondered briefly about its source. A small potbellied, coal burning stove sat in the corner, a fire burning merrily inside, its pipe headed out to vent on the deck above. Along the walls were bunks, twelve of them. They reminded Reinhold of the niche he slept in at the bunker in Altona. Thinking of the bunker reminded him that he had left his suitcase with his few socks, wooden clogs, and a change of shirt there.

"I left my suitcase at the youth center, in Altona." Reinhold said quickly before he lost the nerve.

The Captain scowled at him. "You should go get it then."

He pulled a gold watch on a chain out of the front pocket of his wool coat. He flicked it open, scowling again.

"We leave for the other side of this island to load grain in one hour. If the ship is not here when you get back, keep walking down the river until you see it. Whistle and Dirk will come get you. Now, go, and be quick about it."

Reinhold hurried up the ladder onto the deck. He trotted back down the walkway to where Dirk was leaning against the rail, picking his teeth with a splinter of wood.

"I need to get back to the shore."

Dirk simply nodded and swung his leg over rail, jumping into the small, battered rowboat.

On the trip back across the river, Reinhold paid close attention to the movement of the single oar. Dirk seemed to be moving his hand in an exaggerated figure eight motion. The oar didn't leave the water, acting more like a fishtail than a real oar. Without the extra weight of the Captain, the boat moved all the faster. Once again, before he knew it, Reinhold was climbing up the frozen metal rungs of the concrete pier. He thanked Dirk with what he hoped was a manly nod and took off for the youth center.

It took longer to retrieve his suitcase than he thought. When he returned to the pier, the ship was gone.

Verdammt! He thought to himself.

Following Captain Hermann's instructions, Reinhold headed further east, staying close to the shoreline, avoiding a heap of crumpled metal and a roped off construction zone. He kept an eye trained on the river, looking for the *Eos*, hoping that he would know it when he saw it. He was quickly approaching a series of bridges that crossed one of the many branches of the Elbe to the small island where the *Eos* was going to load grain.

I wonder if I should cross, he thought to himself, eyeing the other riverbank.

Deciding against it, he picked up his pace to almost a run, passing the first bridge. Where the second bridge should have been was just a series of pylons and twisted, blackened metal. Reinhold shivered as a gust of wind ripped through his thin coat. Then he spotted the *Eos*. It was slowly approaching a third bridge, its masts lying horizontal across the deck and extending a few feet beyond the point of the bow. It made sense to him in that instant why the sneering kid was greasing the winches so thoroughly.

Reinhold broke out into a run, trying to cover the hundred and fifty feet to the next bridge as fast as he could, chasing the drab grey vessel like it was loaded with gold, or food. Captain Hermann spotted him from the deck of the ship and waved his arms to get Reinhold's attention.

"I'll go slowly!" He called. "Get on the bridge."

Reinhold sped along the shore, passing the ship, and tearing up on to the bridge. He didn't know what Hermann meant by "go slowly". He came to stop in the middle of the bridge just as the bow of the ship slid silently beneath him, cutting the murky water, sending ripples to the shores on either side.

"Climb down on to the girders!" Capt. Hermann called. "Throw down the suitcase! Hurry!"

Quickly, Reinhold judged that there were fifteen or twenty feet of clearance between the road surface of the bridge and the ship. Deciding against further thinking, he pitched his suitcase onto the deck of the slowly passing ship. He heard it hit with a loud, hallow bang. Thinking of the coal cars back home, he threw his leg over the metal fencing that served as a barrier, twisting so he landed on the other side facing the same direction the ship was headed. Gripping the cold metal, he started feeling around under the deck of the bridge with his foot for the first set of girders. Securing the first foot on a strip of metal, he lowered the second. He repeated his process once more before running out of strips of metal to stand on but still feeling like he had too far to drop on to the deck. Bending down awkwardly he grasped the cold metal girder securely with both hands before letting go with his feet, lowering himself. He was hanging, his feet dangling into empty air, hands gripping the cold metal, when he heard Capt. Hermann yell.

"Ok, now let go. Quick!"

And he did, falling a much shorter distance that he had anticipated, landing heavily on top of the wheelhouse.

Chapter 21: The New Deck Boy

Looking back from a more experienced position on a massive ship in the Caribbean Sea, Reinhold had to chuckle at his younger self. He could still remember the sensation of hanging from that bridge, the cold wind flowing around him, the site of the teak wood deck under his dangling feet. He remembered the stomach twist as he fell, the pain in his shoulder and hip as they hit the roof of the wheelhouse. Spying Max a few dozen yards down the gangway, Reinhold called him over. Max put down his paintbrush and bucket to sauntered over.

"How did you get on your first ship?" Reinhold asked Max, a smile playing on his lips.

Max looked confused for a brief second. This wasn't what he was expecting.

"What do you mean? How did I get on my first ship? How did I get the job?" Max asked.

"No, no." Reinhold shook his head. "How did you get on the ship? You walked up the gangplank?" He clarified his question for his befuddled shipmate.

"Well, yeah, of course. I walked right up on to the deck like I owned the damn thing. Then the First Mate smacked me in the head and told me to stop being so arrogant." Max snickered to himself. "That guy never liked me." He added.

"I jumped on to my first ship." Reinhold laughed again. He wasn't sure if it was the heat or the trip down memory lane, but he was feeling a bit giddy.

Max blinked at him, even more confused. "You jumped? Like a pole vault over the rail?"

"No." Reinhold answered looking past Max into the sands of time, still smiling. "From a bridge."

"Now I've heard some *scheiße* in my day," Max laughed, "but never has someone told me that the first time they got on a ship they jumped from a bridge. What? Were you stowing away?"

"No. I was late getting back from an errand. The ship was already on the move. I jumped from one of the bridges to Hafenstadt in Hamburg."

Max stared at him for a second trying to gauge whether he was being toyed with before asking, "Why?"

Reinhold shrugged. "Captain told me too."

"You're something else, Scholz, you know that, right? I have to get back to work before another First Mate smacks me in the head."

Max laughed as he walked away, returning to his painting. Reinhold's smile faded as he watched his friend settle down in front of the ventilator he was painting, the same one that caused them so much trouble on the Atlantic crossing.

His memory took a dark turn. Silently, contemplatively, he wondered what would have happened to him if he hadn't jumped on to that ship.

Would I have starved to death? He thought. *It was hunger and desperation that led me to jump.*

Slightly dazed, a younger, more naïve Reinhold rolled to the edge of the flat roof of the wheelhouse and jumped down to the coal box before landing on the deck. Captain Hermann strode over to him, clapping him on the shoulder, and grasping his hand enthusiastically. He was equally as frightening when he was happy was when he wasn't.

"Good job, Reinhold, good job!" Turning to the rest of the crew on the deck, he boomed, "Now, that's how you get on a ship!" A muttering of assent went through the few men. "Now, get your suitcase below board." Herman looked hard at Reinhold again before asking, "Are you hungry?"

"Yes." Reinhold responded limply.

His stomach tied itself into empty knots at the mention of food. He hadn't eaten anything yet that day and was sure everyone on board could hear the loud rumbling coming from his midsection.

"Get yourself something to eat. There should be something in the galley. There is a pot of pork and beans on the stove."

Captain Hermann turned back to his crew. They were slowly approaching a dock and he starting shouting orders to the crew. There was a scrambling of men moving in different directions.

Gathering up his suitcase, Reinhold headed down to the crew's quarters. As he traversed the length of the ship, he took notice of the crew he would be working with. They were a rough, wild looking bunch: bushy beards, squinting eyes, cigarettes and cigars clenched between yellow teeth, reddened and wind burned faces under ratty woolen hats, course voices spewing crude language.

Once below deck, he had no idea where to put his stuff so he simply stowed it in the corner. Standing alone in the room, Reinhold felt another wave of apprehension wash over him. He started to shake, reliving what he realized now was a terrifying drop from the bridge, and seeing the worn, sketchy looking crew. It was the thought of food that pulled him out of his emotional tailspin.

Things will get better, he told himself before leaving the room. *They have to get better. There is food here.*

Alone in the galley, Reinhold looked around the grey space. His eyes fell on a battered metal pot on the stove. Lifting the lid, he found the beans and pork. Instantly, his mouth watered. He opened the nearest drawer, winching at the sound of metal on metal. Inside there were several utensils, including a large spoon. Taking the pot and the spoon over to the worn and pitted wooden bench, he sat and ate. It was delicious! Before he realized it, the entire pot of beans and pork was gone. Reinhold was standing at the sinking, pumping water into the empty pot, when the Captain entered the galley.

"The men will be hungry soon. Give them the beans and pork for now. Starting tomorrow, you will be cooking. Remember the salted food has to be soaked overnight before you can use it."

He headed for the stove, not really looking at Reinhold until he realized the pot was gone.

"You ate the whole thing!" The Captain roared.

Reinhold nodded meekly.

"Then you have to make something else for the crew. And make it now!"

The Captain left the galley in a fury.

Make something? Reinhold thought to himself, a bit panicky. *Make something from what? Where is the food?*

He opened the wooden cabinets above the counter and found only pots. The drawers underneath the counter held only the utensils. Looking around, Reinhold spied a cabinet set into the iron wall of the bulkhead. Opening it, he was relieved to find a variety of foodstuffs: salt pork, salt beans, milk, eggs, bread, flour, butter, oil, mustard, salt, potatoes, and other staples of cooking.

What can I make with this? He thought to himself.

One of the first dishes his stepmother had taught him to make was an *Eierkuchen*[18]. It was easy and filling. He had all the ingredients so he quickly decided to make it.

Grabbing the eggs, butter, flour, and milk, Reinhold quickly whisked together a batter. He checked to make sure there was a good fire going in the stove but there wasn't. Nobody had stoked it today and the flames were flickering pathetically. To make the *Eierkuchen* he needed a really hot pan which meant a good fire. Grabbing the small coal bucket off the hook on the wall next to the stove, he ran to the coal box. Lifting the lid, he noticed that it was full almost to the top. Someone had gotten coal. Filling the bucket, he ran back downstairs.

Once the fire was burning hot, Reinhold poured some oil into the pan and proceeded to make a dozen thin, crepe-like pancakes. He stacked them on a plate he found in the cabinet. Surveying his work, he thought the cakes looked flimsy, not nearly enough to fill up a man who had been out working in the cold. Going back to the pantry, he pulled out a loaf of bread. Carefully, he folded the pancakes and stacked them between slices of bread, effectively making a kind of egg sandwich. He wondered briefly if he should add some mustard, but decided against it. Then it struck him that he didn't know how many people he was feeding. He went in search of the Captain.

"There are ten men on this ship, including yourself."

Running back downstairs, Reinhold made eight more egg sandwiches so everyone could have two, including himself.

He was still washing the pan when the first of the crew wandered in. He was a large man in his fifties with a bushy, graying beard below wind burned cheeks and nose. The man said nothing to Reinhold as he helped himself to two of the sandwiches and left. It occurred to Reinhold that he had no idea where they were supposed to eat. There was no table in the galley, just the bench. Trying to seem as casual as possible, he followed the man with the sandwiches up the stairs to the deck. He watched the man enter the wheelhouse and hand a sandwich to Capt. Hermann.

Reinhold wandered to the rail of the ship, still trying to seem casual. Several of the men headed below deck only to emerge a few minutes later holding a sandwich or two. Reinhold watched as they

---

[18] *Eierkuchen* is an egg pancake much like a crepe.

settled themselves on the deck. He quickly came to the conclusion that you eat where ever you wanted to eat.

Reinhold saw that the wooden panels had been pulled off the platform on the deck. A large pipe of sorts was dangling above the hole, spewing grain into the ship. Walking over to the platform, Reinhold looked down into the hull. It was just an empty space with grey iron walls half full of grain.

"...leave tomorrow if the weather holds. How many others are leaving? Do we have a large enough group?"

Capt. Hermann was emerging from the wheelhouse with the man who had brought him the sandwich. They were approaching Reinhold. They came to a halt at the edge of the platform, watching the grain pour into the hull. Reinhold didn't hear the response of the bearded man to the Captain's questions.

"Erik, this is Reinhold, the new deck boy." Capt. Hermann gestured toward Reinhold. Erik looked at him and grunted something. "Reinhold, this is Erik, the First Mate."

Reinhold nodded at the man in response. The two men left to inspect the other side of the hull. It seemed to have gotten colder to Reinhold, a weird kind of chill hung in the air.

Shrugging it off, he wandered to the rail, following the pipe that was feeding the grain into the hull. The pipe extended over the narrow concrete dock into a huge warehouse. The building still displayed signs of the bombing. Most of its windows were missing and there was a coating of greasy soot on the side. Somewhere inside there was a motor running.

Turning, he wandered across the deck to the other rail. The setting sun was reflecting off the uneven surface of the Elbe, creating rainbows of colors. Looking up and down the river, Reinhold noticed a huge ship with people streaming up and down the gangplank. It was docked on the opposite bank near the skeletal remains of a large building. Looking back at the shore from his vantage point on the ship brought the condition of Hamburg into a whole new light. The terrain sloped gently uphill from the river revealing layers of the city, layers of destruction.

He didn't know how long he had been standing there when he heard the Captain start barking orders. Reinhold turned from the rail to see the crew taking up positions on the deck. The pipe that had been shooting grain into the ship was retreating back to its building.

Steel lines were being secured. Wood panels were being hoisted. A large piece of heavy canvas had materialized from somewhere and was being dragged across the opening of the hull. A hook on a rope appeared from an overhead pulley to lift the panels into place over the piece of canvas.

With the panels in place, a new wave of orders came from the Captain. Men scrambled to the lines securing the ship to the concrete pier, pulling them back on to the ship, releasing the ship from its confinement. A few minutes later, the engine started to chug and they were moving slowly down river, the bank slipping lazily past. Reinhold had a brief moment of panic, thinking they were headed for the sea, but they dropped anchor again near the long stone building with the domes. Reinhold could feel the current in the river pulling gently on the ship, trying to carry it away.

The men busied themselves with jobs around the deck. The young guy that had sneered so hatefully at Reinhold earlier went back to greasing the winches, this time on the front mast, while others got out paint brushes and buckets or blowtorches. Reinhold watched as a man with huge hands carefully applied a red substance to a small hole in the solid iron rail. He was amazed the man could see in the gathering darkness. The Captain seemed to be reading his mind.

"Reinhold, come with me. I'll show you how to light the lamps below deck." He called from the wheelhouse doorway in a loud gravelly voice.

Reinhold followed the large man below deck, watching as he pulled a pack of matches out of his pocket. As he lit the lamp, the Captain explained Reinhold's daily treatment of the brass oil lamps.

"The brass has to be cleaned every day. Once you are done with the kitchen, you will start shining. It is quite simple. On this ship we use spit and newspaper."

The Captain lit the rest of the lamps, leaving the hallway with a soft grey glow. Turning to Reinhold, Hermann added, "When we hit rough seas, the lamps have to be extinguished, immediately. Understand?"

"Yes, sir." He responded dully.

The day was taking its toll. The soft movements of the ship coupled with the dimly lit hallway were lulling him into a kind of stupor. The Captain seemed to sense the heaviness in the boy's head.

"You should go ready your bunk." He turned to leave but stopped. Turning back to Reinhold, he said sternly, "Five o'clock tomorrow morning" before continuing upwards.

Chapter 22: Get Up, Boy

Reinhold awoke with a gasp, his eyes flying open to stare at an unknown obstacle just inches from his face. What was that noise? A loud metallic booming was still resounding in his head. Was he dead? Did they bury him alive? Why was he in a coffin? Turning his head to the left, he saw a strange room. Where was he? Nothing outlined in the semi darkness looked familiar. Why was he rocking? Before he could come completely to his senses a rough, disembodied voice reminded him of his situation.

"Get up, boy," it said.

And Reinhold did, quickly swinging his legs off the bunk, because the voice scared him more than his unfamiliar surroundings. The memory of the day before was filtering its way back into his sleep addled mind. He fumbled in the semi darkness for his suitcase in the corner, pulling out his wooden clogs. They would have to do for now. He couldn't remember what he had done with his other shoes last night before falling asleep.

Swinging open the heavy metal door, Reinhold gasped again. Framed against the doorway was Erik, the First Mate. He looked angry and carried a pail of water.

"It's a good thing," he snorted. "I was coming to wake you."

He turned and stalked off, the pail sloshing water. Reinhold hurried along behind him, pulling on his thin coat, thankful that he had escaped whatever fate Erik had planned for him.

Once in the kitchen, Reinhold got to work. He built up the embers in the stove into a decent sized fire and located the coffee pot in the cabinet above the sink. There was a moment of panic when he had trouble finding the coffee but it was short lived. The coffee was boiling away as he thought about what to make for breakfast. Someone had left salt pork soaking in a big pot of water. Quickly judging the amount, Reinhold figured he could use this for breakfast and for lunch later on. Pork and eggs fried up together with some bread sounded like heaven to a very hungry Reinhold. The eggs and pork were sizzling in a pan, wafting delicious aromas into the air, when Capt. Hermann walked into the galley.

"We are leaving today. After the crew eats, make sure everything is secured in the cabinets and bank the fire. We call that 'sea tight'. Understand?" He instructed, helping himself to pork, eggs, and a slice of bread. "Then start cleaning the brass and don't forget about my cabin."

The next half an hour was a parade of sleepy, irritable men collecting a plate of breakfast and a mug of coffee and leaving to find somewhere to eat. The galley was small enough without two or three additional people trying to move around, pouring coffee and dishing out food. Reinhold took his pork and eggs up to the deck, settling himself on the raised wooden platform called the 'hatch'.

The ship was dimly lit by a few scattered oil lamps with most of the illumination coming from the wheelhouse. He saw that most of the crew was gathering inside the wooden building out of the cold predawn air swirling around the deck. Everyone except the guy that had sneered at him the day before. He was sitting on the coal box, eating breakfast, and sneering once again at Reinhold sitting fifteen feet away.

What is this guy's problem? Reinhold thought to himself as he shoveled food into his mouth.

When a half chewed piece of bread hit him in the chest, he looked up, surprised, to find the sneering guy laughing at him. He decided that it was time for him to get back to the kitchen.

"Running away?" The sneering guy asked sarcastically as Reinhold passed.

Flabbergasted by the stranger's contempt, Reinhold just stared at him as he passed. By the time he got back to the kitchen, his confusion had turned to anger.

Who did that guy think he was? He asked himself as he scrubbed pans, plates, and mugs.

His anger propelled him through the rest of the cleaning in the kitchen. He made sure all of the utensils were secured in the cabinets and that the fire was banked before heading out into the hallway. He stopped short just outside the galley door. There a rumbling coming from somewhere below him. As he stood there listening, a kind of chugging started, a very loud chugging. He was thrown slightly off balance, but recovered quickly.

We must be moving, he thought to himself.

Reinhold came across a flurry of activity on deck. Men were running everywhere securing lines, getting the sails ready for use.

How can they see in the dark? He questioned to himself.

The eastern sky was tinged with the pink of the coming dawn but it was still night on the ship. Turning toward the shore, Reinhold saw that it was a sea of small lights spreading in all directions. He wasn't sure which were other ships and which were buildings. They were slowly moving past as the *Eos* headed up river.

Reinhold was seized by the desire to throw himself overboard and swim for it. What had he been thinking?! They were headed for the ocean and then he didn't know where. Where were they going to end up? But he didn't make a break for it. He stood there glued to the spot with men bumping into him, cursing him, as they went about their business.

"Reinhold!" He heard the Captain bellow from the wheelhouse. "Come get this newspaper and start shining the brass!"

Reinhold broke his gaze away from the moving shoreline and hurried to the wheelhouse. The Captain handed him several sheets of yesterday's *Hamburger Abendblatt*[19] and sent him to shine the lamps.

It was strange, walking on the ship, even though it was moving so slowly. The river was rough, as it usually was in the winter months. He staggered a couple of times when his footfalls were out of rhythm with the rising and falling of the deck. Thankfully, the rail was there to help him steady himself. As he started cleaning the first lamp, he had thoughts of stumbling and falling over the short metal rail. He wondered if it would be bad for that to happen. Not long into his chore, with four lamps shined, he started to wonder if he was going to have enough spit to clean all the brass. His mouth was already dry and his fingers were numb from touching the cold metal through wet newspaper.

Turning away from the lamp on the wall to head back to the galley to get some water, Reinhold saw that the ship was moving through misty countryside. Then he noticed that they were not traveling alone. Counting quickly as he staggered back toward the wheelhouse, he came up with eight other ships chugging along the narrow, choppy river. They seemed to be moving in a herd, like deer, with no distinguishable arrangement.

On closer inspection, Reinhold noted that these ships were no bigger than the *Eos*. Some were in worse condition. The one closest to the *Eos* on what Reinhold learned was the port side, was the rustiest thing he had ever seen. The original grey of the hull was barely

---

[19] *Hamburger Abendblatt* is a daily newspaper published in Hamburg.

visible under the stains. Some were in better shape, a bit newer. Most of them had masts on which men were working, raising sails. The men on his ship were positioning themselves to do likewise.

Looking back, Reinhold could still remember his first experience on the open seas. How could he forget it? It was horrible, a nightmare. Everything was fine when they reached the mouth of the Elbe River and traveled out into the North Sea. He was nervous, but strangely excited to see what was going to happen and where they were going to go. The further out to sea they went, the rougher the winter seas became, the more he felt bad, just really bad. At first, he thought he was getting sick because his ears won't stop clogging up and they hurt. Then came the nausea. Reinhold heard of seasickness so he knew what it was, but knowing didn't make it any better.

The *Eos* sat like a duck on the water. It rolled with the waves and Reinhold's stomach rolled right along with it, up and down the twenty foot swells. At the bottom of each swell, the rebelling organ attempted to empty its contents. He remembered next to nothing of his first journey by sea. When he wasn't concentrating on each task in front of him, be it cooking or cleaning, or just walking from one place to another, he was in the toilet room with his head in the bowl, not caring about the filth accumulated on the cold metal. He was ashamed now, as an experienced sailor, to admit that more than once in his first couple of weeks on a ship he had awoken in the bathroom, having passed out where he laid. Sleep, he remembered, had been the only relief. He would go to his bunk at night and pass out from the effort of being sick. At five o'clock every morning, the loud metallic booming jolted him awake.

The sneering guy, who Reinhold discovered was called Klaus, didn't make things any better. He pointed out constantly that Reinhold didn't feel well, calling him a *schwachling*, a weakling, asking if he wanted to run home to his mommy. Reinhold was too sick to do anything but ignore the insults. No one else but the Captain or the First Mate spoke to him. Captain Hermann seemed to recognize that concentrating on a task was the best way for Reinhold to keep moving. He sent the poor seasick boy to fetch and return the same shackle to the bow of the ship half a dozen times in one night.

Reinhold couldn't even remember the name of the first port he had visited as a sailor. He just remembered that it was in Holland- Amsterdam, maybe- and he was relieved that the ship stopped rolling.

The closer they got to the shore, the better he felt, but he was completely exhausted and severely disorientated.

The *Eos* didn't stay in port in Holland nearly long enough for Reinhold. He never wanted to go on the high seas, as they called them, ever again. It seemed like the day after they arrived, the ship was on its way again. He kept hearing pieces of conversations about having to take advantage of the clear weather and the calm seas.

Calm seas! Reinhold thought to himself in exasperation. *What on earth are rough seas?!*

This time, Reinhold remembered, they headed for Sweden. His stomach went up and down with the swells for the five days that it took them to get there. This time, instead of sending him back and forth with a shackle, the Captain sent Reinhold out on the deck with a chisel to de-ice the rails and rigging. It kept him busy and when a wave of nausea washed over him, the sea was conveniently placed to be the recipient of the contents of his stomach.

In these conditions, he had the cold as well as the sea pitted against him. The wind ripped right through the flimsy jacket and threadbare shirt the boy wore while the spray from the crashing waves covered him in dampness making the task even more difficult. By the time he had to go start dinner he was wet, frozen to the bone, blue, and shaking. Once in the galley, he stood, swaying and clutching his stomach, in front of the fire for a good ten minutes before attempting to do anything.

Reinhold also remembered this trip because they were carrying coal. As soon as it was unloaded at a small port on Sweden's west coast, Reinhold and the crew spent the rest of the day cleaning the black, oily coal dust from the hull and deck. It was a messy job. Scowling, the sailor remembered it was while they were docked in Sweden that Klaus kicked him in the butt for the first time. He was bent over, scrubbing the deck, when suddenly he was lying face down on the wet wood.

Looking over his shoulder, he saw Klaus sauntering off toward the other side of the deck with a bucket in his hand. He was shocked that someone touched him, let alone knocked him to the ground. Shaking it off, Reinhold went back to work, ignoring the sneers from Klaus across the hatch. He didn't know if he would get in trouble for doing something in retaliation. And, when it came right down to it, he was just too tired and raw to fight with someone.

Glancing around, he saw that the Captain was watching him from the wheelhouse. Putting his head down, he went back to work.

Chapter 23: Terror and Humiliation

Almost three weeks after he left, Reinhold was back in Hamburg, thankful for being in port, not on the seas, and watching the shore workers unload the lumber the *Eos* delivered from Sweden. He wondered, as he scrubbed the windows of the wheelhouse, if they were going to use it to rebuild the ruined city. He also wondered where the *Eos* was going next. He wasn't entirely sure he wanted to be a part of the crew anymore. Actually, he was pretty well set on not going anywhere else with the ship ever again. Tonight, he would ask Captain Hermann for his sailor's book back and he would leave. Hopefully, he was going to leave with half a month's pay so he could get home and be able to survive while he looked for other work.

Maybe, he thought to himself, *I'll stay in Hamburg and get a job in construction, help them rebuild the city.*

"No." was all Captain Hermann said when Reinhold approached him.

"Why? It is mine!" Reinhold retorted angrily.

"Because you have not fulfilled your commitment yet." Capt. Hermann growled menacingly back at him. "You will stay until I say you are done."

Seeing further argument as futile, Reinhold turned on his heel and clomped his way back to his bunk in his wooden clogs. Once in the room, he kicked off the clogs and flung himself into his bunk. He felt trapped and the coffin-like hole in the wall where he slept didn't make it any better. Tears stung his eyes. He didn't like the feeling of being trapped. The tears spilled down his cheeks.

Stretching his mind, Reinhold began to see the whole ship as a coffin, a rusty, leaky coffin. And he was trapped inside, suffocating. Suddenly he wanted nothing more than to go home. He wanted it so bad that the desire seem to be a physical lump in his chest, pushing down on his lungs, making his breath come in ragged gasps. He missed his sisters. He missed his friends and their trips to the beach. He missed his crappy little town and the forests that surrounded it. Most of all, he missed his warm feather bed in the attic.

Reinhold tried to pull his coat tighter around his stocky frame. The room was freezing even with the fire going and he had no blanket. Curiously, he reached out to his right and laid a hand on the metal wall of the room. He drew it back quickly. It was absolutely the coldest thing he had touched all day. Realization dawned quickly on him. There was nothing between him and the sea besides this wall, this flimsy wall of rusting metal. He hadn't noticed this before when he was so sick he could barely stagger around to get his work done. The tears became a torrent of hot liquid down his face.

How do I get out of here? He thought helplessly to himself.

He turned onto his side, facing the offensive wall, blinking back tears, and thinking how he was going to get off this ship. He half expected the wall to burst open and the icy river waters to come rushing in as he lay there.

I could just leave, he mused, *I don't really need the book back, do I? Not if I am going home to be a farmer.*

The thought of the cows and their tails gave him pause. That didn't sound any better than staying on the ship.

An hour after Reinhold had retired to his bunk, the rest of the crew started filtering in for the night. He didn't turn around to face them, pretending to be asleep. All around him he heard the creaking of bunks, the thud of shoes hitting the floor, the grunts and sighs of men settling down to sleep. Someone added a coal to the fire causing the soft luminousness of the metal to brighten for a few moments but not really adding any warmth to the room.

"Who left their damn clogs in the middle of the floor?" Klaus asked angrily.

Reinhold didn't turn or answer him. A second later, he felt something solid slam into his lower back. As stunned as he was that Klaus had most likely thrown a clog at him, he still didn't turn around.

It was sometime later, as Reinhold lay there contemplating his situation, that a horrible smell wafted into his nostrils. Tears formed anew in his eyes as he realized that he was surrounded by stinking bodies. He pulled the collar of his jacket over his nose, but it was barely big enough to reach the appendage, never mind cover it with any kind of protectiveness. How he wished there was a window he could open. Sleep could not come fast enough that night.

Reinhold would have liked to chuckle about his time on the *Eos* but he found it was not possible. His first six months on the high seas were amongst some of the worst of his life.

I jumped out of the fire and into the frying pan, he mused to himself.

He worked, boy did he work, from the time he got up until it was too dark to work anymore. He spit shined brass, cooked, cleaned, painted, repaired holes in the metal, chipped ice, washed the ship down, and whenever he was brave enough, he would fill a bucket with water from the pump in the kitchen and try to wash himself behind the winch for the middle mast. But it wasn't the work that he found disheartening. He actually liked the work. It made him feel like he had a purpose.

The ship was a constant source of terror and humiliation for Reinhold. The first time he saw a storm at sea was dreadful. The winds howled causing the sails to snap loudly, menacingly. The rain came in sideways and the sea became a rutted road with thirty foot swells. Waves roared over the wheelhouse, leaving cascades of foamy water in their wakes and throwing the small craft sideways. In those seconds, Reinhold had the fleeting thought that the ship was never going to resurface and that he was going to drown in the middle of the North Sea.

He remembered distinctly the first time he tied himself into his bunk so that he wouldn't roll out of it as the ship tossed and pitched on rough seas. He thought as he tied the knot that if the ship went down, he was going with it, reinforcing the kernel of an idea that had sprouted in his head about the ship being a coffin. On stormy nights, he lay in the narrow bunk, listening to the pounding of the waves on the other side of the wall and crying silently to himself. He also remembered being completely unnerved by the amount of water that had accumulated in what they called the bilge when the Captain sent him to help pump it out.

And what work that had been, thought an older Reinhold on a newer ship.

With no electricity onboard, they had to pump it by hand but the water level never stayed down for long. Every couple of days, Reinhold found himself in the hull with a grumpy, hairy sailor, cranking a pump handle.

Humiliation came in the form of stupid mistakes, the First Mate Erik, and Klaus. It took several knocks on the head for Reinhold to gain instinctual knowledge of the location of the boom when moving around on the deck. Not one, but two buckets were thrown overboard by Reinhold in attempts to gather fresh water for washing down the ship. He had simply forgotten to keep a hold of the rope tied to the handle so that he could haul it back up to the deck. The Captain was not happy with him and both times threatened to take the cost of the bucket out of his pay.

Then there was the development of sea legs. It took months for his knees to give and take with the ship. More than once, he ended up staggering into the rail or the wheelhouse or down a ladder because the ship pitched unexpectedly. A month into his time on the *Eos*, the First Mate awakened a still slightly sea sick Reinhold at quarter after five in the morning by dousing him with freezing seawater and snarling, "You're late". Four months into his time on the *Eos*, Erik backhanded him across the mouth for chiding him about not purchasing enough eggs to feed the crew on the five day trip to a tiny port in Sweden north of Stockholm.

It seemed Klaus was always there to mock him when he made one of these stupid mistakes. *Schwachling, dummkopf, arschloch, hinterwäldler*[20], Reinhold heard it all. Klaus would scream obscenities and insults from across the ship purposefully so the rest of the crew could hear. As the months progressed, the older boy's physical attacks become more frequent. Every day, Reinhold ended up face down on the deck after being pushed or kicked in the butt by Klaus, the latter laughing maliciously as he sauntered away.

Every day, he bit back the retorts and quieted his raging blood, resorting to simply staring coldly through narrowed eyes at his attacker. He knew he could take Klaus if need be. He had not forgotten the combat skills he learned back home or in the *Hitlerjugend*. Not to mention that he was stronger. Klaus was a wiry, lanky city boy where Reinhold was short and stocky, all solid, farm built muscle. Reinhold hesitated to retaliate. He didn't know what the consequences were for fighting. As much as he wanted to get off the ship, he didn't want to go on bad terms or be arrested for assault.

The compensation for the tribulations were the wonderful new things he saw. The *Eos*, as a small ship, never went far from the shore. The rugged coastlines of Europe are full of lighthouses, castles, and strange rock formations housing all kinds of sea birds and sea mammals. There were small fishing villages with colorful buildings and huge cities bustling with commerce. There was an innumerable amount of ships to gawk at from individual crafts to huge luxury liners to other cargo vessels.

---

[20] Hinterwäldler in German translates to 'hillbilly' or 'country boy' in English.

The wildlife was like nothing Reinhold had seen before. Dolphins travelled, jumping and leaping, with the ship, small whales swam past, moving faster than the little ship, and sea lions floated lazily around when they were in port. When something caught his attention, he would turn to point it out to someone, but rarely was there anybody there. Once, he even tried to start a pleasant conversation with Klaus about a particularly huge lighthouse off the coast of the Netherlands only to be called stupid and told to shut up.

In the ports, there were tons of interesting things to see: the huge cranes, the huge ships, the people selling their wares, food carts selling all manner of delicious smelling edibles; and the multitude of different kinds of people with their various cultural habits from all over the world. He quickly learned that ports attracted a lesser quality person. Lowlifes, he called them, pimps and hookers, thieves and liars.

A month after coming aboard, when they were docked in Hamburg, he received his first wage payment of 7.50 *mark*. Reinhold was ecstatic. As soon as he could, he got on shore to peruse the selection of clothing that the port sellers had at their stalls. He was in desperate need of a new pair of pants. The hem was nearly up to his knees. His elation was quickly dashed and replaced by dismay. A new pair of pants was twenty *mark*! The blanket he also desperately needed was thirty *mark*, while a jacket was thirty five *mark*. He couldn't afford anything and it would be several months before he would be able to at the wage he was making. He wondered if there were cheaper products to be found outside the fenced off section of the port. He wandered over to the gate only to find it closed. A young man in a blue port security uniform came out of the gatehouse.

"Can you open the gate, please?" Reinhold asked, expecting the security officer to comply with the request.

"Where are you coming from?" the officer asked, suspiciously.

"The *Eos*. I work on the *Eos*. I want to go see if I can get some pants cheaper outside the port." Reinhold answered.

The guard's eye went automatically to Reinhold's pants, a small smile flickered across his features.

"You work on the *Eos*?" The guy chuckled. "How are the Frisians treating you?"

"Frisians?"

"Yes, the Frisians, Hermann and Erik."

Reinhold made no response, baffled by the term. The gateman saw his confusion and explained.

"They are from Friesland. Emden, I think. They say that Frisians don't waste words or smiles."

Reinhold had never heard the saying before but it was accurate enough.

"How old are you, young man?"

"Fifteen." He fibbed. There was actually just over a month until his fifteenth birthday. "Why?" he asked, getting annoyed that the guy wouldn't just open the gate.

"Do Hermann and Erik know where you are? Did one of them give you permission to leave the port?" The officer questioned but before Reinhold could answer, he continued "Because you are underage. I can't let you go without someone from the *Eos* accompanying you or without permission from Captain Hermann."

"Oh." replied Reinhold, anger rising in his chest.

He was about to open his mouth to protest, but something told him not too, to keep his mouth shut. Instead, he turned and walked away hunched shouldered, back to where he could whistle for Dirk.

As it turned out, he didn't have to use his still lamentable whistling abilities to call the big, silent, scary man to come get him. Dirk was just arriving with three of his fellow shipmates. He was disturbed to see Klaus amongst those climbing up on to the pier.

"Look who it is. Out for a stroll?" Turning to the other two men, Klaus continued, "We should take Reinhold with us. He is probably a cheap date. How much could someone so tiny drink?"

It was obvious to Reinhold that they had already gotten into the *Eos's* 'medicine' rum. He could smell it. The noxiously sour aroma made his stomach turn.

"I am not taking responsibility for him." Edwald said and walked away toward the gate.

"He can't leave the port. Come on, if you're coming Klaus. I have wages to drink and women to bed. Stop dilly dallying with that boy." Gerhardt said before following Edwald.

Klaus sneered condescendingly at Reinhold before following the older men.

Reinhold felt his anger rising as he climbed into the little row boat for the trip back to the *Eos*. He marched straight to Capt.

Hermann and asked for his sailor's book back so he could leave. The captain merely shook his massive head.

"I cannot let you leave. You are not done with your job yet. I still need you to work."

Captain Hermann turned away from Reinhold, the radio catching his attention. The Küstenwache[21] was reporting heavy seas and a *windstärke*[22] of nine on the North Sea. There was a storm coming from the west. The Captain cursed softly.

Turning back toward Reinhold, Hermann said, "Seems we are going to be here awhile. Go have Dirk teach you how to row the dingy. We could use someone else to ferry the crew."

He turned away, back to his radio and maps, leaving Reinhold to follow orders or stand there, silently fuming. Feeling awkward and dismissed, the boy went to Dirk and told him Capt. Hermann's order. He spent the rest of the day rowing the little one oared boat back and forth between the ship and shore. When Klaus, Edwald, and Gerhadt returned to the ship several hours later it was Reinhold who rowed out to get them. He endured Klaus' drunken, ridiculing comments on the slow ride back to the ship, his shoulder and arm aching from the effort of rowing.

---

[21] Küstenwache is the German Coast Guard.
[22] The German term for measurement of wind speed or velocity.

Chapter 24: Lessons

There were many weeks that winter and early spring that the *Eos* sat in port, unable to leave due to high winds or seas. The crew kept busy during daylight hours with the constant maintenance the ship needed. At night, they gathered in the wheelhouse or left the ship to go drinking at the port bars. Klaus suggested everytime they left that Reinhold tag along but none of the older members of the crew wanted the responsibility. He didn't understand why Klaus had this weird obsession with getting him intoxicated. The thought of drinking made Reinhold's stomach turn, initiating his gag reflex. He could still taste the spiked punch at Muuss' harvest party more than two years ago.

On those nights when the rest of the crew was away on shore drinking, Reinhold would go to the wheelhouse to pass the time with the Captain. At first, he spent a good amount of time trying to convice the huge, neckless man to release him from his service to the ship but gave up when he realized this tactic just lead to tearful nights laying in his bunk, fustrated and rageful. Once he resigned himself to his circumstance, mostly by reminding himself that he had asked for his position, his nights with Captain Herman become more interesting.

The Captain began showing him how the strange instruments in the wheelhouse worked and what the maps had to say about the sea. The maps of the seafloor detailing reefs and sandbanks fascinated Reinhold. He couldn't imagine how they had gathered all of the information represented. When he asked Captain Hermann, the older man simply grunted, "Lots of sinkings."

Slowly, the brass instruments he spit shined everyday began to make sense in the wider world of sailing. Reinhold easily grasped the purpose of the big compass but it took a month or so before he fully understood how a sextent functioned. By the time summer bloomed, he was able to figure out Greenwich Mean Time, as Captain Hermann showed him, using the moon and the horizon line. He could then apply this to the maps in front of him to figure out where they were in relation to Hamburg.

It was during one of these lessons, three months after Reinhold had come aboard, when the *Eos* was docked in Cuxhaven and the crew was out drinking, that Captain Hermann presented Reinhold with a wool blanket.

"Erik told me you don't have a blanket. Like everything else right now, they are not cheap. Damn price gougers are a scourge on decent people. I had my wife bring this from home. I am also giving you a raise to fifteen *mark* a month."

He handed Reinhold the worn grey blanket, turning away with the excuse of being tired and leaving the wheelhouse before Reinhold could thank him. He stood, gripping the precious item to him, for a minute before unfolding it, wrapping it around his shoulders and leaving the building to sit on the deck. It smelled faintly of a wood fire. He wondered why Hermann and Erik had been talking about him not having a blanket as he watched lights dancing in the darkness on the shore.

On nights when the lessons in sailing were not possible because there were too many people congregated in the wheelhouse, Reinhold would practice splicing lines while the rest of the crew told stories about women and sailing or organized arm wrestling competitions. One of the old timers, Edwald, told him that the only way to get promoted on a ship was to prove you mastered the needed skills. Reinhold was at the bottom of the hierarchy as a *Decksjunge*, a deck boy.

"All you have to do to get promoted from a deck boy to a *Jüngemann*[23] is not get killed or quit. But if you want to make *Matrose*, a full sailor, you are going to have to learn to do some things. The biggest is splicing lines. We splice alot of lines on this ship. To become a *Matrose*[24], you have to be able to splice one behind your back. And be quick and neat about it."

So Reinhold practiced, practiced, practiced. Weaving, weaving, weaving. His fingers were becoming more nimble with every rope that passed through them. When one line became to unwoven for him to use it anymore, he would hunt around for another. On several occasions, Captain Hermann presented him with a new rope before the old one was completely worn. Short splices didn't take him long, but long splices could take him an hour to complete properly.

"Practice your knots while you're at it, boy" was the only comment he got from the First Mate, Erik. "You never know when you're going to need one."

---

[23] *Jüngmann* translates to 'young man'. It is a junior sailor title.
[24] *Matrose* translates to 'sailor' It is the equivalent of an Able Seaman.

Reinhold took Erik's advice and added knot making to his nightly practicing. He was sitting on the hatch, involved in an intricate sailor's knot one night in early summer when some of the crew returned from the shore, drunk and looking to display their masculinity. A good, old fashion arm wrestling competition was quickly suggested by Captain Hermann.

Reinhold stopped making knots and splicing lines to watch. Arm after arm banged down on the top of the coal box, the most convinent place for the competition to occur, according to the Captain. Reinhold got the feeling that Hermann didn't want the agitated, drunken men in the wheelhouse tonight. Dirk quickly beat everyone and was declared the champion. But this didn't satisfy the men. They went for a second round to establish second place. Then, it went a third and a fourth.

"I want to take him on." Klaus said loudly, as he rounded, pointing, at Reinhold.

No one had ever gotten Reinhold involved in the arm wrestling before. They perceived him always as being to young to participate in their antics. Klaus, obviously, was through with this perspective. He was drunk and losing consistantly to the older guys. Reinhold had the feeling Klaus was looking to redeem himself. No one said anything to discourage Reinhold. Instead they waited for his response to the challenge.

Reinhold stuffed his ropes in the pocket of his pants and took a position across from Klaus. He put his elbow up on the cold, grey coal box and waited for Klaus to grasp his out stretched hand. Klaus sneered condescendingly at Reinhold as they locked hands, muttering *schwächling*, under his breath. Reinhold felt his anger rise.

"Go!" Edwald called.

Reinhold wasted no time. He put all his strength into his wrist and slammed Klaus' hand down on the coal box. A cheer went up from the assembled men. It had really been no competition at all. Reinhold realized in that moment that it was Klaus who was the weakling.

"Again!" cried Klaus, red in the face. "That was beginners luck! He moves faster than he thinks. It won't happen again."

Reinhold shrugged and put his arm up. They locked hands.

"Go!" Edwald called.

This time Klaus was not taken off guard by Reinhold's quick reflexes. He held his own for a minute or two, struggling to keep his arm straight up in the air. Reinhold watched as a vein began to throb in Klaus' neck. He reached down into his reserve strength and slammed the other man's arm down. Another cheer went up from the assembled men. They came forward to clap their deck boy on the back.

"Again!" Klaus cried, purple with rage and embarassment.

"No," said Captain Hermann. "That is enough for tonight. This ship is leaving tomorrow for Holland and I don't need a worthless crew. To bed with all of you. Reinhold, come with me."

Reinhold followed the Captain into the wheelhouse, watching out of the corner of his eye as Klaus headed for the bow, loudly defending his losses.

"Here." Captain Hermann said as he handed Reinhold a new practice rope. Reinhold nodded his thanks and left for bed.

Chapter 25: Enough!

The next morning was a busy one for the crew of the *Eos*. After breakfast, they made their way to the pier near the grain elevator. They were preparing for an evening departure from Hamburg with their usual escort of ships. After cleaning the galley and the Captain's quarters, Reinhold made his way above board to start cleaning the brass. He had finished two of the lamps and had just started the third when he heard the First Mate bellow his name.

"Captain wants you to learn to repair the sails. When you finish that lamp, find Gerhardt. He'll show you what to do."

"Yes, sir."

Reinhold quickly finished the lamp and headed for the hatch, thinking that would be the best place to find Gerhardt. Several men, Gerhardt among them, were just replacing the wood panels when Reinhold arrived for his lesson. He was only standing there a second when he saw, out of the corner of his eye, a foot flying at his head. Without thinking, he grabbed the foot before it could make contact with his skull, twisting it away from him. Klaus landed on the deck a few feet from him with a thud and yelp of surprised pain. A few more inches and he would have smashed his head on the metal rail. Reinhold looked down at him, realization releasing a flood of adrenaline into his blood.

This guy just tried to kick me in the head! He screamed to himself, feeling the rage course through him again.

"Enough!" He bellowed.

Klaus had just regained his feet when Reinhold strode the four steps between them, rounded back his arm, and punched him square in the jaw with all his strength, knocking him to the ground again.

Reinhold delivered two swift kicks to the abdomen before throwing himself on top of Klaus and punching him repeatedly with both fists. He could hear Klaus' head bouncing off the deck as he tried to block the onslaught with his forearms but Reinhold just aimed around them. When Klaus covered his eyes, Reinhold punched him in the chin or the chest, landing a solid hit square on his chest, knocking the wind out of him.

It was like someone had replaced Reinhold with a cursing, spitting demon in men's clothing. He knew for a brief second in his rage that his face was contorted and red with the release of months of bottled anger. Klaus sputtered and coughed but Reinhold kept drawing back and releasing his fist, hitting him again and again without humanity, without mercy. He didn't even feel the few punches of Klaus' that made contact with his body and face. He was too intent on destroying the person who had made his life such a living hell for six months now.

The rest of the crew gathered around to watch the fight, making no move to seperate them or stop the action. Reinhold continued to punch Klaus. Blood was flowing freely from the latter's nose and mouth. It was landing in thick drops on the wooden deck. Something about the blood made Reinhold think of the water. He suddenly became determined to throw Klaus overboard, to get rid of him for good.

He stood up and grasped the front of his enemies shirt with his bloody hands, hoisting him to his feet. A fresh stream of blood flowed from Klaus' nose and his head fell to one side limply, his eyes glazed and half open. Reinhold was pushing him the two feet to the rail when he felt someone grab his arm. Turning in his rage to strike this new attacker, he came face to face with Erik's hairy countenance. It was like someone turned off the anger switch. He released the front of Klaus' shirt, letting his body fall back to the deck. The bloody face let out a soft moan of pain.

Reinhold searched Erik's face, trying to read how much trouble he was in. The First Mate looked impassive as always. But there was a new glint in his eye that hadn't been there before.

"What did I tell you to do?" He asked Reinhold almost kindly.

Reinhold blinked at him, feeling blood trickling down his face from a cut throbbing above his eyebrow. What had Erik asked him to do?

"See Gerhardt about repairing the sail." He responded hoarsely, the adrenaline causing his throat to constrict.

Erik pointed at the limp, bleeding face of Klaus. "Is this Gerhardt?" he asked.

"No." Reinhold responded simply.

"Go clean yourself up and find Gerhardt."

Erik released his arm, turned on his heel, and left the scene, returning to the wheelhouse. Reinhold followed the man with his eyes. He saw Captain Hermann watching him from the windows of the wheelhouse. The Captain met Reinhold's gaze for a second before turning away.

Shifting his gaze, Reinhold found the rest of the crew frozen in place, staring at him, cigarettes hanging forgotten from slack lips. One by one, they too turned away and went back to work. Gerhardt caught Reinhold's eye, nodding at him as he pulled the butt of a cigarette from his mouth, seemingly acknowledging the task that Erik had set for the two of them.

Reinhold looked down the front of himself and saw a great deal of blood. He felt the cut on his forehead, winching as his fingers grazed it. He looked at his hands. They were covered in blood and his knuckles were scraped. In a daze, he made his way to the galley where he used the pump to wash his face and hands.

His shirt was destroyed. He would never get the bloodstains out of it and it was ripped where Klaus had grabbed at him. Luckily he had saved some money. He would be able to purchase a new one. Looking further down his body, he examined his pants. They had made it through the skirmish unscathed, thankfully.

I wonder when they will fire me, he thought to himself as he made his way back to the deck to find Gerhardt.

He didn't know how he felt about the prospect of being thrown off the ship for fighting. On one hand, he kind of hoped that would happen. He would finally be able to get off the *Eos*. On the other hand, he didn't want to be fired. He didn't think he deserved to be fired for defending himself.

That guy has been asking for it since I got onboard, he said to himself indignantly. *It is not my fault! I have put up with a lot from him. Was I supposed to just let him push me around forever? Was I supposed to let him kick me in the head?*

Reinhold felt the anger raising again and quickly calmed himself down. He found Gerhardt on deck and spent the rest of the afternoon with the dark, bearded, chainsmoking sailor learning how to use a huge, curved, steel needle with a very sharp point to repair tears in the heavy canvas sails. He was waiting for Captain Hermann or Erik to come fire him but it didn't happen.

That evening, Erik started barking orders to the crew. Everybody jumped into action, including Reinhold. He knew that he had to have dinner ready by the time they were under way, out of the port, but before they reached the North Sea. He hadn't seen Klaus since their altercation.

Looking back at his fifteen year old self, Reinhold realized that his brawl with Klaus was a turning point for him. The firing he expected never came and Capt. Hermann never mentioned the incident to him. Lessons in the wheelhouse continued as if nothing happened.

In fact, Reinhold thought to himself, *they expanded.*

It was only a few weeks after the fight, on their way to Sweden from Bremenhaven, where Reinhold finally saw the lights he sung about, that the Captain told him to take the wheel so he could learn to steer the ship. It was an exhilerating feeling being behind the wheel of the ship, feeling the spiky handles, knowing that he could direct it anyway he wanted. The Captain wanted Reinhold to feel how the ship moved through the water, to feel the rudder, to learn how to control it, and to stay on a course.

He also learned that proper positioning is important when handling the wheel. Trying to be a wise guy one night he decide he was going to handle the wheel from the side, facing out the starboard windows as opposed to the front. He was quite surprised when it jumped on the rough seas. And even more surprised when one of the spikes grabbed his belt, swinging him up and over the wheel head first. He was hanging by his belt, twisting, trying to release himself when the Captain strode over. With his massive hands, he grabbed Reinhold by the shoulders, jerked him off the wheel, and threw him in the corner. He growled that Reinhold should be more careful in the future. A ship is no place for fooling around.

There was also a change in the way the rest of the crew treated him. It was so subtle that he hadn't really noticed it at first. He was offered more respect. The rough and tumble men were more tolerant of his incessant curiousity. They began to speak with him more, asking about his hometown and the farm where he had worked. Edwald even asked if Reinhold would like to join them one night when some of the crew were headed out drinking in Hamburg. One of them, Wilhelm, was suddenly particularly interested in Reinhold's friendship with the gate man at the port in Hamburg.

"What is that guy's name? The one you talk to at the gate?"

Reinhold was surprised by the question. No one had ever expressed the slightest interest in the man at the gate or Reinhold's friendly relationship with him. He was convinced that the only person who knew that he went to hang out with the port official was the Captain.

"Henry." Reinhold responded, his eyebrows drawn together in a suspicious frown. Wilhelm noticed Reinhold's reaction and quickly explained his question.

"I have some friends coming to visit me. I want to talk to the gate man about letting them in so they can come aboard, see the ship. They are not sailors themselves so they are interested to see what it is like. You'll probably get to meet them. Might even be the one to ferry them out here."

Wilhelm went back to work repairing a hole in the metal of the rail. The explanation seemed logical to Reinhold so his suspicion about Wilhelm's curiousity was pacified.

Later that night, after work was done for the day, Reinhold went ashore to visit with Henry, to see if Wilhelm had spoken to him about his friends. As he approached the gate, he saw Wilhelm involved in conversation with Henry. Both men seemed tense and Wilhelm was gesturing repeatedly toward the ship. Henry saw Reinhold before Wilhelm and gave him a slight wave of acknowledgment. Wilhelm followed the movement, calling to Reinhold.

"Will you tell this guy that I am not trying to pull tricks?" Wilhelm gestured toward a very irritated looking Henry. "He thinks my friends are going to try to rob the place."

"It doesn't matter, none of what you have said matters. I cannot let unauthorized people into this restricted area. In order for your friends to gain access you have to go speak with the security office or you have to ask one of the officers on the *Eos* to fill out the appropriate forms. I have no control over it." Henry replied angrily.

With a tip of his hat to Reinhold and a scowl at Wilhelm, Henry disappeared into his little booth, slamming the door behind him. Wilhelm blinked in surprise.

"I wasn't done talking to him." He said to Reinhold.

"I think he was done with you." Reinhold replied before turning to leave, thinking he would see if the port sellers had anything good to eat.

He was in the mood for something sweet. That was one the few good things about sailing. He could have candy and cookies anytime he felt like paying for them. Wilhelm fell into step next to him.

"I don't have time to go to the security office. We are leaving for Holland again in the morning." Wilhelm complained loudly.

"Then when were your friends coming to visit? Tonight?" Reinhold asked, browsing the selection of butter and sugar cookies at Frau Keller's booth.

He noticed that the cookies were still expensive but he dared not comment about it. Last time he pointed out that three *mark* was a lot for three small cookies, Frau Keller had told him that he was lucky she had cookies at all seeing as she had to fight for every ounce of butter and sugar, when she was lucky enough to find it. If he didn't like her prices, he could go without a cookie.

"No." Wilhelm replied. "They were going to come when we got back."

"Then why don't you talk to security now so that everything is in order when we get back?" Reinhold asked him.

Taking his precious cookies, Reinhold headed for the pier to call Dirk to go back to the ship. He didn't understand why Wilhelm was insisting upon carrying on with this conversation. It had nothing to do with him and the guy had never really spoken to him before. He hoped that Wilhelm would decide to go somewhere on shore instead of accompanying him back to the ship.

"Yeah, maybe I'll do that." Wilhelm responded thoughtfully.

He followed along with Reinhold for another minute, deep in thought, glancing sideways at the younger man several times before announcing his departure.

"See you around."

Reinhold nodded in response and kept walking.

The next morning the *Eos* set out once again for Holland. Reinhold was in the Captain's salon gathering up dirty glasses, emptying ash trays, sweeping, and collecting change from the floor when they left port. He was trying to come up with reasons why the Captain's room always seemed to be littered with coins.

Must have a hole in his pocket, Reinhold mused to himself.

He had just tossed a fifty *pfennig* piece into a newly emptied ashtray when Wilhelm's head appeared around the half open door.

"Good breakfast this morning, Reinhold." He said before vanishing again.

It was so quick, Reinhold wondered if he had imagined it.
That was weird, he thought to himself.
Shrugging, he went back to work.
The trip to Holland was uneventful. Reinhold went about his work, thoroughly enjoying being able to move around the deck without Klaus' shenanigans. The summer season also raised his spirits. The sea was a pleasant place to be during the warm months. He was beginning to enjoy the salt air whipping through his hair and the sun beating down on him.

One evening after leaving Holland, headed for Stockholm, he was sitting on the deck, splicing lines and watching the sun set in a dazzling show of orange and red when Wilhelm sat down next to him. Reinhold wasn't entirely thrilled with this invasion of his private moment. There were so few of them on the small ship and its cramped spaces.

Since they left Hamburg nearly a week earlier, Wilhelm had been complementing his cooking and offering him pointers about how to patch holes and pump water out of the bilge faster. Reinhold wasn't entirely sure he liked Wilhelm.

"So, Reinhold, how much is the old man paying you these days?" Wilhelm asked.

"Eighteen *mark* a month." Reinhold replied, more interested in the rope in his hands than Wilhelm's question.

"What would you say if I offered you a month's salary in return for a small favor?"

Reinhold turned to look at the older man. He noticed that Wilhelm was looking a bit older today, a bit shaggier, and a bit greyer in hair and skin tone. The lines around his eyes were etched more deeply than usual and his lips were pursed as though he was angry but his blue eyes were twinkling with mischief.

"What would I have to do?" Reinhold asked cautiously.

He watched as Wilhelm pulled out two cigarettes, waving away the one offered to him. He watched as the cigarette was replaced in its case and a small box of matches was pulled out of a pocket. It seemed to be taking forever for him to light the cigarette. Wilhelm was stalling about something, Reinhold knew. He waited patiently, curiosity keeping him quiet and attentive.

"You would have to talk to your friend Henry for me. Maybe get his key to the gate."

"Henry? Gate?" he asked, brow furrowed in confusion. "In Hamburg?"

"That's the one." Wilhelm replied, flicking ashes from his smoke. "Maybe you could even distract him for me for a few minutes."

An expression of confusion flooded the boy's face.

"Key? Distract him?" He repeated thoughtfully.

Wilhelm looked around, making sure they were alone, before continuing a bit more bluntly.

"I want to get something out of the port without anyone noticing. I need to be able to open the gate and I need the guard distracted. You think you can do that?"

"What do you want to get out of the port? Why can't you just take it out? Why are you sneaking it?" Reinhold asked.

"Never mind about that right now. Are you in or not?"

Wilhelm was getting fidgety. He was always one of the sailors who didn't like to be questioned. Reinhold couldn't count on all his appendages how many times the older man had told him to shut up before this new found friendship.

Reinhold mulled this request over for a minute before answering. It sounded easy enough. All he had to do was distract Henry and he would make a month's wages? Why not? He could put the money toward a new coat for the winter, a new coat that he needed desperately if he was going to be sailing the North Sea in winter again.

"Okay. I am in." He said. Wilhelm beamed at him.

"I'll give you more details as you need them." Wilhelm clapped Reinhold on the back and left him gazing, distracted, at the waning sunset, the rope limp in his fingers.

Chapter 26: Ninety Kilos

The man on the *Brandenburg* in the Caribbean Sea shook his head at his younger self.

I should have asked for more money, he thought as he light another cigarette. *How young and stupid was I?* He grinned at the question. *I was very young and very stupid. Am I all that more intelligent now? Definitely more experienced. That's more important than intelligence, isn't it?*

Looking back, he saw that he had made the classic mistake of not getting enough information. He should have asked a lot more questions, regardless of whether Wilhelm wanted to answer them or not.

But that's experience speaking, he thought to himself.

The younger Reinhold arrived with the *Eos* in Stockholm expecting it to be just another stop in the bustling city. He liked Stockholm although he wasn't really sure why. He hadn't ventured into the city but he had explored around the port. The people seemed friendly enough, the food was good, and there was always lots of bikes lying around just waiting for him to ride. He was sitting on the deck, watching the lights come on in a darkening Stockholm when Wilhelm appeared beside him out of the darkness.

"Tomorrow we load on one hundred and fifty bars of copper. When they start the loading, meet me in the cargo bay."

Without saying anything else he melted back into the shadows leaving Reinhold to stare quizzically after him.

The next day, as Wilhelm instructed him, he headed into the hull via the now quiet engine room. There were three pallets of copper already arranged in a neat line to his right. Reinhold wondered how many more were coming. Wilhelm was leaning against the cold metal bulkhead in a corner behind the first pallet, smoking a cigarette. At his feet was a long hole in the floor. Moving closer, Reinhold realized that the tank cover had been removed as if they were going to pump the water out of the bilge.

"You're late." Wilhelm growled at him as he approached.

The older man extinguished his cigarette by dropping it into the hole in the floor, a slight hiss announcing the presence of sea water under their feet. Without another word, Wilhelm began undoing the ropes holding the canvas in place around the pallets. Pulling back the material, Wilhelm revealed three foot long bars of lustrous copper stacked neatly on top of each other.

"Grab that end."

Wilhelm grasped a hold of the end of a bar nearest to him, gesturing with his chin for Reinhold to grab the other end. The metal was exceptionally cold and not as smooth to the touch as Reinhold thought it was going to be. It had tiny bumps and pits that his eye couldn't see but his fingertips could feel.

"When I tell you to, lift it and move it toward the-"

"Coming down!" Edwald's voice barked from the deck.

"Get down!" Wilhelm hissed at Reinhold as he ripped the canvas back in place, covering the precious metal, and scrambled to the center of the hull to guide down another pallet of copper bars.

It was quickly added to the line of pallets and the empty hook was send back up. Edwald's head appeared, outlined against the sky above.

"Good down there?" He asked, his gruff voice echoing of the metal walls.

"Good." Wilhelm confirmed. "What else is coming?"

"Two more pallets of copper. Then some lumber and some other odds and ends. All headed for Hamburg."

Wilhelm nodded his understanding and Edwald's head withdrew. He had not seen Reinhold or the removed floor boards.

"Quick!" Wilhelm hissed. "Grab it!" Reinhold grasped the bar again. "On three!"

Wilhelm instructed before beginning a count. On three Reinhold lifted the bar with both hands. It was far heavier than he was anticipating. He immediately dropped it back into place, panting with the effort.

"What is the matter with you?" Wilhelm asked. "I thought you were strong."

Reinhold detected a hint of taunting in the man's voice and didn't like it. Not one word of warning about the weight of the copper bar had passed Wilhelm's lips. Reinhold glared at the man as he counted again.

This time, on three, Reinhold put every ounce of strength he had into getting the bar off the stack. Together they managed to lower the copper to the open gap in the floorboards. They rolled it into the bilge where it landed with a hollow bang and a small splash.

Nervously, Wilhelm glanced up toward the deck. No one was looking down on them.

"We need to rearrange the bars on the pallet." Wilhelm said as he turned back to the pallet. "Quickly." He reiterated to Reinhold.

The two men moved the copper bars on the top row of the stack, spreading them out slightly to make it appear that the missing one was never there.

"Get out of here. I'll finish up myself." Wilhelm said tugged the canvas back into place. "And Reinhold, don't tell anyone about this. I'll know if you talk. You and I are the only two involved here."

He gave Reinhold a menacing warning look before turning his attention back to the piece of canvas.

Reinhold left wondering what he had just done. It was obvious that Wilhelm was stealing the copper bar. It was also obvious that Reinhold had just helped him.

What if he gets caught? He thought to himself. *Will I get in trouble to? Am I an accomplice? What would the punishment be? Could they send me to jail?*

Trust was not something he had for Wilhelm. He quickly decided that getting back to work was the best thing for him to do. He also decided that speaking to as few people as possible was best. He didn't want to be tempted to say something.

The *Eos* left Stockholm and returned to Hamburg. On the return voyage, Wilhelm spoke sparsely to Reinhold about mundane topics such as the weather and the quality of the food. Once the ship arrived in Hamburg, Reinhold expected Wilhelm to come find him so he could distract the gate man but that didn't happen. Instead, he found himself standing with some of the crew in the gathering dark watching a dramatic scene play out before him.

"We'll keep counting until everything adds up." Captain Hermann said to a man wearing a suit. The first count of the copper had come up one short.

Big surprise, Reinhold thought to himself.

"Can you trust your men, Captain?" The suit asked a bit testily as the second count began.

"I can trust my men. Can you trust yours?" The Captain growled in response, taking a small, almost imperceptible, step towards the suit.

The suit backed up a step, jerking his head back at the Captain's implications.

"I guess we'll see."

"I guess so." Capt. Hermann said before turning back to the job at hand. "Reinhold!" He bellowed, "Get down here!"

Reinhold felt his palms slicken at the sound of his name. He glanced quickly at Wilhelm before moving only to find the other man's attention was on the pallets of copper bars. He was counting the second of the five stacks as Reinhold made his way down the gangplank.

"Yes, sir?"

He looked at the man in the suit. The suit seemed amused but he also relaxed visibly. Reinhold knew that the man thought he was just an innocent boy with blond peach fuzz on his chin. How could someone so young be anything but honest?

"Reinhold, count these bars. Tell me what you come up with." Capt. Hermann turned to the suit. "Surely, you don't think that young Reinhold here is trying to rip you off? What would he do with a copper bar?"

Panic seized Reinhold. He started to count. Before he had finished the first stack, he decided that he would be honest about whatever number he came up with. They didn't suspect him of stealing anything so why would he lie? Wilhelm finished his count as Reinhold started on the second stack.

"One hundred and fifty." He announced to the Captain and the suit.

Both merely nodded at him in recognition of his findings. They were waiting for Reinhold.

"One hundred and forty nine." Reinhold announced when he was done. He saw the suit sighed heavily.

"Herbert, get over there and count." He said to one of his associates. A small group of men was hanging behind near two large trucks, smoking and watching the scene. "I want an accurate count, damn it, enough of this fooling around."

"One hundred and forty eight." Herbert announced several minutes later.

"You have got to be joking me! I'll count them myself!"

The suit stormed to the stacks and started counting. Reinhold's palms were becoming slicker. He really wanted them to load the copper into the trucks and drive away.

"I get one hundred and fifty." The suit announced several minutes later, straightening up from his crouching, counting position.

"Then there is no issue here. Sign the invoice so I can move my ship before they charge me for the dock space."

Captain Hermann produced a piece of paper and handed it to the suit with a flourish. But the suit still seemed reluctant.

"I want the boy to count it again."

The suit looked at Reinhold. Reinhold saw the Captain roll his heavily lidded eyes.

"Very well," he said. "Reinhold." He gestured toward the line of pallets.

Why can't this guy sign the paper? Reinhold thought to himself as he started to count again. This time he would count one hundred fifty.

"One hundred and fifty," he announced several minutes later.

"Very well," said the suit.

He took the invoice from Captain Hermann and signed it quickly before shouting orders to his men to start loading the copper. One of the men raised his hand and whistled. A hook appeared above the scene and slowly lowered to the pallets. The first one was already in the air, moving toward the back of one of the trucks when Reinhold heard the Captain bellow for him to get back on the ship.

"Captain, how much does one of those bars weight?" Reinhold asked as he trotted up the gangplank after Hermann.

"Ninety kilos. Get supper together."

The Captain was in a foul mood. Deciding against further questions, Reinhold headed for the galley.

The *Eos* left Hamburg again the next day carrying a confused Reinhold. Wilhelm never came to tell him that it was time to distract the gateman. As far as he knew, the copper bar was still in the bilge. Reinhold didn't understand. If it was him, he would have wanted to get rid of that thing as soon as possible. The suit was bound to find out sooner rather than later that he was a bar short.

I wonder what they will do when they find out they are one short, he wondered to himself as he swept the ashes off the carpet in the Captain's salon.

163

They were almost to the mouth of the Elbe when Wilhelm appeared in the door.

"I only have a minute. We are docking in Cuxhaven shortly. You did well counting those bars. You went along with the confusion and managed to look innocent the whole time. Good job. When we get back to Hamburg in ten days I will need your help with the gateman."

"When do I get my money?" Reinhold asked.

He surprised himself with the question almost as much as he surprised Wilhelm. Recovering quickly from the bluntness of the question, Wilhelm smiled at Reinhold.

"You get your money when I get mine."

With that, he left the doorway and made his way back to the deck. Reinhold could hear the First Mate shouting orders. Wilhelm's response made him realize that he had no idea how much copper was worth. How much could someone get for ninety kilos of copper?

Chapter 27: Unlock The Gate

Ten days later the *Eos* arrived back in Hamburg carrying lumber from Sweden. Reinhold was standing on the sunlit deck watching the shore men unload it onto flatbed trucks when Wilhelm appeared at his side. They stood in silence for a minute before Wilhelm spoke.

"Later tonight when the crew has gone drinking and the Captain has his wife onboard, I need you to distract the gateman. Got it?"

"Yes. How will I know when exactly?" Reinhold asked.

"I'll let you know. Just stay on deck. I'll come get you." Wilhelm explained.

They stood for another minute in silence before Wilhelm nodded at Reinhold and left, headed for the wheelhouse. Reinhold watched as his partner in crime approached the Captain and say something. Even through the Captain's rough exterior and impassive manner, not to mention the full beard and bushy eyebrows, Reinhold could see that something Wilhelm said had surprised him. He wondered briefly what could have surprised the stoic old man. Shrugging, he went below deck to start dinner. The crew would be grumbling for food soon.

As Wilhelm had requested, after dinner was served and the galley cleaned to spotless, Reinhold took up position on the deck. He settled on the middle hatch under one of the brass lamps he had shined that day. His back was to the mast and he was facing the rear of the ship. He had a new piece of rope for practicing splicing. He had gotten good at it and had decided that he was going to ask the Captain to let him go or make him a *Leichtmatrose*, a junior sailor. It was doubtful that the Captain would let him go. The old timers said that he just had to work hard and be able to splice behind his back. He thought he could fulfill those requirements. He was just starting his second splice when Wilhelm appeared at his side. The sudden arrival made Reinhold jump. He would be glad when this business was over. He had just about enough of Wilhelm's mysterious appearance and hasty departures.

"It is time," he said. He seemed a bit nervous and was sweating despite the cool night air. "I am going to shore. You follow in a few minutes and go right to the guard. Don't waste any time. Remember, I need the key. Get the key. Unlock the gate. Understand?"

Before Reinhold could answer Wilhelm was gone, disappeared into the darkness. He passed a few minutes finishing his splice before getting up to leave. He wandered down the deck to where Dirk was standing in his usual spot against the rail. The glowing ember and cloud of smoke told Reinhold the man was enjoying a cigarette even though all he could see was a silhouette against the lights coming from the wheelhouse.

"Evening, Dirk." Reinhold greeted him.

"Evening," Dirk grunted in response.

It had taken the better part of seven months, but Reinhold now understood the words that escaped Dirk's lips disguised as his characteristic grunts.

"When you are done with your smoke can you take me ashore?" Reinhold was always polite to Dirk because the man still scared the crap out of him.

"We can go now." The man said, flicking the butt of his cigarette into the river.

Quickly and nimbly, he jumped down to the small boat. Reinhold followed and before he knew it he was climbing the ladder up the concrete seawall. Even on his best days, Reinhold couldn't row the little dingy as fast as Dirk.

Reinhold wandered towards the gate. Until now, he had never really thought about how he was going to distract Henry's attention. He racked his brain as he walked. What could he say? What could he do? What would cause a gateman to leave his post? How long would a gateman abandon his post? How was he going to get the key back once he was done with it? He turned his mind inside out thinking, thinking. It had to be some kind of emergency or suspicious person or activity.

Reinhold realized he had been lost in thought for too long. He was in Henry's view. The man was waving at him from the doorway of the gatehouse. He looked older than usual, kind of haggard. Reinhold wondered if he was getting enough food.

"Reinhold, how are you?" he called. "I'd heard that the *Eos* had docked. Some of your mates just left for the nightlife."

"Yeah, they'll be worked up when they get back. Was Wilhelm with them?" Reinhold asked coyly. He hadn't forgotten the argument Henry had with Wilhelm.

"No." Henry snorted. He had not forgotten either. "What brings you this way? Out for a stroll?"

"Yeah, fresh air and solid ground." Reinhold responded.

He saw something move out of the corner of his eye. Glancing to his right, he saw Wilhelm briefly materialize out of the shadows before fading back into them. He appeared just long enough for Reinhold to know that he was waiting. It was time to hold up his end of the bargain. Returning his attention to Henry, Reinhold stammered for a second, thinking. "Slow night?" he asked, buying time.

"It has been at that, now that you mention it. Boring, really. To be expected. It's Saturday. No Captain wants to be in port on Sunday morning."

Reinhold decided in that moment that he would enliven Henry's night and went for a bald faced lie that would distract the man for at least four or five minutes.

"You know, on my way here, I thought I saw someone climbing the fence over there." Reinhold pointed down the fence line to the east, back the way he had just come. "It looked to me like he was wearing a dark coat and dungarees."

Henry's eyes widened. "Why didn't you say something right away, Reinhold? I have to go check it out! Watch the booth for me, would you? Don't open the gate for anyone. If anyone does come, tell them to wait. I shouldn't be gone long."

He grabbed a flashlight as he spoke, flicking it on to be sure it worked. Then he hurried off into the night.

As soon as Henry was out of sight, Reinhold pulled the gate key off the wall and dashed to the lock. With shaking hands, he unlocked it and pushed open one half of the obstruction. Seconds later, Wilhelm and a man that Reinhold had never seen before appeared from behind the gatehouse carrying the copper bar wrapped in a wool blanket. They struggled under the weight. Once they passed, Reinhold closed the gate and secured the lock. Dashing back to the gatehouse, he returned the key to the hook on the wall next to the door.

Wanting to appear casual, not at all like a troublemaker, Reinhold leaned somewhat cockily in the door of the gatehouse. His heart was pounding in his ears and he had broken into a cold sweat.

Verdammt! He cursed himself. *Stop sweating! It is all over now.*

He took several deep breaths to steady himself. He ran the sleeve of his new coat under the brim of his new wool hat and around his face. Looking out the gate, he saw no sign of Wilhelm and the copper bar but a little ways up the street a car roared to a start and headlights pierced the dark. Slowly, it turned around and headed away from the port. Reinhold thought he saw an arm come out of the window in a kind of waving gesture.

"I didn't see anyone but there are more foot prints along the fence then there really should be." Henry arrived back at his post, scaring an edgy and distracted Reinhold. He jumped at the sound of the man's voice.

"It is just me." Henry laughed at the surprised look on Reinhold's face. "Everything ok?"

"Yeah, yeah. Fine. It's a little creepy here at night all alone."

Reinhold hoped that covered his edginess. He moved out of the doorway so Henry could replace the flashlight.

"Yes, it is." Henry responded. "You should be here when the fog comes in and every sound seems magnified by the mist." Henry gave a slight shudder.

"What do you think happened to the guy I saw coming over the fence?" Reinhold asked desperately trying to sound casual.

Henry scratched his chin, thoughtfully. "I don't think you saw someone coming, Reinhold. I think you saw someone leaving. A ship jumper probably. Most likely from Easy Germany. We get ships from Rostok and Wismar here all the time." He shrugged indifferently. "Why they would want to jump here is beyond me what with no food, the place still a ruin, and barely any jobs to speak of. Don't worry, they'll get him outside the port and return him. I'll just alert the police to be on the lookout."

Henry picked up the phone on the desk in the small gatehouse and dialed a number. Reinhold thought this was an opportune moment to make his exit. He had just about enough excitement for one night.

"See you later, Henry." Reinhold said while Henry waited, receiver pressed to his ear.

"See you, Reinhold." He responded absently.

It was too early and he was too jumpy to go back to the ship so Reinhold wandered the port. One of his favorite things to do was watch the lights mounted on ships move up and down the river. In the darkness, they seemed disembodied and were full of mystery and intrigue. Where were they going? Where had they been? What were they carrying? He especially loved when the really big ships came in covered in electric lights and sending out huge wakes. One of the crew of the *Eos* had told him that ships that size were rare because of the war. So many of them had been taken by the government and then were sunk while on missions and such. The big ships never failed to make Reinhold think of the ships that sunk in Lübeck Bay. He shivered involuntarily.

A real treat awaited him that night. As he circled back around the port, having gone as far west as he could, he caught sight of a huge white yacht lit up like a Christmas display. He stopped to watch it head toward Hafenstadt probably to dock for the night. Music drifted across the river in his direction. He realized it was coming from a party on the deck. He could see people moving between the deck and the large main cabin. Snippets of laughter wafted along with the music. The ship moved off quickly and quietly, leaving a decent wake. Reinhold wondered who owned the yacht.

It wasn't much later, after doing a full lap of the port, that Reinhold decided he would head back to the *Eos*. The adrenaline released by his caper with Henry had worn off leaving him tired. He had wandered past Henry's post to see if there were any repercussions from his lie about the man or his snatching the key but all was quiet. Henry was sitting on his stool outside the gatehouse reading a newspaper. Reinhold didn't dare bother the man again. Instead, he wandered to where the *Eos* was at anchor and whistled for Dirk. A few minutes later, the little dingy bumped into the side of the *Eos* and Reinhold vaulted over the side of the ship on to the deck.

He wandered into the wheelhouse and slumped down on one of the benches lining the wall. The room was empty. Everyone had other things to do tonight. Even the Captain, who was almost always in the wheelhouse, had his wife aboard. Reinhold met her earlier. She was as salty as her husband, grim faced and serious.

She must be Frisian, too, he thought.

He sighed to himself, wondering if it wasn't best for him to turn in for the night. Then movement in the dark on the deck caught his eye. Someone was climbing over the rail. The next minute, Wilhelm appeared in the circle of light surrounding the wheelhouse. He gestured for Reinhold to meet him at the front of the ship.

"Good work, Reinhold. Here is your money."

Wilhelm handed Reinhold fifteen *mark*. Reinhold rattled the coins around his hand to count them. Satisfied with the amount, he shoved them into the pocket of his dungarees. Nodding his thanks to Wilhelm, he turned to leave, considering their dealings to be done.

"Hold on a minute." Wilhelm requested. Reinhold turned back to him, wondering what else this guy could possibly want of him. "I was thinking of going to Reeperbahn to celebrate. Maybe you can come with me."

Reinhold was caught off guard by the offer. None of the crew had ever been keen on him tagging along with them when they went out. Too much of a hassle, they said. Until now, he really hadn't cared that he was confined to the port and the ship. However, with the offer on the table such as it was, Reinhold realized that he would love nothing more than to see something new and exciting.

Besides, he reasoned to himself, *just because I go doesn't mean I have to drink.* His stomach did a flip at the thought of alcohol.

"Okay." He said simply, before his nerve failed.

"That's my boy!" Wilhelm said, clapped Reinhold on the back of his shoulder somewhat awkwardly.

Chapter 28: Reeperbahn

If I knew then what I know now, Reinhold thought wistfully to himself.

The sun was slowly sinking into the Caribbean, creating fractured rainbows on the water and painting the fluffy white clouds shades of pink and apricot. It was truly a lovely sight to behold. Sighing, he glanced at the watch on his wrist. His four hours of standing watch were almost done and he was looking forward to getting something to eat.

If I only knew then what I know now, he thought to himself again. *That trip to the Reeperbahn wouldn't have been so dreadful.*

He could remember it more clearly than he wanted to.

Strange, he thought, *how the bad memories seem to last longer and be more vivid than the good ones.*

He and Wilhelm set out from the port, Henry looking suspiciously at them as they left, and walked the several blocks up Davidstraße to Reeperbahn. On their way, Wilhelm talked excitedly about their destination while Reinhold looked around the battered city. Nothing really changed since Reinhold last walked these streets.

As they walked up the hill from the port, Reinhold peered into side streets, curious to see what was going on. One street, he noticed, had a gate up and a sign posted. Beyond the gate, the street was bathed in red light. He was going to ask Wilhelm but the man never shut up about the Reeperbahn.

"You're going to love the Reeperbahn, Reinhold. It has everything a man could want: drink, food, shows, women, everything. *Die sündige Meile*[25], that's what they call it and for good reason. The shows alone would make a man forget the yammering of his priest. But the women are the best, the heart of Reeperbahn." Reinhold saw Wilhelm look sideways at him. "Maybe we will even get you a woman tonight. How about that? Have you ever had a woman?"

Reinhold felt himself blush. He had never had a woman. How could he? The age restraints kept him confined to the ship and the immediate port area around it. Before the ship, he had more pressing issues to worry about than girls. Playing doctor with Isolde didn't

---

[25] *Die sündige Meile means 'The Sinful Mile'.*

count, in his option. The other guys on the crew thought it was quite amusing, used it as fodder for jokes and comments. Wilhelm must have seen the blush even in the semi darkness of the street.

"It is no big deal. Maybe we will make tonight your first in celebration of our success! Do you have a preference? Blond, brunette, redhead? Surely, you have thought about that." He said with childlike excitement. Before Reinhold could answer, Wilhelm sighed, "Ah, here we are."

Reinhold's eyes were dazzled as they turned the corner on to the wide avenue of Reeperbahn. There were signs everywhere advertising food, nightclubs, taverns, shops, and hotels. He stared into the windows of these tightly packed and obviously very old buildings as they walked. The restaurants were full of well-dressed people laughing and raising glasses. The nightclubs' windows were blacked out, leaving Reinhold to wonder what was going on that needed to be hidden. The shop window's held items that he had never seen before.

"You have to be dressed to go to most of the restaurants and nightclubs here. We have to keep moving." Wilhelm continued down the street a few more yards before stopping and turning to Reinhold. He had a mischievous look on his face.

"On second thought," he said, "I think we will go back to Herbertstraße."

Heading back the way they had come, Wilhelm led Reinhold to the street with the gate and the red light. The gate was a mute gray color that almost made it disappear into the buildings around it. The sign posted informed people that men under 18 and women were not allowed to enter. Reinhold turned to point out to Wilhelm that he was not eighteen, but the older man anticipated the comment and waved him off saying, "No one cares and no one checks," as he pushed open the barrier and motioned Reinhold through.

Reinhold didn't know what he had been expecting but what was on the other side of the gate was not it. It was a quiet, narrow, city street with tall buildings on either side. Miraculously, they didn't look damaged. A few men were wandering down its length, looking in the windows. One or two stood in front of a window, talking to someone on the other side of the glass. Red light came from every building and every fixture giving the place an eerie glow.

Wilhelm started up the street and Reinhold moved to follow him when something caught his eye. Focusing through the red gloom, he saw a girl in the window of one of the buildings to his right. She was half naked! Shocked, he stared for a few seconds. The girl motioned for him to come over. Instead of heading in her direction, Reinhold hurried behind Wilhelm.

"Where are we?" he asked.

"The *puff*[26]," Wilhelm answered. "You get girls here. They stand in the windows and you walk around to pick the one you would like to take to bed. Come on, we'll see what is being offered tonight."

The man and the boy wandered down the street looking in the windows. Women of all types watched them pass, motioning for them to come over.

"Don't commit too early," Wilhelm advised. "Look over the whole selection first. Look for what you like. Do you like blondes or redheads or brunettes?"

Reinhold shrugged in response. He really hadn't thought about it. What did he like?

They walked to the end of the street in silence, looking at the half dressed ladies in the windows. Reinhold noted that many of them looked bored, only half-heartedly trying to interest the browsing men. Half way down the other side of the street, one of the girls caught his attention. She had opened a smaller window in her picture window and was calling to him.

"Oh, little boy!" she taunted. "What are you looking for, little boy? I bet I could help you find it. You are such a sweet looking little man."

Reinhold felt himself blush again.

"That one likes you. You should go talk to her." Wilhelm nudged Reinhold toward the window.

"Why don't you come inside? We'll chat." The girl asked.

"Yeah, why don't you go inside and chat?" Wilhelm encouraged, mimicking the girl's flirtatious tone.

He wasn't entirely sure how it happened, but the next thing Reinhold remembered was standing in the dimly lit foyer of the *puff* while Wilhelm wished him luck and left.

"Come sit over here on the couch. What is your name?"

The girl from the window was guiding him toward a worn red velvet couch. Her voice was soft, silky almost. He felt it curling around his belly like a living creature.

---

[26] *Puff* is a German slang term for a brothel.

"Reinhold."

"Oh, that's a good name, very grown up."

She was sitting almost on his lap, petting his hand, and leaning so that her half naked breasts were pressed against his arm. Her blond hair fell lose around her face. She smelled faintly of something sweet and floral.

"Are you a sailor? You smell like the sea."

He nodded, conscious for the first time in a long time that he probably smelled like more than the sea. He hadn't had a washing in two weeks.

"Tell me, Reinhold, how much money do you have?"

"Fifteen *mark*."

"Fifteen *mark*! Well, you should give that to me and I will take care of it and you."

Reinhold lost the ability to think and reason. He had never had a woman, a real woman, sit so near, touch him so intimately, and speak in his ear in such a seductive whisper. His heart was racing and his mouth was dry. He watched himself reach into his pocket and handed over the few coins it contained.

"Good, good," she whispered. "You should follow me."

And he did.

She led the way up the steep, narrow staircase from the foyer to the third floor. He couldn't help but focus on the semi-exposed female rump bouncing before him. Something was happening to him that had happened before but never in such circumstances, never this powerful. There was a strong sense of urgency and need coursing through his blood.

Down the hallway went the bouncing bottom and Reinhold followed it blindly into a small room that contained only a large bed. It was lit with the same red lights as the street. He stood on the threshold for a second, letting his eyes adjust to the light.

"Close the door."

With dramatic flair, the girl whirled on him and started to take off the few clothes she was wearing. The sheer silk robe went first. It was followed tantalizingly by the scrap of fabric that qualified as panties and the flimsy bra. Reinhold swallowed nervously, unable to blink his staring eyes, his heart hammering against his chest. He and his manhood were painfully aware of her actions, her nakedness. She laid herself out on the bed, spreading her thighs to revel her world to him.

"Come here," said the soft, silky voice.

Reinhold went into sensory overload. He took a step forward, with every intention of getting into the bed but never made it. Without further ado, the little Reinhold in his pants erupted in a flood of warmth. Surprised, he looked down.

What the hell? He thought to himself.

His thoughts must have shown on his face plain as his nose. Laughter began slow and soft from the bed.

"Did you get off without me?" The laughter started anew, louder and more haughty. "My, goodness, little one, you were my easiest customer ever. I wish all I had to do for everyone was show myself."

Again, the laughter. It pierced through Reinhold's surprise and nervousness to bring him shame and belittlement. He didn't like the feeling of shame and he had never liked being belittled. Turning on his heel, he made for the door.

"There is a wash room at the end of the hall. No sense walking around with the evidence in your pants."

The laughter came again, haughty and condescending. Reinhold left the room, striding stiff backed and red faced to the washroom. He wanted to get out of this place as fast as possible.

Minutes later, he found himself back on the street. Disappointed and humiliated, he wandered back to the *Eos* alone. He was glad that Wilhelm hadn't stuck around. How embarrassing would it have been to have him witness a whore laughing at him? He swore to himself as he shuffled along that he would never return to that particular *puff*. At the entrance to the port, he gave Henry a wave. The guard looked at him in confusion.

"Where's the *arschloch* you left with? Wilhelm?" He called.

Reinhold shrugged indifferently. He wasn't in the mood to stop and talk. It had just been too long of a night.

Chapter 29: Don't Ever Change

The rest of Reinhold's time on the *Eos* was uneventful, boring even. The only excitement was when they went to a new port, which rarely happened. Every week or so he would ask Capt. Hermann if he could have his sailor's book back so he could leave the ship. Every time he asked, he was declined and dismissed to continue his duties. Routine ruled his young life. Get up, make coffee, make breakfast, clean until he could see himself in the metal, fill rusty holes, make knots, splice lines, make lunch, make dinner, and finally, sit around at night in the wheelhouse with the crew listening to stories about sailing, drinking, and women.

The stories about women interested Reinhold in a different way now than before his experience at the *puff*. His first attempt had been an embarrassing failure but he was determined that the next time would be better. Now he was listening for pointers, for information on how the deed was supposed to be done so he would be better prepared in the future. He never told anyone what happened at the *puff*. Much to Reinhold's relief, and dismay, Wilhelm never appeared on the *Eos* again. He was able to keep his secret, this time. When the crew got on his case about never having been with a woman, he played along, laughing about his innocence. They weren't so wrong after all. He was never with that woman.

Things changed for Reinhold in October, eleven months after boarding the *Eos*. The *Eos* arrived back in Hamburg after a trip that took them along their usual route from Holland to Sweden. It was payday and most of the crew was on shore at the bars and brothels. Capt. Hermann called Reinhold into the wheelhouse. He figured it was just for his pay. He was right about the pay but was taken by surprise when the Captain also handed him his sailor's book.

"You haven't given up your quest to get off my ship, have you?" Captain Hermann asked him when he saw the shock on Reinhold's face.

"No," Reinhold responded quickly, "I'm just surprised. I didn't think you were going to let me go yet."

"I don't want to let you go but you are so persistent about leaving. I think it is time you move on."

A stunned "Thank you" escaped his lips. As he turned to leave, he realized that he wasn't sure of the protocol in this situation.

Turning back, he asked, "Do I leave now? Or can I wait until morning?"

Capt. Hermann laughed, a deep hearty laugh that made his massive head totter on his wide shoulders. It was a strange sound coming from this man. "You can wait until morning."

His laughter threatened to resume. Reinhold turned to leave but he had only taken a step when he felt large, powerful fingers dig into his shoulder, preventing him from going any further. "One second, Reinhold. I want to say something to you before you go."

Reinhold faced the older man again and waited. The Captain cleared his throat, his eyes looking off into the distance toward the shore and the lights of Hamburg.

"Don't ever change, Reinhold," the Captain said. "For eleven months now you have worked for me and I think I know you well enough. You are an honest man and a hardworking man. I have an ashtray full of coins to prove it. Don't let anyone change that. It is more important in this life to be honest and trustworthy than anything else."

He released his grip on Reinhold's shoulders and gave him a friendly clap on the shoulder.

"Thank you. I won't." It was all Reinhold could think to say.

He wished that he could have said something in return to the Captain but his mind was blank except for the repeating refrain: *I am going home, I am going home, I am going home, I am going home.*

He was so excited that he packed up his stuff immediately. It didn't take him long. He had the same plywood suitcase he had arrived with except instead of containing just a pair of clogs, few extra knit socks, and a ragged shirt, now it held a brand new shirt, an extra pair of pants, and a heavy wool coat in addition to several pairs of new socks. One thing he would be going home with, which he hadn't arrived with, was a small stack of *mark;* seventy of them, to be exact. He counted the bills and coins twice before stashing them back in his boot. Then he lay on his bunk, thinking it would be great if he could just fall asleep and wake up in the morning.

Sleep would not come. After turning several times in his narrow bunk, he got up, retrieved his clogs from the suitcase, and went up to the deck for fresh air. He had gotten used to the stale, foul odor that lived in the bunkroom and was more than happy that this would be his last night having to endure its presence.

On deck, Reinhold gulped down several lungs full of cool, fresh, salty air before making himself comfortable against the center mast on top of the hatch. There was a bit of light coming from the wheelhouse but he was almost completely in shadow. He pulled the newest bit of rope from his pocket and began splicing. Really, he was only half paying attention to the rope. His mind was thinking of home. He wondered if he would find a job that would allow him to stay in Ratekau.

Maybe Lübeck, he thought to himself. *There has to be something going on in Lübeck by now.*

Reinhold knew better than to count on things being better in Lübeck than when he left. Looking toward the shore, he was reminded that even here, in the great bombed out metropolis of Hamburg, there was little opportunity.

Goddamn war, he cursed to himself his hand balling involuntarily into a fist. *It left nothing but crap for us that survived it. No jobs, no food, and bad memories. What a bunch of* scheiße*!*

The first of the crew began to arrive back to the ship not long after Reinhold took up his spot against the mast. The first couple noticed Reinhold sitting there and nodded at him as they passed, headed for bed. They made their way the length of the ship arguing about something involving a woman and a pig. It wasn't hard to decide to spend a bit longer on the deck after the passing of the drunks. They needed time and space to get themselves into their bunks. Half an hour later, with a sigh, Reinhold got up and headed for his bunk.

The next morning, Reinhold woke before everybody else, as was his custom. He hadn't heard the loud banging that usually roused him. At first, this confused him, but then he remembered that, technically, he didn't work for this ship anymore. He leapt out of his bunk, dressed quickly, grabbed his suitcase, and left the bunkroom with a parting nose wrinkle. He headed first to the galley to see who was cooking breakfast. The sight of Erik lumbering around the narrow room, cracking eggs and slicing bread was almost comical to Reinhold.

"Morning, Erik," He greeted the man from the door.

Erik grunted in response without turning to look at him. Nonplussed by the hostility Reinhold asked, "How can I get to the shore?"

"Dirk will be up in a few minutes. You can wait for him."

"I'll take you, Reinhold."

Whirling in surprise, Reinhold saw the Captain standing behind him at the foot of the ladder to the deck.

He followed Capt. Hermann to the dingy. The small boat always seemed smaller when the Captain was in it and today was no exception. The trip to the shore was quick and silent.

"Thanks for everything," Reinhold said before he climbed up the metal rungs set into the concrete pier.

"Remember what I told you, Reinhold: never change. You are good the way you are."

"Yes, sir."

With that, the Captain was gone, rowing his way back to the *Eos*. As he walked toward the gate, Reinhold couldn't help feeling a bit guilty. Captain Hermann had no idea about the copper bar.

What would he say if he knew about that? Reinhold wondered to himself.

He quickly decided not to think about that anymore. He felt bad enough about his dishonesty without adding the Captain's hypothetical disappointment to the mix. At the gate, Reinhold had to show his sailor's book and passport to the guard. He only just barely recognized the man and had never spoken with him before. With a very official nod and a stately opening of the gate, Reinhold exited the port of Hamburg and made his way to the train station. With any luck, he would be home by evening.

Luck was not with him that day. He wandered a bit too much on his way to the station and missed the morning train. The next one wouldn't be until the late afternoon or early evening.

While he sat on one of the hard benches in the still roofless and cavernous station, Reinhold took out his sailor's book to see the first completed page. To his great surprise, he noted that he had been promoted twice while on the *Eos*. He made *Jungmann* not long after his altercation with Klaus. It coincided with a raise he received but the Captain never mentioned that it came with a promotion. The second promotion to *Leichtmatrose* had been just two months ago. It coincided once again with a pay increase but, once again, a promotion was never mentioned.

Talk about men or few words and fewer smiles, he thought. *They didn't even tell me I got promoted. I am a* Leichtmatrose!

A feeling of satisfaction flooded through him.

It was two in the morning when Reinhold walked up the steps to his kitchen door. Turning the handle, he found it locked.

Verdammnt! He cursed to himself. *Now I am stuck on the porch!*

He put his suitcase down, ready to settle down to wait when the door swung open and his father's frame was silhouetted against the dim light coming from the stove. He had a fire poker in one hand.

"Reinhold?" he questioned.

"Yes."

"What are you doing here?"

"I left the ship I was working on, decided to come home."

"Did you bring money to live here?" Reinhold's stomach clenched at the sound of his stepmother's demanding voice.

The older Reinhold waved away her words and ushered his son into the kitchen.

"Are you hungry?"

"Yes. I haven't eaten since breakfast."

"Sit down. We don't have much, some bread and milk maybe."

Reinhold watched his father pull a half a loaf of bread from the cabinet and cut off a slice. The milk jug was on the table so he helped himself to a mug from another cabinet and poured the milk. They sat at the table together for the first time in almost a year.

"What do you mean you left your ship?"

Reinhold shrugged as he chewed on the bread. "I left."

"Are you going back?"

"No."

"What are you going to do?"

"He is not staying here without paying!"

The older Reinhold waved off the voice from the bedroom. Reinhold noticed that his father looked much better than the last time he had seen him but older somehow, greyer.

"I am going to get a job, I guess."

"You didn't like sailing?"

Reinhold shrugged in response and yawned.

"Your sister's aren't here anymore. You can stay in their room, if you want."

"That's ok. I'll stay in the attic."

Honestly, he was looking forward to a ventilated room after sleeping in the coffin for eleven months.

"See you in the morning, Reinhold."

His father left, returning to his bedroom and his wife. Reinhold climbed the stairs to the attic. It was exactly how he left it, sparsely furnished and drafty with a soft, warm feather bed. He wondered where Lisa and Isolde were.

Chapter 30: Why Did I Come Back Here?

Reinhold didn't have the opportunity to speak with his father the next morning. With no responsibilities to tend to, he slept well into the morning. The house was empty when he went downstairs to the kitchen. Helping himself to a slice of bread and some milk, Reinhold took a seat at the table by the stove. He looked around the kitchen expecting something to be different, better so how. But it wasn't. Everything was the same if not a bit shabbier. There was dust piled in corners and the curtains were streaked with old cobwebs.

Mama never was one for cleaning house, he mused to himself.

With Isolde and Lisa gone all the housekeeping fell to her. Shrugging his indifference, Reinhold got up from the table. He was going to do some cleaning today but it was not going to be the kitchen.

Out back, he found the washing tub exactly where he left it almost a year ago. Next to it was the bucket yoke for collecting water from the pump down the street. Reinhold set to work and two hours later was the cleanest he had been in months. It took several trips to the pump and lots of boiling water from the kitchen stove, but he felt that he washed away the dirt of the *Eos* and the smell of the sea.

Once he finished with himself, he got started on his clothes. He borrowed a shirt of his father's and a pair of pants so that he could do all of his own at the same time. He hung two shirts, two pairs of pants, and a dozen pairs of socks on the line to dry.

"Did you rob a bank while you were gone?"

Reinhold whipped his head around in surprise to see Paul Easberger leaning on a fence post, picking his teeth with a small scrap of wood.

"No, of course not."

Reinhold went back to emptying the laundry kettle, somewhat insulted by the insinuation.

"Did you find yourself one of those rich fancy women to buy you all those socks and that new pair of pants?"

"No." Reinhold couldn't help by laugh. "I was working on a ship. I bought all these socks. You have to keep your feet dry on the seas."

"So I have heard. See you around, Reinhold."

The older man threw away his toothpick and departed. Reinhold wondered for a minute if he had offended *Herr* Easberger by laughing at his question about the socks.

Probably never seen so many at one time before, he thought to himself.

His washing done, Reinhold set out to find his friends. It was late afternoon already and they would be finishing with work soon. He was looking forward to seeing them.

"Well, look who has returned from the high seas." Willie called with a grin when he saw Reinhold entering the farmyard.

He and Abby were just finishing up with the cows. Reinhold couldn't help but grin at his two friends. They were covered from head to toe in dirt. He hadn't seen anyone quite that dirty with real dirt in a long time.

"How are the cows, boys?" Reinhold called to them.

"Same as always: temperamental and hungry." Abby answered, slapping the nearest beast on the hindquarters.

"Did you make it on to a ship, Reinhold?" Willie asked.

"Yup. The *Eos*. I got a job cooking and cleaning. We went to Holland and Sweden mostly. Spent a lot of time in the port in Hamburg, too. It is all bombed out there still. You should see it, it is incredible. People are living on ships on the Elbe because there are so few buildings."

Reinhold stopped talking even though he was going to say more. The faraway looks on Willie and Abby's faces told him that they didn't want to hear anymore. He changed the subject quickly.

"How are things here? How's everybody?"

"Same as always. Kule is away at school so are Bernard and Heinilaken. We haven't seen Arnold or his dad for months. He must have left too." Willie answered with a deep shrug.

There was an uncomfortable silence before Abby spoke up.

"We are going to go to Köster's. Want to come with us?"

"Köster's? For what? There is nothing to do there but drink." Reinhold was surprised by the invitation.

"Exactly. We are going to get a beer."

"No, thanks. I don't drink."

Abby grinned at him. "I remember a time that you drank."

Reinhold blushed under his collar. "That's the reason why I don't drink now. Every time I think about it, my stomach turns.

Besides, that stuff is just a waste of money. I watched guys drink their whole month's pay away in one night in Hamburg."

The strange look returned to his friend's face at the mention of his sailing experiences. Baffled, he decided it was time to leave them.

"Well, have a good time at Köster's. I'll get with you later."

"See you, Reinhold."

Reinhold didn't understand why he had gotten such a cool reception from his friends.

This time last year I was their leader, their go-to guy. What happened? And why were they going drinking? Were they even old enough to get served at Köster's?

Shrugging, he kept walking. Hadn't he gotten into Reeperbahn even though he wasn't eighteen?

"Reinhold! What brings you here?" Walter Muuss was emerging from the cowshed carrying an armload of feedbags. Reinhold trotted the few meters to him to help but was waved away.

"I am ok here. I can still move some feedbags. I am not that old yet."

Reinhold backed off.

"I am home from Hamburg. I am looking for work, actually. Do you have any here?"

"I thought you wanted something bigger and better than farming."

"Yeah, well, turns out I don't like sailing very much."

"I am sorry Reinhold but I have all the help I need right now. It is a bad time of year to be looking for work in farming, you know that. The harvest is in already and I haven't gotten my herd back to where it was during the war."

Reinhold was disappointed by the response.

"Ok. Thanks anyway, Herr Muuss."

"You might have better luck in Lübeck. I hear they are looking for construction people there, builders and such."

"I'll look into it. Thanks again."

Reinhold turned his footsteps to the street to head home.

What a miserable trip home that had been. His stepmother made a point of questioning him about his financial situation. He had tried to hold out and not give her any money but in the end her hostile persistence beat him and he handed over twenty of his fifty *mark*.

Finally, after he had given her money, she decided to answer the questions he had been asking.

"Isolde ran off to Sereetz with a boy. Paul is his name. Do you know him?"

"No. I never met anyone here with that name."

Reinhold scratched his chin. He wondered who his guy was that had so smitten his sister. What kind of man would Isolde run off with? He had to smile.

"Well, they got married almost two months ago."

"What? She's married?"

"That's right. Probably expecting by now. And Lisa is in Lübeck."

"Oh. Do you know where in Lübeck?"

His stepmother shook her head in response. He had the feeling she was lying to him. Reinhold didn't have to ask why his sister's left. Hadn't he left as soon as he could?

Looking back, Reinhold also remembered that trip home being boring and disappointing. His father was working or drinking and showed little interest in his son. In an attempt to reconcile his relationship with his father, Reinhold went to Köster's his fourth night home. He didn't drink even though he was offered many mugs of beer. People treated him like a stranger, an outsider, even his friends. They asked him questions about sailing but when he answered them, they didn't seem to like the answers. Their eyes glazed over and they became more interested in their beer. They never openly challenged him, but he could tell they didn't really believe what he was saying. The only part of his experience that they seemed to find remotely interesting was his horrible seasickness. Reinhold went along with their laughter, happy that he had broken the ice. After that, Willie and Abby convinced him to attend a *Damenwahl*[27] the following night.

"We're all going to be there. And there should be lots of ladies. It is a *Damenwahl* after all. Maybe you could get lucky again, Reinhold."

He had embellished his Reeperbahn story to his advantage. He couldn't help being a bit cocky about his time away from the small, tired, boring town.

---

[27] A *Damenwahl* is like an American Sadie Hawkins dance where the girl's invite the boys.

The following night, Reinhold went to the dance at the public house only to find that his friends had not come. Determined not to take it personally and have a good time anyway, he danced and flirted with the girls, telling them how beautiful they were and what graceful dancers. One girl, a pretty blonde wearing a heavily patched blue dress, was particularly interested in him. Reinhold convinced her to leave, wanting another shot at what had gone so wrong at the Reeperbahn, but they didn't get far. The girl failed to mention that she had a boyfriend. After a brief back and forth of words with the boyfriend, Reinhold excused himself and left. He had a bad feeling.

Outside Köster's was a thorny hedge, tall and thick with age. Reinhold hid himself behind this hedge and thought about his situation. He knew that the boyfriend was gathering his friends. He could run home and lock himself in the house but would they come after him? He could stay here and fight but he didn't know how many friends the boyfriend had and whether he would be able to defeat them all. When a guy came out of the gap in the hedge, Reinhold knew that his decision was made for him. He had to stay and fight.

He grabbed the guy by the back of his shirt and swung him into the hedge. What a racket the victim sent up! The second guy to come through the gap was the boyfriend. He was wearing a set of brass knuckles. They came soaring at Reinhold's temple but he stopped them with his hand and punched the guy in the face, sending him to the ground. He grabbed the back of the boyfriend's shirt and threw him into the hedge and again a racket erupted. The girl was the next person to come through the hedge. In his adrenaline fueled and defensive mood, Reinhold almost punched her too but stopped just in time.

"Here," she said, holding out her hand to him.

Focusing on it, Reinhold saw a handkerchief. "What do I want with that?"

"It is for your hand, silly. You're bleeding!"

Looking at his hand, Reinhold realized he was, indeed, bleeding where the brass knuckles hit him. With a mumbled "Thank you" he took the offered rag and wrapped it around his injured hand. He was very glad that it wasn't broken. No one was going to hire anyone with an injury. It was then that he noticed that there were people watching him, Willie and Abby amongst them.

How long have they been here? He wondered.

"Scholz had a fight over a girl!" He heard someone say.

There was someone else here that recognized him.

Ah, crap, he thought to himself, *now the whole town is going to know that I got in a fight over a girl.*

Without a word to anyone, Reinhold turned and left, headed for home.

Why did I come back here? He questioned himself. *Stupid, nothing was going to change here! Only five days home and I get into a fight over some girl. I can't stay here. There is no work anyway.*

He made up his mind before he reached his house to leave Ratekau in morning. He figured there had to be something going on in Lübeck. Maybe Lisa or this boyfriend of hers could help him.

That night Reinhold dreamt of the sea. He was on the deck of a ship, not the *Eos*, but a bigger vessel. He was staring at the sun setting over a watery horizon. He could feel the salty breeze on his face and hear the seagulls crying over head. He felt that they were calling to him. He woke up with an overwhelming desire to go to the sea. He lingered long enough at home that morning to find out from his father where he could find Lisa.

Chapter 31: Experience

Reinhold surprised Lisa when he showed up on her doorstep that evening. Over a meager dinner, she and her new boyfriend, Willie, listened intently to his stories about sailing, even interrupted to ask questions.

"So, it doesn't sound like you had the best time of it. Did you make any money at least?" Lisa inquired.

Reinhold reached into his pocket and pulled out his remaining *mark*, forty of them, to be exact.

"Reinhold, you can't walk around with all that money on you! You should get a post book."

"What is a post book?"

"You get it at the post office. They hold on to your money and give you a book so you can keep track of it. That way you are not walking around, like I said, with all that money. If someone hits you in the head and knocks you out, they take it all from you."

Reinhold put up a hand to stop her.

"Okay, I get it."

"What are you going to do now that you are back, Reinhold?" asked Willie, changing the subject.

"I don't know. I was hoping to find something here." He looked hopefully from Lisa to Willie but neither of them looked confident.

"That's going to be rough, Reinhold. There is little work. You might be able to get some construction job."

"Maybe I'll look around for a few days. Do you know anywhere I can stay?"

"You can stay with us, of course," Lisa said.

Reinhold looked around their apartment. It was just one room with a curtain separating it into two sections, one living and one sleeping.

"Ok," he agreed.

He didn't want to hurt Lisa's feelings by refusing but he hoped that it would be very temporary.

Reinhold poked around Lübeck for a few days with no luck finding employment. He tried carpentry shops, construction firms, bakeries, and warehouses but no one was looking to hire any more people. A man at one bakery told him he would be better off leaving

Lübeck, trying Hamburg or going further afield to Frankfurt or Munich, maybe even further than that. He said lots of people were headed to America in search of employment. Reinhold wasn't opposed to the idea of going to another city, he just didn't have enough money to make the trip.

Sighing as he walked along a partially burned out street, Reinhold decided that he would have to go back to the high seas. After making the decision, he admitted to himself that he was looking forward to watching the sun sink into the sea and feeling the salty breeze against his face. He wasn't looking forward to the company of his fellow sailors.

Three days after arriving in the small city, Reinhold found himself standing at the head of Clemensstrasse, a narrow, tightly packed street that ran into the Trave River. He remembered the name from talk on the *Eos* and on the farm in Ratekau. This was a street of *puffs*. He stood on the corner for a minute debating with himself before deciding that he could spend a little of the money he had on a girl. He didn't want to go back to the sea without the experience. It would just be too embarrassing.

He started off down the street expecting to see show windows like the ones in the Reeperbahn but there were just plain windows with curtains and shades drawn. Only one building looked at all inviting and that was because it had a sign on the facade. It was a short street and Reinhold quickly came to the end at the river. Doubling back, he went to the only building that looked inviting. He entered into a good sized parlor with couches, chairs, and tables. A small bar stood along one wall and there were two men occupying half the bar stools. There were three scantily clad young ladies circulating around the room.

Unsure what to do, Reinhold made a beeline for the bar but didn't make it far before he heard his name.

"Reinhold! Is that you?"

A pretty blonde girl wearing next to nothing was hurrying across the room toward him. It took a minute, but he recognized her from the farm. She was one of the kitchen maids. At least she had been when he was there.

"Emma?"

She threw her arms around him and gave him a big, warm hug.

"Yup. What are you doing here?"

"What am I doing here?" Reinhold couldn't help being a bit incredulous. "What are you doing here?"

"Come sit down and I'll tell you." She maneuvered him toward the bar where there were now three stools available. "Do you want a drink? A beer or something?"

"No, thank you. I don't drink."

She looked taken aback for a second then pressed on with the conversation.

"I came here to make more money. It is that simple. We didn't make much money on the farm, you know that. Muuss preferred to pay us in grain and milk. It is like you said Reinhold, when you left, where is the advancement in that? It is just survival. Cash is freedom."

"Yeah, it was just survival." He agreed thinking back to those days of hunger and back breaking work. It reinforced his decision to go back to sailing.

"What about you? How have you been?"

"Good, I guess."

He didn't know what to say. He was becoming more aware of Emma's half naked body, particularly her large breasts. He couldn't help thinking back to the farm when the older boys played games with the girls, terrifying them by lifting their long skirts to expose their bare womanly places. He felt the blood rush to his face. Emma noticed the blush. She must have read his thoughts.

"You can look all you want here, Reinhold. I know it is not as much fun as lifting my skirts when I was pulling weeds. Anything more than a look will cost you." She laughed coyly at him, leaning her breasts closer. "And you always were a handsome devil. I wouldn't mind taking you as a customer. That's why you are here, right?"

He blushed again. "No. I think I am ok. I couldn't do that with you. You're like my sister, a friend at least. It wouldn't be right."

"Oh. Alright. We'll just have to catch up while you look around at the other girls then. Did you get hired on by a ship? That is what you were going to do, right?"

"Yup. I got hired. I spent almost a year on the seas. It was very interesting. I saw lots of things that I never saw before: big lighthouses, different ports, huge fish."

"That's great! Is there any money in being a sailor?"

"Some. You get paid by your station. I was the lowest ranking because I was new. I'll make more as I move up."

He didn't want to get too specific by calling out numbers. Wilhelm and the copper bar came to his mind just then. "There are ways to supplement your income, too, if you know the right people."

"I see. That's good. When are you headed back out?"

Reinhold shrugged.

I have to end this conversation soon and go somewhere else to get the experience I need, he thought to himself.

"I am going to go to the sailor's office tomorrow. Hopefully, I'll be back out there in a few days." Changing the subject, he asked, "Is it true that this whole street is full of *puffs*?"

"Yes. Almost every house. This one is the most popular but the one next door is pretty busy too."

Reinhold nodded. "I think I should be going. My sister is expecting me."

"Ok. Take care of yourself, Reinhold. Come visit anytime," Emma purred the last few words and rubbed her ample breasts on his sleeve. His level of discomfort rose and he made a hasty exit.

The *puff* next door was set up much the same as Emma's: a good sized parlor with a small bar. The sitting area held a few girls looking for customers and a couple of guys hanging about. Reinhold took a seat at the bar and looked around. Meeting Emma like that had thrown him off his guard. But he didn't let it spoil his determination. There was a girl in particular he had his eye on, a petite brunette with an ample bosom and a soft voice. When she came over and spoke to him, they struck a deal fairly quickly. He handed over six *mark* and off they went upstairs to somewhere more private.

Looking back, Reinhold couldn't even remember her name. Actually, he remembered very little of their intimate involvement that day. She had been very nice to him, especially after she learned that he was new to the art of lovemaking. She guided him through the basics and this time he didn't expend himself before making contact. Afterwards, he left that house feeling like he had just conquered the world. This was something he was going to like doing, eventually, he knew.

That night over dinner, he told Lisa his decision to go back out on the seas. She took it much better than he had expected.

"Promise me that you will get a post book before you go." It was her only real comment.

"I already did," Reinhold produced a small, blue ledger from his pocket. "It is all taken care of."

The next morning, Reinhold set out to the sailor's office. He wondered how long he would have to wait this time to get a ship.

Lübeck is not Hamburg, he reminded himself, but he wasn't sure what that meant. Did that make it easier or harder for a sailor?

The sailor's office was just a one room shack, no bigger than twenty by twenty feet. A lone man in a wool cast off army jacket sat behind a desk. He glanced up when he heard the door shut.

"Good morning," Reinhold greeted him and was rewarded with a curt nod. "I am looking for the sailor's office."

"Looks like you found the sailor's office, young man. What can I do for you?"

"I am looking for a ship."

"For work, I presume. You have a book?"

The question was somewhat sarcastic. Reinhold didn't like the tone. Instead of responding, he reached into his pocket and pulled out his sailor's book and his passport, handing them over for inspection.

"Signed on in Hamburg as a *Decksjunge*, a deck boy, and left just a couple of weeks ago as a *Leichtmatrose*. Are you looking to continue as a *Leichtmatrose*? With a cargo ship out of Lübeck?"

"Yes, sir."

"Okay, let's see what I have."

He shuffled through a stack of papers on his deck, pulling one from the pile. He looked over his half-moon shaped glasses at Reinhold. "You have a preference where you go?"

"No." Reinhold answered quickly but thought about that question for a minute.

Could I have a preference? Is it possible that I could pick where I want to go?

"Would you mind going back to being a *Jungmann*?"

"No, I guess not."

He didn't know he was a *Leichtmatrose*, so what difference did it make?

"Here it is. Are you ready to go now?" Reinhold nodded. "There is a small cargo vessel called the *Stina* docked three hundred yards north of here on the east side. The Captain is looking for a

Jungemann. He wants to leave tomorrow morning regardless of whether or not he fills this position so get going."

He handed Reinhold a piece of paper with the information on it. With a nod, Reinhold left the office headed for the *Stina*.

Chapter 32: Stina

Stina
Photograph Courtesy of 7seasvessels.com

The *Stina* was a small ship, no bigger than the *Eos*. It had a single mast set near the bow but it wasn't a sail ship. The mast held lines and booms for loading and unloading. The man on the deck of the *Brandenburg* spit in repugnance at the memory of the ship.

His time on the *Stina* was short. The ship was just as boring as the *Eos* but, as a whole, a completely different creature. The Captain was a younger man and, in Reinhold's opinion, had a bit of a chip on his shoulder. Baummann was his name. He was in his mid-thirties, a good twenty years younger than Capt. Hermann and young, in general, for the profession.

"I don't take any lip on this vessel. You will do what I say when I say and you'll keep your mouth shut about it."

The well groomed Captain said as he showed Reinhold were the crew's bunks were located.

"We do runs to Sweden for lumber and iron ore, mostly. We go no matter what the conditions. Don't go thinking that because winter is setting in that it is going to be easy work until spring. This is a business, after all. I don't make any money if we are sitting tied up in some port somewhere. Actually, it costs me money."

Turning to speak directly to his audience, his brown eyes peering menacingly into Reinhold's blue ones, he continued, "I particularly don't expect trouble from my *Jungmann*. Understand?"

"Yes, sir," Reinhold responded.

He understood perfectly. Working for this guy was going to be like living with his stepmother.

It didn't take long for Reinhold to conclude that not only did Capt. Baummann have a chip on his shoulder, he had something to prove. The more cargo delivered, the more money came his way but also the more recognition he got from his superiors. This Captain was looking to move up the ladder. He ran a tight ship and was less tolerant of Reinhold's periodic inability to control his tongue than Capt. Hermann. More than once, he wiped blood from his mouth after receiving "discipline" from Capt. Baummann for something he had said, usually something as simple as saying "Aye, Aye, Captain" instead of the more polite, and less amusing, "Yes, Captain".

Reinhold didn't like the cuffs he received but he was not so immature as to deny that he probably deserved them. He was warned, after all. *I don't take any lip on this ship*, he heard in his head. A good smack to the head or a sharp insult weren't the only ways Reinhold was reminded who was in charge. It seemed every time there was something remotely dangerous to do, Reinhold was singled out for the task.

"Scholz!" The Captain would bellow, "Get a sledgehammer! Get out there and clear the ice from the prow."

And there he would be, standing on the ice next to the prow of the tiny ship, pounding away with his sledgehammer, hoping the ice would crack. There was always someone on the other side of the prow from Reinhold, banging away with their sledgehammer, but that person changed port to port. Reinhold was always on the ice. When he landed a good hit and sent a fissure through the frozen barrier, he signaled the Captain, who in turn rammed the prow against the ice sheet.

Inch by inch, Capt. Baummann forced his way out of a port while the Captains and crews of the other ships watched from the windows of the portside taverns. Once the last crack was sent racing through the ice, Reinhold would grab a rung of the ladder and hope to get on the ship before Baummann hit the throttle.

He also spent a lot of time dangling over the rail to paint the seaward side of the ship or to patch small holes in the hull. At first, it was frightening, almost paralyzing frightening. When he looked down at the waters of the Baltic Sea just a few feet below him, churning and pitching, swelling and heaving, capped with bone crushing chucks of ice, his seasickness threatened to come roaring back. On several occasions it did come back, leaving a limp and beleaguered Reinhold hanging on for dear life while he tried to work.

After a few days hanging from the boom in the bosun's chair, painting, he became accustom to the view and the noise. Much to the Captain's consternation, Reinhold quickly grew to enjoy it, swinging around, using his feet to push off the side of the ship and move to a different position. One day it dawned on him that he probably looked a lot like a monkey with a paint brush. He tried to make what he believed was a monkey sound.

"What are you doing?" Huber's head appeared above him. He was been painting the other side of the rail.

"Being a monkey," Reinhold responded flippantly.

Huber grinned at him and disappeared again. Reinhold spent the rest of the day trying out his monkey sounds. The crew thought it was hilarious but the Captain was less than pleased. Reinhold knew that at the next port, he would be on the ice again, banging away with his trusty sledgehammer.

While the Captain was a bit more tyrannical, his fellow sailors on the *Stina* were less scary than the crew of the *Eos*. They were younger, all of them in their twenties, but mature enough not to single Reinhold out for his youth, and that made a big difference. They actually spoke to him and were pleasant enough. They liked a good joke, particularly at the expense of their snippy Captain. And they liked a good story, especially ones about girls.

Of course, they liked to drink when they had the opportunity. Reinhold quickly realized they were not deep thinkers but they were cleaver in their attempts to break up the monotony of their routine. Mostly they turned to money making schemes. Hartmann, for instance, was notorious onboard for buying coffee in Sweden and selling it to some mysterious dealer in Lübeck where coffee was as scarce as gold and almost as expensive.

"Coffee: my retirement fund," he said only half joking.

Huber did a good business in bicycles, which lay around the ports in Sweden like rocks. He threw them onboard and sold them in Lübeck or Kiel.

"Bikes: not good enough to be a retirement fund but enough to get me drunk," he joked in response to Hartmann. "And all profit, no initial investment," he said with a self-satisfied grin.

Reinhold thought they were brilliant.

"Everyone does this," Huber told him. "I learned from the guys I worked with when I was about your age."

He leaned closer to Reinhold in a conspiratorial fashion. "The trick is to know what people want and where to get it, cheap."

It was from Hartmann that Reinhold learned there was a reading club for sailors. Reinhold happened upon him one night engrossed in a copy of the Brothers Grimm. He said that reading was a great way to pass the boring times on the ship and keep the mind from getting old.

"Don't tell anyone, but it is also helping me with my writing. I didn't learn a lot in school but the reading is filling in some holes, so to speak, in how to put a sentence together."

Hartmann blushed under his collar as he spoke but Reinhold understood perfectly what he meant. He became a member the next time the ship docked in Lübeck. Once you signed up, they sent you one or two books at a time. Reinhold got his first book a couple of weeks after signing on the *Stina*. It was Mark Twain's *Adventures of Tom Sawyer*. He thoroughly enjoyed the story even though it took him almost his entire time on the *Stina* to finish it. The tale reminded him in some ways of his own life back in Ratekau. There was even some sailing in it. It made him wonder what life was like in America with all the different types of people. According to the book, they didn't get along so well all the time.

"Why don't you go find out?" Hartmann asked one night while they sat on a bench in the ship's tiny, grey galley. He also read the *Adventures of Tom Sawyer*. "You can get a ship that goes to America. Not a lot of fun in America for sailors, though, from what I hear. I have never been there myself but I know guys that have sailed that way. And there are not a lot of companies that haul there. Hapag is the biggest."

"Hapag?"

"Yeah, you know, the big company in Hamburg next to Blohm & Voss, used to be Hamburg Amerika. They do passenger ships too. Maybe you can go become a waiter for the rich old women going to visit America. Eh, you know, serve them their tea and cakes, take care of all their needs."

Reinhold laughed at the ludicrous innuendo. He had an image of himself wearing a white tux and white gloves, carrying small trays laden with silver tea pots and laughed all the harder.

"That'll be the day." He shoveled some salt pork stew into his mouth along with a bite of bread before speaking again. "I didn't know Hapag, Hamburg Amerika, was so big. I thought they only had a few ships, big ones, to be sure, but not many."

"They got their fleet wiped out in the war. They are building more. They have to salvage the ones that sunk first. That's cheaper than starting from scratch."

"One sunk near me, near my hometown anyway. In Lübeck Bay."

"You lived near Lübeck Bay?" There was excitement in Hartmann's voice.

"Yup, in Ratekau." Reinhold didn't know what the big deal was about the bay.

"Wow! That was supposed to be something to see. That was a huge disaster. I heard the ship was there for years before they took it away. Actually, I heard it was more than one ship. A guy I worked with on the last ship I was with had worked on the salvage ship that broke them up for removal. He said that three of them went down around there."

Reinhold thought about it for a minute. "There were two that I saw. One sunk completely further out and one sunk in the shallow part. It was there for years. We used to swim to it and climb up the side to play and lay in the sun. It washed ashore, finally, just before I left."

Hartmann was staring open mouthed at him. He felt compelled to add in a hushed whisper, "A lot of people died there."

"Yes, I heard that thousands of them were on the ships when they sunk; prisoners of war mostly that were moved from the camps. The *Braunenpatie* didn't want anyone to know what they were up too."

"What do you mean, what they were up too?"

Hartmann looked at him in surprise, "What do you mean. You don't know what they were doing to people? To the Jewish people in particular? And the gypsies? All the killing?"

Reinhold felt his stomach twist. He remembered the horribleness of the sinking and he was afraid that he was about to find out something worse. He debated for a second whether he wanted to know what Hartmann was talking about. In the end curiosity won and he asked, "What killing?"

"The *Braunenpatie* was trying to wipe out the Jewish people. Hitler ordered that they be rounded up and sent to camps where they were killed. They were all over the place, those camps. I heard that millions of people died."

It was Reinhold's turn to stare open mouthed. As Hartmann's words sunk in, his stomach twisted even more, becoming a throbbing knot of disgust and horror. He didn't speak for a long minute.

"Germans did this? They killed other Germans?" He finally questioned. "What about the whole Aryan race thing?"

"Jewish Germans, yes, because Hitler didn't think that they were real Germans. They also sent anyone who spoke against him to the camps. My cousin's husband disappeared in the dark of the night during the war from his own backyard. She never heard or saw a thing but she is convinced that the *Braunenpatie* took him because he had written a story questioning why Germans were obeying the orders of an Austrian."

"That's the most heinous thing I have ever heard," he muttered to himself.

He put his unfinished bowl of pork stew on the bench next to him. He wasn't hungry anymore. He was completely bewildered.

How can people do that to other people? He questioned himself. *How can people be so evil?*

Then he remembered that his town wasn't evil. Most of the people there had been Communists during the war and they suffered for it.

Hitler, he thought to himself, *that goddamn son of a bitch!*

He felt anger rising in him. He hands were clenching and unclenching of their own accord and his breathing became ragged. Hartmann must have sensed the anger rising in Reinhold because he quickly steered the conversation back to ships and sailing.

"It was Hapag ships that sunk in the bay near you. One was a luxury liner. That's the kind of ship that goes to America, not these little ones." Hartmann looked around him with thinly veiled contempt. "This one wouldn't even make it halfway across the Atlantic. Maybe I'll go be an attendant on one of those floating cities myself. I could met a nice rich woman who wants to go slumming. Maybe she would even take me home with her, you know, like a lost dog. I'd be eating out of crystal bowls in no time!"

He winked at Reinhold before departing with his empty dinner bowl.

That night Reinhold sat on the deck, deep in melancholy, watching the lights of the Swedish coast come and go in random clusters and listening to the chugging sound of the engine echoing off the coast. He knew they were getting close to Stockholm when the lights became more frequent. He watched as the islands of the archipelago slipped past, replaced once again by darkness. He found himself thinking a lot about America and the other side of the Atlantic. This was in part because of his reading of *The Adventures of Tom Sawyer* but mostly because he didn't want to think about the grim reality that Hartmann exposed him to earlier. He wondered if there was work to be had in that country.

Lots of people have been going there lately, he thought.

Just the other day he had a letter from Lisa that, amongst news of the family, had mentioned her neighbor leaving for America. The book made it seem like there was a lot of strife but it was a big place, if he had his facts straight. Maybe it was better in another part. New York seemed like the place to be, if you listened to people talk. He had heard of Los Angeles, a town on the opposite coast from New York where they made movies. But, in the back of his mind, Reinhold remembered the wolf's head in his classroom and he wondered what Hartmann meant when he said that America was no fun for sailors. Did he mean German sailors? Surely, the world knew what he had just found out today.

He sighed heavily, watching the lights on shore slip by and thought about how great it would be to find somewhere to go where everyone respected each other and enjoyed life rather than plotting death and destruction. A place where there was plenty of food for everyone.

Boredom set in quickly on the *Stina* for Reinhold. The back and forth trips to Sweden became routine, even the ice breaking became commonplace and irritatingly tedious. He became a sailor because he needed a job, yes, but he had been looking forward to some adventure also. He wanted to see new places. The *Stina* only went to a handful of ports. The port of Ljusne, Sweden where they picked up lumber and spent most of their time away from Lübeck was just a sawmill. According to what Huber said, there were less than a thousand people living in the town and most of them worked for the lumber mill.

The same was true for Gävle and Oxelösund, also in Sweden, where they picked up iron ore. The rest of the crew shared in his frustration.

"Lord, I wish we were going to Stockholm this trip. You can't even get a decent drink in this place," Huber lamented one night as, once again, they docked in Ljusne. "I guess it is the local *tivoli* again tonight, boys."

A less than enthusiastic groan went up from the five other guys on the crew. There was very little to do in the rural areas of Sweden so people gathered to talk and socialize at the town *tivoli*. Even though the guys weren't overjoyed at the prospect of another night of this, Reinhold was envious of their freedom. He had been on the *Stina* for three months and his restlessness was growing almost as quickly as his sense of confinement. He watched them head off from the deck of the ship.

Verdammt! He cursed to himself. *Why do I have to be sixteen to leave the ship? My sixteenth birthday is still more than a month away!*

Sighing, he resigned himself to another night with Tom Sawyer but Hartmann and Huber had other plans for their young crewmate. They were back earlier than usual this night.

"We know you are bored and don't get to go ashore with us, so we brought the shore to you," Huber told him as he pushed a girl in his direction. They had also brought girls back to the ship for themselves. "You just have to go somewhere else to have her since the bunk is going to be full. I suggest, from personal experience, that you visit that park over there."

Hartmann pointed towards a small seaside park not far from the pier where the ship was docked. It took Reinhold a minute to comprehend what they had done, why there was a girl there for him, but once the realization set in he was more than interested in indulging in the gift they had brought. He was also very apprehensive. This would be only the third time that he had attempted intimacy with a girl. Looking at her, he saw a certain wisdom in her eyes as they wondered appraisingly over his stocky frame. With a shrug to hide his nervousness, Reinhold took the girl's hand and tugged her after him.

On the way to the park, he took an appraising look of his own at the young woman. She was pretty enough with shoulder length blonde hair and deep blue eyes. Her skin was perfectly white with just hints of pink on the cheeks that came, most likely, from the steady winter wind that blew off the sea. She looked to be a bit older than him. He tried to ask her name but she just shook her head. She didn't understand a word of German.

Deciding that it was best just to get down to business, he started to kiss her. She understood this and responded in kind. Before long Reinhold was removing the layers of clothes that prevented close contact between them. The cold, winter air of northern Sweden cut short his attempts to get them both naked. Instead, he bared only the parts that were necessary to accomplish his goal.

To his surprise, it was the girl that decided he should have her from behind. This was something new to Reinhold. Not only was it easier to get at her in their semi dressed state, it felt so good! He tried to make it last as long as possible but the cold and his lack of experience worked against him and it was over way too quickly. Looking back through the sands of time, Reinhold figured that encounter was the most exciting thing that happened to him on the *Stina*. He also understood why the girl gave him a nasty look before departing.

Reinhold also remembered trying his hardest to think like the guys on the crew, to endure the boredom by thinking of schemes for making money but he just couldn't focus. The days marched passed in cyclical lassitude. His less than amiable relationship with Capt. Baummann didn't help matters. At least on the *Eos* he could alleviate some of his doldrums by hanging out with Hermann.

It was a rough decision because he knew that work was scarce on the shore but after three months and two weeks of traveling back and forth to Sweden with the *Stina*, Reinhold asked for his sailor's book back and the Captain Baumann was more than happy to give it. He didn't think the sailing life was for him. It was just too confining, too routine. At least on the shore he could wander and find new things instead of being a living piece of cargo bound to the daily grind of a supply route. He left Lübeck after a brief visit with Lisa and Willie and headed home to Ratekau somewhat crest fallen and not looking forward to the welcome that he would receive from his stepmother.

Stina
Photograph courtesy of Reinhold Scholz

Chapter 33: Shore Life

"Why did you leave a paying job? What are you going to do for work?" She shrilled at him.

He knew it was a legitimate question but he also knew that she was only asking because she had wanted him to go away and never come back. Reinhold had been home for four days and had not had a moment's peace from her incessant questioning. He had, however, noticed the dynamic of their relationship had changed. Yes, she wasn't any nicer but he detected an element of apprehension in her. She kept her distance now. There was always a table or a chair or some piece of furniture in between them when they were in the same room. He laughed to himself. He knew that the hard work and food on the ships had changed his physique but he didn't realize that he had become so scary.

She is just being dramatic, as usual, he told himself.

"Maybe Pa can get me a job at the fish factory," Reinhold offered weakly, knowing that wasn't going to happen.

He was grateful when she merely snorted at him. The sound of her voice grated on his nerves. Sighing, Reinhold rose from the table where he had been sitting, eating his breakfast.

"I'll go back to Lübeck and find something."

"I certainly hope so. Do you expect us to just support you for the rest of your life?" She asked the question as she moved closer to the door that led down a short hallway to her bedroom.

Reinhold felt the anger surge in him. "I have always found a way to bring home money so don't go wasting your questions on me. I handed you fifty *mark* four days ago. What happened to that?"

Judging it best for him to leave before their war of words continued, Reinhold strode across the kitchen and out into the cold morning.

Looking backward from the deck of the *Brandenburg*, Reinhold remembered his determination not to go back to sailing.

That worked out well, he taunted himself.

Shrugging to the wind, he reminded himself that he had been incredibly bored on the shore. He found a job in Lübeck, just as he told his stepmother he would, in the warehouse at a glass factory. It actually hadn't been as hard as he had thought it would be. Germany was beginning to return to life. Everywhere buildings were being rebuilt, cities were coming to life again. There was an industrious spirit bolstered by the population's disgust with lethargy. People wanted to work and now, finally, work became available. His first day as an employee at the glass factory fell two days before his sixteenth birthday.

"I don't even remember the name of it now," he laughed aloud.

His musings were answered by a passing seagull. He watched it circle above the ship, held aloft by its outstretched wings on the updraft before gliding off in the direction of a small island to the east of the ship.

For three months, Reinhold worked in that glass factory. At first, it had been interesting watching the glaziers at their work, especially with the silver powder, to make mirrors out of sheets of glass. As a novice, he was assigned the task of cutting the glass to specific sizes.

He liked it at first. The tools were new and like nothing he had working with before. One was a sharp wheel on a stick that was used to cut the glass. It took several tries for him to know how to handle it so that the incision was straight. It was also a bit of a challenge getting the right dimensions and not cracking the glass. He found grinding the edges with a stone tedious right from the start but recognized the need for the step in the process.

After about two weeks, Reinhold's interest in the job waned and he became bored again. It was very repetitive and there was no one to talk to while he worked. The owner of the glass factory didn't want them interacting with each other during work hours.

"Not on my time," he would say. "Distract yourself on your own time."

To make matters more unbearable, he couldn't afford to live in Lübeck so he stayed in the attic in Ratekau. To make it to work on time (and God forbid he was late!), he would leave at six in the morning and travel an hour by bike to the warehouse. Into his second month, he got lucky and was offered a motorcycle for a ridiculous price by a guy that was leaving to go to America. The commute was easier after that.

The worst part about the glass factory was that it wasn't the sea. He admitted to himself late one night as he lay in his feather bed in the attic that he missed the sounds and smells of the sea. He missed watching the spectral lights that appear and disappear on the sea at night without notice or explanation. He missed trying to guess the source. Was it a lighthouse on an island or maybe another ship passing beyond sound but not sight? He missed watching the birds flying above the ship, guiding them almost, to the port. He missed watching the weather change when the clear blue sky would suddenly be flooded with black, threatening clouds. He missed the little white capped waves on a breezy day. He missed the food sellers at the ports in Sweden with the delectable pastries. He had to remind himself that he hated being on the ships. The people had not really be agreeable. At least at the glass factory, nobody was scary and irritable. Not that he would really know anyway since he wasn't allowed to talk to anyone.

  One day at the end of May, things changed for Reinhold. He hit his limit with the glass factory, and his family. Driving home from work on fine spring evening, he slid a slick muddy spot in the road and went careening off the road into a very sturdy tree. Needless to say, his motorcycle was destroyed. The frame was bent so badly that it almost folded itself in half. He didn't even bother picking it up from where it lay in the grass. He wandered along the road in a sullen mood, kicking at rocks, and cursing the countryside and himself for not seeing the mud. It was dark when he arrived at the tiny house he called home. He intended to go straight to his attic and go to bed but his family had other plans for him. His stepmother rushed him as soon as he walked in the kitchen door. She had been waiting like a snake to strike, to throw bad news in his face.

  "Well, that sister of yours has done it again. It was a disgrace when she ran off and married the way that she did but who would have thought that he would turn out to be a murderer!"

  She couldn't hide the smug she was feeling. It radiated from her like the rays of the sun.

  Sighing, Reinhold knowingly bit at the line she dangled in front of him. He knew it was about Isolde. Lisa wasn't married.

  "What in the name of all that is holy are you talking about?"

  Undaunted by the edge in his voice, she launched on a tale of woe.

  "Your sister's husband, Paul, has killed someone, of course. What else would I be talking about? He meant only to rob the poor man, one of his co-workers and on pay day no less, but it went all wrong. He hit the guy with a wooden board that had a nail in it! The man is dead and Paul is in jail. They say he is likely to get the maximum penalty of thirty years in jail. Your father had to go down there, to Sereetz."

Reinhold felt something snap inside his mind. His brain was screaming at him to leave, to go back to Lübeck, get a new ship, and sail away from all this nonsense. He didn't understand why the situation with his sister's husband meant anything to him but he knew there would be repercussions for it that he didn't want to think about.

Goddamn small town, he cursed to himself. *By tomorrow night, I am going to be the guy with a murderer for a brother-in-law. That is quite the label to have at sixteen years old. And Isolde a prison wife at eighteen. That is just too young. Holy Jees, I don't even want to think about this.*

Without further comment on the matter to his gloating stepmother, Reinhold went to his attic room and packed his things: work boots, a couple of shirts, a couple of pairs of dungarees, wool coat and hat for winter, a pair of work gloves, and a dozen pairs of socks. Tomorrow, instead of going to the glass factory, he would go to the sailor's office and get a ship. With the decision made, he looked forward to getting back to sea. It was the beginning of June, the best time of the year to sail.

Chapter 34: The Lifestyle Of A Sailor

Pagensand
Photograph courtesy of 7seasvessels.com

For the third time, Reinhold went down to the sailor's office to enquire about a position. He handed the guy behind the desk his sailor's book, noting that it was the same man who had been so curt with him so many months before.

"You were a *Jungmann* on the *Stina*?"

Obviously, the man didn't recognize Reinhold.

He must see hundreds of sailors a week, he reminded himself.

"Yes. I wanted to ask about Hapag. How do I get a position with them?"

The man looked at Reinhold for a second before replying.

"I would wait to apply with them, if I were you. Not because you couldn't get a job and not because they aren't looking but because it won't be the job that you want."

Seeing the puzzled look on Reinhold's face, the man continued. "As a *Jungmann*, you would be performing tasks that I don't think you would like, at least most people don't like."

Curious, Reinhold asked, "What kind of tasks?"

"Serving food, cleaning, cooking, stuff that you have been doing with the smaller companies, but on a larger scale. If you become a M*atrose,* or even a *Leichtmatrose,* then you can apply with Hapag for an equivalent position. It is just faster. Guys have been known to be *Jungmann* with Hapag for years before being picked to move up. Or they get transferred to the passenger ships and end up as porters or stewards. You don't look like that type." The man eyed Reinhold sharply. "Are you?"

"No."

"Then I have a *Jungmann* position with a ship called *Pagensand*. It is an official mail ship but they haul other cargo as well. The Captain's name is Meyer. He was docked a mile south of here on this side of the Trave yesterday. If he is not there, come back and I'll look for something else for you."

Reinhold found the *Pagensand* still docked along the Trave. It was a bigger ship, twice as big as the *Eos* or the *Stina*. It was painted a festive color grey, if there was such a thing, above the waterline and a matte black below. He found the Captain on the bridge and signed on as the *Jungmann*.

"We are leaving in a couple of hours. Are you ready to go?"

Captain Meyer was an older man with salt and pepper in his beard and a ruddy complexion under his cap. His voice boomed when he spoke but he was good natured, it seemed, and Reinhold liked him immediately.

"Yes, sir."

"Good, good. Let me introduce you to the First Mate. Ackermann!" The Captain bellowed into a handheld radio.

A moment later a tall, thin, severe looking man appeared from below deck and quickly made his way toward the bridge. He held a clipboard.

"Ah, here he is. Ackermann, this is Reinhold Scholz, our new *Jungmann*. Reinhold, this is Adam Ackermann, the First Mate of this ship."

Reinhold extended his hand in greeting and was met by a raise of the First Mate's eyebrows. There was a split second of awkward tension before Ackermann took Reinhold's hand.

Great, Reinhold thought to himself, *we've another pompous arschloch*.

"Ah, just in time, as usual," The Captain said as another man appeared on the gangway.

Opening a window of the bridge, he called to the man.

"Gerold, come meet our new *Jungmann*."

The man hurried into the room, looking quizzically at Reinhold.

"Reinhold, this is Gerold Gärtner, the ship steward. Anything you need you just ask this man and he will get it."

The two men shook hands. Reinhold thought the steward seemed nice enough with a pleasant face and a strong grip. He had heard of ships having stewards but he did not fully understand what the Captain meant by "anything that you need." He made a mental note to question the steward further.

"Let me give you a quick tour before you go get your things."

The Captain turned to Ackermann. "Ackermann, show Reinhold where he will be working and sleeping. I have a quick errand to take care of on shore."

Touching the brim of his cap in goodbye, the Captain left Reinhold standing with a sour looking Ackermann.

The *Pagensand* was a different ship than either the *Eos* or the *Stina*. The cargo was already on board and the hatch was closed leaving a wide, elevated space on the metal deck that measured about fifty meters long. This elevated space was disrupted in the middle by the mast. Ackermann led the way past this space to the foredeck. Lifting a small round hatch, he motioned Reinhold down the passage. Descending the short ladder, Reinhold found himself standing in a short, grey hallway with five doors, three on left side, and two on the right. Ackermann lead the way to the last door on the left.

"This is your bunk."

Opening the door, Ackermann revealed a cramped, plain, grey room with four bunks, two sets, one on top of the other, on either side of the door. Between the bunks was a wooden truck of sorts that he could only assume belonged to one of his new roommates. A porthole let in a bit of natural light.

"You will be sharing this room with Herbert and Arnold. They are in the hold right now so you will have to meet them later. You will have to ask them which bunks they are using."

Crossing the hall, Ackermann threw open the first door on the right side of the hallway reveling the bathroom.

"It is part of your responsibilities to keep this bathroom clean. Since only you and the rest of the crew use it, you can decide what level of cleanliness you all can live with."

The tour moved to the deck and the common areas. In addition to the increased size, the *Pagensand* had several features that Reinhold had not experienced before. First, there was a mess hall. It was just a small room with a table but at least he wouldn't have to find himself someplace to eat anymore which made him extremely happy. It was no fun eating dinner on a cold, wet deck or cramped into a tiny galley with the cook trying to work and men trying to shove past you to get their dinner. Second, there was running water in the bathroom and electricity. This made him even happier. No more sponge baths on a cold, wet deck. No more oil lamps.

The *Pagensand* was a good ship. The work was the work and didn't really change all that much from ship to ship. He didn't care so much about that but he did care that he felt at home. The crew seemed like normal people, with the exception of one guy, a *Matrose* named Franz, who was a bit strange and crazy eyed. Reinhold decided to keep an eye on him as soon as they met. He made a good friend in his bunkmate, Herbert. The two hit it off immediately over a game of chess one of his first nights onboard. He had never met anyone else who played, especially on the ships, where most men had never even heard of the game. It quickly became routine for the two of them to indulge when they were not working. These matches got intense sometimes with both men pondering their moves as if the fate of Europe depended on it. The rest of the crew would watch them with passive interest but never asked to join them. From Herbert, Reinhold learned about the role of the steward, Gerold.

"Gerold will get you whatever you need," Herbert shrugged one night while they sat in the mess hall, a chess board between them.

The *Pagensand* was docked in Stockholm. It was Reinhold's first trip with the ship. Everything went like clockwork with fine early summer weather and the crew was in good spirits. Herbert had immediately challenged Reinhold to a celebratory game in honor of his "maiden voyage", as Herbert put it. Reinhold tried to protest, saying he made the trip from Lübeck to Stockholm dozens of times, but the other sailor wasn't hearing it.

"That was with other ships," he pointed out with a mock disgusted look. "You sail with this ship now and this was your first voyage with this ship."

Reinhold couldn't argue with Herbert's logic. After the business of the day was done, Herbert and Reinhold settled down to play.

"But what does that mean, 'get you whatever you need'? What would I need that I couldn't get on shore for myself?" Reinhold sent one of his pawns forward to be taken immediately by one of Herbert's.

"You can get what you need on shore but Gerold can get it cheaper through the company. You have to wait a few days, maybe even a week sometimes, but then he delivers it right to your bunk. They take the cost of the goods out of your monthly wages."

Reinhold's forehead was furrowed in confusion and concentration. Herbert must have noticed that his confusion had nothing to do with the game before them because he elaborated on his explanation. Reinhold saw him look around quickly.

"The steward gets you, cheaper than on shore, stuff that a lot of people can't get right now or can't afford. I am talking about liquor, beer, chocolate, cigarettes, Lucky Strike in particular, you know, stuff like that. There are limits, of course, but who cares when you can get a bottle of cognac for one *mark*, thirty five *pfennig*? There are people who make a lot of money from that small investment."

Herbert winked at his opponent as he moved his knight to take one of Reinhold's pawns. Reinhold mulled this new information for the rest of the game. He wondered how a bottle of cognac was an investment. Obviously, Herbert was not telling him everything. He shrugged in indifference. Herbert had his reasons for not divulging all his secrets.

Herbert was three years older than Reinhold. He had been sailing since he was sixteen. Much the same as Reinhold, he started out on small, coast hugging vessels as a deck boy and then a *Jungemann*. Now, at nineteen, he was an accomplished sailor, a full *Matrose*, working the spring line of the ship.

"The most important line," he would say as he went to his position on the deck.

The spring line, Reinhold knew, was the most important line. It was the first one to throw when docking and the last one to reel in when setting sail. Herbert had a good throwing arm and accurate aim so he worked the position well. He promised to show Reinhold how to handle it.

"I don't want to be a *Jungmann* forever," Reinhold complained one night during a game of chess.

He was thinking about what the man at the sailor's office in Lübeck had said about Hapag.

"You won't be but, you have to learn how to do the job of a *Matrose* before you can move up," Herbert had answered.

Reinhold understood what he meant. It was like on the farm. Tasks and positions were doled out according to experience and seniority. He needed more experience. He needed time to gain that experience but he knew that eventually, if he didn't change things, that he would get bored with this ship that same way he got bored with the farm and the glass factory.

"We're going to make you a sailor, a full *Matrose*. You'll make more money and have more options when it comes to companies and destinations. You could go work for Hapag and sail all over the world on one their huge new ships. We'll get you the experience but you have to learn to appreciate the lifestyle of a sailor. That way, you won't get bored and go running home just to come back to a ship."

Reinhold felt himself blush at the concise summary of his sailing career so bluntly put from the mouth of one of his colleagues. It made him feel like a petulant child.

"The lifestyle of a sailor? Does that mean I have to drink a lot?"

He asked the question to cover his self-consciousness. He sort of understood but was not entirely sure he did. Being underage, he didn't get to participate in much of anything. Now that he was sixteen that would change.

"Yeah, the lifestyle and no, it doesn't mean that you have to drink a lot. Not all sailors are drunken louts. Look around you. What do you see? A cold, smelly, cramped room on a shitty, leaking, tub of a ship. You get up in the morning and do your job. You go to sleep at night looking forward to the same thing the next day. That's one way of looking at it. I see opportunity, opportunity to make money. Opportunity to see what is going on in the world. To live, in other words, before you settle down and start having kids."

Reinhold fell asleep that night thinking about what Herbert said. It was a different perspective on sailing. He decided to commit himself to trying to make the best of his career choice, to look at it like Herbert, as an opportunity; maybe not to make so much money right now, but to learn as much as he could, and to live.

A few days later, Reinhold was standing on the sunlit deck of the *Pagensand,* spring line in hand, absolutely transfixed by the most alluring and curious of sights. It was a beautiful day in late June and the ship was maneuvering its way through the archipelago of

Stockholm into the port when Reinhold noticed there were people sunning themselves on the rocky islands. After focusing on one island in particular, he was astonished to see that the sunbathers were girls and they were naked! He forgot what he was doing and stared, open mouthed, at the sight.

"Reinhold! What are you doing?" Herbert called to him from the other end of the spring line.

Reinhold answered with a nod of his head in the direction he was gazing. Herbert followed and broke out laughing.

"Yes, it is a magnificent sight, isn't it? Like rocky islands full of mermaids. But we need to finish your lesson before we get to Stockholm."

Herbert gave the rope a tug, almost knocking Reinhold off his feet. Coming back to his senses, Reinhold turned his attention back to the spring line hanging limp in his gloved hand but not without giving a wave to the girls on the island closest. He felt a blush redden his cheeks when one of them waved back.

An hour or so later, Reinhold was standing on the deck, watching Herbert at work as the ship docked in Stockholm.

"I have an appointment to keep after we get the hatches open," Herbert told Reinhold as he took off his greasy work gloves. "You don't have a watch scheduled right now, do you?"

Reinhold shook his head, "I am on later, eight to twelve. Franz is going on now."

"That crazy *dummkopf*! Did you hear he swung a wrench at Fredrick? He was coming around the corner into the mess hall this morning for breakfast and bang! A wrench hits the bulkhead just in front of his face. He follows the arm and finds Franz staring at him. Fredrick had to wrestle the wrench away from him!" Herbert shook his head before continuing, "Good, you have a few hours then. I want you to come with me. You may learn something. Then I'll kick your ass in a game. Meet me here in an hour."

Herbert winked at him as he left to take his position for the opening of the hatch. Reinhold went to his own position wondering what Herbert had in mind and what he was going to learn from it. He had a strange flashback to Wilhelm and the copper bar on the *Eos*. He hoped it wasn't something like that again.

An hour later, the sailors left the ship together. The Pagensand was docked along the shore of one of Stockholm's many islands.

Herbert led the way along the crowded streets, a clanking pack on his back, as Reinhold looked around him in fascination. He had never been to this part of Stockholm and he had never been allowed to wander to see the city. The *Pagensand* was docked on the same island as the palace. Reinhold had to stop to stare at the structure for a long second. It was a wonder of architecture, stately and official looking but not garish. It was one of the most elegant buildings he had ever seen. He made a mental note to himself to come back and take a better look when he had time. Then he hurried after Herbert who hadn't stopped walking.

They crossed a short bridge in front of the palace to another island where Herbert hung a right and followed the street to another bridge to another island. Reinhold saw a sign for Skeppsholmen and wondered what it referred to, the island or the big, old church with the domed roof. Herbert hung a left, passing in front of the domed church and several streets with buildings that had a military feel to them. He looked neither right nor left, uninterested in his surroundings, while Reinhold's head swiveled constantly. They headed directly for the waterfront where several tugboats were docked and a large blonde man smoking a cigarette stood reading a newspaper at the foot of one of the gangways.

"That's Göran," Herbert said, using his chin to gesture towards the man. "I am going to introduce you, but don't say anything. The Swedes aren't big on talk."

Herbert whistled softly and the man peered around the side of his paper not emerging fully until he recognized Herbert.

Herbert introduced Göran to Reinhold as a tugboat operator, which explained the location. The large blonde man nodded at him and gestured for them to follow him up the gangway. Once aboard and inside the wheelhouse, Herbert emptied the backpack he carried with him of its clanking, and clandestine, contents: 3 bottles of cognac, 2 cartons of Lucky Strike cigarettes, and two bars of what looked like chocolate. Göran inspected each item then reached into his pocket and counted off several bills from a folded wad. Herbert counted the bills before shoving them in his own pocket.

"Are you looking for another supplier?" Herbert asked in Swedish as he gathered up his backpack.

"We are always looking for more product," Göran looked at Reinhold suspiciously through narrowed eyes. "Is this the supplier you have in mind?"

It was a surprise to Reinhold that he could understand some of the Swedish the men were speaking. It was also a surprise that he was mentioned as a potential 'supplier'.

A supplier of what, he thought to himself, feeling a bit panicky.

"I thought the two of you could do some business." Herbert shrugged casually.

Göran continued to regard Reinhold through narrowed eyes, making him angry and uncomfortable. The moment stretched into two minutes. Reinhold was just about to ask what the hell the guy was staring at when Göran answered.

"Ok. Come see me when you are back in Stockholm. Same time, same place, as always. Explain the schedule to him."

"A pleasure, as always, Göran," Herbert said in parting before exiting the wheelhouse.

"What was that all about?" Reinhold asked as they headed back across the bridges to the *Pagensand.*

"I'll tell you later. We have to hurry. Meyer wasn't docking at the Gamla Stan for long. Just to drop off some special delivery or something for the government. If he moves, we'll never find him. And if we do, he might not let us back onboard."

They made it back to the ship just before it shoved off for cheaper docking space. As promised, Herbert whipped Reinhold in a chess game. Also, as promised, he explained the day's excursion.

"The tugboat guys, regardless of the country, are deep in the black market. I have been doing business with Göran for a few months. I was recommended to him by the guy I used to work with on another ship when he retired. I bring him whatever I can, whenever I can. Usually, it is a couple of bottles of cognac and a cartoon of smokes. I get eight *krona*[28] for the cognac and six *krona* for a cartoon of Lucky Strike, only Lucky Strike. The other brands are worthless. So today, on a six *mark*, eighty *pfennig* investment, I made thirty nine *mark*. That is thirty two *mark*, twenty *pfennig* profit." He checked Reinhold's queen effectively winning their current match. "And the best part is, I didn't even have to go buy anything. I got that stuff

---

[28] A *krona* is a Swedish dollar.

from Gerold. You should think about doing some business with Göran. It is a great supplement to the company pay."

On watch that night, Reinhold pondered this new information, this new opportunity. He remembered Hartmann and Huber on the *Stina* with their schemes and sales. *Everybody does it*, he heard Huber say in his head. They had never gotten involved in the math with him like Herbert did, but Reinhold knew they also made some good scratch on the black market. And they didn't have a steward to do half the work for them. *You have to get into the lifestyle of a sailor*, he heard Herbert say again. Reinhold mind turned the topic over and over again, like he was kneading bread dough.

And why shouldn't I? Herbert made a bunch of money today for nothing! Smuggling some stuff that people want and can't get for some reason that probably only makes sense to the government?

It didn't take long for him to realize that not getting involved with Herbert would be stupid. By the time his watch was done at midnight, Reinhold was thoroughly committed to making as much money as possible.

At breakfast the next morning, Reinhold told Herbert he was in.

"I am glad you decided to get onboard. Get it, onboard? Ha! Anyway, we'll get you started today. All you have to do is get a piece of paper from Gerold and write on it what you want. I would recommend, since it is your first time, that you start small, maybe a bottle of cognac and a carton of cigarettes. You don't smoke, do you?' Reinhold shook his head. Herbert continued, "Well, maybe Gerold won't realize you are not actually smoking them. If he ever asks why you are getting cigarettes, just tell him you lost a bet to me and have to give me a carton of smokes."

"Gerold doesn't know, then, about the smuggling?" Reinhold asked.

"He probably knows or at least has an idea that something is going on. Hell, he probably has a side gig of his own. I assume everybody does, but nobody talks about it. Keep your business to yourself."

"Yes, keep your business to yourself. Nobody wants to hear it anyway." A menacing voice said from behind them.

Turning, Reinhold saw Franz standing there, a wrench in hand, and a strangely delighted smile on his lips.

"Who keeps giving this guy a wrench? What is he, a mechanic or something?" Herbert called to the mess hall at large.

A ripple of nervous laughter went through the few assembled men. They were all wondering what the unstable man was going to do.

"Keep it to yourself," Franz repeated quietly before losing steam and wandering off.

"We have to get rid of that guy," Herbert sighed as he returned to his plate, finishing his eggs and bread in a few bites. "Anyway, we can get some coffee today and see what happens when we get back to Germany. Now, if you excuse me, there is a pastry cart on the next pier that has the most delectable *Kanelbulle*[29] you'll ever taste. I want one before we head back to Germany."

Reinhold got the hang of the black market quickly. It was nothing really. He wrote a note to Gerold requesting what he needed and it appeared on his bunk a couple of days later. Once they got to Stockholm, he and Herbert would visit Göran and that was it. They would walk away with their cash and go on about their business. It was a good way, as Herbert said, to make a few extra dollars. He deposited the money into his post book when they got back to Lübeck. He was quite proud of the little bit of savings he had accumulated in just a few short weeks.

He was so proud, that he rarely spent any of it. The rest of the crew would go out to the port taverns to drink and look for girls on off hours from the ship but Reinhold didn't join them, at first. He found himself getting bored again. When he mentioned it to Herbert, he was reminded that he had to find his own excitement.

"Get off this ship, Reinhold. Just because you live here doesn't mean you have to stay here all the time and pass the time reading. And just because you go out doesn't mean you have to spend a lot of money. If I didn't know better, I would think you were an old man! The only person you visit with is your sister."

Taking Herbert's advice, Reinhold went out with the guys. And it was fun. The port taverns were small, dark places that catered to hardened men of the sea and were populated by a whole host of characters. There were many different nationalities and several different languages spoken. As long as you could say *bier*, you got served. He was surprised by how many girls congregated there.

---

[29] *Kanelbulle* is a Swedish pastry that closely resembles a cinnamon roll.

The first time he ordered a soda, he expected a hard time from the other sailors, but no one seemed to care. Their attention was on the girls. The guys flirted, bought drinks and dinner, tried to impress with tales of the sea. The girls giggled and accepted the offerings. A couple liked to drink very much and got very drunk before they were "escorted home" by a "chivalrous sailor".

Soon, Reinhold's attention was on the girls, too. He thought maybe he could find someone to escort home. He was chatting with a pretty redhead and thought he was doing well but the whole thing broke down and he didn't understand why. He complemented, offered drinks and dinner, but she had refused all of it, saying she was tired and wanted to go. That didn't seem like a good sign and Reinhold felt like he was missing something. Frustrated by the girls insistence that she didn't want to stay, he gave up and wished her a good night. Equally perplexed, the girl flounced off to the other end of the bar and began talking to another sailor, further confusing Reinhold.

"You didn't handle that right, boy," Reinhold turned to see a grizzled older man sitting on the stool next to him, sipping a tall beer.

"What?" He asked, thinking he hadn't heard the man right.

"You didn't handle that girl right. She was looking for you to leave with her, but for a price."

Reinhold was surprised. "You mean she was a prostitute? She didn't look like one. She didn't act like one."

The old man smiled. "It's a different world then the one I grew up in. In my day, that girl like that wouldn't have been selling herself to sailors. She would be home with a husband and children but the wars changed all that. Now, any girl will sell herself. She was looking for you to offer her some money. She didn't handle it well either. She must be new to this. Judging by her looks, I would say that she is no more than sixteen years old, about your age." The old sailor went back to sipping his beer.

Reinhold stared off toward where the girl was talking with a tall, dark man in a dirty tee shirt, thinking about what the old man said. A prostitute? So, all he had to do was offer money? It seemed too simple.

"What ship are you with, kid?" The old man asked.

"*Pagensand*," Reinhold answered.

"*Pagensand*. Never heard of it. What kind of ship is it?"

"Mail. To Stockholm. We pick up here and in Kiel."

The old man's eyes lit up. "You go regularly to Sweden?"

"Yes," Reinhold answered, getting annoyed.

The old man took a pen from his pocket and a napkin from a nearby stack. He jotted something down and handed it to Reinhold. It was a name and a series of days and times. He looked at the man, prepared to ask questions when he was cut off.

"That is my name, Adam, and the times when I am in this bar. If you happen to come across some extra coffee, I might be willing to buy it from you."

"Ok."

Reinhold shoved the napkin into his pocket and left the man in search of his friends. An idea was brewing in his head that would make him a lot more money. He just hoped Herbert would go for it because he couldn't do it alone.

The *Pagensand* was a busy ship during the fair sailing summer and early autumn months and Reinhold was quite happy to be on the move more often than not. The more money the ship made, the more money he made. Every time they docked, there was business to do, either buying or selling and more often than not both.

In Stockholm, they sold cognac and cigarettes along with some other odds and ends they came across to Göran. Then, they took their profits and visited the *kaffe haus* to buy coffee. Pounds at a time they purchased at four *krona* a pound. Reinhold followed in his ex-crewmate, Huber's, footsteps and started bringing bicycles from Sweden to Germany to sell.

It was a no brainer, he thought. *They just lay all over the place. It takes no time to pick one up and throw it over the rail onto the deck. It would have been lazy not to do it. And who cares about a bike? Not like Customs was going to fine them over it. They were too busy looking for the alcohol, contraband, and stowaways.*

In Lübeck, or in Kiel, Herbert had contacts that were more than happy to buy almost anything. Of course, it was the tugboat operators, same as Stockholm. They had their finger on the pulse of the ports, they were the ringleaders in the underground market of smuggled goods. Business was done while they maneuvered the vessel through ports, accepting merchandising and paying for it simply through the drop of a bucket. They had no problem buying coffee at thirty two *mark* a pound and Reinhold had no problem selling it.

The bicycles fetched anywhere from five to fifteen *mark*, depending on how beat up they appeared and how straight the wheels looked. Fellow sailors were the best market for bikes. Fifteen *mark* for a bike was cheaper sometimes than calling a taxi.

One evening after dinner in early August, Reinhold sat on his bunk, counting a good stack of money.

I have to do something with this, he thought. *I can't have this hanging around. I have to deposit it in my post book.*

He was also thinking that there had to be a way for him to increase his profits when the door swung open. Herbert entered muttering to himself.

"What's your problem?" Reinhold asked. "Didn't get enough beans with your dinner?"

Herbert snorted as he threw himself on the bunk on top of Reinhold's, his head hitting the cans hanging there. "You better hope I don't get any more beans in me. It'll be a rough night for you tonight."

"Holy Jees, I have to complain to Otto. Tell him to stop using so many beans when he cooks or my bunkmate is going to melt my face off."

Herbert snorted again. Leaning over the side of his bunk, he said seriously, "Franz is going to have an accident one day. I might even be there to see it."

He winked at Reinhold before withdrawing his head. Reinhold paused for a second, wondering just how serious he was, before deciding that changing the subject was the best thing to do.

"We should think of a way to make more money."

Herbert's head reappeared over the side of the bunk but he was smiling this time. "I created a monster when I got you into the black market. However, I was thinking the same thing earlier. Any ideas?" His head disappeared again.

Reinhold thought for a second before answering. He wasn't sure how his suggestion was going to be received. "I was thinking that we should sell more stuff, more liquor to Göran, more coffee to the guys in Lübeck and Kiel. Actually, I was going to suggest Adam, a guy I met in Lübeck. He'll buy whatever we bring in and we can bring it to him instead of trading right on the ship. I want to start selling more than what fits in a bucket."

"Of course that would make us more money and once again you are reading my mind. I was thinking that we should buy cases of cognac instead of just bottles. It would be a bit more of an initial investment but we would still make good money off the deal. Then we could increase the amount of coffee. Göran will buy whatever we bring him. They are desperate for a drink in Sweden same as they are willing to sell their first born in Germany for coffee. Who is Adam?"

"Why is that? Why are the Swedes so desperate for our cognac? He is a retired sailor, tugboat guy, I think. He gave me his info. Seems alright."

"Well, your highness, not all of us are as opposed to a drink as you are, first of all. Second, someone, probably King Gustav, maybe their Parliament, decided that rationing alcohol was a good idea. They can only legally purchase something like two liters a month but they are required to give a beer with dinner in restaurants, whether the patron wants it or not."

"That sounds like a good amount for one person in a month."

"Not the way the Swedes drink. They just don't get drunk, they drink until they can't function anymore. They wake up the day after wondering what happened to their stash."

Reinhold snorted. "That doesn't really seem possible."

"Just wait until you have one of them on a ship with you. You'll see." Herbert's grinning face reappeared over the side of the bunk. "But that is a good thing for us, isn't it?

"Yes, yes it is."

Reinhold thought about the Swedes and their drinking habits for a minute. He wondered if the girls drank like that too. "What about the girls? Do they drink a lot?"

"Some do. Not very many though. The Swedes are too stuffy for that much fun. You are thinking of Danish girls. Boy, can they party!"

Herbert's eyes glazed over for a second. He was obviously remembering a night, or maybe just a girl, in Denmark. Coming back to himself, he continued, "What about the cognac? We can get it anywhere in Kiel or Lübeck. But we can't have it on the ship. A couple of bottles purchased through the company for our personal use is different than having a case purchased from a liquor store. If Customs ever comes on board we would be in a world of trouble."

"Customs? I thought they only cared about the cargo, not the personal property of the crew."

"They do care about the cargo and usually they only check the cargo but if they think there is something going on, they will search the whole damn ship. We have to worry about the First Mate and the bosun. We can't have them finding a bunch of stuff in our bunks. Smuggling is illegal no matter how you look at it."

"So then we should stow the cases of cognac in the hull with the cargo. We just have to get it out before the shore guys come to unload."

Herbert was silent for a long minute, his eyes searching the room in thought. "Yes, I think that will work. We can get the cases on to the ship easy enough. No one goes in the hull once the cargo is in, except Ackermann. We just wait for him to be done with his infernal counting, then we can stow our goods."

Just then the door opened, putting an abrupt end to their conversation. Arnold, the third guy in their room, came sauntering in, a bottle of rum in one hand and two glasses in the other.

"I was going to drink this by myself but I thought you might want to join me," he said as he settled himself on the bunk across from Reinhold. "Not you, though," he continued, addressing Reinhold. "I know you don't partake."

He laughed as he cracked open the bottle and handed a glassful of the amber liquid to Herbert.

"Never met a man, especially a sailor, that didn't drink," he said, shaking his head.

After pouring one for himself, he raised the glass in a toast, "To the Puerto Ricans and their amazing ability to turn sugar into alcohol! *Prosit!*"

Both men drained their glasses.

"Another?" Arnold asked Herbert.

Herbert handed over his glass and accepted back the draught that Arnold offered.

"Let's drink to Danish girls this time," Herbert offered.

"Oh, that's good. I'll always drink to the Danish girls. I'll always drink with Danish girls, too! To the lovely ladies of Copenhagen!"

Both men downed their drinks again.

Reinhold watched in curious fascination. The *Eos* and the *Stina* hadn't allowed drinking on board and they were too small to try to sneak it. When he mentioned this, Herbert and Arnold both agreed that what the Captain and officers didn't know, wouldn't hurt them.

After they had toasted a fourth round, to standing watch instead of sleeping, his curiosity got the better of him.

"Why do you drink that stuff?"

"Why don't you drink this stuff?" Arnold threw back at him.

Reinhold's nose wrinkled involuntarily and his stomach lurched just a bit. "It made me sick, really sick."

"What? You mean you drank too much and it made you sick?" Arnold questioned. Reinhold nodded. "That was your own fault. Don't go blaming the drink for your own mistake."

Reinhold was instantly insulted by Arnold's bluntly honest statement but he realized that the man had a point. It was his fault. He did drink too much. As a result, he learned a valuable lesson: know how much you can drink without getting sick.

One shouldn't hurt, he thought to himself.

"Next time, maybe, you should bring another glass," he said to Arnold.

Arnold raised his eyebrows in mock surprise. "Oh, my, is the boy ready to move past his belly ache? Here," he said, pouring a shot of rum into his own glass and offering it to Reinhold. "You can have mine."

Reinhold took the glass. His nose threatened to wrinkle again but he fought it, forcing his features to stay smoothly in place. He brought the glass to his nose and willed it to inhale the sweet yet medicinal smell of the rum. His stomach lurched a bit but he fought that, too.

It was my fault, he told himself. *I can do this. I can't be the only one not drinking anymore. That's childish. I have to embrace the lifestyle of a sailor.*

"Well, are you going to drink it or ponder its fruity bouquet?" Arnold sneered at him.

Without thinking, Reinhold tipped the glass and let the contents slide down his throat. He immediately started to cough. His eyes watered and leaked down his cheeks. He felt like he couldn't breathe and gasped for air. But he kept the rum down. Something like a shout went up from Arnold and Herbert.

"Holy shit, he did it. He didn't throw it back up!" Arnold exclaimed and started slapping him on the back. "That's the way we do it, Reinhold! Now we just get you to come out to the bars with us and you'll be a regular sailor!"

Reinhold beamed at them with a small amount of pride. It was only one drink, after all.

Two drinks later, Reinhold surrendered Arnold's glass, thinking that he would see how he felt after the three. Herbert had done the last two with him and was feeling pretty good himself. Arnold downed another before questioning his bunkmates.

"You guys were talking about something when I came in. What was it? What are you planning?"

"To make lots of money!" Reinhold blurted.

Herbert burst into laughter above him.

"Look at this! Give the boy a drink and he gets loose lips!"

"So he is serious. I thought that was a joke." Arnold looked puzzled for a second.

"It is serious," Reinhold was surprised when he slurred his words. *Oh no*, he thought to himself, *I think I have done it again.*

Herbert laughed again, mimicking Reinhold's slurring. "It is serious!"

Arnold and Herbert dissolved into fits of laughter and Reinhold couldn't help laughing at himself.

"Anyway," Herbert said, wiping his leaking eyes on his sleeve, "We are, were, talking about making more money. Reinhold here suggested that we smuggle more cognac into Sweden."

"Hey! Why are you telling this guy about the smuggling?" Reinhold questioned Herbert.

"Don't worry, Reinhold. The whole crew smuggles something. We just don't tell the brass. Arnold here does the cognac gig as well as some other side projects that he will have to tell you about himself because he has never told me."

Arnold made a locked lips pantomime, saying "My lips are sealed. But what are you talking about getting into?" He poured himself another drink.

"Nothing new, just more of what we do now." Herbert said, vaguely.

"So, what? Out with it, man!"

"Cases, Arnold. We are talking about smuggling cases of cognac instead of just bottles. When you came we were talking about where we could hid them."

Arnold shrugged drunkenly. "The hold, of course. There is nowhere else you could hide cases of cognac where they wouldn't be found."

"That's what we were thinking,"

The numb feeling that had been centered in Reinhold lips was making its way across his face and into his fingers. He wanted very much to go outside. "I am going to go."

Herbert and Arnold laughed as he left the room.

"Don't go getting sick over the side! You'll get us all fired if Ackermann sees you!" Arnold called after him.

The thought of getting sick almost made Reinhold get sick. He steadied himself and gulped back the memory of puking all night in the cow barn.

Don't think about it, he told himself sternly. *Think about something else. The girls on the rocky island. The girls on the rocky island. The girls on the rocky island.*

That did it. The nausea passed leaving him feeling like he was floating on the surface of a cool pool. He closed his eyes and imagined himself surrounded by half naked mermaids, as Herbert had called them. They bobbed along on the pool with him, diving and surfacing in a teasing ballet of wet, naked skin and flowing hair. It was wonderful.

He didn't know how long he was standing there when he heard a bell somewhere mark the hour. At the twelfth toll, there was a sound from below the deck followed by the distinctive clanging of the hatch opening. Frederick appeared out of the gloom to Reinhold's right.

"Stargazing?" He asked as he brushed past, headed for the bridge to stand his watch.

Reinhold just nodded, finding that speaking was a problem. A minute later, there was another clang as the hatch opened again. This time Herbert appeared out of the gloom.

"I am going to the *tivoli*. There might still be something going on there. It is Saturday after all. You want to come with me?"

Reinhold nodded. Both men threw their legs over the side of the rail and jumped a bit unsteadily on to the pier.

Chapter 35: Partners In Crime

Taken on the deck of the *Pagensand*
Photograph courtesy of Reinhold Scholz

The next time the *Pagensand* arrived in Stockholm, Reinhold and Herbert filled their packs with cognac and headed out to see Göran. The Swede was surprised but not shocked by the thirty six bottles that filled the counter in the bridge of his tugboat. He grinned, shaking his head, as he pulled a wad of bills from his pocket. He handed them each their share, one hundred and forty four *krona*. Reinhold felt his pulse quicken a bit. It had been a long time since he had held so much money. Never had he worked so little for so much. They arranged with Göran for a tugboat to meet the *Pagensand* when she arrived in port. Once this was sorted, they thanked the Swede for his business and left. They got a few paces away when Herbert grabbed Reinhold's arm and tugged at him.

"One hundred and forty four *krona*!" he said. "How much did those cases cost us? Twenty *mark*?" Reinhold nodded. "That's one hundred and twenty four *krona*!"

Reinhold thought for a moment that Herbert was going to start dancing.

The next stop for them was the *kaffe haus* where they turned their cognac money into coffee after a quick debate about how much to purchase.

"Turn the whole thing into coffee, all one hundred and twenty four *krona*. What are you going to spend it on in Stockholm? There is no way you could eat that much pastry and that's the only thing they have that's good here! Well, I guess you could visit the *puff* but even that won't cost that much. I could get Katie something nice. Her birthday is coming up."

In the end, they purchased thirty pounds of coffee costing one hundred and twenty *krona*. They hauled their merchandise back to the *Pagensand* and went about their business as sailors. Reinhold even took Herbert's suggestion and visited the *puff* with Arnold and Frederick. It was his first visit to the Swedish institution. Herbert, Reinhold learned, didn't partake in the *puff* because he had a girlfriend in Kiel, a girl he obviously loved enough to never mention her very often.

"It's right next to the palace!"

It was the only comment Reinhold had about his experience when they got back to the ship.

Three days later, they met Adam at the port tavern where he and Reinhold had originally made acquaintance. He was already there, sipping a beer, and watching the sailors flirt with the girls.

"Did you bring coffee?" He asked as Herbert and Reinhold sat down next to him.

Herbert ordered a beer and Reinhold got a soda.

"We did. We have thirty pounds for you." Herbert motioned to the backpacks at their feet.

Adam was surprised. "Good, good. The price right now is thirty two *mark* a pound. Is that a deal?"

"Yes, yes it is," Reinhold piped up. Herbert also nodded his agreement.

Adam did some quick math with a pencil and a napkin. "That's nine hundred and sixty *mark*. I don't have that kind of cash on me right now. I wasn't expecting you to have so much. Can one of you bring the coffee to my tugboat later tonight? From now on, you will bring what you have directly there. Actually, I'll have one of my guys met you when you get to port. No more meeting in the bar. Not a good place to exchange cash."

Herbert went alone to get the cash from Adam. Reinhold was standing watch when he got back to the ship. Herbert merely grinned at Reinhold as he headed for the bunk.

That's when the money really started to roll in, he thought to himself as he stared into the turquoise Caribbean Sea. *I wish I was making half that now! I wish I had saved more of what I made then.*

He sighed to himself. He knew better than to believe that he would have saved that money for all these years. Not after what happened.

A brush with death will change people, won't it? He questioned himself.

Doing a quick calculation, he realized that his brush with death had happened almost exactly six years before. Then he chuckled to himself.

One of my brushes with death.

The rest of the summer and the autumn on the *Pagensand* progressed without incident. Actually, it went to well, it was too easy. At first, Reinhold squirreled away his money in his post book. When the balance reached over a thousand *mark*, which didn't take long, he stopped saving and started spending.

I went girl crazy, he told himself, smiling.

He quickly learned how to talk to the girls at the bars. He bought them dinner and drinks and then offered to take the evening to the next level. He finally succeeded in bringing his first girl back to the ship after spending time chatting with her at the bar. She told him she wanted to know what it was like to make love on a ship and he was more than happy to oblige.

He learned that night that you have to tell your roommates when you have a girl in your bunk or other people walk in on you. Then it takes weeks for the comments to stop. He can still see Herbert humping the wind and telling him that it is all in the hips.

In Stockholm, Reinhold learned that Swedish girls were passionate in bed, when you could get them there. Meeting girls at the *tivoli* wasn't the easiest thing to do, especially if their parents were around. Then there was the language issue. Reinhold was quickly learning Swedish, just not fast enough. He bought a couple of comic books from the company via Gerold written in Swedish that were helping with the grammar and Herbert knew it almost fluently so they would speak it to each like it was a secret language.

The Swedish girls weren't interested in money the way the German girls were and they didn't want you to buy them anything. They just wanted their partner to be a good lover. A Swedish girl would go all night where a German girl was done after an hour or two. It had to do with interest, Reinhold figured. The German girls were after money or material gain and wanted to do the minimal amount to get it. Swedish girls wanted pleasure, as much of it as they could get.

It was during one his romps with a Swedish girl that Reinhold had his first real scare on a ship. They were in his bunk, having a somewhat awkward time as the girl kept pushing his head down, toward her naval, saying the word 'lick', when there was a booming sound. The ship shuddered horribly. Jumping out of his bunk, Reinhold threw on a pair of pants and ran up to the deck to find a ferry had rammed them on the starboard side as they lay at anchor.

"Go make sure we are not taking on water." He heard Captain Meyer bark to Ackermann.

The ferry pilot was desperately trying to reverse his vessel while Captain Meyer hurled insults at him. Ackermann reported back that the ship was taking on water. Reinhold could feel it listing beneath his feet. He was afraid that they were going to have to abandon ship but Ackermann assured the assembled group of curious sailors that this was not the case. The breach in the hull was minor. Reinhold went back to his girl who had so patiently waited for him in his bunk. He spent the rest of the night doing some ramming of his own.

Pagensand docked in Stockholm after accident with a ferry
Photograph courtesy of Reinhold Scholz

To Reinhold's eternal surprise, Herbert liked to go shopping in Stockholm. The Swedes had better quality clothing than the Germans.

Herbert liked to bring pretty things home for Katie and Reinhold tagged along to look for stuff for himself. He was developing quite the wardrobe for a poor sailing boy. He had two pairs of boots now and a shirt and dungarees for every day. Herbert even taught him how to do his laundry faster than hand washing every article. He simply tied the clothes in a bundle and threw them into the wake behind the ship. The bundle went around a couple of times in the propeller and came out clean. He learned the hard way not to leave the bundle near the propeller for too long or all your clothes would come up shredded.

It was in Stockholm that Reinhold saw his first pair of colored underwear. There was pink, green, blue, and red, all the colors of the rainbow. It led Reinhold to believe that Swedish men were a bunch of queers.

"No wonder their women are so desperate for a good man! The Swedish ones are all queer!" He exclaimed to Herbert as he held up a pair of pink briefs.

Herbert laughed and bought a pair to see what Katie thought of him wearing pink panties, as they called them.

It was in October that he and Herbert got too cocky for their own good. They were doing so well smuggling coffee and cognac that they decided they would try something riskier.

Adam and Göran were partial to certain products but were willing to purchase almost anything they could sell for a profit. One day in Lübeck a package containing silk was loaded onto the ship. Reinhold was standing in the hull when he heard Ackermann comment that it had to be stacked on top of everything else and kept very dry as it was fragile and worth a lot of money. He got the idea in his head that maybe he would take that package and sell it to Göran. Herbert was all for it. They came up with a plan to sneak it into their bunk and hide it under their beds until they got to Stockholm. They figured that they could have it off the ship by the time anyone would notice that it was gone.

They were wrong. It was a more precious package then they had imagined. When its owner appeared to collect it and discovered it was missing, he went straight to Customs. Customs, in turn, came straight to the ship. Herbert was on the deck, splicing a broken line when he saw the agents approaching.

Feeling that it had something to do with the silk, he gestured for Reinhold to follow him below deck. They had to act fast. It wouldn't take Customs long to search the hull. Then it was unknown whether they would go to the bridge and the Captain's quarters next or the sailor's quarters.

Once in their bunk, the two sailors desperately pushed the package of silk out the porthole in their room. It took several nerve racking minutes because it was almost the same diameter as the porthole. They barely made it back to the deck before Customs was in their bunk, searching. They decided it was best not to try to do that again, no matter how much money they could make.

"It was a good thing that they didn't find the cases of cognac." Reinhold mentioned as they set out to visit Göran.

Herbert nodded his agreement. "I am not sure how they missed them but thank God they did or Captain Meyer would be even more pissed than he is now!"

It was a month later, almost two weeks into November, when the strange good luck that Reinhold had experienced on the *Pagensand* finally ran out. They left Stockholm against the advice of the harbor pilot who came to steer the ship out into the Baltic Sea.

"There is a big storm coming, the first of the season. The *windstärke* is picking up and should be about a seven very soon. Are you sure you want to leave now?" Reinhold heard the pilot say to Captain Meyer.

"Yes, we need to get back to Kiel and then on to Lübeck. I should be able to make it to Kalmar Sound to shelter against the wind before it gets too bad." The pilot shrugged and took his place at the window, ready to deliver orders.

Not long after leaving Stockholm, while Reinhold was standing watch at the bow, the wind picked up and the heavens burst, lashing the ship with rain that blew in sideways with a lot of sting behind it. The Captain had been mistaken about making it to Kalmar Sound before it got bad. The ship tossed and pitched on the waves for an hour before they finally sailed out of it.

Out of the frying pan and into the fire, Reinhold said to himself as he watched a wet, heavy, dense fog almost instantly surround the ship as it reached the sound.

They slowed down, chugging along at a snail's pace, not able to see what lay in front of them. Kalmar Sound was notorious for reefs and Reinhold was glad he was leaving the bow for the rear of the ship. It was no longer his responsibility to look for them.

Reinhold took his place at the whistle turn feeling as if a feather pillow was smothering him. He spent the first couple of minutes of his watch drawing designs in the mist. Then a feeling of dread descended upon him. He strained to see into the mist, wishing it would just go away and let them sail in peace. Had they passed Kalmar yet? He hadn't seen any lights but the fog was too thick for him to see the bow so how was he supposed to see the shore? He stood there, gripping the rail, uneasy, trying to use his ears since his eyes weren't helping. All he heard was the lapped of the sea against the metal hull and the soft chugging of the slow moving engine.

They had sailed through the fog for a tense hour when there came a bad noise, the wrenching sound of metal hitting and scraping along stone. A cry went up from Arnold at the bow.

"REEF!"

Almost instantly, the ship listed port.

Holy Jees! We are going down! Reinhold screamed to himself as he made for the lifeboats hanging off the back of the ship.

He whipped out his knife and began cutting away the ropes that secured it. He could hear men yelling and the sounds of hatches opening. There was a strange banging coming from below. By the time he got the first lifeboat free the second was half submerged and unreachable. He turned to look at what was going on, why no one had come yet. He saw the Captain emerge from the bridge, followed by the first mate.

"Get in the boat! Everyone in the boat!" Captain Meyer was yelling to the crew. "Everyone in the boat!"

"Sir, we couldn't get to Otto," Frederick and Herbert emerged from the fog, looking panicked and grey.

"What do you mean?" snapped the Captain.

"His door won't open! It is jammed shut! We tried! We tried!"

Frederick was nearly hysterical. The deck pitched to a greater degree sending the men stumbling. They could hear a banging coming from below deck and a faint voice screaming for help.

"Everyone in the boat!" Captain Meyer commanded.

The men scrambled toward the small boat.

"We all won't fit and the other one is gone." Ackermann pointed out as he jumped into the lifeboat.

"Half in the water and hold on. Ackermann, you and I go first. Get in the water!"

Numbly, Reinhold jumped into the lifeboat and settled onto the seat next to Gerold. Taking up an oar, he and Arnold rowed the boat a little way away from the sinking ship while the Captain, Ackermann, and Herbert held on to the side.

"Did you get an SOS off, Ackermann?" The Captain asked.

"Yes, sir." The First Mate stammered through chattering teeth.

The water couldn't be any more than 40 degrees. The lips of the men in the water quickly turned blue and the sound of chattering teeth filled the silence.

Thirty feet away, the last bit of the *Pagensand* slipped below the surface, sending a boiling turbulence to the surface.

Goddamn, that sunk quickly. We couldn't have hit that reef more than six minutes ago.

Reinhold was about to voice his thought when the Captain spoke.

"Let us have a minute of silent prayer for the soul of our dedicated cook, Otto. If we had not been carrying iron ore maybe we would have had more time to save him. May he find peace forever on the seas of heaven."

The assembled men hung their heads in grief, guilt, and respect.

Glancing at his watch, the Captain announced to his crew, "We'll spend an hour in the water and then you in the boat will trade places with us. Ackermann got off an SOS. Hopefully the Kustbevakningen in Kalmar got our signal and have a ship on the way to pick us up."

Reinhold sat in the life boat shivering, willing the coast guard to come before he had to take his turn in the water. But that didn't happen and after an hour the Captain gave the order to switch. One by one, the frozen men climbed out of the water to replace a dry man. Reinhold's breathe caught in his throat as he slipped into the water. It was colder, it seemed, than he was expecting. Instantly, he started to shiver violently. His teeth chattered. He felt the last bit of warmth drain from his blood. He gripped the side of the life boat and rested his forehead against the wood. He tried to remain hopeful that the coast guard would be here soon.

"Try to keep moving, lads," the Captain said to his men in the water. "It keeps the blood flowing."

Reinhold started to tread water with his legs while holding on with his arms, praying for the arrival of a rescue boat.

Reinhold's hope that the coast guard was coming was gone when he slipped into the water for the second, and not last, time. His body was completely numb and his joints were not cooperating. It was not going to be easy this second time to keep his legs moving and he almost instantly gave up. He was shaking violently and could feel his mind starting to slow down, to go numb.

Looking back, he remembered thinking that this was how he was going to die.

Sixteen, he thought, *I am only sixteen. Who gets my money then? The money I saved in my postbook? God, I hope my father doesn't get it! He doesn't deserve my money. Besides, he'll just give it to her. There is no way that woman deserves my money!*

He felt a surge of adrenaline warm his veins at the thought of his stepmother inheriting his hard earned money and was momentarily grateful for hating her so much.

Lisa should have it, he thought hazily.

It was the last thing he remembered until lights appeared out of the murky black, piercing the fog, and coming to rest on the little life boat. He heard men shouting in Swedish and felt himself being dragged out of the water on to something metal.

A blanket was wrapped around him. He was carried down a flight of narrow stairs and ushered into a bright tiled room where he was stripped naked. A large Swedish officer rubbed him with cold salt water. Reinhold's mind came back to him for an instant, just long enough to comment on his situation.

"What," he said, "you don't have any women who can come rub me?"

The Swedish man smiled at him before wrapping a blanket around him again. Then everything went black.

Chapter 36: "Vacation"

Reinhold remembered being completely disorientated when he regained consciousness. He was in a hospital in Kalmar and not in his bunk on the *Pagensand*. It took a few minutes for his unwilling mind to recall the reality of the situation. The nurse assigned to the sailors told him that they were in the water for four hours. They were lucky to be healthy and sound. The guys were jovial enough about their survival but Reinhold couldn't help feeling that they had been very, very lucky. He was feeling very subdued. He reminded himself and this fellow crewmates that they had not all gotten out alive.

"Reinhold, you can't keep reminding yourself about that. We all feel bad for Otto. We all know that these are the dangers we face when we get on a ship and we do it anyway because what else are we going to do? Otto knew the risks." Herbert tried to help Reinhold take his mind off the Otto but there was no cure for his melancholy.

It wasn't just Otto, he thought to himself. *I thought I was going to die. I haven't lived enough to die just yet. What if that had been me trapped in my own bunk on a sinking ship?* The thought made him shudder violently and break out in a cold sweat.

Not long after they were all conscious, Captain Meyer came to visit his crew. He returned their sailor's books to them, officially releasing them. Reinhold stared at his like it had returned from the dead. He had never expected to see it again. Already, the thought of having to reapply had crossed his mind. But Ackermann managed to send the SOS and retrieve the important papers from the *Pagansand* before it went down. Reinhold had a bit more respect for the man after he learned this. That was a lot to accomplish in so short an amount of time in a bad situation.

The Captain told his men that the Kustbevakningen[30] had sent a representative to take an official statement. It had been determined that the crew would not have to give statements of their own. Reinhold was grateful for that. The company, on the other hand, wanted to talk to everybody. He didn't mention that he had heard the pilot in Stockholm warn Captain Meyer about the storm. What good would it do to tell them that? He had always been a fair man, jolly almost, in his dealings with his crew.

---

[30] Kustbevakningen is the Swedish equivalent of the Coast Guard.

"You are welcome to come back and work for me when I get a new ship," Captain Meyer told Reinhold and Herbert when he returned their sailor's books to them. "I don't know how long that will be but I can send you word if you give me an address."

Herbert gave the captain his address in Kiel.

Two days after hitting the reef, Reinhold boarded a train in Kalmar bound for Malmö. He took the window seat and stared at the passing Swedish countryside for at least an hour before Herbert spoke.

"Why don't you come to Kiel with me instead of going to Lübeck? You can get another ship there. But before you do that, we should do something fun. Something to celebrate that we are still alive."

Reinhold thought for a minute. Herbert was right.

"Ok," he agreed.

From Malmö, they took the ferry to Copenhagen. In Copenhagen, the crew split up. Arnold decided to stay in Denmark for a couple of days and enjoy the Danish girls he loved so much. Frederick immediately got a train to Hamburg, muttering something about wanting to see his sister. Franz melted away into the crowd before they even got off the ferry. Reinhold was going to stay a night with Arnold and see these Danish girls, but Herbert wanted to get home to Katie so they hopped a train to Kiel.

On the way to Kiel, Reinhold thought about what he was going to do with himself. Herbert kept insisting that he could stay with him and Katie but Reinhold didn't like the sound of it. Like Lisa, Herbert and Katie lived in a one room apartment. There was not alot of space and privacy. At first he agreed, but as they got closer to their destination he decided that he had to do something else.

As the train pulled into Kiel, he came to the conclusion that he was going to get a hotel. A nice hotel. He had a lot of money, over a thousand *mark*, in his post book. It was just sitting there, waiting for him to die so that someone else could have it. He decided that saving was stupid. It was his money and he was going to spend it!

Reinhold checked in to a hotel in Kiel, a nice hotel, like he planned. His first day in the seaside town, he didn't leave the hotel. He ordered room service and read a book he picked up in the lobby. The first night, he went to the hotel bar and sipped a beer while watching the people dance and talk. He pondered his future. What was he going to do now?

It was not an appealing idea to go back to the high seas. What if the ship sank again and this time he didn't get off? But what else was there to do? He could work on the docks as a longshoreman. Through his coffee smuggling he knew some guys that could help him get a job. Business was picking up in Germany. Maybe he could find something else to do. Deciding that tomorrow he would poke around and see what was going on, Reinhold left the bar and went to sleep in a real bed with clean sheets in a room not on a ship. It was heaven!

The next day he met Herbert at the Nord-Ostsee Kanal in Holtenau. Herbert and Katie lived not far from the canal in Holtenau. There was a sailor's office nearby. It was Herbert's plan to get another ship. They stood on a bridge over the canal, watching the ships move through the locks, and discussed their future.

Reinhold and Herbert in Holtenau
Phtotgraph courtesy of Reinhold Scholz

"I would rather stay on shore, with Katie, then go back to the seas but that doesn't mean that it is possible. What would I do? The only thing I have done is sail."

"There are jobs now, from what I heard on the way here this morning. We could do construction or something. I just don't know about going right back to a ship. I want some time to think about it, to see what else is available out there."

"Yes, I guess that is best, to look for other work. I have some money saved but only enough for a couple of months. After that, I have to have a job."

"Lets see what is out there then," Reinhod responded.

"Why are your shoes so clean? Did you clean them?"

Herbert was eyeing Reinhold's worn and sea water stained boots.

Reinhold shrugged. "I put them out last night at the hotel. Someone picked them up and cleaned them. They did my laundry too."

He gestured to his wool coat, heavy sweater, and dungarees.

"The hotel seems to be agreeing with you. You are the cleanest I have ever seen you."

"Yup and the best part is I didn't have to wait days for the sweater or the jacket to dry after washing it. I don't know how they did it, but I put them out last night and got them back this morning clean and dry. Oh, and there is hot running water and a magnificent shower in my room."

Reinhold, it turned out, wasn't nearly as motivated to find a job as Herbert. He loafed around the port in Kiel or the canal in Holtenau most of the day. The longshoremen were sure they could get him a job, all he had to do was say the word. He hestitated to say the word, afraid that he would hate it and quit. That wouldn't be good for the guy that got him the job. Finding a job of his own accord was the best thing for him to do, he concluded. He hung out in the portside taverns, waiting to hear that someone was looking for new employees but mostly listening to the old timers talk about the rough life of a sailor before the first war when only the newest of ships had electricity and diesel motors.

"Ever shovel coal for ten hours?" One guy asked Reinhold as he sat on the bar.

"No," was the only response he could give.

"Its a hard, dirty job. You guys have it easy these days with the electricity and diesel engines," the old timer muttered into his beer. Reinhold figured he must have been a stoker.

Herbert joined him most days. He too thought it was better if he found a job of his own accord. He, like Reinhold, had been told by the longshoremen that they would put a good word in for him but, also like Reinhold, he didn't want to be in debted to someone. Herbert didn't listen to the old timers in the taverns. Instead, he made acquaintance with the sailors working for different companies. He talked to the tugboat guys and the government agents. He learned that while jobs were becoming more plentiful on the shore, they were not paying any more than a sailor earned.

When Herbert went home to Katie at the end of the day, Reinhold would pick a girl from the selection at the tavern. If there were none there that interested him, he would wander over to the *puff*. There was always one hanging around the parlor that he found attractive. He had a girl every night of his 'vacation' as he took to calling it later. But he was just bragging. He had to admit to himself that he envied Herbert for having Katie. The two of them were hopelessly in love. Reinhold knew that it was for Katie that Herbert was looking for work on the shore. He hated leaving her to go sail.

But that is what the sea does to you, he thought. *She locks you in her grip and won't let go. Not even if it kills you.*

A cold mistress, he had heard the old timers call the sea and he thoroughly agreed. Even as he tried to convince Herbert not to go back he was himself contemplating whether it would be better to get a ship here in Keil or in Lübeck.

"I think I am just going to get a ship and get back to work," Herbert said one day while they sat in a tavern in Holtenau. Reinhold knew Herbert was a bit drunk because he always said that when he got a little drunk. "I am running out of money. I haven't worked in four weeks."

Reinhold understood the dilemma. He was also running out of money. Between the hotel, the food and drinks, and the girls, he had blown through all his savings. The fifty *mark* in his pocket was the last of it. No cash, no savings left in his post book. Grinning to himself he had to admit that he had enjoyed himself the last few weeks.

It was worth it. No more saving, he thought. *Whats the point? I earned it, I am going to spend it!*

Slapping Herbert on his back, Reinhold told his friend, "Let us go get a ship then! Maybe we can even hire on to one together."

Early the next morning, Reinhold meet Herbert at the seaman's office in Kiel. There was a *Matrose* position for Herbert but no *Leichtmatrose* position for Reinhold. The officer behind the desk shuffled through his paperwork several times to arrive at the same conclusion: there was just not two positions available on the same ship. Reinhold was disappointed. The hotel had reminded him to take all of his belongings and politely asked him not to come back this morning. The money he had given them was gone and he had none left to extend his stay. He was hoping to get right on to another ship. As it stood now, he would have no where to sleep tonight.

"You should take that ship and get back to work, Herbert," Reinhold told his friend. No sense in both of them being out of work anymore.

"No, I think I'll wait. It was more fun to sail with a friend then with just any old crew."

Turning to the officer, Herbert asked, "Can you send me a message when a ship comes in that is looking for a *Matrose* and a *Leichtmatrose*?"

Nodding, the officer handed him a clipboard with a sheet of paper attached to it already baring a list of addresses. "Add your name to the list and specify what positions you are looking for. I'll see what I can do."

Reinhold and Herbert left the sailor's office and went next door to the sailor's club. Once they had ordered a drink, Reinhold reveled his predicament. Herbert immediately offered his place to Reinhold.

"Katie won't mind. It is not as if you would be staying there forever. Besides, she likes you."

"No, I don't want to intrude on you guys. I'll just find a girl to take me home." Reinhold grinned wickedly.

Herbert laughed at his friend's audacity. He thought for a minute. "You could stay in the sailor's office. You know, in case you don't find a girl to take you home. Do you have ten *pfennig*?"

Reinhold was puzzled. "Yes, I have a bit of money left."

"Go there today before they close. Tell them you need a place to stay. They'll let you stay in one of the rooms above the office. It is not comfortable but it is warm and dry. I had to do it a couple of times when I was on the bum. Be thankful you are not in Hamburg on the bum. They stretch a rope across the office and you hang your head over it to sleep while sitting in one of those wooden chairs."

Reinhold spent the night in the sailor's office. He decided he didn't want to do that again. No word about a ship came to Herbert's place. Reinhold began to think that they weren't going to be able to get a ship together. He told Herbert so and Herbert agreed.

"I need to get back to work, Reinhold," he said four days after putting his name on the list. "It is bad enough that I have to go stand by the canal and beg a pack of smokes from the ships going through the locks. I don't want Katie to have to go back to work."

He look of disgust on his face told the whole story of how he felt about Katie having to go back to work.

"Then go take a ship. Get going."

"What are you going to do?"

"I am going to visit my sister. I'll get a ship in Lübeck."

"How are you going to get to Lübeck?"

"I have just enough money left to get there. I'll stay with her for a night and take the first ship that comes along."

The two men shook hands and parted ways at the train station with a promise to keep in touch. Reinhold wasn't looking forward to taking a ship without Herbert but it couldn't be helped. It did make him feel better to know that he had a friend on the high seas, looking out for him.

Chapter 37: **Fona**

Fona
Photograph courtesy of 7seasvessels.com

Fortune favored Reinhold. He got a ship the day after he got to Lübeck. He spent the night with Lisa and her now husband Willie. They passed the time catching up on what had happened to Reinhold. Lisa was not happy that he spent all his money but she was thrilled that he didn't die in the Baltic Sea when the *Pagensand* sunk. She made him promise that he would start saving again. Reinhold was grateful that she did not ask for too many details. She seemed to sense that he did not want to talk about it and chose not to push the matter. The next day, December 15, he left Lübeck on the *Fona*, a coal ship, as a *Leichtmatrose*.

Reinhold remembered it being a filthy ship, so filthy he could write his name in the layer of coal dust that coated everything. Looking back, he wished he could say that it was the dirtiest ship he was ever on but, unfortunately, that was not the case. They cleaned and cleaned and cleaned but never really made a dent in the buildup. How could they? Every time the hold was unloaded or loaded, a grimy, greasy cloud enveloped the ship, coating everything it touched. Even his skin felt different on the *Fona*. Water seemed to run off him like a duck. Coal had never been his favorite cargo. If he had not been broke and determined not to go home again he would have waited for a different ship.

The Captain of the *Fona*, Captain Meyer (another Meyer!), was almost non-existent. Reinhold barely ever saw the man. He spent most of his time in the bridge or in his salon. The First Mate was a prick, as most First Mates were, for some unknown reason. Reinhold thought for a moment but could not come up with the man's name. The Third Mate had been a nice guy. Kahn was his name. He was fair with the crew, unlike many Third Mates.

The crew of the *Fona* was ok. There were fifteen men on the ship, not including the Captain and the mates. Five of them were stokers. This was Reinhold's first experience with stokers. They were not young men, which surprised him. It was a hard job shoveling coal for hours on end but these men were tough, hard as steel. They were a hardworking and a hard drinking lot. As long as they had a pair of dungarees and a tee shirt and somewhere to lay their head when they were done drinking, they were happy. They didn't spend their money on anything but booze and women. It did not take long for them to notice that Reinhold had no tattoos.

"What kind of a sailor has no tattoos?" They questioned him.

"This kind," he retorted.

He had no desire to get a tattoo nor did he believe that he had too. The guys on the crew didn't agree with him. One night in Amsterdam, they arranged for a tattooist to come visit Reinhold. The guys held him down while the image of an anchor was permanently etched on his left forearm. For good measure they also had a sailboat tattooed on his right forearm.

It was almost impossible for him to work for days afterwards because of the pain from the ink. He kept this too himself, however, as the crew was watching to see if he was going to be a man or a bitch. Reinhold chose to show them that he was a man.

Of all the crew, Reinhold got along with well enough with two of them: Keller and Manfred. Both were older than Reinhold. Keller was in his mid-twenties and Manfred was almost twenty. The three of them became drinking buddies, spending their time in port at the local watering holes, picking up girls.

Not long after he joined the *Fona*, Reinhold had his first experience with the legendary Danish girls. He was not at all disappointed. He remembered it clear as day. They got into Copenhagen two days before Christmas. Keller suggested they celebrate Christmas that night since they would be on the high seas on Christmas proper. After they finished with their work for the night, they headed out. Manfred suggested that they go to the Carlsberg brewery since it was not far from where they docked. They decided against this because the stokers were headed that way. They ended up at a port tavern and had a few drinks into them when a group of ladies entered the bar. In a matter of minutes, Reinhold had several hanging on him. They were a bit older than he was, but he did not care. His friends were very jealous, but he did not understand why. They had all the girls they could handle themselves.

"Look at this face!"

"Forget the face, look at those arms! I love a sailor's arms!"

"How old are you? 16! My goodness, I bet you could go all night. How about you show me?"

Reinhold spent a couple of hours enjoying the attention before deciding which one he was going to take back to the ship. He chose a pretty brunette with incredible assets and a soft voice. After the first go around, he was surprised that she was ready to go again so quickly. Usually he had to be the one to initiate the second time but this girl was on him before he could regain his breath. All night it went like that and at dawn she left without so much as a "when are you back in town" or a "can we keep in touch?" or "can I have some money?" It was a sailor's dream! As he fell asleep that night, he asked that, if there was indeed a God, he bless the girls of Copenhagen. He also wondered where his bunkmates were. He hoped that their absence meant that they got lucky too.

A week later, on New Year's Eve, the *Fona* steamed into a port in France. Reinhold had never been to the country before and certainly had never been to a port like the one he encountered there. Manfred explained to him that some of the highest and lowest tides in France, in Europe, happened at this port.

"It is tiny, when you compare it to other places. Cargo ships don't come here much, especially the big ones."

They went through a series of locks and a short way up a river to get into the port. Once docked, Keller was quick to suggest that they go out and celebrate a new year. They thought they were all set to have a good time. None of them had to stand watch that night and the company was sending an agent to exchange money for them. It was 9:30 when they docked.

At 10:30, the agent had not shown up yet and the night was wearing away. It looked like they were doomed to a boring New Year's Eve on the ship with the damn stokers but Keller had an idea. He had a briefcase of cigarettes.

"I keep them around for just such an occasion. We can barter some drinks for the cigarettes! Let's go!"

Off they went to find a local bar. The selection was dismal. They chose one for its proximity to the ship, definitely not for its ambience.

"We can crawl from here," Manfred pointed out. "Like the stokers do." They laughed.

The owner of the bar was behind the bar when they entered. He was a big guy, tall and wide. Reinhold guessed that he was an ex-sailor or longshoreman. He had a build that suggested that at one time he had done hard work. As best as he could with the limited French he spoke, Keller worked out a deal with him. They would get two glasses of wine for one pack of cigarettes. Keller ordered the drinks and paid with the cigarettes. The sailors toasted the New Year.

"To a new year! May it be better than the last but not as good as the next!"

"And to Lucky Strikes! May they never stop making them!" Keller added before they downed their glasses of wine and ordered another round.

"I didn't know that you could get drinks for cigarettes." Reinhold mentioned as they started sipping their second glass of wine. "I thought only cash bought things."

"Things are cash," Manfred pointed out. "This guy will just take the Lucky Strikes and sell them for cash or barter them for something else or smoke them himself."

"Not all currency is cash," Keller summed up neatly.

Leaning over, he pulled up the cuff of Reinhold's sleeve, noting that it was bare. "You should get a gold watch. Gold watches come in handy on the seas."

Reinhold did not have to ask why. Gold, duh!

Looking around the bar, Reinhold noticed that there were not many people there.

"What's the deal here, Keller? People don't go out on New Year's Eve in France? Or did we just pick the wrong spot?"

"New Year's isn't as big here as it is in Germany. They are probably all in church or something pious like that. Damn Catholics!"

"And New Year's isn't as big in Germany as it is in Australia. They throw huge parties down under, whole towns get together for fireworks, beer, girls...." Manfred's voice trailed off as he thought.

"You have been there?" Reinhold asked.

"Yup, a couple of years ago," Manfred answered. "I was going to jump ship and stay but we left port a day earlier than I was expecting. I am going to try again this spring. Screw these ships! I want a career on the shore, you know, a wife and family, maybe a business. I am a pretty good carpenter. Australia is looking for people, skilled people, like carpenters and mechanics."

"I don't believe that you will do it," Reinhold said, a bit flippantly. "You didn't do it the first time, I don't think you'll do it the second time. And if you do, you have to write and tell me where you are so I can visit."

"You'll see," was the only answer Manfred gave.

They were having a good time, drinking and joking about Manfred's plan to go to Australia when the owner of the bar announced that it was midnight and wished the bar a Happy New Year. The sailors toasted the New Year again and ordered another round of drinks.

"Man, I wish there was some girls here!" Keller lamented.

It had to be near one o'clock in the morning when the bartender approached the sailors with a new deal. For the rest of the cigarettes in the briefcase, they could drink all night, anything that they wanted. Keller agreed to the deal and handed over the Lucky Strikes. Reinhold did not have the best feeling about the deal but he went along with Keller's judgment. His drink was the first to be finished. He signaled for another but the owner just started yelling at him. Not understanding French, Reinhold looked to Keller. Keller was red in the face and getting redder.

"You lying, cheating *arschloch*! We had a deal! You took my cigarettes, damn it!"

Keller was standing now, leaning over the bar and screaming in the man's face. The owner stood his ground, arms folded across his massive chest, a look of indifference on his face. Reinhold quickly surmised that they were being thrown out of the bar. The guy was trying to rip them off. Looking around, he noticed that they were the only patrons left. There was just a few friends of the owner hanging out by the door.

Before he could think or act, Keller threw a punch at the French thief, knocking the man back. He regained his feet and went after Keller while Manfred and Reinhold tried to stop the owner's friends from interfering. The situation escalated quickly into a brawl. Reinhold took several punches to the face and chest but managed to give back exactly what he got. Then the police showed up. Reinhold knew that the owner called them before the fight broke out. There was no way they could've gotten there that quick!

With their clubs, the law beat down the Germans, cuffed their hands behind their backs, and hauled them into the back of a waiting truck. They raged and screamed and kicked the walls of the vehicle, but it was all for naught. It was Reinhold's first arrest and he would never, ever forget it as long as he lived.

For two days, 48 hours, Keller, Manfred and Reinhold sat in a small, dark cell. The police took off the handcuffs, which was a relief. The wine had worn off just as quickly as the adrenaline, leaving them tired, hungry, and thirsty. No one brought them food or water. For two days!

They tried to attract attention to their plight by banging on the door of their cell. All it attracted was a beating by the police. They flooded into the cell half a dozen times, wielding their clubs, and beat their prisoners into submission. After the sixth time, the sailors gave up. They were too weak to care anymore that they were thirsty. Instead of making noise to attract another wave of violence, they laid on the floor of their cell and waited, for what they had no clue. Would they have a hearing in front of a judge? Would the company have to bail them out? Why hadn't the company come looking for them? Reinhold began to wonder if the company had left them for dead in a French jail.

After two days, they were dragged, dehydrated, bloodied, bruised, and half dead, from the cell and thrown into the back of the truck again. Before the doors closed, a man who bailed them out introduced himself as a representative of Stern Linie, the company that owned the *Fona*. In perfectly annunciated German, he explained what was going to happen next.

"You are not allowed to touch French soil again on this particular trip to this country. They are going to back this truck up to the gangway and you are to get out and get on the ship without speaking or looking at anything. Understand?"

The sailors nodded their ascension.

"In the future, when your occupation brings you to France, you will not leave your port of arrival. If you do and you are caught, you will be deported back to Germany, immediately. Understand?"

Again, the sailors nodded their ascension.

"Do you know what they did to us in there?" Keller asked the agent.

The man looked at them for a second before answering. "I have a good idea, but it doesn't matter. This is settled. You are leaving France within the hour. The only reason why you are free to go is that the *Fona* is set to sail. I suggest you don't do anything like this again."

Keller tried to say something else but the agent disappeared and the back of the truck slammed shut.

It was a short drive to the Fona. The truck backed up to the gangway and the doors opened to show a very angry Captain Meyer. Reinhold, Keller and Manfred got out of the truck and limped the rest of the way to the deck. The stood bedraggled and abused in front of the Captain. They could feel the eyes of the rest of the crew on them as they awaited further punishment.

"Your bail was paid by the company. The amount of one hundred *francs* apiece will be deducted from your pay until the amount is repaid. As further retribution to the crew that had to do your work while you lounged in jail, you will clean the slag out of the furnaces for the next two days."

With a last disgusted look at his sailors, the Captain turned and left them in the care of the Third Mate.

"Well, why are you still standing there? We have a ship to getting sailing." Kahn dismissed them without further comment.

The next day, as he cleaned the slag out of furnace number three, Reinhold vowed never to set foot on French soil again. They didn't want him in their country and he didn't like their way of conducting business. He suspected they received the treatment they did because they were German. Manfred pointed out that Germany occupied France during the war and destroyed a lot of stuff.

"And that is not to mention the stealing!" Manfred had told Reinhold. "My cousin was in a division of the army that carried big paintings and statues out of a museum in Paris after the occupation. It is not really hard to see why they hate Germans."

Reinhold thought about this as he scooped and scrapped the thick, grey dust that had built up in the furnace. He could understand why the French hated the Germans. Hitler had done horrible, horrible things not only to France, but to several nations in Europe. But Hitler didn't speak for all Germans, especially those from Reinhold's part of Germany.

The man never even came to northern Germany, he thought to himself. *He knew that he had no support there. Sure, there were people like the Draves and Herr Klausen, but how many of those types were there? And how many of them followed the* Braunenpatie *because they didn't want to starve?*

What he couldn't understand was why an individual person would treat another individual person as the Frenchmen he encountered in that port had treated him and he friends. They weren't causing any trouble. They weren't doing anything that a Frenchman would have done. It was a bar, for Christ's sake! Drinking and joking were human behaviors. The Swedes, the Danish, the Dutch, all of them had treated him like a person, with respect. Why had the French been such poor hosts in their country?

"Stop thinking about it," Keller told him when he brought the topic up later that day. "That guy just wanted to go home and bury his French dingy in his boyfriend. He thought the easiest way to get rid of us was to have us arrested. It worked, didn't it? We were gone pretty quick and he got all my Lucky Strikes."

Reinhold shrugged. "I guess so but what about the beatings in jail? Do they beat all their prisoners that way? They were really enjoying themselves."

This time it was Keller's turn to shrug indifferently.

Reinhold knew he was irritating his friends. They didn't care about the social problems and injustices of the world. They were simple people with simple goals and ambitions. If the French hated them, then they were fine with hating them right back. He dropped the subject but it continued to eat away at him. When he thought about his stay in the French jail, his pulse would quicken and his fists would involuntarily clench. It was very hard for him to get past the insult on his dignity.

He became very interested in Manfred's plan to jump ship in Australia. Unfortunately, he did not have a lot of time to talk with him about it. The winter was in full swing and the *Fona* was very busy shuttling coal around. She didn't stay more than a single night in any port she visited. Luckily, they didn't pick up anymore cargo headed for France.

They did go to England, Boston to be exact. Reinhold had never been to England. He was excited to see what the country was all about. He quickly learned that he was not a big fan of the British sensibility. The women were snotty to him, even the hookers at the port, the few he could find. Their pimps were demeaning and insulting. Reinhold had learned early, very early, that he hated pimps and refused to deal with them, for the most part, but the ones in England were particularly bad. The crude way they advertised their women contrasted mightily with the attitudes of the women themselves.

Then there were the longshoremen. He had never seen a group of people take so many breaks! The tea wagon would show up and work would halt for an hour. He wondered how many times a day a person could stop working to drink tea. Giving up on the whole scene, Reinhold retired to his bunk early at night to read the book he had just received about Klaus Störtebeker. It reminded him of trips to the beach when he was a kid. On a whim, he decided to write a letter to Bernard Muuss. He wondered if his father was still an engineer on the high seas.

It did not take long for Reinhold to become bored and restless with the routine on the *Fona*. After three months, he called it quits. It was time for something else. He heard from one of the new guys that the sailor's office in Kiel was desperate for men. They had more openings on ships then there were people to fill them. He had to get to Kiel but the *Fona* didn't put into Kiel. They had not even been to Lübeck since Reinhold got on. Hamburg had been their German port for three months now.

Close enough, I guess, Reinhold thought to himself. *I'll hang out in Reeperbahn for a night, then get a train to Kiel.*

Chapter 38: Ever Consider Being A Diver?

Back in Kiel, Reinhold learned from Katie that Herbert was sailing to Finland with a Swedish ship he picked up a couple of weeks before. She invited him to stay and chat but he didn't feel comfortable hanging around with his friend's girl so he left her and went to the sailor's office.

The agent behind the desk had a couple of *leichtmatrose* positions for Reinhold to consider. One was another mail ship to Sweden. The thought of another mail ship gave him the chills. Another was a coal ship, which didn't sound appealing either.

"I just got off a coal ship. I would prefer not to get another. Do you have anything else, something different?"

After shuffling some papers, the man came up with something different.

"I have a salvage ship, the *Pakistan*. I can't say there would be a lot of sailing to do, but it is different. They need a sailor and watchman. The Captain is leaving tomorrow to head back to their salvage site about a day's sail from here in the Baltic Sea. Are you interested?"

Reinhold thought about it for a minute. "I'll give it a try. Why not?"

He took the paper with the information and left the office in search of the *Pakistan*.

Reinhold on the wheelhouse of the *Pakistan*
Photograph courtesy of Reinhold Scholz

The *Pakistan* was, indeed, different. It had a short nose and a low back. Fore of the bridge, it was a normal ship with a common height rail. At the bridge, as is common with ships, the rail dropped several inches. Aft of the bridge, the rail dipped to just a foot. The rear of the ship was just a platform.

The platform was crowded with equipment that Reinhold had never seen before: tanks and hoses and lengths of wire and cables. A huge crane was there, dominating the mid deck, arms folding like a cricket at rest. At the rear of the ship was a huge metal tank with a heavy door and a porthole-sized window. Reinhold wondered what it was for.

Where the ship's equipment was different, everything else was the same. The Captain, Herr Lahücha, was a brisk man who barely looked at his new sailor before sending him off to the bow to find his bunk, reminding him to be quick about because they were leaving momentarily. His bunk was a copy of previous bunks, a narrow slip of space with bunk beds built in to the bulkhead. Not sure which was taken, Reinhold simply threw his new sea bag in the corner and reported to the deck.

There were only a couple of other sailors on the crew. They quickly introduced themselves before they all took their places for shove off. Reinhold noted that there was a group of men hanging around the crane, smoking and talking, that had no part in the sailing of the ship. They were all older men, a bit arrogant, he could tell, but not sailor arrogant. He didn't get the feeling that one of these men was going to swing a wrench or a fist at him. Instead, he got the feeling that this group wasn't even going to bother with him.

They left Kiel as part of a convoy, something Reinhold hadn't experienced since he was on the *Eos*. One of the other sailors, Rolf was his name, informed Reinhold that the barges accompanying them were to hold the ship parts that were salvaged using the crane. This answered the question that was brewing Reinhold's brain about where they store what was salvaged. A day's sail from Kiel, the *Pakistan* came to a halt in the middle of the Baltic Sea, another new experience for Reinhold. The sailors anchored the ship in place. It bobbed on the surface like a buoy, quickly becoming a stopping point for sea birds.

It was from Rolf that Reinhold learned the specifics of work on the Pakistan.

"We have dynamite on board and according to the law, it has to be watched at all times, especially at night. That is our job."

Reinhold thought about that for a minute while he ate his steak and beans. "So, we don't move for two weeks? And all we have to do is stand watch?"

"Yup. If they need help with the big pieces of metal that come up, they might ask us to lend a hand but that's about it. Oh, and, sometimes, if there is going to be a big explosion, we retreat a few hundred meters to allow space. You know, so we don't get exploded too."

Reinhold was silent for a few minutes so Rolf continued. "Do you read?"

Reinhold nodded. "A bit. I have a book I just got before I came aboard. I guess I am going to need it, huh?"

Rolf nodded. "Let me know if you finish it. I have a good collection after being with this ship for two months now. I've been reading one a week since I came onboard."

"Ok. Thanks. Do you play chess?"

"Play what?"

The blank look on Rolf's face told Reinhold everything he had to know.

"Nothing. Never mind."

It didn't take long for Reinhold to know how Rolf was reading a book a week. There was more down time than working time on the *Pakistan*. During the day, there wasn't much to do but paint, scrap paint, clean up bird droppings, and watch the other men work. At night, he stood watch on the roof of the bridge, making a circuit of the ship every fifteen minutes or so.

The group he had seen clustered around the crane turned out to be a bunch of divers and an explosives expert. By the time Reinhold got on deck after catching some sleep, usually around noon, the divers were already suited up and in the water. He stood by the rail for a bit and watched the fountain of water that was proof the explosives detonated. A short time later, the crane hoisted the metal chunks of the sunken ship out of the sea and onto the waiting barges.

"That steel has to be a foot thick!" He exclaimed the first time he saw one of the chucks of metal.

He knew that the hull of the ship he was currently on, as well as the hulls of the ships he had been on previously, was not that thick.

"When I was on the *Eos*, I could feel the sea through the iron walls of my bunk."

"Yeah, well, the *Eos* wasn't designed to take torpedo fire," Rolf responded sarcastically. "Not that the thick hull helped this girl. A torpedo got it anyway."

He flicked his cigarette into the sea and walked away toward the crane.

"No, I guess it didn't help this ship," Reinhold said aloud to himself.

What a stupid waste of steel, he thought to himself. *And what for? They only thing that changed was now my grandparents, and a whole lot of other people, are, what, Russian? Soviet? Was that an actual thing to be? Soviet? What if they hadn't gotten out when they did?*

He thought about his elderly grandparents walking the whole way from Silesian to Ratekau and couldn't help being angry. He bore them no real strength of love but thought that it was wrong, just plain wrong, for people to be forced from their homes and made to be beggars in a foreign land.

And for what, he asked again.

And, again, he came up with no good answer.

At night, Reinhold stood watch, 8:00 pm to 6:00 am. It was a surreal experience at first. The ships were bathed in the strange glow of red emergency lights while around the ship, reflecting off the water, was the glow of the white, green, and red lights that let other ships know the *Pakistan's* position. It made him feel a bit anxious at first, like there really was an emergency, but he quickly got over that and settled into the routine.

Reinhold read Rolf's books about mechanics and shipbuilding or about fictional adventurers. He paused every hour to do a round of the ship but everything was always the same: quiet. He wasn't even sure what he was supposed to be looking for when he did his rounds. Another ship approaching would never have escaped his notice and gotten so close that he would have to come across it on a sweep. And there is no way that a small dinghy or other craft could make it all the way out here.

Whatever, Reinhold thought to himself. *It's a paycheck at least.*

It was one night about two weeks into his stay on the *Pakistan* when something happened that Reinhold never expected. He was sitting on top of the wheelhouse, completely engrossed in a chapter about the uses of sonar, when a siren ripped through the quiet night, sending him jumping to his feet.

He looked around frantically for the source, trying to remember what he was supposed to do when he heard the siren. But he had no recollection of a siren. No one had mentioned anything about it and what to do if he heard one. He was still rooted in the same place, trying to decide what to do when the hatch to the lower level slammed open and a group of men came pushing out on to the deck. It was the divers, Reinhold noted, and they were carrying something. Or somebody and that somebody let out a blood curdling scream that was quickly muffled by something placed over his mouth and nose.

Reinhold scurried down the ladder and ran to where the divers were trying to shove the writhing body of their colleague into the metal tank with the porthole window. A decompression chamber, he learned it was called.

"Can I help?" he asked, breathless.

He saw that the diver had an oxygen mask on his face that was stifling his screams. Above the mask, his eyes were bugging out of their sockets. Pain was written in them like the words in the book Reinhold was reading. He recognized the man as one of the divers that had actually spoken to him a couple of time during meals, unlike the others.

"Grab his feet! He won't stop struggling! Get him in there!"

Reinhold grabbed the man's feet. Using all his strength, he guided them toward the open door of the chamber. The man tried kicking but Reinhold held them firm. Instead, he wrenched his head in his agony, dislodging the oxygen mask and letting the screams come back to full volume.

"Quick! Push him in!"

"Someone get the crane!"

"Someone get that mask back on him! Get it secured!"

They managed to shove the diver's body unceremoniously into the decompression chamber and shut the door. He lay motionless for a second.

Maybe the cold is helping the pain, Reinhold thought, hopefully.

A second later, the writhing started again. Thankfully, the metal was so thick that his screams could barely be heard. Another diver was climbing the side of the chamber, reaching for a hook that the crane arm was lowering. He attached it to the chamber and the whole thing was lifted off the deck and slowly lowered into the sea. Reinhold watched it go, confused and shaken.

"What was that all about?" He asked a diver that was standing near him, also watching the chamber sink.

The diver blinked at him as if he was just noticing there was someone else there.

"He has the bends. We have to get him back under pressure for a bit and then bring him back up."

"The what?"

"The bends. Decompression sickness. It means that he has too much nitrogen in his blood and not enough oxygen. It happens to divers sometimes. It has to do with the pressure underwater and breathing gases that are under pressure for long periods." He frowned to himself, "It took a while to show up in Winkelmann tonight. Judging by his writhing, I would say that it hit his joints and his brain. That is most commonly where it shows up."

"Is he going to be ok?" Reinhold asked.

The diver smiled tiredly at him. "Yes, he should be fine. We caught it in time. We'll pump oxygen down to him and bring him up in a couple of hours."

Reinhold nodded, still staring at the bubbles that were surfacing in the wake of the chamber.

Thank goodness that only happened once. He didn't ever want to see that again. He didn't ever want to hear a man scream like that again.

The silver lining to Winkelmann's bout of the bends was Reinhold was no longer invisible to the divers. They appreciated his willingness and speed in helping them with their colleague. They began to talk to him when they saw him on deck or in the mess hall. It made life on the *Pakistan* less boring but a bit more uncomfortable. The rest of the sailors on the crew didn't understand why the divers spoke with Reinhold but not with them. Reinhold didn't understand what the big deal was. He was polite and respectful to the divers and they were nice to him.

"Look at you," said Handel, the self-proclaimed head diver one night as they stood on deck smoking and passing a bottle of rum. "You are so young! How old are you?"

"I just turned seventeen, sir," Reinhold answered.

"Just turned seventeen! And so polite! We could have you out here with us underwater by the time you are twenty!"

Handel laughed but Reinhold was caught off guard by the comment. Immediately, his mind began to turn over this new piece of information, to familiarize itself with the implications.

At first, Reinhold considered it, seriously considered it, planned on it, actually. It certainly was not a boring job. What could be more exciting than spending the day underwater, blowing things up? What about the bends? That guy was fine now, but that night, the screams in particular, still haunted Reinhold's dreams.

He was standing at the rail, soaking up the late April sun one day, when he paused in his thinking about becoming a diver. The *Pakistan* moved a couple of hundred meters away from the salvage site to allow for a large explosion. When the geyser of water settled down, they resumed their original position. Reinhold was waiting in anticipation to see the size of the piece they were bringing up. To his horror, the hull piece dangling from the hook was not empty. Two skeletons were plainly visible in the twisted metal. They still wore what was left of their German uniforms.

"We've got passengers!" He heard the First Mate shout.

Instead of swinging the crane to the barge to unload, Christophe, the crane operator, swung the hook toward the *Pakistan*. Rolf and another sailor, Vogt, worked the remains free and carried them off somewhere. Reinhold never knew where and he didn't really want to know where. He thought about two families, somewhere in Germany, that never got their children, husbands, brothers back because they went to the bottom of the Baltic Sea with the ship they were serving. Again, he found himself asking why.

He mentioned his thoughts about the pointlessness of war to Rolf, but the other sailor just blinked at him. Sensing he wasn't going to have the conversation he was looking for, Reinhold dropped the subject and asked instead what plans Rolf had for when they returned to Kiel the following day. Rolf launched into a monologue about getting drunk and finding a woman.

"And if I can't find one willing to give it up at the bar then I am going to walk down to the *puff* and get one there!"

Reinhold had to laugh at the determination Rolf displayed.

"Maybe I'll go with you," he said.

"You guys should come hang out with us when we get to Kiel," a voice said from behind Reinhold.

Turning he saw that it was Winklemann. The invitation surprised him and stunned Rolf. The divers never associated with the crew onshore, ever.

"No thanks, Herr Winkelmann," Rolf mumbled, obviously self-conscious.

"I'll go with you guys," Reinhold said. "What did you have in mind?"

Winklemann smiled conspiratorially at Reinhold. He had a hard time believing in that instant this was the same man he had seen screaming and writhing in pain a few weeks before.

"We have our fun, Scholz. You'll see."

The next evening the *Pakistan* sailed into Kiel with two laden barges in its wake and a load of men who wanted to get off. The tugboats were left to deal with the barges and it took extra time to dock the ship because the harbor was particularly busy. A huge passenger ship was trying to maneuver its way out against the flow of traffic. By the time they were docked and the crew was done working for the day, Reinhold was almost twitchy with anticipation of his shore leave. He could not wait to get a drink and flirt with some girls. He was heading to his bunk to change his clothes when he ran into Winkelmann leaving his own bunk.

"You still up for a night out with us?" The diver asked.

"Of course. I was just going to change my clothes."

"You do that and meet me at the gangway."

That was a night to remember. The divers really knew how to party. Winkelmann took Reinhold, dressed in his newest suit, from the ship to Holstenstraße where the guys were renting rooms for the week it would take to unload the barges. Better than sleeping on a ship, he said and Reinhold agreed. If he had a room to sleep in, he definitely would not be sleeping on the *Pakistan*. After they had unloaded their stuff, they took Reinhold to their favorite watering hole, a hotel not far from the largest *puff* in Kiel.

"It's your turn, Handel!" Winkelmann cried as they entered the hotel bar.

"Yeah, yeah. I know, it's on me tonight, boys!"

Handel opened his wallet and withdrew a stack of bills and threw them on the bar. "Get my guys whatever they want."

A cheer went up from the five men and the bartender started pouring drinks. Reinhold settled himself on a stool and ordered a beer. After the first round, the bartender took orders for their dinner. Reinhold wasn't going to order anything, figuring that he could just eat on the ship, but the divers insisted he have dinner with them. He ordered the roast pork and sat back to sip his beer.

The divers were in high spirits. Most of what they said and joked about went over Reinhold's head but he enjoyed the atmosphere of the hotel. There was music playing somewhere and people were dancing. Girls crowded around them, attracted to the rambunctious demeanor of the divers, and to their money. Handel bought them drinks also.

A couple of the guys, after a couple of drinks, took to the floor with the available ladies. Reinhold even took a spin around the floor himself with a lovely redhead who didn't speak a word of German. He doubted that she would have agreed to dance with him if she didn't think that he was with the divers as a colleague and not just a tagalong. Divers had better reputations than sailors.

The schedule he kept on the *Pakistan* accompanied by the weeks bobbing around in the ocean without a scrap of land in sight played havoc with his sense of time. It was hard to believe that he stayed at a hotel very much like this just a few weeks ago. The three times they put back into Kiel he expected the world to be radically different but it wasn't. The divers didn't seem to have this problem. They didn't seem to care about time or the day of the week or the world changing. They carried on, ordered food and drink, and joked with the bartender who just took the cost of it all out of the stack Handel threw on the bar. It wasn't long before they turned their attention to Reinhold himself.

"Look at this guy. We have get him in the water! He would be perfect for diving!"

"Can you swim?"

"Yes, I can swim," Reinhold answered. "Would I make more money than being a sailor?"

The divers burst into almost hysterical laughter. The youngest of the divers, whose name Reinhold had just learned was Astor, was the first to speak.

"Make more money than a sailor? We make in a month what you make in year, maybe more, I don't know. Depends on how much you make right now, I guess. But we make lots of money." The others nodded in agreement.

"What about the bends?" Reinhold asked.

"Every profession comes with its hazards, right?" Winkelmann said. "You could fall overboard from one of those ships and never be seen or heard from again, right? The whole damn ship could sink and you could freeze to death waiting for someone to come rescue you. Everything has its compromises. The more danger you are exposed to the more someone is willing to pay you."

"And the longer you expose yourself, the more money you make but we are not likely to live long," Handel said before he ordered another drink. "That's why you have to enjoy yourself while you can."

"What do you mean?" Reinhold asked.

Winkelmann spoke up this time, cutting off Handel with a wave of his hand.

"Divers don't exactly have the longest lives. Handel is exaggerating a bit but it is a fact. We breathe a lot of chemicals that mess with our blood and the pressure underwater and the exposure to cold is bad for the old ticker."

"Oh, I don't know about that." Reinhold knew he sounded disappointed by this new information. That sounded worse than sailing. At least he could prevent himself from going overboard or getting his hand chopped off or breaking something by being careful. The divers had to breathe those chemicals and had to be exposed to underwater pressure.

"What, kid?" Winkelmann questioned. "Are you looking for the perfect profession? Where? You set out on the wrong foot with sailing for that."

"Australia," Reinhold said without thinking.

"Australia!" The divers were surprised by the obviously unexpected answer.

"Australia," Reinhold repeated. "A guy I know told me they are looking for all kinds of craftsmen for jobs on shore. And you can jump ship there and get away with it."

"Do you know anyone in Australia?" Winkelmann asked. "It is a lot harder than that to move to another country. Can you speak English?"

"No, but I'll learn." Reinhold said before adding, "I just don't want to live where there wars anymore. Look at those skeletons that came up with the ship. They were people and now they are dead because of Hitler. I've also heard about other things he did, horrible things."

"Enough of this depressing talk," Handel said before anyone could comment. "Let's get out of here and get Reinhold a girl. He doesn't look or sound like he has had nearly enough of them and the ones here just want free drinks and food."

Handel scooped up what remained of his money off the bar and led the way out of the hotel. They walked the few dozen meters down the road to the *puff*. They ordered more drinks in the parlor while the girls swarmed around them, smelling money. Reinhold was amazed by the reception they received.

Reinhold was the drunkest he had been since that night in the barn on Muuss' farm when he was twelve. He staggered back to the *Pakistan* and fell into his bunk just before the sun came up. His last thought was of the girl he had been with that night. She had not been the prettiest but she made up for it by teaching him some new ways to pleasure a woman. He finally understood why women pushed his head toward their navels. He only hoped that he would remember in the morning.

Morning came entirely too quickly. Reinhold swore he was only asleep for five minutes before Rolf was shaking him awake.

"Get up, you drunken *dummkopf*! We have to change all the rigging and grease the crane arm today."

Reinhold forced his eyes to open, terrified that he was going to feel horrible. To his surprise, he didn't feel that bad, a bit of a headache and the worst thirst ever. Sitting up, he realized why he did not feel so bad. He was still drunk! Sighing, he pulled on some clothes and headed to the mess hall, hoping there was lots of food and lots of coffee. He made it through the day and spent the night trying not to fall asleep as he stood his watch.

Five days later, the divers reappeared on the *Pakistan* and the ship headed back out to their salvage site. It was back to business as usual. The divers didn't mingle with Reinhold like they had on the shore. He understood. This was business and that was pleasure. To his surprise, the following Sunday during breakfast, Winkelmann asked if he wanted to try to go into the water with the diving suit.

"Not a full dive, of course. You're not trained for that, but we could get you into the suit and put you in the water, so you know how it feels."

"Hell yes I want to do that!"

Winkelmann laughed at his enthusiasm. "We'll see if you still feel that way later. Meet me on deck when you are done working for the day."

As the sun was getting ready to sink in the west, the divers helped Reinhold into the drab tan suit. He had never touched one before. It had a strange rough and smooth texture when he ran his hand across it and was surprisingly heavy. Whenever he had seen it on the divers, it had appeared light but the material was several layers thick. On top of this, they put straps, belts, and hoses that made no sense to Reinhold at all. They skipped the weight belt, explaining that he just didn't need it since he wasn't going down too far. They did not, however, skip the weight shoes.

"It is just not the same experience without them," Astor said as he pulled the straps tight.

Lastly came the helmet, the hat they called it. They placed it over his head, twisting and screwing it into place. The view through the faceplate was obstructed by the grillwork of the outer shield but they showed him that he could flip that open and have a clear view. Then they attached hoses that supplied air. When they were all done, Reinhold felt like he was packaged for shipping.

"You control the air flow with your head," Winkelmann told him, gesturing to his head and moving it to show Reinhold the upper and left motion that was necessary to reach the control switch. He tried it and succeeded in touching the switch.

"Now, let's try to walk."

Winkelmann and Astor grabbed his arms and helped him up while Handel straightened his hoses and straps. Reinhold picked up his foot to take a step and almost fell forward. The weights were not that heavy but they were awkward.

"They weigh 18 pounds each." Winkelmann still held his right arm.

He was guiding Reinhold towards the small platform that hung over the side of the ship. The divers called it the launch. Before he even got to the platform, Reinhold was feeling claustrophobic. The slow motion way of moving was strange and uncomfortable and he was a bit panicky about being able to breath underwater. His breathing was already irregular. Winkelmann told him just to relax and breathe normally but he could not do it. They turned him around on the platform and helped him put his foot on the first rung of the ladder into the water.

When the lower half of his body was in the water, Winkelmann told him to get his airflow started. In his nervousness, he must have nudged the switch too hard. There was a horrible rushing noise passed his ear and within seconds the whole suit blew up like a balloon. This aggravated Reinhold's already panicky nerves and he freaked out.

"Get me out of this thing!" He cried to the divers and frantically started to climb the ladder again. As frantically as someone can in lead shoes.

"Ok, calm down. We'll get you out of there just relax. You have to sit down again." Astor and Winkelmann guided him slowly back to the diver prep area.

Astor quickly unscrewed the bolts securing the helmet and twisted it off. Reinhold took several deep breaths of the salty sea air and was relieved. They got the rest of the suit off him. Thankfully, it took less time to get it off then to put it on. Reinhold was a bit ashamed by his reaction but he couldn't help it. He wasn't diver material. Handel seemed to sense Reinhold's sense of embarrassment.

"At least you made it to the water. Some people freak before they even stand up. The helmet can be scary the first time you have it on."

"And then there's the shoes. Many people don't like the looks of them, won't even put them on," Astor commented as he gathered up as much of the suit as he could carry and headed off to the storage closet.

"I don't think I want to be a diver anymore," Reinhold said. "I think I was meant to stay on the surface of the ocean."

Winkelmann laughed. "Most of us started out thinking that. You really have to want to dive, to go under the water, and see what's going on. Let us know if you want to give it another shot."

Reinhold was sure that he didn't want to give it another shot.

With the fascination of the diving gone, it didn't take long for the boredom of the job to set in for Reinhold. He had been on the *Pakistan* for almost three months when he decided that it was time for something else.

Another ship, I guess, he thought to himself.

Rolf tried to convince him to stay but gave up when he saw that Reinhold's mind was made up.

"Why don't you get another ship and get out of here?" Reinhold asked his fellow sailor as they sailed toward Kiel late in May.

Rolf shrugged. "What if I can't get another ship? I don't want to be like those bums that hang out by the canal, begging cigarettes and money from passing ships."

Reinhold understood Rolf's point of view. No one wants to be a bum. "But there are lots of ships right now. I got this one the same day I went to the office. A guy I was on the *Fona* with said that there aren't enough sailors to fill the openings."

"I don't know, Scholz. I guess I am not as adventurous as you are but I will keep it in mind. This tub is reliable and every two weeks, I get an extended shore leave."

"Suit yourself," was all Reinhold could say in reply.

On the morning of May 30, 1952, Reinhold walked away from the *Pakistan* with the best wishes of the crew and divers.

"If you ever change your mind about diving, you know where you can find us," Winkelmann said as he shook Reinhold's hand farewell.

"Thanks and I'll keep it in mind."

Chapter 39: Together Again

Getting another ship wasn't as easy as Reinhold thought it was going to be. The agent at the sailor's office in Kiel didn't have anything he was interested in taking and he wasn't desperate enough yet to take anything that was available. He wanted nothing to have to do with coal ships and he wasn't taking another salvage ship, not yet anyway.

"They might be your only option. Every day, we get a call or a visit from a salvage ship looking for men. Well, maybe not every day but close enough. Not really surprising though, with all the salvage activities out there right now, pulling Hitler's damage out of the water."

"I'll wait for something. Can you let me know when you get a *Leichtmatrose* position on a bulk carrier?"

"Sure, have a seat," the agent said, gesturing to the room at large.

Reinhold settled himself in a chair and pulled the book he was reading out of his bag. He was about to get comfortable and wait when it dawned on him that he could go to the canal office in Holtenau.

Reinhold shouldered the backpack carrying all his worldly possessions and left the office. He headed to Holtenau in hopes of picking up a ship headed through the canal. But it was the same story there: salvage and coal.

"If you give me your address, I can contact you when we get a *Leichtmatrose* position," the agent behind the desk told him.

"I don't have an address," he frowned at the man. "Is there a boarding house near here?"

The agent gave him directions to a boarding house that catered to sailors and said he would send along any positions that came in. The boarding house was easy to find. It was a white, four story old wooden building that fronted on the canal. Its wooden steps, front porch, and front door were salt stained and weather worn but the old woman who answered the door was pleasant enough. Reinhold couldn't help thinking that in easier times that she would have been a very beautiful woman but hardship was etched into her features. She showed Reinhold to a back room on the second floor that contained nothing but a bed and a small wood stove. After confirming that he knew how to operate a wood stove, she left him to "settle in". Settling in consisted of putting his bag down and testing the bed.

With his hopes of getting another ship right away dashed, Reinhold headed out to the sailor's club to see what was going on, and to get a drink. It was mid-afternoon when he arrived and several fellow sailors had already congregated at the bar or around the scattered tables. One table of old timers near the door was playing an intense game of *skat*[31]. They all looked at Reinhold as he loudly closed the door behind him. He crossed the room to the heavy wood bar and ordered a drink before settling on a stool. The drink hadn't even materialized yet when someone grabbed him by the shoulders and spun him around. Reinhold's clenched fists were in front of his face, ready for a fight, when he realized he was staring at Herbert.

"Are you trying to get punched?" Reinhold laughed as he clapped Herbert on the back. "What you doing here?"

"I got off ship yesterday. Haven't found another one yet."

"Me neither. I got off the *Pakistan* this morning. Nothing at the sailor's office but salvage and coal ships. No thank you. I'll wait a few days. Have a drink with me." Reinhold gestured to the empty bar stool next to him.

"I thought you would never ask."

Herbert took the stool and the two sat on the bar for several hours exchanging tales of their respective tours. Herbert had just left a Swedish ship.

"Great work schedule, great food, just the best, but the damn Swedes drink too much. One of them stole and drank a bottle of perfume I picked up for Katie in Helsinki! Another one went overboard, fell from the swing while chipping and painting, and did not remember it the next day! If you asked him today, he probably couldn't tell you why he got fired. Probably doesn't remember being fired!"

"Most boring shit ever," Reinhold concluded after telling Herbert about the Pakistan.

"The diving sounds interesting. Too bad you freaked. It may have been a good career change."

Reinhold shook his head. "They don't live long. One of them told me so. I want to live a long life, Herbert, with a good wife and a bunch of kids running around, eventually." He said with a grin.

---

[31] *Skat* is a three player card game based on taking tricks.

Herbert laughed at him. "You're in the wrong profession for that, my friend. Sailors don't live long either. And where do you think you are going to meet this woman that is going to give you these children?"

Reinhold scoffed. "That's why we need to not be sailors anymore. There has to be something on shore that won't bore me to tears. Maybe we should go into business together, Herbert. You don't want to sail anymore, do you?"

Herbert shook his head. "No, no I don't. I would like to have my own business so I can make my own rules and go home to Katie every night."

"Then let's do something else. Anything, as long as it means that we don't have to get another ship."

"I have to get another ship. I am broke. Well, not broke, but definitely not in a position to go starting a business."

"I guess I don't really have the money right now either. Back to the seas we go," Reinhold said as he raised his glass to Herbert.

"Back to the seas," Herbert responded, raising his own mug of beer.

For more than a week, Reinhold waited in Holtenau for "the right ship", or so he said. He didn't know what he was waiting for really. The sailor's office sent several jobs his way but he rejected all of them. Nothing seemed right and something in his head told him to wait. He was getting a bit anxious, thinking he was going to end up one of the guys by the canal begging for food from passing ships, when his patience paid off.

He was sitting in the sailor's club on the afternoon of June 11th, listening to the old timers talk about their experiences at sea and wondering why the sailing profession attracted such characters, when Herbert walked in looking for him. He ordered a beer. The bartender placed it on the bar in front of him and he took a long swallow before speaking.

"I got a ship," he said quietly. "The *Govan*. It leaves tomorrow for London."

Reinhold was disappointed. "Oh, that's great for you. What kind of a ship is it?"

"Cargo. Just straight cargo. And Swedish, which is nice." He took another long swallow.

Reinhold finished his drink and ordered another. He was going to miss Herbert.

"Have you been practicing Swedish?" Herbert asked.

"The language? Not really. I understood enough of it to get by in Stockholm on the *Pagensand*."

"You'd better start practicing if you are going to sail on a Swedish ship."

Reinhold was confused. "I am not sailing on a Swedish ship. That's your gig. And don't worry, if a Swedish ship comes along, I'll pick the language up pretty quick."

"You'd better because, like I said, we are leaving tomorrow."

Reinhold thought for a minute that Herbert had lost his mind. Then he saw the sly smile spreading across the other man's face.

"What are you talking about, Herbert?"

"The *Govan* is looking for a *Matrose* and a *Leichtmatrose*. I told Martin down at the office that you would be interested in the job. Are you?"

"Hell yes!"

Herbert laughed at his friend. "Then you should go tell him before he gives it to some other miserable sailor."

Reinhold downed his drink and took off for the office. He took the job on the *Govan*, set to dock at Holtenau later that night. The vessel was scheduled to pick up a canal pilot and leave in the morning, bound for London. He and Herbert were to report to the Captain when it docked. Reinhold spent the rest of the afternoon getting his things together and saying goodbye to the pleasures of female company.

"Shipping out on a ship full of men to a country where the women are cold warrants a trip to the *puff*," he told Herbert before they parted to their respective agendas, agreeing to meet at the *Govan* later that night.

In his near decade of sailing, Reinhold had heard fellow sailors recant tails of the perfect ship. Whenever he joined these conversations, he spoke of the *Govan*.

What a great ship, he thought to himself. *If only all ships were like the* Govan, *maybe I wouldn't have spent so much time looking to get onshore.*

Govan
Photograph courtesy of 7seasvessels.com

Reinhold signed on to the vessel before Herbert. The watchman at the top of the gangway introduced himself as Raimo and directed him toward the bridge at mid ship to find the Captain. As soon as he walked on the ship, he sensed a difference. She was the same old tub that he was used to sailing on but it was a clean old tub and looked well maintained. The Captain was a salty old dog who stank of liquor. He took Reinhold's book, confirmed he could communicate in Swedish, and sent him below via the aft house to stow his stuff. A few minutes later, he was settled in the tiny room they would be sharing with three other guys for the duration of their stay on the vessel. He didn't have long to get acquainted with his room. The Captain had assigned him night watch. He was to relieve Raimo at 8:00pm sharp. Herbert showed up on the gangway a few minutes after he took his position.

"Working already, huh?" Herbert clapped him on the shoulder. "How's the Captain?"

"Seems ok. I think he was drunk."

"Swedes." Herbert rolled his eyes. "They'll drink anything, anytime. I should go report before he is so tanked he doesn't remember me."

Reinhold watched Herbert enter the bridge then turned his attention back to his watch. It wasn't long before boredom set in. He was wondering where the coffee was located when Raimo appeared on the catwalk passing the wheelhouse. He was cleaned up and dressed to go ashore. Reinhold smiled at the man's swagger as he approached. There was someone following that he had not met yet.

"Reinhold, this is Otto. He is the cook."

The two men shook hands, surveying each other from under their eyelashes.

"You from around here?" Raimo asked in Swedish. Reinhold didn't understand the full meaning of what he said. Seeing the puzzled look on his face, Raimo rephrased his question. "You live here?"

"Not really," Reinhold responded in Swedish.

Raimo laughed and Otto snickered. Reinhold wasn't sure he liked the man, fellow German or not. There was something about him that didn't sit well. He hoped that this guy wasn't one of his bunkmates.

"You know the town?" Raimo asked for clarification.

"A little. Are you looking for a place to go?"

"You know it. It was a three and a half day trip from Helsinki staring at a bunch of ugly mugs like this guy."

He gestured toward Otto with his thumb. Reinhold smiled at him, understanding the feeling.

"The sailor's club is just down this street, over there." Reinhold pointed toward a cluster of buildings to the west of the ship.

"Thanks."

Raimo and Otto continued on their way, down the gangway and up the short wooden pier. Reinhold watched them go, intrigued by his new crewmate. He seemed like a genuinely nice guy. Those were hard to come by on the ships.

"Since I got here after you, I get the watch after you, even though I outrank you, *Leichtmatrose*." Herbert was headed to stow his stuff.

"Yeah, yeah, *Matrose*. You don't outrank me by much or for long. You watch, I'll be a full *Matrose* before I sign off this ship."

"Did you meet a couple of the guys? How are they?"

"So far so good."

Reinhold kept his misgivings about Otto to himself. He learned that first impressions can be deceiving. He would give the man another chance before he wrote him off as untrustworthy. Instead, he pulled out a cigarette and lit it before offering one to Herbert. The two men stood with their backs against the rail, facing the harbor, puffing their Lucky Strikes in silence. The sun was hanging low, getting ready to set, and turning the sky and water lovely shades of orange and yellow. Herbert flicked the butt of his smoke into the sea and picked up his bag.

"I am going to try to get some sleep before my watch. See you later, Reinhold."

He walked off to the aft house.

Poking around just after sunset, Reinhold located the mess hall and helped himself to coffee. He noticed there were cupboards along the bulkhead that were unlocked. Opening one, he found it full of food. There was cans of sardines, loaves of bread, boiled eggs in pickling water, pickled herring, and crackers amongst other delectables. He was tempted to help himself to some sardines and crackers but thought he would wait and ask if that was acceptable. He headed back to his post at the gangway with a mug of green coffee. Sipping it, he was thankful it didn't taste as bad as it looked.

The *Govan* left Holtenau the next morning via the canal. They had a load of lumber to deliver to London. Reinhold watched the first locks of the canal fade away in the early morning light. He was looking forward to breakfast. Herbert said that the food on Swedish ships couldn't be beat and Reinhold was ready to judge for himself. An hour later, he agreed with Herbert. The food was delicious and he learned that there was a coffee and pastry break at mid-morning. He could smell the pastry baking during breakfast. He couldn't wait to try it.

The rest of the crew seemed OK to Reinhold. He didn't trust them, of course, but he sailed with worse. Raimo, it turned out, liked to talk. Reinhold found this both comforting and unnerving. He was unfamiliar with chatty men. At first, he wondered if the guy was gay. Then Raimo offered to let Reinhold borrow one of his girly magazines, blowing the gay theory out of the water.

"He is Finnish. I have sailed with a couple. They like to talk," Herbert reassured him. "You have to remember that this is not a German ship. We're not even through the canal yet and I have come across five nationalities between sailors and stokers."

Nine hours after shoving off in Holtenau, the *Govan* reached the end of the canal at Brunsbüttel, sailed past Cuxhaven, and on into the North Sea bound for London. The weather was fair with no rough seas in sight, so far. Summer sailing was the best sailing, especially on the temperamental North Sea. Reinhold was enjoying the sun and the breeze while painting the fantail near the aft house when the Third

Mate approached him. He knew immediately that something was wrong.

"Scholz, right?" the mate asked.

Reinhold nodded. "Nylund, right? Sir."

The mate eyed him sharply but ignored the questionable respectfulness of Reinhold's comment.

"Sir will suffice. I have a question for you regarding the cook, Otto. Have you seen him lately?"

Reinhold thought for a minute. When had he last seen Otto? In the two and a half days they had been at sea, he hadn't seen much of the cook.

"Supper last night, I think. I could hear him telling the mess boy to bring food to the tables. I don't remember him at breakfast this morning."

"He wasn't at breakfast this morning. We can't find him. If you see him, come directly to me and let me know."

"Yes, sir."

The mate spun on his heel and stalked off. Reinhold resumed his painting thinking that the cook was going to be in a world of trouble when they found him.

Probably passed out drunk in the cargo hold, Reinhold thought to himself.

He forgot the subject until his stomach grumbled and he realized that it was dinnertime. He had completely missed his coffee break. Entering the mess hall, he found the crew helping themselves to sandwiches from a platter. He took one and sat down with Herbert.

"The cook is missing," Herbert informed him.

"I know. The Third Mate came to question me about it. If he was here, I would be complaining about the lack of food at dinner."

"He is probably dead," Herbert stated nonchalantly, causing Reinhold to stop mid chew.

"Why do you say that?"

Herbert shrugged. "Raimo says he was gay."

"Oh."

Reinhold had never been on a ship where someone had "fallen" overboard but he had heard stories. It was not common for this to happen to suspected "gays", but it did happen.

"Well, I wish someone had told the Captain that they were going to shove him off. He could have ordered another cook before we left Kiel."

Herbert laughed. "Always thinking with your stomach."

"Not always," Reinhold laughed.

Later that evening, as they made their way up the Thames, Jensen the bosun gathered the crew to inform them that they were not to leave the ship.

"Scotland Yard is coming to investigate the disappearance of Otto. You are to answer their questions as completely as you are able. Watches we be covered as needed by anyone that is available and able. Do you understand?" A rumble of assent went through the assembled group of seamen. "It's not that bad," the bosun continued. "Most of you don't like England anyway. The quicker we get this done, the quicker we can get going. Our next stop is Copenhagen."

A small cheer went up from the men.

Reinhold was called to the bridge for his questioning around 10:00pm. He entered to find the Captain, the First Mate, and two English men in dark suits waiting for him. Introductions were quickly made. There was a brief conversation in English that Reinhold didn't understand before the English men addressed Reinhold. The taller, paler, older man with glasses spoke first, in German.

"You are German?"

"Yes, sir."

"You have been on this ship for three days?"

"Yes, sir. I signed on in Holtenau, at the canal."

"Do you know why you are here?"

"The cook disappeared, from what I understand."

"Do you know anything about it? When was the last time you saw him?"

"I don't remember when the last time I saw him, but I heard him yesterday at dinner giving the mess boy orders."

"Are you sure it was him? I mean, if you didn't see him, how could you be sure?"

Reinhold thought for a minute. He was going to say that he was sure because the cook had a distinctive way of elongating his 's' sounds, almost like a hiss, but thought better of it.

"No, I guess I can't be sure. I didn't actually see him."

"Did you ever speak with the cook?"

"No, not really. Just hello and goodbye. I haven't had the time."
"Did you hear anyone say anything about him?"
"No, sir."
"Have you heard a fellow sailor say anything that could be construed as hateful towards another sailor?"

Reinhold laughed. "You have to be more specific."
"Never mind."

The Scotland Yard agent studied him for a long second. Reinhold studied him in return. He wondered how long he was going to have to stay here. The bosun had changed his mind and informed them that once they had been questioned, they could go ashore if they weren't scheduled to stand watch. It was a minute before the English man spoke again.

"How old are you, son?"
"Seventeen."

The agent smiled at him before dismissing him. "You can go. Thank you for the time."

Reinhold nodded and left the bridge before the agents could change their minds. Five minutes later, he was leaving the ship with Herbert to check out what London had to offer for entertainment for the night. It turned out to be not much. England was too rich for his poor sailor's blood. He and Herbert ended up having a couple of drinks at the sailor's club before taking a stroll around London to looking at the architecture. It was a beautiful city full of old buildings. Reinhold couldn't help noting that there was still a lot of construction going on. The facades on many buildings were obviously new. He heard that London was bombed heavily during the war. He wondered how many architectural wonders were gone from this town, never to be seen again.

Everybody has to rebuild what that ridiculous war destroyed, he thought to himself.

On their way into the port, just passed the security gate, Herbert and Reinhold ran across a group of men playing cards on a over turned crate. They were focused on their game, surrounded by a cloud of pipe and cigarette smoke, until Herbert tripped over a curb, cursing loudly. The attention of the men turned to the two German sailors. Reinhold's hair stood on end as they passed the group. He heard them muttering amongst themselves but didn't understand what they were saying. He felt threatened and mentioned this to Herbert.

In hindsight, that was a bad idea. It confirmed the British men's suspicion that they were Germans. Almost immediately, a bottle smashed at their feet. Herbert and Reinhold took off running for the *Govan*. Hostile shouts followed them but the men did not. The bottle was just a warning.

"They would love to draw some German blood," Herbert panted on the deck of the *Govan*.

"What the hell happened to the two of you?" Raimo asked from his post at the top of the gangway. He had only just missed being run down by his fellow sailors.

"A group of Brits threw a bottle at us," Reinhold told him in his halting Swedish.

Raimo looked perplexed. "Why would they do that? Did you have an argument with them?"

Herbert laughed bitterly. "Yeah, it was a war that ended damn near a decade ago."

Raimo's face clouded with anger. "Did they try to roll you 'cause you're German? Those bastards! Let's get'em!"

Reinhold put a restraining on Raimo's arm. "Forget it. We are leaving soon, right? It's not worth it."

"We're not leaving soon. Look at the deck! Those lazy longshoremen spent more time drinking tea than hauling lumber. We're going to be stuck here for at least another week just to unload. Then, we have to load coal!"

Raimo gestured angrily down the deck at the stacks of lumber still piled there.

"I thought we were going to Copenhagen next," Reinhold questioned.

He remembered the bosun telling them their next destination earlier that night.

"That guy was lying to shut us up," Raimo spit over the side of the rail into the Thames. "He is a real piece of work, that one, just wait. You'll see."

Sighing, Herbert turned and headed for the galley, muttering something about being hungry. Reinhold followed, looking forward to sardines on crackers.

Chapter 40: Jensen

While the crew on the *Govan* was easy to get along with, the mates were a different story, the bosun in particular. Raimo was right to warn them about him. He was a miserable, drunken, wall of a man with a bad attitude. One never knew when he was going to come across Jensen in the course of his day and what kind of hostility would be hurled at them. Reinhold quickly became disgusted with the sullen man and his belittling habits. Two months after he joined the ship, the guys who had dealt with the abuse longer decided to teach Jensen a lesson.

Reinhold was standing four to eight port watch in Amsterdam when the situation played itself out. He was at the head of the gangway, sipping his first cup of coffee, when Jensen returned to the ship with a case of Heineken. He saw that they were the larger sized bottles, not the usual twelve ounce size.

"You stocking up for winter?" Reinhold asked as Jensen passed him.

The bosun turned and looked at his underling, merely a *Leichtmatrose*, and threatened, "Watch your mouth, Scholz, or it will be your permanent job to clean the toilets on this vessel."

With that he stalked off to his room. Reinhold shrugged and pulled a cigarette out of his pocket.

Sometime later, he and Raimo were chatting and smoking when a man appeared on the gangway, asking for Jensen. He explains that the bosun arranged for him to come tattoo him.

"A tattoo of what?" Raimo asked.

"A fly."

"A fly? Where does he want a fly?" Reinhold laughed.

"On the tip of his penis. Where can I find him?"

The man was getting irritated by the delay. Raimo stopped laughing long enough to tell the man where he could find Jensen.

"Aren't you done with watch in a few minutes?" Raimo asked, lighting another cigarette. Reinhold nodded. "We should go get a drink."

"Sounds good."

Later that night, Raimo and Reinhold returned to a ship in an uproar. Herbert explained to them that the tattoo guy asked a couple of guys to keep a hold of Jensen while he worked. Jensen was so drunk that he fought with everyone that came near him, including the tattoo guy. Eventually, Jensen tired himself out and the tattoo guy finished his work, leaving the ship as fast as he could.

"That guy was thankful to be getting away from Jensen, said so twice. Never had a worse appointment, he said. We thought Jensen was going to kill him when he took out that needle and tried to grab his little soldier. He went completely berserk, started screaming, and grabbed the guy by the throat. He managed to break free and come find us in the mess hall. Lucky for him, there were still enough guys left on the ship to subdue Jensen."

"But that is what Jensen wanted, the tattoo guy told us that Jensen hired him to put a fly on his penis."

Reinhold was not surprised that Jensen had freaked out. He was a ticking time bomb.

"Yeah, well, apparently he forgot after drinking that case of beer." Raimo laughed.

"Now," Herbert continued, "Jensen is lying in his bunk in a puddle of his own piss, too drunk to move and we're going to get him." He eyes gleamed as he spoke. "It's payback time for that miserable Swede."

"Let's go then," Raimo said, the same devious gleam in his eyes as Herbert.

It all happened so quickly that Reinhold still had a hard time believing that it did happen. The deck crew all took turns exercising their repressed anger with the hard ass bosun. They dragged him out of his bunk and held him up so their fellow mates could get their licks in. By the time they had burned out their madness, the bosun was bloody and ugly bruises were developing on his face and body. They threw him back in his bunk and left his room like nothing happened.

The next morning, Jensen stormed into the mess hall, almost ripping the sea door of its hinges. It hit the bulkhead with a bone shuddering bang.

"Who did this!" he demanded pointing at the purple bruises on his face.

No one answered him. He asked the question louder, screaming it to the room at large.

"WHO DID THIS?"

Again, no one answered. Jensen picked up a plate from the table closest to him and sent it flying across the room. It smashed just above the head of one of the stokers, showering him with pieces of ceramic. The man was making to get up, but the guy next to him put a hand on his arm to restrain him.

"Let's see what happens," he said.

Glancing around the room, Reinhold noticed that the men involved in last night's events were on the edge of their seats, not taking their eyes off the enraged bosun, ready to defend themselves if Jensen rushed them. The others just looked amused.

"I am going to get all of you! You think you are going to get away with this? I'll throw every one of you into the drink, one by one, if I have to! I'll have all of you painting the seaward side of the rail during heavy seas. I'll make you paint the stack with no chair! What about the latrines? Who wants to deal with them?"

From the back of the room a voice spoke up.

"I wouldn't threaten us, Jensen, if I were you. You are just going to get drunk again and we'll get you back. Maybe next time, we'll throw you into the drink. You'd never know, would you? Do you think you can swim when you are so drunk you can't even get up to piss?"

The huge bosun paused in his anger. His eyes darted back and forth across the room, searching for a target to lash out at, weighting the consequences of his actions. He was questioning whether or not this group of men had the nerve to throw him overboard. Reinhold wondered if the bosun had ever been threatened before. A man that huge probably had his way his whole life. Instead of lashing out at his attackers, Jensen wheeled around to leave the mess hall, smashing his fist into the iron bulkhead next to the door before exiting.

"Now we are in for it." Herbert said as the tension left the room and everyone returned to their breakfast. "That guy is going to have us doing nothing but dirty work for the next month."

"No," Raimo said. "Just until he gets drunk again and forgets what happened. It won't be too long."

Jensen didn't forget right away. The trip to Stockholm from Amsterdam was almost intolerable. Jensen stalked around the ship, looking for sailors doing anything, anything at all, except working diligently. Herbert and Reinhold were chatting idly while chipping old paint off the forward hatch cover when Jensen came along the catwalk and screamed bloody murder at them for goofing off.

To accent his point, he picked up the bucket of paint they were going to use and hurled it off the ship, forcing them to spend half an hour locating and mixing another in the supply closet. In a fit of self-righteous rage, Jensen punched a *Matrose* in the jaw after the man supposedly mouthed off about the watch schedule. Raimo was a witness to the incident and said the *Matrose* hadn't said anything, hadn't even made a sound, when the bosun attached him.

The pressure proved too much for some of the crew. Upon reaching Stockholm, five guys quit. The ship stayed in port an extra day to fill the positions.

"I am going shopping later, after quitting time. I want to find Katie something nice." Herbert said over breakfast as they lay for anchor in Stockholm.

Since they were waiting for new arrivals and neither was schedule to stand port watch that night, they ventured out into the city in search of the gift. Even though it was only six o'clock in the evening, all the lights in the city were on and shining merrily in the face of the sinking sun.

"We should treat ourselves to a good dinner, something fancy. We deserve it after dealing with that *arschloch*," Reinhold suggested. Herbert looked like he was going to say no but to Reinhold's surprise, he agreed.

"Do you have a suit? I haven't seen you wear one since the *Pagensand*," Herbert asked as they walked through the narrow streets of Stockholm.

Reinhold frowned. "I haven't replaced the one that went down with the ship. I guess I should, huh?"

Herbert shrugged. "If you want a nice dinner, you are going to need a suit."

Reinhold had his eyes open for a new suit as they walked and eventually found a grey one that fit and looked nice. It was also half of what he would have paid in Germany. In the shop next door, he found a pair of shoes that matched and fit nicely. They were also half the price of what he would have paid in Germany.

I love Sweden, he thought to himself.

They had dinner that night at a local hotel. They returned to find they had a new roommate. His name was Rouger.

The older version of Reinhold on the *Brandenburg* in the Caribbean sighed to himself. It was the first time that he went out with Rouger that he met Anya. He, Herbert, Rouger, and Raimo went to the *tivoli* in Kalmar. There wasn't much else to do in Kalmar. It was a nice *tivoli* at least. The locals treated the sailors like family, which was nice. He spied Anya across the empty open space where dances usually occurred. She was beautiful with blonde hair and an angel face. There was something melancholy about her, something which transcended innocence. She was like a mythical nymph creature brought to life. He was drawn to her almost against his will.

It didn't take him long to convince her to come back to his ship. Once there, he was in for the surprise of a lifetime. She was experiencing her womanly time of the month! And didn't know what was happening to her! Apparently, no one had ever told her this would happen even though she was fourteen years old.

Reinhold spent the rest of the night cleaning her up in the ship's shower. Then taking her to an all-night drug store near the port where he purchased her tampons and maxi pads. He explained their function while Anya listened attentively.

Afterwards, he taught her how to satisfy a man with her mouth. She was a natural talent with her tongue. It became habit for the two of them to get together when Reinhold was in Kalmar. He would arrive in port and find her waiting like a sad, beautiful puppy.

Chapter 41: Message In A Bottle

"You're going to love Helsinki, Reinhold."

Raimo said as he tossed his paintbrush into a nearby bucket. The *Govan* arrived in Finland's capital city the night before. It was Reinhold's turn to stand watch and he missed the crew outing to blow off some steam at the local watering holes. Tonight, Raimo promised him an experience to remember.

An hour after quitting, Raimo, Reinhold, and Herbert were clean, dressed, and leaving the *Govan* for the saunas of Helsinki. Reinhold was looking forward to it. They hit some heavy seas and gusty winds, not unusual for the North Sea, but it turned out to be a bit more than a summer squall. He had some pain in his knees from the jarring he took in the wheelhouse standing Quartermaster. Raimo said the best thing for him was to relax in a steaming sauna. Everybody, he explained, went to the sauna at least once a week in Finland.

"It is not a place to pick up chicks," Raimo emphasized, an eye on Reinhold. "You go there to relax and release the stress of the day."

"I understand you, Raimo. I'll behave myself." Reinhold grinned at his companion.

"It is also not a place for bad language. If you curse too much, the older folks yell at you, tell you to respect the sauna. 'It is not a toilet', I have heard that more than once."

Four hours after leaving the *Govan*, Reinhold understood completely why the Finnish people loved their saunas. He, Raimo, and Herbert relaxed in the steamy, wooden room, slapping themselves with birch branches. It was a bigger room than Reinhold had expected, measuring some 15x15 meters, and there were more people there then he had expected, numbering a couple of dozen, all men and all naked. When the heat became too extreme, they jumped into the cold water of the adjoining pool and then went back into the sauna for another round. After the sauna and a shower they put on soft robes and went to the lounge to enjoy a shot of the locally brewed spirit and wait for their turn on the message table.

A woman in a thin paper robe came to fetch them for their messages. She was obviously nude under the robe. This intrigued Reinhold. She instructed him to lay down face down on the table and she set to work on his back and legs. It was the most glorious feeling!

All the tiredness and tension in his muscles melted away under the woman's skillful hands. When she finished with her back, she rolled him over to work on the front.

Reinhold was able to stand the touch of the woman when he was lying on his stomach, but the sight of her ample breasts moving in time with the strokes of her hands on his flesh was too much. He felt his excitement rising, embarrassingly, and didn't know what to do about it. A thought flashed through his mind that she might take care of it for him. She did, but not how he was hoping. Without losing her rhythm, she smacked his manhood so hard that he thought she broke it, that he would never be able to use it again. The massage came to end without her having to smack him again.

Back in the lounge, Reinhold had a couple more shots of the locally brewed spirit and relaxed. He felt like he was floating in the womb, surrounded by warm, soft water, weightless. Way to soon it was time to go back to the ship. Reinhold wondered when the *Govan* would put into Helsinki again.

Back on board, he opened the door to his bunk and was hit with a noxious odor that was somewhere between a barnyard and a filthy toilet.

"Rouger," Reinhold said the seagulls gliding above the *Brandenburg*. "What a pain that guy was."

He couldn't help but chuckle to himself. The beginning of their relationship was a bit rocky but he and Rouger still kept in touch, visiting whenever they had the chance. He was serving on a Swedish ship somewhere in the North Sea.

Rouger didn't have much sailing experience when he turned up on the *Govan*. He grew up in a coastal village surrounded by people related to him. He spent the warm months on fishing boats and pleasure cruisers. The cargo ships turned out to be a different experience then he was anticipating. Much like Reinhold, he started on a ship of old timers that didn't speak much and would rather spend their off time drinking then teaching a new guy how to handle life on a ship. Reinhold sensed Rouger's ignorance and tried to help him learn the ropes, literally. He took the Swede under his wing in the same way that Captain Hermann and Herbert had done for him.

Rouger learned quickly and was soon pulling his own weight on the deck but his personal hygiene was bordering on offensive. Reinhold learned that he was an only child with a doting mother who catered to his every whim. He never cooked a meal, cleaned a room, or did his own laundry. Luckily, he did not have to cook for himself and he learned most of the standards of cleanliness that were expected on the ship without complaint. Laundry was the point of contention between Rouger and his bunkmates. Reinhold showed him how to clean his clothes.

"All you have to do," he explained, "is take your dirty clothes, bundle them up, tie a piece of line around them, and throw them into the wake of the ship, near the propeller."

Reinhold demonstrated with his own bundle. He pitched the clothing into the sea, waited a few seconds, and reeled the bundle back in with the line.

"Only leave it in the water for a few seconds or the propeller will shred everthing."

He untied the bundle and shook out the extra water before hanging the individual garments over the boom to dry.

"See," he concluded gesturing toward his handy work, "it is that easy."

Rouger watched the demonstration with rapt attention, nodding his understanding, and then did nothing. His bucket in their washroom filled with clothes that didn't get washed. When he ran out of clean ones, he dug through the bucket to find replacements that 'weren't that dirty'. Soon, the whole room was full of the stench of musty body odor and moldy fabric. Two weeks after Reinhold gave his lesson on washing clothes; he pulled Rouger aside after breakfast and issued a very serious threat.

"If you don't wash your clothes today, I am going to pile them in your bunk and shut the curtain so that they fester there. Then you will have to sleep in your own filth. Understand?"

He nodded good day to his speechless bunkmate and left to get started with the days round of checking lines and tightening valves. The bosun, surprisingly and most likely on the orders of one of the mates, had promoted him to cobblescot man. He was excited to get his new job underway, to prove that he could handle the responsibility. He knew that it meant a promotion to full *Matrose* was soon to follow.

Later that night, as he went to the bridge for the eight to twelve watch, Reinhold saw Rouger standing at the fantail, fooling around with a large bundle of clothes. He was tempted to stop and help but decided against it.

He needs to learn how to do things for himself, he told himself firmly. *There is no room for a mama's boy on this ship.*

Guiltily, he remembered his own experience on the *Eos*, how he had cried silently in his bunk at night, hoping that no one would notice his tears, and wishing like hell he could get off at the next port. Shrugging, he stopped thinking about it. They were almost to the Kalmar Sound and the harbor pilot would be coming aboard soon. He had to be focused, not half distracted by an incompetent crewmate and his dirty laundry. Besides, if he was going to be distracted by something, it was going to be thinking about cradling an angelic Anya as they lay in bed together.

In spite of the laundry difficulties, Reinhold came to like Rouger very much. The Swede had a good sense of humor and liked to talk, something that Reinhold was growing more accustom to. Rouger told him about his childhood in a small village near Saltor.

"The whole town is related," Rouger exclaimed. "That's why I had to leave. I don't want to marry one of my cousins. And that is probably what happened to your girlfriend, Anya. Her parents are probably brother and sister."

He wrinkled his freckled nose in disgust and ran a hand through his bushy brown hair. Reinhold had to laugh at the candidness of the statement.

"So you are looking for a wife? You are not going to find one out here on the seas, unless you are looking for a mermaid."

Rouger's eyes widen in astonishment. "Do you think they really exist? Have you seen one? Do you know anyone who has seen one?"

Reinhold snorted. "Of course they are not real. Probably just a dolphin or something that some drunk, horny sailor thought was a woman."

Rouger thought for a minute. "I have heard that an uncle or great uncle or somebody in my family met his wife after he put a letter in a bottle and threw it overboard in the Mediterranean. He lives on one of those islands down there now."

"A message in a bottle, huh? That sounds like fun. We should do that. Maybe we'll meet our wives." Reinhold grinned at his crewmate. "I have an old vermouth bottle that will work perfectly."

"Vermouth," Rouger wrinkled his nose again. "How can you drink that stuff? It is way too sweet!"

"It's cheap. There is a place in Kiel that will refill your old bottle for ninety *pfennig*. It is sweeter than hell. That's why we call it 'wawa' juice because after a night drinking that, you wake up the next day saying 'wawawawa, my head!'" Reinhold laughed.

Reinhold found the idea of a message in a bottle amusing. While going about his work he thought about it. What if he threw a bottle in the sea and someone actually found it? What if they responded? Actually sent a letter? It would be nice to get some mail. The only person who wrote him was his sister Lisa. Mail call was a painful reminder that he had very little family. He remembered his stepmother saying that keeping in touch with people was a great way to keep her writing skills honed. She once wrote to Hamburg to get their genealogy information because, as she said, she wanted practice writing a formal letter. In actuality, Reinhold suspected now, she was trying again to get rid of her husband's children. She wrote to Hamburg to see if they had a Jewish background. It didn't take him long after learning about Hitler's atrocities to put those pieces together.

Maybe I should do that, he thought. *Reading has been helping my language abilities. Maybe I should start writing more. What could it hurt anyway?*

The next port the *Govan* visited was London. Reinhold groaned to himself when he learned their destination. If he left the ship, he would be risking a beating to drink overpriced beer in a stuffy port tavern while being propositioned by either old hag hookers or pushy, abrasive pimps drumming up business for younger, prettier, snottier hookers that he couldn't afford. Sighing, he couldn't help thinking it might be a good time to write a letter and put it in a bottle.

"Where do you want to drop them?" Rouger asked as he pounded the cork into his bottle, sealing it tight.

"Nowhere near here," Reinhold answered, gesturing with his chin toward the Thames. "Once we are in the North Sea, we'll drop them."

Several weeks later, while the *Govan* lay at anchor in Stockholm, Reinhold's name was called during mail call. He fully expected the letter to be from Lisa. When he read the sender's name, he was surprised to see that it was not. Instead, it read 'Marta Braren,

Föhr, Germany'. He tore it open and read the first line. His eyes widen.

"Bad news from home, huh? The only time I get mail is when there is bad news from home," Raimo said shaking his head sadly.

"No, it's not from home. No one writes from home. This is from a girl. She got my message in a bottle and wrote back!"

Reinhold grinned at his friends. They stared at him in disbelief for a second.

"That's a bunch of lies!"

Herbert snatched the letter from Reinhold and read. His eyes also widened. "Well, I'll be damned! This guy can even get lucky with a bottle thrown in the ocean!'

"Give me that!"

Reinhold snatched the letter back. He folded it carefully and stuck it back in the envelope. Then he crammed it into the pocket of his dungarees. He felt eyes on him and looked up from what he was doing to see his friends staring at him.

"What?"

"You're not going to read it?" Rouger questioned.

"I'll read it later," he answered.

Later that night, when the rest of the guys were busy elsewhere, Reinhold drew the curtain across his bunk and read Marta's letter with a battery operated book light. She was sixteen years old and lived on the island of Föhr. Reinhold had never heard of it and made a mental note to check the navigation maps next time he was on the bridge. Germany didn't have many island so it wouldn't be hard to find. She found the bottle containing his letter on the beach not far from her family's farm. She was swimming, she wrote, and saw something glinting in the sun.

"I'll be your pen pal if you tell me how exciting it is to sail around on a ship," Marta wrote. "I don't get to leave this island very often but I would love to see the world! My father says it looks just like here. Do you know Föhr? Does it look like the rest of the world? Write back and tell me."

After her signed name, Marta printed in neat letters her address. Reinhold was contemplating writing back immediately when he heard a scraping noise outside the curtain of his bunk. Pulling the fabric back a bit, he peered out into the semidarkness of the small room. At first, he saw nothing. The noise changed from a scraping sound to a rustling noise. Opening the curtain wider, Reinhold saw one of his crewmates, a Swede named Jan, rummaging around in his locker.

What is this guy doing in my stuff? He was about to say something but thought better of it.

Let's see what he is up to.

Reinhold watched as Jan pulled a small bottle of ink out the locker. He shook it to confirm that it was liquid before unscrewing the cap and taking a sniff. It must have smelled good to him because Jan downed the contents in one gulp before putting the bottle back in the locker.

He just drank my ink! Reinhold exclaimed to himself.

Jan closed Reinhold's locker and went to open another but Reinhold decided that this had gone far enough and made a loud, phlegmy snoring noise. Jan jumped two feet in the air and made a hasty retreat out the door without even looking to see if he was discovered. Reinhold chuckled to himself. The look on Jan's face was worth the loss of a bottle of ink. But now he would have to wait until they came to their next port before he could write Marta back. Sighing, Reinhold pulled his new Swedish comic book from under his mattress and started reading.

The next morning the mess boy told Reinhold and Herbert there was something wrong with Jan.

"He is pissing all blue!" The boy told them, completely mystified.

Reinhold roared with laughter, smacking a hand on the table. The boy and Herbert looked at him like he was a crazy person. After regaining his breath, Reinhold told them the story.

"He drank my ink! I was reading in my bunk last night and this guy comes in looking for something, I don't know what, but he drinks my whole bottle of ink! Now he is pissing blue."

Reinhold started laughing again but Herbert joined him this time. The mess boy was still a bit mystified.

Chapter 42: An Eerie Feeling

The fair sailing of summer passed into the chill of autumn. The Captain ripped the September page off the calendar. The crew of the *Govan* grumbled. They paid closer attention to the weather. The infamous North Sea winter rough sailing was just around the corner. Suddenly the white caps on the water no longer represented a cool breeze but a possible gathering gale. Reinhold wondered when his promotion to full *Matrose* was coming. He was cobblescot for three months but hadn't received his promotion or the pay raise that would come with it. He was in the dumps, thinking about changing careers again, when they put into Kiel for the first time in a month.

Reinhold had the idea in his head that he wanted to rent a room somewhere and Kiel seemed like a good spot. The incident with the Swede drinking his ink had gotten him thinking. He knew that people weren't trustworthy but he had underestimated their audacity. Since the *Pagensand* sunk, he had acquired some things, a small collection of books, some clothes, a small radio, and a camera, that he didn't want to get damaged or stolen. The *Govan* kept a busy schedule so he had little use at the time for most of his things. Over a rare dinner at Herbert's small apartment, Reinhold mentioned his idea.

"I know a guy that is renting a room just down the street," Herbert's wife Katie said as she served them. "I clean his neighbor's house. I'll tell him you are interested."

Katie was true to her word and the next day, Reinhold met and agreed to rent a room from Herr Plaut. Reinhold liked the man as soon as he met him. It didn't take long for them to work out an arrangement. Herr Plaut appreciated that Reinhold was a sailor and wouldn't be around all that much. They agreed that Plaut's young daughter could use the room when Reinhold was away. On occasions when Reinhold would be using it, he would send Plaut a telegram so unfortunate situations were avoided. Reinhold got a key and he moved his few belongings in the same day.

"Good, that's settled. Do you want to go to the opera tonight?" Raimo asked.

He helped Reinhold carrying his things to his new room. The question surprised Reinhold. Raimo hadn't struck him as the opera type. Raimo noticed the look on his friend's face.

289

"What? I noticed the opera house is playing Wagner's *Flying Dutchman*. I've never seen it."

Reinhold snorted. "Wagner, huh?"

He didn't have the fondest memories of Herr Wagner. Whenever he heard the composer's work, he thought of Herr Klausen and the basement of the schoolhouse in Ratekau.

"Come on, it will be fun. It beats sitting on the ship or drinking the night away."

Again, Reinhold snorted. "Does it?"

"Yes it does. Get your tuxedo on. We are going."

Reinhold sighed in resignation. He liked operas and it seemed pointless to continue arguing with his friend over a stupid childhood memory. "Ok. But I don't have a tuxedo. A suit will have to do for this."

Raimo grinned and smacked his friend on the back. "That will be fine. But next time we go to Helsinki, you have to get a good Finnish suit."

"I hadn't realized the Fins were so well dressed." Reinhold couldn't pass up an opportunity to tease his friend.

"I'll show you just how well dressed a Fin can be later!" Raimo retorted.

Unfortunately for Raimo, a stop in Helsinki would have to wait. The *Govan* picked up a delivery for Oslo in Kiel and headed to the city via a stop in Copenhagen. Reinhold had only been to Oslo a handful of times and never for more than an overnight stay. He was looking forward to seeing the hauntingly dramatic Oslofjorden again.

Upon arriving in Copenhagen, Reinhold was pleasantly surprised to receive a letter from Marta. He had written back after acquiring a new bottle of ink and some good paper. He told her of life on the seas, the great food he was served, the good men he worked with, the beauty of the coastlines, and, of course, the constant painting, chipping, and repair work.

"We mix our own paints. Then we start at the front of the ship and work our way back until we reach the fantail. Then we go back to the front and start all over again. Sometimes we can do the whole ship in a couple of weeks, sometimes it takes a month, depending on how fast we move and how much attention the bosun is paying to what we are doing." Reinhold had written her.

He knew that it wasn't very exciting but he didn't have anything else to talk about because he certainly wasn't going to tell her about his questionable activities on shore.

Ladies don't want to hear about hookers and drunken bar fights, he told himself as he picked up his pen.

He decided to write what he knew about, which was work and the ocean.

He knew that a good pen pal asked questions about the person with whom they were communicating. He was also familiar with farming so he asked about what kind of farm her family owned. He asked if she liked farming. He asked if she liked living on an island. Reinhold scoured the maps in the bridge looking for Föhr and finally found it tucked along the west coast of Germany not far from the border with Denmark.

"Interesting place, Föhr," the Second Mate commented when he saw where Reinhold was studying.

"Why do you say that, sir?" Reinhold questioned.

"It used to be part of the mainland but a storm washed away most of the coastline. That was six hundred years ago. Now those islands are mostly rock and mud. The winds off the sea keep most vegetation from taking hold but not on Föhr." He pointed to the islands north and west of Föhr. "It is protected by Amrun and Sylt. Föhr is like a beautiful, green sand dune."

"Have you been there, sir?" Reinhold questioned. "What kind of farms would they have there?"

The Second Mate regarded him suspiciously for a second. Reinhold had to admit it was a strange question for a sailor to ask. He wasn't even sure why he asked it. The mate was short when he answered.

"I have been there but just to the harbor at Wyk. I know nothing of its farms."

It was Reinhold's turn to stand port watch so he was unable to read Marta's letter until the *Govan* was underway to Oslo. The ship was riding heavy seas as Reinhold sat in the mess hall and opened the letter. Marta's lovely handwriting stared up at him, telling him that she lived on a plain old farm.

"We have chickens and a few pigs. We also grow potatoes and beans for the winter and greens for the summer," she wrote. "I have a horse. She was a gift for my sixteenth birthday last year. I like to ride her on the beach."

She went on to describe her island almost exactly like the Second Mate, as a green spit of land off the coast of Germany.

"The wind blows constantly here, but not as bad as on Amrun. And it is always green, even in winter, and it almost never snows."

It sounded like a fairyland to Reinhold, with farming. Marta expressed again her desire to leave her island and do new things, meet new people.

"I often think that I am related to everyone here by blood or marriage. I've met everyone there is to meet."

She implored him to write back and "brighten the boredom" of her days.

Reinhold began composing a letter to her almost immediately but got nowhere. He didn't know what to say, sitting instead with the pen in his head staring out the mess hall window at the growing fog. They had entered the Oslofjorden just a few minutes ago and a pilot had come on board to guide them up the island dotted waterway. The man had a grim look on his face as he passed the mess windows on his way to the bridge. Reinhold didn't blame him. He was scheduled to go on watch in a few minutes and was hoping that the fog would let up before he went to the bridge. Sighing, he gathered up his pen and paper and headed toward his bunk to stash them.

From the moment Reinhold remerged on deck and took up his position at the bow there was an eerie feeling in the air. The fog swirled around him with ghostly fingers. He couldn't see a thing a foot off the bow and the fog was stifling everything he could hear. Somewhere off in the distance, he could hear the mournful bellowing of the buoys accented by the closer, yet muffled, slow chugging of the ship's engine.

It put Reinhold on edge. He listened for other, more comforting sounds, like the laughter of his crewmates or banging as they opened valves, sounded tanks, and removed rust or a sneeze even from somewhere behind him on the deck. He heard nothing but sounds that put him further on edge. The lapping of water against unseen objects was the most distressing. He was having flashbacks to the fog in the Kalmar Sound when the *Pagensand* sunk. Every one of his nerves was taunt, waiting to hear the scraping of metal on rock, waiting to feel the lurching of the ship as it struck ground. Those sensations never came. Instead, the ship's bell tolled, telling him it was time to head to the bridge to continue his watch.

Thankfully, Reinhold headed astern, silently wishing the next guy to take the bow watch lots of luck being able to see anything. His apprehension grew as he passed hatches one and two. He tried to shake it off as he passed the dark and deserted mess hall. Reinhold paused at the bottom of the narrow metal ladder to the bridge. He wanted to compose himself before appearing in front of the pilot and the mate on duty. Slowly, he started up, the fog still swirling around him.

Something screamed, scaring the living hell out of Reinhold. Before he had time to react, something sharp pierced his face below his left eye and two somethings smacked him in both sides of his head. A grey shadow covered his face. Adrenaline flooded his veins and a strangled scream escaped his lips, carrying dully across the deck of the ship. Without thinking, he reached up and grabbed whatever was attached to his face and heaved it away from him with an involuntary shudder. He thought he had felt feathers. The object landed against the rail on the bridge wing and fluttered away a few feet. Following it with his eyes, Reinhold focused on a seagull. The bird cowered on the metal deck, shaking. It was immediately obvious to the sailor that the animal was injured.

Relief replaced the adrenaline and laughter erupted from his lips. Reinhold stood almost doubled over on the ladder, laughing hysterically. He felt the tension leave his body and laughed all the more.

A seagull, he cried to himself, *a seagull!*

"Sailor, is everything okay out here?"

Reinhold looked up to see the Third Mate staring down at him. His laughter slowed enough for him to answer.

"It was a seagull, sir. I was attached by a seagull. It flew into my face. See," he pointed to face where the bird's talons had dug in. "And see," he pointed to the culprit itself, still cowering on the deck.

The Third Mate smirked, almost smiled, in amusement as he ordered Reinhold to the galley to clean his face.

"Be quick about it," the mate snarled at him, remembering his authority.

The seagull, it turned out, had an injured wing. Reinhold took it inside the bridge and put it a spare crate. For several days, whoever went to the bridge brought a little something for it to eat. When it succumb to its injuries a couple of days later, they buried it at sea.

Chapter 43: North Karelia

"Great news!" Raimo said excitedly as he stuck his wool covered head into the rigging closet. "We are going to Helsinki!"

Reinhold grinned at his friend. "You need a trip to the sauna, huh? I can't say I blame you. Colder than hell out there and it is not even December yet."

"You better believe it! And, it gets better!" Raimo paused for dramatic effect. "We are going to be there for four days!"

Reinhold was surprised. "Four days? Why so long? And how do you know this already?"

"She needs maintenance," Raimo answered, patting the iron bulkhead fondly.

"Maintenance?" Reinhold questioned. He was about to ask more questions when Raimo interrupted him.

"Why are you asking so many questions? What does it matter? I just heard the Third tell Jensen that we are putting into Helsinki when we leave this beautiful city of Kalmar. Once there, the ship is scheduled for maintenance. Who cares what kind? We are not the engineering department. Let them worry about it. We get three of those four days off!"

Reinhold laughed at his friend's enthusiasm. "You are absolutely right, Raimo. Who cares? We can go to the sauna every day until our muscles are like veal."

"No, not this time, Reinhold. I am going to go home for a visit. I haven't seen my family in six months. I want you to come with me."

"Go home with you? Where do you live?"

"I am from Karelia, North Karelia, a small town not far from the airport at Joensuu. We have a plane. I'll radio my father and we can fly up there."

"Okay, Raimo, what the hell? I'll go with you."

Five days later Reinhold stood on the deck of the *Govan* watching the city of Helsinki grow larger in the distance. An icy blast of wind hit him full in the face. He shoved his chin down into the collar of his wool jacket and pulled his wool cap lower over his ears until the only part of his face exposed to the cold were his tearing eyes.

Holy Christ, he thought to himself, *it is going to be a bad winter. It is only the middle of November and I already can't feel my nose.*

He and the rest of the crew were on standby for docking. The pilot on the bridge was maneuvering the ship in the wake of a tug that came to walk them in. The islands they passed were covered a thin layer of ice crystals that reflected the light of the rising sun and made the land sparkle. As they approached the docks, the bosun started yelling orders and the flurry of activity that accompanied the docking procedure began. Once they were tied up, Jensen gathered the crew to make an announcement.

"As you girls may or may not know already," he began with a glaring look at Raimo, "the ship requires some maintenance that will keep her in port for the next four days. You will work the rest of today as usual and have the next three as shore leave. If you decide to leave the vessel, you are required to be back on the 18th by 8:00am. Ok, back to work. Let's get those hatches open. Move it!"

Reinhold had to admit he didn't remember all that much about those days he spent with Raimo. He knew they were amongst the three coldest days he could remember in his life. He apprehensively boarded a tiny plane at the Helsinki airfield and flew with Raimo and a pilot he introduced as Einar the two hours to Joensuu. It was already dark when they left Helsinki so Reinhold saw nothing as they soared over the Finnish landscape. Raimo told him he was missing the most beautiful sight in the world.

"When we go back to the ship, we have to leave in the daylight so you can see the land. Einar says it has already snowed a lot. It is truly magnificent when you see the white stretched out before you and the herds of reindeer running from the plane."

They arrived in Joensuu close to midnight. They jumped out of the plane into powdery snow that covered Reinhold's boots and crept almost to his knees. The cold was not bad at first, but as they made their way across the landing strip, it seeped into the seams of Reinhold's clothing and went right to his bones. Raimo's father, Noak, was waiting for them with the strangest vehicles Reinhold had ever seen. It looked like an army jeep but with tracks instead of tires.

"It is better for getting around in the snow," Raimo explained when Reinhold questioned him about it. "We don't move the snow they way they do further south. We would do nothing but move snow all winter, so we just pack it down and wait for spring."

The soft forward motion of the vehicle accompanied by the muffled sounds of Raimo and his father talking in the front seat quickly lulled the tired sailor to sleep. When Raimo woke him, they were stopped in front of a long, low building with a steeply pitched roof. There was light burning merrily in long, narrow, paned windows. Sounds drifted toward them. The light flooded out of the door as it was opened and a woman called to them.

The next thing Reinhold remembered was kids, lots of kids. He didn't know where they had all come from but they were everywhere. They were of all ages. There were small ones and big ones and ones that probably weren't really kids anymore. A woman with silver blond hair and kindly wrinkled face took his coat and sea bag before guiding him to a room lined with bunk beds. He remembered falling into one and passing out before his head hit the pillow. He slept straight on through to the next morning, finally dragging himself from slumber around nine o'clock.

Opening his eyes and finding himself in a wooden room brightly lit with winter sunlight was not at all familiar. It took a couple of seconds to remember where he was. He heard the door open and Raimo's face appeared above him.

"Are you ever going to get up? You have already missed breakfast. Now there is just coffee."

Reinhold laughed. "Yes, sir."

They went out into the main living area of the house. It was lovely with beautifully upholstered chairs and couches.

"My family makes furniture," Raimo stated simply when Reinhold admired the pieces.

Somewhere in the back of his sleep addled brain Reinhold recalled Raimo telling him that once before.

The silver blonde woman from the night before was introduced as Raimo's mother, Agnis. She welcomed Reinhold to their home and Raimo gave him a steaming mug of black coffee. Reinhold took a big swig of the beverage. It was hot, sweet, and delicious. There was a different quality to it then coffee he had elsewhere. He listened to Raimo tell him about his family and the factory. He helped himself to another mug of coffee and was almost done drinking it when he realized he was drunk. He wasn't just drunk, he was really drunk.

"Raimo," he slurred to his friend, "why am I drunk?"

Raimo laughed at him. "Because the coffee is spiked with my father's *korpiroju*."

"With what?"

"Wood alcohol. He makes it near the factory."

Reinhold was so drunk by 10:30am that they put him back to bed. He woke up again in the afternoon still feeling blurry.

"That is some wicked stuff you guys drink. Holy Jees! I don't think I am going to be any good for anything today!"

"Nonsense," Raimo snorted as he handed Reinhold another mug of coffee. "We'll go for a drive. It will be fun."

Reinhold shrugged and sipped the coffee.

"As long as we're not working, right?" Raimo grinned and raised his own mug, toasting the solid ground beneath their feet.

The two men headed out into the cold to the jeep. They drove into the countryside east of Joensuu. Raimo took a turn down a road that led them through a pine forest. The ground and the trees were coated in a layer of snow creating a wall of white and green. It reminded Reinhold of Christmas cards he had seen as a child.

In between the patches of forest were wind swept plains dotted here and there with stunted, twisted pine trees. There were the lakes, huge and half frozen, surrounded by white banks and dotted with small fishing crafts. For several hours, they drove around, chatting and sipping spiked coffee out of a thermos to keep the chill away.

Reinhold didn't remember what they chatted about as they drove. He remembered the dramatic scenery and an equally dramatic moment when Raimo stopped the jeep in the middle of a road, at a spot where it became more of a trail and wound off into the distance across a wide plain.

He pointed toward the white horizon and said, "That's Russia, the new Soviet Union. If I was to continue down this road for another thirty miles or so, we would get shot at before we even saw a single person. There are snipers everywhere, on every road that leads to the border."

"Have you ever been close?"

"Once, my brother and me, we were out drinking and got too close to the checkpoint. They sent a couple of warning shots our way. They weren't really trying to hit us but they wouldn't have been sorry if they did."

The two sailors headed back to Raimo's for dinner and more coffee. Noak, Agnis, and some of the children entertained the group with music and singing. At some point, Reinhold made his way to the room with the bunks and fell asleep. He awoke the next morning to Raimo's face and mug of coffee that he was very careful to sip. They ate a hearty breakfast before either one spoke again.

"Come on, I'll show you my father's factory," Raimo suggested and off they went in the jeep.

The factory was not what Reinhold was expecting. It was smaller and had less workers. It resembled the house where Raimo's family lived in design having the same low profile and steeply pitched roof. The room was packed full of wood and fabric. In the corner stood an old potbellied wood stove burning brightly, a pot of coffee on top. Each man worked intently on one piece of furniture, hammering small nails into the wood with robotic precision. Then they fixed themselves a drink with coffee and the wood alcohol. Reinhold was handed a mug of coffee and tasted the now familiar quality. He was surprised. Raimo said that all the guys drank coffee all day, especially in the winter.

"Watch them," Raimo said. "They never miss a nail. The hammers have magnets in them."

Reinhold watched the upholsterers. Each man held a hammer in one hand and the fabric he was tacking in the other. They spit a tack out of their mouths onto the hammer. The magnet held it in place and with one hand they hammered the tack into the wood, tightly securing the fabric. Most of the tacks only required one or two strikes of the hammer to embed them completely and securely. It was a steady rhythm of spit, strike, and repeat. Reinhold was amazed and mesmerized.

"They never swallow those nails after drinking all day?" Reinhold asked.

"Never," Raimo responded.

Too soon, it was time to return to the *Govan*. The afternoon sun was shining, reflecting blindingly off the snow, when Noak dropped Raimo and Reinhold off at the airport for the return flight to Helsinki. Before departing in the jeep, Noak handed Reinhold a ceramic jug.

"Something to remember your trip," he said, simply, before tipping his cap and climbing back into the jeep.

"Don't drink that all at once," Raimo grinned at him. "That's a month's supply."

The plane took off into a perfect cloudless sky. They were airborne for only a few minutes when Raimo pointed down. Following his friend's finger, Reinhold saw one of the most spectacular things he had ever witnessed. A hundred feet below them, a herd of reindeer was fleeing in panic from the shrill noise of the plane's engines. There were hundreds of them, a moving mass of brown against the white backdrop of the snow. They ran toward a forested patch of land in the distance, the leaders pulling away from the main body followed by the slower animals, creating a streaming effect. Reinhold fancied he could see the whites of the eyes as the plane zoomed overhead.

"What now?" Raimo asked as they walked through the small airport. It was still early in the evening when Einar dropped them off on the tarmac in Helsinki.

"Like you have to ask? We head out to sea again tomorrow. I say we head downtown and look for some women! I can't have a whole shore leave pass and not get laid."

Reinhold smacked his friend on the back. The *korpiroju* they sipped on the plane was making him feel very frisky. "If we don't find any willing girls in the bars then I will buy you any one you want on Aleksis Kiven katu. I think I want a brunette tonight. How about you?"

Raimo thought for a second. "Redhead."

It was after 2:00am when Reinhold and Raimo stumbled back to the ship.

"Where have you two been?" Rouger asked, half-heartedly.

He stood at the head of the gangway with a mug of steaming coffee in his head and the collar of his wool coat pulled up around his neck. Reinhold couldn't resist the temptation to knock the mug out of Rouger's hands. He laughed as it tumbled down the gangway a few feet, spraying coffee everywhere, before it bounced over the side into the water.

"We've been out," Raimo answered.

He headed straight for the mess hall and started pulling open cabinets. Reinhold joined his friend in a buffet of sardines, crackers, pickled eggs, and pickled herring before stumbling below deck and falling asleep face down on his bunk.

Chapter 44: Eva

The next morning was unpleasant, to say the least. The *korpiroju* caught up with Reinhold and his head was pounding. He had no idea how much he had drank the night before but he was sure it was probably too much. To make matters worse, the bosun was in a miserable mood. He was prowling the deck like a wild animal, looking for someone doing something remotely wrong.

"Jensen spent the last three days drunker than I have ever seen him," Herbert told Reinhold and Raimo as they left the mess hall. "Even the hooker he hired last night wanted nothing to do with him. She left the ship without keeping her end of the deal. Jensen was naked and screaming obscenities at her as she ran down the pier. I think if we had been at anchor, she would have jumped overboard."

The men laughed at the thought but then Herbert became very serious and added, "He hit Malmgren in the head with a chipping hammer. Luckily, he is ok.

"Malmgren, the stoker?" Reinhold asked. Herbert nodded.

Nobody bothered to ask why Jensen would do something like that since he had no authority over the stokers. The answer was obvious: that is what psychotic people do. Reinhold shrugged away his disgust with Jensen. His head hurt too much to think about it. He said as much to his friends before they headed to their positions to make the ship ready to sail.

The sky was growing dark to the east even though it was early morning. Heavy, black clouds were making their way across the city. From Reinhold's perspective, it looked like they were skimming the tops of the tall buildings to the west. A gust of wind hit the ship, moving it against the lines that secured it to the pier.

"I don't like the look of those clouds," Reinhold muttered to himself.

Glancing over the side of rail of the ship, he noticed the harbor waters were becoming a bit choppy. Further out, in the Gulf of Finland, he could see white caps moving from east to west, running in front of the wind. He wondered if the Captain would hold them back or put out in spite of the impending bad weather.

A shuttering vibration went through the ship followed quickly by two short blasts from the ship's whistle and Reinhold knew they were leaving.

The *Govan* was barely out of the Gulf of Finland when the clouds burst above them. Torrents of cold rain pelleted the crew and gusts of wind threatened to send them overboard. Every two minutes or so, a cold wave of seawater washed over the deck. With water coming from above and below, it was pointless trying to stay dry. The storm persisted until they reached the Baltic Sea a few hours later, finally petering out and leaving them to contend with just the deep swells of the post-storm sea.

Late that next night, the *Govan* docked in the small northern Swedish port of Sundsvall. Reinhold was scheduled to stand the twelve to six watch and was not looking forward to it. After getting the ship tied up, he went to the galley for a fresh mug of coffee before heading to the gangway to start his shift.

He hadn't been standing there long when a strange noise caught his attention. It sounded like someone was moaning in pain. Listening, he decided it was coming from the bridge and went to investigate but found nothing out of the ordinary. Shrugging his indifference and assuming the noise must be coming from somewhere on shore, he headed back down the ladder to the gangway to resume his watch.

The next thing he knew he was lying on the deck of the ship on his back, throbbing pain beginning to well up from several impact spots on his body.

"What the hell?" He said aloud to the iron ladder.

He had slipped on the wet metal and fallen back down the few rungs. He pulled himself back to his feet feeling a bit silly for falling. Unconsciously, he rubbed his wrist, which seemed to be throbbing the most. He had smacked it on the bulkhead in his tumble. It grew more uncomfortable as the night worn on but Reinhold just shook it off.

Just a bang, he thought. *It will be fine in a few days.*

A week later, the *Govan* arrived in Bremerhaven and Reinhold's wrist was making work more difficult and more painful. Now that he was back in Germany, he considered getting it looked out but was distracted by an invitation to go to the local tavern for a drink.

I'll do it tomorrow, he told himself.

He couldn't turn down the opportunity to go look for a girl. He missed a visit with Anya when they were in Kalmar a couple of days before because the Third Mate gave him port watch as punishment for mouthing off.

The watering hole in Bremerhaven wasn't anything special, just a room with a bar and some tables. It was near the tracks and therefore wasn't a quiet place. He, Herbert, Raimo, Rouger, and a couple of other guys got comfortable at a table and ordered rounds of drinks while the available ladies made their own rounds, offering everything from company for dinner to quickies in the parking lot to a full night of making the sailor's dreams come true. The other guys invited a few of them to join their table but Reinhold wasn't impressed with the selection or the offers. He wanted a regular girl tonight and he had the feeling that if he gave it another hour or so, a pretty girl would show up, at the very least a younger hooker.

Five drinks into the night, Reinhold was feeling pretty good. He was laughing at his friend's attempts to get an olive out of a woman's cleavage using just his teeth when the wooden bar door opened and in walked a beautiful blonde. Reinhold figured she had to be in her mid-twenties, a bit older than his seventeen years. She greeted a table of longshoremen on the other side of the room but didn't join them. She went to the bar instead and ordered a drink. As she sipped, she looked around the bar, her eyes glancing at the tables and moving on without interest until she saw Reinhold staring at her. She smiled shyly at him. Reinhold was immediately enchanted. Without a word to his friends he got up and went to the bar, taking a seat next to his enchantress.

"Hello," he said, staring into her deep blue eyes.

"Hello," she responded.

They locked eyes for a minute before Reinhold spoke again.

"What's your name?"

"Eva."

"Your name is almost as beautiful as you are," Reinhold complimented.

He noted that a light blush spread across her cheeks and was very happy. "My name is Reinhold."

He picked her hand up off the bar and lightly kissed the back, keeping his gaze focused on her face. He noted that the blush deepened in color and spread down her neck. It was exactly the response he was looking for.

"Can I buy you another drink?" He asked, signaling the bartender without waiting for her to answer.

They spent the next two hours drinking and staring into each other's eyes, chatting idly about their lives. Eva was a secretary for a shipping line that operated out of Bremerhaven. She hadn't been here long and was originally from a small town named Beverstedt.

"I had to get out of there. It was just so boring!" She said with a bit of exasperation.

Reinhold thought he fell in love with her in that second.

"I left home because I was bored," he confided. "Sailing is a lot more fun than farming."

Eva giggled at him and the sound of it was magic. "I couldn't picture you as a farmer." She looked him over. "I think you look better in sailor's grease than farmer's dirt."

Reinhold was definitely in love now. He could feel the pent up hormones coursing through his system.

"Want to see my ship?" he asked huskily.

"Yes, I would like that," she answered somewhat huskily herself.

Reinhold didn't know if it was her or the cocktails that were talking and he didn't care. He left some money on the bar, took Eva's hand, and pulled her off her stool. Glancing over his shoulder, he saw his friends still gathered at the table. He caught Rouger's eye and winked as he guided Eva toward the door. Rouger grinned at his friend and nodded his head toward the woman next to him indicating that it would not be long before he was headed to the ship with a lady himself.

Eva turned out to be pretty good in bed, eagerly accepting whatever Reinhold did, which wasn't much really. He was saving his good moves for the second and third romp. They managed to get one good go around in before Rouger returned with his own lady.

"I only get one turn on this ride." Rouger whispered to Reinhold as he lay with Eva on his bunk. "Why don't you and your lady go somewhere else for an hour?"

Reinhold turned to Eva. "What do you say? Want to let my bunkmate have the place to himself for a few minutes?"

Eva smiled enchantingly and nodded. "Sure. It's time I get home anyway."

She started to lift herself out of bed but Reinhold held her in place.

"You are leaving?"

"Yes. It is time to go. I have to work in the morning."

"So do I. You don't see me calling it quits so early. I still have some things I want to show you."

Eva smiled at him again. "I need my beauty sleep and I've seen your 'things'," she purred. "Why don't we get together again next time you are in Bremerhaven?"

Reinhold let her rise and dress but couldn't hide his disappointment. He walked Eva to the gangway and gave her a kiss good night. They agreed to meet again but he doubted that would happen. He watched her walk away, down the concrete pier and into the darkness, and sighed heavily.

"Fall in love again with a girl that was just looking for free drinks?" Lars grinned at Reinhold over the rim of his coffee mug.

Reinhold couldn't help laughing. "I guess so. It wasn't even really worth it. I still want more! German girls!" He snorted. "You never know what you're going to get. When do we go to Denmark again?"

Lars caught his friend's meaning. "Not nearly soon enough for me. I hope to God that I am not standing port watch when we get there!" He thought for a second. "The girl I had last time we were there was incredible. Beautiful, with an ass that was made for smacking."

Reinhold remained on deck, chatting and smoking with Lars. His wrist was throbbing again and he cursed himself for not going to the doctor like he planned.

After work tomorrow, he told himself, *I am definitely going to get it looked at.*

He stayed on deck with Lars, exchanging stories until he saw Rouger's lady leave. He was tempted to ask if she was up for another go around but decided against it. He had no idea how many men she had been with that day. Sighing, he got up and headed to bed. Tomorrow was another day of splicing lines. He needed to do another five, three hundred foot sections before they got into London in a week's time.

Chapter 45: Is It Broken?

Reinhold sometimes envied stokers. Sometimes. On certain days in particular. Today was one of those days. He sat, surrounded by line, outside the rigging closet in the forecastle, splicing lines and watching the cranes unload the pallets of canned fish in hatch one. They picked it up in Stockholm before sailing to Sundsvall where the pallets were covered with the lumber they finished unloading yesterday. The stokers not assigned to clean the furnaces today were lounging, drinking bottles of cheap vermouth, on the foredeck like it was a summer day and not a very cold day at the end of November.

Malmgren was the exception. He set his easel up on the pier and sat blissfully painting something as the crane swung the pallets over his head and longshoremen shouted and cursed. From time to time he would lift his head and stare at the ship before continuing his work. After a couple of hours, curiosity and the desire for a change in scenery got the best of Reinhold. His wrist was throbbing something fierce from applying pressure to the lines to make the splices tight. He rubbed it as he went down the gangway to the pier to see what Malmgren was painting.

"Hey Malmgren. What are you painting today?"

Malmgren looked up, a paint brush between his teeth, one in his hand, and a pigment laden piece of sheet metal in his hand. He grunted something in response and went back to painting, moving his hand in short and rapid strokes over the canvas.

Reinhold sauntered over, positioning himself behind Malmgren as another pellet flew overhead. Looking over the man's shoulder, he saw the *Govan* sailing on a white capped sea. The ship was almost a perfect representation of the real thing. The artist even included a trail of black smoke emitting from the stack, a reminder that there were men in the furnace room, shoveling coal. But, there was something not right about the two dimensional ship. Glancing back and forth between the ship and the canvas, Reinhold noticed that the ship's name was missing from the painting. The *Govan* was labeled twice, once as is customary, on the bow near the hawse pipe, but also right below the bridge castle in big letters along the hull. He was about to point it out but he was became mesmerized by the movement of the stoker's brush.

"The *Govan*" by Malmgren
Photograph courtesy of Reinhold Scholz

He watched as Malmgren made the sea look more storm tossed by adding more white caps before switching brushes and adding colors like black and dark green to the front of the waves. This made them appear more realistic, deeper, more threatening. Reinhold stood behind the stoker for almost twenty minutes, watching the man work. He liked this painting very much and he had no idea why.

"Malmgren, do you sell these paintings?" Reinhold asked when the stoker's hand stopped moving so he could contemplate his work.

The man jumped and turned toward the sound of the voice that had spoken, like he had forgotten that Reinhold was there.

"Ah, Scholz, what are you doing here?"

He reached down for the bottle next to the easel and took a long gulp of the vermouth it contained.

"I've been standing here for twenty minutes, watching you paint."

"Oh. Well, what do you think of it?" The stoker asked, wiping his mouth on his sleeve.

"It is very good. I like it very much. Do you sell them? Because I would buy this one from you."

The stoker seemed surprised. "I do sell them. I'll let you have this one when I am done for twenty *mark*."

"Are you going to add '*Govan*' along the side like it is on the real ship?"

Malmgren thought about it for a second. "I guess so. It would be more realistic, wouldn't it?"

As Reinhold watched, Malmgren picked up a small brush and quickly outlined the word *Govan* on the hull of the painted ship. He reached into his pocket and pulled out twenty *mark*.

Malmgren took the money. "I am almost finished with it. I'll leave it in your bunk when it is ready. Maybe next week, depending."

"What do you think you are doing, Scholz? Don't you have lines to be spliced? What the hell are you doing onshore?"

The sound of Jensen's voice snapped Reinhold back to the reality of his situation. He was supposed to be working but had been on the pier for nearly a half an hour.

"Get your ass back to work or I swear you will be chipping rust off the stack for the next week!"

"Well, that's my cue," Reinhold said to Malmgren and sauntered off to the ship.

He half expected Jensen to meet him at the top of the gangway to continue his verbal assault, possibly even deliver a physical attack but it didn't happen. Jensen was busy overseeing the cargo unloading, which was at a feverish pitch because the old man wanted to leave tomorrow night. Not willing to push his luck that day, Reinhold went back to splicing. It wasn't long before his wrist started to throb again.

After a painfully long trip to London, the *Govan* headed for Sweden. Everyone on board was happy to be leaving England. It had been another tedious trip interrupted by teacarts and two hour lunch breaks. Reinhold's wrist was causing him a lot of pain but he skipped going to the doctor in London mainly because of the language problem. When someone told him what was wrong, he wanted to be able to understand what they were saying. Besides, if something was really wrong, he didn't want to get put off the ship in London.

The *Govan* docked first at Kalmar, arriving late. After finishing his eight to five day shift, he went to Jensen and asked to be referred to a doctor in Kalmar.

"Why, what is the matter with you?" The bosun slurred at him.

Apparently, Jensen had not waited until five o'clock to start drinking today. Reinhold noted that he had a flask stuck in his belt. He held up his wrist his superior.

"I have been having some pain in my wrist. I think I should get it checked out."

Looking closely at the throbbing body part, he noted that today it looked swollen. He added this observation to his request with Jensen. "It is actually a little swollen today."

Jensen stared at Reinhold's wrist, just inches from his face, without focusing on it. "Swollen you say? I don't see what…"

"What is going on here?" the Third Mate was standing at the top of the ladder to the bridge, staring down at the scene.

"I need to see a doctor," Reinhold blurted before Jensen could respond. "My wrist is swollen and has been hurting for weeks."

"Then go see Dr. Larsson. His office is there," the Third Mate pointed to a row of squat wooden buildings just outside the port, probably a bit more than 300 yards from where they were at anchor. "Aren't you the eight to twelve watchman tonight?"

"Yes, sir."

"Be back in time for the twelve to four. Jensen here will stand your watch for you." Jensen snorted in drunken surprise and protest.

"Thank you, sir," Reinhold replied politely.

The Third Mate didn't look to be in the best mood. He was staring moodily at a swaying Jensen. Nodding to his superiors, Reinhold left to get cleaned up before catching the pilot boat to shore to see Dr. Larsson.

Dr. Larsson, it turned out, was an old sailor himself. His office was decorated with memorabilia of the sea: old fishing nets, model ships, a sextant, and rope tied into various types of knots. He explained while he examined Reinhold's wrist that he had liked the medical training he received during his sailing days. After they were cut short by an accident, he went to medical school. He kept long hours so he could be available for injured sailors coming in from sea. From what he said, he did a very brisk business.

"You never know when something is going to go wrong." He chuckled cheerfully as Reinhold winced in pain. "Every day brings new surprises."

The doctor's brow knitted in furrows of concentration. "You are going to need an x-ray, son. I think there may be something fairly serious going on here."

While they waited for the machine to spit out the image of Reinhold's wrist, the doctor asked what happened. Reinhold gave him a brief explanation.

"And you continued to work after the accident?"

"Yes, sir. I can't not work onboard."

"No, of course not," The doctor said with an understanding smile but Reinhold knew the man was thinking that he should have gotten this looked at weeks ago.

Thankfully, he didn't voice his thoughts. The doctor left to check on the x-ray. When he returned, he had a serious look on his face.

"Herr Scholz, I am going to have to put you in a cast. My assistant is preparing the plaster and it shouldn't take long to apply but you will not have full use of your hand and arm once it is in place."

"Does that mean that I won't be able to work?" Reinhold was a bit alarmed by the possibility of being out of work.

"Not necessarily. You could probably still perform your duties but it will be extraordinarily difficult with the cast. You will not have a good range of motion."

"What is wrong with it that it needs a cast?"

"You broke one of the small carpal bones when you hit it against the bulkhead. I am surprised, knowing the physical labor you do, that you lasted this long. It should have swelled long ago."

"It is broken?" Reinhold questioned, surprised. "How can I still work at all with something broken?"

"It is a small bone, no larger than your thumb nail. The others around it have been compensating for its disability."

Reinhold could only grunt in response. Something was definitely compensating somewhere. He could feel it throbbing.

Half an hour later, Reinhold emerged from Dr. Larsson's office with a new cast and a bad mood.

Six weeks, he thought to himself. *How am I going to last six weeks with this thing on?*

He started toward the ship but changed course and headed for Anya's house. The doctor gave him nothing to lessen the pain in his wrist, which had gotten worse after the bone was set. He didn't need pain pills, he just needed was a stiff drink and a girl. Then he would feel loads better. He frowned when he looked down at the cast. Dr. Larsson, being a former sailor, understood Reinhold's dilemma and tried to make it as unobtrusive as possible but it still encompassed his thumb and wrist, making it difficult to maneuver. He was determined not to leave the *Govan* because of a wrist injury.

The mates and bosun were not thrilled when Reinhold appeared with a cast but he waved them off, saying it was nothing that would prevent him from working.

"Guys work in casts all the time," he rationalized with them. "It's nothing and will be gone soon."

They didn't believe him, but they let the issue drop. He had always done his job and worked with the injury for a month already. What was six more weeks? Reinhold thought everything was fine until the Captain paid him a visit the day after getting the cast. He was splicing lines, with some difficulty, near the aft castle when he saw the old man walking toward him. Out of surprise and respect, he stood and took off his woolen hat.

"Captain Köppel, sir."

"Scholz, I hear that you are injured and I see that you are in a cast. What happened?'

Reinhold quickly recounted the slip on the ladder. The Captain listened patiently, once reaching into his pocket for a flask that he sipped from quickly before returning it to his pocket. Had the story been longer than a few sentences, Reinhold was sure that the Captain would have had a few more sips from the flask.

"Well," the Captain said when Reinhold finished his explanation, "I can't have a man on his vessel that is injured. It is too risky. I am afraid I am going to have to sign you off."

He put a hand out and patted Reinhold's shoulder before turning to leave.

Reinhold watched the Captain start to walk away in stunned silence. He was losing his job! No, no, no! That can't be. It took a couple of seconds for his mind to process the new information.

"Wait!" he called to the retreating Captain. "Can I at least stay until we go back to Germany?"

The Captain turned to look at him. "Okay. That won't be long. We head for Kiel next, for the canal. You can get off there."

"Yes, sir."

Reinhold was panicking. He knew he wouldn't be able to get a new ship with his wrist in a cast. The agent at the sailor's office won't even put your name on the list if you have a visible injury. As he stood there, staring across the deck toward the bridge castle, he saw Jensen encounter the Captain on the catwalk. They conversed briefly. Then the bosun made a beeline for Reinhold.

"I hear you're out of here when we get to Kiel." The bosun sneered at him. "Good riddance, I say. I don't care that the Captain thinks you are such a good sailor. You're nothing but trouble, Scholz."

Reinhold felt the rage rise in him when he saw the triumphant look on Jensen's face. He had to try very hard to suppress it. He knew that Jensen would destroy him. He weighed more and was taller, not the kind of guy that Reinhold wanted to fight alone and no one was going to come help him beat up their superior. Instead of striking the man, he opted for sarcasm.

"I'm going to miss you too, Jensen. Now I have to find some other hopelessly drunk moron at the bar to torture while he is passed out." He grinned at the shocked look on Jensen's face. "It is a shame. You were so easy to have fun with."

Jensen's face was turning purple in his fury. "You are going to regret that, Scholz."

Blinded by his madness, Jensen took a wild swing with a fist the size of a small ham. Reinhold knew the blow was coming and easily sidestepped it, sending his own fist square into the man's stomach, using Jensen's forward momentum against him. Jensen crumpled up on the deck at Reinhold's feet. Just for good measure, after looking to make sure no one was looking, he kicked Jensen with the toe of his heavy work boot right in his massive chest. He heard the air leave the prone man. Reinhold couldn't help feeling satisfied after all the terror he had endured. What did it matter if they kicked him off the ship now for assaulting a superior or in Kiel for being injured?

"What do you mean, you have to leave?" Raimo questioned, flabbergasted by the turn of events.

Reinhold left Jensen writhing on the deck to find his friends. He came across Raimo making ready to climb the bridge castle to paint the stack.

"I have to go because of my wrist," Reinhold held up his hand in illustration. "The Captain told me himself."

There was a hint of pride in his voice. At least he had been fired by the Captain and not one of the *arschloch* mates or the drunken bosun. "But he said I could leave after we get back to Germany. Our next port is Kiel."

Raimo searched Reinhold's face for signs that his friend was joking. When he found none, he said the only thing that made sense. "Then we will have to make the most of the time you have left."

Every moment not spent laboring on the ship was spent ashore, drinking and looking for women. The *tivoli* in Kalmar wasn't as big as the one in Stockholm, but it was still provided enough entertainment for the sailors. Rouger was becoming quite the ladies' man and was fun to watch in action. Raimo spent his time trying to get Reinhold laid by a girl who wasn't Anya, saying they were too young for just one woman. Herbert, as always, played the role of casual observer. He was never going to be unfaithful to Katie. As the *Govan* steamed toward Kiel and the canal, Herbert and Reinhold played one last game of chess. Reinhold won and was convinced that Herbert lost the game on purpose.

On the morning of December 9, 1952, Reinhold collected his seaman's book from the First Mate on the bridge and left the *Govan* on the pilot boat. The ship wasn't loading or unloading in Holtenau, just awaiting their clearance through the canal.

"Enjoy your time on the bum!" Herbert called to him from the bridge.

Reinhold raised his hand in salute. They promised to keep in touch. Raimo and Rouger were nowhere in sight. He had promised to keep in touch with them also.

Chapter 46: On The Bum

Once ashore, Reinhold headed straight for the agent office in Holtenau, hoping to get another ship.

On the bum, my ass, he thought to himself as he waited his turn to put his name on the list.

With any luck, he could have a ship in a few days. He tried to hide his wrist from the agent on duty but it was no use. The man saw through his attempts.

"You know that I can't put you on the list with an injury. How long have you had that cast?"

"Three weeks," Reinhold lied.

"Hmm," the agent responded skeptically, examining the relatively new cast. "I still can't put you on the list with an injury. Come back when you get it off."

Reinhold left the sailor's office, resigning himself to an unplanned vacation. He tried to look on the bright side. Maybe he could find a job that would keep him ashore. He knew better than to even look in Holtenau but thought maybe he would have some luck in Kiel. He made a pit stop at his room to drop off his stuff. Not really being in a rush, Reinhold stood in the middle of his space and considered where to hang his new painting. He quickly decided that over the small chest of drawers was a good spot, mostly because there was already a nail there.

Once settled, he left the house on the hill and headed south, across the canal to Kiel. He could still see the *Govan* anchored in the bay. There were men in the rigging. He wondered who had taken over his spot as cobblescot. He hoped it was Rouger. He was good with the lines and wasn't a full *Matrose* yet. Cobblescot would bring a few extra *krona* in his paycheck. Reinhold stopped in his tracks.

Verdamnt, he thought, *I only have krona on me. No one here is going to take krona!*

He considered backtracking to the sailor's club but decided he would visit the one in Kiel. Thinking about money made him realize that he had very little cash on him. He had spent quite a bit in the last week of goodbye celebrations with the boys. A trip to Lübeck was in his future. He sighed to himself. Lisa was going to scold him for needing to take money out of his post book but it would be good to see her and Willie.

Reinhold stopped at the sailor's club in Kiel and exchanged his money. He had a beer while he was waiting and listened to the old timers talk about the news of the day. Much of the city was still in ruins after the intense bombing during the war but they were making head way in the cleanup. The old timers were talking about an old bunker that was bombed by the British in 1945, Kilian bunker, they called it. There was some debate about what to do with what remained of the cement structure.

"They should get rid of it. It's an eyesore." One old man was slurring over his beer.

Another old man huffed. "You have no respect for the seaman who died there, the U-boat guys. That is their tombstone, you old *arschloch*."

"Don't you tell me I have no respect for sailors!" The drunk old man became irate. "I am a sailor!"

He slammed his mug on the bar, spraying beer all over himself. Reinhold was glad when he saw the man reappear with his cash. He hightailed it out of the club while the two old men bickered loudly. Once outside he laughed to himself. The old men at the clubs were always good for entertainment. If he wasn't on a mission to find a job he may have stayed to see how the debate ended.

Later that evening, Reinhold returned to his room in Kiel a defeated man. He couldn't put his name on the agent's list in Holtenau or Kiel. The shipyards in Kiel were not looking for labors. All the construction jobs were filled. The sailor's clubs weren't looking for help. Several of the people he spoke to said they won't hire a guy in a cast anyway. He was in a bad position until he could get the cast off.

Sighing, Reinhold stretched out on his bed, enjoying the feel of a real mattress under him. It felt weird that he wasn't swaying and it was so quiet. He took stock of his situation. He was going to be out of work for five more weeks. There was little cash in his pocket but his post book had some money in it, funds he had been saving for a while. Lisa had his post book. Tomorrow, he had to go to Lübeck. Reaching in his pocket, he pulled out his meager wad of cash, counting it quickly. The exchange rate for Swedish *krona* had been in his favor and worked out to forty-five *mark*. That would get him to Lübeck in the morning and would get him a few beers tonight. He cleaned up and dressed in his suit deciding that he would go early, get to bed early, and get the early train to Lisa's in the morning.

Getting to bed early was out of the question once Reinhold got to the sailor's club. He met a gorgeous Russian girl with raven black hair, olive colored skin, and wide blue eyes. She just arrived in the country and couldn't speak German. George, the old timer behind the bar, had spent a number of years on a Russian tramp ship before the revolution and still remembered some of the language. From him, Reinhold learned that her name was Tatiana and she came from a town near Riga. She had made her way to Holtenau as a stowaway on a cargo ship before she was discovered and ejected by the Captain. Now she was stuck and waiting for a sailor to sneak her on to a ship going west.

After hearing her brief story, Reinhold felt bad for Tatiana. They spent the night sipping cocktails from tall glasses, signing to communicate, playing footsy under the table, and staring into each other's eyes. He bought her dinner at a restaurant around the corner from the sailor's club. She repaid him with a night of uninhibited passion between the sheets.

In the morning they parted ways and Reinhold felt bad for her again. She had nowhere to go. If he had a ship, he would have considered smuggling her aboard so she could continue her westward journey.

Instead of planning and executing the romantically dangerous mission focused on helping Tatiana escape the oppression of the Soviet Union, Reinhold found himself on the ordinary noontime train to Lübeck. Three hours later, he was knocking on Lisa's door.

"What happened to your hand?" Lisa asked after she ushered him into her small apartment, both surprised and happy to see him.

Reinhold summed up his injury and confirmed her suspicion that he was there for money. She retrieved the book without comment. What could she say? He was clearly unable to work.

After a trip to withdraw money, the siblings spent some time catching up. When Willie came home, the three of them went out for dinner at the Red Cat. Reinhold kept them entertained with stories from the high seas. Lisa demanded he speak a bit of Swedish to prove that he had taught himself the language by reading comic books.

Finally, after a month of unemployment, Reinhold had enough. He was out of money, well almost out of money, and bored out of his skull. He felt like he had no purpose, which actually bothered him more than the monotonous boredom. The doctor recommended that he keep the cast in place for another two weeks.

Screw that, Reinhold thought to himself. *I'll lose my mind in two days, forget two weeks.*

In defiance of his doctor's orders, he got out his knife and sawed at the cast that imprisoned his wrist and thumb until he was able to wiggle out of it. Gingerly, he tested to see if there was any pain by putting his hand flat on the table in front of him and slowly applying pressure. He felt nothing.

Good, he thought, *now I can go get a ship and get out of here.*

On January 10, 1953, after three twenty four hour shifts waiting at the sailor's office, he was called for a *Leichtmatrose* position on a German ship called *Midgard*. He gathered up his belongings and headed for the docks where his new ship was awaiting clearance through the canal.

Chapter 47: Introductions

Midgard
Photograph courtesy of Reinhold Scholz

A stern faced First Mate met Reinhold at the top of the gangplank. The man was probably in his late twenties or early thirties with a wind-reddened face below the brim of a wool, navy blue sailor cap.

"What's your specialty, sailor?" the First Mate barked.

Undaunted, Reinhold replied, "Spring line, sir, and cobblescot."

He handed the mate his sailor's book. He looked around as the mate thumbed through the document and saw the crew assembled on the deck, smoking and observing the scene with causal interest. He could only figure that the ship was getting ready to sail.

As if to confirm the sailor's thoughts, the First Mate said "We are getting ready to sail. Stow your sea bag in the mess hall and present yourself on deck for assignment."

The mate shoved Reinhold's sailor's book into the pocket of his coat and stalked off to the bridge.

Reinhold threw his bag on a bench in the mess hall and returned to the deck as the mate reappeared on starboard bridge wing. He started shouting names and orders and men got moving, headed to their positions.

"Schultz!" he shouted. "Get the spring line! Koch, get up to the hawse."

Reinhold watched as a man who had been reclining against the bulkhead of the wheelhouse sauntered off toward the front of the ship, towards the fore hawse. He didn't see anyone else move.

Looking around, he wondered who Schultz was and why he wasn't taking the spring line.

"Schultz!" The First Mate screamed. "What are you waiting for? Get to the spring line! Nietzsche, get aft and take Hein with you."

Two men moved to obey orders. One looked back over his shoulder at Reinhold before disappearing around the bulkhead.

Nobody moved toward the spring line. The thought flickered through his head that the mate might be talking to him but he dared not make the assumption. It was his first day. He didn't want to screw it up by questioning the man.

"Schultz!" the First Mate roared.

He was getting really pissed now. His face was a brighter shade of red. When no one answered him again, he snorted in disgust and disappeared into the bridge. He appeared on the deck and walked briskly to where Reinhold was standing. He stopped inches from Reinhold's face.

"What's your name?" He screamed.

His breath was a foul mixture of coffee, cigarettes, and sleep.

"Scholz," Reinhold replied.

The First Mate's brown eyes narrowed in anger and his lips drew together in a thin line. Reinhold could feel the anger rolling off him. He could feel the crew still assembled staring at them.

"Get your ass on the spring line, Scholz."

The mate's voice was calm and controlled but overflowing with bitterness. Reinhold couldn't help thinking that he had managed to get in trouble his first fifteen minutes on this new ship without even opening his mouth.

Another old tub, he thought to himself, surveying his new home.

It had the telltale signs of a hard life: hasty patch jobs, thick paint, and lots of rust stains.

Once the ship was under the direction of the canal pilot and was sailing smoothly through the rolling farmland that surrounded them, Reinhold retrieved his sea bag from the mess hall and went to find the bosun.

"Schultz, is it?" The bosun asked when he saw Reinhold approaching.

"The mate seems to think so." Reinhold tried and failed to keep the sarcasm from his voice. "My name is Scholz, Reinhold Scholz."

"Well, Scholz, you're bunking with Hein." The bosun looked around, spotting a guy across the deck, repairing a corner of the canvas covering the hatch opening.

"Hein!" He shouted, motioning for the man to come over.

Hein was the same stocky build as Reinhold, but a few inches taller. He was as dark as Reinhold was blonde and walked with a fighter's gait. Reinhold had the feeling he was going to like this man.

"Hein, show Reinhold where to stow his stuff. Then get him to work repairing that canvas. It has to be done when we get to Cuxhaven tonight. We start loading first thing tomorrow morning."

The bosun turned and walked away.

"What do we pick up in Cuxhaven?" Reinhold asked as he and Hein made their way aft toward the castle.

Hein shrugged. "This old gal is owned by a coal company, Poseidon Coal Import, so I would guess it has something to do with coal."

He pulled open the door leading below deck to the accommodations. Reinhold was surprised by the size of the accommodations space. There were more rooms than he was expecting, than he had ever seen on a ship before. There had to be at least a dozen doors in the dimly lit space.

"How many men are on this ship?" He asked Hein.

"Thirty, if you include the stokers and engineers."

Reinhold whistled. "That's more than I was expecting."

Hein swung open the sea door with a flourish. "Welcome home."

The room was exactly what Reinhold had expected. A grey, narrow slip of space with a set of bunk beds, a spare chair lashed to a pipe, and two closets. Sighing, he swung his bag on to the bottom bunk and turned back to Hein expectantly.

"Do you want to settle in?" Hein asked tentatively.

Reinhold was confused. He looked down at his bag on the thin bunk mattress and then back at Hein.

"I just did."

Hein laughed uproariously, smacking Reinhold on the back. "I am going to like you, Scholz." He laughed again. "Come on, there is canvas to repair and people to meet."

That night, after the *Midgard* docked in Cuxhaven, Reinhold was assigned port watch. It was only fair. He was the new guy. A steady stream of people flowed passed him as he stood at the top of the gangplank. There were sailors in their going out clothes some of whom returned later in the evening drunk and clutching women, eager to get below deck. There were also sailors in their work clothes that had no further plans than a couple of drinks at the local taverns. They also came back drunk. One mistook Reinhold for an intruder on the ship and tried to throw him over board. He was a little guy that Reinhold hadn't met yet. Helmut, Reinhold learned was the man name.

At least a third of the stream of people were stokers in their dungarees and cleanest dirty tee shirts headed to the port side bars. Some of them also returned clutching women, some of them were so drunk when they came back to the ship that they crawled up the gangplank. None of them bothered with the sailor on watch and Reinhold didn't bother with them. He had already noted that there was a separate mess hall for the stokers. He could only assume that this meant there was past trouble on this ship between the stokers and the sailors.

Even the Captain was part of the stream of people. Reinhold had not met him yet. His name was Müller. He eyed Reinhold suspiciously as he approached the gangway, a bit unsteadily, from his salon at mid ship. The First Mate and two other men were with him. Reinhold noted that all four officers, even the relatively young First Mate, were old salty dogs with wind-weathered faces, particularly the Captain. The Chief Engineer, at least he assumed it was the Chief Engineer, was a huge man with a scowl etched on his face.

He watched the old man and his companions head up the pier. Hours later, the men returned staggering worse than before and singing old sea songs about wooden ships and mermaids. They ignored Reinhold as they passed but the Chief Engineer stopped a few yards from the gangway, wheeling on Reinhold.

"You will wake me at six o'clock. Not a moment sooner or later. Understand?"

The scowl deepened on his face and his eyes narrowed as he assessed Reinhold.

After a second's shocked silence, Reinhold responded, "Yes sir."

The chief wheeled back around and stalked off. Reinhold checked his watch. It was three am.

He still going to be drunk at six am, he thought to himself.

Reinhold's first port watch with the *Midgard* passed without excitement. The boredom sucked the energy out of him. It had been a month since he experienced the monotonous inactivity of standing watch. After apprehensively waking the Chief Engineer, he fell into his bunk to get two hours of sleep before he needed to be on deck to help with opening the hatch covers.

Chapter 48: Life On The **Midgard**

After Cuxhaven, the *Midgard* sailed for Boston, England. This didn't make Reinhold happy. He was broke and England was expensive. He resigned himself to indefinite ship confinement and was very happy when, upon docking in Boston, he was handed a letter from Marta. Winter was in full swing and she was bored and cold. Her father was getting ready for the spring birthing, which could start anytime and would consume his days until the last calf was born. She wanted him to come visit her, to keep her warm. There are no good men on this island, she wrote. Not that their worth matters because I am related to almost all of them. What was a girl in her position to do for a husband?

Reinhold spent the first five days in Boston composing a letter to Marta and comparing it a book he picked up in Holtenau on proper lexicon. He explained that he couldn't get away right now as he had just taken a new job with a new ship. He wanted more than anything to see her, he wrote, but time and money were never on his side. He spent free evenings reading his latest book club arrival, a Hemingway novel called *The Sun Also Rises*.

He also accompanied Hein and another guy, Nietzsche, into town to do some shopping. Hein was looking for something for his mother's birthday. They browsed the shops and chatted idly about the pretentiousness of the British. Each of them had a story or two about a Brit who tried to hurt them in some way.

"The women sure are beautiful." Reinhold reminded his friends.

He had his eyes on a petite red head in a tight tee shirt and flared skirt with a jaunty kerchief tied around her slender, elegant neck. She was across the small shop from where the sailors were standing but departed quickly when a friend came and said something to her. He watched them flounce down the street, giggling about something.

"Isn't the coronation coming up here? That woman, Elizabeth, she is the queen now, right? That's what all this stuff is? Memorabilia for her coronation."

Hein was holding a statue of Big Ben in his hands. The clock face bore a portrait of Elizabeth II. Reinhold wrinkled his nose in disgust at the little figurine. Glancing around the table, he saw a gold plate. On the face was a scene showing three men sitting at a table, drinking, and playing music under a tree near a building. It was happy and joyful. He liked it immediately.

"Now this is better for celebrating a queen," Reinhold said, holding the plate up for his friend's inspection. "Something gold and heavy."

"But it doesn't have anything to do with the coronation." Nietzsche pointed out.

"All the better." Reinhold said. "What do I care about that?"

"You should get it for our room, Scholz. Really class up the place," Hein grinned.

"I am broke," Reinhold stated flatly.

"No, you're not," Hein looked puzzled. "Pay day was yesterday.

Didn't you get anything for the time you have worked?"

"No."

Nietzsche whistled in alarm. "That's not good. You should talk to the mate."

Hein snatched the plate out of Reinhold's hands. "In the meantime, I'll buy this ugly plate and you can repay me when we get to Copenhagen."

Reinhold laughed when Hein winked knowingly at him.

Reinhold was still chuckling when they left the shop with their purchases. He was not looking forward to talking to the mate about his missing pay and he didn't have to. There was an envelope waiting in his bunk when he returned to the *Midgard*.

Reinhold still counting his pay when Hein burst into their little room. He was purple in the face.

"That *arschloch* just made up a rule against women on the ship!" He shouted at Reinhold.

Reinhold was stunned. "What *arschloch*?"

"Hofstadter, that *dummkopf*! Does he really think this is going to work? That we are going to just let that happen? Where are we going to bring women?"

"Who's Hofstadter?"

"The First Mate, of course!"

Reinhold thought about this for a second. "He can't do that! Why would he want to do that? Does he mean here, in Boston, or everywhere from now on?"

"Because he is a miserable *arschloch*! And yes he means everywhere from now on!"

Hein was screaming now. Other sailors in the accommodations heard him and came to investigate.

"And the Captain supports this?" Reinhold questioned.

"The Captain is a drunken jerk," Hein spit. "He supports whatever the First Mate tells him too. He is tired and old, too old to be at sea anymore."

There was a murmuring of agreement amongst the few men present. The rumor of the rule spread like wildfire through the ship. Men were angry, very angry.

Reinhold was sure that Hofstadter had his reasons for not wanting women on board. He was sure that they were all selfish and ridiculous. The ship was a sailor's home.

You can't tell a sailor they can't bring a girl home for some fun, Reinhold thought to himself.

The rest of the *Midgard's* time in England was tense, the crew grumbling as they worked. They worked slower than usual, often stopping all together. The First Mate got no respect and he didn't care. He handed out punishments without thinking about it until someone spit off the top of the wheelhouse, landing a direct hit on the officer's shoulder. After that, he threatened to fire them all when they returned to Germany. This attitude just made the crew hate him more. The bosun had no choice but to be the middleman between the brass and the sailors. He didn't pretend to support the new rule and he didn't pretend to have any control over the two dozen sailors under him. Reinhold felt bad for the man.

Four days after the new rule took effect the *Midgard* left Boston for Amsterdam. The crew was restless. They were looking forward to the red light district after the monotony and sexual boredom of more than two weeks in England but the "no women onboard" rule hung over their heads. What if they got lucky without having to resort to the professional ladies of the night? Someone, no one knows who, finally broke the news to the stokers that they would not be allowed to bring women on board in Amsterdam. All those not actively engaged in shoveling coal flooded on to the deck to protest in front of the wheelhouse.

It was quite the scene: large, muscular, grimy men in dirty tee shirts and dungarees shivering in the cold North Sea wind, shouting obscenities at the bridge castle like it was the cause of their anger. They dared the First Mate to come out and speak with them but Hofstadter didn't appear. He ordered the Chief Engineer to get his men back in order. Of course, it didn't work. Half of the stokers quit on the spot. Another quarter vowed to quit once they reached Amsterdam. Still the rule stuck.

The sailors decided they had to plead their case to a higher authority than the officers of the *Midgard*. They held an impromptu meeting in the mess hall to discuss the situation on the night they arrived in Amsterdam. Someone suggested, half-heartedly, that they go to their union. This idea was immediately flatly rejected. The corruption in the union was not a secret. The Captain and First Mate would hand the union rep a briefcase of cigarettes along with a couple of bottles of cognac and the complaint would be settled in favor of the Captain. Someone else suggested they mutiny. They tossed this idea around for a few minutes. It was more viable than the union but was too dramatic for most of the crew. One of the stokers suggested that it would be best for everyone if the First Mate disappeared. No one could deny the truth to the statement but no one openly supported it either. Finally, the bosun spoke up.

"We could just go to the company."

He stated it flatly and simply. Every pair of eyes in the room settled on him.

"What are you all staring at? It is a simple solution. Plead your case to the company."

Slowly a murmur of assent went through the crowded room.

"Who is going to go? And where do we go?" Reinhold asked.

"As your boss, I will go. I'll take Hesing and Nietzsche with me."

He thought for a minute before continuing. "We have to load some cargo here, nothing major. We'll be shoving off in a couple of days. Bremerhaven is our next stop. Poseidon has an office there. We'll go there and talk to someone."

Several days later, Reinhold was sitting in a portside tavern with Hein and Nietzsche, laughing about the First Mate's reaction to the company's repudiation of his ridiculous 'No Women Onboard' rule.

"He had a face full of vinegar," Nietzsche hooted. "You should have seen it Reinhold. I wish I had a camera with me so I could take a picture. I would take it out every time I needed a good laugh."

"Yeah, that will show him," Reinhold responded automatically.

He was distracted and kept watching the door. He hoped that the girl he met last time he was here would walk in. What was her name? Reinhold couldn't remember. He did, however, remember her being beautiful and captivating drinking companion. She had been so-so in bed, but that was the first time. Maybe she was one of those girls that opened up the second or third time.

"Look at this guy watching the door," Hein said to Nietzsche. "He wants first crack at any girls that come in."

Reinhold smiled at his friends. "You better believe it. Not that the two of you offer any competition."

"Oh, you don't have to worry about Nietzsche here moving in on your girls," Hein said. "He only beds fat chicks."

Reinhold was shocked. "What are you talking about?"

"They're cheaper," Nietzsche shrugged.

It took a second for the meaning to become clear to Reinhold. Then he almost fell off his chair laughing.

"You cheap bastard!"

An hour later, the door opened allowing a cold draft to penetrate the warm, smoky interior of the tavern. Reinhold glanced at the door from his table in the middle of the room. He saw a woman enter, a beautiful brunette woman with smooth skin and a confident stride. She was wearing a fur coat and high heeled boots. His glance became an outright stare.

That's not a girl, he thought to himself, *that's a woman right there*.

She caught him staring at her and smiled seductively as she crossed the room to the bar. Reinhold left his table and followed her. She was still shrugging off her jacket when he reached the bar. Smoothly, he grasped the collar of the heavy fur and gently peeled it off her arms, laying it across the back of her bar stool. She was surprised by his actions but smiled warmly, thanking him for the assistance. Their eyes met for a fleeting second and Reinhold felt that familiar sensation in his stomach. He could fall in love with this woman. Maybe he would.

"Can I buy you a drink?" He asked.

"Sure. I'll have a champagne." She smiled slyly at him.

He raised an eyebrow at her. This wasn't the kind of woman he usually encountered while in port. Reinhold ordered the drink. The bartender looked amused but poured the bubbly with all the dignity the old guy could muster. Reinhold ordered another beer for himself. He looked her in the eye again as she took the first sip of her champagne.

"What is your name?"

Her name was Kristal. She lived in Bremerhaven, not far from the port. She loved where she lived because she got to meet sailors from all over the world. And she really loved sailors.

"They are adventurous and always ready to please a woman." She teased Reinhold as her hand inched up his thigh.

He liked Kristal, her vivaciousness. It was still early, just about ten o'clock, but Reinhold was ready to go and he was sure that Kristal was also ready.

"Why don't you finish your drink and I'll show you just how ready I can be?"

His own hand was working its way up her thigh. She drained her glass and slid off her stool. Reinhold helped her with the fur jacket. "My ship is docked just across the train tracks."

"Oh! Your ship! How exciting!" Kristal shivered visibly with anticipation.

Reinhold thought it was a bit odd that she was so excited about his ship but didn't say anything. Why ruin the moment?

Reinhold nodded to his fellow sailors as he and Kristal passed their table. He got grins in return. He guided her out the door and across the tracks to the pier where the *Midgard*, awaiting resumption of cargo loading in the morning. Helmut was on port watch. He sneered at Reinhold as he passed. Reinhold really couldn't understand what that guy's problem was but every time they encountered each other there was a bad vibe. It reminded him of Klaus on the *Eos*. Kristal paused as they passed the rows of open hatch covers, peering over the side into the cargo holds of the ship.

"It is so far down, I can't see the bottom," she observed.

"It is about 35 feet down to the bottom. Of course you wouldn't be able to see it."

"What is down there?"

Reinhold shrugged and pulled her close in an embrace and kissed her deeply to remind her why she was on his ship. She responded eagerly, running her hands through his hair and up and down his back, squeezing his butt playfully. They resumed their trek to the rear castle to go below deck.

"My room isn't much." Reinhold said as he swung open the door, reveling the tiny space and the bunk beds all swathed in grey.

"I don't care about that," Kristal said seductively.

She grabbed the front of Reinhold's shirt and dragged him into the room behind her. He tripped over the threshold and barely had time to kick the door shut before they tumbled into his bottom bunk.

Kristal was the kind of girl Reinhold liked. There was no room for error with her because she told him exactly what she wanted and when she wanted it. He knew when he was doing what she wanted the way she liked because she moaned with a passion he had not heard before, deep and primal. Kristal was also equally as giving as she was taking. She took direction as well as she gave it.

The lovers had managed to have two romps through the land of ecstasy when Reinhold heard something outside the door to his room. He went to investigate, throwing open the door, and reveling a crouching Nietzsche.

"What the hell are you doing?" Reinhold asked, shocked.

"Nothing. What are you doing?"

"Were you listening to us?" Reinhold didn't need to ask the question. The answer was evident on the other sailor's face. "Did you even hear anything through the metal door?"

"Yes, a little. The door wasn't closed all the way."

Reinhold shook his head in amused and disgusted resignation.

"Go get your own girl, Nietz."

When he turned back into the room, Kristal was out of bed and dressing.

"Whoa, what are you doing? I thought you would be spending the night. What is left of it, anyway."

He reached out to caress a still naked breast.

"No, that is not possible. I have to be home before the sun rises. I can't have my neighbors gossiping about me." She had all of her underclothes on now and was pulling on the outer ones.

"Who cares about your neighbors?"

"I do. I can't have them telling my husband I don't come home at night."

Reinhold was stunned. "Husband?"

"Yes, my husband."

She pulled a set of rings out of her purse and slipped them on to the fourth finger of her left hand.

"Why didn't you tell me that you are married?"

"Would you have done this if I had told you?"

Reinhold considered the question for a second. "Yes."

Kristal burst into laughter. "That is why I love sailors and I think I like you best of all the ones I have met."

She threw her arms around his neck and gave him a big kiss.

"I have to go," she whispered in his ear.

A shudder ran down his back.

Reinhold walked her to the gangway where they kissed again. He wished that she was staying for just a bit longer. He wished she wasn't married.

This one could have been the one, he thought.

She promised to see him again when she had the chance. Somehow, he didn't doubt that he would see her again. He watched her walk down the gangway and onto the pier, following her with his eyes until she was out of sight.

"That was a pretty piece you had there." Helmut remarked from the shadows surrounding the wheelhouse. "Maybe I'll follow her and see if she is up for another go."

Reinhold whirled in the direction of the voice, startled out of his trance. Something in Helmut's voice made Reinhold's blood boil. He took a stride toward the man, reaching to get a hold of him, but stopped before he made contact. It took him a second to get his anger under control.

You can't afford to get kicked off this ship, Scholz. Not yet anyway.

"Are you always such a shithead, Helmut, or do I just bring out the best in you?"

Reinhold's voice shook with the anger he was repressing with a great deal of effort. He wanted to pick the little guy up and throw him overboard.

"Must be you," Helmut spit back.

Reinhold glared at him as he walked away.

"Ignore that guy," said a voice from the shadows of the aft castle.

Reinhold jumped out of his skin in surprise and whirled in the direction of the voice. In the darkness, the end of a cigarette grew bright, illuminating the face of the bosun. He was leaning against the castle, smoking and breathing deeply of the night air. Reinhold immediately took the comment as an order.

"Yes, sir," he said stiffly. "I'll do that."

Reinhold was happy to learn that, upon leaving Bremerhaven, the *Midgard* was headed through the canal and on to Kalmar and then Stockholm.

"Did you bring a tux with you?" Nietzsche asked Reinhold over breakfast.

"No, but I have one in my room in Kiel. Didn't think I would need it. It would easy enough for me to pick it up when we pass through. Why?"

Reinhold shoveled bread and eggs into his mouth. He missed the food on the *Govan* terribly. It had been so much better than the *Midgard's* offerings.

"Because eventually we are going to go back to France, maybe soon, and I want to go to the casino at Biarritz. You should go with me. But they like you to dress up."

Reinhold was a bit surprised. "I thought you were cheap, Nietz."

"I am not cheap. I am frugal." Nietzsche put his nose in the air in mock indignation.

At first, Reinhold had only heard 'casino', but as the comment settled in his brain, he processed the rest of its meaning. He paused with his fork in midair.

"This ship goes to France?"

"Sometimes," Hein shrugged.

331

Reinhold resumed eating, a bit sullenly. "I can get my tux. I'll go to this casino with you but I am not much of a gambler."

And I would prefer not to get off the ship in France but that is another matter entirely, he added to himself.

The sail through the canal was uneventful. Once the ship was secured in Holtenau, Reinhold ran up the hill to get his tux. On his way back, he ran into Katie. She told him that Herman was away at sea and she expected him back for a short time in a few days. She offered to make him a home cooked meal and keep him company for the evening but he declined. She waved off his objections but he wouldn't hear it. He left her with the promise to come to dinner when Herman was back, if he was still around, which was doubtful.

The *Midgard* picked up no cargo in Kiel but did have to undergo a routine inspection so the crew got two entire days off. Reinhold used one of them to visit Lisa in Lübeck. He had some financial matters to straighten out. She was taking good care of his money while he was away but he wanted to speak with the banker himself.

Confident that everything was good with the family and his money, Reinhold returned to Kiel and got completely snuckered at the sailor's club before wandering over to the *puff*. He hadn't met anyone good at the bar and was in the mood for a professional. He wandered the street until he found what he was looking for, a black haired girl with crystal blue eyes and a tenacious attitude. They negotiated a price. He handed over the *fifteen* mark she wanted and they went upstairs.

The next morning over breakfast, Reinhold tried like hell to remember what had happened and if he had liked it but just couldn't get a hold of it in his mind. He knew that he had been at the sailor's club and he kicked himself for it. He had just gotten his finances in order and then he spent the cash he had on drinks.

I should have gotten a damn bottle of vermouth and a hooker and called it a night but no, I had to go try to find a real girl.

To make matters worse, his head was throbbing and his eyes didn't want to stay open. Every wave that hit the ship rolled right through Reinhold's stomach, threatening to liberate the undigested breakfast.

Why did I drink so much? Sailing is going to be bad today.

He jumped, a pain slicing his head, when a plate landed on the table next to him.

"Did you hear that the Polish guy, Jerzy I think his name was, almost got his hand cut off this morning?" Hein asked rather nonchalantly, not noticing his friend's pained look.

"No," Reinhold started to shake his head but stopped immediately. "What happened?"

"Don't know exactly," Hein continued after shoving some bread in his mouth. "He was up in the crow's nest doing something last night. Next thing, the bosun is hollering for someone to get the boom going 'cause that the guy is hanging by just his hand. They got him down before he fell and rushed him off to the hospital."

"No word on how he is?"

Reinhold had not really spoken with Jerzy but had also never had a problem with him. He felt that if there hadn't been a language barrier, he might have liked the man.

"No, but he is not coming back. I heard the First Mate call for a new man before he left the bridge this morning."

The new man appeared on the ship before lunch. Reinhold was repairing the canvas covering the hatch when he saw a huge man saunter up the gangway, a piece of paper in his paw, and a sea bag slung over his shoulder. He paused on the deck, looking around, his eyes coming to rest on Reinhold.

"Where can I find the First Mate," The new guy asked.

Reinhold took off the freezing metal glove he was wearing, flexing his frozen fingers, and sizing up the large man in front of him. He was older than Reinhold and at least a full head taller. "The First Mate is on the bridge, most likely." He gestured toward the wheelhouse with his chin. "You the new guy?"

The new guy nodded. "My name is Werner." He stuck out his huge hand a bit awkwardly, hesitantly.

Reinhold took it and they shook. "Reinhold. Nice to meet you."

Werner touched the brim of his wool hat and walked away. Reinhold had the feeling he was going to like Werner. He had no idea why, it was just a feeling.

Chapter 49: Anya

The *Midgard* docked just after seven o'clock at the lumber loading dock in Kalmar. Off to the west, Reinhold could see the lights in Kalmar Castle. Seeing the castle at night, without the visual interference of the modern world, always had a strange effect on him. He felt that at any moment, a squad of medieval knights on horseback would come pounding out the huge main gate, riding to some long forgotten battle with a long diminished threat. Being a knight had always appealed to him; the fighting, the nobility, the damsels in distress, the land, the castle, and someone else to care for your horse. It was all terribly exciting.

Once done working for the day, Reinhold had dinner with the crew before heading below deck to shower and change. He was anxious to rekindle his love affair with Anya. An hour after quitting time, Reinhold was knocking on the door of her small home. Anya's mother answered. A strange look crossed her face when she saw Reinhold standing on the doorstep.

"Reinhold, we were not expecting to see you again." She ushered him into the kitchen of the house.

"I broke my wrist. I had to wait for it to heal to sail again. Is Anya here?"

"Yes, she is in her room. Would you like some coffee?"

"Please."

"Sit. I will call Anya."

Reinhold sipped his coffee at the table in the kitchen, waiting. He was thinking that tonight was going to be a great night. A movement at the end of the hallway caught his attention. Anya came running into the kitchen and flung her tiny frame into his arms. He wrapped his arms around her and inhaled the perfume of her soft hair.

Thank God she's taking care of herself, he thought.

"Where have you been?"

Her voice was as soft and sweet as always. It went straight to his chest and nested there, like a warm ball of liquid. Anya pulled away and looked at him. Her eyes were full of hurt and her angel face wore a worried expression.

"You remember my wrist, right? The last time I saw you I had a hurt wrist. They put me in a cast and I got kicked off my ship. I had to wait for it to heal to get another ship. This is the first time I have been back to Kalmar."

Her face relaxed. "Oh. Then it is better, your wrist?"

She took his hand and examined the offending wrist.

"Yes, yes, I am fine." He took her hand in both of his. "I missed you."

He kissed her long and deep. He felt her respond to his lips and was relieved. She was too beautiful. It would kill him if she had not wanted him anymore. In a whisper he asked, "Can we go somewhere private?"

Anya took his hand and led him back down the hallway to her room. Her parents were in the sitting room. Once in her room, he undressed her slowly, savoring the perfection that was this girl. She hadn't changed. Her perfectly pert, firm breasts; her flat, soft stomach; her toned, plumb bottom; her well-muscled arms and legs; and, not least of all, her warm, moist love canal. Everything was the same. It was glorious. They spent three hours reacquainting themselves with each other's bodies. She was the same in bed too. If she had found someone else, they hadn't taught her anything. Reinhold didn't even bother telling her what he would like. Instead, he guided her hands where he wanted them to be. As usual, he couldn't tell if she was enjoying herself or not. He set his tongue to work and she moaned in response.

They lay in bed together for some time, enjoying the afterglow. She was twining his thickening chest hair around her fingers, pulling gently. He always found it relaxing for some reason. He was on the verge of falling asleep when she propped herself up on one elbow.

"How old are you, Reinhold?"

"I'll be eighteen soon." It was an odd question. "Why?"

"I was just wondering." She thought for another minute. "Do you want to sail forever?"

He thought about the question. It was a tricky one.

"No, not forever. I want to buy a house and settle down. I can't do that if I keep sailing. I want a family of my own one day."

Anya smiled at him. "That's good to hear."

"Why?"

Something in the tone of her voice scraped away the lazy, comfortable feeling he had and made him pay closer attention.

"I am pregnant."

She whispered the words to him. He didn't think that he had heard her right. He looked into her eyes, searching for the truth. Was she just joking with him? But no, she wasn't. She couldn't lie to him. He knew her too well.

So, she has been with someone else.

"Who's the father?" He asked, half wanting an answer, half not wanting an answer. He felt anger growing inside him.

She giggled at his question. "You are, Reinhold."

Impossible, he thought to himself.

"How long have you known?"

"I didn't get my monthly last month."

"In January?"

He sat up in the bed, leaning back against the pillows, and rubbing his eyes with his fists.

"Yes."

"What about December?"

He was trying to think back. When was the last time she had her monthly when they were together?

I don't know! I am not here that often. I can't keep track of stuff like that. This is her job!

"December?"

"Yes. Did you have your monthly around Christmas?"

She looked puzzled. "I don't remember. I just know that it didn't come last month and I get sick in the mornings. Mama says that means I am pregnant."

She looked happy at the end of the sentence. He fully expected her to say something like 'Aren't you happy? We are going to have a child.' A chill went through him, destroying the warm ball of liquid that she had planted there earlier.

"Who else have you slept with?" He hadn't wanted to ask but it seemed impossible not to.

Again, she looked puzzled. "I haven't slept with anyone else. Just you."

He didn't want to believe her. His anger was mounting. He looked at her and felt his anger melt a little. She was gorgeous and sweet, but a child? She was practically a child herself. His anger rose again. He had to get out of here before he said or did something stupid.

"I am very happy for you," he said gently, kissing her lightly on the lips. "I have to get back to my ship. We have a busy day tomorrow."

Anya looked stricken. "You can't stay? I was hoping you would stay."

He shook his head. "Not tonight. We'll talk again tomorrow night. I'll come get you and we'll go to the *tivoli*."

He gave her another deep, lingering kiss. His anger was subsiding again. He wondered seriously for a second if he should stay. He could sign off his ship and get a job here in Kalmar. His subsiding anger turned to a rising panic. A vision of himself chopping wood in the forest flashed through his mind, spurring him to action. Quickly, he got out of bed and dressed, throwing clothes on in his haste to leave.

"I'll see you tomorrow."

He pulled his wool hat on and down low over his ears and left the room, pacing quickly through the darkened house and out on to the street. He headed for the port without a glance backwards, his mind racing.

A father!

The bar near the port was still open and Reinhold turned his steps in the direction of the lighted windows. He quickly got very drunk. It didn't dull the thought of being a father. When the bartender finally threw him out, he crawled back to the ship like a stoker. Still the thought of being a father plagued him. Lying in his bunk, in the darkest hours of the night, the room spinning around his head, he made what he made a decision. He would never see Anya again. He didn't believe that it was his kid; he convinced himself that it wasn't his kid. She was with someone else.

His thoughts kept him awake that night and the alcohol wearing off made his mood in the morning surly. Without thinking, he mouthed off to the First Mate, informing his superior that he didn't really give a damn that there was rust developing on the outer rail of the port side of the ship. As a reward for his surliness, he was assigned port watch for the rest of their time in Kalmar and at the next port. It also became Reinhold's and only Reinhold's job to use the bosun chair to eradicate the rust on the rail and fill the resulting holes.

When they left port several days later, Reinhold was still hanging over the side, covered in rust dust, patching the hole, which irritated him. As they steamed out of Kalmar, Hein informed him that they were headed for Copenhagen, which made him angry. He was going to have to stand watch the whole time they were there.

On one of his nights standing watch while the rest of the crew was out enjoying Danish hospitality, a palm reader came on board the ship. She offered to read the sailor's palm for five *mark*. There wasn't much he could do for entertainment, so Reinhold took her offer.

At least, he thought, *it will be fun to see how far from the truth a palm reader can be.*

The gypsy took his hand and examined it closely, running her fingertips over the lines etched in his skin. She chanted a few words and looked at him.

"You are going to make a great journey across a wide and tossing sea," she began.

Reinhold could not help but snort. She looked sharply at him.

"It will not be for work. It is a spiritual journey." She continued to stroke his palm. "You are unhappy here and you know it. You struggle with the future. It will become clear to you one day, what you are supposed to do. You will accomplish your goals, but it will not be easy." She stroked a few more times, chanting again. "You will have four children."

Then she abruptly dropped his hand and left him standing at the top of the gangway, blinking in surprise, while she went off to find another customer.

Looking back, Reinhold was not proud of his decision. He wasn't proud of running away from his problems. He was not stupid, he knew the right thing to do but he couldn't bring himself to do it. The palm reader freaked him out. After her prediction, he told his friends what she said and about Anya. He was considering going back to Kalmar to take responsibility for the child. They were sitting in the mess hall, drinking a case of Carlsberg that Hein picked up at the brewery the night before. Reinhold had only an hour or so before he had to report for port watch.

"Four?" Hein had repeated, incredulously. "That is a lot of children."

"It's not so many," Nietz pointed out. "I come from a family of seven children. Now that's a lot of children."

"You Poles are good breeders," Hein said. "Almost as good as the Irish. I worked with an Irish guy once who said he had eleven brothers and sisters. Where does a person find time to have so many children?"

"Sometimes they come out more than one at a time." Nietz said. "How many do you think Anya will have?"

"I don't want any children right now!" Reinhold exclaimed, bringing them back to the more important subject at hand.

He didn't want to talk about large families right now. But the mention of so many kids made him think of home and his neighbor Anna Easberger.

"I can't have a kid right now. I am not even eighteen years old."

There was just about a month until his eighteenth birthday.

"You're not even eighteen yet?"

Werner was sitting quietly in a dark corner, drinking a beer. He took a liking to his bunkmate, Nietz, and to Hein and hung out with them, drinking beer but rarely joining whole-heartedly in the conversation. Reinhold had almost forgotten he was there.

"No, not yet."

"Then you have no business having a kid. You're still a kid yourself." He took another gulp of his beer.

"But it is the right thing to do." Reinhold sighed.

"No, its not. Why would you say that?"

Werner drained his beer and grabbed another, nodding a thank you to Hein as he gripped the cap in his teeth and twisted it open.

Reinhold thought about the question for a minute before answering.

"Because that's what a responsible person does. They take care of their children. They take responsibility for their actions, right?"

He was close to convincing himself that he needed to go back to Kalmar when Werner spoke again.

"That's a bunch of nonsense. What good are you going to be to a child? You don't know anything and you have no skills to earn a living on shore unless you want to be a laborer. In Sweden, that means chopping wood all day, every day. Or going underground to the mines. We all know that. That girl would be better off putting that kid up for adoption or giving it to the church." He swigged his beer again. "If she can't take care of it, the state will take it anyway."

"How old are you, Werner?" Reinhold was curious.

"Twenty five." He swigged his beer again. "And I am too young to have a child. I don't know anything yet either." Another swig. "I'll go so far as to say that if you leave this ship and go to Kalmar to be with that girl, I'll beat the crap out of you."

Reinhold was shocked by the comment. "Are you threatening me?"

"Yup. It is for the betterment of all society that I do. Stupidity shouldn't be tolerated and you're thinking about being stupid. No one should have kids before they are ready. That just makes you a bad father."

Werner downed the rest of his beer and excused himself to "return the beer to the ocean."

"The man has a point," Hein said. "How are you going to take care of a child? You can barely take care of yourself."

Reinhold scoffed at him. Then he shrugged. He suddenly felt very tired and was not looking forward to standing watch. Since it was punishment, he wasn't even getting overtime for it. Sighing, he got up and went to the coffee maker to make a fresh pot. He was going to need it.

Some of the crew of the *Midgard*. Werner is far right.
Photograph courtesy of Reinhold Scholz

Chapter 50: Rostok

Reinhold never knew what cargo they loaded in Copenhagen on that trip. He was too wrapped up in his own problems to care. Whatever they were carrying was bound for Rostok, a port Reinhold hadn't been to before. It was located in East Germany, a place that was not friendly to West Germans or to anyone else. The bosun informed the crew that when they arrived, before they reached the docks, an agent with the Soviet government would board with the pilot to check passports and accompany the ship to the dock. They were not to leave the port. Stepping even a few feet outside the perimeter, marked by an impressive looking fence complete with barbed wire and guard towers, would result in hostile fire. Unloading the cargo would be done as quickly as possible meaning that they could be underway, headed back to Sweden, in as little as two days.

"If you have any reason not to go to East Germany, I would get off the ship before it leaves Copenhagen in two days' time," The bosun concluded and dismissed them.

Reinhold was disappointed. He was hoping they were going to Bremerhaven.

The night before they left Copenhagen for Rostok, a sailor Reinhold didn't know very well called a meeting on the accommodation deck. His name was Niemec and he wanted the help of his fellow sailors to get a girl he knew out of East Germany. At first, the crew was not thrilled about it.

"What if we get caught?" Hein asked. "I am not going to a *gulag*[32] for your girlfriend."

A mutter of assent went through the group.

"Will we get paid? Does this girl have any money?"

"What about the bosun and the mates?"

"How do you plan on getting her on the ship?"

"Is she pretty?"

"Is she your girlfriend or can anyone have a go?"

Niemec waited patiently for the guys to stop calling out questions. Then he explained his plans.

"We will smuggle her on to the ship dressed as a man. Whoever is on watch will just let her walk passed. Then we'll hide her down

---

[32] *Gulag* is a Russian word for 'jail'.

here, behind a hatch. No one will know she is there. After Rostok we sail for Stockholm. It is a two day trip at the most. I think we can keep her hidden for two days. The mates and the bosun never come down here."

"Why does she want to leave her country?"

The group turned toward the voice, surprised by the question. The speaker was the deck boy, a lad of just fifteen years old, named Dieter.

"Because it is not her country. She is German, not Russian, and doesn't want the invader telling her how she has to live her life."

"And what do we get?" Another voice called.

"She can repay you as she sees fit. She is my girlfriend, yes, but not my wife."

The meaning of the statement was obvious to the sailors. After a few more questions, centered mostly on her appearance, they agreed to help. Niemec was so grateful to his fellow sailors that he offered to buy the first round at the port tavern in Rostok.

True to the word of the bosun, a Soviet official presented himself with a small group of underlings and the port pilot at the ladder of the *Midgard* promptly after it entered the port at Rostok. Passports were checked, papers signed, warnings issued, and the entire ship was searched thoroughly.

They can't honestly think that we're trying to smuggle something into this country, do they?

Reinhold watched as the official lackeys searched his bunk. He wondered if the men were ethnic Germans, forced into service of the Soviet regime or if they were transplants from Moscow. Once the men were done with their business on the ship, the ship was allowed to proceed to the dock.

"I hope we aren't here long," Hein said as they took their positions for docking. "These are not friendly people." He was eyeing the guard towers manned by soldiers with automatic weapons. "It is like everyone has their finger on a trigger."

He shuddered visibly. Reinhold held his tongue.

They met the young lady they were to help escape East Germany at the local port tavern. Her name was Hildy and she was a very attractive brunette with a button nose and grey eyes. Reinhold and several other sailors including Niemec, Hein, Nietz, and Werner sat in a corner of the tavern and listened to her story while she pretended to flirt with them. She was desperate to get out of Rostok. The new government had arrested her father and brother for treason and confiscated the family's butcher shop. That was three years ago during the transitioning and restructuring. The Soviets were trying to make examples of people, to assert their new authority. Hildy watched as her father and brother were executed in the town square. To support herself she became a prostitute and cleaning lady.

"I can't thank you enough for helping me." She told the sailors, tears welling up in her eyes.

Quickly, she brushed them away and laughed, plastering a smile on her face and flinging an arm around Niemec's shoulders. She cast a guarded glance at the bartender. He wasn't paying any attention to the table. Over drinks and Hildy's laughter, they worked out all the details to get her out of the country.

When the time came for the *Midgard* to leave port, Hildy was safely ensconced behind the hatch that led to the accommodations. To hide her feet, the only part of her that was visible, a resourceful sailor named Heinrich suggested they use the dustpan. It would look natural, he said, to have a dustpan propped against the wall. The sailors themselves tried to act natural, to go about their duties and not be on guard but it was very difficult when the Soviets came aboard to carry out their inspection. Everyone was very tense, not daring to look at each other. When the official descended into the accommodations, the tension reached an almost palpable level. But, the Soviets emerged empty handed and gave the OK for shove off. They accompanied the ship to the mouth of the harbor before disembarking. The crew breathed a small sigh of relief. One trial was over, but another was beginning. They had to keep the girl a secret for two days until they reached Stockholm.

Hildy, in order to avoid detection, was forced to stand behind the hatch door to the accommodations until they were out to sea, which was several hours. When Niemec went to free her, he found that the poor girl had passed out. She fell hard to the deck without the metal to support her. They installed her in Niemec's bunk and spent the rest of the trip to Stockholm taking turns in bed with her. Hildy didn't seem to mind but she also wasn't that interested. Reinhold only visited her once because he didn't like the vacant look staring back at him from her adorable little face. He liked his girls to enjoy themselves.

When they approached Stockholm, just before the pilot climbed up the ladder to guide them in, Hildy retreated behind the hatch, the dustpan was propped against her feet and the crew prayed that everything would be OK. The Swedish authorities weren't nearly as in depth as the officials in Rostok, being more interested at the time in contraband, not stowaways.

Once the ship was secured to the pier and the crew was freed from work for the night, they dressed Hildy up in an extra set of men's clothes and walked her off the ship as part of the shore bound sailors. Reinhold chuckled to himself at the memory. Hildy became like a bunny. As soon as her feet were on Swedish soil outside the state run port, she thanked the sailors and took off into the night, darting between groups of people and cars. The guys spent the rest of their night congratulating each other on a job well done. None of them, including Niemec, ever saw her again. Reinhold always hoped that she found a way to make a living for herself. He hoped that she wasn't caught and sent back to East Germany.

In Stockholm, the bosun gathered the sailors and informed them that the engineers had found something wrong with one of the ship's engines. They were leaving the next morning and heading directly to Hamburg where the ship was to enter dry dock at Blohm and Voss Shipyard. The crew was laid off with pay while the repairs were carried out. Of course, the bosun told them, they were free to sign off and find another ship, if they were so inclined. Reinhold had the feeling that the company wanted the sailors to sign off. That way, they didn't have to pay employees for not working. He chose to stay signed on and enjoy a few days relaxation in Hamburg. It had been a while since he visited the Reeperbahn. Hein, Nietz, and Werner also stayed on.

"I have a sister in Hamburg," Werner told them as they gathered up their gear in Hamburg and made to disembark. "I wired her to tell her I was coming to town. I usually stay with her."

Reinhold ended up staying with Werner and his sister for a few days. They went to the Reeperbahn and got obscenely drunk their first night in town. They browsed the selection of women in the windows before settling on one *puff* in particular.

"It's going to be nice to bed a woman without Nietz listening," Werner slurred as they followed their ladies to the upstairs rooms. Reinhold had to laugh.

Wait until he found out that Nietz took photos of him with one of his ladies and tried to sell them to the other sailors on the ship, he thought.

Nietz probably would have sold them too if he had gotten more of the lady and not so much of Werner. The photos shed a new light on the sailor. The huge man was huge in every way. Reinhold wondered if he noticed the new respect the others paid him.

Reinhold left Werner at his sister's and moved to a cheap boarding house for the last few days of their layup. Gisa, Werner's sister, took a strong liking to Reinhold and followed him around every minute that she could spare. He admitted that he liked the attention and Gisa was not a bad looking woman but she was his friend's sister. Reinhold had always considered the sisters and wives of friends as off limits. He left her place because Gisa was very encouraging and he was tempted to break his own rule.

Chapter 51: "Watchman!"

Life on the *Midgard* after the engine repair continued in its own strange way. Most of the crew returned, having thought of the break as a paid vacation. They were all eager to get back to work having spent a lot of money in their pursuit of happiness. The first port the *Midgard* visited after leaving Hamburg was Helsinki. Reinhold found himself standing port watch again as punishment for a charge of insubordination against the First Mate. He thought he was completely respectful when he pointed out to the mate that the *Midgard* was an old rust bucket and no amount of chipping, scraping, and painting was going to make it look any better than it did at the moment. He addressed the man as 'sir' at least. It was the middle of March and a cold wind was blowing in from the sea as Reinhold stood at the top of the gangway, shivering and trying to stay awake. Thinking that a fresh cup of coffee was in order, he headed to the kitchen.

Back on the deck, he leaned against the rail and sipped the hot coffee, watching another ship, a smaller vessel, glide into the harbor, lights a blaze. The Captain's voice screaming for the watchman made Reinhold jump in his skin and drop his mug of coffee as he ran off to find out what was going on. Upon reaching the Captain's suite, he stopped dead in his tracks. The sight was just too bizarre.

The old man was standing outside his salon in his nightclothes. In either hand, he held the collar of a fur coat worn by a completely naked woman, if you didn't count knee high boots. The women were chattering in Finnish. Reinhold blinked in surprise as the Captain yelled at him.

"Did you let these women on the ship?" He roared. "What is the meaning of this?"

"No, sir. They must have snuck on when I went to get a mug of coffee."

"Get them out of here now and never leave your post again! I'll put you off this ship right here and right now, watchman, you better believe it."

The Captain practically threw the women at Reinhold before disappearing into his salon, slamming the door behind him.

Reinhold took each woman by the arm and guided them none too gently toward the gangway. They chattered at him in Finnish.

347

Reinhold didn't understand a word nor did he try to communicate with them. He was so angry that they got him in trouble that he contemplated seriously just tossing them over board.

At the top of the gangway, he shoved them toward the pier, then took up a position that prevented them from getting around him, placing a hand on the rail on either side of him. The women continued chattering, trying to get him to let them back onboard. He knew that they were thinking of the crew and the money that could be made from them. After a few minutes of their pleading, Reinhold got very angry.

"Get the hell out of here!" he roared in Swedish.

That got their attention but they didn't move. He repeated the command in Swedish and in German. It wasn't until he removed his hands from the rail and made to remove them bodily that they finally left.

"What do you mean you kicked two naked women off the ship? *Dummkopf!* Why didn't you send them down to us?"

Hein was flabbergasted by the story Reinhold recounted to them in the morning. He wasn't surprised by the Captain's reaction but he was shocked by Reinhold's.

"I thought you were a playboy, a real ladies man, a fellow sailor, always on the lookout for *pflaume*."

Several other sailors agreed with Hein.

Reinhold hadn't thought of the women as possible entertainment for the crew. He was so taken aback by the situation that he blindly followed the orders of the Captain.

"The old man wanted them gone, so I got them off the ship. What else was I supposed to do? He threatened to put me off right then if they weren't gone fast."

Hein snorted. "What he doesn't know won't hurt him, right? In the future...."

"I know, I know, think of my fellow sailor," Reinhold interrupted. "And the *pflaume*." He added with a wicked smile.

Hein couldn't help but laugh. Reinhold's transgression was forgiven and plans immediately laid to go looking for beautiful and exciting Finnish women after work was done.

"Maybe one will try to cut you up with her razor blade," Hein joked, making a slashing motion across his own face and grinning.

Before breakfast on the day the *Midgard* was scheduled to leave Helsinki, the bosun informed the crew that they had cargo going to Spain.

"Yes, this is what I've been waiting for!" Nietz was the most excited Reinhold had ever seen him.

"Spain has an abundance of cheap hookers?" Reinhold chided.

"Yes, and they have a casino and you're going to visit it with me, smart ass."

"Oh, right, the place I need a tuxedo for. You know, I am not big on casinos."

Reinhold settled himself on the hatch covers to start splicing the lines they would need to unload the cargo in Spain.

"They are a waste of money."

Nietz snorted. "You bet they are but they can also be a lot of fun. And Biarritz is the biggest casino outside of Monte Carlo. They have food and shows and pretty girls."

It was Reinhold's turn to snort. "There are pretty girls everywhere. What do you care about pretty girls? I thought you thought they were full of themselves, and expensive."

"I wasn't talking about hookers! I mean the eye candy is outrageous."

"Eye candy?" Hein asked. "Who the hell wants eye candy? I want hand candy."

Reinhold laughed in agreement.

"Whatever." Nietz was getting frustrated with his friends. "You'll see when we get there."

"Do you even know that we are going anywhere close to Biarritz?" Hein asked. "The bosun said Spain, not France. Spain is a big country with a coastline on the Mediterranean and the Atlantic. What if we end up on the other side of the country?"

"I know we are going to Biarritz. We are going to be there for two days. I heard the mates talking about it this morning. Hold 3 has cargo for Biarritz. They don't want to tell us. They think we'll lose our minds or something. Then we'll go to Spain."

"Hold 3? There is just coal in there." Hein didn't believe him. "We'll see. I don't remember bringing coal to France before this."

"So that means that we can never bring coal to France?" Nietz shook his head. "I'll bet you a case of French beer, not Spanish, that we go to Biarritz."

"We'll see," Hein repeated.

It occurred to Reinhold that they might not be dropping off coal in Biarritz. They might be picking it up and loading it into Hold 3 on top of what was already there.

We'll see, he thought to himself. *There has got to be more there than just a casino.*

Chapter 52: Biarritz

It took longer for them to settle the argument than it should have under normal circumstances. For some reason unknown to the crew, the Captain ordered them to take the Skagerrak instead of the North Sea Canal. The *Midgard* wasn't even fully into the straits when they encountered a wicked windstorm. The seas picked up, tossing the ship around like a cat playing with a mouse.

Reinhold wished he could just wait the storm out like the off duty stokers, in the comfort, relative comfort, of his cabin, reading a book and smoking. He tried to sleep on the benches in the mess hall but was constantly shaken out of slumber by the movements of the storm and by the bosun.

Where there is a storm, there is problems on deck, he thought.

Twice at the height of the storm he volunteered to go out to refasten the canvas covering the hatches or catch a ventilator that had come lose and was rolling around the deck. The bosun tied a rope around his waist and sent him out from the wheelhouse. It took only about twenty minutes to repair the canvas or a few minutes to capture the ventilator but it felt like an eternity. An eternity filled with pitching metal, roaring wind, and smashing waves.

The first time out Reinhold paused to look around him only to discover that they were in a trough. On either side were thirty foot waves that hit the deck with the force of a train hitting a tree. The trip to the offending hatch cover was up hill part of the way and downhill part of the way. It was amazing how fast the ship was riding the swells.

Reinhold survived the outings without going overboard but one of his crew mates wasn't so lucky. Helmut went overboard with a washer, a wave that comes across the deck at knee level and sweeps you off your feet. He was trying to reposition a steam pipe that had come lose when it washed him right along with it over the side. Luckily, the rope and the reaction time of the bosun prevented him from drowning or even spending too much time in the frigid water. The crew hauled him back on deck and smacked the water out of him.

Niemec had the worst luck of all the crew. He went out to reattach a lose steam pipe when a washer took him right into one of the stout iron cleats, breaking his leg. To make matters worse, he was unable to stop himself from moving with the water towards a drainage scupper. The broken leg went through the opening in the rail and got stuck. Several sailors had to retrieve a screaming Niemec and get him into the mess hall. The Second Mate did the best job he could under the circumstances setting the broken leg. Niemec spent the rest of the trip around the Skagerrak alternating between drunk and sleeping.

It was another two days before the storm blew itself out. By the time they were on their way again, on some of the calmest seas Reinhold had ever seen, the crew hadn't had a hot meal or a dry sleep, or any sleep really, in damn near eight days. The trip around Denmark took nine days when it really should have taken less than half that time.

"They just had the worst flooding they have seen in many years along the coast in Belgium and England." Werner pointed out as they surveyed the damage to the deck from the storm.

There wasn't nearly as much destroyed as they anticipated. A few lose steam pipes, a ripped canvas cover, some dented ventilators, a few frayed lines.

"We were lucky." The bosun announced. "That could have been much worse than it was. We should have all of this repaired long before we get to Spain. But, first we have a stop to make in Bremerhaven, where Niemec requested we let him off."

At the mention of Spain, Hein looked pointedly at Nietz, his eyebrows pulled up in a questioning manner. Nietz ignored him.

The crew was rewarded for their endurance, and the extra work, through the windstorm by rising temperatures as they traveled south. By the time they docked in Bayonne it was like a beautiful summer day in northern Germany.

"Ha! You were wrong!" Hein said triumphantly to Nietz when the ship turned to make for the Adour River. "We are going to Bayonne!"

"Yeah, which means we are going to Biarritz!"

"They are two different places. What are you talking about?"

"Bayonne is the port for Biarritz."

"No it's not. Biarritz is the port for Biarritz!"

"My God, you two sound like a bunch of women!" Reinhold interjected. "Will you shut up if I get you both a case of beer?"

"Save your money, Reinhold," Nietz responded. "You are going to need it when we go to the casino."

"You are going to Biarritz, not we. Have a good bus ride." Hein sauntered down the gangway to the mess hall.

"Bus?" Reinhold questioned.

That didn't make him very happy. He had no desire to get off the ship in France at all, let alone get on a bus and travel around.

"It'll be fine." Nietz assured him. "I know the routes here. It is half an hour to the casino from the port."

Reinhold had not seen this part of the world yet. It was Basque country, Hein told him. A group of people as old as Europe itself, he claimed. Reinhold wasn't sure he believed all that, but it was beautiful country. He stood at the rail for a few minutes and watched the landscape on the starboard side of the River Adour. It was green even in late March and dotted with grazing animals. It wasn't the same kind of green as Germany, he noted. The color was a more washed out and under toned with brown. The approach to the city of Bayonne interrupted the rolling hills with red tile roofs and white washed walls. Dotted amongst these newer buildings were stone fortresses. They looked like something out of a fairy tale.

The town was like something he had seen on a postcard. The main part of the city reminded him of Amsterdam or one of the other cities in the Netherlands with their tall, narrow buildings displaying brightly painted moldings. They lined the river almost right to the bank. Low stone bridges prevented the *Midgard* from traveling too far along the waterway.

"You know, the men here fight bulls."

Reinhold turned to see Helmut behind him, leaning on a ventilator, spitting tobacco juice.

"What do you think, Schultz? Are you man enough to get in a ring with an angry bull?"

Reinhold felt his anger rise. "I know I am. I don't think you are."

Instead of continuing the conversation and making himself more angry, Reinhold went back to work. The pilot was guiding them towards a slip not far away and the tugs were approaching. They would dock soon. He kept Helmut's comment about bullfighting in the back of his mind. That was something he would like to see.

The harbor in Bayonne was like no other Reinhold had encountered. It was almost medieval in its appearance. The industrial machines seemed out of place amongst the old buildings and bucolic setting. The women were like nothing he had seen before either. They were dark in every way: hair, skin, and eyes. They wore long, brightly colored skirts and sandals. Reinhold found the idea of a new kind of woman very exciting. He couldn't wait to get off the ship and really see the place. He didn't even care so much that he was in France. This was a different kind of France than he visited with the *Fona*.

The Biarritz, as Nietz said, was half an hour by bus. They got their tuxes on and headed out for some shore life. Hein even decided to join them, saying there was nothing better to do.

Everything started off good. Biarritz was beautiful, just the right mix of coastal and desert, making it have a blessed oasis feel. The bus dropped them off in front of the casino Barrière, near the beach. There was still plenty of daylight and a whole night ahead until work the next day so the sailors decided to see the beach and the waterfront before committing to the gaming tables.

The beach was full of beautiful women in bathing suits lounging under umbrellas on blankets and towels. The guys wandered down the sandy strip, gazing at the 'eye candy', as Nietz said. They hiked a little ways up on the rocky coastline to get a better look. The sea was an emerald green with darker, bluer patches just under the surface and lines of white foam rippling across it. It was lovely. As the sun sank, the guys tired of people watching and dune climbing and wandered back toward the casino Barrière.

Reinhold didn't want to think about the rest of that day. What an idiot he became once inside the glitzy building.

Twenty five hundred mark, *gone in four hours!* He thought to himself. *Damn Nietz and his casino!*

As first, Reinhold was winning. The roulette wheel kept hitting his black 21. Unfortunately, that luck didn't follow him to the craps table. When he ran through his winnings and the cash he brought with him, Nietz convinced him to dip into his post book.

354

It was too damn convenient that they could take money out of it at the casino, instead of me having to actually be in Lübeck to get it. He shook his head sadly at his younger self's lack of self-control.

They stumbled back to the *Midgard* late that night drunker than hell and broke, not a *mark* between them. Over the next few days, Nietz told the rest of the crew about Reinhold's epic loss at Barrière.

He poured a lot of salt in that wound, Reinhold thought, still annoyed by Nietz's lack of couth.

Chapter 53: Pasaia

A dolphin pod appeared off the starboard side of the *Brandenburg*. They kept pace with the ship for a few minutes, playing in the turbulent water kicked up by the prow. Reinhold watched the creatures. He never ceased to find them amusing. Having had their fun with the ship, the dolphins moved away and out of sight. Reinhold lit another cigarette and blew some smoke rings. It was a poor entertainment substitute for the dolphins. He learned on the *Midgard* that the waters around the Iberian Peninsula were full of dolphins and other colorful fish.

Instead of heading back north as the crew expected, the *Midgard* traveled around Spain and Portugal. The weather was beautiful, the work was hard, and the girls were exotic. Reinhold would never forget his first trip into the Pasajes River in the Basque country. He was Quartermaster and the ship was traveling parallel to a sheer rock face section of coastline. When the Second Mate called for hard to port, Reinhold instinctively did what the mate instructed but his heart skipped a beat thinking they were going straight into the rock. Then he noted the lighthouses, brightly colored and separated by about two hundred and fifty meters. The mate continued to bark orders that resulted in Reinhold steering the ship between the lighthouses into a wide river mouth.

"Wow."

The word escaped Reinhold's lips before he could stop it. The mate turned away from the bridge windows to look back at him.

"First time to Pasajes?"

"Yes, sir."

His eyes were scanning the wonder in front of him. On all sides, the river mouth was surrounded by high, rocky mountains that sloped steeply to the magnificently blue river. Here and there, they were covered in short pine trees and tall grasses which created a patchwork of dark green against the reddish brown of the native turf. Winding around the steep slopes ran roads connecting clusters of red roofed villas. It was one of the most beautiful, most tranquil feeling spots he had ever seen. It reminded him of the story of Don Juan. He read the book a couple of years ago while sailing around the Scandinavian countries and tried to picture the scenery described by the author. Now he felt like he understood.

As he stood gaping and trying to keep the ship on course, a small motorboat pulled up beside them and two men climbed up the ladder.

Every river has a pilot, Reinhold thought to himself as as two black haired, olive skinned men appeared on the bridge.

They took up their positions and the pilot began calling orders. Reinhold watched the scenery glide passed. The clusters of houses were getting closer together. It didn't take long for the town to come into view around a bend. It was lovely. The red tiled roofs sat atop white and tan buildings lined with balconies. They were varying shapes, some short and squat, other tall and narrow. They ran right up to the water's edge. Scattered amongst them, some high on the sides of the hills, were solid stone constructions that recalled an earlier time. Reinhold wondered what awaited him on shore.

"But she looks so young," Reinhold said as he sipped his beer at one of the many small waterfront bars in Pasaia.

The *Midgard* docked earlier in the afternoon, releasing about thirty men into the small town of Pasaia. Reinhold was overjoyed that the local ladies were quick to make their acquaintances. Werner, Hein, Reinhold, and a few other guys found their way to a lovely water side bar to enjoy a few beers, the wonderful climate, and the company of a few ladies.

As the night progressed, the sailors started disappearing with ladies for further, more private entertainment. The lady sitting on Reinhold's lap was a young one. He was concerned that she was probably too young for him.

"That's because you like older women," Hein teased.

"Yes, yes I do. They're better in bed."

A thought of Anya slipped unwelcome to his mind and he quickly banished it.

He eyed the girl on his lap as she sipped the beer he bought her.

Hein laughed at his friend. "Who cares as long as they say it's ok?"

"Let's switch then. You take this one and I'll take yours."

"Not a chance. I like this one." Downing the last of his beer, Hein continued. "Come on. Let's get out of here and see what they can do."

Reinhold was too drunk and too in need of the company of a woman to argue further. "Ok. Let's go."

Hein's girl led them to a nearby boarding house where they paid for rooms. Before going upstairs, they each paid their girls. The older girl said something in rapid Spanish to Reinhold's younger girl before they parted ways.

Looking back, Reinhold remembered his experience with that girl being very awkward. She didn't know anything. She stood in the corner of the room, frightened and wary of him while he undressed. It wasn't until he removed his watch that he felt that he had her attention. He got her to come to him, to touch him even. She was staring at the watch and gestured in a manner that indicated she wanted to see it more closely. He handed it to her, drunkenly, without thinking. It felt so good to have a woman's warm hand on his manhood. He closed his eyes and pretended she was Kristal.

After a few minutes, he coaxed her into bed, which wasn't easy since he didn't speak Spanish and she didn't speak German. She didn't relax. Reinhold decided that the best way to approach this situation was to treat her as he would any girl he had paid for a night's entertainment. He went ahead enjoying himself while she lay there almost like a dead fish. He couldn't help noticing that her body was soft and rounded like a child's. He wondered if it was because she was Spanish. She was so tight, that he wouldn't have been surprised if this was one the first times she had been with a man. In the back of his head, Reinhold knew this could be bad. Since he paid for this ride, he intended to enjoy it so he stopped thinking and concentrated on feeling.

Later, in the courtyard of the building, while exchanging anecdotes of their experience, Reinhold noticed his watch was missing. He didn't see it laying on the dresser when he got dressed. The last time he saw it was right before the girl started playing with him.

"You had it when you went upstairs?" Hein asked.

"Yes. I gave it to the girl to look at it. She sort of asked to see it."

"Did she give it back to you?" Hein features darkened.

Reinhold thought. "I don't remember. She was playing with me at the time. It was hard to concentrate. Especially since I was wondering the whole time how old she is."

"She is twelve."

Reinhold's stomach lurched. "What? How do you know that?"

"My girl told me. At first, she tried to say that she was sixteen but when I pressured her a bit, she told me that she was really twelve. They are sisters."

Reinhold was floored. "Twelve. And what do you mean by pressured?"

"Don't worry about it. They start them early in Spain. You just helped her support her family. It's no big deal. Stealing your watch is a big deal. Let's go ask her about it. She is still in that room up there."

They went to the room and knocked. The girl opened the door. Her eyes widened in surprise when she saw them standing there. Hein said something in broken Spanish. The girl shook her head. Hein raised his voice and asked roughly the same question. Again, the girl shook her head.

"Wait here," Hein said, walking into the room and shutting the door behind him.

Reinhold leaned against the wall, waiting. He heard voices inside. They got steadily louder. He didn't understand the words. Then he heard the sound of a punch followed by the crash of objects hitting the floor. He heard Hein's raised voice and the whimpering sound of the girl's voice. Again, the sound of a punch and objects, this time unmistakably a human body, hitting the floor. More raised voices. Hein was half shouting. He didn't want to call attention to himself, Reinhold knew. The next sound of a punch landing came before the girl could have gotten off the floor. There was the dull thud of something hitting the wooden floor.

Reinhold was sickened by what was going on. He was about to intervene when Hein opened the door and strode into the hallway. He handed Reinhold the missing watch and walked away toward the stairs. Reinhold stood there for a second, staring at the watch. He glanced into the room and saw the girl picking herself up, wiping blood from her nose and mouth. She looked at him, miserable and defiant. Their eyes met for an instant before she kicked the door shut.

Sighing, Reinhold followed his friend down the stairs and accepted his suggestion that they see if the bars were still open before they went back to the ship. Reinhold thanked Hein for getting his watch back. Neither of them ever mentioned it again.

Chapter 54: Viana do Castelo

The *Midgard* sailed the lower extremities of the Bay of Biscay along the Spanish coast. After a few weeks, she made her way into the North Atlantic and down the coast of Portugal. They port hopped for several days, never staying in one spot long enough to get any time ashore. Reinhold was getting sick of the grey of the ship and the sound of metal under his feet. He wanted some time on solid ground.

Finally, on Thursday, April 23, 1953, the *Midgard* sailed into Viana do Castelo. The sailors were to have a few days break while the shore crew unloaded the cargo. Since they were carrying fertilizer, the shore crew was also tasked with cleaning the corrosive substance out of the hull, a job that would take them at least two days to complete. Reinhold was a happy sailor because not only were they staying put for a few days, he didn't have to stand port watch. The bosun gathered his crew just after the one of the two tugs the small port operated nudged them into the pier.

"The First Mate has volunteered to take some of you guys up the river tomorrow on a sightseeing expedition."

He pointed inland toward the hills beyond. "Anyone interested who is not scheduled to work tomorrow needs to let the mate know now. He is going to get the small boats down tonight so there will be no delay in the morning. Dismissed."

Reinhold went directly to the First Mate and told him to save a spot in the boat for him. The mate looked a bit disappointed that Reinhold intended to join them. Reinhold shrugged him off and went to get showered. There was a new town to explore tonight.

The town turned out to be beautiful, not a lot of fun, but rustic and romantic. Reinhold half expected the characters from the fairy tales he had read to materialize in the main square only to disappear down one of the many narrow, winding alleyways. There were old stone churches and monasteries with pillared cloisters that looked out on stone paved squares that were laid down a hundred years or more prior. The squares were lined with buildings ornately carved with figures and designs. There were large, mansion like structures that had to be hundreds of years old built entirely out of stone; and, of course, the red tiled roofs and white washed walls of the villas.

High on a hill overlooking the small town, and accessible by a long flight of stairs, was a magnificent square church with a rose window and a dome. A sign said it was called Santuário de Santa Luzia Erica. Behind the church was an equally spectacular building that Reinhold thought would be a fitting place for a governor to live. The group of sailors came across several watering holes, but Reinhold didn't drink too much. Just sitting in the cafes, absorbing the new sights and smells was enough for him that night. He was particularly enthralled with a pair of dancers performing in one of the squares. They were so energetic and graceful and the music so haunting that everyone had no choice but to watch them. When their dance ended, there was a brief silence before an eruption of applause from the audience scattered around the square at the cafes and restaurants. It was almost magical.

The next morning, Reinhold loaded into one of the small boats and headed up river with some of the crew and the First Mate. They left the town of Viana do Castelo, maneuvered around the shifting, semi-solid sand bars of the delta, and passed into rolling farm country, green and tan. In the distance were large dusty looking mountains, shaping the landscape into a broad river valley. Reinhold felt transported back in time to a simpler lifestyle, something akin to the way he grew up in Ratekau. They passed small villages where children ran with chickens and goats. People trudged along country roads, driving herds of sheep and cows from field to field. His fellow sailors made off color jokes about the farmers sexual preference for animals as opposed to women but Reinhold didn't find the jokes funny. He felt bad for them and their ignorance.

Damn city boys, he thought. *Sheep fuckers, my ass. What would they do if they ever had to milk a cow or pluck a chicken?*

The small boats with the sailors stopped in Ponte de Lima for lunch at a small eatery near the river. Over lunch, the First Mate recounted some history of the region. Viana do Castelo, he said, was once a great port, even though you would never know it now by its backwater appearance. Portugal, he reiterated, was a very poor country. However, during the Age of Exploration, Viana do Castelo was an important, thriving center.

"That is why there are so many big mansions in the city," the mate continued. "The explorers wanted to be close to their ships so they built magnificent homes. They say that Alvaro Velho set sail from here on the expedition that found the Congo. With the rich folks, came the poor folks and slowly a town grew. They say that millions

of *mark* in gold and sugar and wine and other foreign products went through this port at the height of its prosperity. The big, beautiful buildings, if you noticed, are all of two styles: Renaissance and Baroque. They were mostly all built around the same time. Today, it is an excellent place to buy fish or to go fishing. There is deep water not far off the coast."

There was a pause while the First Mate took a swig from his Portuguese beer. The silence was filled with Hein's voice.

"How do you know all this, sir?"

The First Mate looked disgusted for a second before smoothing out his features and answering. "I read, Hein, and I paid attention in school."

"My school got bombed," a voice from the end of the table exclaimed.

Glancing, Reinhold saw Manfred, a guy about his age that he didn't deal with too much. Manfred was a kitchen boy who had signed on when the ship was in for engine repair. He mentioned once that he grew up right in Hamburg, near the port. Instead of addressing the comment, the First Mate got up from the table, telling them that the boats would leave in five minutes.

The sailors went to take a look around the small village and smoke a cigarette before getting back on the river. They met a group of local kids outside the cafe. They crowded around the men, begging and gawking. Reinhold gave the kids some coins before shooing them away. One older boy asked with hand gestures for a cigarette. Reinhold laughed as he handed it over. He didn't laugh when he caught an adorable little girl trying to pickpocket him.

They continued up river as far as Ponte da Barca. The landscape was the same, but even more bucolic. The amount of farms had increased greatly but so had the amount of trees. Reinhold thought it was just lovely.

If I could spent my life here, on one of these farms, with a nice wife, maybe I would mind being a farmer.

These pleasant pondering were interrupted by the sounds of gunfire that echoed off the rolling hills, sharply and ominously. Reinhold jerked upright in his seat, alert.

What the hell was that all about?

"That is our cue to go back to the ship." The First Mate announced from the other boat.

The small vessels made hasty turns in the river and accelerated back the way they had come.

"What was that? Gunshots?"

"Yes, yes. We all know it was gunshots." The First Mate was tense and irritated. "It could be anything. A farmer putting down a lame animal, a hunter shooting a duck, anything."

He sounded like he was trying to convince himself of this.

"Isn't there fighting around here?" Hein shouted over the drone of the outboard engines.

"No, Hein," the First Mate said. "You are thinking of the Basques in Spain."

He turned his attention back to the river, ignoring Hein's further questions.

"What are you talking about?" Reinhold questioned Hein.

"There is trouble with the Basques." Hein said somewhat flippantly. "They want an independent country. They feel, from what I have heard, that they were treat unfairly under Franco, a target, you know, of discrimination. So, they are starting to fight back. They are quick to defend themselves against anyone they think are outsiders." Hein ended his explanation with a shrug of indifference.

Reinhold was deflated. His opinion of the beautiful country they had been traveling in was destroyed by this new information.

There really is fighting everywhere, he thought. *In Europe at least. I really have to get out of here.*

He sat quietly in the boat the rest of the way back to the *Midgard*, contemplating the future, his future. Again and again, his thoughts turned to what he had heard about Australia and America.

"America?" Nietz exclaimed. "You've never been there, have you?"

Reinhold mentioned at supper that night that he had good things about America.

"No, never been there. I have read a bunch about it."

Nietz snorted. "Expensive country filled with snotty people who have a bad opinion of Germans. You'd be better off in Australia."

"It's a boring place for sailors, America," Werner added. "The women are stuck up and prostitution is illegal. You're lucky if you can even get a woman to speak to you never mind getting one into bed. Nietz is right, you'd be better off in Australia."

Reinhold sighed. That was the opinion he always heard. Australia would be better. One day he would find out for himself. Seeing new vistas in Southern France and Spain had made him begin to think that he should do longer hauls to see more of the world. He went to sleep that night thinking of where he would go first. He came up with Australia.

Chapter 55: A Very Bad Thing

The morning of April 25, 1953 dawned clear and beautiful. Reinhold dragged himself out of bed at 6:30. He had a rough time sleeping. His mind was running with thoughts of his future in Australia. He got a coffee from the galley and stood at the rail, watching the sunrise over the mountains in the distance, tinging the sky with pinks and lavenders. It was one of his favorite times of the day. He could hear the quiet lapping of the calm water against the pier and, in the distance, the morning calls of the mating birds. All around him, the port was coming to life with muffled, sleepy sounds.

By 7:30 he was standing, yawning still, beside hold three on the starboard side of the ship, waiting for orders. The cargo had been unloaded the day before and Reinhold was one of the cleaning crew.

At least it's not the fertilizer hold, he thought to himself.

The bosun appeared on the port side, whistling and gesturing for the scattered sailors to join him. Without thinking, Reinhold started across the hatch beam traversing the open hull. The beam was no more than a support for the iron planks that covered the hatch. It was about a foot wide. About halfway across, Reinhold realized his feet were no longer touching the metal. He was falling.

Looking back, Reinhold remembered nothing. He didn't remember hitting the bottom of the hatch. He didn't remember the desperate scramble on the part of his fellow sailors to get down to him. He didn't remember being placed on a stretcher and hoisted to the deck. He didn't remember being rushed in an open backed, port owned truck to the local hospital in Viana do Castelo. He didn't remember the doctors and nurses working on him. Standing in the intense heat of the Caribbean sun on the sweltering deck of the *Brandenburg*, far from the accident scene, Reinhold was sure he didn't want to remember any of what happened that day.

He remembered blinking open his eyes to find he was lying in a strange room. It was empty save the bed, a white enameled cabinet, and a chair. On the wall to his left was a framed picture of the Virgin Mary next to a closed white door. On the right was an open door. Sounds drifted in from the hallway. There were voices speaking a language he didn't understand. There were sounds of pain, moaning and whimpering, but there was also laughter. He had no idea where he was or the time of day.

Then he felt pain. It started somewhere in his side and radiated outward, hitting every nerve as it moved, making him want to wraith but he wasn't able. Looking down at himself, he saw a rubber sheet covered him. There was blood on the sheet. As he breathed out, he saw the tiny speckles of red increase. He couldn't move his arms to his face to prove to himself that he was bleeding out his nose and mouth. Somewhere, deep inside, a panic took hold. He opened his mouth to call for help and realized that he couldn't. A tube was restricting his vocal cords. The noise that came out was pathetic: a rasping wheeze that loosely formed the word 'help'.

To his surprise, a woman's face appeared around the corner of the doorframe. Just as quickly as it appeared, it disappeared. He tried to call for help again but got only the rasping wheeze. He tried to move, to get up but couldn't. He was in excruciating pain and an awful panic.

What the hell happened? Why am I restrained?

He questioned himself, trying to remember why he was in a hospital. Was he still in Portugal? He was pursuing these thoughts in his pain clouded mind when a man in a white coat and a colorful tie appeared in the doorway. He smiled at Reinhold as he approached the bed. A nurse came behind him with a needle. She moved the sheet and jabbed it into Reinhold's right thigh. Almost instantly, the pain in his lower extremities began to subside. So did his panic. He relaxed against his pillows and looked warily at the doctor who had made himself comfortable in the chair next to the bed.

"Reinhold Scholz," the doctor said questioningly.

He had a thick accent but good German pronunciation and limited vocabulary. Reinhold simply nodded.

"You fell," the doctor continued. "Do you remember?"

"No," Reinhold rasped in response.

"Better like that," the doctor said, struggling a bit with the German words. "You fell three days ago. You sleep since."

Reinhold's eyebrows went up in surprise. "Three?"

"Yes. Very bad condition." The doctor shook his head gravely. "You almost died."

Reinhold let that sink in to his drug laced mind.

I almost died.

"Am I going to be ok?" He rasped.

The doctor avoided the question, asking questions of his own instead. "Herr Scholz, you know where you are?" He got out a pen.

"Portugal. Viana do Castelo, right?"

The doctor smiled at him before making notes on his clipboard. "Yes, Reinhold. You know how you got here?"

"I sailed here on a ship, the *Midgard.*" Reinhold thought for a second. "We brought fertilizer from Spain or France, maybe further away, Germany, perhaps. We are to go to Italy next."

He frowned. He didn't want to admit it, but something told him he wasn't going to Italy.

The doctor nodded, still making notes. "The Captain of your ship will be here later with paperwork. He says you have a sister in Germany. You get mail from her. Is that true?"

Reinhold nodded. "Lisa. She lives in Lübeck."

"We will contact her, if you give us an address, to let her know that you are here."

Reinhold nodded. He was concerned greatly that the *Midgard* was leaving port without him. This was bad, very bad. "When can I leave?"

The doctor looked surprised. "Herr Scholz, Reinhold, you are to be here for a long time. You have extensive injuries. The right side of your body was completely...." He groped for a word. "shattered."

The doctor reached into his pocket, taking out a pack of cigarettes and a lighter.

"Shattered?"

"Yes. Your knee, hip, wrist, ribs, and shoulder are all damaged. Your lungs bleed. One is ruptured. Very bad." The doctor shook his head again. "Very bad. But, you remain alive. You will recover but it will be a slow thing."

Reinhold's eyelids were getting heavy. He had one more question to ask before succumbing to the morphine coursing through his veins. "Who are you?"

The doctor stood and removed his glasses, looking down at Reinhold as he puffed his cigarette. "My name is Dr. Lubidos."

Chapter 56: Like A Canned Herring

Reinhold had very few recollections from his first days in the hospital in Viana do Castelo. He remembered Capt. Müller coming to visit.

"Scholz," he began, "you are not in good shape. You are lucky to be alive."

The expression on the Captain's face was depressing. Reinhold knew he must look bad, covered with a bloody sheet, blood seeping out of his nose and mouth, and his face bruised.

Reinhold could only nod in response. He wanted to scream that this was impossible. He ran across that beam hundreds of times, thousands if you count the hatch beams on all the other ships. The Captain must have known what he was thinking.

"Accidents happen."

Capt. Müller went on to explain that the *Midgard* was leaving port the next day.

"There is no way that you will be able to travel. The doctors think you are going to be here for a couple of months. When you are well enough to move, go down to the sailor's agent at the port and tell them who you are, that you work for Poseidon. They will contact the office and arrange for you to get home. Get a ship back to Germany, whatever ship is going to where you want to go. The company will take care of everything. You just have to get back in shape, sailor, so you can rejoin the *Midgard*."

Reinhold knew that it was inevitable, but hearing the news that the *Midgard* was leaving from the Captain's mouth was depressing.

A couple of months, he thought, his depression deepening.

After Capt. Müller's visit, the nurse gave him more morphine and he slept a painless sleep. In his mind's eye, he saw the *Midgard* sailing out of the port in the brilliant light of a perfect sunset.

It was not easy for Reinhold to look back at those early days in the hospital. The pain was so bad that he would scream in helplessness, begging for something to make it go away. Every breath was agony, every twitch of his body a nightmare on his nervous system. The nurses shot him up with morphine and he drifted away on the comforting cushion of the drug.

Dr. Lubidos and his colleague, Dr. Amico, came to check on him, nodding to themselves and making notes on clipboards. They would say a few encouraging phrases to Reinhold before leaving him. A week into his stay, a pretty nurse with very black hair removed the rubber sheet. Reinhold was encouraged. He soon realized, however, that the removal of the sheet didn't change his position.

For weeks, Reinhold laid in bed like a canned herring, alternating between sleeping and staring at the wall, to drugged to focus on anything in particular. The most exciting part of his day was when the pretty nurses came to administer his medications and painkillers or when the orderlies came to change the sheets and empty the bedpan. He tried to communicate with the nurses but they just made soothing noises to him like a child. The orderlies just ignored him.

After a few weeks, when the pain began to subside and his body began to mend, he found that he was just plain bored. The hospital had no readable books or magazines. They were all in Portuguese or Spanish. He asked if his sea bag had a book in it but the doctors said they didn't think so.

Nietz probably kept my books, cheap bastard!

With his shoulder all taped up and immobile, he wondered if he could even hold one in front of his face and turn the pages.

Reinhold spent some of his waking time testing his body. He remembered lying in bed with his eyes closed, concentrating his morphine filled consciousness on one joint at a time. Dr. Lubidos said that he had shattered the right side, so he began with his right knee. He told his knee to bend and it tried, moving as much as the tight tape around it would allow. The pain was evident through the layer of painkillers. Once his knee stopped responding, he moved to his hip and repeated the process. The hip's response wasn't as good as the knee's. He didn't know what was holding his hip together, whether it was tape like the knee or something else. Whatever it was didn't allow for much movement. He moved on to his shoulder. The shoulder twitched in response to Reinhold's requests that it move. The tape was very tight. He ended his efforts with his wrist, which responded nicely. It hadn't been as badly damaged. Luckily it wasn't the same wrist he had problems with in the past. The hip, it appeared, took most of the impact from the fall. This exercise always left him exhausted and discouraged. As far as he could judge for himself, there was more damage to his right side then the doctor had let on. So, he laid there, drugged and dazed, waiting to get better.

Just when Reinhold thought he couldn't take another second of confinement to bed or to the plain room, Dr. Amico arrived with a chess board. He displayed the game questioningly and Reinhold nodded his approval enthusiastically, so happy he could have cried. Finally, something to do! The two of them sat and played a game of chess. Reinhold was rusty and lost mightily to the doctor, the first time. It became a ritual for them to play whenever the doctor had a few minutes.

Soon, Reinhold was back in top form and beating Dr. Amico soundly. Reinhold suspected it was because the other patients he was tending preoccupied his opponent's mind. They had a few exchanges that were close to actual conversations. Looking back, one in particular stood out. On this day, both Dr. Amico and Dr. Lubidos came to see him.

Reinhold had been in the hospital for four weeks and was recovering nicely. They stopped his morphine cold turkey three days earlier and he was experiencing withdrawal symptoms. He was sure these symptoms were the reason why he had the pleasure of both doctor's company on this day. He played chess with Dr. Amico while Dr. Lubidos looked on, making notes on his clipboard when Reinhold's hand visually trembled or when he wiped sweat from his forehead and upper lip or when he cursed loudly in anger at an ill-conceived move. Reinhold lost the first match to Dr. Amico. They were setting up the board for a second game when Dr. Lubidos spoke.

"How are you feeling, Reinhold?" The doctor's German had improved from their first conversation.

"Fine, just fine." Reinhold answered.

He was lying, of course. There was still a good amount of throbbing in his joints and he desperately wanted a shot of morphine. He also began to dread the changing of his bandages. It took all his will power not to react to pain, to just let them do their work and be done with it.

"You know why we had to stop the morphine?"

"I assume that you don't want me getting addicted to it."

"Yes, that is correct. Are you in pain?"

"A little," Reinhold said cautiously.

He hoped that the doctors would reconsider and give him a dose.

"It will pass with time."

Reinhold was disappointed. It was not the answer he had been looking for at all.

"When can I leave? Rejoin my ship?"

The doctors laughed. Dr. Amico spoke first.

"We like your determination, Reinhold, but you will not be leaving for several more weeks."

"First," continued Dr. Lubidos, "we have to get you up and walking. Do you think that you are up to this?"

"Yes."

Reinhold hadn't even hesitated to think about the question. Anything that would get him out of bed sounded great.

"Good," Dr. Lubidos continued. "We will start that tomorrow. We will take away...."

The word escaped him. He pointed to the bedpan on the floor next to the bed.

"The bedpan?"

"Yes, bedpan. Maybe you can even wash yourself in the tub in the bathroom." He gestured toward the closed door.

"This that what that is in there? A bathroom?"

Dr. Lubidos nodded before lighting a cigarette. The room was silent for a minute while Reinhold and Dr. Amico started their next game of chess.

"Why are you so eager to go back to your ship, Reinhold?"

Dr. Amico looked questioningly at his colleague.

Reinhold was surprised by the question.

"Because it is my job."

"There must be other, less dangerous, things you could do instead of sailing?"

Reinhold frowned at the pawn in his hand, deciding where to move it, but also buying time to answer the doctor's question. He placed the pawn and turned his attention to Dr. Lubidos.

"I like sailing. I have seen some beautiful places and met some great friends. There are other places I want to see before I settle down."

"Where do you want to see?"

Reinhold moved another pawn, taking one of Dr. Amico's pawns.

"Australia and America." He answered the question without thinking.

Dr. Lubidos snorted, startling both Dr. Amico and Reinhold.

"I don't know about Australia. Many sheep ranches, I hear. But America! Why would you want to go there?"

"I don't know." Reinhold moved another piece. "People say it is nice, a good place to live. Peaceful and good jobs."

"Hmmmm," Dr. Lubidos thought for a second, his eyes scanning the room in agitation. "I like you, Reinhold, and I was hoping that after you leave us that you would write me and let me know how you are doing."

Reinhold was happy to hear this and was about to say so when the doctor continued. "But, if you move to America, you can forget about speaking with me again."

Reinhold was shocked by the hostility in the man's voice. He didn't understand.

"What do you mean? You don't like America?"

"It is not that I don't like America. It is hard to explain what I mean. If you understood Portuguese, I could explain, but in German, I cannot. It is a feeling, an idea that I don't know the words for."

There was silence for several minutes. Reinhold moved his pieces to counter Dr. Amico's moves. The doctor lit another cigarette. In his mind, he was wondering why the doctor had such a bad opinion of America.

"Have you been to America, Dr. Lubidos?"

"No," he responded. "I don't need to go there. I have heard enough."

He and Dr. Amico had a rapid, although brief, conversation in Portuguese before he addressed Reinhold again.

"I'll be back tomorrow to get you up and walking again. We'll get you out of here as soon as we can so you can continue your world tour. Hopefully, you go to Australia before you go to America."

With that, he excused himself.

Chapter 57: Portugal

True to his word, Dr. Lubidos was back the next day and Reinhold's days lying in bed like a canned herring came to a painful end. With the help of orderlies under the direction of the doctor, he made it to the bathroom only to be disappointed by the room. There was a toilet, yes, but it didn't flush without assistance from a bucket of water. There was an old tin tub and a bucket for filling it.

At least there is water in the sink, Reinhold thought, scratching his month old beard.

He was looking forward to shaving. The hospital returned his sea bag to him so that he could use his own personal effects. He suspected it was because they couldn't afford to get him any others. The shaving had to wait for another day, however. The trip to the bathroom sapped his energy.

By the end of the week, with a lot of determination and equally as much anger, Reinhold made it outside. The hospital had a small courtyard with benches. He made it to one and collapsed with the effort. The nurse that escorted him left to run an errand, leaving him to relax. His knee, hip, and shoulder all throbbed while his lungs flamed but it felt good to be outside in the fresh air.

He breathed deeply despite the pain. His arm was in a sling, but that was nothing compared to where he had been recently. Nurses and orderlies, priests and doctors passed him sitting there and they all nodded their hellos, staring in curiosity. At first, he thought people were just being nice. Then he realized that he stuck out like a bad potato. His blond hair, blue eyes, and fair skin were far from ordinary.

Everyone in town has probably heard of me, he thought to himself. *The German guy who fell and almost died and is now laid up in the hospital like a limp, pathetic herring. That's how you get famous. Thank God those ugly bruises are gone.*

He couldn't help snickering sardonically, trying to pull his pride together. His mood had not improved when Dr. Lubidos joined him on the bench. They exchanged greetings. The doctor obviously sensed Reinhold's discomfort.

"I was wondering, Reinhold, if you would like to join my family and I for a meal this Sunday. My wife is a good cook."

He paused for a second. When Reinhold didn't answer he continued. "There are some people who would like to meet you, the wives of the other doctors mostly. I think it would be good for you to get out of the hospital."

"That sounds nice." He added, remembering his manners, "I would be honored to meet your family."

Reinhold thought that the doctor was just taking pity on him. Once again, his pride was wounded. He reminded himself that it would be nice to get the hell out of the hospital; even if it was just for the afternoon.

"Good, good. Maybe we can take you on a bit of a tour and show you my beautiful country. It will be good for you."

Dr. Lubidos clapped Reinhold on the back and excused himself to his rounds.

Looking back, Reinhold recognized his afternoon with Dr. Lubidos and his family as one of the most relaxing days of his life. Miraculously, his familiar grey suit appeared in his room that morning, washed and pressed complete with the white scarf he liked to wear with it. There was also a freshly laundered white strip of cotton to serve as his sling for the day.

Dr. Lubidos picked him up in his car and drove to his home where Reinhold met some of the other doctors, their wives, and their children. There were so many of them that their names became a blur. It was a blessing that he didn't speak the language because he would have embarrassed himself by not remembering names.

The doctors' wives prepared a huge picnic supper which they loaded into Dr. Lubidos' car and drove to the hilltop where Santuário de Santa Luzia Erica stood stout and stately. They spread the picnic on the lawn while the children played amongst the trees and buildings. The food was delicious. Reinhold had no idea what it was but it was good and that was all that mattered. Someone got out a camera and took pictures, posing Reinhold and the doctors on a retaining wall in front of the massive stone façade and rose window of the sanctuary.

After lunch, the doctors' wives packed up the remnants of lunch. The wives and several of the doctors said their goodbyes, leaving Dr. Amico and Dr. Lubidos to take Reinhold on a tour of the countryside. It was just as beautiful from the car window as it was from the lifeboats of the *Midgard*. It seemed a lifetime ago that Reinhold traveled up river with the First Mate and the crew.

Reinhold with the doctors
Photograph courtesy of Reinhold Scholz

His joints protested at each bump in the road but he tried to ignore the pain and concentrate on the scenery. The farmers were hard at work on the year's crops of wheat and corn. Reinhold saw them moving in their fields, inspecting and pruning. Dr. Lubidos pointed out the various types of non-traditional farms that Reinhold wasn't familiar with, being from a more northerly climate. There were vineyards that would provide grapes for the year's wine and groves of olive trees for oil. There were also orange orchards, which smelled wonderful. Everything was green and verdant.

As well it should be, Reinhold thought to himself, *it's the end of May already.*

That was truly shocking. A month had passed so quickly, yet so slowly and strangely.

"They make a very special type of wine here, in this country, called Vinho Verde," Dr. Lubidos told Reinhold as they bucked along down a dirt road between two vineyards. "It means 'young wine' in your language. The French and the Italians like to age their wine. But here, we drink it fresh. It is delicious, sweet and fruity, like sex with a beautiful, full bodied woman."

Dr. Lubidos pulled a pack of cigarettes out of the breast pocket of his suit jacket, removing one with his teeth before offering one to Reinhold.

"What color is it?" Reinhold asked, puffing on his cigarette.

He liked the Portuguese cigarettes. They weren't as harsh as the Lucky Strikes he usually smoked. They were more refined. Dr. Amico told him that they grew their own tobacco in Portugal. It was Salazar's goal, he told Reinhold, not to be reliant on other countries for anything that the Portuguese people needed. Salazar was the country's dictator, as Reinhold understood it although Dr. Amico had used a different word to identify the leader.

It doesn't matter what you call the person, a dictator is a dictator, he thought, shuddering.

He didn't trust people who wanted absolute power. It reminded him too much of home. He had crossed Portugal of his list of possible places to settle down for good once he heard about Salazar.

"It comes in all colors: red, white, pink. It is good for pain."

Dr. Lubidos grinned and Reinhold had to laugh. He pointed out the window at a field they were passing.

"You see, the high fences with the grape vines on them? The farmers do that so they can still plant vegetables on the ground."

All too soon it was time to return to the hospital. The next day, Dr. Lubidos informed Reinhold that if all continued the way it was going, he and Dr. Amico were prepared to release him in just over a week.

"Probably on the 10th of June," Dr. Amico said.

Reinhold couldn't hide his surprise. He sputtered out a few words but didn't say anything. The doctors grinned at his incoherence.

"We think you will recover better if you can go home and be amongst your own, your family."

Reinhold nodded in response, thinking. The last place he wanted to be was amongst his family. The throbbing in his shoulder reminded him that he was going to need help, but dreaded the idea of going back to Ratekau.

Maybe it won't be so bad, he thought.

He hoped that his stepmother had fallen down a well or been hit by the train, but he knew that wasn't going to be the case. Evil never dies.

Reinhold spent the remainder of his stay in the hospital hobbling around or visiting with the doctors and their families. The hospital was poorer than he originally thought. There was no landscaping to beautify the premise. The benches and outdoor furniture were from a different time, one before he was even born. Reinhold remembered when he happened upon a lawn that stretched down a hill toward the sea. It was covered with linens. They lay all over the ground, billowing and blowing in the breeze off the ocean.

He had heard that you could bleach linens with the sun, but he had never actually seen it before. Women moved amongst the linens, spraying them with water. Reinhold wandered through the field of material to the other side where he found a small creek where the hospital laundry was being beat against rocks in the creek. The sun and the fresh air explained why his sheets smelled so good.

There were many rooms in the hospital that served as offices and storage, operating theatres and maternity suites, but the general populace, people like Reinhold who were just hurt, or worse, dying of a non-communicable illness, were housed in just two rooms. There was one for men and, on the other side of the building, one for women. He had a private room because he was a minor VIP. Sometimes he wished he could be in the communal room so that he could try to learn Portuguese but the doctors scoffed at him when he asked.

"Why do you want to be in that zoo when you have a private room all to yourself?" Dr. Amico asked. "Those people out there would like to be you."

Reinhold didn't bother trying to explain that he was bored and lonely. He wrote a letter to Lisa instead. It took all night to compose because he had to write it with his left hand as his right was still in the sling. He told her that they were going to release him soon. He got her response the day before he left the hospital. She invited him to come stay with her for a while. He thought about it. Lisa didn't have a lot of space. Maybe he would. Maybe he wouldn't.

In the end, Reinhold went to the port in Viana do Castelo and got a ship to Lübeck, heading for Ratekau. Leaving the hospital was easy, and hard. The staff wished him well, smiling and awkwardly shaking his left hand or clapping him on the uninjured shoulder. It was hard for Reinhold to say goodbye to Dr. Amico and Dr. Lubidos. They were good to him and his only real companionship for the last six weeks. He counted them almost as friends. Dr. Amico gave him several packs of Portuguese cigarettes.

"Something for the journey home," he said.

Reinhold thanked him and shoved the smokes into his sea bag.

"Don't close that suitcase yet," Dr. Lubidos called to him.

He was striding down the main corridor with something in his hand. When he was within arm's reach, he handed Reinhold a bottle of wine, white Vinho Verde.

"It is not as fresh as it should be but it still good."

He dug a piece of paper out of pocket and handed it to Reinhold. "Don't forget to keep in touch."

The two men shook hands as best as Reinhold could manage.

He was a bit apprehensive. The joints on his right side still throbbed. A sudden movement or the placing of a foot wrong sent shooting pains through him that brought tears to his eyes. The completely imagined picture of him being on the ship home and hurting himself worse ran through his mind like a memory.

Reinhold scolded himself for being weak and whiny. He was getting what he wanted, he reminded himself as he walked confidently with his cane up the gangplank of the cargo ship that was to carry him to Germany. He couldn't remember the name of that ship. This was evidence of his distressed mental state, he knew. A sailor never forgets the name of a ship. He remembered it being a nice cabin with a clean mattress and sheets, a private bathroom, and a porthole to look out. It was the best cabin he ever had on a ship.

Chapter 58: Shore Leave

It was strange to be a passenger as opposed to a sailor. When he heard the bells toll, he had to stop himself from reporting for duty. The guys on the crew were all very nice to Reinhold, reverent almost. Whether they liked to admit it or not, they all feared what he had survived. On their first night out to sea, Reinhold sat on the raised hatch cover and cracked open the bottle of wine Dr. Lubidos gave him. He had no glass, so he slugged it right out of the bottle, watching the moonlight play on the fractured surface of the sea. It was good to be back on the sea. The chugging of the engines, the shouts of the sailors, and the splashing of the waves were comforting, a confirmation that he was alive and life was continuing just as it had before his accident.

The trip home passed uneventfully. The ship made several stops and Reinhold joined the crew for some fun on shore. It felt good to be back amongst his fellow sailors. On board ship, no one asked him anything about his accident and he was grateful for that. But after a few drinks at a local watering hole in Copenhagen, that last port before Lübeck, one sailor, Peter, asked Reinhold what happened.

"I fell off a hatch beam," was Reinhold's only response.

He wasn't sure what else to say. He didn't think he knew these sailors well enough to elaborate.

"We know that," Peter said. "But what happened to you when you fell."

Reinhold looked at the guy more closely. He was young, about Reinhold's age, maybe a bit younger. Obviously, he had not been sailing long. There was a bright eyed naiveté about him. If Reinhold had figured correctly, this guy was still just a *jungemann*.

"I got hurt really bad and almost died," Reinhold told Peter bluntly. "What do you expect would happen to someone who fell thirty five feet?"

An awkward silence descended over the table of sailors and Peter squirmed uncomfortably.

"I don't know. I guess I was just curious."

Reinhold smiled at him. "The moral of the story is to remember not to fall."

He looked around at the men gathered, sensing their anticipation. He raised his glass.

"To all those who went before and all those to come after. May Poseidon watch over us all."

A cheer of approval went up from the men and everyone drank the toast.

"Now, if you boys will excuse me, I see a beautiful blonde at that table over there that I would like to get to know better."

Laughter spread around the table. Several men wished him luck.

"I don't need luck," he retorted. "Women love a guy with an injury."

He gestured to his sling and made an exaggerated hurt face before leaving the snickering sailors.

Over breakfast the next morning, the Third Mate struck up a conversation about Reinhold's future plans. It was the first time the two had spoken.

"Are you going back to your ship, Reinhold?"

"That's the plan. Doctors say that I need more time to recover before I can go back."

"What ship were you with?"

"The *Midgard*."

"Ah ha, yes, Capt. Müller, right?"

"You know him, sir?"

"Yes, I sailed with him on the *Artus* a couple of years back. A miserable man, if I remember correctly, who drinks a bit too much for my taste. He used to piss off the bridge wing. Didn't even look to see if anyone was standing under him first. Did he tell you to get up and stop being a loafer when you fell?"

"I don't know, sir, I was unconscious for three days afterward."

The Third Mate blinked at Reinhold in mild surprise. "Three days?"

His brow knit in a frown. He stared briefly at the sling Reinhold wore around his right arm before returning his eyes to his plate of food.

"I don't think I would go back to my ship if that happened to me. I would be looking for a job on the beach. I probably wouldn't even have sailed home. I would have gotten the train. You're a lucky man, Reinhold."

"The company told me I had to go by ship if I wanted them to pay for it. It is tempting to look for work in a shipyard or something but I like the *Midgard*. I have friends on that ship." He paused for a second before continuing. "Besides, I haven't seen everything I want to see yet. I haven't made it to Australia."

The mate laughed. "Australia, huh? You looking to be an emigrant?"

Reinhold shrugged. He wasn't surprised the mate guessed his intentions. "Maybe. You know anyone who has gone there?"

It was the mate's turn to shrug. "Maybe. And maybe he has been there for a few years now. Maybe he is even a very successful blacksmith" A bell tolled from the bridge marking the eight o'clock hour. The mate rose and picked up his plate. "That's my cue. See you around the ship Reinhold."

He left Reinhold sitting there by himself. He stared out the windows at the heaving sea and the men passing on the gangway. They left Copenhagen close to three hours earlier at high tide. A storm was brewing; he could smell it. The crew was going to have their hands full tonight. Reinhold's blood coursed with impotent anticipation at the thought of a good storm.

It is not my ship, he sighed to himself. *Soon, maybe, I'll be back on my ship.*

Two mornings later, Reinhold walked down the gangplank on to the pier on the Trave in Lübeck. He was expected at Lisa's for the night but there were a few things he needed to do before heading to her place. First, he had to report to his company's office. Poseidon Coal Imports wanted to speak with him about his condition and about his paycheck. They had continued paying him while he was in the hospital. Now that he was out, the company was taking him off the payroll and handing his case over to the government. He was going to be collecting disability while he was out of work.

Then, he had to get his finances in order. He didn't know where he stood after his ill-fated trip to the casino with Nietz. Once the money was in order, Reinhold was looking forward to going to a restaurant he knew for a good breakfast. It was a bit of a shock to him when he realized he hadn't had a good German meal in two months.

He was also toying with the idea of applying for his license. Since he was eighteen, he had every right to drive a car. The thought of getting behind the wheel and driving around the countryside made him involuntarily smile. He knew that it would take him awhile to get

 through the classes and learning, but applying would get him closer to having the license.

Maybe then I'll go drive a truck or something.

He adjusted the sling to a more comfortable position on his right shoulder. Sighing, Reinhold set off into Lübeck to the Poseidon Coal Import Company. He noted that the city was looking better.

Even though Lisa insisted that it was ok for Reinhold to stay with them, he left after two days, taking the train to Ratekau. He felt like he was intruding on Lisa's limited space and taking advantage of her unbounded kindness. If he were to stay, she would dote on him like a mother and that was not what he wanted.

Reinhold boarded the train in Lübeck, settling himself into a window seat. He watched as the familiar landscape rolled past. Nothing had changed. The fields were dotted with men toiling under the sun. It was time to cut the clover, he noted, seeing a man swinging a scythe while others picked up the grass with pitchforks and threw it into the waiting wagon. He didn't miss farm work at all, not in the least, not even in his current state of occupational injury. The train rumbled into Bad Schwartau and Reinhold exited. He was not looking forward to the walk to Ratekau.

By the time he arrived at Blüchereiche, Reinhold's hip was throbbing with an intense, dull pain and his knees were stiff and achy. He settled himself on the front steps of his childhood home to take the pressure off his destroyed limbs. Somewhere inside the house the radio was playing. He knew his father wasn't home and he was in no rush to see his stepmother. The house was falling into some disrepair. The steps were sagging and the spaces between the shingles on the roof were bigger. His old neighborhood was deserted but he could hear voices coming from the Easberger's backyard. It was oddly pleasant to sit on the porch and listen to the domestic sounds of the people. His stepmother disrupted his momentary solitude. He knew the door had opened because the voices from the radio got louder

"Well, what are you doing here?"

She stood in the doorway with her hands on her hips. She surveyed him, her eyes lingering on the sling and his sea bag. Obviously, they ignored the telegram he sent.

"You're not coming to live here if you have no job and can't work. What did you do to yourself?"

Sighing, Reinhold pushed himself off the steps and picked up his sea bag.

"I fell. I'll be back later when my father is home."

He limped off in the direction of Küster's with the idea in mind that he would get a beer.

Reinhold wasn't surprised to find a few old timers occupying tables at Küster's. They looked suspiciously at him when he entered. He dropped his sea bag near the door and walked up to the bar. The bartender was an old timer that Reinhold knew from his days at Muuss' farm but he didn't recognize him at first. It wasn't until Reinhold ordered his beer that recognition dawned.

"You're Scholz's boy," was all he said. It sounded more like an accusation than a friendly icebreaker.

"That's me," Reinhold responded with more attitude than he had intended.

"What happened to you?" The old timer was eyeing Reinhold's sling.

"I fell."

"Where?"

"Into the ship I was working on," Reinhold gulped down his beer and ordered another.

"That's right, you ran away to sea. That's why we don't see you around anymore."

"I didn't run away. I got a job." Reinhold sighed.

"What brings you back here?"

Reinhold gestured to the sling. "I can't work so I am home for a visit." He took another gulp of his beer.

"Home?" The bartender's brow knotted in a strange way that Reinhold couldn't interpret. "Don't you sailor's think your home is your ship?"

A man at a table snickered and Reinhold turned to see who made the noise, ready to exchange words, but nobody seemed to be paying attention.

"Yes, when you have a ship, it is your home." He answered cautiously, feeling his anger rising.

"So does that mean that you are homeless right now?"

Again a snicker came from behind. Reinhold didn't bother trying to see who made it.

"No, you ignorant *arschloch*. I have a home in Kiel." Reinhold sighed. This wasn't going to be fun.

And it wasn't. His whole trip home was a fiasco. The men at the bar rejected him, again, just as they did a couple of years before. They asked him questions about his travels and then told him he was lying about the things he had seen. They didn't believe him that the city of Stockholm was powered by waterfalls. Nor did they believe that there were snipers on the Russian border. But, Reinhold noted, they had no trouble believing that English people were condescending and rude to Germans.

When he returned home, his stepmother greeted him by saying that if he was hungry, he could make his own supper. Then she disappeared into her bedroom carrying a plate with her own supper. It was an awkward attempt at best considering his sling and the general lack of ingredients. Nothing much changed since the last time he was back. His father was pleased to see him but all around indifferent to his presence. It was a disappointment for the sailor when his father didn't object to his stepmother demanding compensation for his stay in the house. It was from his father that Reinhold learned that none of his old friends still lived in Ratekau.

The icing on the cake of his visit home was the roof of the attic. Reinhold laid in bed at night, staring through the holes, praying like when he was a kid that it wouldn't rain. He tried pushing the bed to another spot, but it didn't change anything.

He lasted a week before he decided that Kiel was a better place for him. Hoping to find help at home was a mistake and he should have known better. If he was going to fend for himself he might as well do it in his own place. He walked the five painful miles back to Bad Schwartau and got the train to Kiel. He arrived at his room in pain from the exertion of the day but far happier than he had been in weeks.

Luck was with him on this occasion. Herbert signed off a ship just two days before Reinhold got back to town with plans to spend a couple of weeks on shore with Katie. Reinhold ran into him at the seaman's club the day after he returned to Kiel. They embraced like brothers, thrilled by the happy coincidence. Over a few rounds of beer, Reinhold told Herbert about his fall and his stay in the hospital.

By the time the story was done, Hebert wasn't the only one listening. Many sailors bought him a beer, most offered their best wishes and prayers, and some just looked at him in sympathy. An old timer with one eye and three fingers on his left hand gave him a medal of St. Michel, patron of sailors, for protection, he said, when Reinhold returned to sea. Even the sailors from foreign countries instinctively understood that Reinhold had survived some horrible calamity. He left the club that night feeling the best he had since he fell.

After returning to Kiel, Reinhold's injuries improved rapidly. The camaraderie he felt was worth a week under doctor's care. His joints throbbed less. His breathing improved. He stopped using the sling. It felt good to walk with his arm free. Overall, he felt whole and undamaged, for the most part, instead of broken and physically powerless.

His financial situation, however, did not improve. The government gave him only a percentage of the fifty *mark* a month he was bringing home when he was working. The amount left in his post book was appallingly small for someone who was facing indefinite rehab. Fear set into Reinhold's mood. He was afraid he was going to run out of money before he was well enough to go back to work. As much as he didn't like doing it, he went down to the canal to hang out with the guys on the bum to beg food and cigarettes off the ships that passed. It was easier to do when he had the sling. He felt legitimately in need of assistance. When the sling was gone, he just felt like a bum even though he knew he was still not in good enough shape to go back to work. To conserve money, he stopped frequenting the seaman's club opting instead for a bottle of 'wawa' juice and the kitchen table at Herbert and Katie's place.

Herbert decided at the end of June that he had to go back to work. Reinhold tried to convince him to stay ashore and start a business with him. When ideas were slow in coming or unsustainable, Herbert went down to the sailor's agent and got a ship, another Swedish flag, and left the same day. The minute he sailed away, boredom set in for Reinhold. It was no fun drinking alone or with strangers at the sailor's club. He felt confined by his broken body and lack of funds.

Two days after Herbert left, a stroke of fate blindsided him. He was standing by the canal, smoking and watching the ships when he saw the *Midgard* appear from the east. She was sailing for the canal's docking area. Reinhold met her when she docked, shocking the crew with his presence in Kiel.

"It's like seeing a ghost!" Nietz exclaimed.

"Are you signing back on, Reinhold?" Hein asked.

"No. I just saw her coming and thought I would come say hi, see if guys want to get a beer."

"Of course we want a beer!" Werner said. "More than one preferably."

Over drinks at the sailor's club, Reinhold learned that the *Midgard* was down a man, a *Matrose*. A guy named Günther who had signed on after Reinhold's departure got badly beaten on shore in Helsinki.

"No one knows what happened," Hein explained. "He came back to the ship, oh, a week ago now all banged up and bleeding badly. He was holding his side when he staggered up the gangplank." He paused to take a swig of his beer.

"Yeah, I was on watch at the time." Werner picked up the thread of the tale. "I asked him what happened but he wouldn't tell me. Just kept saying that he deserved it." He shrugged. "Probably some deal gone bad. He had a strange feel to him, that guy. He was small and quiet. He and Helmut got along great. I wouldn't be surprised if he was the type to smuggle drugs up his butt or something."

"Point is," Nietz continued, "we are down a sailor. The old man was planning on filling the spot here. That could be you. You just have to go talk to him."

It all sounded too good to be true. Reinhold frowned.

"But I am not a *Matrose* yet. And I don't know if I should go back to work yet."

Hein scoffed at him. "You are one of the best cobblescots I know and you are on your way to becoming an excellent Quartermaster. Not as good as me though."

He winked at his friend. Then something clicked in his brain making his face light up. "And, you're favorite person left. Walked off the ship in Cuxhaven a month ago and haven't see him since."

"Who? Helmut?"

"No, that *arschloch* is still with us. The First Mate left. We think he took over his own ship. But who knows. At least he is gone."

"When do you leave?" Reinhold expected the answer to be tomorrow.

Nietz shrugged. "The old girl needs some maintenance. She goes to the shipyard where the U-boat bunkers used to be tomorrow. I forget the name of it."

"Winckler?" Reinhold asked.

"Yup, that's the one. She shouldn't be there more than a couple of days. Why don't you sail down there with us? Stay on the ship tonight." Werner signaled for another round of drinks.

"Like one of your girls? Forget it. I have a room here with a real bed."

"Oh, fancy guy here is too good for his old bunk." Hein grinned at his former bunkmate.

"That's right," Reinhold raised his fresh glass of beer in a toast. "To real beds."

Everyone drank to that.

After drinks and a trip to the *puff* in Holtenau with the guys from the *Midgard*, Reinhold wandered up the hill to his room thinking about what he had learned. He wondered if he should go back to sea.

I could definitely use the money, he thought. *Better to earn the full fifty mark than to lounge around and have the government give me fifteen mark.*

Then, as he twisted the key in the door of his room, a sharp pain in his shoulder reminded him why he wasn't working. He flopped down on his bed and kicked off his shoes.

I have to go back to work, he thought. *I am going to go crazy if I don't find something to do with myself. This is the perfect opportunity.*

Unconsciously, he rubbed he injured shoulder.

Reinhold didn't remember falling asleep that night, but he remembered the dream he had. It was set on the deck of the *Midgard* the day he fell. Except, he didn't fall. He ended up cleaning out the hull that held the fertilizer. It was a nasty job and he was pissed because the charterer was supposed to send someone to do it. There was no good reason why that didn't happen. When he was done for the day, he headed ashore to find his wife, a faceless brunette woman, and their infant son waiting for him. Strangely, he wasn't in Germany.

He didn't know where he was or who these people were but it felt right for him to be there with them.

Reinhold was awaken by the sound of a ship's whistle in the canal. He pulled himself out of bed and looked out the window. It was a beautiful summer morning with blue skies, and soft breeze, and sea gulls calling. The sailor felt the call of the sea to strongly to ignore. Checking his watch, he saw it was just after nine o'clock. Doubtless, the *Midgard* was down at Winckler's already. He washed and changed clothes and headed to the seaman's agent to check if the *Midgard* had requested a new sailor.

The guy behind the desk told him the captain of the *Midgard* had been in and made his request. Reinhold explained his situation to the agent, who wore an incredulous expression through most of the tale.

"You mean to tell me, son, that you had this horrible incident on the *Midgard* and now you want to rejoin that ship?"

"Yes."

The agent began shuffling papers, looking for the *Midgard's* order.

"Don't believe in bad luck, huh?"

"Not really. It was an accident."

The agent snorted. "I'll say. If everything you say is true you're lucky to be alive. I had a guy fall and land on the hull deck like you on a ship I was with, oh, going on twenty years ago now. He died, alright, but not before he spent two days bleeding out in a hospital in Galway. Nothing they could do for him except keep him drugged."

The agent pulled a paper from the stack. "Ah, here it is. Says they're looking for a *Matrose*. According to your book, you're a *Leichtmatrose.*" The man looked up from the form to Reinhold.

"Oh," was all he could think to say. But hastily added, "I am due a promotion. I've been a *Leichtmatrose* for two years now."

The agent eyed him carefully. Reinhold could see the debate raging in the man's mind. Technically, he couldn't find the position with an inferior sailor, regardless of their experience or past traumas.

But I have a history with this ship! Reinhold screamed at him in his head.

As if he heard him, the agent said, "Hold on. Let me leave this decision to Captain Müller. He should be with his ship."

The agent got up from his desk and went to the radio. He sang a line of code into the hand piece, ending with a "copy?" No answer. Again, the singing code and "copy". No answer. Just crackling and popping noises issued from the black box.

"One last time," the agent said to Reinhold. He began to sing the line of code but was interrupted before he got to the "copy?"

"*Midgard*, go ahead."

"*Midgard*, I have a sailor here who says he was to rejoin you. He wants to fill the position you filed with us. Name is Scholz."

There was an extended silence from the *Midgard*. Then there was a snap and the voice that Reinhold recognized as the Captain came through the speakers.

"This is Capt. Müller. Is he sea worthy? Over."

The agent looked at Reinhold, who nodded vigorously, ignoring the soreness in his shoulder. "Yes, Captain, he says that he is sea worthy. He is not a *Matrose,* as you requested. Herr Scholz's book indicates that he hasn't progressed past *Leichtmatrose*. Over."

Again, the dead sounds of crackling and popping.

"Send him down sea ready. We'll take him on. Over."

Reinhold was elated. He could barely contain his relief to be going back to sea.

"Well, you heard the Captain, Scholz. Get going."

The agent handed him his orders, making his job official.

Reinhold went to his room, collected his things, told the homeowner he was leaving, and was back out the door before he had time to question whether this was truly a good idea.

On July 3, 1953, seventy days after leaving the *Midgard* unconscious on a stretcher, Reinhold found himself standing on the familiar bridge, handing his seaman's book to Capt. Müller while the Second Mate watched from the map table. The Captain looked him over as he opened the book to an empty page and began writing. Reinhold could have sworn he saw respect hidden in the older man's eyes.

"I didn't think I would see you again on this ship, Scholz." He glanced up from the book.

"Yes, sir."

"A fall like that would keep most men on the beach for a long time." Again, a glance.

"Yes, sir." He said, adding, "I don't like the beach."

The Captain laughed, signing Reinhold's book with a flourish and snapping it shut.

"I don't like it either. You were just promoted to full *Matrose*. This means your pay rate just went up to seventy *mark* a month with the possibility of raises in the future. Congratulations, *Matrose*."

He rose and extended his hand to Reinhold, who hesitantly took the offered hand in his own. He hadn't shook hands with a Captain since Hermann on the *Eos*.

"And welcome back."

"Thank you, sir."

Reinhold picked up his sea bag and made to leave but was stopped by the second mate.

"You still play chess, Reinhold?"

Reinhold hadn't realized the mate knew he played chess.

"Yes, sir, when I have someone to play with."

"Why don't you meet me in the mess hall tonight and we'll play a game."

Reinhold hid his surprise and answered. "Yes, sir."

"Good. After dinner then."

Reinhold nodded his agreement and left the bridge for his new old bunk.

Chapter 59: Return

The return to the *Midgard* was bittersweet. Reinhold was happy to be back to work amongst friends with sea breezes ruffling his hair and the smell of salt in his nostrils. Hein, Nietz, and Werner gave him a hero's welcome. It was a double celebration because he was returning as a full *Matrose*. The guys got into their tuxedos and went to the Kiel Opera House to see *Don Giovanni* by Mozart.

The venue was still in a state of partial destruction and the acoustics were horrible. Reinhold had read in the paper recently that two important architects, from Frankfort if he remembered correctly, were commissioned to restore the structure to its former beauty. They sat in the back of the small auditorium, passing a flask, and listening to the haunting strains of the musical accompaniment. Reinhold watched as Giovanni was hauled under the earth by a living statue as punishment for his immorality and his arrogance. Briefly, he wondered if he too was being punished for immorality and arrogance. He quickly shrugged it off. There was no morality to life. It was just life. His accident was just an accident, nothing more. He scowled to himself for reading more into it than what it was. He applauded loudly when the curtain went down.

On the way back to the *Midgard*, the sailors stopped at a local port tavern for a round of drinks. There were more people, including a good number of women, then usual. Everybody stopped to look at the four of them in their tuxes. Women quickly gravitated their way over until their table was surrounded. A round of drinks quickly turned into a few rounds of drinks. It was hours after they entered the bar that they left, each with his own lady. Nietz had even found himself a hefty girl.

The *Midgard* returned to sea two days later with Reinhold on the spring line. He assumed that they would be heading through the canal, but learned from the Second Mate during an intense game of chess that they were sailing for Copenhagen. This was excellent news for Reinhold for more than one reason. He hadn't had a lot of fun recently and Danish girls were good for fun. Reinhold was also glad that Copenhagen wasn't that far away. If his body wasn't ready to be back at sea, he could sign off and get home without too much trouble.

He could even bum around Denmark for a few days and see all the things that he missed.

And I almost did that, Reinhold thought to himself, unconsciously rubbing a sunbaked shoulder, watching a tiny tropical island slide by about a mile away. *That first trip was hell. Everything seemed heavier, further away, just plain more difficult.*

His shoulder ached with every movement. His knee and hip throbbed with the pressure of fighting the roll of the ship on the sea. He had never noticed before that his sea legs were actually centered in his hips and knees. It made him angry, this weakness and injury.

I should have just died, he thought in a second of intense rage fueled self-pity.

Werner, in particular, noticed Reinhold struggling sometimes under the weight of a shackle or the tension of a boom line. One of the first jobs back on board was rebuilding a cabinet in the galley that was damaged by rough seas. Wielding the hammer and saw left Reinhold's elbow and shoulder in agony. Werner saw Reinhold struggling and took the hammer from him.

"Go do my painting for a bit, Scholz."

Reinhold stared at him, wondering what had gotten into the tough guy. Werner rolled his eyes.

"You have to change the motion. You can't just do the same thing over and over again."

"How do you know that?"

"Do you think you're the first person to get hurt on a ship?"

"I guess not," Reinhold admitted.

He left Werner to build the cabinet while he painted. After an hour, he returned to the galley, reclaiming his hammer. The two sailors followed this pattern for the entire trip except when Werner spent the better part of an afternoon hanging over the starboard side in the bosun's chair welding a gaping seam.

Upon arrival in Copenhagen, Reinhold, much to his consternation, was put on port watch.

"I thought as a *Matrose* I didn't have to stand port watch anymore," he questioned Werner and Nietz, both full *Matrose*.

"That's not true." Nietz said. "I stand port watch whenever I am told to. Besides, you just signed on, Scholz, you know the ropes. The new guy stands watch at the first port we arrive at, regardless of rank.

The rest of us were standing at the top of that gangplank, swilling bad coffee, while you were bleeding in a hospital."

"Cheer up, Reinhold," Hein added. "We are loading a lot of cargo according to what I heard on the bridge. We are going to be here for a while, at least a week. The old man isn't going to make you stand watch for the entirety. And the First Mate is a much better man then the last *arschloch*. You'll stand two nights, tops, before you are out with us."

His second night standing watch, Reinhold watched Werner escort a tiny little lady up the gangway. She was adorable, with freckles and a button nose, but the top of her head only reached his chest. They made an odd pair. Reinhold tipped his hat to them as they passed.

It couldn't have been more than half an hour later when Reinhold heard commotion coming from the aft castle followed by a splash. Running toward the noise, he saw a stark naked, sexually excited Werner pulling a life ring off the wall.

"What happened," Reinhold gasped, coming to a dead stop by hitting the rail.

Peering over the side, he saw Werner's lady friend treading water about twenty feet from the ship.

"Crazy broad jumped overboard," Werner explained as he threw out the ring.

"Watchman! What is going on out there?" The Captain bellowed from his salon below the bridge.

"Captain, a woman jumped overboard." Reinhold called back.

"A woman? Whose woman?"

"Werner's, sir."

"Tell him to get her back on board and to keep her on board or she has to leave. Understood?"

"Yes, sir," Werner and Reinhold answered in unison.

Reinhold helped Werner pull the girl back onboard.

"Why did she jump?"

"I don't know. Why don't you ask her?"

"Why did you jump?" Reinhold called to the girl, who was about half way up the side of the ship.

"He is huge. Look at him! He'll split me open with that thing! He is not coming near me!"

The girls' eyes held genuine fright. Reinhold stole a quick glance at the offensive body part and burst into laughter, almost losing his grip on the ring's lifeline. Once she was aboard, Werner wheeled on Reinhold.

"What are you laughing at?"

"This." Reinhold gestured with his hand to cover the entire situation. "You're too big for her, so she jumps overboard."

He burst into laughter again. Werner also had to smile, somewhat sheepishly. He turned his attention to the naked, wet, shivering girl.

"Come on, we have to get you warm or you'll get sick. The showers are down here." He guided the girl toward the aft castle again, throwing a grin over his shoulder at Reinhold.

Reinhold smiled to himself, shaking his head, as he return to his watch. A sound in the mess hall stopped him in his tracks. It was a soft banging noise. Sticking his head into the room, he saw a man in tattered clothes trying to break into the galley. He was trying to be quiet but wasn't succeeding.

"Ho there!" Reinhold called, scaring the man.

He whirled, pulling a switchblade knife out of his jacket. He made slashing motions in the air as Reinhold approached, his hands held out in front of him in defensive posture.

"There is no need for the knife. I am not going to hurt you but you have to leave."

The man lunged drunkenly at Reinhold. He easily sidestepped the man, grabbing his collar as he passed. He swung him around once by the collar, grabbing the back of his jacket with the other hand. Now, with two hands guiding the drunk vagrant, Reinhold propelled him through the mess hall, out the door and over the side of the rail. There was a loud splash, followed by sputtering. Reinhold looked down to see the man swimming awkwardly for the pier ladder.

"Watchman! What now?" Bellowed the Captain again.

"Vagrant, sir!"

"Is he gone?"

"Yes, sir."

"Well done, watchman."

Reinhold returned to his post. His shoulder was throbbing. He was jealous of Werner who he knew at this very moment was in the shower with that tiny little girl.

Chapter 60: Those Girls

"What are you daydreaming about?"

The sound of a voice jolted Reinhold out of his sundrenched stupor. The deck of the *Midgard* melted away, replaced by the deck of the *Brandenburg*. He turned to see Max standing next to him, a canteen in his hand.

"Figured you could use a drink, Scholz."

Reinhold nodded and took the canteen. "Copenhagen."

"What?" Max was confused.

"You asked what I was daydreaming about. The answer is Copenhagen."

"Oh, right, yeah, Copenhagen. What a place. Those Danish girls. Gold bless every one of them."

"I was remembering this one trip. I was with the *Midgard*, oh three years ago now, and we spent nine days at pier loading cargo. My bunkmate and I went out looking for women. We found them, of course, and spent the night riding them like the champion stallions we thought we were. They find us the next night and start telling us how they didn't appreciate us not giving 110%."

Reinhold laughed at the memory, taking another cigarette out of his pocket.

"Hein's girl starts telling me that they only did it four times. How could that be enough, she asks. So, my girl pops up and says that we only did it five times, she didn't feel that her experience was any better."

Reinhold laughed again and Max joined him.

"Do you know, we took those girls back to the ship and tried again? We did better, in their opinion, the second time. The best part of the story is, the next night, those girls are waiting for us on the pier! Hein and I had enough of them. Neither of us wanted another go so we get the lifeboat down and row to the other side of the port. They never saw us leave!" Reinhold roared with laughter while Max chuckled.

"Danish girls," Max sighed wistfully. "Anyway, Reinhold, keep the canteen. There is some problem on the bridge or something. The First Mate wants you to take Michel's turn back here at whistle turn. OK?"

Reinhold had been looking forward to his turn on the bridge as Quartermaster, out of the sun with a better view of what the Caribbean had to offer.

"Yup, whatever the First says, right?"

"Right."

Reinhold thought Max would be leaving then but he didn't. He made himself comfortable against the rail and lit two cigarettes, handing on to Reinhold.

"The *Midgard*, huh? What company was that?"

"Poseidon Coal Imports, or something like that. I don't pay much attention to the company." He took a long drag, blowing out a plume of smoke. "So long as the pay keeps coming, I don't care who I work for."

Max snorted. "That's the truth. I sailed with a guy from the *Midgard*. His name was Nietz."

Reinhold stopped mid drag, shocked by the smallness of the world.

"A cheap Polish German?"

Max laughed. "That is the guy. Always brought the worst girls back to the ship."

It was Reinhold's turn to laugh.

"He did. I have a good story about Nietz and his girls." He picked a bit of tobacco out of his teeth. "So, we're in Cuxhaven. I have the port watch, punishment for something or other. The Captain could be a real prick. Anyway, Nietz brings this girl back to the ship. She's a heavy one, and old and drunk. Even by his standards, this was bad. They go below deck and do whatever they do. An hour later or so I hear a bunch of commotion aft. I go check it out. Wouldn't you know, it's Nietz's girl, running around split naked, flopping all over the place, covered in red paint." He took a drag of his cigarette.

Max looked confused. "Red paint?"

"Yup, red paint. It was the only one we had mixed at the time or else she may have been wearing grey or black. Nietz painted circles around her nipples, like a bull's eye, colored in the nipples, and painted a line down her belly, you know, following the happy trail, to her *pflaume*. Then he painted that too." Another drag.

"You have got to be kidding."

"I wish. She was running around, drunker than hell, dancing, all her rolls jiggling. Guys came out of the wood work to watch the show. One guy, a stoker, comes back to the ship and sees this. She runs over to him and tries to grab him. 'What are you doing?', he asks. 'I'm working,' she says and the guys all think it is the funniest thing ever." Another drag. "The whole time she's running around, Nietz is taking pictures of her. He tells me that he took pictures of her while they were doing the deed too." Another drag.

"Pictures?"

"Yup, he got them developed before we left Cuxhaven. They were pretty bad. It was more of Nietz then I wanted to see. And don't you know that he tried to sell them at every port we went to after that."

Max burst into laughter. "That's Nietz for you. Did he sell any?"

"I don't think so. Not to anyone on my crew, that's for sure. Well, maybe a stoker."

"What happened to the girl? Did they wash her off?"

Reinhold shrugged. "Last I saw her, the stokers were taking her below deck. She must have left the ship after I got off watch."

"I'd love to stay and exchange Nietz stories with you Scholz, but I have to get back to work before one of the *arschlocher* see me just standing here."

Max sauntered away. Reinhold watched him go, thinking about that trip to Cuxhaven. He had an amazing time with a girl the night after Nietz's show. He met one of those rare wild child girls in a bar portside. They got to talking. She asked him quite frankly if he wanted to bed her. Never one to ignore a direct question, Reinhold answered yes. Taking his hand, she pulled him off his barstool, saying something about the high tide coming in soon.

"Come on we have to go now or we won't have enough time."

"Enough time for what?" Reinhold followed her out the door.

"To do it on those benches under the old wooden pier before they are underwater."

"Oh," Reinhold was intrigued and excited. "You're right, we have to hurry. The tide is coming."

They rushed down to the waterfront and got down to business. She rode him like the American cowboys he had read about in his books. All she needed was a ten gallon hat and some spurs to dig into his flesh. She kept looking behind her at the approaching water, telling him to hurry and to slow down at the same time. When she finally let him finish, the water was covering his ankles. His pants were soaked through with seawater and his injured hip was pulsing with a hot achy pain. It had been worth it.

It wasn't long after the stop in Cuxhaven that they picked up fertilizer in Lübeck to deliver to Spain, the Mediterranean side. They had just one stop, in Bremerhaven, between the Nord-Ostsee Canal and their delivery point. Then it was more than a two week sail. Kristal was standing on the pier when the *Midgard* docked at the small port town. She took him home with her since her husband was gone. She wanted him to take her to bed but he refused.

Never sleep with another man's wife in his own bed, he thought. *That is truly disrespectful.*

They took their time getting reacquainted. Kristal was tender and loving with his scarred and sore body. She traced the stitch lines with a fingertip as he told her what happened. Reinhold could have sworn that she looked genuinely concerned about him. It made him feel good. Their visit together was brief because the ship had only one night in Bremerhaven before leaving for Spain. They kissed goodbye. She promised to meet him the next time he was in town.

They were two days out when Reinhold noticed his food tasted weird. He questioned Werner about it.

"Does your food taste strange?"

"It is not the food, Scholz, it's the salt peter."

"The what?"

"Salt peter," Werner answered.

"Why are we eating salt peter? Isn't that what they put in gun powder to make it explode?"

"Something like that," Hein responded since Werner's mouth was full. "They put it in sailor's food to keep them from killing each other on long trips. It makes it so your dick can't get hard and you have no manliness in your blood."

"Yup, it should cool that temper of yours, Scholz." Werner said, gesturing with his fork toward where Reinhold's enemy Helmut was sitting, brooding like a snake. "Maybe we'll make it to the Mediterranean without you killing that guy."

Reinhold turned to see who they were talking about.

"Screw that guy. I'll kill him no matter how much salt peter they put in my food if he pushes me far enough. Lucky for him he decided to be quiet since I got back."

"He thinks your bad luck." Nietz laughed.

"Bad luck?" Reinhold's eyebrows went up in interest.

"Yup, since you fell and survived and came back. He thinks you've cursed the ship with bad luck."

All Reinhold could do was laugh. "Good, let him think that."

Chapter 61: Straits of Gibraltar

It was just after sunrise when the *Midgard* entered the Straits of Gibraltar. The seas were choppy and had been rolling for hours. Reinhold gave up sleeping in his bunk half way through the night. He woke up lying on a bench in the mess hall, the face of the kitchen boy standing over him. He blinked several times to clear his vision.

"It's time for breakfast, sailor," the cook called from the entrance to the galley. "Get up."

"You should see it, sir," said Henry, the wide-eyed kitchen boy. He had a Bavarian accent. "It's beautiful."

"What?"

"The Straits of Gibraltar, sir. We sailed in about an hour ago."

This got Reinhold off the bench. The morning sun was still weak in the sky, casting long shadows across the iron deck and the hatch covers. The white caps were rolling across a blue expanse of sea bracketed on each side by tan and green hills. It was the bluest water Reinhold had ever seen. The first feature of this new body of water to strike him was the pod of dolphins. The sleek slate blue creatures jumped and played near the bow of the ship, their chirps and squeaks floating over the *Midgard* on the warm morning air where they joined the calls of the seagulls.

He turned his attention to the broader landscape. The hills, he reckoned, couldn't be more than fifteen nautical miles distant from each other and the gap was narrowing. On the Spanish coast, he saw a good sized town spreading up the hillside from the sea. There were many other ships of all shapes, sizes, and flags sailing in well-organized lanes. One huge carrier, obviously one of the newer models, sailed passed on her way to the Atlantic. The shipping lanes brought them so close, Reinhold could see her crew working on deck.

Pleasure boats and yachts were darting in and out of the paths of the larger cargo carriers, making their way to different marinas along the Spanish coast or sailing majestically in the lanes, headed for distant locations. Fishing boats were easily identifiable by their lack of movement and small structure. The Spanish coast was loaded with them. The details of the Moroccan coast were barely visible but Reinhold was sure that there were lots of fishing boats there too. As the ship sailed further into the stretch of water, he saw his suspicions were correct.

Last night, over a game of chess with the mates, Reinhold learned that the strait was less than ten nautical miles at its narrowest. Fassbinder, the Second Mate and navigator, was positive that it was only seven nautical miles from Europe to Africa. This, he told Reinhold, made sailing tricky. The Mediterranean was very salty and warm. This water met the colder, less salty Atlantic waters causing the choppiness he saw now. He also learned that the famed Rock of Gibraltar wasn't at the narrowest point, as he had assumed. It overlooked the busiest shipping lanes in the world to the east of the narrowest point. There were several huge ports in this small section of sea. *The Midgard* would be stopping briefly to refuel and unload at the port of Algeciras, the largest one in the area. It was located, as he learned, in the morning shadow of the Rock. Having been to Spain and Portugal before, Reinhold wasn't expecting much from Alegcirca. He was expecting quite a bit from the Rock of Gibraltar.

Reinhold stood at the rail watching the straits pass by, listening to the sounds of the wakening ship, until he figured he should go into breakfast or lose the chance to eat. The crew was in a collective weird mood, a byproduct of the rough seas overnight. No one spoke over breakfast. They spoke only when needed as they took their places for docking. Alegcirca was approaching quickly. The tugs and pilots were coming to greet them at the mouth of the large cove where the port was sheltered. Reinhold took his position at the spring line. Docking went smoothly.

Once the ship moored safely, Reinhold allowed himself to gaze in wonder at the huge rock that dominated the horizon to the east. Its size was not what impressed Reinhold the most. He had seen sheer cliffs, rocky outcrops, and barren islands in abundance in Scandinavia. It was the unmistakable position and composition that instilled awe in the sailor. This rocky outcrop seemed like a mistake, like someone forgot to pick it up and put it away when they were done with it. It looked very much like it didn't belong.

"Impressive, huh?"

Reinhold jumped, surprised by the sound of the Second Mate's voice.

"Yes, sir. Very impressive."

"The Romans called it the Pillars of Hercules. Its twin is on the other side of the straits."

He pointed across the channel. In the distance, Reinhold could make out a double peak rock formation. "They believed these two rocks marked the boundaries of the known world. There was nothing beyond to them but gods and monsters. People have been using this port since they first set foot in a boat."

"Oh" was all Reinhold could say.

"Too bad we won't be here long enough for you to see it closer or go to the beach or to take the ferry to the other side, to Africa. We leave as soon as we unload the coal in hatch one. Better get down there and help them get the cover off, sailor."

"Coal, sir? I thought we were dropping fertilizer."

The Second Mate eyed him coolly before responding.

"The fertilizer is for the next port. Today, we unload coal here. Understand? Now get your ass down to hatch one."

"Yes, sir."

Somewhere he had missed that they were stopping at multiple ports in Spain. He was very disappointed that he wouldn't be going to a beach in this beautiful spot on a hot summer day.

It is probably full of beautiful Spanish women, he thought glumly to himself.

The port's facilities were a bit more modern than the other Spanish ports Reinhold had visited. This one was outfitted with many large cranes for bulk unloading that would have been at home in Rotterdam or Hamburg. As soon as the hatch covers and beams were gone, the operators dug in, scooping up the sooty black energy source and stowing it safely aboard train cars. He was pleasantly surprised by how efficient the longshoremen were but he noted that they looked at the crew of the *Midgard* suspiciously. They were dark men with dark eyes in loose fitting, almost billowy, shirts and short black pants. Many were bare foot. Reinhold couldn't image touching the sun heated metal of the deck with no shoes.

The ship very rarely came to this port and therefore had no relationship with the shore men. They wanted to get the strange ship and its crew on its way as soon as possible so they could move in another, more trustworthy vessel, that might have goods to trade or sell on the vast black market. They were underway again by suppertime. A crew of sailors was already in hatch one, cleaning the coal dust.

The *Midgard* headed east out of Alegcirca, passing the Rock of Gibraltar, and heading further into the Mediterranean. As far as Reinhold could gather, they were headed for the Ebre River, some two days sail away. They were to drop the fertilizer off in-land, at a town called Tortosa, wherever the hell that was. Reinhold kept an eye on the landscape as they traveled and he worked in the sun.

The Spanish coast was dotted by small towns, larger cities, and lone villas on hilltops with the occasional fortress recalling days gone by. It was lovely against the backdrop of the blue sea. But it was hot! It was the hottest weather Reinhold had ever encountered. By the end of the second night, the crew was looking for ways to cool off. One of the old timers who sailed these waters before said that they tried on his ships in the past to waterski without much luck. It was a great way to cool down, he said.

By the time the ship reached the Ebre River in the province of Catalonia, Nietz, Hein, and couple of other guys had worked out a system of lines and found a flat board for water skiing. They were going to try it on their way back to the Atlantic as they all assumed they would be leaving the Mediterranean after Tortosa.

They took the turn into the Ebre River and headed up river through a dense and beautiful delta area packed with fields of what looked like wheat and vegetables. They passed a through a sleepy village that took up space on both sides of the river. It was like looking at a postcard complete with chickens in the street and children running around with no shoes or shirts. They stopped to watch the ship float passed, wide eyed and curious. Some followed for as long as they could, waving to the sailors and shouting things in Spanish. One sailor threw a candy bar, barely making it to the shore. It was picked up by a little girl in a tan colored dress. She quickly stuffed it in her pocket and ran from the other children who threatened to take it from her.

The *Midgard* pressed on out of the lush delta into the Spanish countryside. The crops still grew on either side of the river but it was noticeably less fertile and there were irrigation systems at work, large trenches siphoning off water from the river. They passed another small town and again children ran after the ship. Reinhold was surprised when it was Nietz who threw a candy bar to the shore.

"Sun and heat getting to you, Nietz?" Reinhold questioned.

He didn't get a response. The other sailor simply shrugged and shuffled away.

A short way further up the Ebre, the *Midgard* came to the town of Tortosa. It was smaller than Reinhold was expecting. The town had only two piers big enough to hold the *Midgard*. They docked quickly with the aid of an ancient tugboat and got the hatch covers open so the unloading could begin. The only crane in sight was a smaller model that could be moved as needed. The operator maneuvered it into place with expert skill and slowly began hoisting out buckets full of fertilizer.

"Looks like we are going to be here for a couple of days, boys." Werner pointed out.

He was standing next to hatch three, arms folding, gazing into the open pit before his feet.

"That it does," Hein agreed.

He turned his gaze to shore. A group of children had gathered to watch the excitement as well as a few adults. "I bet there is nothing to do in this place."

"There is always a bar." Reinhold pointed out.

The bar had cheap, warm beer and a good selection of prostitutes. The sailors took a table and ordered while the locals stared at them over the rims of their glasses. The owner spoke a bit of German. He told them the big activity in the town was the daily market. It took place in the town square, not far from what the town called a port, which was really just the two piers and a boat launch. Bored and not interested in the girls (must have been the salt peter!), Reinhold headed back the ship and read the night away.

In the morning, after breakfast, the bosun informed them that they had the day off. The unloading was the primary focus so they could stay and help to earn some overtime or they could get the hell out of his face. Reinhold chose the latter and left the ship with Hein and Werner while Nietz stayed to help with the cargo.

They wandered over to the market area not expecting much and were pleasantly surprised. There were booths full of fish he had never seen before. The colors were astounding: yellows, blues, reds, and oranges. There were eels like he had never seen before. The sailors bought some of these fish with the intentions of cooking them on the deck of the ship. The locals watched them and the children followed them. The town was obviously very poor. Many of the children looked half starved. Reinhold wondered if it was neglect or lack of resources. He slipped a couple of coins to children that got close enough. They roasted the fish over a fire in an old bucket. They were delicious.

It was a lovely, quaint place but the crew of the *Midgard* was happy to leave it. The bosun informed them they were headed to Italy, Sicily to be exact. What the cargo was, Reinhold didn't know and didn't care. On the way to the island, the guys perfected their water skiing technique and Reinhold played chess with the mates. He learned that they were to be in port at Sicily for less than four hours to pick up "a package". From there they were bringing said package directly back to Germany, Hamburg to be exact.

Chapter 62: The Soviets?

Back in Hamburg, Reinhold got the surprise of his life. Bernard Muuss was standing on the pier waiting for him and he had a car.

"What are you doing here?" Reinhold asked his childhood friend, shaking his hand, and smacking him on the shoulder. "How did you find me?"

"It is not that hard, Reinhold. My father was a sailor, remember? I just went to the agent and asked where you were and when your ship was expected back."

Reinhold laughed in happiness and at his stupidity. Of course, that is how Bernard found him. That's how everyone finds him.

Reinhold introduced Bernard to Werner, Nietz, and Hein before they took off to get food and catch up. Bernard was going to school to be an engineer. To make money, he was working as a roofer. There was a ton of work going on in Hamburg so he was doing really well for himself.

"Sometimes I regret not meeting you that morning, Reinhold."

It was late and the two had been drinking since dinner at a little pub on the outskirts of Hamburg, Bernard's favorite. Reinhold was convinced that he liked it because he was sweet on the bartender. Or maybe just her breasts. Reinhold didn't blame his friend. They were the girl's more prominent feature. He called for another round just so he could watch her walk it over.

"Don't regret the past, Bernie. You did what you did and that is fine."

"But maybe I should have gone with you. It sounds like you have had some fun."

"Yeah, and I've worked my ass off." He took a mouthful of beer. "And I almost died. Recently. I got a guy on my ship right now that likes to listen when I bring a girl home."

"But you didn't. And why does he listen?"

"Who knows. Cheap son of a bitch. Sneaky, too I have to keep an eye on my clean shirts or he'll take them."

Bernard laughed. "Sounds like a stand up guy."

Reinhold shrugged. "He's alright. That's just people for you, right? We all have our something. It's the Captains that are the worst. Drunks, most of them. And the mates? Jeez, would think someone anointed them. Do you know just last week the Chief Engineer on my ship punched me so hard, I went flying through the galley?" Reinhold paused to light a cigarette. "Just because I didn't wake him up on time."

"Really?"

"Well, not exactly. I actually forgot to wake him up all together but the point is......"

He trailed off because Bernard was laughing at him again.

"You're something else, Scholz."

"If I had a *mark* for every time I heard that line."

Reinhold frowned. He was just being himself. Why did it seem so incredulous?

The Reinhold standing on the deck of the *Brandenburg* smiled to himself. That had been a great night and the beginning of many. Bernard met him, and still meets him, on the pier in Hamburg whenever he has the time. That was in September, 1953. He remembered because that night ended with him going home with a girl who was celebrating her birthday. She was seventeen on the seventeenth of September. A bit young for him, usually, but she had just been so charming, with a beautiful handkerchief that Reinhold's innards had melted on sight. The good news was she had a friend for Bernard.

"Where are you headed next Reinhold?" Bernard asked as they drove back to the port.

"Rostok, I think. I heard the mate say something about cement. We get that it Rostok."

"East Germany? You've been there before?"

"Yup."

"They give you any problems? The Soviets?"

Reinhold shook his head. "No, but there are a lot of rules. We can't leave the port, or else."

He drew his finger across his throat and then laughed half-heartedly. He knew that it wasn't a joke. They probably would kill him. The two friends parted ways at the pier.

Reinhold's assumption was correct. The *Midgard's* next port was Rostok, in all of its Soviet cheerfulness. Once again, a boat met the ship as they entered the port bearing a pilot and engineer and an officer with the Soviet army. The officer scrutinized their passports while the pilot took up his position at the bridge window. Nietz received extra attention because he was a Polish German, born in Anklam. He was called to the bridge to meet with the officer, who was concerned he was a defector. Nietz, spitting obscenities and threatening an international incident, was the angriest Reinhold, Quartermaster at the time, had ever seen him. It was a joke on the ship that Nietz was a Polish German but to Nietz, he was just a German.

"A defector, my ass!" He yelled at the officer. "You are the invaders, you self-righteous *arschloch*. Or maybe you are just a coward, working for the people who have a boot on your neck. Afraid that you'll let something slip past and get yourself shot so you harass the innocent...."

"Enough!" The Captain had to get involved to quiet the situation. "What is the problem here, officer?"

"I suspect this man is a defector."

"He is a sailor, not a 'man', first of all. Second, aren't there enough people defecting from this place in truth? You have to make up these charges? Get off my bridge. Continue your 'inspections' elsewhere. Sailor, you stay here."

The soldier sputtered in response but knew he had no recourse. He pulled himself up to his full height and came to attention with such ferocity that his heels actually clicked together. He saluted the Captain before leaving the bridge. Reinhold had to stifle a snicker and got the evil eye from the Captain.

The Soviets didn't want non-Soviets, outsiders, hanging around their ports for too long. The *Midgard*, thankfully, was loaded with cement and ready to go in two days' time. The night before departure, Werner and Reinhold sat in a portside tavern, drinking, when a young woman approached them. She brazenly offered her body to them for passage on their ship. She didn't care where they were headed. Reinhold had a moment of déjà vu, remembering the girl they took aboard before he fell. He couldn't remember her name but he remembered the anxiety of being caught and the excitement of being caught.

"Sure, we'll sneak you out of here. We just have to go talk with our crew and get you some men's clothes. We can't sneak you out of here as a woman."

Her eyes lit up with hope. "I don't care if you dress me as a fish!"

It didn't take long for the crew to agree to the clandestine activity. Most of them were involved when Niemec brought his girlfriend aboard. Nietz was one of the holdouts, which was surprising considering there was free *pflaume* in his future. His confrontation with the Soviet officer rattled him worse than he was letting on. Finally, he consented. All agreed that the stokers, mates, Captain, and kitchen staff would remain blissfully ignorant.

Werner and Reinhold met the girl back at the bar, leaving the clothes outside. They sent her out to change and wait for them. It looked less conspicuous this way. After a couple of rounds of Polish beer, the sailors left, picking the girl up on their way. The three of them headed for the tracks, avoiding the port patrols, acting like the drunk sailors they were supposed to be. One patrol crossed the tracks too close for comfort, forcing them to hide under a freight car that Reinhold was pretty sure had last carried livestock, judging purely by the smell. They swayed, under the hard stare of another patrol, on their way across the open freight yard to the pier where the launch boat would pick them up. The waiting was agony. It seemed like an hour before the small craft bumped against the pier. For good measure, Reinhold was sure to stumble and fall into the boat when it arrived. The patrol moved on, obviously convinced they were just drunken sailors.

On the short trip to the ship, the girl, whose name Reinhold couldn't remember, gave Werner a brief demonstration of her oral abilities, which were considerable given Werner's endowment. Once on board, they went below to continue getting to know each other while Reinhold hung out on deck. He scanned the dimly lit harbor, looking to see if they had been followed or for any other signs of alarm from shore. When he was satisfied they weren't under suspicion, he also went below deck to collect his payment from their stowaway.

Looking back, Reinhold was glad that he could smile about the situation. The *Midgard* left Rostok and traveled to Helsinki without incident. They helped the girl to the port entrance where they said goodbye. Like the previous defector, she scampered away like a bunny and disappeared into the hustle and bustle of the Finnish waterfront wearing her sailor's clothes. The sailors treated themselves to a trip to the sauna. It could have turned out much worse.

Reinhold had to question himself as to why he left the *Midgard*. It was a great ship. Why had he left? The pain from his injuries never abated completely while he was with her but that wasn't the reason. Instinctively, he ran his tongue along the inside of his upper teeth. Then it dawned on him.

"Helmut," he sighed aloud to himself. "That bastard."

The incident returned to him crystal clear and just as enraging now as it had been then. The *Midgard* was on her way to Amsterdam from Stockholm. It was a beautiful late October evening. Reinhold and his friends were hanging out on the deck, enjoying the brisk breeze and a spectacular sunset when Helmut stumbled into their midst, obviously drunk. Of course, the guys couldn't let that one go without a good verbal flogging.

Nietz started it with Werner and Hein quickly picking up the line. Reinhold chose to remain silent, which, he had to admit, was unusual for him. On this night, he felt bad for Helmut. In the months since he had returned to the ship, the man had deteriorated into a hopeless drunk who shook violently. He was also completely paranoid; sadly so, seeing and hearing things everywhere. There were more alarms when Helmut stood watch for a night then Reinhold had heard on all his previous ships combined. He said nothing as Nietz laid into the drunk little man.

"What's this?" The tone was snide. "A fly in our web? What say you, boys, shall we suck him dry."

Helmut just looked confused for a moment. "What are you guys doing out here……" His voice trailed off.

"Did you hear that?" Werner chimed. "He tried to form a question. What do you want to know, Helmut? Why you are so pathetic, maybe?"

Reinhold thought that was a little harsh. Pathetic was a hurtful word.

"Who are you calling pat—peth—pis," Helmut slurred, stumbling on the word, becoming more angry.

"You hear that?" Hein asked. "He can't even get the word out! It's pathetic, Helmut. P-A-T-H-E-T-I-C. Try to get it right."

Reinhold shook his head and turned his attention to the sea, watching the waves swell passed the ship. A storm was brewing.

"What are you shaking your head at?" Helmut sounded almost sober.

A commotion erupted suddenly and Reinhold turned his attention back to the men. An iron pipe made contact with the side of his face. Pain exploded in his eyes and his mind turned red and black with streaks of bright yellow. Before he knew what he was doing, he had Helmut by the neck and he was punching him in the face, aiming for his nose and eyes. He felt hands trying to pull him back and heard voices screaming in his ears but he continued to make contact. In his defense, Helmut put his arms up to block his face. Reinhold responded by aiming his blows at the man's ribs.

Reinhold didn't know how long he had been assaulting the drunk man when his friends finally succeeded in pulling them apart. Werner had his arms pinned behind his back, putting burning pressure on his injured shoulder. The red glare slowly drained from Reinhold's mind, leaving the ship's deck in its place. Hein and Nietz had Helmut in a similar position as Reinhold. He tasted blood. With his tongue, he probed his front teeth. One was very loose. When he exerted more pressure on it, it popped right out of its socket. Rage filled him again. He spit the tooth at Helmut, sending a spray of blood with it that speckled the other man's face and chest.

"You fucking pig! You knocked my tooth out! I should kill you right here! Let me go."

He struggled against Werner's grip but couldn't dislodge his arms. Helmut's face, still speckled with blood, went white with fright. He too struggled against his captors. Hein and Nietz couldn't hold him. Helmut ran from the scene, stumbling and tripping his way aft.

"Get back here you fucking coward. I'll rip you apart with my bare hands! This is it for you, *arschloch*! When I get a hold of you, you're dead! Let go of me, goddammit!"

He stopped screaming when the hatch slammed behind the retreating man. Shaking off Werner's slackened grip, he looked around the deck, feeling oddly self-conscious. Many other sailors heard the commotion and came to see what had happened. There were a dozen people standing there, all staring at him. His friends' faces looked apprehensive. They were waiting for him to go after Helmut again. Instinctively, Reinhold's tongue sought out the hole where his tooth used to be. Anger welled in him again and pain surged through his body both from the new injury and the aggravating of the old ones.

"What the hell are you all staring at?" Reinhold bellowed before stalking off toward the galley to wash up and rinse with salt water.

The men assembled on the deck parted so he could pass. The bosun, he noticed, was amongst those gathered but the man said nothing as Reinhold walked away. He didn't dare go down below to the sailor's washroom. If he ran into Helmut down there with no one to stop him he might bang the man's head against the iron bulkhead until it squished like an over ripe plum.

Helmut was smart enough after this incident to keep his distance from Reinhold. Upon arrival in Amsterdam, he was smart enough to sign off the *Midgard*. Reinhold was disappointed. He had been looking forward to beating the crap out of the little man on shore. The Third Mate, having heard about what happened over a game of chess, sent Reinhold to the see a local dentist. The doctor put in a temporary bridge, temporary being the important word. The first meal out to sea, the damn thing fell out leaving an ugly, gaping hole in its place. No one dared say a word about it.

Reinhold remembered the trip from Amsterdam to Germany feeling like a long one. When the *Midgard* turned into the mouth of the Elbe, he figured they were going to Hamburg. Surprisingly, the ship sailed across the bay to the canal entrance. There had been no chess games since they left Amsterdam so he had no idea why they were headed for the canal or what their final destination was when they were through. Eight hours later, he had his answer when the ship sailed passed Holtenau into the Baltic Sea, hugging the German coastline. He had hoped they were going to stop in Holtenau for the night. He wanted to sleep in his bed in his room on the hill. A night of chess with the brass informed him they were to put in to Lübeck.

Reinhold laid in bed that night, thinking, his tongue playing idly with the gap in his teeth. It made his heart race to know that he would never get to teach Helmut the dangers of being a drunken *arschloch*. His shoulder was throbbing dully and there was a sharp pain deep in his knee. He had noticed that the joint was creaking today and seeming to catch in its socket, causing him to have a halting gait. Sighing, Reinhold rolled over on his side, bending his knee, hoping to relieve some of the pain while blocking Hein's snoring out of one of his ears.

The next afternoon, as he stood waiting to throw the spring line, his knee throbbing, Reinhold decided he was done. He was signing off and going home. Involuntarily, he shivered in the rising wind, a reminder that another Northern Europe winter was coming. He didn't want to know how the winter was going to affect his injured body.

First, he had to go get his tooth fixed. If he left before doing that, the company might not pay for it. The Third Mate got him an appointment with a dentist and Reinhold was pleasantly surprised when he found that what he expected to be a he was actually a she. She explained to him very matter-of-factly that the company only paid for porcelain replacement but for an additional sixty *mark*, she would make him a gold replacement that would be more durable and, of course, more befitting a sailor. When Reinhold explained that he wasn't going to be a sailor all his life, she countered by saying that he would always have the scars and tattoos from his time as a sailor so he might as well make them as good as he can.

"Who wants to be with a bland ex-sailor?" She asked him.

He had no reply so he forked over the sixty *mark* and she made him a gold tooth. It was a damn good tooth; just as efficient for opening beer bottles as the real one.

Once that was done, Reinhold broke the news to the guys that he was leaving.

"What do you mean you're leaving?" Hein demanded. "I don't want another bunkmate, again! The last one sucked."

Reinhold shrugged. "It is time for me to move on. I want to spend the winter some place warm like the Mediterranean. It was great there."

"We were there in the summer," Nietz pointed out. "You have no idea what it is like down there in January."

"Do you?" Reinhold asked, already knowing the answer.

"Well, no but…"

Werner eyed him knowingly. "Beware the Greek ships, Reinhold. They do strange things with each other and with animals, if you get my meaning. Try to get an Italian one. They're a bit better. Good food from what I understand."

Reinhold nodded. "Yes, you've mentioned in the past." He still thought his friend was exaggerating.

"You are determined to leave?"

"Yes, Hein, I am determined to leave."

"Then there is only one thing to do. Who's going out for drinks tonight?" A cheer went up from the group. "Then the Red Cat it is!"

The sailors went out, got entirely too drunk, and ended up at the *puff* where Emma worked on Clemensstrasse. She was there and they intrigued her with stories of Werner's legendary size. They made a deal that if he was the biggest she had ever seen, he could have her free. The specifics of the deal were laboriously finalized and the two went off upstairs to be alone. In the end, Emma didn't charge Werner and he spent the rest of the night being an egotistical nightmare.

Reinhold said goodbye to his friends and signed off the *Midgard* on November 2, 1953.

Chapter 63: Are Those Sheep?

Standing in the shade of the bulkhead of the *Brandenburg*, Reinhold sighed to himself. He tapped another cigarette out of the rapidly emptying pack and rolled it around in his fingers for a minute, staring at the horizon. Finally, he stuck it between his lips and lit it, taking a long draw, exhaling slowly, enjoying the burning sensation in his chest.

The winter of 1953- 1954 was a difficult one for him. After signing off the *Midgard*, Reinhold went home to his room on the hill. He spent two days being a bum, sleeping and drinking. Herbert's wife, Katie, told him that Herbert was off with the German company Hapag. It reminded Reinhold that he wanted to work for them. Somehow, he had lost sight of that goal. Now that he was a full *Matrose*, he could probably get a job with them. He was hesitant because of his physical condition. The pain in his knee didn't subside. The cold kept it cramped up and achy.

A debate raged within his mind. Should he go back to sea or stay on shore? Every whistle or horn that drifted up the hill to his window or found him sitting on a bar stool in the seaman's club called him back to the sea. Again, he began hanging around the canal, bumming cigarettes and food from passing ships, hoping that it would quell the sea longing. It didn't. Katie tried to convince him on one of Herbert's trips home that he should find a nice girl and settle down on shore.

"There are jobs now." She said. "Kiel looks more and more like it's old self every month. The opera house is a big project. Maybe they need help there. You know how much you like the opera. They probably pay enough to support a family."

Reinhold smiled politely and agreed with everything she said. It wasn't hard. What she described was what he wanted. He just didn't want it there, in Germany. It wasn't long before Reinhold found himself in the seaman's office. He put himself on the list for a warm weather bound ship.

Two days later, the agent at the office woke him out of a deep slumber to tell him that a Greek ship had called. They needed a sailor and Reinhold's name was next on the list.

"Where is it going?" Reinhold asked, rubbing his eyes and groping around for his wool cap.

"It is headed to its home port, Thessaloniki, I think the guy said. I could barely understand him with the thick accent." The agent looked at Reinhold searchingly. "Are you going to be able to understand Greek? I can't really send you out if you are going to have language problems."

"I'll be fine." Reinhold waved the man away. "Just give me the marching orders."

"Ok."

The agent didn't seem convinced. The big man lumbered back to his desk and scribbled down the name and location of the ship.

"Good luck."

Reinhold wasn't sure at the time why he needed luck but now, three years later, he understood. The ship its self was unimpressive. It was the same size and build as the *Midgard,* maybe a bit newer. There was a crew of swarthy men busy scrubbing down the deck with stiff brushes on long sticks and buckets of something Reinhold didn't recognize. Nodding to the sailors as he passed, he made his way to the bridge stairway. No one stopped working to stare at him, but they did stare. He didn't like the looks of several of the men. They made him uncomfortable in a way he hadn't experienced since he was a younger man.

As he mounted the ladder to the bridge, a strange sound caught his attention. It was something like a cow getting strangled. Looking over the railing, he saw, strangely enough, a small pen, maybe 10x20, holding several sheep. They were chewing lazily on a pile of hay and making loud, doleful noises.

Why would a ship have sheep? He asked himself before coming to a dead stop, Werner's comments about Greeks coming rushing back to him.

Good Lord, maybe he was right.

Shaking it off, Reinhold continued to the bridge where he found the Captain, a small old timer with a thick accent and liquor on his breath. There was a bottle of something clear and licorice smelling on the map table in front of him. He seemed nice enough if a bit drunk.

The Captain sent Reinhold down to the deck to meet the bosun, a man that didn't speak a word of German. Through hand communication and facial expression, Reinhold gathered that the ship was leaving soon to traverse the canal. With a sharp toss of his head, the bosun told him to go below and stow his things. Nodding his understanding, Reinhold headed below deck, feeling eyes on him as he walked away. He felt like an animal in a field.

Below deck, he swung open the third hatch on the port side and came face to face with a small, dark man with a two-day-old beard and a cigarette clenched between his teeth. There was a colorful handkerchief tied around his neck. In his hands was a small, black gun and a dirty rag. He rubbed the gun with the rag and glared at Reinhold without saying anything. Reinhold nodded a curt greeting and threw his sea bag on the bottom bunk, deciding quickly to leave the room and explore the ship.

As he searched for the washroom, he couldn't help thinking that it was odder than odd that his bunkmate had a gun and didn't speak. In all honesty, he was a bit freaked out. Greeks were heavy drinkers, he knew from running into shiploads of them in Sweden, Spain, and Hamburg. He didn't trust a drunk man with a gun.

He found the washroom but didn't go in because he heard voices issuing from inside. They weren't conversational voices. It sounded something like an argument. Turning on his heel, he headed back above deck. Half way up the ladder, a bell sounded. If it meant the same thing on this ship as it did on the other ships Reinhold had served with it meant it was time to leave. He exited the small forecastle and made for the spring line position. The shore crew cast off the lines and the ship headed for the canal entrance. No turning back now, Reinhold thought, looking around at the crew he had just signed up to work with for an indefinite amount of time.

Normally, when a ship is in the canal, the crew relaxes a bit. There is nothing for them to do. A canal crew handles the ship. This was usually a time for making acquaintances but none of the Greek sailors approached Reinhold to introduce themselves. They all stared moodily at him as they went about their work. Rapidly, the feeling of being an animal in a field was replaced by the feeling of being a steak on the table of a starving man. He decided to sign off this ship before they passed the Audorfer See at Schacht-Audorf. Going to the bridge, he explained to the Captain that he was sick, that his old injury had flared up at cast off and there was no way he would make it to Greece in his condition.

For the life of him, Reinhold couldn't remember that Captain's name and couldn't look it up in his seaman's book because he had been on the ship so little time that he was never properly signed on. He thought it was something like Ladas or Latos. Either way, the Captain was not happy with this new sailor but he acquiesced. The Second Mate set a course for Brunsbüttel. The canal pilot was not happy with the alteration either. It upset the flow of traffic. Now they had to figure out if there was space for them to lay anchor until a replacement for Reinhold was found. After an hour of back and forth on the radio, the pilot informed Reinhold that he would leaving the ship on the pilot's launch boat. Everything else was worked out, a replacement sailor had even been found. Lucky for the Greeks, it was one of their own.

"Are you really hurt?" The pilot asked on the ride to shore.

"Yes, but not that bad. I just wanted to get off that ship. Did you see the way they looked at me?"

The pilot laughed. "Why did you sign on to a Greek ship in the first place?"

Reinhold shrugged. "I wanted to go someplace warm."

Again the pilot laughed. "Go to the Middle East then. With a German ship. Or South America. Or Africa. Might want to avoid the Mediterranean. They have a different idea about acceptable ship board behavior."

Looking back, Reinhold laughed at the situation. He had lasted eight hours onboard with the Greeks.

They wanted to get me into bed so bad they could taste it, so to speak, he mused to himself. *How often had they seen a blonde haired, blue eyed young guy on their ship? Probably about as often as I've seen a mermaid.*

He laughed again. Thinking about the bunkmate with the gun dulled the laughter. He hadn't trusted a Greek since and he had run into plenty of them. He wondered why that sailor was allowed to have a firearm onboard. A German or Swedish ship would never have tolerated it. Shrugging, Reinhold let the thought go.

Chapter 64: Back To Salvage

The rest of the winter passed without incident or interest. Reinhold lay around, nursing his injuries and keeping bar stools warm all over Kiel and Holtenau. He met several attractive and interesting young ladies and he paid at least three of their electric bills with his disability money. Half-heartedly, he looked for work on shore doing construction or working in a factory but everything sounded so boring that he passed over most opportunities. He visited Lisa several times to get money from his post book. Willie, his brother in law, was starting to joke that the only time they saw Reinhold was when he needed money. Lisa wasn't joking when she told him that Isolde had tuberculosis.

He wrote to Marta on Föhr twice. She was saying that she loved him and wanted him to come visit so he could make her a woman, which she was saving for him and, oh, how she wanted to get rid of it! It was very tempting to get a train up there and take the ferry across to the island. He had never had a virgin before. Fear prevented him. He didn't want to get stuck being a farmer, no matter where the farm was located. Instead, he wrote how much he loved her too and how much he wanted to see her but he was wounded and unable to get around well. Maybe in the spring, he suggested. She seemed to believe him and sent many good wishes for a speedy recovery.

In January, he got talking to a guy at the seaman's club in Kiel. It turned out he worked for Winckler Shipyard. The yard was looking for two guys with sailing experience to accompany a scuttled ship from Kiel to Hamburg to Blohm & Voss Shipyard. There would be no actual sailing involved. The two men would really just function as a security detail, making sure nothing happened to the ship en route. Reinhold said he was interested and two days later he and another guy named Karl left Kiel in the shell of a ship being towed by a much bigger ship and a hundred yard long line. It took eight days for them to get around the Jutland Peninsula and into port at Hamburg. It was uneventful except for a massive storm in the Skagerrak that reminded Reinhold of the seven days he spent swirling around in the straits on the *Midgard*. He and Karl took turns standing watch. They cooked their food over an open fire in a barrel since there was no galley. The fire was also their source of heat since there was no coal or furnaces. It was a cold, boring trip.

Upon reaching Hamburg, the sailors were paid cash by the agent at Blohm & Voss. Reinhold treated himself to a trip around the city, meaning the Reeperbahn, and an evening hanging out with Bernard Muuss. He spent the night in the seaman's office with a bunch of other drunk sailors, sleeping with his arms over a cord hung between the walls of the room.

In the morning, an agent woke them all up by cutting the line. Reinhold hit the floor with all the others. Thankfully, he didn't land on his right side. He considering hanging around Hamburg for a few days but decided against it when it took several hours to get the proper circulation back in his arms after a night hanging on the rope. He got a train back to Kiel instead.

By February, he was restless. Two months of sitting around with just the scuttled ship to break the monotony had taken their toll on him. He wanted to go back to work and paid a visit to the agent office. It was packed! There was forty guys sitting around dozing, playing cards, reading, chatting, and waiting.

"I suggest you take the first ship that comes around, sailor."

The agent was a new guy that Reinhold hadn't dealt with before. He was the youngest agent he had ever seen and was missing an eye. Reinhold was beginning to think it was mandatory to be old or maimed to work in the agent's office.

"We have a lot of people waiting, as you can see." He gestured toward the room with his chin.

Reinhold took a seat and pulled a book out of his jacket pocket. He wasn't sure what to hope for so he didn't hope at all. His ship turned out to be a salvage ship. Not glamorous, as Marta would have said, but a ship that came with a paycheck. She was in town refueling but was destined for anchor in the canal not far from Holtenau near the Gross-Nordsee lay-by. She was salvaging a ship that sunk due to a collision. He reported at the Holtenau canal entrance to the *Hiev*. Almost immediately, they cast off for the accident site. On the sail there, Geoff, the bosun, explained the situation.

"We got a vessel underwater, a team of divers trying to patch the rip in the hull, and three support vessels, including this one. There are six sailors on this ship including you and me. There is also a cook and a team of divers with their support people. But they move from ship to ship as the fancy strikes them. You ever work salvage before?"

Reinhold nodded. "I was with the *Pakistan* out in the North Sea. We salvaged navy ships. It took several months, if I remember correctly."

"So you are familiar with what is going to happen. Once we get to the site, the Captain is going to leave, the lazy bastard, and I am in charge. There are no other mates right now. The First Mate got drunker than hell one night last week and fell into the canal from the bridge wing. Almost froze to death. They took three of his toes and two fingers at the hospital. Once they release him, he'll be back. We have to be prepared to sail at any time even if it is just to reposition the ship. Other than that, you will be standing watch, assisting the divers, and doing maintenance. Any questions?"

Reinhold shook his head. He had the fleeting thought that now the First Mate could go work for the agent's office.

"Seems pretty straight forward."

"It is. You'll only be out here for two weeks. Captain is afraid that if you stay longer than that, you'll go crazy. Don't take it personally. You'll understand once you are on site."

Reinhold understood quickly. The salvage site was almost as boring as not working. He got up in the morning, had breakfast, and went to the deck where he threw some lines around in an attempt to pretend to work before heading back below deck to read until it was time to eat again. The most interesting part was talking to the divers. He was half hoping he would know some of them from the *Pakistan* but that wasn't the case. They told him the ship they were trying to patch was a Soviet ship.

"The Reds are making it hard for us to do our job because they won't let us into the hull to repair the damage from inside," explained one of the younger divers. He was giving the crew of the *Hiev* an update on the operation over lunch.

"Why won't they let you inside?" Reinhold questioned.

The diver looked around suspiciously and lowered his voice, forcing the assembled sailors to lean in.

"They say that there is gold in that ship. It was bound for the banks in London when she got side swiped by a Dutch flag. The Soviets don't want us to see it. They are afraid that we'll get gold fever like those people in Africa and South America."

"You're making that up! Gold? Right, sure." Geoff rolled his eyes at the outlandish story, unconvinced.

"It's true!" asserted the diver. "Ask anyone around here. They say that it is from the war. The Soviets confiscated all the gold the rich people had in Germany and Poland and Czechoslovakia. Some of it is on that ship right there in the canal." He nodded knowingly.

There was silence for a minute as the sailors contemplated this information. It sounded plausible but was it true? Satisfied that he made a lasting impression, the diver gathered up his dishes and left the silent sailors chewing thoughtfully. Reinhold could buy it, he figured. They did steal a lot of stuff from people.

Why wouldn't they have shiploads of gold? Why else would there be a heard of nasty looking armed guards stationed at all times around the site?

Deciding in the end that it didn't make a difference what was in the ship, Reinhold left the mess hall. It was a sunny day, perfect for pictures. He decided to take his camera ashore and document what was going on. If nothing else, it was a story he could tell his grandkids one day.

At the end of his uneventful two weeks, Reinhold sailed back to Holtenau. Once again, he found himself unemployed. For the hell of it, he went to Lübeck to see Lisa. He learned that Isolde wasn't doing any better. They put her in a sanitarium for lack of knowing what else to do with her. Her latest husband, the loser that he was, had divorced her and taken their children. But, Lisa was happy to say, Isolde met another man in the hospital and they were thinking about getting married. Isolde was still sure she was going to be cured of her tuberculosis somehow. Then she would lead a normal life again, as she called it. Reinhold wasn't so sure. He left Lisa's heavy hearted and depressed. To get over it, he spent several days drinking 'wa-wa' juice and playing cards with the sailors at the club. A favorite topic of conversation amongst them was the rebuilding of Germany. The old timers seemed convinced that once everything was rebuilt that they were going back to war.

"Somebody has to pay for it!" said one guy. "They bombed it, they should pay for it."

Reinhold was amused by the sentiment. "Who is 'they'? The British? The Americans?"

"All of them that bombed us!"

The man had a Bavarian accent. Reinhold suddenly wasn't sure he was a sailor. "Have you ever sailed to England? To London?"

"No, I ain't never been there. Why would I go there?" The man leaned over and spit on the floor in disgust. "Limey bastards."

"Are you a sailor?"

"Hell yes I am a sailor!" The man bellowed his response and people turned to look at him.

"I meant no disrespect," Reinhold said quickly, trying to calm the man down before the bartender threw them out.

He really wanted to yell back at the man for his ignorance. Reinhold saw many times for himself the devastation in London.

Goddamn Bavarians, he thought. *Always putting country before common sense. Bunch of hillbillies.*

In the beginning of March, he decided he had enough of laying around. Injured body or not, he was getting out of Germany. The rhetoric was getting worse. Everybody was talking about the next war. Who the perpetrator of this war would be differed depending on the company. Some thought it was going to be the Soviets trying to take over Europe. Some thought it was going to be the Americans who, unable to control their greed, were going to invade Europe the way they invaded Korea. Some thought it was going to be the British seeking reparations for Hitler's bombings. Reinhold didn't want to hear any of it. He couldn't wrap his head around why people were so eager for the next war when they were still cleaning up from the last one.

Over drinks one night, Reinhold asked Herbert, who was home on a two night shore leave, what he thought. His friend just shrugged.

"I hear the same stuff on the ship. Guys running their mouths, just asking for another war. All southerners. I think they put something in the water in Bavaria that makes them all crazy."

"Yeah, and what about you?'

"I am not Bavarian. I am from the Black Forest, you know that. There is a difference."

"Oh, that's right." Reinhold teased. "You're almost French, aren't you?"

Herbert responded by punching him in his bad shoulder.

Chapter 65: **Christoffer Oldendorff**

On March 10, 1954, Reinhold put his name on the list in the seaman's office. He specifically requested a long haul and went as far as to request a ship under the Hapag flag. He was done with sailing around Europe. He wanted to see the rest of the world. The agent looked at him indulgently before sending him off to take a seat. Five days later, on March 15, Reinhold walked up the gangplank of the *Christoffer Oldendorff*. It was his nineteenth birthday.

Christoffer Oldendorff
Photograph courtesy of Reinhold Scholz

The *Oldendorff* was a huge ship, the biggest he had ever worked on. It was one hundred and fifty eight feet from bow to stern and nearly thirty feet wide, weighing more than forty seven hundred tons. The hull was black while the rail stood out a gleaming white, except where the rust spots turned it a dingy shade of red. As with the *Midgard*, there were two masts with several booms each. The bridge sat four stories above the deck.

The Captain, his name was Broplin, took Reinhold's book and signed him on briskly, dismissing him almost immediately. The only information he imparted was the location of the sleeping quarters, below deck and fore. Obviously, he was the sort that didn't take a lot of interest in the crew. Reinhold learned quickly from his bunkmate and the other sailors that there was a crew of forty.

The first stop on the *Oldendorff* was the port of Gdynia, Poland. It was a grey industrial wasteland dripping with the feel of Soviet rule. It was exceedingly appropriate to him that they were loading three holds of cement. The place seemed to ooze cement and steel. The people looked harsh and harassed and the guards looked stern and cold. He didn't even bother to get off the ship, not trusting the Soviets or their citizens to leave him alone.

As he sat on the deck, smoking a cigarette, watching the activity on the shore, Reinhold thought of the girls in Rostok and how desperate they were to get out the country. He flicked the butt of his cigarette into the bay in disgust. He was very glad when they cast off. They went back to Germany for a stop in Rotterdam before continuing non-stop to the Mediterranean.

Reinhold grimaced at the thought of that stop in Rotterdam. He went ashore with some of the other guys in hopes of finding a woman to keep him company. They were going to be out to sea for two weeks before they reached Morocco, the first stop in the Mediterranean. He wanted to have a night with a girl before the saltpeter diet began. They went to a port tavern, nothing special, most of them were still dressed in their work clothes. Half of them, including Reinhold, got an early start and were already a bit drunk when they got to the bar. A beautiful woman approached Reinhold not long after they arrived. She was tall with silky blonde hair and grey smoky eyes. Considering himself lucky, he closed the deal as quickly as she opened it and they were on their way back to her place within the hour.

They were hot and heavy in the cab, lips locked, tongues intertwined, and hands wandering. She was an excellent kisser and she knew how to please a man. Her hands stroked the front of his trousers, expertly finding the sensitive spots. She was rearing to go. Reinhold wanted to gage just how ready this woman was so he slowly inched his hand up her thigh until he found the sweet spot.

Before he knew what he was doing, he was rolling out of the still moving taxi, trying to protect his injured right side from touching the pavement. He was unsuccessful. When he got to his feet, his knee buckled under the weight. He stood there, shocked, watching the cab as it drove away. A head was stuck out the window on the driver's side, blonde hair flowing in the breeze. A shudder went through him, sending rippling waves of revulsion down every nerve.

I almost went home with a guy, he remembered thinking, shocked. *I almost went home with a guy. I almost went home with a guy. I kissed a guy! What the hell? I kissed a guy and a guy was touching me! At least I got a good shot in before I jumped out of the car. I hope I broke one of his teeth! Bastard!*

He could still smell 'her' perfume on him and taste her lips on his. He spit on the sidewalk in disgust.

The shock wore off quickly and anger took its place. Reinhold had a strong desire to run after the cab, find where the thing lived, and beat it to a bloody pulp but he couldn't run. Instead, he stood there fuming, his fists clenching and unclenching while he cursed in his head, asking rhetorical questions to no one.

Did he think I wasn't going to notice? How far did that arschloch *think this was going to go? Did he think I was gay? Holy fuck, that thing thought I am gay!*

Reinhold quickly assessed where in Rotterdam he was and headed for the nearest *puff*. There was no way he was returning to the *Oldendorff* for a two week sail to Morocco with the taste of a man on his lips. He needed a stiff drink and nice set of breasts in his hands.

The saltpeter diet started as soon as they left Rotterdam. Reinhold recognized the change in the food immediately. He mentioned it to the other guys but no one seemed to notice the difference or care. This was a different crew then the *Midgard*. They were nice enough but less intelligent. Reinhold wondered why this would be the case but shrugged it off. A sailor couldn't be too particular about the company they were forced to keep onboard. Thankfully, there were no Helmuts on this ship.

The Captain, on the other hand, quickly showed himself to be a drunken narcissist. He was an old timer, not as old as the Captain of the *Eos* or the *Midgard*, but close. Reinhold had an image of Capt. Broplin stuck in his memory that was both cartoonish and malevolent. He strutted, in a staggering kind of way, around the ship, barking slurred orders to the crew that no one could understand, and the whole time being trailed by a tiny, yipping dog named Twist. It didn't matter that the crew couldn't understand him because he quickly forgot that he had issued any orders at all. He drank so much that he was in bed every night by 8:00 and dead to the world until 5:00 in the morning. If there was an issue to deal with, the First Mate was the go-to man.

The First Mate, Musil, was the complete opposite to the Captain. He was sober, organized, down to earth, and genuinely friendly with everyone he met. Reinhold learned a bit about him over a few chess games on their way to the Mediterranean, but not too much. He was a tight-lipped Polish German who had survived the war by hiding out in the wrecked train yard of the Polish port he was sailing out of when the Germans attacked. Reinhold hadn't recognized the name at the time and now couldn't remember which one it was. Musil managed to get out of East Germany on foot across the fields and open country when he learned that the Russians were closing the borders and annexing the east. Once in what is now the west, he hired on to the first ship that would have him and never looked back.

The Second and Third Mates were non-descript men that Reinhold remembered little about. The Second Mate seemed OK but they only interacted when Reinhold was Quartermaster. The Third Mate was OK too but distant and cold. He didn't get involved with anyone or anybody. Reinhold remembered him rarely speaking unless it was to issue an order or deliver a message. If his memory served correctly, they were both Frisian and everyone knows the saying about the Frisians: They don't waste words or smiles.

By the time the ship arrived at the Straits of Gibraltar, Reinhold had learned that it was the bosun, Herr Baumhauer, who had the Captain's ear. He insisted people address him as 'Herr Baumhauer' or 'Sir'. Nothing else was acceptable. The evil man reported everything he saw and heard to the Captain. He was just a little guy with a big fish in a small pond mentality.

Another goddamn little guy with a big freakin' mouth, Reinhold mused to himself.

Many harsh punishments were dealt out to sailors who made the mistake of commenting on the Captain's drinking or leadership abilities within earshot of 'Herr Baumhauer'. Tensions quickly mounted. Before the ship reached its first scheduled stop at Morocco, there was a deep divide between the bosun and the crew. The First Mate became the go-to man for the sailors not just for issues and problems, but for day to day communications.

Reinhold was extremely disappointed when he learned there would not be time to get off the ship in Morocco. He spent their day in port working, repairing a hairline crack in the stack, watching from the deck during lunch as the vendors pedaled their exotic wares. There were handmade baskets that Lisa would have loved, fruits that Reinhold would have liked to try, cooked dishes that made the food on the *Oldendorff* look like it was only fit for a dog, and, oh, the women! They were beautiful with brown skin and dark eyes, so like the women in Spain but so different at the same time. He wanted to run his fingers through their glossy black hair to see if it really was as soft and thick as it looked.

He was struck, as in Spain and Portugal, by the old fashion, almost primitive, nature of the port. There were several pylon style piers but there was only one set of tracks and one crane. It was not even a heavy lifting model. It was busy unloading a ship flying a French flag. Reinhold took a break to smoke a cigarette and watched while tall, scrawny longshoremen unloaded bags of cement by hand, carrying them on their heads down the gangplank to a waiting ex-army truck. In the distance, no fences or barriers marked the boundaries of the industrial area because there wasn't much of one. Chickens roamed and goats bayed. Reinhold was fascinated and repulsed by the simplicity of the place.

The same situation played itself out in Sicily except this port had two cranes and one was quite large. There were also fences and barriers of the flimsy sort, but they were there. This time they loaded provisions instead of cargo. The guys had only a few hours to explore. They chose to hike to the top of a hill to a church for a bagged lunch and some picture taking. Then it was back on the ship, headed for Port Said, Egypt.

Reinhold realized as they journeyed through the crystal blue and strikingly turquoise waters of the Mediterranean that the *Oldendorff* was a filthy ship, worse than he expected. Every ship has its difficulties: rust, bilge water, bugs, questionable refrigeration, dirty bathrooms and showers, etc. The *Oldendorff* had all of these in excess.

As the ship left the colder waters of Northern Europe and entered the warmer waters of the Mediterranean, the roach population became a problem, a big, big problem. He woke in the middle of the night, feeling something tickling him, only to see one of the insects running away from his bunk. It made his skin crawl. When the crew complained to the First Mate, just before they reached Sicily, he assured them he would speak to the Captain. They were approaching Port Said when the crew spoke with the First Mate again. The temperature was in the 90s and it was very dry. In other words, perfect roach conditions. He kindly told them that the Captain had been informed. Then he reminded them that they were not paid to stand around and complain about roaches.

Their stay in Port Said was brief, just a few hours. They were really only waiting for their turn to approach the canal. The *Oldendorff* never even threw a line ashore. They laid for anchor until they saw the pilot's launch pull up to the ladder. Reinhold was surprised by the amount of people the launch carried. Usually the pilot arrived with one or two, in extreme circumstances there might be three, other people. There were seven people crammed in the small speed boat. Four of them carried large bundles. He was on the bridge at the time as he was scheduled to Quartermaster through the canal. The Captain cursed long and loud when he saw the pilot's gang climb up the ladder. He went out on to the bridge, trying to shout for the departing launch to stop.

"Get back here and get this rabble off my ship!" He screamed. "This isn't a bazaar, goddammit!"

The launch kept going and the pilot arrived on the bridge. Immediately, orders started flying. Reinhold was relieved that the commands were familiar and recognizable. He had been concerned he wasn't going to understand what the Arab man said.

The *Oldendorff* drew anchor and took a place in the line of ships headed into the Suez Canal. The crowd of men the pilot brought with him turned out to be pulling double duty. They were there in an official capacity to help guide the ship, sort of, but they were also vendors looking to sell all manner of small, carved wood and ivory knick-knacks and textile goods. They displayed their wares on blankets spread on the deck. Guys visiting the bridge for one reason or another brought all sorts of purchases with them to show off but Reinhold wasn't interested in the wares. He was very interested in the canal.

It was immediately obvious that this canal had no locks. It wasn't very wide and it wasn't very deep. It was going to be slow going. The top speed in the canal was posted at seven knots. This, the pilot explained, was to prevent heavy wakes from eroding the sandy banks. Even the small wakes, Reinhold observed, caused mini collapses. The sand slide like it was in an hourglass down the slanted bank and into the waters of the canal. It caused an optical allusion, making it seem like the banks were alive.

Port Said and its hinterland faded away into a haze of heat and dust, leaving only the monotonous desert to slide passed. In some spots the view of the desert was blocked by large retaining walls that looked like pyramids with the tops cut off.

The *Oldendorff* sailed slowly down the slip of blue water in the line of other cargo vessels and passenger liners all flying various flags and all moving south. The ships in formation were not the only vessels in the canal. Small, simple fishing boats, more rowboat than fishing boat, bobbed on the surface while their operators cast nets and hauled in the day's catch. Speed boats piloted by men in long, white robes and head scarfs zipped passed, weaving in between the ships, the material of their garments blowing in the wind. Reinhold began to wonder if the guys in the long robes were wealthy people. Their choice of boat would suggest that he was right.

Reinhold kept his eyes open for another German vessel but didn't spot one.

Strange, he thought, *there is always another German flag around.*

He voiced his thoughts to the Third Mate who was on bridge duty at the time.

"We are in virgin territory, sailor. There is only one other company sailing to the Middle East. The ports we are headed to, from what I have told, don't even have docks and piers. We are going to be unloading cement in Kuwait while laying anchor. Oldendorff bought this ship to start runs down here because they see it as a burgeoning market. Don't expect to see a lot of folks from home."

Reinhold thought about this. He already felt like he was in another world with a bleak, hot, rocky landscape and oddly dressed inhabitants. The Third Mate's information gave him an ominous feeling. He wasn't sure why. Laying for anchor to unload cargo was nothing new. It didn't happen in Europe very often but it did happen, especially if the port in question was a busy one. Hearing that this was the situation they faced made him feel like an explorer from years gone by, like Robinson Crusoe. It also explained why the Second Mate spent so much time on the bridge with his nose stuck to the map table. He was trying to figure out where they were going because he had never been there. It was very exciting.

Through the fog of his daydreams and under the chugging of the slow moving engine, Reinhold made out a strange, faint scrapping noise coming from somewhere below board. He listened for a moment, narrowing the source down to the stern. It didn't sound like part of the engine noise or engine trouble and no call had come from the engineers in the engine room to report anything. It was definitely something. Reinhold shrugged it off and forced the sound from his ears. He had to keep his attention on the pilot.

He didn't know how long it was before the phone from the engine room rang. They had also heard the noise and went looking for its source. The canal was so shallow that the ship's propeller was scrapping the sandy bottom. One blade in particular was touching ground. There was no way for them to assess the damage until they reached a port.

Chapter 66: Hot and Dry

Nine hours after leaving Port Said, the pilot directed the *Christoffer Oldendorff* into a small lake on the west side of the canal. Reinhold balked for a second before turning the wheel in compliance with the order. The lake was shallow and filled with sandy islands. It looked like a puddle on the surface of the desert. It was one of the most beautiful landscapes he had ever seen but didn't change his feeling that he was about to beach the ship. Forcing down his own sense of foreboding, he turned the wheel and nosed into what the pilot referred to as a lake but he was not comfortable terming it. It was a lagoon paradise in the middle of a harsh landscape. The water was like crystal blue gemstones melted by the sun over the desert. Palm trees swayed on the shoreline. It was difficult to keep his eyes on what he was doing and not stare open mouthed at the wonder of it all.

"This is Ismailia." The pilot told the crew on the bridge once he had positioned them and ordered the anchor dropped. "It is just a small lake with a small port but it is a good bypass."

He pointed across the lake to an assembled group of ships.

"Those ships were headed north but were stopped and directed here, same as you headed south. They will continue their journey now. The canal is just one lane so these breaks are necessary and frequent."

"How long will we be here?" The Captain asked.

"It is hard to say. It depends on how many ships are heading north. Probably not more than a day."

"A day?" The Captain was obviously not happy.

"Yes, a day. It would have taken you weeks to get around the continent of Africa."

The pilot bowed his head to the Captain and left the bridge without saying goodbye. The Captain grumbled his dissatisfaction but did not follow the man. He dismissed Reinhold with a wave of his hand.

Reinhold headed to the deck to get some food and his orders for the rest of the day. Instead of finding men working, he found them grouped around the First Mate. A sight he had never seen before. Usually it was the bosun that had a crowd around him. Something was a foot. He joined the group to find out what was going on.

"...they stole everything that wasn't sea tight!" Exclaimed a sailor named Pieter.

Those grouped were nodding their agreement and all started speaking at once. The First Mate waved his hand for silence.

"We have bigger problems, at the moment, boys," Musil was saying. "We have a bent propeller blade and no way to fix it."

"What do you mean?" asked Remy, the sailor in the bunk next to Reinhold.

The two had become friendly and had formed a group of associates with their bunkmates and a couple of others. Reinhold knew how the propeller got bent, thinking of the scrapping noise.

"Port Suez is just ahead, isn't it?"

Remy looked a bit uneasy, as if the journey through the Suez Canal had taken them somewhere off the map, a canal to the center of the earth or something. They had been talking about stealing when he joined them. Reinhold wondered what he missed on deck while he was on the bridge.

"Yes, but we can't pull her out of the water here or anywhere. Captain doesn't want to and the company won't let him. It is going to cost too much to fix it here. When we get to Suez, the Captain is going to send down divers to check it out."

"What a pile of junk this ship is," commented a sailor in the back of the group. "Why did this company buy a ship specifically to go to the Middle East that is roach infested and has no refrigeration? How did the propeller even get bent? All we have done is sail through a canal?"

It was a good question. Reinhold turned to see who had asked it. Turns out, it was a stoker. His name was Henry and he was the nicest, most soft spoken stoker Reinhold had ever encountered. He honestly liked the man.

The First Mate sighed. "I know, I know. And it's only going to get hotter. You just have to deal with it unless you want to get off in Suez and sign on to another ship. The propeller got bent as we sailed through the canal. The canal is a shallow body of water. We scrapped the bottom the whole way here. You didn't hear that, sailors?"

A grumble went through the guys standing around. It sounded almost like a threat. It was a threat.

Nice guy or no, Reinhold smiled to himself, looking around at the men assembled, *he still has to maintain control of the group and a motley crew is it. It is not his fault that a bunch of cheap bastards own the company. They could have at least put a refrigerator in the kitchen. It is also not his fault the canal is shallow. I heard the scrapping. Looks like these guys didn't.*

The good news about the bent propeller was it gave the crew a couple of days in Port Suez. They wandered around the bazaar and the port, looking for women, sampling local food, taking pictures like tourists, and trying to stay out of trouble. The condition of the place and the people struck Reinhold. They were overdressed he thought for the climate. The women were all wearing long black robes; some had their faces completely covered. The men preferred white. Some wore long robes, some had on lose knicker style pants with loose tunic shirts, and some just a garment that Reinhold could only call a loincloth.

Everywhere they went there were chattering, hungry looking locals, many of them were dirty children, trying to sell them something: knick knacks in the shape of the pyramids, photo albums made of leather, carved wood figurines, rugs, food, fruits of various types, objects made of reed and papyrus, hats, and loads of other stuff. Reinhold bought a leather photo album from a young boy wearing a loincloth. The boy had his younger sister in tow. It made Reinhold think of his own childhood, wandering around with Isolde. He thought, since they were going to be away from Germany for so long, that he would dedicate the entire album to his trip with the *Oldendorff*. As he sailed with the *Brandenburg*, that album from the *Christoffer Oldendorff* was safely stored on a shelf in his room in Kiel.

A cultural difference Reinhold noticed was the interaction between the men and women. More than once, he saw a man slap a woman who was with him. Whether these were wives, children, friends, mothers he had no idea. He didn't like it. When a man hit a woman very close to where he was standing, knocking her to the ground, Reinhold tried to help her up. Immediately, the man and several others were on him, pushing him back, yelling at him in a language that he had no hopes of understanding. Getting the hint, Reinhold walked away from the situation but was angry, very angry. He didn't like that way these men treated their women. It made him want to hurt them. To keep out of trouble, he went back to the ship and shut himself in his hot bunk to read. He wasn't entirely sure he liked Egypt.

The divers in Suez were, thankfully, Dutch men. They found that, yes indeed, the propeller was bent but not to a degree that would keep the ship from sailing. It was just going to be a slow trip. They joked with the sailors about being virgins in the Middle East.

"It is going to be like your first time all over again, boys: slow, awkward, and bouncy."

"Not to mention hot and dry!"

The *Oldendorff* was still in Suez when Reinhold encountered one of the strangest things he had seen in nature. Looking back, it was as much a nightmare in memory as it had been in reality. The ship went to sleep the night before leaving the port town thinking that nothing could go wrong. At dawn, they were awoken by a droning noise that no one could place and a shouting watchman. A dark cloud shrouded the horizon. Surprisingly to the sailors, it was moving toward the sea. As it got closer, the sailors saw that it was insects, huge insects. There must have been millions of them.

"Locusts," muttered the sailor standing at the rail next to Reinhold. Punchy was his name.

"Locusts?" Reinhold questioned.

"Yup."

Reinhold watched the first of the cloud come rolling off the shore and land on the deck, on the rail, on the ventilators, on the pipes, on the lines, everywhere there was a space for an insect to stand. They looked like huge grasshoppers just more of a yellow color than the green and brown he was used to in Germany and they had brown spots. Some were as long as his middle finger.

"Like from the bible?"

He squished one with his heavy work boot, the crunching as loud as if he had stepped on a mouse.

"Yup."

Punchy walked away, swinging his arms above his head to fight off the critters, and returned a minute later with a broom. He was coated in bugs and Reinhold could only imagine he looked the same. A glance down the front of himself confirmed the thought. Punchy started sweeping the bugs off the deck into the sea. Using the side of his foot, Reinhold attempted to help him as he tried to knock the bugs off his clothes and hair. He wasn't getting far.

"Have you seen these before?"

All over the ship, men were yelling and the sounds of running came from all directions. Orders were shouted toward the stern by the bosun and the First and Third mates appeared on the bridge, wildly throwing their arms around their heads.

"No, not in person. When you read the bible, you encounter them some. The Plagues and all."

"Oh." Reinhold hadn't pegged Punchy as a religious man. "Where do they come from?"

"Don't know really. The Bible says they come out of the desert at the command of God to ruin the crops of sinners."

"So does that mean that Gods thinks were sinners? Is he punishing us for our bad deeds?"

Punchy shrugged and swept. "That's what they told us in school."

"Where are you from Punchy?"

"Stuttgart."

"That makes sense."

Punchy took offense to the remark. "What makes sense?"

"The Bible talk from you. Bavarians are Catholic, aren't they?"

Punchy calmed down. "Yup, I guess we are."

Attempts to sweep the locusts off the deck turned out to be futile. They continued to arrive in a great, clicking, chirping swarm. The ship was on lock down, all hatches and holds closed as tightly as possible but not in time to keep the insects at bay. They were everywhere. They flew in through open portholes, slipped into the bulkhead through cracks. The ship was prevented from sailing that morning because the swarm caused visibility issues. The sailors disagreed with this decision, thinking it would be better to get underway, to get away from the bugs. Reinhold spent a sleepless night covered in locusts. It was disgusting, more disgusting, he thought, then the roaches. The locusts were so big, he was afraid they would attack his face and try to eat in eyes.

When the ship finally set sail, the swarm seemed to follow them. Sailors started asking aloud how long a swarm could last. The feeling of bug legs on his bare skin sent shivers of disgust down Reinhold's back but it was too hot to wear a shirt. The sailors dealt with the locusts by throwing buckets of warm, salty water at each other. As they sailed, he overheard the mates in conversation saying it was one of the worst locust seasons Egypt had seen in recent memory. The radio on the bridge was noisy with Captains discussing what to do, how to proceed.

Reinhold was thankful when they finally set sail and left the swarm behind. It took days to eradicate the bugs from the nooks and crannies of the ship. Soon enough, they were left with just the roaches again.

It is a shame that locusts don't eat roaches, Reinhold thought to himself. *That would have helped us out some.*

If memory served Reinhold correctly, the next ordeal for the *Oldendorff* was the flying fish. This was even more amazing to Reinhold than the insects. The locusts had just been doing what they were made to do: eat and travel. It wasn't unheard of in Europe to have swarms of flies or bees scare the hell out of a town somewhere. While anchored off the coast of Saudi Arabia at the port of Jeddah, the first fish jumped on board. It was night and the watchman didn't see it or hear it. The next morning, the ship awoke to a deck full of strange dead fish baking in the already hot morning sun.

"Would you look at this mess? Aren't fish supposed to stay in the sea?"

Reinhold's bunkmate Freddy questioned as they made their way to the utility closet for brooms.

"Yup. That's why these are dead." Reinhold replied dryly.

He was in a bad mood. Sleep had eluded him again. It was just too damn hot to sleep. He read somewhere that pirates in the Caribbean used to hang their sleeping hammocks wherever they could find space. In the summer when it was hot, they would hang them on the deck to take advantage of the cool night breezes. It was tempting to sleep on the deck, dead fish or no dead fish. This whole situation would be more interesting if he wasn't so goddamn tired. Especially since the fish looked like nothing he had ever seen before.

They looked more like planes than fish, Reinhold thought to himself as he lit another cigarette on the deck of the Brandenburg. *Never seen anything like it since. Fins like wings and tails like rudders.*

"Smart ass." Freddy retorted before pointing towards a ship approaching. "Look."

It was a small launch boat and it was flying a Greek flag. Reinhold and Freddy watched as it pulled up to the ladder. An old timer in Captain's stripes climbed up on to the deck. He went straight for the bridge, not even bothering to look at the sailors working to get the fish off the deck.

"Do you think we can eat these?"

Freddy had a fish in his hands, examining it carefully.

"It doesn't look poisonous. Aren't poisonous things usually bright colors? This is just a blue fish with big fins."

Reinhold shrugged. "I don't know. There aren't a lot of poisonous things where I come from, just mushrooms."

He plucked a fish off the deck and smelled it. He was more concerned about its freshness than whether it was poisonous.

"Smells OK. Let's clean some and see what they look like inside."

"I was just thinking about that myself."

Reinhold turned to see Punchy's bunkmate Alex approaching carrying a bucket of fish.

"Let's get the rest of them off the ship before the Captain slurs loudly at us then we'll clean these and take them to the cook. They'll make a great lunch!"

"Captain has company, another Captain, probably from that old girl over there."

Reinhold pointed toward what looked like a Liberty ship judging by the seam work. It was flying a Greek flag same as the launch that brought the Captain.

"Greek, huh?" Alex spit over the rail. "You know what they say about them, right?"

Reinhold snorted. "I don't have to know what they say about them. I signed on to a Greek ship before this one."

Freddy and Alex looked surprised and amused.

"And? What happened? Where did you go?" Alex asked.

"I went from Holtenau to Brunsbüttel and got the hell off. I faked sick and got my book back."

He pulled a cigarette out of the pack and lit it before continuing.

"The guy that I supposed to bunk with was black as night and cleaning a gun when I dropped my bag. They, the sailors, all looked at me like a steak in the butcher shop window. The strange part was there were sheep in a pen at mid deck. Why did they need sheep?"

Freddy and Alex didn't respond. There was a few seconds of silence before they burst into laughter.

"See," Alex gasped. "The stories are true!"

"Why did they need sheep? That's a good question!"

Freddy nodded his chin toward the Greek ship anchored not far away.

"Why don't you go ask them?"

The laughter began anew.

"Very funny, guys. At least I was willing to give it a shot. Come on, let's get these fish off the deck."

The sailors topped off Alex's bucket of fish before pushing the rest off the deck into the Red Sea. Almost immediately, the ship was surrounded by sharks. Reinhold had never seen so many in one spot before. The crystal clear, almost motionless water made it possible to see all the way to the bottom of the shallow cove in which they were anchored. Most of the sharks were larger, two meters in length, and were a smooth grey color and texture. Reinhold reminded himself not to fall overboard in these waters.

"I am not touching those things. Get them out of here. Lunch is already cooking. I don't have any room for those nasty things."

Reinhold didn't understand then and he didn't understand now, on a completely different ship in a different area of the world, why cooks were such blatant *arschlocher*. They cleaned and filleted the flying fish in such a manner that cooking them should have been a one-two-three procedure. But, the cook wouldn't do it, for whatever reason he was being stubborn. The baker wouldn't touch them either, probably out of fear that the cook would make his life a living hell. The kitchen boy wouldn't cook them either. He was definitely afraid the cook would beat him on the spot. Reinhold dumped the cleaned fish overboard to the sharks. It ticked him off to waste food and the energy it took to clean it but he had no choice. If he had the time, he would have started a fire and roasted the fish himself.

Later that night, the bosun ordered the lights remain off over night. The watchman for the night protested, saying he couldn't watch anything in the dark.

"Too bad," the bosun spat. "I am not spending another day clearing fish off this deck. The lights attract the fish, the fish jump on to the ship and die, leaving us with a huge mess. You are going to have to watch with your ears tonight."

The explanation for the attack of the flying fish made perfect sense to Reinhold. He didn't know why he hadn't thought of it in the first place. It was so natural to have lights on that it just never occurred to him.

Chapter 67: He Left You?

The next stop in the Middle East for the *Christoffer Oldendorff* was Aden, Yemen. By the time the ship dropped anchor in the somewhat modern port, Reinhold was restless. He hadn't stepped foot on shore in almost two weeks since they left Suez. When Wolfgang, a guy Reinhold barely knew, said he was looking for someone to go ashore with him for a night out, Reinhold jumped at the chance. Since they were in unfamiliar territory, they adhered to the buddy system with a new level of seriousness

They left the ship via the launch boat and headed into town. Looking back, Reinhold didn't remember how they ended up at the rooftop hash bar; he just remembered it ending badly. The trek through the city to get to the bar hadn't been the most pleasant either. The women who passed them stared curiously while the men glared suspiciously. Reinhold couldn't help but stare at them in return because the open hostility took him by surprise. He was used to encountering rough, hardened types in the ports around Europe but usually, once away from the riff raff around the port, the regular inhabitants didn't care much that there were foreigners around. Here, though, the Germans stuck out like rotten potatoes. The locals didn't trust them, which was evident on their faces. Reinhold had an uneasy feeling before they even made it to the hookah bar.

Maybe it was the city itself, too, he thought to himself, puffing on his cigarette, drumming his fingers thoughtfully on the bulkhead of the *Brandenburg. There was something unwelcoming about the whole place.*

The buildings were the same color as the land, a shade of khaki that reminded Reinhold of the uniform he wore in the *Hitlerjugend.* Here and there, on more impressively sized buildings, there were hints of color but it did nothing really to break up the wash of tan. The sounds of camels in the distance were ominous. Reinhold didn't know they made such doleful noises. The most notable, and unwelcoming, feature of the place to him was the language. It was harsh. The body language and facial expressions of the speakers seemed to reinforce the harshness of the words. Everything just looked and sounded hostile. Reinhold was ready to go back to the ship just a few minutes after leaving it but Wolfgang wanted to experience the hookah culture he had heard so much about. Reinhold was honor bound to stay ashore.

They found the hookah bar. It was on a rooftop not far from the port area in Aden. They took a flight of stairs to the roof where they were immediately the focus of the attention of the men assembled there. Reinhold knew there was going to be a problem when all conversation ceased and a dozen pairs of eyes turned to look at him. He didn't know what they were smoking. Wolfgang told him as they strolled the city that it was hashish, a byproduct of opium, but it smelled like tobacco, a pungent and spicy tobacco with the underlying aroma of hot of tar. It was frightening to think that the rooftop was full of aggressive foreigners all hopped up on drugs.

"They're testing us," Wolfgang said to Reinhold. "They wanted to see what we are going to do. We should just sit down and start smoking. They'll calm down."

Wolfgang made for the table closest. Reinhold followed. They were about to sit down when a tall thin man with wild eyes stood up and started yelling at them, gesturing wildly. Several other men got to their feet. The first man pulled out a knife and approached Wolfgang first. Reinhold thought he was asking questions as he came at them. He wished he spoke the language.

The rest of the incident happened so fast that it was difficult to put it together. The man with the knife lunged at Wolfgang, who dodged and took off down the stairs, leaving Reinhold to fend for himself. Wolfgang's fleeing took Reinhold by surprise and he dropped his guard for a split second. The man with the knife, however, didn't hesitate and turned his weapon on Reinhold, throwing himself at the sailor.

Reinhold tried to fight him off, but his hesitation worked against him. As they struggled, Reinhold felt the blade of the knife stab his left thigh. He screamed in anger more than pain, fighting the man off with a few blows to his ribcage and a well-placed kick to his balls. The man howled in pain and stumbled backwards. Reinhold pulled the knife out of his leg and threw it at the man who attacked him, landing a hit in his shoulder.

The man's howls doubled in volume to a high-pitched screech. The others assembled rushed toward Reinhold, who turned and fled down the stairs, running as fast as his injured leg would carry him towards the port. He was never so happy to see a ship as he was at the moment he rounded a corner and saw the *Christoffer Oldendorff* laying at anchor in the bay. Without slowing, Reinhold jumped into the water and swam for the ship. The salt stung like hell in his new wound.

The sound of a loud splash drew the attention of Willie, the watchman that night. He met Reinhold at the top of the ladder with a look of confused and amused surprise.

"Out for a swim? I know the waters are warm and inviting here but swimming at night isn't the smartest with all those sharks around...."

"Is Wolfgang back?" Reinhold cut Willie off.

Willie blinked in shocked surprise this time. "I think I saw him come aboard when I was getting coffee. Why? Wait, wasn't he with you?"

Reinhold started to stalk off, wet, angry, and bleeding.

"Where is he? I am going to kill that bastard!"

"Are you dripping blood?" Willie said as he followed.

"Yes, I am dripping blood because that son of a bitch left me and ran like a coward. I got stabbed by a crazy Arab!"

"Oh," Willie gasped. "That *arschloch* left you? And you got stabbed?"

Reinhold didn't answer but kept walking. He figured that Wolfgang would be in his bunk, hiding like the coward he was. Below deck, he flung open the hatch and found him lying on his bed as if nothing had happened. He dragged the sailor out of bed and threw him against the wall. Neither man said a word. Wolfgang didn't protest or beg Reinhold to stop hitting him. Reinhold managed to punch him a dozen times before Freddy stopped him.

"You're bleeding all over the place, Reinhold!" Freddy grabbed his arm and spun him around. "We'll take care of this guy. You go see the Second about your leg."

Reinhold saw the wisdom of having his wound looked at even though his anger. Lord only knew what was on the knife that was festering in the wound now. He punched Wolfgang square in the mouth one more time, feeling very satisfied when the man's head bounced off the metal behind it, before leaving the bunk.

The Second had bridge watch from 12:00- 4:00am. Lucky for Reinhold it was 11:00. He won't be interrupting anything the mate in the course of his duties. When asked to explain himself, he told the story exactly as it happened.

"He left you?"

"Yes, sir."

"That's in violation of a direct order. None of you were to leave the ship unaccompanied and you definitely weren't supposed to leave your buddy behind."

"Yes, sir." Reinhold knew better than to push the subject. The mate was already on his side.

"The wound doesn't look infected. Come back tomorrow and I'll change the dressing. I would suggest that you don't go ashore again, but we'll be leaving this God forsaken land in the morning. Just keep it clean, will you?"

Reinhold nodded and put his pants back on and went to his bunk. Freddy was waiting for him.

"I can't believe that guy left you. He's plenty beat up. Don't worry, he won't last much longer."

Too tired to care, Reinhold slumped into his bunk and fell asleep immediately. The next morning, the *Oldendorff* was underway to Kuwait where, they were told, there was no port.

Chapter 68: Strangers In A Strange Land

The *Oldendorff* dropped anchor off the coast of Kuwait City just over a week after leaving Yemen. With every passing mile, the trip wore more and more on the sailors. The temperature climbed into the 100s with the promise of going higher. The lack of refrigeration was becoming a big problem. After a long day working on the deck in the blazing sun there wasn't even a cold beer to look forward to. There was no form of air coolant system so sleeping was nearly impossible. Reinhold just laid in bed, sweating, in a kind of heat-induced stupor.

The roaches were out of control. They were everywhere. Countless times Reinhold bit into a hunk of bread to find half a roach or poured condensed milk into his coffee to find a roach had gotten into the can and was now floating in his cup. The sailors gave the cooks hell for the lack of sanitary food preparation because it made them feel better but they knew there was nothing to do about it. The baker was in a worse position because the bread had to proof, exposing it to the mercy of the insects. By the time they docked, once again, Reinhold was itching to get off the ship, to find something cold and bug free, somewhere.

Kuwait was more desolate than Yemen. Aside from the lack of a port, there was a lack of anything modern. The boats lining the waterfront looked like the pictures of gondolas Reinhold had seen. They were short and narrow with high scrolling bows and sterns. There were a few small fishing boats scattered around the bay were they were anchored. From time to time, a speedboat whipped past or a large yacht that looked completely out of place slid placidly by. A single radio tower adorned the landscape amid a cluster of sand colored buildings. A sand colored wall that Reinhold could only imagine was a good old-fashioned city wall like in Europe surrounded these buildings. Unlike the examples in Europe, this city wall had a camp outside full of camels and colorful cloth structures. Men and women circulated around this camp, cooking food, playing with children. The steward, Welke, said that these people were "real desert people" and called them Bedouins.

"They are not allowed inside the city, for some reason," he explained while taking Reinhold's order for chocolate, cigarettes and beer.

"Desert people?"

"Yup, they wander around the desert with their families and camels, looking for watering holes called oasis. They graze their animals near them. And then move on when the grass is gone."

"Sounds like a rough life. What do we do around here for money?"

The steward frowned. "We have to wait for the official to come aboard from shore. He'll bring currency. From what I understand, it is called *rupees*. I am surprised you want to go ashore after what happened in Aden, Scholz."

Instinctively, Reinhold touched the healing wound on his leg.

"Can't let a little knife wound stop me, Welke. When do you expect the beach official?"

Welke shrugged. "Who knows? We dropped anchor two hours ago and no one has been out to see us yet. I expect that means they'll be around soon. Good luck with the platform and the awnings."

Reinhold snorted. "Simply done, my friend, simply done."

The platform was a new piece of equipment for Reinhold. Essentially, it was a floating pier. The sailors attached it to the hull of the ship at the ladder. Small boats tied up to it, unloading the longshoremen. The boom lifted the bags of cement out of the hulls and lowered them to the platform. Longshoremen loaded the cargo in to the waiting small boats. These small boats ferried the cargo ashore.

The awnings were another new piece of equipment. They were made of sail canvas and supported with a wooden framework that attached to the bulkhead and the rail of the ship. They spread out over the gangways around the wheelhouse. They were supposed to provide shade for the sailors, a place to retreat to when the sun became unbearable.

The shore officials arrived in a small speedboat. The details of unloading were worked out, the platform was put in place, and it was agreed that the longshoremen would arrive the next morning to begin work. The sailors hung out on the deck of the ship that night, drinking warm beer and telling stories until Freddy got out his button box to play a tune or two.

"It cools off a bit a night, at least," observed Punchy, his eyes closed, leaning against the boom support.

Reinhold snorted. "Not nearly enough."

Sweat was trickling down his back. He wondered how long they were going to be here. With no cranes or modern equipment, he suspected that this was going to take a long time.

The longshoremen arrived with the sun the next morning. They were a hard faced lot draped in white cloth with red-checkered headwear. The sailors opened the hatches and stood aside to let them work. They broke into three teams, one for each of the cargo bays to be unloaded. Each team had a leader. This was nothing out of the ordinary, but when one guy started chanting, all the sailors stared open mouthed at him.

He sat in the middle of the deck, eyes closed, and sang his strangely rhythmic chant undeterred by the Europeans staring at him. At certain points, every thirty seconds or so, the longshoremen working responded to something he had said. It made sense to Reinhold after a few minutes that he was chanting a work song. He had heard his fair share of them while he was working in the fields as a kid.

It would be less annoying, he thought to himself, *if I understood the words and could join in. Answer him at least.*

"What do you think they're saying?" Punchy stood next to him, sipping a mug of tea.

"I have no idea what they are saying but I know it is to keep the pace. We used to do it during threshing season back home. How can you drink that stuff in this heat?"

"I never pegged you as a farm boy, Scholz. What else am I supposed to drink? The water is just as hot as this tea and God knows what is swimming around in it. It is too early for beer. Not that the beer is any colder either."

"I am not a farm boy. Do you think it is any colder in the water? Could we send the beer down?"

Punchy thought for a minute. "When we put out that platform, the water seemed pretty warm. Like the Caribbean. Maybe if we send it down deep it is colder."

"You've been to the Caribbean?"

"Sure. I was there last year. Great place with lots of women, lots of rum, great food, and excellent weather, until it rains. Then you get drenched." Punchy took another sip of his tea. "Did you hear? The First Mate said the Captain gave us all the day off so we could adjust to the heat before he set us to work. Want to go ashore and see what this place is like?"

"Yup," Reinhold grinned wolfishly at Punchy. "I always want to go ashore."

Punchy snorted tea out his nose, laughing. "Hold on there, Scholz. It is doubtful you are going to find a woman here. These Muslims aren't like our European women. They don't know how to live here. I heard the First Mate saying that women are the property of men. They can beat them, sell them, or kill them, anything."

Reinhold thought about this for a second. "That can't be right. That sounds like slavery, doesn't it?"

Punchy shrugged, obviously done with this conversation. "How about we go ashore and see what is going on. I'll see if Freddy and Alex want to go."

Freddy and Alex did want to go. Reinhold suspected it was more to get away from the chanting then out of curiosity about this new, strange place were men could own women. They took the launch boat to the beach.

The waterfront and the city astounded the sailors. Where Europe had metal structures and high rise buildings, Kuwait had sand, rock, and squat buildings. Here and there were tall, thin towers with pointed tops. There was very little waterfront development, but the plans were in the works for something.

"That must be what the cement is for," said Freddy, pointing toward an area where a jetty had been prepared. It looked like the beginning of a pier. "Their building a modern port and getting rid of these wooden docks."

He pointed to where an ancient looking dock system stood surrounded by small boats.

"I thought there was a lot of shipping in the Persian Gulf. Where are all the ships?"

The sailors all shrugged. They headed into the city via a newly asphalt paved road.

On the walk into town, Reinhold felt like the sun was trying to burn his skin off. He was thirsty like he had never been thirsty before. When he mentioned he needed a drink, everyone agreed. He wanted to take off all of his clothes and walk around naked in hopes of cooling down. The dungarees he was wearing seemed to weigh a ton. It started to make sense why the natives dressed in loose fitting, white clothing.

As he stood on the deck of the *Brandenburg*, recalling his time in the Middle East, he wondered why there was such a difference between the sun in Kuwait and the sun in the Caribbean. They are located at roughly the same latitude.

The sailors looked for a bar on the walk into Kuwait City but didn't see one. The main part of the city was paved in stone and had wooden planks and pieces of cloth stretched between the buildings over the street. The sailors were thankful for the shade they provided. They didn't encounter a single vendor or store selling anything to eat a drink until they reached what must have been the marketplace.

"Look, that guy has bottles of Coke."

Freddy pointed across the open space at a small cart selling foodstuffs and drinks.

"Let's go get one. Then maybe we can find a beer."

They encountered few people on the way into town but that changed now in the marketplace. There were groups of men standing around talking and groups of women browsing the few stalls that were there selling edibles, spices, and household goods. They all turned to stare at the sailors as they passed. They weren't hostile stares but they were guarded, to say the least. Reinhold started to get a bad feeling, as if he did not belong and was not wanted.

The sailors purchased their Cokes with a series of hand gestures and a few *rupees*. Thinking nothing of it, Reinhold opened his Coke bottle with his teeth and drank deeply. The sweet beverage was not exactly refreshing but at least it wet his mouth again and washed away the grit accumulated there. Grit seemed to be everywhere in Kuwait. His head was starting to ache a bit from the sun. He barely even registered that a commotion had broken out until Freddy jabbed him in the ribs.

A group of heavily clothed women was coming at them from the left. Their fingers were in the air, their voices were high pitched and unpleasant. They were yelling in the unfamiliar language.

"Um, I don't think their stopping," Alex noted. "I think they're going to hit us!"

His voice was incredulous. And he was right! The old woman in the led smacked the Coke out of Alex's hand and pointed a gnarled and lined finger in his face. Before the sailors knew what was really happening, they were surrounded by yelling, pushing the women. One of them hit Reinhold with a stick she picked up off the ground. Glancing at his friends, he realized all the women had makeshift weapons. In self-defense, the sailors lifted their arms in front of their faces and tried to retreat.

"Let's just get out of here," yelled Punchy over the women. "These people are crazy!"

"What are we supposed to do, Punchy?" Reinhold questioned as he covered his face with his hands and inched his way across the open plaza of the marketplace.

"We can't hit them back. Their men will kill us."

He vividly remembered the crazed look on the face of the man that cut him on the rooftop in Aden.

"Make a run for it!"

Freddy was physically pushing the women away, dodging sticks, with the intent to run once he made a path. The others followed his example. A few seconds later, they were sprinting down the stone paved street. Thankfully, the launch boat was still there. They jumped aboard and fired up the outboard motor, hightailing it back to the *Oldendorff*.

"What the hell was that all about?" Freddy asked, making an obscene gesture toward the few women who had followed them the whole way to the port.

"I've never been run out of a town before and I've been all over the world!" Alex was gingerly touching a spot just above his left eyebrow. "That old woman hit me right in the face with a stick!"

"Obviously this place doesn't like foreigners." Reinhold said. "And that is OK because there is nothing to like about it for us foreigners. I'd take the worst place in Europe, even France, over this place any day."

The First Mate was observing the longshoremen working when the four sailors arrived back at the ship. The chanting echoed across the deck in an unbroken mantra.

"What the hell happened to your face, Alex?"

"Some God forsaken women hit me with a stick!"

"A group of women attached us in the plaza in town." Punchy clarified.

"Why?" The First Mate looked puzzled. "What were you doing?"

"Standing there, drinking a Coke."

Alex went back to rubbing the spot above his eyebrow. A good bruise was developing.

"That is why they attacked you."

The voice startled all of the sailors standing on deck, including the First Mate. The Captain rarely addressed them as a group.

"It is Ramadan, according to what the beach officials told me. These people are forbidden to eat or drink anything before sunset. That is why it took so long for them to check us in yesterday. It was feeding time."

"Ramadan, sir?" The First Mate still looked puzzled.

"Yes, some religious observance. It lasts a month and consists of prayer and fasting."

Almost in response to what the Captain was telling them, a voice drifted across the bay to the anchored ship. They could barely hear it over the chanting of the man on the ship. The Arabs on the ship heard it. They stopped in their tracks, turning to the southwest, and knelt as if in unison. For several minutes, they went through a sort of routine that consisted of them lowering their foreheads to the ground and sitting back up again. They spoke few words but every phrase contained the word "Allah". In the same sudden manner they began, the men went back to work and the chanting began anew. The sailors were left staring open mouthed at each other.

"As I was saying, it is a religious thing."

The Captain turned and went back to his salon.

"So we got beat for drinking a Coke?" Freddy asked. "Is that what I am supposed to believe here?"

"Looks like it." The First Mate responded. "This is a different place then we are used to, boys. Let's just try to make it as easy on ourselves as possible. Perhaps you don't want to go ashore again."

"We would definitely like there to be less roaches in our food, sir." Reinhold ventured out on a limb by broaching the subject again. "Any chance of that happening?"

The First Mate sighed. "I know, I know. It is disgusting. But what can we do? Look at where we are."

He gestured toward the platform floating off the port side of the ship. An Arab longshoreman was squatting there, robes bunched around his waist, a strained look on his face.

"Is he shitting?" Alex asked bluntly.

"Yup."

The sailors watched the man finish his business and splash some water on himself in an attempt to wash away the evidence. He returned to work as if nothing happened. The sailors were speechless in shock.

"Have they been doing that all day?" Freddy looked a bit green.

"Yup."

The First Mate responded as he pulled a pack of cigarettes out of his pocket and offered them around. He lit his before continuing.

"The worst part is that the shit is attracting sharks."

The shit attracting sharks, as Reinhold remembered it, wasn't a bad thing. Sure, they had to be careful when swimming to stay as far from the toilet area as possible (and not just because of the sharks) but the fishing was excellent!

In addition, it turned out, Henry the stoker, who was from Eckernförde, was an excellent fisherman. He showed Reinhold some new techniques with bobbins and a way to keep his line from tangling when casting. The two spent many happy evenings drinking piss warm beer and catching sharks. They never kept them. What was the point? They threw them back and kept on fishing. It became a

 competition to see who could reel in the biggest shark and who could reel in the most in an evening.

The working hours aboard the *Oldendorff*, however, weren't so happy. The chanting, and the 120-degree temperatures, drove the sailors crazy. Reinhold would be busy, painting or welding or building a new cabinet for the galley or slicing lines, and hear a loud crash or an indistinguishable scream from somewhere on the ship and know that someone had just lost their mind for a second. He didn't blame them one bit and came close to punching an Arab man in the face himself for no good reason other than annoyance. The chanting didn't cease as long as there was work to do. It was like a big, buzzing fly that you couldn't catch and couldn't shoo away. It was just there, buzzing in your ear, driving you mad with its presence.

There were also problems with theft. The sailors quickly learned that nothing, nothing, could be left lying around unattended. Even the tiniest bit of line would walk away from where someone left it. It was the Suez Canal all over again. The ship lost two buckets, a wrench, approximately 60 feet of line, a fire extinguisher, an assortment of canned goods, two dozen eggs, and a good bit of canvas before they noticed there was an issue. Afterwards, there was someone posted on guard duty at several points on the deck and on top of the bridge. The mates took turns patrolling. They ordered everyone to keep their eyes open. The cooks kept the kitchen in sea tight condition at all times in hopes of thwarting pilferage attempts.

To make matters worse, Captain Broplin lost his own mind. His drinking was really out of control since there was essentially nothing for him to do while the ship was laying for anchor. Every morning, he demanded the crew be on deck at 6:00am so he could talk to them.

Talk to us my ass, thought Reinhold, *that drunken* arschloch. *He just wanted to lecture us like children.*

The talk always started out the same way.

"You boys today have it too easy……"

The rest was a tirade of 'in my days' and 'you don't understand how it used to be' and 'none of you would have made it'. Reinhold stood there with the rest of the crew staring at the horizon, watching the sky become lighter, waiting for the sun to make an appearance and drive the temperature back up. The only good thing about having to up so early was the cooler morning air. A comical aspect of these morning lectures was Twist, the daschund. He scampered after his master, getting under foot. The Captain often stepped on the dog, causing it to yelp horribly and making the men cringe but he took no notice of it himself. He just kept walking and the dog just kept following.

"They're made for each other." Freddy noted one night as they drank warm beer on top of the bridge under the stars.

It was a cool night and the sailors were thankful for it. They were also thankful for the quiet.

"That dog is just as stupid as his master. You can almost hear the wind blowing through its ears. You know, like one of those shells in the Caribbean that you can hear the ocean in."

"A conch," Henry said quietly.

Henry had taken to hanging with Reinhold's group at night along with a stoker friend of his named Alfie. They were both soft spoken and polite and had traveled together often because they worked for the Oldendorff Company for many years. Neither of them were young men, which surprised Reinhold. He had noted over the years that stokers were not young men. It was hard work shoveling coal for hours at a time. He often wondered if the profession aged a person prematurely.

Reinhold remembered this particular night not because it was pleasant but because he witnessed one of the most disturbing sights he had seen in his young life. The *Oldendorff* had been at anchor for just over a week. The Captain delivered his third tirade that morning. None of the men had been off the ship since Reinhold, Alex, Freddy, and Punchy told them that the women attacked them with sticks. They were musing about the Captain and his dog when another sailor, Schindler, came almost bounding up the ladder. He said one word.

"Look."

He pointed toward the bow of the ship where some of the longshoremen made a kind of temporary camp with brightly colored woven rugs and fabric lean-tos. Another first. Reinhold had never seen the dock guys sleep on the ship. The 'camp' at the bow was smaller than the 'camp' at the stern due to space restrictions.

The sailors followed Schindler's finger toward the front of the ship and stared open mouthed at what they saw. There were two sets of men having sex with each other. It was as clear as day. They didn't care, apparently, that the ships spotlights were on, illuminating the scene with diffused light. They also didn't seem to care that they were on a ship full of other men, foreign men.

An urge is an urge, Reinhold rationalized to himself but the image burned itself into his brain.

He didn't know what to do, how to respond, or where to look. A disgusted feeling welled up in his chest, making his face twist. He couldn't take his eyes off the men having sex.

"Are they gay?" Freddy asked.

"I don't know." Schindler responded. "This isn't the first time I've seen this. The other night, the guys at the stern were going at it, I mean really giving it to each other. I thought I drank too much so I didn't say anything. I haven't had anything to drink yet tonight. This is definitely happening."

"That is disgusting!" Alex yelled. "Go stop them! What are they doing? Only animals do this!"

Angrily, he slammed down his beer and got up. He slide down the ladder and headed straight into the bridge.

A few minutes after he left, Reinhold could hear Alex yelling. Then he heard the Third Mate responding in softer tones. He kept his eyes glued to the scene in front of him. The one guy was plunging against the backside of his partner, oblivious that there was yelling on the bridge. Maybe he couldn't hear. He definitely didn't understand the language. Obviously, he had his mind on other matters.

The other couple was still in what looked like the foreplay stage. One was giving the other an oral performance. Once again, not a scrap of attention was diverted to Alex's yelling. Reinhold could not move, speak, or look away. He was horrified and uncomfortable but not shocked the way his fellow sailors were. It almost made sense to him that the men in Kuwait were gay.

All the more reason to avoid them, he thought. *Had they even showered since working? And no wonder the women are so cantankerous! The men are more interested in satisfying each other! They are all gay!*

The next morning, as part of his daily tirade, the Captain reminded the sailors that they were strangers in a strange land. The more they just let the longshoremen do their jobs, the faster they would be on their way. It amounted, to Reinhold, to the Captain saying "shut up and stay away from them so we can get the hell out of here without incident."

Chapter 69: Games

The crew was very happy a few days later when a small speedboat flying the German flag came to visit the *Oldendorff*. The boat was carrying a couple of engineers who were working in Kuwait City. They, along with their crews, were responsible for building the new port. The two men went to visit the Captain and afterward stopped to chat with a few of the sailors. They invited all aboard to come use the beach and the other facilities at their club.

"We know it must be hard for you guys out here," one of the engineers explained. "We just want you to know that you are not the only Germans in Kuwait."

They gave directions to the club's dock, which was located on the Persian Gulf side of Kuwait City, opposite where the ship lay anchored in the bay. Eagerly, the sailors gathered up swim suits and towels and piled into the launch boat for the short trip to this magical beach were German people were hiding in plain sight.

They learned quickly that it wasn't just the engineers using the beach. There were women and children there too. They were the families of the men working on the project. There were British people also, not just Germans.

Things went badly. Many of the sailors forgot their manners. Comments were made to respectable women that could never be taken back and should never be tolerated. Comments were made to British citizens that could never be taken back. Reinhold tried to behave himself but it had been so long since he had seen a woman, especially one in a stylish bathing suit, that he stared openly at breasts and rumps. He called a few over to talk to them and could not prevent himself from leering. He wasn't the only one leering.

One outspoken, and very shapely, woman was the subject of many of these uncomfortable looks and inappropriate comments. She asked the sailors to leave. At first, they protested and tried to make amends, but it was too late. The damage was done.

In retrospect, Reinhold was ashamed of his behavior. He realized, however, that he was under a great deal of strain. The tension on the ship was getting worse. The cultural differences between the Arabs and the Europeans were deep and fundamental. The heat and the intensity of the sun exacerbated these differences.

To break the tension, the sailors came up with a variety of games to ease their minds. There was wrestling, both full body and arm. There were strength contests, which consisted of someone saying 'I bet you five *mark* you can't lift that shackle over your head'. They played name that tune on the button box. They threw parties, got drunk on warm beer, dressed up like women, and pretended to go on dates. However, the most original game, one that could probably only be played on the *Oldendorff,* was roach racing.

Roach racing was simple. One found a roach, which wasn't hard. The contestant just had to look down. They put the roach in any empty matchbox that had the short side modified to open like a gate. The next step was to irritate the roach by scratching the box or shaking it lightly, not to hard or you would kill the insect. Then they lined the matchboxes up at the end of a table and 'opened' the 'gates'. The roaches came flying out to escape the box. They were so disorientated, they usually just ran straight ahead and off the table. The sailor whose roach went over the edge first won. The minimum bet was five *mark* a race. The drunker the sailors, the more fun this game. Reinhold won three races in a row one afternoon. The only person to top three races in an afternoon was Musil, the First Mate. He won four.

Musil turned out to be a much more down to earth man than Reinhold gave him credit for at the beginning of the trip. He liked to hang out with the crew in his bathing suit, drinking warm beer, and fishing for sharks. At first, this put the sailors on edge but gradually they relaxed. They relaxed so much that they had no fear of joking about mutinying over the roach situation and were not as shocked as they should have been when he produced some of his own jokes. It was from the First Mate that Reinhold and his friends learned that the Captain was a flyer in Hitler's army.

"He likes to brag about it." Musil told them one night as they were sitting on the deck enjoying the cooler temperatures and some button box music.

"If you are near him after he has been drinking, he'll tell you all about it. He has a plane still, somewhere Nuremburg."

"What about Herr Baumhauer?" Alex asked, more snidely than he would have if he wasn't drunker than hell.

"That guy is a different story. Broplin is a drunk with a military history. Baumhauer is a drunk with a sadistic history. They flew together, the two of them, and became friends. It was probably easier for Broplin to overlook or not recognize Baumhauer's nature during a war. Now, he just keeps him under wraps as best he can."

"Under wraps?" Reinhold was curious.

"The last ship they were on, Broplin caught Baumhauer carving his initials into the backside of a drunk prostitute." Musil spit over the rail into the sea. "Stopped him and got rid of the girl, from what I understand." Musil shrugged, signaling an end to the story.

Almost on cue, Reinhold remembered as he looked back through the hazy sands of time, Twist the daschund showed up, poking his nose around and looking for attention from the sailors. Freddy got the bright idea to get the dog drunk. Nobody thought it would work but they were wrong. Twenty minutes later, the animal was stumbling around the deck, yipping stupidly.

"You should get rid of him before he throws up," Punchy suggested.

"Hold on," Reinhold stopped them shooing Twist away. "I have an idea."

He ran to the galley and asked the cook for an open can of condensed milk. Grudgingly, the cook handed it over, explaining unnecessarily that it probably had roaches in it. Reinhold spilled some of the thick milk into a shallow bowl and brought it to Twist. The dog slopped it up and ran away before the sailors could shoo him.

Minutes later, they could hear the Captain screaming for Baumhauer. Apparently, Twist threw up all over the Captain's salon. The sailors rolled in laughter. Reinhold was quick to get rid of the milk and the dish by throwing them overboard. They discovered a new game that day. Twist came to visit them frequently, looking for beer, and they were more than happy to oblige. Almost every time, the dog threw up on the carpet in the Captain's salon. After the second or third time, a new theme made its way into the morning lectures. The Captain threatened to skin alive the person who was getting his dog drunk. Nothing ever came of the threat, however, because the person who made it was drunk beyond comprehension by the middle of the afternoon himself.

It was by mistake that the sailors discovered another game to play. He didn't remember exactly how it happened but one afternoon Reinhold was in the mess hall, trying to escape the heat and read a chapter of his book, a collection of short stories, when the kitchen boy came flying out of the galley and streaked through the mess hall with the cook close on his heels. The fat old cook didn't stand a chance against the lanky, young boy and stopped running a few feet short of leaving the mess hall. Instead, he threw the egg he was holding at the fleeing youngster before turning and going back to the galley. The one eyed stoker on the other side of the mess hall, 'the stoker side', said something that Reinhold didn't quite grasp about the cook before going back to his whittling. The guy kind of gave Reinhold the creeps and it wasn't because he was a stoker, or that he had one eye. There was something almost sinister about the man, something he couldn't put his finger on. Shrugging, Reinhold went back to reading a story by a writer named Edgar Allen Poe about a man who is entombed in a wall.

A few minutes later, Shorty, another guy in Reinhold's bunk, stuck his head in the door.

"Why is there an egg out here?"

"Cook threw it at the boy," Reinhold explained.

"Oh," Shorty looked down at the egg again. "I didn't know you could throw a cooked egg. How did he do it?"

Reinhold and the one eyed stoker looked at each other in surprise. Obviously, the heat was getting to Shorty.

"I think you should get out of the sun, Shorty."

"Why?"

"Because it wasn't a cooked egg that the cook threw. It was still in the shell. I saw it and heard it smash."

"Oh, well, that explains why there are shells in this egg."

Truly baffled, Reinhold got up and went to see what Shorty was talking about. The stoker got up too.

"I'll be damned. It is a cooked egg."

Reinhold turned on his heel and went to the galley, returning a minute later with another egg and the cook. He stepped out of the mess hall on to the deck and strode to a spot baking in the relentless Middle Eastern sun. He cracked open the egg, letting it fall on to the deck. The men stood there, watching for a few seconds before anything happened. Then the edges of the egg started to bubble. After a minute, the distinct aroma of a frying egg filled the air.

"I'll be damned." Reinhold said again. "The deck is so hot, we can fry eggs."

The phenomenon quickly spread through the crew and soon there were fried eggs everywhere. Luckily, they were one of the provisions they could replenish in the desert. The Captain added a new thread to his 6am speech, causing the sailors to redouble their egg frying. If it weren't for the fact that the baker and cooked needed them, the Captain would have cut eggs out of the provisions list.

By the sixth week of unloading in Kuwait, the crew's nerves were stretched to breaking. Tempers were short and no amount of beer could lengthen them. The Captain was having a hard time controlling the crew, keeping them busy. One sailor flat out refused to paint the stack, calling it a death sentence since temperatures on the ship had climbed into the 130s. Reinhold didn't understand how it could be so hot but Musil explained that the metal absorbed the heat and trapped it, making it hotter.

"Probably not this hot on the beach." Musil finished with a gesture toward the shore.

They were standing on the deck outside the mess hall, enjoying the cooler early morning temperatures. The Captain finished his tirade for the day and breakfast was still going on in the mess hall. The longshoremen were starting their work for the day. The chanter was just beginning his mantra.

"How much longer do you think we'll be here?"

Musil thought for a second. "Maybe a week, week and a half. Depending on how the next couple of days go. They are down pretty deep into the hull now."

Reinhold was about to say something when a high pitched scream erupted from the deck near the mess hall, just around the bulkhead from where he was standing with Musil, Alex, and Freddy. Before they could move to see what the scream was about, Henry came trotting out of the mess, a grim look on his face. It was an unusual look for Henry and it immediately concerned Reinhold. He followed the stoker.

The scene that followed was one of the touchiest Reinhold had ever seen. He didn't think, for a few minutes, that they were going to get out of it. One of the stokers, Levi, had a fit of madness brought on by the heat, the filthy conditions of the ship, and the constant stream of high-pitched verbalizations from the chanter. Reinhold understood completely. Just the day before, he thought he was going to rip his eardrums out because he just wanted to read in quiet or hear some good music, something melodic, instead the droning chant filled every corner of the ship. All Levi wanted this day was to drink his tea in peace but couldn't because the chanter was positioned under the mess hall window, facing Hatch 3 of the *Oldendorff's* mid-deck. The sound of his voice echoed off the metal bulkhead. In frustration, and the afore mentioned momentary madness, Levi threw the tea over his shoulder, out the porthole, hitting the chanter in the shoulder. The Arab man was scalded down his back.

The Arab men viewed this act of tea flinging by Levi as an insult, a direct insult, an act of willful violence. The tensions that existed between the Europeans and the Arabs, that had been building for weeks, came exploding out of the bottle like champagne. They dropped what they were doing and rushed toward their injured colleague, chattering in their language, and gesturing toward the window. They were incensed, so angry that they were almost smacking themselves in the head. Someone sent for the Captain, someone sent for an interpreter. Levi was called out. The chanter was given a salve from the ship's medical kit for his burns. He continued to howl not so much in pain as embarrassment and anger.

From what the interpreter said, the injured Arab, and the uninjured ones also, thought it was appropriate for Levi to be beaten for his transgression. The Captain didn't agree. He felt an apology would be sufficient. Levi apologized through clenched teeth. The Arabs weren't satisfied. For four hours, the negotiations went on without the parties seeing eye to eye on a punishment. Finally, Levi was let off the hook with an apology that he delivered on his knees in front of the injured chanter. He had, literally, to beg forgiveness.

Completely ridiculous, Reinhold thought to himself. *Even after all these years, it was stupid. I have never seen anyone be so insulted over something so trivial. If I got that upset so easily, I would never have made it as a sailor. What are those Arabs made out of? They are definitely not iron men.*

The following week, when the announcement came that the last bag of cement had been unloaded, a cheer went up from the men. They didn't care that the relatively easy days of port maintenance were done. They wanted to get the hell out of Kuwait. Most were hoping like hell to head back to Europe but Musil told them the *Oldendorff* was going to India to load copper ore. Reinhold was excited. He was looking forward to seeing somewhere new.

Chapter 70: India

Getting to India was more exciting than being in India. The *Oldendorff* was still down a propeller blade and ambled its way across the Arabian Sea to the west coast of India. Reinhold could have sworn that the ship was trailing dust behind it or that the dust was following them. He could see the grit swirling around and feel it in his mouth and lungs. The other sailors were experiencing it as well, judging by the amount of spitting going on.

They encountered a massive, raging storm along the way that made the North Sea look like an angry bathtub. The seas swelled, creating forty-foot waves and the winds blew hard, registering a *windstärke* of eight. Many Captains in Europe wouldn't leave port with such conditions. The Second Mate, on one of the rare occasions when he spoke, said that it was because of the difference between the water temperature and the air temperature, like in all parts of the world. Unique to the area were the wind patterns. Since it was the summer, the wind was blowing toward the land, bringing rains and turbulence. In winter, it blew away from the land, causing dry conditions. Looking back, Reinhold remembered thinking that this wasn't all that interesting. Now, he found it fascinating. All the winds of the world were intertwined in a huge system of airflow.

During the storm, Reinhold misjudged the timing of the pitching of the deck while trying to secure some rigging and fell forward, landing heavily on his right knee. He didn't need the explosion of pain to know that he did some damage to it. Sighing, he continued his work, his knee throbbing, knowing that this could be troublesome in the future.

Reinhold was surprised by the amount of traffic in the Arabian Sea. It was refreshing to see other ships after being docked alone in Kuwait City for seven weeks. Sure, other ships came and went, but they were almost never from European countries. Only once did a Dutch ship slip into port and that was only overnight, less than twelve hours it had been there. Now, on the high sea, through the looking glass, Reinhold spotted British, lots of British, as well as Dutch, Swedish and Spanish flags. No other German. When he mentioned this to Musil, he was reminded that the Oldendorff Company was in virgin territory for Germans.

"This is the beginning, Scholz, you'll see."

He pulled a pack of Lucky Strikes out of his breast pocket, offering one to Reinhold.

"Ten years from now this is going to be the place to be. There so much oil in the region that they are going to have to design new ships just to carry it all back to consumers in Europe." He took a long drag in his cigarette. "You think Hamburg and Rotterdam are big ports now? Just wait until this area opens up. They're going to have to dredge the Elbe to make it deeper."

Reinhold didn't know if he believed Musil or not but it was something to think about.

There were ships sailing these waters that flew flags Reinhold didn't recognize but the Second told him they were from places like Nigeria, Libya, Madagascar, India, Indonesia, Australia, China, Pakistan, and Iran. Most of these ships were smaller than the *Christoffer Oldendorff*, with the exception of the Australian ship. He wondered how far they were from Australia.

Nine days after leaving Kuwait City, the *Oldendorff* dropped anchor in Mormugoa, India. Once the ship was settled, Reinhold surveyed the port. It wasn't as bad as he had anticipated. It was small in area and shallow in depth but there were piers, real piers, and a rail line with trains that obviously were for transporting cargo. There were no cranes but there were other ships! Several with European flags and one was German! It was like a homecoming to see another German vessel. There were many Portuguese flags.

"That's because the Portuguese run this place," Musil said when Reinhold voiced his observations.

"Portuguese?"

"They have owned this land for hundreds of years. The Indians are trying to kick them out now."

He pointed to a pair of heavily armed and armored soldiers patrolling the waterfront.

"We'll see how far they get. The Portuguese like having this territory. There are lots of resources here such as the copper ore we're picking up and iron ore not to mention wood, spices, cashews, and rice." He lit a cigarette before continuing. "The town up there, according to the maps, is called Vasco de Gama."

He nodded to a point above the bay to a hilly hump of land. Buildings littered the side and there was a good-sized church in the Spanish style at the top.

Reinhold was surprised.

Good Lord, the Europeans are everywhere! Is there anything they don't own? Anywhere they haven't taken over?

He watched the people on the shore going about their business. It was by no stretch of the imagination a wealthy looking place, nothing like Viana do Castelo with its impressive architecture. The people were dressed in rags and some had rags tied around their heads. The rags the men wore were mostly all white with very little color. The women wore blues and purples with the occasional orange. The buildings were ill kept and ramshackle with the exception of the large, white, Spanish style church and a few large, old, official looking buildings. There were also a few older villa style homes that looked like someone took care of them but even they had seen better days.

The strangest structures to Reinhold were the ones that looked like they were made out cement. They looked like the bunkers in Hamburg but with windows and balconies. The whole place had a different character to it, more exotic and tropical then he had encountered before but with the same kind of industrialization he was more than familiar with. There were chickens and palm trees everywhere. The poverty came rolling off the place like a smell. It was depressing.

The *Oldendorff* had to wait two days for a spot on a pier to open up. When it did, with the help of an ancient looking tugboat, they maneuvered their way to the cement pylon and secured the ship. Happily, the ship behind them was a German flag out of Cuxhaven. Reinhold wished he could remember her name. The sailors on board called out greetings to the new comers and the crew of the *Oldendorff* responded in kind. The other ship had been there for two weeks loading copper and was getting ready to ship out soon. They were more than happy to tell the *Oldendorff* that the best place to buy beer was just a few hundred yards away. After his last two experiences on the beach, Reinhold was more than happy to stay on the ship and let others go find the beer.

Looking back, Reinhold remembered a sense of lost worldness coming over him in India. It was like a scene out of a movie about exploring unchartered areas of the globe. Everything was so different. The behavior of the nineteen-year-old Reinhold amused the twenty-two-year old Reinhold. He grew a beard, stopped trimming his hair, and spent most of his time in his bathing suit. His stepmother would have beat him for his lax attitude toward personal appearance but he couldn't help it. It was so hot and humid that wearing long pants and a shirt was next to impossible. They just got soaked when it rained anyway and he'd have to take off his wet clothes and change. The bathing suit was just more practical. There were no women to impress or Captains to keep happy with a clean-shaven face and cut hair so why bother? He was very foppish and the older Reinhold envied the younger Reinhold just a bit.

The ship was docked at the pier for two days when the sailors finally decided to make an excursion to find cheap, local beer. Reinhold stayed behind and was lounging on the hatch cover behind the bridge when a strange European man came strutting up the gangplank. He spotted Reinhold and crossed the deck towards him, extending his hand in greeting. Albert was his name and he was a *Matrose* on the ship docked behind the *Oldendorff*. He and his ship were leaving in two days. Before they left for the long trip back to Germany, they wanted to throw a party and invite the crew of the *Oldendorff*.

"Everyone is invited, even your stokers and mates," He grinned at Reinhold who chuckled knowingly.

"I'll spread the word. Some of our guys just went to get beer, so we'll be able to contribute some. I'll ask the cook to do something. It might even make him happy to cook for people besides us."

At that moment, a roach shuttled across the deck just behind Albert. Reinhold was momentarily appalled by his ship.

Luckily, and due mostly to the cook's pride, no roaches ended up in the food the *Oldendorff* took to the party that night. Reinhold didn't know how it happened, he was just very glad that it did. It would have just been to embarrassing. The other ship was clean and orderly, like it should be. Luckily also, Captain Broplin, who heard about the party somehow, disappeared with the other Captain and no one saw them for the rest of the night. The mates all congregated at a table in the corner, only interacting with the sailors when they needed something. Herr Baumhauer, the bosun, disappeared with the Captains.

All in all, it was a nice night. There was good music from the musicians on board with button boxes and guitars. There was good food thanks to the prideful cooks. Moreover, there was good company. Reinhold even learned something shocking. Somehow, he ended up talking to the one eyed stoker from the *Oldendorff.* The man took his glass eye out and put it on the table, prompting a quick back and forth about manners that led to the stoker asking if Reinhold was Bavarian or something.

"Because only the Bavarians care so much about manners," the stoker spat at Reinhold in disgust.

"I am not from Bavaria," Reinhold spot back. "I am from the north, near Lübeck. Do I look Bavarian?"

"Lübeck?" The stoker was intrigued. "I know the area. What town near Lübeck?"

"Ratekau."

"Ratekau!" Reinhold thought the stoker was going to fall off his chair in surprise. "Ratekau! I am from Techau!"

Now Reinhold thought he was going to fall off his chair.

"Techau! That's the next town over from Ratekau. What the hell are you doing here?"

"The same thing as you, fool. Trying to earn a living before I die."

He became thoughtful for a second, polishing his eye in silence while Reinhold processed that this guy was his neighbor in a town that seemed like it was on the other side of the world at that moment.

"There are some great women in Ratekau." The stoker said quietly, sticking the eye back in the empty socket.

"Women?"

Reinhold was shocked. He couldn't think of a single great woman in Ratekau. Most of them were old cows.

"Yup. I used to visit one and I will visit her again before I leave this world."

"Who?"

The stoker blushed slightly. It was strange because he was such a tough guy.

"Anna Easberger," he sighed.

"Anna Easberger!" Reinhold's shocked came rushing back three fold. "Anna Easberger? You are joking? That's my neighbor!"

The stoker's one functioning eye opened in surprise. "Your neighbor? I don't believe it."

"Believe it. I'll prove it. She is a big women with a husband named Paul and eleven children. Hitler gave her an award for being such a good breeder and contributing to the population of Germany. Two of her sons died in the war."

"I'll be damned. Maybe she is your neighbor!"

The stoker, whose name was Schiffer, and Reinhold spent some time talking about their hometowns. The one eyed tough guy turned out to be a much more personable man than Reinhold had figured. He told Schiffer about his uncle. He had been a sailor before the war and jumped ship in India, probably in this port.

"So you have an uncle floating around here somewhere?"

"I guess so. I don't know where else he would have jumped. He was working on a ship hauling iron ore. Hitler was getting ready for war and needed lots of iron to build equipment."

He paused to swig his beer. He had already drank entirely too much but why bother stopping? Tomorrow, the longshoremen would show up and do all the loading work while Reinhold stood on a scaffold in Hatch 3, painting the interior walls with a sealant.

"Why did he jump ship?"

Reinhold focused on Schiffer. "Why wouldn't he have jumped? When he got back to Germany they were going to draft him into the *Kriegsmarine*[33]. Who the hell wanted to be on a ship during the war?"

"I was in the *Kriegsmarine*. That's where I lost my eye. Never even saw battle. Lost it during a training maneuver in the Baltic Sea. One of the big guns misfired."

"War is a terrible thing." Reinhold slurred.

He looked around before continuing, leaning in and keeping his voice down.

"That is why I am going to jump in Australia."

"What is so great about Australia?"

"No wars and no one cares you're there."

The rest of the night was a blur. He stumbled back to his ship at some point and fell into his bunk without taking his shoes off. That night, he dreamt of Ratekau and Anna Easberger. He remembered the doctor's car parked outside every week and it made sense. He had

---

[33] *Kriegsmarine* is the German Navy.

loved the doctor's car. It was an old time model that needed to have the engine cranked. The crazy old man fueled it with ether. Oh, how it would backfire! Suddenly, the happy memory of seeing the car became corrupted. He was witnessing cheating and Anna Easberger wasn't the kind of woman Reinhold wanted to picture as a temptress.

The next morning Reinhold awoke early in spite of not having slept long. He tried to lay there and go back to sleep but the sound of Freddy's snoring was unbearable. Sighing, he got out of his bunk and went to the galley to get a mug of coffee, taking it to the deck to wait for breakfast. The sun was still low over the horizon. His head was throbbing a bit and he thought he was still a little drunk.

He turned away from the sun and found himself facing the shore. The sun was playing off the different colors of the vegetation and buildings, bringing to prominence the whitewashed structures. Reinhold stared groggily at the brighter colors, drawn to their luminousness even though it hurt his eyes, like a moth to the flame.

It took a few seconds for him to realize that the snaking white line he was staring at was moving. Focusing painfully, he saw that it was people, dressed in white, making their way down the hill toward the port. They weren't alone. Traveling with them were goats, chickens, and dogs. It was a sight. Reinhold watched as they made their way to sea level. The white line continued to the train not far from the ship where it became a moving puddle of white. One at a time, white figures broke away from the group and headed for the *Oldendorff*. They were carrying large plate like objects on their heads. He watched, mesmerized, as the white figures walked up the gangplank to Hatch 2 and dumped the contents of their plates into the hull. The parade of figures continued like ants, a constant stream of workers all fixed on one goal.

"Reinhold," He heard Freddy say in his ear. He started out of his hung over trance.

"What?"

"Breakfast."

"Oh. Right. Coming."

He threw another glance in the direction of the white figures before following Freddy to the mess hall.

Over breakfast, Alex told them that at the party the night before a sailor from the other ship told him where to find girls. All the sailor's ears perked up at this new information. Somewhere along the shore, not far from where they were docked, was the outlet of a creek. If they followed the creek inland, they would come to a house were women could be bought. They quickly devised a plan to go later that night.

Climbing out of Hatch 3 later, Reinhold noticed the stream of workers was still flowing. They weren't white anymore. They were red now, from head to toe. Even their faces were coated in a red film from the copper ore they carried in the plates on their heads.

After a quick dinner and an even quicker shower, Reinhold, Freddy, Alex, Punchy, Henry, and a couple of guys Reinhold didn't know very well set out from the ship, following the beachy coast line until they found a creek outlet. It was a nasty, filthy creek full of garbage and emitting a strange, rancid smell that fell somewhere between cow dung and industrial waste.

"What is that smell?" Alex asked.

"The creek," Punchy answered him.

"What's wrong with it?" Alex wrinkled his nose in disgust.

"Probably sewage," Freddy answered him. He walked a little closer to the bank and sniffed. "Yup, that's sewage."

They followed the dirty creek inland several hundred yards, passing small hut-like homes with children and old people hanging around, until they came to a wooden house that had to be what they were looking for because there were half-naked girls hanging around outside. When they appeared, the girls started calling to them but nobody understood what they were saying. Everyone, however, understood what everyone else wanted. The girls presented themselves in a haphazard kind of line near a dilapidated porch, displaying what they thought were their best features. There were more than enough to satisfy all the sailors. Reinhold chose a tiny little thing with a tight body and a pretty face framed by waves of raven black hair. She had to have been fifteen years old and Reinhold was glad for it. All of her parts were firm and perky, just waiting to be squeezed and messaged.

Looking back, Reinhold had to say that she had one of the best bodies he had ever seen. Moreover, she was good in bed, which was exactly what he wanted. After several months with no companionship, he wasn't looking for a wilting daisy. He wanted a thorny rose.

The language barrier vanished once they were alone in one of the tiny, dirt-floored rooms of the shaky wooden structure. There was no bed, just a kind of woven grass mattress on the floor and Reinhold didn't care. They spent a glorious hour together before she ended it by satisfying his needs and hastily getting dressed. She put out her hand for payment as soon as Reinhold had buckled his pants. He put a couple of the *rupee* coins in her hand, wondering if it was enough. She snatched her hand away so quickly that he figured she was happy with the amount.

As they were leaving, Reinhold noted that the women were in the creek, washing themselves. He shuddered. One woman looked like she had a bloody nose and a swollen mouth. Reinhold wondered if one of the guys had gotten rough with her. It made him angry to think about it. Shrugging, he decided that it was none of his business. There was nothing he could do about it. Some men just could not control themselves around women. He would never understand why the attentions of a woman made men feel like they had to be violent.

The sailors took their time walking back to the ship, sharing stories of their women. Most of them were very happy, giddy almost. It had been a long, long time for all of them. They were making a lot of noise as they passed other shacks along the creek. People stared indignantly at them but they didn't care. They continued carrying on. Only one guy wasn't happy. When they asked him what was wrong he said he thought his girl had been "dirty".

"They're all dirty." Punchy told him. "Did you see how they were washing? They're all coated in sewer water!"

Reinhold shuddered again.

Chapter 71: Disgusted

The *Oldendorff* wasn't in India seven days when Reinhold's knee took a direct hit from the scaffolding support in Hatch 2 when it shifted unexpectedly.

What a disaster that was, he thought to himself.

Freddy and Alex helped him out of the hatch and to the mess hall before going to get Musil.

"I have to call the Captain," Musil said with a sympathetic tone. "I can't send you off the ship to get medical attention without his approval."

He looked over his shoulder toward the shore before continuing.

"I don't even know where the hospital is in the place. We'll have to ask the local agent."

The Captain was not happy with Reinhold's condition. He screamed and carried on that he was faking the injury because he didn't want to work, like a child. Not even after both the First Mate and Reinhold pointed out the previous damage to the joint did the Captain relax. He grudgingly consented to take Reinhold to the hospital for x-rays.

"We'll see about this supposed injury," Captain Broplin slurred loudly to the crew. "The hospital is just going to confirm that this guy is faking. Then he'll be cleaning the bilge for the rest of our stay here. There will be no slackers or fakers on this ship! Someone get the goddamn agent so we can take care of this nonsense!"

Reinhold was so angry with the Captain, he could have punched the man so hard he would have gone over the rail. Hearing the splash of the *arschloch* hitting the water would have been extremely satisfying. When he arrived, the agent must have read Reinhold's mind.

"He is just drunk and blowing steam." The agent tried to reassure the sailor. The man was a transplanted Englishman who didn't speak German. The First Mate translated the comment for Reinhold. "He doesn't really think you're faking."

Reinhold stared at him for a second.

"You don't know this guy then. He is a real *arschloch*. Which reminds me, I want to file a complaint against this ship and the company that owns it. It is infested with roaches. They get into our food, even the coffee."

The First Mate translated again.

The agent looked disgusted. He made a quick comment to Musil who then responded to Reinhold.

"He noticed it isn't the best kept ship."

"They buy us crap supplies. They bought the wrong paint."

Reinhold gestured to the bulkhead, indicating the peeling paint and the bare spots where it flaked off.

"This is interior house paint or something. It is not for ships. As soon as we apply it, it flakes off because of the salt or the wind or the sun."

Musil relayed the observances. The agent looked around, nodding, but said nothing further. Nothing would come of the complaints, Reinhold knew. The Captain would just give the agent a few cartons of Lucky Strikes and a few bottles of liquor. The agent would take the goods and say nothing to anyone about anything.

They loaded Reinhold into a taxi at the ship. The taxi was a big old car of British manufacture that easily accommodated the driver, the sailor, the agent, and the Captain. At the agent's direction, the taxi headed for the ferry that took them across the bay to Dona Paula. 'Ferry' was the wrong word. They should have called it a raft because it was a platform with an awning and a flimsy rail. Reinhold was surprised when the taxi drove on to it. He had expected to have to get out and get another taxi on the other side. The trip across went relatively smoothly.

The trip from Dona Paula to Panjim, where the only hospital was located, was a nightmare. The agent said that the hospital was about seven miles from the ship and should take them about an hour, depending. Instead, the trip lasted all day and turned out to be an eye opening experience.

When they departed the ferry in Dona Paula, the scene was lovely. A beautiful beach and lovely homes lined the seashore. Colorful fishing boats dotted the coast. Reinhold thought his eyes were playing tricks on him because he could have sworn there were cows on the beach. In contrast, as they moved further inland, he couldn't help but notice that they were traveling into what could only be described as a slum.

There were half clothed children running around with filthy, mongrel looking dogs. Chickens roamed freely, pecking and scraping in the mud. There were hopeless looking people sitting on the front steps of broken down buildings or just huddled in the streets against the sides of buildings, trying to stay out of the flow of traffic. Some were sleeping propped against buildings or street lamps. There was trash everywhere. There was human waste everywhere. The roads were not paved with anything more than stones that showed a good deal of mud between them. The smell was outrageous, something like a moldy barn.

Then there were the cows. There were cows wandering freely through the streets. Their excrement was everywhere. No one seemed to mind. It was appalling to Reinhold that people lived in these conditions in a Portuguese colony when Portugal itself was so clean and orderly, even in its poverty.

"Why are there cows in the town?" Reinhold asked the agent.

The question was grudgingly translated by Capt. Broplin.

"The cows are welcome and revered members of the community here."

"Revered?"

"Yes, they are scared animals. They don't kill them or eat them. They just let them wander and do what they want."

Even the Captain looked mildly interested by this bit of cultural information.

As if to illustrate the point, the taxi turned a corner and came to an abrupt halt behind another big, old taxi. Up ahead in the middle of the road was a cow. The animal was lying with its whole body blocking the thoroughfare. There were two men trying to rouse the beast. They were not having any luck. Reinhold didn't think they were trying very hard.

"Why don't they just grab it by the head and pull it up?" Reinhold asked, frustrated and in pain.

The agent smiled understandingly.

"It takes some getting used to, this letting animals do whatever they want. They can't touch it. They can't try to change its mind once the creature has decided on something."

"That doesn't make any sense. It is just a cow. They are not even smart animals. If you are going to worship an animal you should at least make it a smart animal like a dog or a cat or a money. You know, something that knows how to take care of itself."

"That's the smartest thing I've ever heard you say," the Captain sneered at Reinhold.

As they sat there, waiting for the cow to move, the agent told the Captain about the uprising going on against the Portuguese areas of Goa. The Captain listened politely and translated every so often for Reinhold. More frequently, he pulled a flask out of his shirt pocket and sipped deeply.

This arschloch *is trying to look like a nice guy after his ranting and raving on the ship,* Reinhold snorted to himself but he appreciated the agent's knowledge.

It wasn't anything like a war, the agent said. It was non-violent in nature, for the most part. Every now and then, there was a skirmish or a few young Indians attacked patrols. Therefore, the Portuguese, the agent explained, maintained a show of power. This explained why there were armed soldiers mingling with the crowds on the street. They looked slightly uneasy despite their firepower. The natives looked at them with expressions of disgusted apprehension.

"I suspect the Portuguese won't last much longer. They don't have the funds to hold on to this colony even though they would love to. There is a lot of wealth to be had from this area."

The agent lit a cigarette with a flashy golden lighter before offering a smoke to Reinhold. He took the cigarette and the agent lit it for him before continuing. The Captain waved the pack away, choosing to sip his flask instead.

"The Goans have rebelled in the past without much success but this time they have the backing of the rest of the Indian nation, who are feeling their independence after the British left a few years ago. I suspect that they will intervene militarily eventually to reunite the country."

"Brits think everybody is theirs to own." Capt. Broplin said to Reinhold in German. He spit loudly out the window.

For hours, the taxi stood motionless in the street, waiting for the cow to move. Afternoon was wearing on when the animal finally got up and left. Reinhold was so happy he left out a shout of joy that drew scathing looks from the Indians passing the car. He didn't care. Getting out of the car was his only goal. The Captain was drunk and slurry. It was only a matter of time before he lost his patience sitting in the car.

Almost five hours after leaving the ship, the taxi finally pulled up in front of the hospital. Reinhold was glad to see that it was a modern institution not a third world medicine man tent. The driver and the agent helped him out of the car and inside where they put him in a wheelchair. After a young Indian man in a white coat took x-rays of the injured knee, Reinhold sat with the agent and the Captain in a grungy room with two dozen other sick and injured waiting for the results.

When they were finally ready, the Captain relayed the results to Reinhold through clenched teeth. Reinhold felt vindicated. He had torn his meniscus and couldn't work. He needed surgery as soon as possible to repair the damage.

A few minutes later, they left the hospital. Reinhold knew he wasn't getting the surgery here in India. The company would never go for that. Not only would they have to pay for the surgery, they would have to pay for his stay in the country and then get him home somehow. This wouldn't be a big issue if the company had regular routes to India but they didn't and wouldn't for some time. He had to wait until he got back to Germany to get his knee fixed. They gave him some pills for the pain in the meantime.

The ride back to the ship was a tense one. The Captain fumed, answering questions from the agent in one word or in grunts. Finally, after a particular comment from the agent, he lost his cool and started yelling. Reinhold figured that he was in need of a drink. It had been a while since he saw the flask. It was probably empty.

"You can't work!" He screamed. "You can't work and you need surgery! I am not going to tolerant this! You hurt yourself on purpose so you can loaf around and not work. This is an outrage! You WILL work. I will see to that. Your arms aren't broken. You don't need surgery on your brain. You can still work."

Reinhold nodded absent-mindedly. Something caught his eye. They were traveling through the city of Panjim. Dusk was gathering and heavy night was visible in the sky to the east. There was a wagon, pulled by a set of horses and guided by a man in an orange robe, moving through the streets a little ways from where Reinhold and his compatriots were waiting for traffic to move. From time to time, the man stopped, picked something large up off the ground and placed it in the back of the wagon before moving on again. It was intriguing because Reinhold couldn't image what the man was collecting off the streets. The peculiar sight was moving toward them and he strained to see what was in the cargo area.

"Holy Jees," he exclaimed as the wagon finally came into full view.

It stopped just ten yards from where the taxi waited. The man stooped down near another man, older and grizzled looking, sleeping in the dirt against the corner of an ugly cement building. He touched the sleeping man on his wrist and neck and put a mirror in front of his face. Then, he picked the man up and put him in the back of the wagon with several other people before moving on. Reinhold turned to the agent.

"What is that?" He asked, interrupting the ranting of the Captain.

The agent shook his head and looked questioningly at the Captain.

Annoyed, the Captain translated the question, his eyes following where Reinhold was pointing. The agent moved in his seat to see what was going on, craning his head around the car's high seat. He sighed.

"That is the cart from the local temple."

He took off his glass and wiped them, reluctant to go on. He took a cigarette from his pocket and lit it. Reinhold waited patiently for his fears to be confirmed.

"They send it out from the local temple at night to collect the dead."

Reinhold knew the Captain had translated the agent's words exactly because he said them in the same quiet tone. He wasn't sure if the gentile Englishman and the Captain were appalled by the public and tragic death of innocent, obviously poor, people or the practice of collecting them off the street in a wagon.

Reinhold was disgusted. Looking back from the deck of the *Brandenburg*, he was still disgusted. How could a country allow people to die in the streets like animals? The temple sent the wagon around to collect them, yes, but why not collect them before they died? Why were people allowed to live like that? It was in that moment that he saw the true horror of humanity, of governments, of business. What he had witnessed in Germany when he was a kid had a larger cause, namely Hitler and the war. There was no reason for this situation in India. It was just greed and ignorance.

No one seemed to care. As the wagon moved through the streets, no one gave it a second glance; no one made any motions of deference. Reinhold felt sick. He spent the rest of the trip to the ship with his forehead pressed against the glass of the window, staring blankly out at a crowded, busy, bustling world that didn't care.

Chapter 72: We Have So Much

Reinhold spent the rest of his time in India preparing the lines for the trip home and repairing any that broke. As the Captain pointed out, his hands weren't broken and neither was his mind. The rest of the guys painted, built, sealed, and pumped and Reinhold would gladly have joined them if it weren't for his knee. The pain was bad but not as bad as he had been expecting. The pain pills helped.

As he sat on the deck under the shade of the awning, splicing and repairing lengths of boom line, Reinhold observed the natives. One of his favorite things to do was to watch the procession of workers down the mountain in the morning. After traveling through Panjim, he felt he had a better understanding of the way these people lived. He felt bad for them. He pictured women in a village on top of the mountain standing over huge boiling vats of soapy water, scrubbing the copper ore dust out of their husband's or father's clothing so she could send them off to work clean in the morning. He pictured the children gathering plants and caring for animals. He watched the workers in the continuous procession from the train cars to the ship's hull. They were loading the copper ore faster than the Arab men unloaded the cement.

One day, as he watched the longshoremen, it occurred to him that he didn't see them stop for lunch or dinner.

No wonder they are all so skinny, he thought. *They don't eat all day and do nothing but walk back and forth carrying heavy loads on their heads.*

He wondered if it was a condition of their employment that there were no breaks or if they just didn't have any food. Over lunch, he asked Musil. The mate had taken to eating with the crew as opposed to the other mates.

"I never thought about it. Not all of us have time to sit around and think." He grinned at Reinhold's discomfort. "I guess I could find out for you."

"Don't bother," Reinhold said. He picked a roach out of his beard. "They look hungry. I think we should give them some of our leftover food. We have so much."

"That is a stupid idea. Who wants to eat our roach infested crap?"

It was one of the guys that had gone to see the prostitutes with them that spoke. Reinhold learned the man's name was Zucker. He had been in a bad mood since their experiences ashore with the girls. Reinhold suspected he had the clap because of the way he was walking and scratching.

"I don't care what you think is stupid," Reinhold retorted, preparing for a fight.

He was ready for it, excited almost. He hadn't had a good fight in a while. To his disappointment, Zucker just picked up his dishes and left.

"I think it is a good idea, Scholz," Alex said.

Next to him, Freddy sat nodding his approval, his mouth full of potato.

"What's wrong with that guy?" Reinhold asked, jerking a thumb toward a retreating Zucker.

Alex snorted. "He's got the clap."

There was a few seconds of silence before everyone at the table started to snicker.

So I was right, Reinhold thought, *he does have the clap!*

"I am surprised you haven't heard him screaming when he pisses."

The snickering became full-blown laughter. Musil quickly silenced it.

"You shouldn't laugh," he warned with a frown. "That could be you one day."

"We know, we know," admitted Freddy. "It just couldn't have happened to a nicer guy than him."

"He should have picked a better girl," Alex said. "He said when we were leaving that he thought his girl was dirty."

"Well, I said it then and I'll say it now, they were all dirty." Punchy snorted.

"Why didn't the Second Mate give him some penicillin?" Reinhold asked.

Everyone looked to Musil.

"We don't have any." Musil looked a bit sheepish at the admission.

"Just when you think it can't get any worse." Alex shook his head in disgust.

After dinner, Reinhold went to the train and got one of the big plates the longshoremen were using to transport the copper ore. He rinsed it off as best he could in the small sink in the galley and piled

the leftover food on it. He wasn't quite sure how to offer food to the workers and was quick to settle for simplicity. He went out to the deck and intersected the line of longshoremen, holding up the plate, gesturing toward the food, then gesturing for them to follow him. He walked to the shade of the awning and placed the plate on an old crate.

It took a few minutes, but slowly the workers came over to investigate. Reinhold gestured toward the food again, bringing his hand to his mouth to tell them to eat. They looked apprehensive but hunger won in the end.

Ten minutes later, there was a crowd of Indians standing on the deck of the *Christoffer Oldendorff*, eating chucks of potato and bread and canned beef. They were under the awning, so the Captain never saw what was going on, thankfully. Reinhold didn't know how he would take it but wouldn't have been good. Some of the sailors and Henry the stoker joined the crowd. Soon, the two ethnicities were attempting communication and laughing at themselves. Even Musil joined them.

"Their boss doesn't care that they are not working?" Musil asked, craning his head to see if the foreman was paying attention.

He didn't spot him and shrugged. No one objected. It became customary for Reinhold to give the leftovers to the Indians. It also became customary for the sailors to come hang out for a few minutes and interact with the natives. It helped bridge the cultural divide between the two groups of people.

Reinhold thought about those days in India with a certain amount of fondness tinged with irritation. The treatment of the sailors by the Captain and the company still made him angry. However, it was because of the company that he had some good times. If they had agreed to let him have his surgery, he would have spent his time in the country cooped up in a hospital room. Instead, he was on a kind of paid vacation. Yes, he worked, but not as hard as the other sailors.

Reinhold also looked back with fondness on the time he spent with Henry. They continued their evening fishing and drinking with Henry teaching Reinhold new ways to catch eels. The Arabian Sea off the coast of India was loaded with them. They wanted to eat them, to compare them to the eels they grew up with but, once again, the cook refused to cook them. Taking matters into their own hands, the pair found an old, rusty metal bucket and built a fire it in. They roasted the eels on skewers made from a broken wooden beam. They were delicious and different than the European variety in the texture and flavor. They handed them out like lollipops to everyone who walked by.

Also in the evenings, there was drinking and singing. Punchy would get out his accordion and make up songs about how the sea was the only woman a sailor needed. They tried to cool their beer in the sea as they had done in the Middle East and they got the same result. The water was just too warm. The Indian beer was ok but Reinhold was positive that it would be better cold. Punchy said the same was true for American beer.

"American beer isn't all that bad, it just has to be cold. I don't know why that would be. It just tastes better." Punchy said one night during a break from playing music.

"You've had it?" Alex asked suspiciously.

"Of course." Punchy helped himself to another Indian beer. "I was sent to America on punishment a few years ago with this very company here." He pointed at the deck of the ship.

"What did you do?"

Punchy shrugged. "Fighting."

"And insubordination," Musil added, appearing out of the gathering gloom and helping himself to a beer. "He is not telling you that he fought with a mate, the First, if I remember correctly."

"You remember correctly." Punchy looked irritated. "And I would do it again. Damn guy called me a low life. Can you imagine? Someone working for this company calling me a low life? My home isn't infested with roaches like this old tub."

"Speaking of which," Alex looked to Musil. "Are we ever getting rid of these roaches? Isn't there an exterminator here, in India?"

Musil looked grim. "Listen, men, it is not going to happen. No exterminator is setting foot on this ship. The Captain doesn't care that your food is infested with roaches, he doesn't care that you have no refrigeration, he doesn't care that you have no air conditioning, and he doesn't care that you are unhappy, especially you, Scholz."

The First Mate took a long gulp of his warm beer while the sailors sat in stunned silence. It was quiet for a solid minute before the indignant noises began. There were half words, snorts, snickers, and sighs but no one seemed to be able to put those thoughts into words until Alex spoke up.

"Then we'll mutiny."

This was something the guys could wrap their heads around.

"Yes, that is a good idea."

"Let's put the Captain and Herr Baumhauer in a boat and set them adrift like they did to Henry Hudson."

"No, let's sail to one of those islands on the map, the Maldives, and maroon them there."

"Can we keep the dog?"

"Let's just hang them off the boom as a warning to everyone else."

"They like to fly so much, maybe we should hang them from the crow's nest."

"We could throw them overboard and take the ship back to Germany. We could tell the company they found girls in India and jumped ship."

"Who would believe that? I say we mutiny on the way to the Middle East and drop them in Aden. It is such a hospitable place they should do fine there."

"We could always just lock them in one of the hatches until we get back to Germany then bring them up on charges."

"Charges? What charges?"

"He is so drunk all the time; we could probably get him for abandoning his post. Baumhauer too. I haven't seen that guy for more than meals in a week."

"Doubtful. We could still lock them in one of the hatches though."

"Maybe we should just drown them in that shit paint they bought."

The group got a bit bigger. A few guys that were passing by and heard the conversation stayed to see what was going to come of it. They cast curious looks in Musil's direction. Musil shook his head in bemusement. He finished an entire beer and grabbed another before speaking, letting the would-be mutineers get the suggestions out of their systems.

"You can't mutiny. You need the support of a mate."

Alex looked confused. "I thought we had your support."

"You do but I still don't think you should mutiny."

"Why not? You said yourself that the company and the Captain don't give a crap about us or about the ship. Why shouldn't we mutiny? They have us living like animals." Reinhold felt his anger rising.

"If you mutiny, you will never get another job as a sailor in Germany, or in Europe, possibly the world, ever again. You will get arrested when you get home for treason. The courts will throw you in jail without another thought. In the past, you would have gotten the death penalty."

"The union won't let that happen."

This time it was the *Leichtmatrose*, Willie, who spoke up. No one said anything in response, but everyone stared at him like he was a crazy person. He became instantly uncomfortable.

"Right? Isn't that why we pay union dues? So they protect us in cases like this?" The poor kid turned bright red.

"You still pay union dues?" Freddy asked. "We have rights as seamen to edible food and a sanitary environment," he continued. "Capt. Broplin is violating our rights by not providing these things. He is not upholding his end of the equation. He has the duty of care."

Musil looked a bit impressed but still shook his head negatively. "Listen, you guys know I am right. You'll all be black listed and you won't get paid for the time it takes you to get back to

Germany. You might not see any pay at all. After, what, four months now, that would be quite a bit of money."

"How long could that really be? Getting back to Germany? Three weeks without pay is nothing. And I'll be damned if I don't get paid for the work I have done this far."

"You are forgetting the propeller, Alex. It is going to take a hell of a lot longer to get home than three weeks. We have been discussing this, the Second Mate and I. We think it is going to take a month to get home if we don't run into any problems."

"So, we would still teach that guy a lesson." A sailor toward the out edge of the group spoke up.

"No," Musil said. "No, you wouldn't. You would be at fault here. Mutinying is the worst, worst thing you could do. Let's just get back home and then we will address this. I don't want to see any of you destroy your lives because Broplin is an *arschloch*. Don't worry, he'll get his eventually."

Reinhold remembered that conversation like it happened yesterday. They were serious about mutinying, really serious. The possibility of a large scale strike continued the rest of the *Oldendorff's* stay in India. There was definitely a work slowdown. Men stopped showing up for the Captain's morning pep talk. They had to be fetched like bratty children. Herr Baumhauer was the only one paying attention to the old man anymore. Reinhold and Henry's evening fishing became whole days and it was more than the two of them sitting on the rail with fishing poles. Half the crew stopped working at noon. Soon, there were four or five cooking buckets going. Luckily, there was lots of dry cow dung around for fuel. There were also more sailors around when Reinhold took the leftover food from lunch to the deck and gave it to the longshoremen. It became a kind of party atmosphere, until the foreman of the Indian workers ordered his guys back to work.

We lost all pride in ourselves and our work, Reinhold thought to himself with a tinge of guilt. *But, we were justified in our actions. Fuck the Oldendorff Company and Captain Broplin, wherever that bastard is right now! Hopefully he got really drunk one night during a bad storm in the North Sea and fell overboard.*

Chapter 73: The Long Trip Home

He was glad, looking back, that they listened to the mate and stuck it out under the Captain. It was hell getting out of India and back to Europe, but it was worth it. The *Oldendorff* shoved off from the pier on the morning of July 24, 1954, headed for Europe. Their first scheduled stop in a real port wasn't until Rotterdam. No one knew how long it would take to get there. The First Mate was anticipating four to five weeks, if the weather stayed good and the currents were favorable. The crew was a bit more skeptical. Most thought it would take six weeks.

"I'm going straight to Reeperbahn when we get back," Alex said wistfully, like he could already taste the beer and feel the skin of a good German girl.

"We're going to Rotterdam to unload the copper, not Hamburg." Reinhold pointed out.

He was going to follow up by saying that they would have to make due with a Dutch girl when Alex's temper flared.

"I am getting off this floating metal Swiss cheese as soon as we drop anchor in Rotterdam and getting the first train to Hamburg. Screw waiting until we unload and sail to Hamburg. The train is faster." He snorted in anger. "I might throw Zucker overboard before we even get to the Suez Canal if someone doesn't get him some medicine. My bunk is next to the head. His screaming echoes off the bulkhead like someone is hitting it with a hammer."

No one ever did get him any medicine, Reinhold thought. *He screamed the whole way back to Rotterdam. One day he mentioned that he thought he was starting to hallucinate. It was not at all surprising when he was the first one to get paid off and disappear with his sea bag and sailor's book. He didn't even say goodbye to anyone. Can't blame him. What kind of ship doesn't keep penicillin onboard? What kind of sadistic people let a man suffer like Zucker did? Cheap crooks, is the answer. We should have had medicine, better materials, and better food but the steward and the Captain pocketed the money. Bastards.*

The *Oldendorff* limped back to Europe, taking the same course it took on the way out without stopping at a single Middle Eastern port. The weather stayed fair, with occasional squalls popping up, but nothing major. The temperatures stayed in the 100s and the heat radiated off the sun washed deck in waves. As they moved closer to the deserts of the Arabian Peninsula, the air got drier and the wind more severe. It was blowing offshore, against the path of the *Oldendorff*, slowing her down. Through the binoculars, Reinhold watched the towers and water front buildings of Aden slid past as they rounded the edge of Yemen, headed for the Persian Gulf and the Suez Canal.

I'll always have the scar to remember it by, he thought.

They reached the mouth of the Gulf of Suez some twenty days after leaving Mormugoa. The thought of traversing the Suez Canal lifted the spirits of the sailors until Herr Baumhauer reminded them that the locals would be coming back on board as part of the pilot crew.

"You all are going to have to be on guard duty the entire time we are in the canal while there are foreigners on the ship." He spat over the rail he was leaning against. "On our way through last time, we lost fifty feet of line, four buckets, three wrenches, a handful of hammers, twenty gallons of paint, and that is just what I remember at the moment. We have to keep a better watch this time."

The crew rolled its eyes collectively at the bosun. They all knew that as soon as the pilot took over the bridge, he and the Captain were going to disappear, not to be seen again until they reached the Mediterranean Sea. And that was exactly what happened. Musil ordered everything not in use stowed and locked down.

In the port of Suez, they took on a pilot and a whole slew of others who claimed to be 'electricians'. Most of them set up their mats with wares to sell and never touched a single line or observed a single function. They were the same scrawny Egyptians they picked up on the way through the first time. Reinhold ignored them this time. He was assigned to watch the ladder, to make sure no one got off the ship that way.

Speedboats raced alongside the *Oldendorff*, waiting for some kind of loot to be pitched over the side to them. As far as Reinhold could tell, nothing went off his side. The speedboats darted around the other side. A few minutes later, they were back. The ship was being circled like a dying animal by hungry crows. It added another layer of disgust to Reinhold's already bad opinion of the people in the Middle East. The boats drew off and disappeared when the big lake at Ismailia appeared on the horizon.

They spent a day at Ismailia before continuing north in the canal in a convoy of two dozen other ships. A new pilot appeared with another gang of electricians in tow. They set up their mats and got to work selling. Reinhold wondered if anyone was buying. As far as he could tell, no one had purchased anything. The sailors were all too disgruntled and all of them were standing guard at strategic places onboard. The speedboats came back and circled. Reinhold knew they were approaching Port Said when, again, they disappeared.

They dropped anchor in Port Said twenty-two days after leaving Mormugoa. The next day, the *Christoffer Oldendorff* was on its way again. The blue waters of the Mediterranean greeted them like an old friend. There was a noticeable decrease in the tension onboard. There was still a lot of anger. Every time a roach scuttled passed or someone picked one out of his coffee, the anger resurfaced.

The Straits of Gibraltar was looming in the distance when Musil called an informal meeting with the crew. He knew there were a few sailors on the verge of mutinying again. They had misunderstood him in India and thought that once they got back to Europe it would be safe to overthrow the Captain. He called them together to explain that he decided to write a letter to the authorities to explain the grievances of the crew.

"I can word this document in a way that expresses the short comings of the Captain, his failure to provide 'duty of care', as they call it, and tells of the hardships you guys have endured so that you are viewed as a dedicated and responsible crew. If you mutiny, I can't do that. There will be no way I can make you look good after that."

"What are you going to do with this letter?" Alex asked.

"When we reach Rotterdam, I will give it to the authorities there. I want all of you to read it and sign it. Then, you can all sign off in protest. This can be noted in the letter."

Musil looked around at all of them to see if the message was sinking in to those that still wanted blood. There were some reluctant looks; Reinhold could see them for himself. The First Mate sighed.

"Do as you will. I will start to compose the letter. I will call you all together to sign it."

He dismissed the meeting and headed back to his cabin with a slump to his shoulders. Reinhold watched him go and didn't envy him. At any moment, a disgruntled sailor could snap and storm the Captain's salon with a mind toward causing as much harm as possible.

The *Christoffer Oldendorff* rounded the Iberian Peninsula, steaming north for Holland. The weather cooled down and the waves got choppier. As they crept up the latitudes, the roach problem became less noticeable. The crew's spirits lifted. It was good to be back in the Atlantic. When they reached a strong storm near the English Channel with twenty-foot swells and wind-driven rain that whipped in sideways, Reinhold was never so happy to be on a pitching ship with waves smashing over him onto the deck. It was a glorious welcome back from the North Sea.

Forty-five days after leaving Mormugoa, India, the *Oldendorff* dropped anchor in Rotterdam. The crew was ecstatic to be home, or close to home. When the ship was secured in a familiar port, a kind of defiant cheer went up from the sailors on the deck. The First Mate on the bridge sounded the bell. Later that day, a tug came out and guided the ship to a pier for unloading. The First Mate called a meeting. He had composed his letter.

"The agent is going to be here in the morning for the pay off. I was hoping to have you guys sign this letter tonight that way you can get paid and leave if you want to without the Captain and the agent knowing about your grievances. I won't mention it to anyone. I am just going to take it over to the authorities and drop it off. They will take it from there."

He looked at the assembled men to see the reaction. Being back in Europe brought out the patience in the seamen. They all nodded in agreement. Everyone took his turn signing the letter. Musil shook their hands and wished them luck in the future. In the morning, they lined up again, this time to get paid. The agent supervised the pay out and the Captain did the counting. Reinhold got just over eight hundred *mark* for his work over the previous six months. The Captain glared angrily at him during the transaction and made a comment to the agent that he didn't think this particular sailor deserved so much money. Reinhold quelled his anger by reminding himself that he never had to see that man or his nasty ship ever again. It was September 8, 1954.

Chapter 74: Welcome Home, Scholz

Reinhold, Alex, Freddy, and several others took the express train from Rotterdam to Hamburg. Just as Alex planned, they went from the Hamburg train station by taxi to Reeperbahn.

"This is going to be an expensive night!" Alex said gleefully.

The sailors were in high spirits. They were back in Germany and had a lot of money burning holes in their pockets. They all agreed with Alex.

"I am going to have to get three girls to get back to my usual stamina." Freddy made a thrusting move with his hips. "I can't wait to practice!"

"First, gentlemen, there is a proper beer in our futures. Not that warm swill we drank for five months." Reinhold reminded them. "I think we should get some good German cooking to go with it!"

The others heartily agreed with him after months of salted meat, canned vegetables, and roach infested bread.

They headed to the first restaurant they encountered on Reeperbahn and ordered almost everything on the menu. They ate and drank until they couldn't eat another bite.

The sailors spent the night hopping from spot to spot on Reeperbahn, drinking, dancing, and flirting. Finally, as the bars were closing for the night, Reinhold met a woman he wanted to go home with. He didn't think she was a prostitute. She was probably one of those women who pick up guys when they need money and Reinhold didn't care. They got a taxi back to her place. She kept him occupied the whole way. He paid for the ride and followed her up the front steps to a first floor doorway. Even in his tipsy condition, Reinhold's sailor's instincts told him something was wrong. It was too dark. The only light coming into the room was from the streetlights outside.

"Why is it so dark in here? I want to see you." He mumbled into her neck.

Something moved just over her shoulder, in the corner of the room. She gave a small, nervous laugh. "My electricity got shut off."

She found his hand and began leading him further into the shadows.

The instinct told him to run for it. He didn't want to run for it. Her lips were soft and her body was warm. She smelled like vanilla. The instinct told him to run. Something moved in the corner of the room again. And Reinhold ran. He went straight to the window, pushed it out and open, and jumped into the street, landing heavily in front of a man in a suit carrying a briefcase. He looked very surprised.

"They are coming out of the windows now!" He said before shaking off his surprise and continuing his morning walk to work.

Reinhold looked back up at the window.

"Come back here!"

The girl was leaning over the sill, screaming. Behind her was the vague outline of a large man.

That was close, he thought. *Six months of work gone in a blow to the head! Welcome home, Scholz!*

Reinhold put a protective hand over the leather wallet in his breast pocket and took off down the street, unsure of where he was, but knowing that he had to get out of there before the neighbors got suspicious. He hailed the first taxi he saw and went directly to the train station. The adrenaline of the situation wore off in the car. His knee started to throb with pain. With every move, a sharp shooting sensation stabbed him in the back of the joint. He limped into the station, retrieved his bag from the locker where he stowed it earlier, and surveyed the big board. The next train to Kiel left in just over an hour. He bought a ticket and settled on a bench to wait, propping his leg up to relief some of the pressure.

"When did you get back, Scholz?" The old timer behind the bar at the seaman's club in Holtenau leaned across the wooden counter and shook the sailor's hand.

"This morning," he took a gulp of the beer that appeared in front of him. "Worst trip ever. I will never go to the Middle East again." He took another gulp. "I might go back to India though."

The bartender nodded. "I have been to India. Poorest place I had ever seen."

"Have you seen Herbert?" Reinhold was hoping to see his friend.

"Yup, he got back a few days ago. He was in last night for a beer or two."

The bartender went off down the bar to help some new comers. Reinhold pulled a pack of cigarettes out of his pocket and lit one. The guy on the stool next to him was looked like he wanted to say something. Reinhold wasn't sure whether to ask him what he wanted or walk away before the guy said something. He decided to walk away, but a second too late.

"You just back from the Middle East?" He asked.

"Yup," Reinhold said as he looked the guy over. "Why do you ask?"

"I was thinking about getting a ship that way. I've never been and I want to see the place."

Reinhold snorted. "There is nothing to see there at the moment. Give it a couple of years. Maybe at least then there will be piers and docks. Maybe even a seaman's club. You can't even get a cold beer there now."

"Why? I heard it was hot in the summer. The refrigeration on your ship couldn't handle the temperatures?"

"We didn't have any refrigeration."

"What?" The guy was shocked. "What company sent a ship to the Middle East with no refrigeration?"

"Oldendorff. I was with the *Christoffer Oldendorff*. Filthy ship."

Reinhold took another gulp of his beer. Back in his adopted hometown, with a good beer, he was feeling better.

If only my knee would stop hurting, he thought.

Unconsciously, he rubbed the throbbing spot behind the joint. He wasn't looking forward to his trip to the doctor tomorrow. If they told him the same thing as the doctor in India, he would be going under the knife to have the damage repaired.

"Oldendorff? I would never work for that company. It's run by a heartless bitch."

Reinhold was surprised. "Why do you say that? Have you worked for them? I thought Egon Oldendorff was head of the company. Who are you talking about?"

"No," the guy spat. "And I never will. Egon is the president of the company but his wife, I forget her name, pulls all the strings. They lost a ship about a month ago, an old one that probably shouldn't have been sailing any more, somewhere in the Atlantic. *Komet*, I think, was the name. Do you know that heartless bitch says that it was no big deal?"

"No big deal? That they lost a ship? What happened to the crew?"

"All were lost at sea." He hastily crossed himself. "They found a life boat with no one in it. She said they were expendable. Ships are valuable, she said, but crews are not. I believe she said we are replaceable."

Reinhold felt is face flush with anger. "Expendable, replaceable, same thing. What a bitch. I can tell you that the company is horrible." He finished his beer and ordered another. "I can tell you that a guy on my ship got the clap in India. There was no penicillin onboard and they didn't send him to the doctor in Mormugoa. He screamed the whole way back to Holland."

"Really?"

"Yup, and the ship was infested with roaches. I heard they put it in dry dock in Rotterdam to fumigate it. The Captain's an ex-flyer with Hitler. He is also a crazy drunk."

"Sounds like you had a great time in the Middle East."

"Middle East? Is that where you have been?"

The voice was familiar. Reinhold turned on his stool and saw Herbert standing there. He stood up and gave his friend a big hug and a slap on the back.

"That's right, baking in the heat like a beached herring and picking roaches out of my food."

"Sounds like a good time." Herbert turned to the guy Reinhold was speaking with. "Reinhardt, how are you?" They shook hands.

"Can't complain. I was telling your friend here about the sinking of that Oldendorff ship over the summer."

Herbert's expression changed. "Oh, yes, that. The Oldendorff Company made a bad impression on sailors. Egon's wife or daughter or someone called sailors expendable and ships very valuable, or something like that."

"I went to the Middle East with the *Christoffer Oldendorff*."

Herbert made a disgusted face. "Really?"

"And I came back with a bunch of money. Let me buy you a drink!"

Reinhold filled Herbert in on all the happenings on the *Christoffer Oldendorff*. He left nothing out: the roaches, the Arabs, getting stabbed by an Arab in Aden, the women in Kuwait City, the Captain, the bosun, the broken propeller, the guy with the clap, their desire to mutiny and throw the Captain overboard, and his own knee troubles. There were good things too, Reinhold remembered. Shark fishing with Henry and music at night on the deck and finding out that one of the stokers had an affair with Anna Easberger. Anna Easberger! Thankfully, it had been a good crew.

Herbert did some filling in of his own. He had been with a German ship doing runs back and forth to the Soviet Union carrying grain.

"I've had my passport checked by the Soviets more times than my wife has checked my balls. I had to get off. I am going back to Swedish ships." He sighed heavily. "If only there was something on the beach to do that wasn't tedious and boring. I hate leaving Katie alone all the time."

"When you make Captain, you can take her with you." Reinhold grinned at this friend.

"That would be horrible for her. She gets seasick something awful."

It was late and the sailors had been drinking steadily for several hours. The conversation turned to Reinhold's appointment the next day with the doctor. He knew that they were going to send him for surgery. There was no way he was going to be able to sail after that. Like Herbert, he wished there was something on the beach to do that wasn't boring and he didn't have to answer to a drunken idiot. He decided he wanted to be his own boss.

"Why don't we go into business? Like I said, I have a bunch of money from my last ship, eight hundred *mark*."

Herbert's head swiveled quickly to see who was lingering around them. There was no one.

"Careful. You'll get jumped on the way home. An injured sailor with a pocket full of money is an easy and rich target."

Reinhold waved him off. "Stop avoiding the subject by lecturing me. We should go into business."

Reinhold laid out the plan that was forming in his head. They would rent a garage, buy a truck, buy some wood and coal, and sell it to people in Kiel. Winter was coming and the demand for fuel would be increasing. He had a picture in his head of himself and Herbert driving around, selling their wares door to door until they built up a business and people started coming to them. They could work out of the garage until they could afford a storefront. He was glad that he had gotten his driver's license, finally, before signing on to the *Oldendorff*.

"What do you say? Sounds good, right?"

Herbert chewed on the idea for a little bit. Reinhold could see him weighing the pros and cons.

"There is a lot of paperwork to do before we can do this."

"Paperwork?"

"Yes, you can't just open a business. You have to go apply to the government for a license and get the permits. Then there are the tax forms."

Reinhold thought. "You can do all of that and I will focus on getting us a truck and the initial product to sell. We'll be partners, you and I. You know the legal side and I know the business side."

Herbert finally consented to give it a try. He had some money saved he was willing to invest. The two of them agreed to meet after Reinhold's appointment to hash out the details.

Chapter 75: I Miss The Sea

Contrary to want he thought was going to happen, Reinhold was not scheduled for surgery. Instead, the doctors put him in a cast from his ankle to his hip to keep the joint straight so it could heel properly. Reinhold hobbled around on his cast, not letting it slow him down.

He and Herbert started their business. They rented a small garage on the Kanalstraße in Holtenau. They bought a cheap, beat up, old truck and some product to sell. They went door to door, working long days, every day. On the weekends, Reinhold went out in search of ladies. He found many that took pity on him because he was injured. And a sailor. They fawned over him. It was magic! In order to dance, he broke his cast above and below the knee. On Mondays, he returned to the hospital where they repaired the damage and scolded him for not taking it easy.

I must have done that three times, he thought to himself with a smile.

He met a girl named Nadine. Her parents owned a produce store near the canal in Holtenau. He liked her. She was a good dancer as well as fun in bed and easy on the eyes. They began a quiet courtship. It was quiet because if Nadine's father found out she was dating 'beneath her station' he would kill Reinhold. She met him at his room and they spent evenings together before she went home before her curfew.

The beached sailors weren't doing a bad business. They built up some customers and had a good reputation but, after a month, they barely broke even. The paper work turned out to be a nightmare of bureaucratic nonsense. They often got stopped in their daily rounds to have their permits and licenses checked. Every day it seemed there was some new form to be submitted or fee to be paid.

"This is ridiculous!" Herbert exclaimed one day after getting stopped yet again. The agent with some office of official business told them their truck didn't fit the standards needed to carry coal.

"We can't afford to keep giving the government all of these fees!" He looked Reinhold in the eye. "I don't think this is going to work out, Reinhold." He sighed. "I miss the sea. I don't want to work on the beach."

Reinhold understood completely. He missed the sea too. Being on shore just wasn't the same. It was better in some ways, and worse in others. It was nice to go home to his own room and not have three other guys there. It was nice to eat, sleep, and drink when he wanted too. It was nice to have a solid, unmoving floor beneath his feet. But, he missed the shifting weather, the cries of the seagulls, the excitement of putting into port after days at sea, and the camaraderie of his fellow sailors. He missed the variety of jobs to be done at sea. He never knew from day to day if he would be splicing lines or building cabinets or fixing the plumbing.

Besides, he needed to get away from Nadine. She was talking marriage and children. That wasn't what Reinhold had in mind for himself with her. She just wasn't the one he wanted to marry. He couldn't picture himself living the rest of his life in Holtenau, running a produce store. It was easier for him to run away to sea than tell her how he felt.

After about five weeks, Herbert caught a Swedish ship and started doing runs with it back and forth to Stockholm and Oslo. He loved the sea but he also loved his wife and didn't want to be away for too long. Slowly, Herbert was building a life that was suitable for him, half at sea and half at home with Katie.

Reinhold had his cast removed three months after Herbert left. He went straight to the agent's office and caught a Swedish ship called the *Windar*. A call came into the seaman's office in the wee hours of the morning and Reinhold was the next in line for a position. The agent woke him up and handed him a piece of paper with his assignment. He signed on in the early hours of the morning on October 23, 1954.

Chapter 76: Windar

Windar
Photograph courtesy of 7seasvessels.com

The *Windar* was an older ship than the *Oldendorff*. It was more like the *Midgard* than the *Oldendorff*, weighing just over a thousand tons. It was also much, much cleaner than the *Oldendorff* could ever claim to be.

Reinhold noticed right away that the ship was a lumber carrier. When he boarded at Holtenau, the deck was stacked high with good Swedish boards. He guessed, correctly, that they were headed for England. The English need for lumber had only increased in the years after the war and the Swedes were more than happy to sell it to them. He noted that the rail of the ship was extraordinarily low in the spots were the lumber was stacked. He wondered if it was a necessity for loading and unloading. Without a metal rail in the way, a crane could scoop up the lumber and avoid the time consuming process of unloading by hand.

Reinhold went directly to the bridge and reported to the Captain. He seemed nice enough, laid back, and not obviously drunk, which was nice. The Captain sent him to the deck to find the First Mate. At the moment, the *Windar* had no bosun. The mate showed him to his bunk, below deck at the stern. He would be sharing it with three other guys.

Nothing was out of the ordinary on the *Windar*. His bunk, the mess hall, the galley, the bridge, the supply closet, everything was exactly where it should be and everything functioned exactly as it should. It was nice to be back on a well-run Swedish ship.

It was also a relief that he hadn't forgotten all the Swedish he learned while aboard the *Govan*. He found a couple of Swedish comic books in the head. He took them to his bunk to read at his leisure.

One aspect of the *Windar* that became clear quickly was the variety of nationalities and the difficulties that came with language barriers. There were sailors from Sweden, Germany, Poland, England, Denmark, Norway, Finland, Estonia, and Holland. Reinhold remembered sharing his bunk with a sullen Polish guy, a happy and clumsy Danish man, and a quiet guy from Norway that didn't inspire trust in Reinhold. Quiet guys spelled trouble in his mind in the same way that he didn't trust little guys after the problems he had with them in the past.

They always have something to prove, he thought to himself.

Fights were commonplace on the *Windar*.

There were so many miscommunications and so many quick flaring tempers, he recalled with a sad sigh. *Territoriality was bad too. God forbid you touched something that didn't belong to you or made the wrong face at the wrong person.*

On one of his first nights aboard, he went to the mess hall for dinner. As he was custom to do, he hung his hat on a nail hammered into a piece of wood next to the door. Then he took a seat at a table, not thinking anything about it. A large Swedish man entered the room and demanded loudly and angrily to know who had put their hat on his nail. Looking, Reinhold realized it was his black wool cap that the Swede was referring to. He quickly got up and removed the hat from the nail with a curt apology.

No sense ruffling feathers over trivialities, he figured.

He moved the cap and was going to return to his seat when he heard the Swede question, once again loudly and angrily, who was sitting in his seat. Once again, Reinhold realized that the Swede was addressing him. He left his plate of food at his seat when he got up to move the hat. The Swede was gesturing toward it now. He stepped forward and claimed the plate, apologizing curtly again. He felt like he was stuck in the story of the three little bears that he had read last year in a volume of children's stories. 'Who's hat is on my nail', 'who's sitting in my chair'. It might as well have been 'who's been sleeping in my bed' and 'who's been eating my porridge'.

"You have to learn your place, boy," the Swede informed him before settling into the spot Reinhold had occupied not a minute before.

Everyone in the mess hall was staring at Reinhold now. He couldn't help feeling a bit self-conscious. He stood with his plate near the door for a good minute, until all the other sailors settled themselves, before choosing another place for himself.

The dynamic was strange. They grouped themselves by cultural identity, or as close to it as they could. The Swedes, Fins, and Norwegians were at one table, the Poles and Estonians were at another. The British hung out with the Dutch while the Germans gathered with the Danish. Reinhold decided it was best for him to stay solo until he knew more about how this ship functioned.

The trip to London from Holtenau was uneventful other than the occasional scuffle between the sailors. The weather cooperated and the sailing was smooth, as smooth as could be on the North Sea. The work was straight forward and kept them all busy from sun up to sundown which was good because free time spelled trouble. Reinhold was enjoying having no cares in the world except the weather and covering his own backside.

No permits, tax forms, or government officials here, he remembered thinking as he welded a seal in the deck, *just good old fashion work.*

The First Mate complimented him several times on his knowledge and technique. When they docked in London, the mate approached Reinhold to ask if he would be interested in taking the bosun position.

"It pays a bit more," the mate told him. "And you have some more authority."

Reinhold was skeptical at first. He wasn't sure he wanted the responsibility.

"What would I have to do? I mean besides keeping an eye on the crew and handing out work in the morning."

The mate shrugged. "Not much. Half an hour before the crew gets up, you will meet me in the mess hall for coffee. We go over the day's work and that's it. I send you off to rely the orders to the crew. You don't have to write any reports or fill out any forms."

"What about the contentiousness between the guys? There are so many fights over stupid nonsense."

The First Mate winked at him. "You have to handle that how you see fit. You have to prove yourself, eh? Get them to respect you."

Reinhold accepted the position, shaking hands with the First Mate to seal the deal before heading out to supervise the unloading. He tried not to let his chest puff in pride in his new position but he stood there gloating for a minute in the new authority.

When the tea wagon pulled up to the ship at ten in the morning, Reinhold was reminded that England was one of the worst places to unload cargo. He watched the workers gather to get a steaming cup of tea and a cake or cookie and sighed in resignation. He headed to the mess hall to get a coffee for himself. No sense rushing to complete his own work. They were going to be in London for a while.

"We have a new guy signing on today, Scholz," the First Mate told him in the galley. "He is going to be the lead stoker."

Later that afternoon, the biggest black guy Reinhold had ever seen walked up the gangplank. He headed for the bridge. A few minutes later, the Second Mate's voice called to Reinhold from the wing of the bridge.

"Scholz, get up here!"

Reinhold put down his welding torch and peeled off his gloves before scrambling up the ladder to the bridge. The black guy was still there, talking with the Second Mate. He was even taller and broader than Reinhold thought. He literally filled the room.

This guy must be almost seven feet tall, he thought to himself.

"Scholz, this is Jack," the Second Mate introduced them.

Jack stuck out a huge paw of a hand for shaking and Reinhold grasped it, not taking his eyes off the man's face. He had the grip of a machine.

"Jack is here to take the position of lead stoker. Can you show him to the bunks?"

Reinhold and Jack became good friends quickly. Jack was a British guy and ex-boxer. He broke his wrists in a freak accident that ended his career in the ring. His size and strength made him the perfect stoker. His soft spoken nature and common sense made him rise to the top of the stoker ladder, so to speak. Jack was promoted to boss after only a year in his position. When he signed on to the *Windar*, he had almost five years behind him managing some of the roughest, most unpredictable men the seas had to offer.

He became Reinhold's enforcer. When a sailor disrespected Reinhold's authority as bosun, Jack stepped in to assist in settling the situation. Physical altercation was the only thing that every sailor respected and Jack was so strong that he refused to make a fist and punch someone. He used an open hand to knock a man off their feet before proceeding to throw them around like a rag doll.

Reinhold remembered one incident in particular with a Polish sailor. The guy was insolent and lazy, always looking for ways to cut corners or pass the buck. One afternoon, when the *Windar* was docked in northern Sweden for loading, Reinhold gave him the job of painting the outer hull. The Polish guy got in the bosun's chair and went over the side. A couple of hours later, Reinhold leaned over to see how he was doing and saw him swinging idly, reading a book. Anger surged through him. He started screaming at the man and an argument ensued in German, which came naturally to both participants. Jack appeared out of nowhere and hauled the bosun's chair up to the deck and smacked the Polish guy so hard in the face that he broke his nose.

Reinhold smiled at the memory.

He hadn't even known what was going on, didn't speak the language, but he immediately took my side.

There was a huge benefit of having Jack as a buddy when they were in England. With the country being a voracious consumer of lumber, the *Windar* docked there often. He knew the spots to get cheap beer and met girls. For the first time, Reinhold walked around London with confidence, not on his toes, ready to defend himself against roving packs of drunken English hoodlums looking to refight the war. They went sightseeing and saw movies, which Reinhold thoroughly enjoyed even though they were in English.

The girls were still stuck up, even with Jack, but they were easier to convince with the big guy around, he reminded himself.

The presence of Jack and his English skills meant local tavern keepers were more willing to take Reinhold's gold watch as collateral even though they curled their lips condescendingly as they poured the drinks. The wonderful things to see in England made up for the disposition of its residents.

Unfortunately, nothing made up for the expense. To save money, Reinhold and Jack would walk the town, looking at the architecture, and tracking the progress in repairing the damage. It became a game for the sailors to compare London to Hamburg and Kiel. Hamburg was beating everybody. The city had come so far in the last few years that Reinhold would never have guessed it was the same rubble filled place he caught his first ship.

It was during one of their trips around the city, during Reinhold's first trip to England with the *Windar* that Jack told him he had trouble when he traveled to Germany.

"They don't like me there," he said gloomily.

"Why?"

"Why do they hate you here?"

Reinhold took his meaning immediately. "Oh, I see, you're British. Of course they would treat you badly in Germany." He thought for a second. "Even in Lübeck? And Kiel?"

"Yup." He was silent for a second. Quietly, he added, "I am also black."

Reinhold eyed Jack for a second.

"It doesn't help that you are huge and scary looking, either." He smacked Jack on the shoulder affectionately. "Don't worry, Jack. When we get to Germany, I'll show you all the good stuff to do, same as you have done for me here."

Before sailing for Germany, the *Windar* took a side trip to Ireland. Reinhold had never been there before. Jack told him he was going to love Galway.

"The Irish are great people," Jack said excitedly. "A bit religious, but, boy can they drink! And the girls are wonderful."

Reinhold quickly learned Jack was right. They had a great time at the bars near the port and a girl picked him up. She was a cute redhead with freckles and a nice set of womanly assets. She had never had a German boy before and 'wanted to see what they were made of'. They had a good time and in the morning, she was gone.

When they got to Germany, Reinhold kept his word and showed Jack the best spots in the cities they visited. In Bremerhaven, he introduced him to Kristal, who managed to come up with a friend for him. In Hamburg, the first trip to the Reeperbahn with a German speaker was eye opening to Jack, who had never had the full experience before. He had no idea that you could ask to see the girls' book of doctor visits. He also had no idea that prostitution had been a legal activity in Germany since the 1200s.

In Lübeck, he introduced Jack to Emma, who immediately took him as a customer for a night, saying she had never had a black man before. In Holtenau, they went to the sailor's club where Reinhold introduced Jack to all the old timers, who couldn't help but notice that the British sailor was huge. There were a few minutes of good natured teasing but Jack didn't seem to mind. After this hazing, the conversation in the bar turned, as it always did, to the sea. They spent several hours listening, with Reinhold translating, to gossip from other ships and companies and to stories, new and old.

Being on a ship dedicated to lumber was another new experience for Reinhold. He had hauled it on other ships, but always as an added cargo. The *Windar's* hull was crammed full and the deck was stacked high with fresh smelling wood. He was aboard the *Windar* for only two weeks when the ship encountered heavy seas off the west coast of Germany. The waves rolled over the deck like the ship wasn't even there. The lumber became saturated, especially the starboard side, which was taking the heaviest onslaught. The ship began to list, alarming everyone onboard. The First Mate called everyone to the bridge.

"Men, we have to get that lumber off the deck," he called above the thunder of the waves. "We are at a twenty four degree list. Twenty more degrees and we are done for. I need someone to go out and free the load."

Reinhold looked around at the crew. No one was moving. Most were staring out the front windows of the bridge in horror at the strange twist to the ship and the foaming waves.

"How do you do that?" Reinhold asked. "Release the winch? That will take forever. There are three of them per stack."

"Yup, we have to release the winch but just one stack." The First Mate pointed to the starboard stack. "We need to get rid of that stack. Someone has to go smack the winches with a sledgehammer to release them."

No one moved. Several men crossed themselves. Several were muttering prayers. Reinhold knew they were familiar with this procedure having seen it before on this ship. It didn't seem so hard but dangerous, for sure. One wrong move would send a sailor overboard into the rough seas. A single wave could wash away a puny human like they were nothing at all. He thought about what would happen if he was to go out there to free the lumber. He would have to climb the pile to get a good hit on the winches. That meant that, when he freed the last winch, he would go with the stack into the ocean. It made sense why no one was volunteering. He stepped forward.

"I'll go," he said loud and proud.

It was the perfect opportunity to prove himself as the new bosun. It was also just plain exciting.

The First Mate nodded in understanding. He led Reinhold to the deck where a couple of other sailors tied a great, thick line around his waist.

"This is to pull you back, should something go wrong," the mate explained. Reinhold nodded. He knew exactly what the line was for.

The huge Swede handed him a twenty-pound sledgehammer and clapped him on the back. The ship was listing badly now as Reinhold approached the looming stack of lumber, dodging a wave by crouching close to the deck. He knew he didn't have long to do what he had to do. He waited for a break in the waves, climbed up, and smacked the first winch with all the strength he could muster. The cable broke, whistling away in the air as the tension released. It barely missed Reinhold's head. He scolded himself for not remembering that the cable was going to snap with enough force to take someone's head off. Quickly, before the next wave could crest, he ran to the next winch and smacked it. Again, the cable whizzed past his head.

He felt a wave approaching and made himself as small as he could while exposed on the top of a pile of lumber. It washed over the top of him, pulling at his clothes and pushing him sideways. He held on, willing himself not to be washed away, until the wave passed then got up and ran to the next winch. He hesitated a second before bringing the sledgehammer down on the third and last piece of equipment that stood between him and the sea.

As soon as the cable went whizzing past his head, the lumber began to move under his feet. There was nothing to hold on to. A wave smashed him in the back, stemming briefly his log roll to the sea but not stopping it all together. He ran along the falling lumber trying to avoiding being pulled down but failed. It was moving too quickly. He plunged with the lumber into boilingly turbulent and freezing North Sea.

The shock of the cold took his breath away and made him sputter when he surfaced. There was barely time to register that he was in the water before a tugging around his waist drew him back toward the ship looming above him. He grabbed a hold of the line and began pulling himself along as his fellow crewmembers pulled from the deck. He arrived safely back on the relatively dryer deck and was immediately ushered toward the mess hall where blankets were wrapped around him and a healthy dose of rum was shoved into his trembling blue hand. He gulped some down. The warmth from the rum ran through his system straight down to his toes.

It was after that first dunk in the sea that the pain returned to Reinhold's knee.

I must have banged it against the wood when I fell, he thought. *It is the only explanation.*

The throbbing returned along with the occasional shooting pain. He began to limp visibly. Luckily, he could blame it on something that happened on the ship, so no one questioned how he got hurt. A few weeks later, while sailing on Christmas between Sweden and the canal at Holtenau, he hurt it again breaking up a fight in the mess hall.

He wasn't quite sure how that fight started. The obvious answer is the language barrier and national differences. It was Christmas Day, 1954, and the crew was sitting down to lunch when the fight broke out between a Swede and a Brit. Both were bad tempered stokers. They were throwing hearty punches at each other when others, excited by the activity, joined in.

Someone threw someone else into the Christmas tree, igniting the dry wood and needles with the candles that were decorating it. The tree went up in flames faster than Reinhold could pull the guy out of the way. He could still smell the burning flesh and see the agony on the face of the burnt sailor. It was a Finnish man that was injured. He got off in an emergency stop at Bremerhaven and his replacement got on, another bad tempered brute of a Finnish man. The whole transfer took less than twelve hours, which was just enough time for Reinhold to do some shopping and pay a visit to Kristal.

He was happy that no matter what happened or how often they saw each other, she always looked, kissed, laughed, smiled, and screwed exactly the same. Reinhold remembered that day in good detail. She wanted to have him in her bed. She insisted, pleaded that it was fine to use the bed. It would be more comfortable, she said. Something about it made Reinhold very uncomfortable. It wasn't right, to have another man's wife in their married bed. It was just too dishonest, too disrespectful. He convinced her that the floor or the couch would be just as good for their needs. He even suggested the shower. Anything was better than her husband's bed. They spent two glorious hours together before she drove him back to the *Windar*.

"This ship looks like it has seen better days," Kristal observed when they pulled up on the pier. "And those days were a long time ago."

"It's a pile of garbage, to be sure, but it's a paycheck. And it makes it more exciting, thinking that you could go down at any minute." He grinned at her rakishly.

They got out of the car, Kristal running her eyes over the dark grey hull of the *Windar*.

"*Windar*?" She questioned. "What does that mean?"

Reinhold shrugged. "It's Swedish for something."

He walked around the front of the Kristal's Ford and pulled her close. She gave him a long, lingering kiss, running her fingers through his blond hair, as his hands roamed down her sides and told him that she would keep an eye out for his return. The guys on the *Windar* saw them return and the very physical goodbye they shared and shouting things from the deck.

"Looking good, Scholz!"

"Are you going to share?"

"Are you sure he's the guy you want, lady? I could give you something so much better."

"Swedes do it better! Especially than Germans!"

The comments continued as he climbed the gangplank. Some of them were accompanied by less than imaginative gestures and hip thrusts. Reinhold couldn't help wishing they had dropped anchor instead of docking. He looked back to see Kristal getting behind the wheel of the car. Before putting it in gear, she held up her hand and extended her middle finger to the ogling sailors in an American gesture of defiance that had become popular after the war. Reinhold chuckled to himself as he headed for his bunk to stow some cigarettes he purchased. Doing some quick math in his head, he figured the ten cartons he had to sell would fetch him about ten pounds next time they went to England which in turn would be somewhere near a hundred *mark*.

"You want me to go make those guys stop harassing your girl?"

Reinhold almost walked smack into Jack as he rounded the corner of the wheelhouse. The big man had a dark look on his face.

"No, forget them," Reinhold shot the guys at the rail a dirty look. They were leaning now, watching the activity on the pier. "They are just jealous. Look at them. They couldn't get laid if they were the only people on a ship full of women lost at sea for years. They would all become lesbians."

Jack burst into laughter and nodded his agreement but kept his eyes on the group, warily and ready to attack.

Reinhold's time on the *Windar* lasted long enough for him to take two more trips into the sea on a moving pile of lumber. One such dip was at the end of December, the other at the beginning of February. He had legitimately earned the respect of his crew by the time they wrapped him in a blanket and gave him a healthy dose of rum for the third time. Hypothermia was a real threat on the North Sea in winter and every sailor was all too familiar with its lasting effects. As Reinhold sat in the mess hall after his third time unloading the lumber, a British sailor named Higgins was assigned to watch him for signs of trouble. The guy was a talker.

"I was on a ship, oh, maybe, three years ago that had a similar situation. A sailor went into the sea in January. He was only supposed to be in there for a few seconds, but the waves were heavy and the ship was pitching wildly. It took us six minutes to haul him in." Higgins shook his head sadly. "It was too long. He was never the same. The doctors said he suffered from brain damage because of the cold. The company fired him not so long after that."

The cook joined them as they sat there. He refilled Reinhold glass of rum from the ship's stock before downing the rest of the bottle himself. Reinhold was too frozen to care that the cook was visibly drunk at three o'clock in the afternoon. He did care, however, that the man wasn't in the galley getting dinner together.

"What's for dinner tonight, Mats?"

"Steak and potatoes," Mats slurred in response.

"Shouldn't you be cooking it?" Reinhold questioned. "Or maybe helping the baker get the bread together?"

"I suppose," Mats answered lazily. He made no move to leave the mess hall.

"Maybe you should do that now," Reinhold said sternly, he anger with the drunk man growing.

Mats, with a casual, drunken wave of his hand, got up to leave. Reinhold felt his patience snap. He got up and kicked the cook in the ass. Mats lost his balance and fell face first into a table, which he slide off, and landed heavily on the floor. Slowly, he picked himself up, giving Reinhold an awkward, apologetic, nod of his head before shuffling off to the galley.

Looking back, Reinhold felt horrible about his treatment of the man. Three days later, when the *Windar* was docked in Boston, England, Mats locked himself in his bunk and fell asleep smoking a cigarette. The cigarette set the thin mattress on fire and woke Mats up. He tried to get out of the room but couldn't. He was drunk and half asleep and the room was full of smoke, making him cough. The sailors, Reinhold included, tried their best to open the hatch, but it was locked from the inside. Mats died. They cut open the hatch with blow torches to retrieve him and buried him without ceremony or service in Boston. It was, to Reinhold, one of the worst things that could happen to a person, to be laid to rest so far from home with no friends or family to say goodbye. The crew did their best to send him off, drinking toasts and placing flowers but it didn't change Reinhold's melancholy.

Reinhold never mentioned to anyone that his knee was more painful than ever. He couldn't walk without limping and ladders now posed a problem. His knee didn't want to bend without sending a shooting, searing pain down his calf and up his thigh. The First Mate, one morning during their daily meetings before breakfast, asked if he was still able to perform his duties. Reinhold assured him that everything was fine. They continued their meeting. Since it was snowing that day, the mate decided it was a good day for interior work. The *Windar's* hulls were currently empty in anticipation of a new load of lumber in Sweden in three days' time.

"I want the hulls cleaned before we load again. Have every available man on it, even the stokers that aren't shoveling coal."

Reinhold nodded. "Yes, sir."

And the rest is history, he thought to himself.

Not four hours later, he was lying in the mess hall, ice packed around his knee, his wrist tightly wrapped in a splint, and the Captain staring down at him questioningly.

"What happen, sailor?"

"I fell, sir."

"How?"

"I was climbing the ladder out of the hull and lost my footing."

When the Captain didn't say anything, he continued. "The rungs are wet as are my boots. It's snowing, so everything is wet and starting to freeze. The First Mate says my wrist is broken."

He didn't mention his knee.

"Indeed," the Captain said. "Where did you get on?"

"Holtenau, sir, at the canal."

"Where do you want to get off?"

"Holtenau, sir."

"You are in luck. We can be in Holtenau tomorrow."

Jack took the news of Reinhold's injury and subsequent departure very badly. He cried like a child and accused Reinhold of leaving him on a hostile ship with no friends.

"Come on, Jack, you can visit me whenever the ship goes through the canal," he reminded the distraught man. "Not like I am going anywhere for a while," he added bitterly.

The *Windar* dropped anchor in Holtenau the following afternoon. Reinhold threw his sea bag over the rail into the waiting launch boat and got ready to climb, slowly and painfully, down after it when a shadow appeared above him. Looking up, he saw Jack standing there. Silently, the huge man handed him something soft and colorful. Unfolding it, Reinhold saw that it was Jack's favorite tie. It was the same one that Reinhold had seen him wear countless times to the movies, restaurant, bars, and brothels. He opened his mouth to say that he couldn't take the gift, it was just too much, but Jack didn't give him the opportunity. He felt himself crushed in a huge bear hug, almost lifted off his feet, and released, a little short of breath. Then Jack walked away, shoulders slumped, hands deep in his pockets. It was February 16, 1955

Looking back, Reinhold realized he never saw Jack again. In fact, he never saw the *Windar* again. He wondered what happened to the ship and to Jack.

Chapter 77: On The Bum, Again

The next nine months were some of the most boring of Reinhold's young life. The only time that was so inactive was when he was recovering from his fall. This made a lot of sense to him because, once again, he was recovering from an injury. The day he signed off, he went and had his wrist set and his knee examined. A few days later, he had a meniscectomy to address the knee injury. Again, he found himself in a cast from his ankle to his hip and taking painkillers to recover.

I was on the bum again, he thought, remembering standing by the canal in Holtenau, bumming cigarettes and sandwiches from ships going through the lock.

His fellow sailors took pity on him more than the others standing around begging because of the casts. They assumed, rightly, that he was injured on the job. Some asked what company or what ship he had been working for at the time he got hurt. He always blamed Oldendorff, which worked to his benefit. Oldendorff had a worse reputation than he thought. After learning he got hurt working for them, one sailor passing on a tanker threw him an entire bottle of rum, saying that those bums that run Oldendorff should be ashamed of themselves for even living, the bitch in particular.

On his twentieth birthday in March, Reinhold got a letter from Bernard Muuss. It had obviously been through many hands looking for him. There were so many stamps on it that he could barely read the return address. Bernard, it seemed, was doing fine. He was still in school in Hamburg. He felt, he wrote, that he made a good career choice with all the rebuilding still going on and all the technological advances in structural engineering that were happening. Reinhold was surprised and proud of his friend's growing sophistication and intelligence. He wrote back immediately and told Bernard about his last round of sailing with the *Windar* and about his injury.

After finishing that letter, he wrote one to Marta on Föhr. He waxed sentimental in his lonely, incapacitated, and medicated state, telling her how much he looked forward to her letters and how much he wanted to come visit her, maybe even make her his wife. It was a letter fit for Cyrano de Bergerac. Then he went to the seaman's club and got entirely too drunk before ending up at the *puff* to have a go with one of his favorite ladies. He just wished he remembered it the next day. It would have made the hang over more tolerable.

The months rolled by while Reinhold languished in Kiel, unable to be productive. His boredom was broke up by Herbert's trips home and by letters from Marta, Bernard, and Lisa. Marta wanted him to visit and he promised her as soon as he was able, he would. On a whim one day in April, after almost two months of laying around, he decided he would go to Lübeck to visit Lisa. He took them to dinner and dancing at the Red Cat. Willie laughed at Reinhold's broken cast but Lisa was unthrilled. She asked more than once how he expected his injury to heal if he was constantly breaking his cast for something as frivolous as dancing. Altogether, it was a good night. He slept on their couch that night. In the morning he was to head back to Kiel when Lisa guilted him into going home to visit his father and stepmother.

What a disaster that was, he thought.

His father wasn't home and his stepmother flat out told him she didn't want him around. She got one look at the cast and became suspicious that he was looking to move back in. Deciding that he didn't want to be in the same building as the awful woman, he limped down to Küster's to see what was going on. It was early afternoon, so he wasn't expecting anyone to be there that he knew, but he was wrong. There was the usual collection of old timers, friends of his father that recognized him. They questioned him about how he got hurt.

"I fell a couple of years ago on a ship I was with and broke it. Then, I reinjured it a few months ago by falling again on a different ship." He gulped down the beer in his glass and ordered another.

"Ship, huh?" Asked an old guy Reinhold didn't know, a new old timer. "You been out there sailing around?"

"Yup. I was in the Middle East this time last year."

"Oh? What was that like?"

"Hot. We fried eggs on the deck. It was almost 130 degrees."

"You're lying!" His father friend accused. "It's not that hot anywhere! You can't fry eggs on a ship deck."

"Yes, you can," another old guy said. "I've heard of other sailors doing this."

"I don't believe it!"

"It's true, you old geezer. Ask a sailor. Go down to Lübeck and ask the guys at the sailor's bar down there. They'll tell you."

Reinhold couldn't help being both amused and offended.

My word just wasn't good enough for them, the old bastards, he thought.

"What else did you do out there, Reinhold?" His father's friend asked. "Did you see mermaids with nice breasts and long hair?"

Reinhold laughed. "No, but we did see flying fish." He took a gulp of his beer. "They jumped on the deck of the ship one night, covered the whole thing. We had to push them off in the morning with brooms and shovels."

"Lying again! Fish can't fly!"

This time, everyone thought he was lying. The old guys had been living near the sea for so long they thought they knew everything about it. There was no way there could be anything in the sea that they hadn't seen or already heard about. Reinhold sighed in resignation and ordered another beer and a side of schnapps. The old timers asked a few more questions and told him he was lying every time he answered. He didn't understand why they asked questions if they weren't going to believe the answers he gave. Finally, he gave up and went back to his father's.

When he arrived, he found his father home, sitting at the table, waiting for him. They had a brief exchange about his injury and his time abroad. It was an awkward conversation that made a half drunk Reinhold feel very uncomfortable. He decided it wasn't worth it to sleep in the attic that night and left, headed to Bad Schwartau where he caught the bus to Lübeck. He just missed the last train to Kiel. Making himself comfortable on a bench, using his wool sea jacket as a blanket, pulling his cap over his eyes, he feel asleep in the train station. In the morning, he caught the first train home to Kiel.

Chapter 78: A Fateful Letter

It was the middle of November, 1955 when, frustrated by boredom and desperate for some kind of excitement, something new and different, Reinhold boarded a train for Hamburg. He was going to visit Bernard Muuss, he decided, and that was the end. The cast on his knee came off a month before and the brace the doctors had put him in was due to come off in a few days. He wanted to get out and see the world again.

This was the first trip Reinhold was planning on making. The other was to Föhr to see Marta. He wrote her a letter just a few days before and said he was going to come visit, maybe even stay with her. Depending on how quickly she answered the letter, he figured that he would head out to see her in the middle of December. The train would get him as far as Husum. From there he would have to take buses and the ferry. After looking at a map, he realized that Föhr really wasn't all that far away, just about seventy miles, and felt a bit silly for not visiting earlier. But not really.

In Hamburg, Bernard, having received the telegram Reinhold sent, met him at the station and they went directly to Reeperbahn. The two old friends spent the afternoon and evening roaming, drinking, eating, and talking. It was later that night, as they were wandering near the huge port on the Elbe that the subject of Reinhold's future came up.

"What are you going to do now, Scholz? Going back to the sea?"

Bernard understood the lure and appeal of the sea to some men. His father had been an engineer on ships his whole life. He only recently retired and took a job at the small port in Travemünde.

"I want to go back. I miss the sea but I don't want to just go back and forth across the Baltic Sea or the North Sea." He pulled out a pack of cigarettes and lit one. "I want to see something new."

"Like what?"

"I don't know. Africa maybe. Or South America. I would really like to go to Australia." He pulled the collar of his wool sea coat up around his ears. "Did you know that you can jump ship in Australia and not get caught?"

Bernard's forehead wrinkled in consternation. "Is that what you want to do? Go to Australia and jump ship?"

"Maybe."

Bernard said nothing in return. Reinhold could tell he was thinking. The unmistakable sound of a large ship traveling up the river drew Reinhold's attention behind them, toward the sea. A huge cargo ship was sailing slowly into port. It was the newest ship he had ever seen so close. There was no way it had been sailing for more than a couple years because there wasn't a rust spot on its black hull. There were also newer style booms and a huge mid-deck wheelhouse.

"Now that is a sight," he said half to himself.

He watched the ship get closer, wanting to see what they called it and what company it belong to. It was flying a German flag. As it approached, Reinhold saw that it was called *Weserstein*. The company flag was blue diamonds on a white field.

"Hapag," he muttered to himself.

"Do you know that ship?" Bernard asked, confused.

"No. She is new from the looks of her. She flying the Hapag flag."

"That makes sense. Hapag has a bunch of new ships. They sail in here all the time. I think they are building some of them in Lübeck and some are being built here, at Blohm and Voss. My father has been watching the test sails in the bay near Lübeck."

"I would love to sail on one of those new ships." Reinhold said wistfully. "They are made for long hauls. I heard that they have only two guys to a bunk."

"Then why don't you apply for a job with Hapag? You have lots of experience. They would hire you."

Reinhold sighed. "That would mean writing a letter to them to see if they are looking for people for these new ships. Or waiting in the seaman' office here until they happen to put in an order for a replacement sailor."

"So?"

"My writing skills aren't as good as yours. And I don't like my chances at the office. It could take months that way."

"So I'll write the letter for you and you just sign your name. I have a typewriter that I can type it on so there won't be any handwriting differences."

That is exactly what happened. The next day, Bernard and Reinhold sat down in front of the typewriter and composed a letter detailing all of Reinhold's experience, including the ships he had sailed with and the fact that he was an accomplished cobblescot and a bosun. They requested a long haul ship, particularly the South Pacific, and accented this request by mentioning that Reinhold was single with no children. Bernard asked why that mattered and Reinhold responded that his friend just needed to trust him on this point. They sent the letter off and went back to Reeperbahn to celebrate Reinhold's potential new career.

A few weeks later, Reinhold, back at home in Kiel, received a letter from Hapag. They offered him a job as a *Matrose*. He was to report to a ship called the *Leipzig* in Hamburg on December 16. She would be sailing to South America and the South Pacific, if time allowed, stopping at several ports in Europe first then sailing to four South American countries. This meant a trip through the Panama Canal. He was so excited, he didn't know what to do.

The date was December 11th. There were five days until he had to be in Hamburg. He thought logically about the situation and decided he needed to go to the seaman's club and find someone who had sailed to South America. There were many questions he needed to have answered, not least of which was about the weather. And the seas. Surely, the Pacific was different than the Atlantic. What about the Atlantic? He had heard horror stories about the crossing. Was it really that bad? Droves of emigrants left Europe every year to go to America. The crossing couldn't be that bad or no one would go.

At least it would be exciting, he thought. Life had been boring enough the last few months.

But first, he had to write a letter to Marta to tell her he wasn't coming. Over the previous month, they had worked out that he was going to visit her little island. She was so excited, she wrote, to see him and start their life together. There was no way he was going to see her now, not when a trip to South America, maybe even Australia, was waiting. When he left Holtenau for Hamburg on December 14, the letter was still not written and sent.

Chapter 79: Leipzig

Leipzig
Photograph courtesy of *7seasvessels.com*

Reinhold arrived in Hamburg on December 15, 1955. He spent the night with Bernard Muuss before reporting to the *Leipzig* docked in Hamburg's enormous port on the morning of December 16, 1955. It was like no ship he had ever served on before. It was huge, 160 feet in length, weighing sixty-seven hundred tons, with a wheelhouse that stood four stories tall. At the top was an observation deck complete with awning and railings. A huge stack painted black, tan, and red loomed over the wheelhouse. There were eight booms covering six hulls, one of which was a fortified and locked vault for carrying precious cargo. This was no tramp ship, wandering from port to port like a feather in the wind, taking on cargo on an as needed basis. This ship had a schedule. She was only a year and a half into her sailing career and had competed four journeys from Europe to South America, each trip taking about four months to compete.

The Captain seemed alright, all business. He signed on the new sailors and sent them to find the mates or the bosun. Reinhold encountered the First Mate as he was leaving the bridge. He was all business too. He had close cropped hair and a short manner to his speech that reminded Reinhold of his time in the *Hilterjugend*. He sent Reinhold to his bunk to stow his sea bag and told him to be on the middeck at 18:00 hours for a briefing.

Reinhold swung open the hatch to his bunk to find three guys already there. They were all medium build guys about Reinhold's age with German features and seamen's gear. They looked him over before speaking.

"You must be the new guy," the blonde said. He took two paces and extended his hand. "I'm Johan. These two are Otto and Wolfgang."

Reinhold shook hands all around saying, "My name is Scholz, Reinhold Scholz." He looked around the small bunk and saw only two beds. "Am I in the wrong bunk?"

"No, you're rooming with me. These two sleep next door," Johan said.

The rumors he had heard about the new Hapag ships were right. The best part was the bunk set up. There were only two people to a bunk on the *Leipzig* as opposed to the three or four or six or more on other ships. And, better yet, each bunk had its own bathroom with shower. It was glorious! Looking back from the deck of the *Brandenburg,* another Hapag ship, as it plowed its way through the tropical waters of the Caribbean, Reinhold remembered thinking that the *Leipzig* was some kind of sea faring heaven. He remembered being instantly proud to be serving on such a magnificent ship with such a reputable company.

"We're going ashore to get a couple of drinks and some food before the bosun's meeting later, Scholz. You want to come with us?"

"Sure. Where are you going?"

"Reeperbahn, of course."

Reinhold learned that day that his crewmates were rambunctious. They went to three bars on Reeperbahn and they almost got into fights in all of them. Reinhold was shocked at first because they didn't look like the types to go getting in fights and raising hell. He had to remind himself that looks could be deceiving. No one would ever think that he was the fighting type. It was his shorter stature and fair looks that tricked people into thinking he was more docile than other guys.

For some reason no one ever suspects a blonde of being aggressive, he thought to himself. *Come to think of it,* he thought, *I am a bit shocked when a blonde guy comes at me with fists raised.*

"Every port in the Low Lands knows the *Leipzig* and her crew," said Johan proudly as they wandered down Reeperbahn to the second bar from the first.

"That's right," said Otto. "We have a reputation to uphold, Scholz. You think you're the kind of guy to help us?"

"I guess we'll see about that," Reinhold answered. He knew better than to blindly agree with strangers.

A bunch of smart asses, he thought to himself as he pulled a cigarette out of the almost empty pack, staring at the crystal blue horizon of the Caribbean.

He clenched the cylindrical tube between his teeth and lit it, sending a plume of blue smoke into the hot air.

I fit right in with that crowd, he thought, *like peas in a pod.*

The boisterous group of sailors got back to the ship from their trip ashore just in time for a mandatory meeting. The bosun, Krause, introduced himself to the group gathered on the deck crew on the evening of December 16. There were five or six new crewmembers not including Reinhold in the fifty or so men present. The bosun told them the *Leipzig's* schedule for the next four months. They were stopping in three ports in Europe: Amsterdam, Rotterdam, and Antwerp. Then they were continuing on to La Guairá before taking the Panama Canal to the west coast of South America. On the west coast, the *Leipzig* would travel to Guayaquil, Callao, and Valparaiso with possible stops at Buenaventura, Arica and Antofagasta. If time and cargo allowed, they would travel across the Pacific to New Zealand and Australia.

Reinhold didn't recognize a single name after Antwerp and he didn't care. The Panama Canal! He couldn't wait to see it. He wondered how long it would take for them to get there. The *Leipzig* had a whole host of equipment to make loading and unloading go much faster than previous ships. They would be in and out of the European ports in no time.

We could have unloaded in half the time in Kuwait if we had all these booms, he thought to himself, somewhat sarcastically. *Maybe they should be sending this ship to the Middle East.*

The *Leipzig* pulled anchor and sailed out of Hamburg on December 17, 1955. As scheduled, it stopped in Amsterdam where Reinhold, Johan, Otto, Wolfgang, and a guy named Gottfried went out drinking their first night at the local port bars and got into a huge fight with a group of Greek sailors. Someone looked at someone funny, insults in foreign languages were thrown around, and finally, a Greek sailor threw the first punch. After that, it became quite the scene. Tables and chairs went flying, people went flying, fists went flying. It was impossible to stay neutral. Other patrons in the bar either joined in the fight or fled. It was exhilarating for Reinhold. He felt invincible, alive! After so many months of lying around, waiting for his knee to heel, this was exactly what he was looking for.

The same scene repeated itself the next night with a group of Russian sailors with Reinhold throwing the first punch. The night after it was a group of French sailors with one of the French guys throwing the first punch. Reinhold loved every minute of kicking French ass. Every punch he threw was pay back for three days and a lot of beatings at the hands of the French police. By the time they left Amsterdam, the *Leipzig's* name was well known.

The fight scenes repeated themselves in Rotterdam. Reinhold and his friends were developing a routine. Reinhold, Johan, and Wolfgang would start the fight with another group of sailors, usually Greek or French but Russian and Italian would do too. They would knock the guys around for a few minutes before passing them to Otto and Gottfried, who would stand by the door, waiting to catch the banged up guys and throw them out the door. The five sailors cleaned out bars three nights in a row in Rotterdam in this way.

In Antwerp, they got in one night of action at one of the port bars before they were banned from all of them. This sent a whoop of victory through the fighting five from the *Leipzig*. They went from being known to having their reputation proceed them to other cities in a short couple of weeks.

"Who cares if we can't drink at those dumps?" Johan pointed out. "We leave for South America in two days!"

"And the girls will take our money no matter how many fights we start," Wolfgang pointed out.

We bonded quickly, those guys and I, he thought to himself with another rueful smile. *Like peas in a pod was right. Friends and shipmates to the end, and all that jazz.*

When the *Leipzig* left Antwerp, Reinhold felt like it was his first ocean voyage all over again. He was almost giddy with anticipation. Crossing the Atlantic was a benchmark for a sailor and crossing the Equator was an accomplishment to brag about. The sailors at the seamen's club who had crossed the equator were treated with a bit, not too much, but a bit more respect. Reinhold knew from listening to them talk that there was some rite of passage that he would have to endure. One grizzled old timer in particular at the seamen's club in Holtenau told him that when he crossed the Equator for the first time, his crewmates threw him overboard and made him swim under the keel. Reinhold was shocked.

"Wasn't that dangerous?"

"Hell, yes, it was dangerous! You had to swim fast or you would get sucked into the propeller or drown. One guy they threw in with me didn't make it. He drowned before he could get to the other side."

"What if you couldn't make it? What if you kept surfacing on the same side they threw you in?"

"They wouldn't let you back on board unless you made it to the other side. That is how the guy drowned. He had no choice. If he wanted to get back on the ship, he had to surface on the other side. He just couldn't make it."

The old guy hadn't wanted to talk anymore after that. Reinhold tried to ask him a couple of question, but got nowhere. The bartender answered the most important question he had.

"They don't do that anymore, Scholz. Don't worry, your shipmates aren't going to throw you overboard at the Equator. Not for any initiation anyway. I can't speak for them teaching you a lesson or two regarding your personality flaws. They are definitely going to shave that pretty mane of hair you have. I can promise you that."

He winked at Reinhold before shuffling off to help a guy down the bar. Reinhold ran a hand protectively through his blonde hair.

On the *Leipzig*, Johan told him one night over a beer or two on deck that in the American Navy, sailors who haven't crossed the Equator are called 'pollywogs' and sailors who have crossed are called 'shellbacks'.

"What the hell is a pollywog?" Reinhold questioned.

"It is a baby frog, I think."

"So what is a shellback?"

"Something stronger than a baby frog. They get stronger by crossing the Equator."

Before Johan could continue, Reinhold blurted, "Are you going to shave my head and throw me overboard?"

Johan laughed. "Maybe. It depends on much beer you donate to our cause."

"Beer?"

"You'll see, pollywog."

Once through the English Channel, the *Leipzig* didn't bother hugging the coast like the other ships in Reinhold's past. Instead, it picked up speed and headed straight out into the Atlantic. Almost immediately, they were greeted by a huge, powerful storm with a *windstärke* of eight. The waves reached almost thirty five feet. It wasn't the best start to his cross Atlantic journey but it didn't matter. It was no different from the storms in the North Sea. After the storm blew itself out, the crossing was uninterrupted by bad weather.

"That's the Atlantic for you," remarked Otto. "You just never know what she is going to throw at you. Have be on your toes."

The crossing took sixteen days. Reinhold and the crew spent most of it refitting the ship with manila ropes. What a pain in the butt that was, he thought. Every foot of the steel lines were stowed neatly in the storage locker for use when they returned to the colder temperatures in Europe. For the duration of their stay in the hot, wet climate of the tropics, manila ropes were they only acceptable material for lines. The *Leipzig* entered the Caribbean Basin, Reinhold's first encounter with the body of water, just after New Year's. They were still switching the lines out as the ship wound its way through the Windward Islands.

It was just as beautiful then as it is now, he thought, gazing at the landscape before him on the deck of the *Brandenburg*.

He thought he caught a glimpse of a large sea turtle swimming in the distance. He remembered the almost instant effect the Caribbean had on him. The place encouraged a slower pace and a more enjoyable way of life.

What the hell am I doing working? Reinhold remembered questioning himself as he hauled rope and swabbed the deck with grey paint. *I should just move here and live on the beach and eat fish. I bet there are thousands of beautiful girls around here that would make good wives.*

The *Leipzig*, unlike the *Brandenburg*, didn't stop at a single Caribbean port. She skirted around the islands and across the warm, shallow, brilliantly colored sea to La Guairá, a decent sized port on the north coast of Venezuela. They docked the ship at a concrete pylon that was serving as a pier and set the booms ready for the shore crew.

Reinhold didn't know what the cargo transfer was in this port and he didn't care. He was more interested in the majesty displayed before him. The port rested on a narrow strip of land, flanked by beaches flowing into turquoise water, and backed by green, verdant mountains. Buildings spread their way up the hillsides, ending only when the terrain became too steep. It reminded him faintly of India but India's hills were not as dramatic as Venezuela's mountains. The two locations, however, did have the same military presence at their ports. Soldiers in green uniforms roamed the piers, brandishing large rifles. The landscape also reminded him of Sweden and Finland, but the mountains here were greener, lusher. They stretched as far as the eye could see in both directions and were cleaved by deep, lush valleys.

"Good stuff grows in those mountains, Scholz," Johan said, joining Reinhold's observation of the terrain.

"Like what?"

"We're loading coffee and chocolate here."

"Chocolate?"

"Not the finished product, but the bean they make chocolate out of. They make it into chocolate back home."

Johan pulled a long, yellow fruit out of his pocket, peeled it, and offered Reinhold a piece.

"What is this?" Reinhold asked as he took the offered food.

Johan looked surprised. "You've never had a banana before?"

"A banana? What is it?"

Johan laughed heartily. "It is a fruit, kind of like a sweet, soft potato." He threw a piece into his mouth, chewed and swallowed. "I can't believe you've never had one before."

Reinhold popped the piece of fruit in his mouth and chewed, experiencing the texture and taste.

Not bad, he thought, *a bit dry, but tasty other than that.*

"Where would I have come across a banana in Europe or the Middle East?"

Johan shrugged. "You can get bananas in Hamburg, in the market near Reeperbahn."

"I don't live in Hamburg. I live in Holtenau. And whenever I am near Reeperbahn, I am not looking for fruit. I am looking for somewhere to put my banana, if you get me."

Johan laughed again. "Fair enough, Scholz. If you like these and want another one, there is a bunch hanging in our bunk."

"Our bunk?"

"Yup, I went out and bought some as soon as we docked. There," he pointed east toward the beach where a group of stalls stood.

The saltpeter must have worn off in his system because he had two things on his mind: food and girls.

"How's the food around here?" he asked Johan.

"Delicious," Johan answered. As if reading his friend's mind he continued, "But not as delicious as the girls." He winked at Reinhold. "We're going to love South America, Scholz."

"Oh?"

"Yup. We're going to get the bus to Caracas, the capital of this tropical wonderland. Otto says it is a site to see and it doesn't take that long to get there. From what he says, it's in the mountains right above us. You want to come?"

"Yes," Reinhold answered. "Of course I want to go. What's with the soldiers?"

Johan shrugged. "Who knows. All these poor countries are like that."

Johan, Reinhold, Gottfried, and Wolfgang left the Leipzig and headed into the small town of La Guairá. Otto said the bus picked up in a sort of town square, near a squat church, about a quarter of a mile from where the ship was docked. They wandered their way in the direction Otto pointed, passing residences and businesses along the cobblestone streets that had seen better days. The other guys thought the place was run down and primitive, but Reinhold thought it was quaint and colorful, even in its obvious poverty. The buildings were a bit ramshackle and flimsy, but really, what else did you need in such a place? Here it was, early January, and the temperatures were in the high 70s.

They found the town square, a stone and dirt paved triangular area dominated by a church painted a white that captured the sun's rays and threw them back at you in all their brilliance. It was almost blinding. There was a group of people waiting near the center of the square. They had bags and packages and animals.

"That must be the bus stop," Johan remarked.

"I don't think so," Reinhold said. "They have animals. Maybe they are waiting for someone to pick up the animals, like a butcher."

No sooner had he said that then the bus showed up, coming to a stop in front of the group of people. The sailors watched as they piled into the green and rusty transport.

"I guess that's it," Johan said, breaking into a trot to catch the bus before it left.

The other guys followed, reaching the doors just as they were closing. They handed over their coins for the ride and found seats in the middle of the crowd.

"Thank God the agent and steward had their acts together today or we wouldn't have been able to pay the fare," Wolfgang said.

Reinhold was amazed by the bus ride. The locals, a short, brown people with liquid brown eyes and black hair, all had livestock with them. There was goats, chickens, ducks, and other birds that he didn't recognize as well as small rodents that looked like beavers without the tails and smaller teeth. What a noise they made! The birds in particular never stopped squawking. The only thing Reinhold could hear above the din was the growl of the bus's engine. Odder still was the lone policeman who sat at the front of the bus with a straight back and an expressionless face.

The trip to Caracas was entirely uphill on a paved road that twisted and turned around the contours of the mountains. As the bus careened around sharp turns, the people and the animals slid on their seats without paying much mind. Reinhold, on the other hand, was enthralled by the scenery. It was breathtaking. The mountain loomed over the road and fell away from the pavement into gorges and ravines. The green of the rainforest around them was brilliant in the sunlight. Perched on the sides of the mountains were whitewashed buildings. It was so like India and so not like India. This place seemed newer and older at the same time.

After about half an hour of climbing, the bus crested the top of the mountain. For a brief minute, the valley were Caracas is nested was spread out before them, city and all. It was beautiful, truly beautiful. The white island of the city was framed by the green of the rainforest and ringed by rippling mountains. The bus descended and the scene was lost but Reinhold could still see it in his mind's eye, a lovely vision like the one he was sure Pizarro was looking for in the story of El Dorado. They sped down the road and the urban sprawl began, turning the vision of El Dorado into a vision of poverty. The bus stopped a few times on the outskirts of the city, picking up more people with their animals. Reinhold was amazed that, even this close to the city, there were chickens and goats.

An hour after they boarded, the sailors disembarked in the center of Caracas near some very impressive looking architecture. They walked the streets, taking in the sights and buying strange food from vendors. It was beautiful and didn't remind Reinhold of India anymore. It felt Spanish to him. It also felt a bit oppressive. Everywhere he looked there were green clad soldiers holding impressive looking rifles and wearing serious expressions. They were on every street corner and in front of every official looking building. Several times, one of these soldiers followed the progress of the sailors through narrowed and suspicious eyes. He sighed to himself.

"That's because it was founded by the Spanish," Johan remarked when Reinhold voiced his observations.

"Otto was saying that the natives had a city here before the Spanish came," Gottfried said.

"Of course they had a city here," Wolfgang said. "It is easier to claim someone else's city than build your own."

The sailors walked and talked for several hours before Johan pointed out that they had no idea had long the buses ran. The *Leipzig* was also schedule to shove off that night with the evening tide. "This isn't Germany, guys. We have no idea how long the bus to the port will run today. And I don't want to get stuck here, labelled a runaway sailor."

They headed back to the spot where they had gotten off and waited for the next bus with La Guairá above the windshield. It was about an hour before one came. They boarded and settled amongst the people and animals for the return trip. They crested the mountain again and started down the steep other side. The bus picked up speed rapidly, whipping around turns and coasting through the straightaways.

The locals and their animals didn't seem to notice the bus's alarming speed but the sailors did. When Reinhold glanced at Johan, he saw a man who looked like he was silently praying. Wolfgang had his eyes closed and was swaying in his seat with the rhythm of the bus. Gottfried was sitting bolt upright, eyes wide open, staring out the windshield like a petrified man. Just when the trip couldn't get more terrifying, the bus driver turned off the engine, cutting the growl that drowned out the noise of the animals. Reinhold's stomach flipped in fear.

"Did he just turn off the bus?" He called to Johan, who simply nodded. "Why would he do that?"

Johan shrugged slightly.

The bus was speeding down the mountain simply on the momentum of its own weight and gravity. All they could do was watch as it swayed around sharp turns and overtook slower moving vehicles, dipping into the oncoming lane to do so. The locals didn't seem to notice any of this. One old man actually slept through the whole ride, a large, red, caged chicken balanced on his lap. The chicken looked as unconcerned as the sleeping man.

Finally, they reached a straightaway that Reinhold recognized as the home stretch to La Guairá. The sea was visible through the trees in the distance. The driver started the engine and the growl filled the bus, drowning out the din of the animals again. They arrived safely back in the small town and disembarked. Reinhold was very happy when he walked up the gangway of the *Leipzig*. The ship, he felt, was definitely safer than the bus.

Chapter 80: Panama Canal

The *Leipzig* didn't leave port that night but early the following morning. The ship struck a course for the Panama Canal. Several days later, they arrived in Límon Bay, a wide body of water littered with ships at anchor. The cranes and equipment of the port of Colon, Panama were visible in the distance. The Hapag ship sailed amongst ships flying flags from all over the world and dropped anchor not far from Colon. They waited their turn to approach the entrance to the canal. Once they were called, a crew would board the ship and take control of its operations. They wouldn't touch a single line for the duration of their sail through the canal.

"Think of it as eight hours off, boys," Krause said. "Scholz, Fuhrmann, you are still Quartermasters. Report to the bridge as usual."

Reinhold and his friends wanted to go ashore to see what Panama had to offer but they were forbidden to leave the ship.

"All hands on deck, Scholz, when you hear the whistle." The bosun stated. "The Canal Authority doesn't wait for anybody. We leave when they call us. Now, go measure the bilge. There is also a short in the electric to the galley. See if you can identify the source of the problem."

The *Leipzig* sat at anchor for an entire day before the signal came for the sailors to take their positions. Reinhold filled the day by organizing the storage closet and measuring lines. That night, he and his friends dropped their fishing lines into the bay and tried to identify all the different flags they saw around them. A German ship anchored to starboard shouted invitations to come drink but the bosun declined the offer.

The call to sail came early the next morning, just after dawn. The sailors did very little to get the ship moving. A crew of Panamanians came aboard and took control. The regular crew was there only to assist the lock crew. They hoisted the anchor, got in line with a dozen other ships, and made their way to the first set of locks, the Gatun Locks. Reinhold stood at the rail and watched the set of sea gates get closer. He saw the terracing in the terrain and in the locks. He watched as, one by one, the ships in front of them entered the starboard gates and were hoisted to the next lock. They were moving along faster than he figured they would.

"We're going up twenty six meters," a voice said to Reinhold's right. Turning he saw Otto standing next to him.

"How long does it take?"

"To get through all three steps, about an hour."

"What happens then?"

"We sail through Gatun Lake to Gaillard Cut then to the Pedro Miguel Locks and the Miraflores Locks then out to the Pacific."

Reinhold nodded his understanding, watching the gates get closer. When they were just a hundred meters away, he felt the vibrations from the propeller stop and the ship slow to a crawl as the sea gate opened to accommodate the vessel. They slid slowly and silently into the metal and concrete chute and came to a stop. A crew of men on the starboard side attached the ship to a small car on a track.

"What is that?" he asked Otto.

"The Panama Canal locomotives. They pull the ship from lock to lock. Watch."

Reinhold felt the ship raising him up as the lock filled with water. Once the lock was full, the locomotive moved on its track up the terraced terrain, towing the ship behind into the next lock. Looking back, Reinhold saw he was looking down on the next ship entering the first lock. It was an odd sensation, like some invisible hand had picked the ship up and it was hovering above the ground. It gave him a strange feeling in his stomach, something like when the ship rode a wave into a trough during a storm. The process repeated itself for the third lock. Then, the *Leipzig* was released like a fish into a huge lake.

It was beautiful, a blue-green lake surrounded by green mountains and dotted with little hilly islands. The early morning sun played across the water, turning it shades of purple and pink that only nature could create. The day was warm and humid without a breeze, making the surface of the lake smooth. Even the wakes of the ship before them seemed to die premature deaths in reverence to the calm atmosphere. Otto disappeared, returning a minute later with a stool. He settled himself on it, took off his shirt, and propped his feet on the rail. A few minutes later, Johan, Wolfgang, and Gottfried joined them. They brought a case of beer with them and some chairs. An impromptu party erupted on the spot. Reinhold declined the beer. He was Quartermaster in two hours, just in time, Otto said, to navigate the Gaillard Cut, a narrow canyon from Gatun Lake to the Pedro Miguel Locks that may or may not accommodate one ship at a time depending on the size of the vessels involved.

As they sailed, Reinhold noticed patches of vegetation underwater, then he picked out contours of land that were more mountainous then subaquatic. He mentioned this observation to Otto.

"Those are the trees and mountains that they flooded when they built the canal."

"So, this is a manmade lake?" Johan asked.

"Yup," Otto replied. "Used to be the largest manmade lake in the world. Largest dam too, but that's changed now."

Reinhold reported to the bridge as the *Leipzig* was approaching the narrowest point of the lake leading to Gaillard Cut. He took the wheel from Fuhrmann and focused his attention ahead. The canal narrowed and he was somewhat uneasy about approaching ships but no one gave commands for him to change course or speed. The pilot stood at the front windows, straight as a mast, hands clasped behind his back, and rocking backward and forwards on his heels. The kitchen boy entered a few minutes into Reinhold's shift, bringing coffee. The pilot took a steaming mug, never glancing at Reinhold behind the wheel.

Wheel, he thought to himself, *there was no 'wheel' on the Leipzig. It was buttons that you pushed, not a wheel that you steered. Kind of takes the fun out of being Quartermaster on these new ships. It is a lot harder to pretend you are a pirate.*

As the ship sailed further into Gaillard Cut, Reinhold realized his apprehension was for nothing. Another ship, equal in size to the

Leipzig, sailed passed with a couple of yards to spare. The terrain here was, again, dramatic. Heavily vegetated jungle slopes angled steeply to the water and craggy rock outcroppings loomed. At one spot, a strange formation appeared that looked like a natural set of stairs for a giant. They were made of stone and were covered in a kind of mossy plant. Reinhold could only guess that the engineers that built the canal made this to prevent the rock from sliding into the canal and blocking the lanes.

The Gaillard Cut was fairly straight, with just a few course alterations needed. At one spot, the pilot turned and informed the Captain in English that they had just sailed across the continental divide. It didn't take long, maybe an hour or two after entering the Cut, for the *Leipzig* to arrive at the Pedro Miguel Locks, which was actually just one lock. Reinhold maneuvered the ship to the pilot's specifications and into the lock without incident. They sailed in and sailed out in a matter of minutes, dropping about nine yards.

A short time later they came to a small lake and the Miraflores Locks. Once again, Reinhold set the course on the pilot's commands, cut the propeller, and sailed into the first lock. The ship was secured to another locomotive that pulled it from the first lock to the second. Then they were released back into the narrow Gaillard Cut and a short time later arrived at the port of Balboa. Here, they dropped anchor and a small boat arrived to ferry the canal crew and the pilot ashore. Reinhold was surprised by the presence of two huge, grey navy ships flying the American flag. They had big guns sprouting off them. It made Reinhold's stomach twist a bit to wonder why those ships were present in the port. The *Leipzig* remained in Balboa for only a couple of hours until she was cleared for departure.

Chapter 81: **Schellfisch**

Reinhold noticed immediately that there was a difference in the Pacific Ocean when compared to the Atlantic Ocean. The *Leipzig* was a day's sail out of Balboa when he mentioned his observations to Otto.

"The Pacific is an entirely different ocean, Scholz." Otto said between forkfuls of the pot roast the cook prepared for dinner. "Just wait until we get down along the coast of Chile. The difference is more than noticeable."

Sometime during the Atlantic crossing, Reinhold decided he never wanted to work for any other shipping company. Hapag was his home now because the food was so good. There were two cooks and two bakers. He silently thanked the bakers heartily for their presence as he grabbed a fresh baked loaf of bread and ripped it in two, taking half for himself to dip in the gravy from the pot roast. Delicious.

"How so?" Reinhold asked.

"The waves are long and slow here. You'll see what I mean." Then a mischievous grin spread across his face. "But, at the moment, you should be more concerned with what is going to happen tomorrow night, Scholz."

"Why?" Reinhold looked around the table at the other sailors.

Johan was also grinning. Wolfgang and Gottfried looked as lost as Reinhold felt.

"Because we cross the equator tomorrow afternoon." Otto answered. "We have to initiate you and Wolfgang here into the club."

"Club?"

He remembered what the bartender at the seaman's club in Holtenau told him before he signed on to the *Leipzig*. The only thing he remembered thinking was that they were going to shave his head and what a disaster that would be in the constant sunshine of the tropics.

"Not every sailor crosses the equator," Johan explained. "My father sailed his entire life and never came close to crossing it."

"I can tell you that when I was cop walking the beat in Hamburg if you told me that one day I would cross the equator, I would have told you to go home and sleep it off." Otto pushed his plate away and stood up. "There are preparations to make, gentlemen. Until tomorrow,"

He doffed his cap with a flourish and left the mess hall followed closely by Johan.

The next day, the five or six who had never crossed the equator were assigned work in the out of the way parts of the ship. Reinhold was placed on sweeping duty. He spent the entire day sweeping the aft sections. It was degrading for a *Matrose* and he figured it was all part of the initiation. By the time he was done for the day, he had blisters in the crook of his thumb on his right hand.

The 'police' came and got him after dinner. They brought him, and the rest of the initiates to the wheelhouse, to the open flying bridge. The 'priest', who was really Otto dressed in a makeshift cassock, was waiting for them. They had a long wait to get started because one sailor, Beck was his name, locked himself in his room, afraid of what was going to happen to him. The 'police' dragged him up onto the flying bridge and made him wait in line. Reinhold didn't understand why he was being such a girl about it. One by one, the sailors were called forward to kneel in front of the 'priest' and pledge something.

"You have to make a donation in the name of the Lord to the Crossing Party. What do you want to donate?"

"Beer." Reinhold answered.

The 'priest' wrote this down on the piece of paper he was holding.

"How much? A case?"

Something in the way the 'priest' asked made Reinhold think he needed to go bigger than that.

"Two."

The 'priest' wrote this down on the paper. He said a quick prayer and made the sign of the cross in the air.

"Bless you, my child, now go in peace to the barber to have that thick mane of yours trimmed to an appropriate length."

Reinhold was guided by his sponsor, a sailor named Richter, to the 'barber', who was a sailor named Peter. Peter was dressed like a barber in a white dress shirt, black pants, a red bow tie, and an apron. His hair was parted in the middle and slicked down on both sides as in pictures Reinhold had seen from the 1920s.

"What did you pledge, sailor?" the 'barber' asked

"Two cases of beer," Reinhold answered. Richter, his accompanying initiate sailor, confirmed his answer.

The 'barber' pulled a pair of scissors and a shaving razor out of the pocket of his apron. He looked from one to the other significantly, making a show of his decision between the two methods of removing hair. After a minute or two, he put the razor back in his pocket. He tilted Reinhold's head from side to side before trimming away a bit of hair here and there, a little off the top, a little off the sides, and a little off the back. Looking back, Reinhold thought that he had done a pretty good job trimming. He wondered if Peter had been a barber before becoming a sailor.

After the 'barber' dismissed him, Richter guided Reinhold to a canvas tube about four feet in diameter that was erected with steel lines from the flying bridge to the deck below. There was water gushing down the tube that was pumped up from the sea via a system of pipes.

Leave it to sailors to come up with a way to pump water five stories into the air from the sea, Reinhold thought to himself. *This has to be the work of the damn engineers.*

It angled downward at a pretty good degree, probably around forty degrees.

"Ok, Scholz, you can go down the tube by yourself or I can push you," said Richter.

"What's down there?" Reinhold asked curiously.

"Only one way to find out," Richter responded before shoving Reinhold into the tube.

Reinhold flew down the incline on the running water. He felt something smack his ass and thought that it was one of the supports for the tube. Two more things smacked his behind. He heard laughter. It dawned on him that his fellow sailors were standing by the tube, hitting the initiates as they passed.

Before he could think anymore, he splashed into a tank of salty water. He surfaced and looked around. He was on the deck in a canvas tank of water. The tank was filled by the water coming down the slide and the runoff was flowing over the sides on to the deck. A second after he surfaced, he was attacked by two black guys. Reinhold knew a moment of real fear. There were no black guys on the ship! Who were these two?

One had him around the neck, trying to dunk him, while the other was grabbing his legs, trying to pull him under. Reinhold reached up to get rid of the guy who had him by the neck but he couldn't a hold of the guy's arm. His own fingers slipped off several times before he realized the black guys were just sailors coated in engine grease. Taking a different approach, Reinhold used the grease to his advantage and slid out of their grip and swam to the side of the tank, throwing himself out of the water and on to the deck like a flying fish in the Red Sea. No one followed him. They greased up guys were distracted by the next sailor coming down the tube.

The sailors on deck helped him up and dragged him to the closet hatch cover where Krause, dressed as Neptune, sat in a chair holding a real trident. They made Reinhold kneel in front of Neptune, his head bowed, while the sailors reported on his behavior during his initiation.

"Scholz here has been a real sport," Richter told Neptune. "He donated two cases of beer for the party."

"Good, Scholz, I knew you would be easy," Neptune said.

Almost on cue, shouting erupted from the tank of water. Whichever sailor just came down the pipe was not happy to be attacked and dunked by a pair of greased up black guys after having his ass smacked. Neptune raised his trident above Reinhold's head and blessed him.

"Fair winds and following seas and long may your big jib draw!" The tip of the trident lightly touched Reinhold's head. "You may rise, my son, and go forth a better sailor than you arrived. Take this to prove that you are one of the privileged."

Neptune handed Reinhold a rolled up sheet of paper tied with a piece of string. It was a handmade certificate bestowing on the sailor, in the name of Neptune, the rank of *Schellfisch*[34]. It also noted the exact coordinates of the Leipzig's crossing: eighty degrees, thirty-five minutes west. Decorating the document were blue and yellow flags on a rope, a very realistic rendition of a ship on an impressionistic sea, and the figure of Neptune himself, complete with trident. It was signed by Neptune and by Captain Jacobs.

A cheer went up from the already initiated sailors waiting to welcome the *schellfisch* to their club. Reinhold joined them and watched the rest of the guys come to get blessed. The one that had been screaming in the tank was Beck. He was thrown roughly down

---

[34] *Schellfisch* literally translated to English means "haddock". The use of this term in an equator crossing initiation is unclear.

on his knees in front of Neptune, who proceeded to smack him around with his trident. Reinhold was glad that he had cooperated.

"When is the crossing party?" He asked the engineer standing next to him.

"Tonight!" The engineer replied. "Unless you're on watch."

"Nope, not me."

Reinhold stayed to watch the rest of the initiates get blessed by Neptune. Everyone was excited about the party later. He knew a moment's panic about the two cases of beer. He had to go find the steward and order it, hoping that the guy would release it immediately and not pull any bureaucratic nonsense. He didn't want to know what would happen if he showed up without his donation.

Later that night, after most of his donated beer was gone, a very drunk Otto came stumbling over to an equally drunk Reinhold. He planted a wet kiss on the side of Reinhold's face.

"Thanks, for the beer, Scholz," He paused to hiccough. "You've never been to the Southern Hemisphere before so you have never seen the Southern Cross."

A swaying Otto pointed to the sky off the port side of the ship to a spot about forty five degrees off the horizon. Reinhold followed his finger, noticing four bright stars roughly in the shape of a cross.

"Every sailor in these waters should know where the Southern Cross is. It is a navigation aid."

Otto undraped his arm from Reinhold's shoulders and stumbled away. Reinhold continued to gaze at the new constellation wondering how sailors of old figured out that this small configuration could help them navigate.

Chapter 82: The Natives

The bosun informed them at their morning meeting the next day that there was a schedule change. Instead of heading straight to Peru, they were stopping in Ecuador at the port of Guayaquil. It barely registered with Reinhold what he was saying. He had gotten no sleep, partying all night instead. Not only had the steward come through with the two cases of beer, he gave him a bottle of rum as a gift for being a good sport about the initiation. Standing in the early morning sun on the rocking boat, Reinhold could have fallen asleep right there.

"It is going to be a short stop, boys, so don't get your hopes up about going ashore or having the beach edition of the Crossing Party. We are picking up bananas and sailing again. There is a pier already waiting for us. We'll be in port no more than four hours."

They entered the gulf of Guayaquil later that morning to the greetings of a group of bottlenose dolphins. They leaped and played in the wake of the ship on the sapphire colored sea the whole way to the mouth to the Guayas River. The *Leipzig* wound its way around islands that dotted the entrance to the river and passed what seemed like hundreds of small, primitive looking fishing boats. These boats were manned by brown, shirtless men that stared as the big ship sailed passed.

What a sight we must have made to the native people, Reinhold thought to himself. *A big, new, European ship manned by a bunch of shirtless white guys. Especially since we had sent Johan over the side in the bosun's chair to repair a seam in the rail where it met the deck. He was the palest of us all, wearing a welding helmet and holding a welding torch!*

On the islands were shacks and sheds that served as homes for the fishermen. Once again, Reinhold asked himself what else a person really needed in such a climate. It was hot and humid. The only time any of them put a shirt on was for meals or to report to the bridge. He remembered distinctly asking himself what he would really need if he were to live there. The answer was very little.

Where the sea had been clear and sapphire, the Guayas River was muddy and brown. There were extensive wetlands along the shore from which a wide variety of colorful birds flew as the ship's wake disturbed their nesting. They traveled a couple of hours up river to a large city and port of Guayaquil. It was a remarkable sight with its brightly colored homes and colonial architecture set against the dark green of the surrounding jungle. Here, just as in La Guairá, were soldiers armed to the teeth with automatic rifles and handguns.

Reinhold was lost, deep in thought about why there were soldiers guarding bananas, when he heard someone let out a piercing cry. Below him, on the pier, the longshoremen were scattering away from the crates, shouting and waving their hands, even the soldiers were backing up.

"What's going on, Scholz," asked Merck, one of the engineers, who appeared at the rail.

"Don't know," Reinhold pointed toward a retreating man. "That guy screamed something and everyone ran."

"It's a snake." Otto and Johan appeared at the rail.

"A snake," Merck repeated. "Is it a huge snake that is going to eat everyone? Like an anaconda?"

"No," Otto answered. "It is a small, green snake that is so venomous it could kill a horse."

"Oh."

"Why are they running away? It is just a small snake. They can't keep working? Who cares if it is poisonous? Just don't go near it." Johan commented.

Otto shrugged. "This snake has killed a lot of people here, from what I have been told. It doesn't kill immediately, either. From what I have heard, the poison eats you from the inside, slowly rotting your limbs off."

"Oh."

A short time later a short man appeared alone on the pier carrying a bag and a stick. The assembled group of sailors watched as the man smacked the wooden banana crates with the stick, waiting silently and still between smacks. Every few minutes, he would move a few feet to a new spot and listen before smacking the crate again.

This went on for more than an hour. Slowly the sailors got bored and left to find more interesting things to do. Reinhold stayed and watched, leaning on the rail, head propped up in his hands, eyes blurry with the lack of sleep. One part of his brain was telling him to go sleep in the supply closet while the other was fascinated by the process of finding the snake.

Finally, the man with the stick dove into a crate and struggled with something. He emerged with a wiggling green snake grasped firmly by its head. As he stuffed the snake into the burlap bag he was carrying, applause erupted from the watchers on the shore.

"Oh, good," Reinhold heard Krause say behind him. "Maybe now these *arschlocher* will get back to work."

Reinhold had to agree. It took two hours to catch the snake, which meant the *Leipzig* was more than two hours off schedule. On the bright side, however, the delay gave him time to visit the food stalls along the pier. He got a stalk of bananas for a pack of Lucky Strike. He also got a good look at the South American women who ran the stalls. The young ones were lusciously beautiful with full lips, breasts, and hips. The kind of women a sailor wants to take directly to the bedroom and get to know better. They seemed to like him, too. They batted their eyelashes and giggled musically while they stared into his eyes or at his hair.

So, they like the pale Europeans, he thought to himself, *this is excellent.*

He returned to the *Leipzig* wishing his stalk of bananas was the girl that sold them to him.

The *Leipzig* sailed out of Guayaquil and headed south along the coast of Ecuador and Peru. Otto's remark that the Pacific waves were long and slow made perfect sense to Reinhold before they reached their next stop at Callao. The sea was like an undulating snake that gave the ship a rhythmic rising and falling. It wasn't like the choppy and violent North Sea where a ship would ride the troughs and smack the surface with force; it was more like the Pacific was trying to lull them all to sleep like a baby in a crib. Reinhold had to regain his sea legs for such a motion. He overheard one of the chief engineers saying over dinner one night that the reason the waves behaved this way was the proximity of the deep-water trenches to the shore. He wondered if this was true or the guy was talking out his ass to look important.

They arrived in Callao on a bright, sunny morning two and a half days days after docking in Guayaquil. Before he saw land, he saw five ships, all flying different flags, equal in size to the *Leipzig*. The only flag he recognized was from America. Otto said one was Australian. Johan said he was wrong. They were debating the topic loudly when a mountain appeared on the southern horizon. Reinhold figured it was the port. A couple of hours later, he learned he was only partially correct.

The mountain that had crested was an island off the shore of Peru. It protected the harbor and port of Callao. It was also home to penguins, lots of penguins. Every soul on the ship could hear their squawking as the ship sailed passed into Callao. Or was that sea lions? Looking back, Reinhold figured it was a combination of animals that welcomed them to port, both the sea lions and the penguins.

Looking ashore, Reinhold felt like he was back in the Middle East. Where Ecuador had been green and verdant, Peru was rocky desert. But, where the Middle East was devoid of ship traffic, Peru was teeming with vessels. The port was packed with all manner of ships: cargo freighters, industrial fishing boats, tankers, military ships, pleasure yachts, and, of course, a myriad of small, native fishing vessels.

"This could be Rotterdam or Hamburg," Johan observed.

Reinhold nodded his agreement.

"We're dropping anchor for now, boys" Krause informed them. "The port officials will call us in a couple of hours."

As the bosun said, they were called only a couple of hours after dropping anchor. They were ushered ashore by an agile tugboat and tied up quickly. After securing the spring line, Reinhold turned his attention ashore and noted that, once again, uniformed soldiers carrying rifles and handguns populated the port.

God God, he thought to himself, *what is going on down here that they need all of these soldiers around. You would think we were in the Soviet Union.*

The longshoremen wasted no time going to work. They came aboard accompanied by an armed guard, who walked laps around the deck of the ship. Two more guards stationed themselves on the gangplank, backs to the ship, eyes on the port. Quickly, the men hooked up the cargo and started swinging it ashore with the booms and crane. One after another, the crates swung ashore, the whirring of the boom motor marking their progress. Reinhold knew they were full of toys from Germany.

He was headed below deck, to his bunk, to get cleaned up when he heard a shout in Spanish then a loud crash and the distinctive ripping sound of splintering wood. Without thinking, he turned and ran aft, toward the noise, fearing that someone was lying, pinned and bleeding, under a broken wooden crate. Peering down into the open hatch, he saw that this wasn't the case. All of the men working in the hull managed to get out of the way. But what a mess! There were toys everywhere! They exploded out of the crate and covered the floor. From forty feet above, Reinhold could make out the shapes of trains, soldiers, trucks, and various types of animals all colorfully painted and hand carved out of good German wood. The men in the hatch were yelling in Spanish and gesturing as orders were given and received.

Cleaning this up is going to take them all night, Reinhold thought to himself. He headed for the showers.

A couple of hours later, as he sat on the flying bridge with Johan, Wolfgang, and Gottfried, Reinhold watched the departure of the longshoremen for the day. The scene playing out below them was nothing like he had ever see before. The soldiers stationed on the gangplank were searching every man as he left the ship. For every three of them, two had toys hidden somewhere: up a sleeve, in the pocket of a shirt, in the leg of their pants, wherever they could stash something. The soldiers were collecting the toys in a duffel bag and letting the men go unmolested.

This went on for about thirty minutes before the soldiers abruptly stopped searching the departing workers. One of them picked up the now bulging duffel bag of toys and stowed it in the army truck waiting on the pier before returning to his post on the gangplank. He got out a cigarette, offered one to his watch buddy, and the two of them stood there smoking as the longshoremen left unmolested with whatever contraband they were carrying.

"That's why some of them were milling around, fussing with winches and double checking corners in the hull." Johan said, puffing on his own cigarette. "They were waiting for the guards to stop searching."

"Yup," Otto confirmed. "Once the soldiers have their share, they don't care why the peons do or what they steal." He grabbed another beer out of the tub of ice. "Unless we are transporting silver. That's a different story."

"Silver?" Reinhold questioned.

"We'll pick it up here before we go back to Germany. They bring a small army with them when they deliver it."

"Did they break that crate on purpose?" Wolfgang piped up. "They wanted the toys?"

"Probably," Otto shrugged.

It was bittersweet and a bit wistful to look back at the *Leipzig's* time in Callao. They spent a week in the port while the European cargo and the bananas from Guayaquil were unloaded and the cargo going to other South American ports was loaded. It was one of the best weeks of Reinhold's sailing career.

The second evening they were there, Reinhold and the guys left the ship to wander around the waterfront. They headed south toward a finger of land that jutted out into the sea, almost, but not quite, touching the island with the mountain and the loud animals. The port area they walked through could have been in any European city. There were trains carrying cargo, trucks lumbering along paved roads, and men hauling, fixing, and yelling. It reminded Reinhold of his stay in Portugal or his visits to Spain. Which made perfect sense because the Spanish set the stage for Callao to be a world-class shipping destination before they left Peru in the early 1800s, according to what he heard around the ship.

Outside the port, there were a collection of cheap port side taverns that were a welcome site to the sailors. They stopped in a couple and learned that they were very different from European taverns. First, there were ladies, but Reinhold wouldn't have touched any of them. They were not the attractive, luscious girls he saw in Guayquil. The women here were short and squat with manly faces. Otto told him they were natives, Incas he called them. The men were not friendly and gave off distinct 'don't talk to me' vibes. They, too, were short and squat with wide, flat-ish kind of faces. They wore interesting, bright colored clothes and never had bare heads, choosing to cover them with a sort of bowler hat.

"You like the Spanish girls, Reinhold." Otto reminded him. "We have to go to Lima to find them."

The bars also only served beer and wine.

Vino blanco and Vino tinto, he thought, *I am never going to forget those phrases.*

Not a big deal, really. The wine wasn't bad and Reinhold could have sworn that it was stronger than European wine. It was definitely cheaper.

The sailors continued their wanderings. The buildings alternated between big, old Colonial structures with Imperial Spanish features to wood and sheet metal shacks that sat near the beaches to desert brown stone structures that Otto said were made by the Incas. There were bright colors everywhere: pinks, blues, yellows, oranges. It was lovely against the blue of the Pacific. The local boats caught Reinhold's eye. They were larger than canoes, made out of wood with high sides and square-ish shaped with no visible mast apparatus.

They must row them, Reinhold thought to himself.

They ended up at the point of the finger of land, La Punta, Otto called it. A huge building dominated most of the land. It looked official, possibly even military. The sailors skirted around and ended up on the southern shore. There, on the rocky beach, they encountered the most usual scene Reinhold had ever witnessed on a beach. He heard that people used to catch big fish in the North and Baltic Seas and prepare them right on the beach, but that was a long time ago. Germany passed laws heavily regulating this kind of behavior long ago. But here, in Peru, this was still the way of life.

A dozen or so people, short, native looking men and women, were gathered around a smoldering fire. Several of them were engaged in the butchering of a large fish while others were cooking pieces of the fish in the hot coals of the fire. The sailors walked their way to get a closer look, loitering around, watching.

"What kind of fish is that?" Reinhold wondered aloud.

Wolfgang shrugged. "Looks like a tuna. I've seen pictures of them, but never one in real life."

"There are tuna in the Pacific, big ones, too. It may be a tuna." Otto agreed.

Reinhold lowered himself on to the rocky beach, thinking that it was as good a place as any to relax for a few minutes. There was a great view of the Pacific, the comforting sounds of waves splashing on the shore, and some interesting activity to watch. Besides, he was in no rush to get back to the ship. Otto, Johan, Wolfgang, and Gottfried must have understood and agreed with him because they settled themselves next to him. The people cooking the fish took notice of the newcomers and their interest in the fish. They made a couple of friendly, welcoming gestures and smiled broadly but Reinhold was very surprised when one of the men turned and made a finger to mouth gesture that indicated he would share some of the catch.

At first, there was some hesitation but the sailors didn't want to be impolite so they accepted the banana leave plates they were handed. Reinhold wasn't sure what to expect from the large, meaty fish. It turned out to be delicious! The cooking technique imparted a smoky quality that was just as good though different from the European traditions of smoking fish. The sailors ate every bit they were given.

They tried to make a bit of conversation with the people, but were unable to communicate more than they had sailed to Peru from far away. The natives understood and repeated the word "Germany", nodding and talking amongst themselves about it. One woman gestured to Reinhold's fair hair, commenting in her language. The sailors departed a little while later after thanking their hosts for the fish. Otto gave the guy that seemed to be in charge a couple of coins to cover the cost of what they had eaten.

On the way back to the ship, the group of sailors decided that since they had the day off, they would go to Lima in the morning. Reinhold devoted the rest of the night to getting the wrinkles out of his suit and shining up his good shoes.

Chapter 83: Lima

It was late morning when the guys finally got off the ship to catch the bus into the city. They passed a variety of types of neighborhoods on the way. There was a large, poverty stricken area outside the port that probably housed the people who worked in the terminals and on the piers.

That is the way it always is, Reinhold thought to himself. *There is always a ring of poverty around the port. After the poor areas come the suburban middle class neighborhoods. There are usually children playing in the streets and shiny cars driving around. Then you get to the city where everyone dwells together, rich and poor.*

They arrived in Lima proper after noon. It was one of the most beautiful places Reinhold had ever seen. The bus brought them from the port at Callao into the heart of the old city. They got off at a square plaza that was bordered by large, old buildings. There were ornately carved stone façades on large, official looking structures. Wolfgang translated some of the designations on them. One particularly stately edifice belonged, not surprisingly, to the Government Palace. Another eye catching building on the plaza had arched niches, like balconies, cut into an almost flat but somehow tastefully embellished façade. Wolfgang said it was where the government met. It reminded Reinhold very much of the old buildings in Spain and Portugal but with a German feel.

"That's because a lot of Germans came to live here," Otto explained matter-of-factly. "There is a rumor in my family that my great-great granduncle came here as a stone mason a long time ago. Supposedly, they were paying good money to skilled craftsmen."

Outside the official government area, Reinhold couldn't help being impressed by the amount of detail on homes and small businesses. Carved wooden adornments were everywhere, adding an Old World flair to the simplest of structures. Of course, there were churches, beautiful, shining examples of the colonial and imperial European presence in Peru.

The only part of Peru that could tear Reinhold's eyes away from the buildings were the girls. They were gorgeous, dark eyed, raven haired, and full bodied. The sailors stared without shame at them as they walked passed. Gottfried walked straight into a tree while ogling one beauty. After this, he suggested they find a bench to occupy so they could stare without risking injury. Otto suggested they find a café with an outdoor patio. This wasn't hard. The city was full of them. The sailor spent a couple of hours lingering over a native lunch of fresh seafood and people watching before continuing their wanderings around the city.

It was near dinnertime when they decided it was time for some drinking. They picked a place with a bar and food. The food was foreign and good with lots of grain accents. After they ate, the sailors sat at the bar and drank wine. Reinhold quickly became a target for the ladies. And what beautiful ladies they were! They wanted to run their hands through his blonde hair and stare into his blue eyes. He only wished he could speak the language!

Looking back, Reinhold wasn't entirely sure what happened that night. The wine he was drinking went right to his head, blurring his memory. There were five girls, he remembered. They hung out at the bar for a while, trying to talk and ended up just touching mostly. It had been a while, an entire Atlantic crossing, since he had a girl and he was more than ready to go!

Sometime, they left the bar and went to the girl's rooms in a nearby hotel. At least he thought it was a hotel. Looking back, it may have been some kind of high-class boarding house. There was a fancy lobby with high ceilings and wide stairs made of marble. The girl's room was lavish with gold gilt wallpaper and a huge, soft bed. Reinhold remembered falling into it and not wanting to leave, ever. It was the softest thing he had felt in months. No one else was there with them but only once did it cross his mind that he didn't know where his friends had gotten too.

He distinctly remembered the girl doing a short striptease for him that ended abruptly when she brought her ample breast to her mouth and licked her own nipple. It was too much. He grabbed her and pulled her into bed with him. They had a wild night together. She taught him things girls could do with their hips that he had never seen before. It looked like she was dancing on top of him. She also responded to him with an abandon that he hadn't seen before and he thought that he had seen the height of response in Kristal back in Bremerhaven. Since it had been so long for him, the first go didn't last long but he made up for it by becoming instantly ready to go again. The sky outside the girl's window was the color of the dark before the dawn when Reinhold passed out in the downy softness of the bed.

A banging on the door awoke him the next morning. The girl, wearing his button down suit shirt, answered and Otto barged in.

"We are late!" He blurted out. "It is already half past eight."

Adrenaline surged through Reinhold. He leapt, naked, out of bed and started pulling on clothes. The girl tossed him his shirt and stood there naked while a stunned Otto stared.

Five sailors went running out of the hotel and frantically looked for the closest bus station. Thankfully, it was only a block away. Once on their way back to the port Reinhold commented on their luck in finding girls in the same building.

"They are all friends," Wolfgang told them. "They are studying at the university here. My girl was actually from Bolivia. Her father does something with mining."

"Were they all rich girls then?" Gottfried asked.

"Probably," Otto shrugged.

"What do you think they will do to us for being late?" Reinhold asked.

His head was pounding now that the shot of adrenaline had left his system. His mouth was dry and cottony and he knew his breath was bad. He had entirely too much wine the night before.

"Dock our pay," Otto responded. "There is nothing else they can do here except give us the bad jobs. Don't be surprised, in this heat and sun, if all of a sudden the stack needs to get painted or the latrines need to get pumped."

On their arrival back at the ship, Krause informed them they were almost two hours late. Their pay was docked accordingly, their access to the goods the steward controlled was restricted, which was bad for Otto because he was running low on smokes, and they were all sent below deck to assess the condition of the bilge. Of course, it had to be pumped and that took all day. But it was worth it.

The *Leipzig* left Callao a few days later. The guys spent the rest of their time there wandering around the port, watching the ships come and go. A German ship docked two pylons from the *Leipzig*. Reinhold and Johan ran into two of her crew on shore at one of the local watering holes. Their ship was a tramp and they had been traveling the coast of South America for three months, stopping in every little port along the way. They suggested that Reinhold and Johan take a bus a couple of towns north of the airport.

"It is really primitive up there," one said.

"The sidewalks are wooden and there is cow dung everywhere." The other said. "It looks like it is right out of the old American West."

Reinhold and Johan took the suggestion and found the town. The sailors from the other ship were right. It looked exactly like something out of a story about the American West. There were dilapidated wooden buildings with wooden sidewalks and the smell of cows. The cowboys were interesting in their brightly colored ponchos and small top hats. The horses must have been a native breed because Reinhold had never seen ones like them. They had small, broad heads, shaggy coats, and short legs.

They stopped at a local bar and had a couple of glasses of wine and tried to talk to the locals but they clearly wanted no part of the strangers. They turned their heads and ignored them. The women were a bit more open but Johan realized they were just hoping for money when he felt one of them put a hand in his pocket. She didn't understand him, but he asked her why she thought she could ever rob a sober sailor.

"You have to get us drunk first," he scolded her.

The tone of Johan's voice attracted the attention of the men and they quickly decided it was time to leave. They wondered on the ride home if the other sailors had sent them there on purpose, as a joke. It was a question that Reinhold never got answered. The other ship was gone by the time he and Johan got back to Callao.

It was about the time that the *Leipzig* was leaving port that Reinhold discovered he had the clap. It made itself known in the usual way: a burning sensation while urinating and a strange discharge. He immediately thought of the guy from the *Oldendorff* who had the clap for two months or more. Fear of being that guy made him immediately visit the Second Mate who nonchalantly told him to bend over and drop his pants. He must have seen the hesitant look on Reinhold's face because he asked a very relevant question.

"There are fifty men on this ship, Scholz, do you think you are the first one to get the clap from some native wench? I've seen a dozen men's asses on this trip."

Reinhold couldn't argue the logic. He took the shot. The Second Mate told him if he had any other symptoms to come back. He didn't have to repeat the experience. The shot of penicillin was enough to knock out the infection. Once it was gone, his thoughts turned to the girl who gave it to him. He was shocked. She seemed so clean, so together, and so mature.

"Just goes to show you, Scholz, you can't trust anyone," Johan said when Reinhold told him what happened.

Chapter 84: Opportunity

Their next stop was the small port of Arica, Peru. They were in and out in less than a day. Then there was Antofagasta, where they spent one night. It was bigger than Arica but neither was bustling by European standards. Reinhold convinced Johan and Wolfgang to go ashore with him to grab a drink at a local tavern. It was a rough looking place. Once again, he was reminded of what he had read about the American Old West. There were warehouse buildings made of wood with turn of the century trains parked amongst them all set against a mountainous desert landscape. The army personnel with modern assault rifles and the white wash on the buildings were only things that destroyed the Old West feel.

The sailors walked across the dusty port and found a row of wooden buildings. One was the customs office. A uniformed soldier with a machine gun guarded it. One was a general store. Two of the buildings were taverns. The sailors went into the first one they encountered. Johan put a pack of Lucky Strikes on the bar, nudging it toward the bartender with his forefinger. The bartender nodded his acceptance and Johan ordered three glasses of red wine. Reinhold surveyed the room. There were several hardened looking men scattered around the tables. Reinhold was disappointed to see there were no girls. He couldn't say that he blamed them for not coming here. It was a rough looking crowd. Johan suggested they settle themselves at a table to have their wine.

"Do you think the Leipzig is going to Australia?" Reinhold asked Wolfgang.

I was tired of sailing, he thought to himself. *There was something about South America that made me want to stay on the beach. But Australia was my goal.*

Wolfgang shrugged. "I don't know. I hope so."

"I don't think it is going there this trip, Reinhold." Johan sounded almost apologetic.

"What makes you say that?"

"Because we've been tramping up and down the coast for too long already." Johan explained. "If we were going to Australia, if there was cargo to go there, we would have picked it up already and been on our way." He looked crest fallen. "I really thought we would go this time. Maybe next time."

"There is still the possibility," Wolfgang said. "We haven't been to Valparaiso yet. Maybe we'll get cargo for Australia there."

"Yes, but, Krause has never said anything about Australia," Johan pointed out.

This made sense. It was another three weeks to cross the Pacific. Reinhold was as disappointed as Johan sounded. He was looking forward to seeing the continent down under, and jumping ship. He decided the best way to work through his growing disappointment was to drink. Johan agreed heartily with him.

The first glass of wine became a second glass. Reinhold went to the bar and repeated the process Johan went through with the first round. He took the wine back to the table and sat down. Before he could put his glass to his lips a shadow fell on him. Reinhold felt his adrenaline surge in anticipation of a fight.

"I couldn't help over hearing you talk about Australia," said a deep voice in perfect German.

Surprised, the sailors looked up to see a large, fair skinned, blue eyed, and blonde haired man staring down at them. He had a slight smile playing about his lips. His huge hands were carrying three glasses of wine and a beer.

"Mind if I join you?" he asked. "It would be nice to speak with fellow Germans."

"Not at all," Johan said. "Sit down."

The man put down the glasses and settled himself at the table. He passed around the wine.

"I took the liberty of getting you your next drinks." He raised his glass in the air. "*Prost!*"

The sailors raised their glasses and responded, "*Prost!*"

"My name is Hans, by the way, Hans Schuster. I live here, in Chile. I am assuming that you came on a ship."

The sailors confirmed Hans' assumptions, telling him a bit about the traveling they had done and how they came to arrive in Antofagasta. Hans was interested in what cargo they were loading, but the sailors were of no use to him for information. They didn't know what they were picking up or where it was going.

"Do you have a vault on the ship?" he asked.

"Why do you ask?" Reinhold's suspicions were raised at once by the question.

Hans backpedaled quickly, explaining himself. "I ask because I own a copper mine here, in the mountains to the east. It is small now but I have plans to expand. I am looking for a ship to haul my ores to Europe."

"You own a mine?" Johan asked, somewhat incredulously.

"Yes, yes I do. It is going to be one of the biggest in Chile in a few years," Hans told them proudly. "I need people, good people that I can trust, to help me run it."

Several glasses of wine and as many hours later, Reinhold, Johan, and Wolfgang had agreed to jump the *Leipzig* and go to work for Hans Schuster at his mine. It was an exciting prospect and the sailors were practically giddy with anticipation. They toasted with Hans to their new future together in this exotic and desolate land.

Reinhold's life was shaping up before his eyes as he sipped his wine. He would go to Lima, find a good woman for a wife, and bring her back here to this barren country. He would build them a house, a big house with floor to ceiling windows with a view of the mountains. Maybe he could even find a view of the teal colored seas. They would have children who would also work in the mine. Maybe he would even have his own mine one day.

The sailors left the bar in the dark hours before dawn, drunk and happy about their turn of luck. They sang songs about Germany on their way back to the *Leipzig*. Reinhold fell into bed in his bunk and was asleep before he could take his boots off. He was no match for the wine and the grind of the *Leipzig's* schedule. He woke the next morning to Krause, the bosun, standing over his bed, screaming at him to get up. He scrambled out of bed and headed for the deck, Krause shouting orders at him as he went.

The events of the previous night came rushing back to him, making him pause. He looked around for Johan and Wolfgang. He saw Johan in the crow's nest, fumbling with some rigging, the navy blue and white Hapag flag snapping above his head in the brisk breeze blowing off shore. Wolfgang was nowhere in sight. Reinhold hoped that he was somewhere on the ship and hadn't jumped. He was relieved when he spotted him on the forward cargo winch with Fuhrmann. Neither of his co-conspirators looked very happy. And neither did the First Mate. He was glaring at Reinhold from the bridge wing.

At lunch, Johan and Wolfgang told Reinhold they had overslept too. It explained why Krause had been so fuming mad by the time he got to Reinhold to wake up.

"You slept right through him screaming at me, Scholz." Johan grinned at his bunkmate. "Krause had to make a special trip to get you up. He was on the verge of getting out the fire hose. It's a good thing you got up when you did."

Reinhold shrugged. "I doubt it would have reached."

They were all hung over something horrible. His head was pounding and he couldn't get enough water. His stomach was sour and empty. He missed breakfast, but he was planning on making up for it at lunch and shoveled potatoes and sausages on to his plate before voicing his concerns about the night before.

"I don't think we should jump here and go work for Hans at his copper mine," Reinhold told them.

Johan looked a bit surprised but nodded his agreement. "I don't think it is a good idea either."

Wolfgang nodded, his mouth full of food.

"We would be completely at his mercy," Reinhold continued. The thought made him shudder. "We wouldn't have any ID or passports or anything."

"And the German embassy doesn't help wayward sailors," Johan added.

"They don't?" Wolfgang asked.

"No, they don't." Reinhold looked grim when he said it. "They don't care. We wouldn't even be able to prove that we are German. For all the embassy knows, we could be Polish or Austrian."

The sailors agreed to stay on the *Leipzig* and wait for Australia. The ship sailed out of Antofagasta with the evening tide. Reinhold watched the mountains fade into the horizon while sipping a cold beer on the aft castle. Below him, the churning of the propeller was sending out white water and a wide wake. Above him, a magnificent sunset was sending out streaks of peach, orange, pink, red, and purple.

Chapter 85: Valparaiso

The *Leipzig* visited several other ports that escaped Reinhold's memory. They didn't spend more than ten hours in any one of them. They sailed back and forth along the coast of Peru and Northern Chile, dropping off and picking up small loads of local cargo. There were days when the *Leipzig* stopped in three or four ports. They were always tiny, mostly consisting of a couple of pylons, a warehouse or two, and a train. The grind was such that most nights, Reinhold fell into his bunk after dinner and passed out with his work clothes and boots still on. This didn't make him very happy because the accumulated sweat on his clothes started making his bunk smell and there was little time for laundry.

One night he awoke in the middle of the night and was disgusted by his own filth. He stripped naked, gathered up all of his clothes and bedding, tied it into a ball and headed for the propeller. He threw his bundle overboard, waiting for a few minutes in the dim illumination of the ship's lights before hauling the bundle back up and returning to his bunk. The next morning, the clothes were still damp, but at least they smelled better, for the moment.

Once, the ship sailed passed Valparaiso without stopping at the city, much to the sailor's disappointment. They went to a small port in the greenest place Reinhold had seen since leaving Ecuador. The terrain, however, wasn't any different.

The Andes are a long mountain chain, Reinhold thought to himself. *They stretch through a variety of climates. Look at how green they are now! And how brown they were north of here.*

"They call this the Lake District," Otto told him. "Lots of livestock here. I bet you that is what we are picking up."

"Animals?" Reinhold questioned. How would they load animals here? There is no equipment."

"It makes no difference to this ship," Johan said one day. "They built it specifically to go to these ports, with its own equipment. We can load and unload anywhere."

"But animals?" Reinhold scratched his chin with a gloved hand. He had been working on the water transfer pipes when he heard the "Land ho!" shout. "What kind of animals? Big ones? Like cows? Or horses?"

"They have cattle here, big ones," Otto responded. "They also have smaller livestock, like sheep. And then there are the llamas."

"Llamas?"

"Yup, we haven't seen any on this trip yet but they are the native pack animal of the Andes. The Incas used to use them to transport goods."

"I am beginning to think you make this crap up, Otto," Reinhold joked. "Especially the stuff about the Incas."

"I can't help it if I've learned a lot." Otto shrugged. "This is my third trip here."

"So then tell me, smart guy, is this what the rest of the trip is going to be like?" Reinhold asked. "Tramping around from country port to country port?"

"No," Otto responded. "We'll get to Valparaiso in a couple of days. You'll like that city, Scholz. Lots of pretty girls."

It wasn't animals the *Leipzig* loaded in the small port under the green mountains. Instead, they took on a load of cowhides. They were unprocessed, rough cowhides. They were stiff with dried fluids and packed in salt. They smelled so bad that Reinhold swore he could smell them in his bunk, in his sleep, in his dreams. They were going to Valparaiso, which made the crew happy. It meant that the city was the next stop.

The *Leipzig* arrived in Valparaiso on a clear, beautiful night in early March, 1956. They dropped anchor in the harbor to await clearance for docking, which everyone knew wasn't going to happen before morning. Reinhold stood at the rail with a beer and a cigarette and gazed at the urban vision before him.

The lights from the city were dazzling after so much dark coastline, so many small, almost lifeless ports. The city was nestled in a sheltered cove not far from the modern port. It was nice to be greeted by cranes, booms, freight trucks, herds of swearing and yelling longshoremen, and the sounds of grinding metal. The ship was scheduled to be here only a few days, long enough to unload the cargo they collected in their travels and to load the cargo going north or to Europe.

In the morning, they were called for docking and a tugboat came out to meet them with a harbor pilot. As they approached the shore, Reinhold noted that here too was a military presence. It seemed to be heavier with a pair of soldiers stationed every dozen or so yards.

He, again, wondered why this was the case. He shrugged it off when he saw the shore man motioning for him to throw the spring line.

"Scholz, we're going ashore later. You want to come?" Johan called from the fore deck once the ship was secured.

"Hell yes!"

Reinhold left the ship later that evening with Johan, Otto, Wolfgang, and Gottfried. They strutted through the port in their suits as if they owned the joint. The *Leipzig*, for some reason, was causing a bit of a stir in Valparaiso. All day, as they worked, the crew would feel someone staring at them only to look up and see a group of Chileans pointing at the ship and talking rapidly. The bosun guessed that it was because the ship was less than two years old. It was launched in June, 1954, making it one of the newest ships on the seas. Ignore them, was Krause's advice. But the sailors couldn't help it, it made them feel like rock stars to have their ship be the focus of so much attention.

They skipped the local dive portside bars and went to the nicer ones inland. Reinhold was surprised, and bit shaken, by the presence of uniformed soldiers in the bars. They stood in corners with machine guns at the ready to shoot someone for what Reinhold couldn't even imagine. He sipped his red wine, which was good, better than in Peru, and observed the soldiers for a few minutes. His attention was soon diverted by the presence of lovely ladies with long, black hair, dark, smoky eyes, and curvaceous bodies, who gathered around Reinhold, gazing at his blonde hair and looking into his blue eyes.

"I think they like you, Scholz," Johan teased. He also had a few interested lovelies. His hair wasn't as blonde as Reinhold's and his eyes weren't as blue but he was still very fair by South American standards.

Reinhold grinned in return, enjoying every minute of the attention, taking liberties with breasts and buttocks when he felt he could get away with it.

The sailors hopped around for a bit, each of them leaving packs of cigarettes behind as payment for drinks and food. In every bar, the girls flocked to them, talking seductively in Spanish. Otto and Wolfgang translated some but they too preoccupied with girls of their own. The men in these establishments, Reinhold noted, were not pleased with the situation but made no moves to stop the girls. The bartenders, Otto told them, were the ones to talk to about arranging private time with the ladies.

"So do that then," Reinhold told him.

No freebies here, then, like in Peru, he thought. *Back to paying for it.*

They were in their fifth bar of the night and time was getting short for them to take the fun to the next level. Reinhold noticed that there were less and less ladies in the bars. Otto had a brief conversation with the unassuming looking guy behind the bar before popping open the briefcase of cigarettes they were carrying with them. The bartender looked please. He took four cartons of cigarettes and left the bar, returning a few minutes later.

"This guy tells me that we are all set. We have rooms upstairs, there are girls waiting, and there is white and red wine also."

"*Vino blanco* and *vino tinto*," Reinhold muttered to himself. "Are the girls pretty?"

"Yes," Otto said, "He says he sent his best up."

"Then let's go!"

The Reinhold on the deck of the *Brandenburg* in the Caribbean Sea smiled at the thought of that night.

What a night! He thought. *South American girls are so accommodating. With the exception of the Danish girls, they are the best.*

The sailors ascended the stairs to the upper level of the bar. He hadn't noticed when they arrived, but the building was set up like the ones in Spain and Portugal with an open floor plan downstairs and an open courtyard overlooked by a balcony on the second floor and a red tiled roof. Situated around this balcony were eight or ten rooms. The bartender gave them all slips of paper with a room number. Reinhold had room number 5. He stopped in front of his door, suddenly hesitant to go in but the many glasses of wine he had drank and his desire to see and feel naked female flesh overcame his hesitation. He swung open the door.

To his surprise, there was not one, but two girls, lounging on the bed. They were indeed beauties, classic South American lovelies. To cover his surprise, he walked into the room and shut the door, locking it. He walked to the stand near the window next to the bed and poured himself a glass of wine. He downed half of it before turning his attention to the girls. He wasn't sure what to do.

Looking back, Reinhold smiled to himself.

I didn't do anything, he thought. *They did it all for me. They undressed me and laid me in bed. They kissed me and touched me and muttered exotic sounding words into me ear. I didn't know what to do with myself! Everywhere I looked, there was a girl, a voluptuous, naked girl with her hand in my hair and her mouth on my ear, my lips, my face, my chest, my stiff soldier.*

His favorite part, however, was watching the girls enjoy each other. This was a completely new experience for him. Never, in all his travels, did he even think it was possible for two girls to want to go to bed together and enjoy it as much as these two girls were enjoying it. He could have watched it all night, and he almost did, but that wouldn't have satisfied his cravings. He stopped their show by joining them in the touching and kissing.

He awoke the next morning, once again, to Otto yelling at him.

"Get up, Scholz!" he yelled. "We're late!"

Reinhold vaulted out of bed and started throwing on clothes. The girls were gone as was the magic of last night. He found himself in an ordinary looking room with half empty bottles of wine and a rumpled bed. The window looked out on the brick wall of the building next door.

"Did you get two girls?" he asked Otto with a dry, scratchy tongue as he pulled on his wingtips.

"Yes," Otto grinned at him. "We all got two girls. And two bottles of wine." He glanced at Reinhold's bottles. "You didn't drink yours."

"I had better things to do."

The bosun met them at the top of the gangplank. He was fuming mad. They were an hour late to work. They didn't bother trying to explain themselves. Reinhold, as punishment, was demoted for a week and made to stand watch every night after his regular work was done for the day. He was also charged with mixing all of the paint they would need for upcoming maintenance. He groaned. It wasn't the hardest job, put it was a messy pain in the ass. He was going to have paint stained hands until they got back to Germany.

"And, you'll be disappointed to know," the bosun informed them, "that we are leaving here tonight. The Captain picked up a time sensitive cargo. It will begin loading shortly."

As he spoke, the bosun gestured toward the shore. The sailors followed his gesture to a pen of cows.

"We're loading cows?" Wolfgang asked.

Without warning, the bosun drew back and smacked him across the face.

"Don't question me, *Leichtmatrose!*" Krause turned on his heel and stalked off.

"I didn't mean any disrespect," Wolfgang said defensively. "I am just surprised to see cows here, in such a port."

The rest of the group shrugged it off, went to their bunks to change out of their suits, and went to work. Reinhold couldn't help watching the loading of the cows. The animals were lifted, one by one, on to the deck of the ship where they would stay for the duration of the trip to Callao. The noise they made was incredible. The whole port seemed to be full of their bellowing.

Sometime after mid-day, the *Leipzig* shoved off from Valparaiso and headed north. Reinhold watched the port melt away into the horizon with only a tinge of sorrow. He would be back, he knew, with his next trip on the ship.

I am staying on this ship until they throw me off, he thought, *or until I get to Australia. Hopefully, that will be the next trip. Hopefully, we stop here again first.*

Chapter 86: Asleep At The Helm

Sailing with cows turned out to be one of the most disgusting things the crew had ever seen. Reinhold didn't know it before hand, but he found out all too soon, that cows get seasick. The long, rolling waves of the Pacific caused them to vomit all over the deck and they shit constantly. They made horrible, loud, strangled bellowing noises and swung their horns wildly. The smell was like nothing else on Earth. It permeated the whole ship in the same way that the hides had just a few days before. The cowboys in charge of them seemed not to notice anything, the smell or the danger of the swinging horns. They silently and placidly hosed the mess from the deck with the ship's fire hose while the animals shifted and pushed around them. The cowboy's horses weathered the trip much better, needing only to be calmed from time to time.

When the ship arrived in Callao, the cows were unloaded the same way they were loaded, with a huge sling placed under their bellies. The longshoreman in charge of the crane wasn't as experienced or maybe just not as gentle as the one in Valparaiso. The transition was jerky and the landings were rough on the cows. Several of the animals vomited again during the unloading while several others broke their legs upon landing on the pier. Reinhold felt bad for the animals as they lay on the ground, bellowing in pain and anger.

When the first one went down, he wondered how they would handle the situation. He got his answer in the form of a cowboy in leather chaps and a pistol. The man walked to the cow, put his gun to its forehead and pulled the trigger so fast that several of the watching sailors gasped in surprise. After being put out of its suffering, the cow was roped around the horns and dragged away by another cowboy on horseback.

The other cows became agitated by the smell of blood and the sound of the gunshot. They tried to stampede on deck and got nowhere. Reinhold's pity for the animals deepened as cow after cow was put down.

This should have been handled differently. Someone should get that guy off the crane, he thought before leaving the deck and the cows and heading to his bunk to wash up.

There was not a long stay planned for the ship and sailors in Callao this trip. Once the cows were gone and deck hosed down, the rest of the cargo was unloaded quickly and reloaded just as quickly, taking just two days to complete. When Reinhold asked what the rush was, Otto said it was because the ship had to be ready to accept a load of silver in the morning and sail immediately afterward.

"A ship can't sit around a South American port with a load of silver in its belly," Otto explained. "That's just asking for trouble. You would quickly find out why there are so many soldiers around here."

"What about the vault?" Reinhold asked.

"They would just kill us all and steal the ship," Johan answered.

"That makes sense," Reinhold thought out loud. "Why bother unloading it if it is already stowed, safe and sound, for you?"

"That's the idea, Scholz," Otto laughed. "You'd make a good criminal."

"No, its just common sense." Reinhold said. "So, wait, that means that this is our last night in South America?"

"For now, yes, but we'll be back."

Reinhold had a moment of misgiving. He knew that life didn't always land you where you wanted to be. This trip, for instance. He was supposed to be going to Australia. Now, he was headed back to Germany.

"I have heard you guys say that the gold here is excellent quality and cheaper than anywhere else," Reinhold said to Johan and Otto. "I think I want to go buy a new watch."

As soon as work was done for the day, the sailors took off to the shopping district. They looked around the shops at all the beautifully crafted gold jewelry. Reinhold didn't see a watch he wanted but he spotted a bracelet that he couldn't let go. It was solid gold but delicate and beautifully crafted out of tiny representations of llamas all linked together. He decided almost immediately to purchase it.

"What are you going to do with that?" Otto asked him as the shop owner wrapped the bracelet.

"I am going to give it to my wife on our wedding day," Reinhold responded. The tone of his voice challenged any of the sailors present to question his sentiment.

"Always the lover boy," Johan said gently with the trace of a smile. "It is for your Australian bride?"

"That's right."

"You know what would be good to take back to Germany?" Johan asked.

"What?"

"Champagne. It is just as good as the French stuff and more than half the price. We could start a trend in Germany. Give people a taste for South American champagne and then import it for them."

"That's an excellent idea," Otto said. "I saw a shop not far from here that sells cases of the stuff."

The sailors picked up a case of wine each before heading back to the ship. They stowed their wares and headed back out to have one last night of fun in Callao. Johan slipped off with one of the Incan girls at some point, violating the buddy system rules. In retaliation for his stupidity, Reinhold and Otto put sauerkraut in his bunk. He came back to the ship so drunk he didn't even notice. Reinhold and Otto were so drunk when they did it that they forgot about it.

All three overslept in the morning and, again, incurred the wrath of the bosun. Krause was particularly angry because of the impending silver delivery. More than once in the few minutes he devoted to screaming at them he called them unreliable and untrustworthy, which, of course, made them bad sailors. He didn't dole out punishment, but he warned them that the First Mate would hear of their truant behavior. Reinhold, Otto, and Johan considered themselves lucky to have avoided punishment.

All hands were called to deck for the silver delivery. It was the sailors' job to stand around the deck and make sure no one stuck over the side. They watched as an old black locomotive pulling a few freight cars arrived in the port and made its way to the pier where the *Leipzig* waited. It was crawling, positively crawling, with soldiers armed to the teeth. There were at least two dozen of them. They brandished machine guns in their hands but carried handguns, knives, and grenades. On top of the first freight car was a machine gun turret. Reinhold hadn't seen anything like it since the war in Germany. It made him vastly unhappy.

The Captain appeared from the bridge, the train came to a stop, and the soldiers climbed down. They lined themselves along the path the silver would take off the train, up the gangplank, and to the fortified vault hold at the front of the ship. Reinhold watched from the fore deck as the old man entered the combination and swung open the small hatch. The longshoremen hauled the boxes from the train in pairs as the Captain of the squad of soldiers paced the length of the shoreward side of the ship, his eyes alternating between scanning the activity on shore and the activity on the sea.

No ships docked near the *Leipzig* for the duration of the loading. No one was allowed to leave his post. They all stood there, the sun blazing down on them. There was no stopping for lunch. The longshoremen were given water and a bread product that Reinhold didn't recognize but they were not allowed to leave the ring of soldiers.

Reinhold's mind wandered. Looking down at himself, he realized how tan he was. He had been working shirt less for months and was as brown as when he was in the Middle East. Looking around, he noted that most of the guys were tanned, even Olsen, the Scandinavian guy.

He wondered if Australia would be like here. Everyone said the place was a desert inland and a bit tropical along the coast. Isn't that what Chile is? Not so tropical, maybe, but less desert-like then other places he had seen.

For hours, the crew of the *Leipzig* and the soldiers stood there. It was late afternoon when the Captain locked the hatch and the First Mate told the crew to prepare for cast off. An hour later, they were underway, leaving Callao behind and headed for the Panama Canal.

"We don't have a single stop between here and Rotterdam," Reinhold heard someone say at the table next to his at dinner.

"Is that true?" he asked Otto, who always seemed to know everything.

Otto shrugged. "Probably. Word spreads quickly about a ship carrying silver."

"Still thinking about Australia?" Johan asked him.

Reinhold nodded. "I'll get there next time."

He glanced at his watch. He had only a few hours before it was his turn to stand Quartermaster. Leaving the mess hall, he headed to his bunk to see if he could get some sleep beforehand.

Sleep didn't come. Reinhold laid in his bunk and stared at the grey metal ceiling. At 11:45, he got up, went to the galley, got a cup of coffee, and headed for the bridge. He relieved Furhmann, who looked as tired as Reinhold felt. After checking the course coordinates and making some adjustments, Reinhold got out a book about repairing ship engines and settled down for a night monitoring the ship's course. With the new technology, there was actually very little for him to do.

He awoke with a start, a bit of drool on his cheek and on the instrument panel beneath his face. His head whipped up, adrenaline flooding his system.

Oh shit, was all he could think. *Where are we?*

Glancing at the map, he saw the ship was at almost the same coordinates as when he last looked.

How is that possible? How long was I asleep? He looked at his watch. It was almost 3am. *I was asleep for almost two hours! Why aren't we further away from when I came on?*

Checking the equipment again, Reinhold noticed that the course was set to draw the ship to the right. As they sailed now, the ship was pulling around, headed towards land to the east. He could only figure that, in his sleep, he had hit the right hand button and altered the ship's course by a few degrees.

Is it possible that we did a complete circle, that we are just coming out of it, and going back into? The course is set that way. That must be what happened. We have gotten nowhere in two hours! We are going in circles!

This was all starting to make sense in his head when the bridge door flew open and Beck came falling into the bridge.

"What the hell is going on?" He demanded. "Why are we pulling to the right? Where are you going?"

Reinhold stared at the man for a second, taking in the situation. Obviously, Beck didn't notice that they were headed into their second pull to the right, their second circling around the Pacific Ocean.

"It's alright, Beck, we are just a bit off course." Reinhold tried to comfort the upset man.

"What do you mean we are off course?" He demanded. "Aren't you paying attention?" Beck examined Reinhold's face and must've noticed the sleep still apparent there. "You fell asleep! How long have we been going to circles? We could have beached or hit another ship! We're in a shipping lane!"

Reinhold felt his anger rise quickly.

Who does this guy think he is, the bosun? The First? Captain, perhaps?

"This isn't the first circle we would be making, *arschloch*!" he screamed at Beck. "I am not the only one who fell asleep, am I? How long were you out for? What do you think the Captain will think of both men sleeping on duty?"

"It doesn't matter what the Captain thinks about me! I didn't fall asleep" Beck responded. "I am going to tell him that he can't trust his *Matrose* to keep the ship on course!"

Reinhold couldn't control himself. He ran at Beck, knocking him to the ground and keeping him there by throwing himself on top and grabbing him around the neck.

"You aren't going to say anything about this to anyone," Reinhold growled. "It would be bad for both of us, you fool."

"Let go," Beck protested feebly.

Reinhold tightened his grip on the man's throat, giving him a good shake to get his attention.

"No, not until you agree that neither one of us is going to say a word to anybody about this."

Beck's eyes were bulging slightly out of his face and Reinhold relaxed his grip, but gave him another shake.

"Agree!" he demanded.

Beck nodded, his voice a raspy shadow of its real self. "Ok, Ok, I agree, you crazy *arschloch*. Now let go!"

Reinhold let go of Beck's throat and got to his feet. He stared at the man on the floor as he straightened his clothes.

"We could have had a good laugh about this, you know, if you weren't such a woman."

"What are you talking about? Laugh about what?" Beck was still on the ground, rubbing his neck.

"We both fell asleep! To most people that would be funny."

"I'm not one of your friends, Scholz. I am sure Johan and Otto and Wolfgang or Gottfried would find this hilarious but I don't. We could have beached or hit another ship because you weren't keeping us on course."

"Yup, we would have because you weren't awake to warn me that something was in our path." Reinhold suppressed the urge to kick the man in the face. "Now, get off my bridge and back to your post, watchman."

When Reinhold was relieved of his post at 4am, he didn't mention the detour. He waited for someone, the First Mate or the

Second Mate, to ask him why the ship wasn't in the right place but no one seemed to notice.

Thankfully, it was only a couple of hours, Reinhold thought to himself.

He didn't want to know what would have happened if someone in command found out he fell asleep at the helm.

Chapter 87: Punishment

The *Leipzig* arrived at the port of Balboa as the sun was descending and dropped anchor. They waited ten hours for their call to sail. Once the pilot and his crew were on board, the *Leipzig's* sailors relaxed, prepared to spend the next eight to ten hours with nothing to do. Reinhold did the math and realized that the trip through the canal was going to be a day off for him. He got a stool and a book, stripped down to his short pants, and sat on the deck, his back to the bulkhead, to read.

"What are you doing, Scholz?" Johan asked when he spotted Reinhold on his stool.

"Relaxing. What does it look like?"

"It looks boring."

"To you, I am sure it looks boring, but I am enjoying the beautiful day and a good book."

"Books are for nerds," Wolfgang joked, joining his friends.

"Smile!"

The three sailors turned in time to see Otto snap a picture of them.

"I say we try that champagne we bought in Callao." Otto said, leaning against the rail with his camera.

"Now that sounds like an idea. None of us has to work until tomorrow."

"I thought we were planning on selling that in Hamburg," Johan questioned.

"One bottle isn't going to hurt," Otto replied. "Think of it as a toast to South American women. Then we can get into the beer."

We finished the whole case, Reinhold thought to himself. *The whole case. We each drank three bottles, roughly. Gottfried showed up when he got done working, but he couldn't have had any more than a bottle himself. Then we got into the beer.*

He didn't remember a whole lot about the trip through the canal. He seemed to recollect a contest to see who could hit the shore from the ship with an empty bottle. It wasn't hard. The shore was only a few yards away. That turned into who could throw it the furthest. Reinhold won that contest but it was only by a few inches. He also remembered visiting the steward to order another case of beer. They drank their way through the canal and out into the Caribbean Sea. It was strange to think about from his current position on the *Brandenburg*, somewhere off the coast of the Dominican Republic headed south to the Dutch islands of Aruba and Curacao.

The First Mate woke Reinhold and Johan the next morning. They were late again and the First Mate was angrier than Reinhold had ever seen him but, oddly, the man said very little. He had sailors drag them out of their bunks and into the bathroom where they were unceremoniously thrown into the tiny shower and doused with cold water. This method of waking didn't help the champagne hangover. Reinhold's brain was throbbing through the side of his skull and his stomach was doing flip-flops. As punishment, they were put on cleaning duty and assigned a week's watches.

And it was the 8pm-12am watch, too, Reinhold thought. *The worst watch. We didn't get much sleep that week.*

The rest of the trip back to Europe was uneventful. The temperature dropped steadily as they traveled north. They hit a good storm crossing the Atlantic that sent thirty-foot waves across the deck and dislodged a section of piping aft of the wheelhouse. The rest of the trip was devoted to getting the piping back in order. It wasn't until two days after the storm that Reinhold realized it had hit on his twenty first birthday. He didn't mention it to anyone. What was the point? What were they going to do on the ship to celebrate? Have the baker make him a cake? Big deal.

When the *Leipzig* sailed through the English Channel, Reinhold resigned himself to being back in Europe.

Not for long, he remembered telling himself. *The next trip with the* Leipzig *is the last one. As soon as this ship docks in Australia, I am gone.*

The very air seemed more oppressive than anywhere else he had been in the last six months. The lighthouses were reminders that there was no where you could go in Europe without someone already having been there. He felt like he was being watched.

The ship dropped anchor in Rotterdam twenty-two days after leaving Callao. Four hours later, they got the call to dock. They opened the hatches and the cargo they picked up somewhere in South America was unloaded. Otto, Johan, Wolfgang, Gottfried, and Reinhold went ashore as soon as they were dismissed. They went to the local seaman's club and drank their fill of European beer and schnapps before picking a fight with sailors from a Greek ship. It was as if they had never left. They picked up right where they left off cleaning out the bars and establishing the *Leipzig* as a ship not to be toyed with.

The next stop was Bremenhaven where Reinhold was surprised to see Kristal standing on the pier when they docked. She looked beautiful. The guys called to her, trying to entice her to look their way, but she had eyes only for Reinhold. She waited patiently while the ship moored and Reinhold could call down to her.

"What are you doing here?"

"Waiting for you. Hapaq said you were due in today."

"You talked to Hapaq?"

Kristal laughed. "Of course. I called from my office a couple of days ago. I told them I am your wife."

The deck erupted in a chorus of 'ohhhsss'. Reinhold tried to shoo the guys away without success. He gave up and descended the gangway to have a private conversation. Kristal wrapped her arms around his neck and pulled him close, not caring about the day's grime on his clothes, and kissed him long and slow.

I wish she wasn't married, Reinhold thought to himself, running his hands down her sides to cup her firm, shapely bottom. *I wish she didn't live in Europe.*

He briefly entertained the thought of sneaking her onboard the *Leipzig* the next time she left port. They spent a fabulous night together, reacquainting themselves with each other's landscapes.

"You are so tan, Reinhold," Kristal observed, running a finger across his chest, pulling on the hair she found there.

"It is summer in South America. It was hot. I spent most of my time onboard without a shirt, sweating in the sun."

"I like it," she purred.

She tried to convince him again that it was ok for them to use her bed, but Reinhold, once again, refused. He was more comfortable now than ever with their adulterous relationship, but there were lines, intimate lines, he would never cross. Instead, they made love on the kitchen table and then the living room floor ending finally in the shower. He said goodbye to her that night knowing that the *Leipzig* was leaving in the morning for Hamburg.

"I'll see you next time," he said, kissing her neck.

"I'll be waiting," she whispered.

He knew that she would be and felt a tinge of guilt. It passed quickly. She was married after all.

In Hamburg, the *Leipzig* docked in the main port, near a large concrete building with few windows and conspicuous, but unarmed, security. Reinhold watched the Captain open the vault. It was the end of the line for the South American silver. There were no armed guards here or machine gun turrets, just a ship unloading cargo surrounded by other ships unloading cargo. They were secure in their ability to blend in to the crowd in Hamburg, the second biggest port in the world. The building, on the other hand, was probably a fortress. Reinhold, standing on the fore deck, was gazing at its imposing profile, thinking it must be one they built for the war, when the bosun called him.

"Scholz, report to the First Mate," he called from mid deck.

The order surprised him and he moved quickly to obey it. His surprise turned to suspicion when he entered the First Mate's salon and found Johan, Otto, Wolfgang, and Gottfried already there, standing stiffly in a line. The First Mate was seated at a large wooden desk, writing something on a form.

"Ah, Scholz, you're here," the First Mate began. "Now we can begin."

He surveyed the men in front of him before continuing.

"I have been sailing for nineteen years. Never in that time have I seen a group so opposed to following rules." He got up and began pacing the floor in front of the sailors. "In the course of our journeys, you have blemished the name Hapaq and the *Leipzig* by engaging in bar fights here in at least three European ports. At least you were smart enough not to do that in South America. I am sure you realized quickly that they would just shoot you there. You have been insolent, tardy, and sloppy due to excessive drinking. More than one of you brought a sexually transmitted disease onboard. This behavior cannot be tolerated on this ship. You are being transferred immediately to other Hapaq ships, ships that are traveling places were you can't cause the trouble you have caused in the last six months. It is a shame because you are not bad sailors. You just have no self-control."

Reinhold remembered feeling like someone had punched him in the stomach. It hurt him and made him angry at the same time. The First Mate handed them their seaman's books.

"Your new orders are in your books. Good luck. Now, get out of my salon."

Reinhold could only hope that his orders were for a ship headed to Australia. They filed out of his room in silence. The rustling of paper was the only sound that followed them. No one spoke until they were on the aft deck out of sight of the bridge.

"Who does that guy think he is?" Otto roared. "He can't just send us away!"

"He's the First Mate, Otto, he can do whatever he wants to us. Do you think the Captain is going to stop him?" Johan said. He turned to Reinhold. "What ship are you on?"

"The *Göttingen*," Reinhold answered quietly. "I have to report there tomorrow morning."

"I am on the ship, too," Johan said, looking slightly relieved. "Also reporting tomorrow morning."

"I am on the *Göttingen* also," Otto said. "At least we'll be together. What about you, Wolfgang?"

Wolfgang looked crest fallen. "I am on the *Augsburg*."

"*Augsburg*?" Otto questioned. "Doesn't that one go to Asia?"

Wolfgang shrugged. "Doesn't matter. The First said it was going to be somewhere boring, right? What about you, Gottfried?"

"I am on the *Augsburg*," Gottfried responded.

"You guys might have lucked out on this one." Otto said. "If the *Augsburg* is going to Asia, you are going to have a great time, from what I have heard."

"You might even make it to Australia," Reinhold pointed out. Wolfgang smiled faintly.

Otto rolled his eyes. "You'll get to Australia, Scholz. You just have to get through this punishment and request a ship going that way. Why are you in such a rush?"

"*Arschlocher!*" Johan exclaimed. "Punishment! They're sending us to North America!"

"No," Otto whispered. "I refuse to believe that."

"Something isn't right about this," Reinhold said, mostly to himself.

"What do you mean?"

"Why aren't they breaking us up entirely? Hapag has dozens of ships. They could send us all to different vessels, right? Why are they dividing us up between two?"

The other sailors thought about this for a minute. No one had an answer but every one admitted it was a good question. The more Reinhold rolled it around in his mind, the more it didn't make sense. Bar fights? Sailors fight in bars all the time. Johan and Otto admitted that they got the idea to build the reputation of the *Leipzig* because other ships they were on had done the same thing. Reinhold had personally witnessed hundreds of fights in seaman's clubs. Excessive drinking? They had to be joking! There were songs about drunken sailors in every language. Sexually transmitted diseases? Ridiculous! Not even worth thinking about. So what was going on? What did his group get kicked off the *Leipzig*.

Looking back at the situation, examining it from afar, Reinhold knew that someone ratted on him and the others. Someone went to the mate and told him they were planning on jumping ship in Australia. He was sure of it. He was also sure it was Beck, that bitch. The thought sent a rage through him. Nothing would have made Reinhold happier at the moment than knocking Beck unconscious and throwing him to sharks. If he ever saw the guy again, he would try to do just that.

The guys went out that night to the Reeperbahn to celebrate their time together. Reinhold had it in his head to recreate the experience of having two girls, but couldn't find two girls that were interested.

"South American girls are just more giving, Reinhold," Johan laughed. They drank a toast to South American girls.

He ended up with a nice, sufficiently pretty blonde with ample assets. For the first time in a long time, he asked to see her medical book. It was paranoia. He didn't ever want to have the clap again.

They spent the night at Wolfgang's sister's apartment in Altoona. Her name was Ursula and she took a liking to Reinhold as soon as she laid eyes on him. He didn't feel the same. In fact, he didn't feel much besides a pounding head and a rumbling stomach. The five sailors parted ways at the port, two headed for a ship named

Augsburg, three headed for a ship named *Göttingen*. It was April 3, 1956.

Chapter 88: New York City

Göttingen
Photograph courtesy of 7seasvessels.com

The *Göttingen* was a new ship, like the *Leipzig*, and it was huge, like the *Leipzig*, weighing in at more than sixty five hundred tons. Johan, Otto, and Reinhold ascended the gangplank and headed for the bridge to find the Captain. Reinhold noticed immediately that the *Göttingen* was almost an exact replica of the *Leipzig*. He wondered if they came from the same shipyard.

The Captain was ashore. They were received by the First Mate, a guy named Rossdam. He was about Reinhold's height and equally as blonde haired and blue eyed. They could have been related.

"The *Leipzig*?" He questioned the new arrivals. "That explains the tans."

He checked them in quickly and told them their bunks were on the second level of the bridge castle, the same place they had been on the *Leipzig*. Johan and Reinhold bunked together again, while Otto was paired with a surly, sour faced old timer named Martens. He was also the guy charged with showing the new sailors around but a tour seemed unnecessary. Everything was in the same spot as the *Leipzig*. Instead, they hung out in Otto's new bunk and drank a couple of beers. They weren't shoving off until the following day.

"What did you do to land yourself here?" Martens asked.

Otto, Johan, and Reinhold all looked at each other, no one quite sure how to answer.

"We had a bit too much fun for the old man on the *Leipzig*," Otto replied.

"I had the same problem with a different ship," Martens winked as he spoke. "Several years ago, Hapaq decided it was best for me to sail to North America and I agree. It keeps me out of trouble. I've been with this ship for about two years now and before I sailed with two others that tramped around Canada mostly."

"Is North America really as bad as we have heard?" Reinhold asked.

"I don't think so. Canada is a great country, especially Quebec and Montreal. We aren't going to Canada this trip. We are doing the east coast of America. I can tell you that it is expensive, especially New York City, and there are no women that are going to want to have anything to do with you. They all put their noses in the air when they see you coming and prostitution isn't legal. They also don't like what I call 'bad behavior' like public drunkenness and talking too loud. I would say that it is more conservative."

When the *Göttingen* left Hamburg the next day, Reinhold resolved to have as much fun as possible before facing the long boring of the United States. Their first stop was Bremen. As they docked, Reinhold was hoping that Kristal would be standing on the pier, waiting, but she wasn't.

The husband must be home, Reinhold thought to himself.

It was a quick stop and they were underway with the next tide.

"The old man keeps a tight schedule," Martens informed Reinhold as they shoved off, headed for Amsterdam.

It wasn't until they got to Rotterdam that Reinhold left the ship. He and Johan had some fun, but behaved themselves, for the most part, and headed back to the ship on the earlier side. They left for North America the next day.

Sixteen days after leaving Rotterdam, the *Göttingen* got her first glimpse of land. It was flat and featureless, protected from the ocean by a set of barrier islands.

"They call it Long Island," Martens told Reinhold. "Just another day and we'll dock in Brooklyn."

"Are we going to see the Statue of Liberty?" Johan asked, his eyes shiny with the possibility.

"Of course," snorted Martens. "You can't sail into New York without seeing that lady."

In the end, they didn't get as good a look as Reinhold wanted of the famous statue. He wanted to sail right past so he could gaze upwards and really look at the wonder he had heard welcomes all the immigrants to America. The *Göttingen* skirted around the end of Long Island with all of its wetlands and an airport, through a narrow stretch of water into New York Bay. They stayed to the right and followed the coastline of Brooklyn to dock at a place called Gowanus Bay. They were more than two miles from the island where the statue stood. The Port of New York covered more area than he thought it would. Looking through binoculars from the stern of the ship, Reinhold picked the emblem out from the buildings behind it.

"We'll see it better without the looking glass when we go up the Hudson River," Martens said when Reinhold noted the distance. "We'll go right past it."

"We're going out tonight Reinhold. Are you coming?" Johan asked. "Otto says there is a seaman's club on 42nd Street, over there somewhere." He pointed west toward a cluster of skyscrapers.

"I'll go," Reinhold shrugged.

The things he heard about America dampened his normally enthusiastic agreement to go ashore. But, it was New York City, a shining example of prosperity and industry. How could he not go see the place?

The guys got cleaned up. Since they were just going over to the seaman's club and maybe to a German restaurant Otto knew about, they skipped the suits and opted for sailor's clothes. They left the ship, picking their way across train tracks and around freight trucks to the port entrance. The port was not well kept. There was garbage everywhere. Reinhold almost tripped over a guy laying by a building as he rounded the corner.

They nodded to the guard on duty at the gate as they left. He looked suspiciously at them. It was a brisk spring night. Reinhold had his hands buried in his pockets and his collar turned up against the breeze coming off the bay. Maybe that was bad in America. They were immediately approached by a guy in rags, his hand out. Recognizing him as a vagrant, they brushed past, ignoring his pleading.

"Where is this subway station, Otto?" Reinhold asked. "How far?"

"Martens said it was just ahead, on 4th Ave."

A man approached Reinhold from the left. He flashed something shiny and said something low and authoritative. Annoyed, Reinhold brushed the guy aside.

I thought New York was supposed to be classy, but here is some guy trying to sell me a watch, he thought.

The next instant he was face down on the ground, his left arm twisted around his back. His assaulter said something loud and very impatient.

"Johan, what is going on?" Reinhold asked, his lips brushing the asphalt.

"I think he is a police officer." Johan responded. "He wants to look at all your clothes."

The officer proceeded to do just that. He patted Reinhold down from his chest to his feet, gripping each ankle in turn to see there was anything in his socks. It wasn't until he got to Reinhold's jacket that he found anything. One by one, the officer pulled a pack of Lucky Strikes, a lighter, a flask, and a passport book out and threw them on the pavement. Once satisfied that he found everything, the officer let Reinhold go and scooped up the contents of his pockets.

"He is looking for drugs, Scholz," Johan said.

The officer had kept up a steady stream of questions that Johan haltingly answered in his mediocre English when he understood them.

"Drugs?" Reinhold asked, surprised. "Like what?"

Johan shrugged. "He didn't find any so who cares."

Reinhold examined the officer as the officer examined Reinhold things. He was dressed in plain clothes, dungarees and a wool jacket, much like the sailors, and a pair of work boots.

No wonder I mistook him for a just some guy selling crap!

Without speaking, he took back all of the things the officer confiscated, including the flask, which was surprising. Reinhold expected him to keep that.

"He says to have a good night and enjoy our stay here," Johan told him as the officer stalked off in search of new prey.

"Yes, it is very enjoyable," Reinhold said sarcastically. Looking down at the dirt speckling his clothes, he was glad they hadn't worn their suits. "What's going on here? Why are they looking for drugs on sailors?"

"That's not a good question," Otto said. "How much stuff have you smuggled while sailing?"

"A lot, but never drugs, everything else."

"He doesn't know that," Johan pointed out. "But it is weird that he targeted us when there is a Panamanian flag docked on the pier next to us. Everybody knows the Germans are drinkers!"

"You want to go back to the ship?" Otto asked Reinhold.

"No. Let's go." Reinhold answered, taking a big swig out of the flask.

They found the subway station, just a railing and a set of stairs going below the pavement with a sign announcing it was the BMT Line. The map on the wall of the filthy subterranean station was color coded and not hard to read. Otto quickly figured out the train, the yellow line, they needed to take to get to the seaman's club on 42nd St. They used the American money the steward gave them to purchase coins from a guy in a booth. The coins went into a turnstile. They stood on the platform with two dozen other people and waited for the train.

Reinhold looked around at the people waiting. They seemed like regular people. Some were dressed for jobs doing dirty things; some were dressed for business in suits. There was a group of school-aged teenagers, girls and two boys, huddled in one corner, chatting amongst themselves. Everyone was speaking English and, although he really didn't understand what they were saying, the language sounded familiar. It sounded a lot like German. Reinhold was about to say something to Otto, the group know-it-all, when a rumbling came rolling toward them. The train was approaching. They piled into a car with the other passengers and took off.

They rode for about fifteen minutes before Otto told them it was time to get off.

"We have to get on the blue train to Grand Central Station. We can walk to the club from there."

He led the way, Reinhold and Johan following behind. This station was bigger, more bustling, and more people were wearing suits. Their train arrived and they piled in with the crowd. A few minutes later they got off and emerged into a huge station with lots of different branches. It was a beautiful interior, all granite and marble with a blue ceiling. Reinhold could have sworn that it was painted to look like the stars but it was hard to say without stopping and examining it.

"This is Grand Central Station," Otto told them. "Lots of trains come in here. It's a hub like the U-Bahn has in Hamburg."

They left the station through a set of doors marked 42nd St. The noise hit Reinhold before anything else. It was a rush of honking horns, car and bus engines, and people. It took a minute for him to realize the noise was bouncing off the high rise buildings and compounding itself into a din that was inescapable. He had never experienced anything like it.

"All Americans have cars," Otto said flippantly. "They drive them everywhere, even into the city. Martens told me that. He noticed the same thing about America. The sound of cars is everywhere."

They headed down 42nd Street in the direction of the seaman's club. The architecture was stunning in its simplicity. There was little here of the ornate stone and woodwork he so loved in other cities. There were elaborate cornices and carved lintels, even panels of relief work but it didn't dominate the structure. Here, the quality of the workmanship stood as the ornamentation. If you relaxed your eye and scanned the edifice, it all came together to create a feeling of power. Combined with the amount of people on the streets and the pace at which they were moving, New York made an impact on Reinhold. He wasn't sure he liked it. It all seemed too big, too busy, too grey, and too loud.

When they arrived at a large, open plaza, the feeling abated somewhat. The space was open but it was far from pretty. It was mostly grey with lots of artificial color on billboards that were stories tall.

"They light up," Johan observed when Reinhold pointed out the billboards. "See, they are covered in light bulbs."

"This is Times Square," Otto said. "They say at night it is so bright here that it is almost daylight."

"Where is the seaman's club?" Reinhold asked after taking another swig from his flask.

"Around here somewhere," Otto replied.

They traversed Times Square and found the seaman's club on the other side. It was an unassuming building with dark windows. Inside, it was just a regular seaman's club like they had seen all over the world. It had a bar and tables. He could smell food so he knew they could eat here. There was also a front desk off to the left so he knew they had rooms for rent. It was a relief to know that this club was like all the others.

Reinhold quickly learned that the sailors who told him that North America was expensive were very right. Otto bought the first round. Three beers cost him three American Dollars.

"Three dollars!" exclaimed Reinhold. "You've got to be kidding! That's twelve *mark*!" He took a sip. "And it's not even that good!"

Otto shrugged. "It's a German beer, according to the name. It is a Budweiser. No big deal. It's New York City!"

Johan nodded his agreement. "It is New York. We can say that we've been here and all that now. We just can't drink that much."

They took turns buying a round. Halfway through their third beer, a guy approached their table. He introduced himself as Erich Ruge. He was German and an ex-sailor a few years older than Reinhold. He told them that New York was full of Germans and had always been full of Germans. He had come to the famous metropolis from his native Wilhelmshaven after the war, when he got tired of sailing and wanted to settle down.

"I met my sponsor here," he told them. "A nice guy. He owns a butcher shop in Brooklyn. I met him at a bar over there and we got to talking. He took me on as an apprentice, trained me with his own son."

"Is everywhere expensive?" Reinhold asked.

Erich chuckled. "Yes, for the most part. What is the exchange rate now?"

"One American Dollar to four *mark*."

Erich winced. "That is not good. It has been worse in the past. Just a few years ago it was double that."

"So, where are all these Germans?" Johan asked. "They are not here."

He waved a hand around the mostly empty bar room. There were some dark and stormy looking men sitting a table on the other side of the room and there was a couple of Latino looking guys sitting at the bar with a few Americans.

"And are there any women?" Reinhold asked.

Erich smiled at Reinhold. "There's women, but not really for hire, not around here. This isn't Europe or South America. You have to have connections here to get a call girl."

"What do you do? Do you have connections?"

Erich's chest puffed a bit with pride. "I have a wife, an American one, so I don't need those kinds of connections."

"Where is this wife of yours?" Otto asked.

"She works here. She is cleaning the rooms upstairs." Erich thought for a second. "You could try the Heidelberg. I have a friend that works there. It is a nice place."

"The Heidelberg?"

"It is a German restaurant on the Upper East Side. The staff all speak German."

"How would we get there?" Otto asked.

Erich thought again for a second. "I think you would take the blue line to 86th Street. I think it is on 86th Street. Hold a minute."

Erich looked over his shoulder and called the bartender. They had a brief conversation. One of the Americans at the bar joined in. Erich turned back to Reinhold and the sailors.

"Yes, you would take the blue line to 86th Street and head toward the water when you leave the station."

Johan looked at his two companions. "What are we for? Let's go find the Germans!"

Reinhold didn't remember how long it took to get to the Heidelberg Restaurant, an hour maybe, and he didn't remember how much it cost, but it was worth it. It was Bavarian in nature but that was ok because the food was excellent, the beer was German, real German, and the staff was all German so there were no awkward communication problems.

Best of all, there were ladies there, German ladies as well as American, who loved the fact that the sailors were just off the boat for the night visiting New York City. They wanted news from home and the sailors were more than happy to oblige, filling them in on the reconstruction progress in Hamburg and Kiel, but unable to speak about what was going on in the southern part of the country.

It was getting late and the sailors were thinking about wrapping up their night when Otto said he wasn't going back to the ship and disappeared with a pretty redhead.

"Why does he get the girl?" Reinhold asked.

"Because it can't always be you, Scholz," Johan laughed at his friend. "You could have one of these ladies if you want."

"No, I don't want to risk getting lost in this city and missing the ship in the morning. Let's go."

They found their way back to the subway station at 86th Street. The map seemed pretty easy. All they had to do was take the blue line to the yellow line to 4th Ave in Brooklyn. They got on the train confident they would find their destination. They switched trains when they saw the sign for the yellow line, confirming their confidence in getting back to the *Göttingen*.

They watched for their stop but it never came. For hours, Johan and Reinhold rode around on the yellow line, looking for 4th Ave. The crowds thinned out until they were the only people left in the car. They began to wonder if the train ran all night or if they stopped at a certain time. Panicked, they decided to get off to find out where they were.

Before they could reach the map, they encountered a couple of uniformed police officers. Out of desperation only, Johan approached them and asked if they spoke German. Luck was with them. One spoke a little bit of German, enough to understand the issue the sailors were having. It turned out they got on the wrong train. They were not on the yellow line at all. Somehow they ended up on the red one and were in a place called Queens. The officers put them on the right train, going the right way. They got back to the *Göttingen* at four o'clock in the morning. There was no sign of Otto.

Chapter 89: Where America Keeps Its Navy

The *Göttingen* left New York for Philadelphia. They sailed out of New York Bay and down a length of coastline protected by a series of barrier islands. Houses and towns dotted the islands. One town was particularly interesting to Reinhold and the other sailors. It was hard to make out from a distance but they were all pretty sure there was a long pier with a Ferris wheel and a roller coaster. It reminded Reinhold of the *tivoli* in Stockholm. Behind these structures, on the beach, it looked like there were huge buildings.

"They call it Atlantic City," Martens told them when they asked if he knew of it. "Some kind of resort town where people go to gamble."

"There are a lot of towns like that in America, from what I have heard," Johan told Reinhold. "I have a cousin who immigrated to someplace called Wisconsin. He says that the Great Lakes are full of German resort towns where people spend the summer."

They sailed passed the interesting town to the end of the barrier islands and made a starboard turn at a head of land into a large bay. The head of land was home to a large recreational boating marina. The bay was full of small yachts and sailboats. The people on the small vessels watched as the big cargo ship slid passed. Reinhold's attention was drawn to a dilapidated, mostly ruined structure in the water, starboard of the buoys marking the shipping lane. The only thing he figured it could be was an old lighthouse. What was odd, however, was that there was not a single light on it and the structure looked like it had been bombed. He wondered why such a hazard was left and not torn down. Not long after this, Reinhold saw the pilot arrive in a small speedboat. The man deftly climbed the ladder and went to take control of the bridge.

"We'll be in Philadelphia soon," Otto said.

Reinhold and Otto were repairing a water pump that had broken while they were hosing down the deck.

"How do you know that?" Reinhold asked.

He was still annoyed that Otto had gone off with some girl in New York, leaving Reinhold and Johan to find their own way home.

"Because Martens said that we would be close when we rounded that head of land into this bay." Otto said, a bit annoyed himself. "From here, we go up that river there."

Reinhold followed the way Otto was pointing and saw the wide mouth of a river on the horizon. He also saw another wrecked lighthouse.

What the hell is going on here? He kept the thought to himself, not wanting to give Otto another reason to speak. *Two wrecked lighthouses in one bay? Seems ridiculous. And dangerous.*

The *Göttingen* made its way across the murky bay and into the river, winding around hidden shoals and marshy islands. They passed a large city on their port side and kept on going, following the urban sprawl.

They rounded a bend in the river near an airport and Philadelphia came into sight. Reinhold knew that it must be their destination because it was almost as impressive as New York with tall skyscrapers and an impressive waterfront. The port was located along the river, making it seem like Hamburg, a hive of activity on all sides. A tugboat approached and nudged them into a spot on an empty pier. He wondered what these guys smuggled, what was valuable in Philadelphia.

I wonder if it is drugs, like New York, he thought.

The crew opened the hatches and turned control of the deck over to the longshoremen, who wasted no time getting to work. So far, Reinhold's two experiences with the longshoremen in North America had been good. They were diligent and worked quickly. Looking over the rail into the port he saw that it was cleaner, more orderly than New York, but lacking in comparison to ports in Europe. Darkness was falling fast now

"We are going to see if there is a place to grab a beer, Reinhold, do you want to come?" Johan asked as they showered and changed into clean clothes.

The idea didn't appeal to him. Beer was available on the ship cheaper than the bars and there was little chance of him finding a girl, so why bother? Instead, Reinhold filled his flask and took a walk through the port, observing how it ran and what kinds of people worked there.

It was very similar to Germany and the rest of Europe. There was one big difference. Vagrants. He could see the less than fortunes panhandling for money and food.

Such a rich country, he thought, *and there are people begging in the ports. At least in other places, they were looking to sell things.*

He had to remind himself that there had been a time, not too long ago, when he was on the bum, begging for cigarettes and sandwiches from ships passing through the canal in Holtenau. Somehow, it seemed different. He had been injured. There didn't look like there was anything wrong with these people.

As he wandered, he caught snips of conversations coming from around him. He didn't understand most of it but he slowed his pace when he heard a couple of guys speaking German. They were longshoremen, he thought, telling one of the beggars that if he learned English, they could get him a job. The beggar responded by saying that he was trying but English wasn't coming easily for him. Reinhold felt bad for him and not bad for him at the same time. He was tempted to stop and talk with the guys about their experiences in America, but decided against it.

The *Göttingen* left Philadelphia less than forty-eight hours after arriving, traveling back down the river and out into the bay. At the head of land, they made another starboard turn and headed south. They were back to the coastline with barrier islands. The glimpses Reinhold got of it as he worked were quite lovely. Martens said the next stop would be Baltimore.

The ship rounded another head of land and ended up in one of the largest bays Reinhold ever seen. It went on forever. It wasn't long before a pilot's ship showed up to take control. Reinhold watched the marshland on the starboard side of the ship slip passed, the wake of the ship disturbing the birds that were nesting there. Dozens at a time took flight to escape the flooding of their nests.

"We're not really going to Baltimore," Martens told them. "The port isn't in the city, like Philadelphia. It is a bit away, in the middle of nowhere. Pretty spot, though."

The sailors quickly realized what he was saying. It reminded Reinhold of his travels to the upper ports of Sweden to get lumber except they could see Baltimore further up the river where in Sweden, because of the mountains, Stockholm wasn't visible. They were scheduled to stay in Baltimore for about three days, two of which were days off. Otto had the idea to take a bus to the city and everyone agreed that would be good. The bus schedule turned out to be a pain in the ass to read and Otto, by the time he was done with it, swore that there was no bus coming their way on the days they had available. Schulz, the steward, told them that getting a ride from where they were to Baltimore was going to be almost impossible.

"Settle yourselves down, boys," he told them, "You're stuck here. But, there is a train station, if you want to go to Washington D.C."

"There is a train that goes to Washington D.C., but not to Baltimore?" Reinhold asked, somewhat incredulously.

"That's right. Strange, huh? I guess they rely on buses to get to the closer city and the train to get to the one further away." Schulz shrugged and left the sailors to their devices.

The next day, Reinhold, Johan, Otto, a couple of other sailors boarded a train to Washington D.C. It was about an hour to the city. The group got off at the station nearest the capital building on the map and made their way to what Schulz told them was the Federal District. In actuality, it turned out to be the National Mall. They walked around for several hours, looking at the buildings and the people.

It was impressive, and cold. The architecture was technically wonderful, exhibiting excellent craftsmanship and quality materials. It felt powerful but it was sterile and distant.

Maybe that's the reason why it feels powerful, Reinhold thought to himself.

It had no flair of its own. He found more beauty in the river that ran close to the National Mall. Many flowering trees planted there made the scene truly beautiful, even though they were in their last days of bloom. He also found the Roosevelt Memorial to be haunting not so much because of the building, but because of its secluded position on an island in the river.

Unfortunately, Reinhold found the whole capital lacking in personality and that was truly disappointing. The other guys were far more impressed with Washington. On the train ride home, Reinhold tried to explain why he was not as excited as them but he got nowhere. They just didn't understand what he was saying.

The *Göttingen*'s last southern stop was Norfolk, Virginia. Where, Martens told them, they would pick up bales of tobacco.

"Real tobacco?" Johan asked.

"Yup," Martens confirmed. "You can go into the hold and rip off a couple of leaves for a pipe, but I wouldn't recommend it. It hasn't been processed so it is bitter tasting and strong. You'd think you were smoking five cigarettes at once."

"I know how to process tobacco," Reinhold volunteered. "You almost have to toast it before you can smoke it. And you definitely have to dry it really well. "

"Why am I not surprised to hear that you know how to process tobacco?" Otto asked.

"I am full of surprises." Reinhold responded coyly.

Martens told them they wouldn't be in Norfolk for long.

"You'll see why when we get there," he said.

Reinhold was beginning to realize that Martens was having fun with the new comers to the North America route. He liked knowing things that they didn't.

Norfolk was a short trip from Baltimore, just across the huge bay. The pilot was in command of the ship the entire way. They got there after dark. Reinhold was so tired he was falling asleep on his feet and went to bed right after dinner. In the morning, he woke to Johan shaking him out of a dream of domestic bliss.

"Scholz, get up!" he yelled. "You have to see this! Quick!"

Reinhold rubbed the sleep out of his eyes, not coherent enough to question his bunkmate. He swung out of bed, not looking forward to another day on the ship. It was mornings like this that made him realize the full extent of the punishment of North America.

I should be in Australia opening a carpentry business or something right now, he thought as he pulled on some clothes. *Or at least on my way there.*

He headed top side still yawning. The yawning stopped when he saw what the fuss was all about.

Sailing past the *Göttingen,* which was docked on the south side of a tributary into the bay, was one of the biggest ships Reinhold had ever seen. It had to be more than three hundred feet long. It towered over the smaller ships it passed, with a flight deck sitting at least thirty meters out of the water. The flight deck was the most impressive aspect. Reinhold counted the tail ends of dozens of aircraft before he lost sight of them. It was as if a building had just sailed past.

"And that, gentlemen, is the reason why we lost the war," said Kladetzke.

Under normal circumstances, Reinhold knew that someone would question the bosun's statement but the impact of such a sight kept most of the men speechless. Particularly when it was accompanied by the sight of dozens of other smaller military craft.

"Where are we?" Reinhold heard the mess boy ask Göllner, the cook. They were standing outside the mess just down the gangway.

"Virginia, boy," Göllner answered. "This is where America keeps its Navy. From what I have heard, there is a river around here somewhere where they keep all the ships they aren't using. It's a reserve fleet, ready to go at a moment's notice."

The mess boy's eyes widen at the thought. He wasn't much older than Reinhold was when he started sailing. He wondered how a younger version of himself would have reacted to such a sight. Shrugging, he headed for the mess to get breakfast.

"The Atlantic part of it, anyway," Kladetzke snorted. "They got a whole other fleet in the Pacific. Enjoy the sight while you can. We won't be here long. The Americans don't like foreigners hanging around for too long." Reinhold heard the bosun comment as he walked away.

The mess boy's eyes widen more. Obviously, his sailing hadn't taken him through the Panama Canal yet. He would have seen a few of the ships of the Pacific fleet there.

The *Göttingen* loaded tobacco, a task that took less than twenty-four hours, and left Norfolk. The ship sighed a collective sigh of relief. The presence of so much military might made the sailors nervous. Reinhold heard someone ask the bosun if there had been any issues with the Americans customs or immigration.

"No," the bosun responded. "They don't care about the Germans anymore now that they have us on our knees, neutered like a stray dog. They have their attentions focused on the Soviets. You can be sent to prison right now in the United States if they even suspect that you are a Communist. A red sympathizer, they call it. Or something like that."

"Really?" asked the other Scholz on the ship. His name was Edgar. He and Reinhold didn't really get along, having very different world views. "How do you know that?"

"Never you mind how I know," Kladetzke told him. "I have sources. The same sources that tell me America is the worst place to jump ship. They send the FBI out to find you. They don't stop looking until they have you in custody. They hand you back over to the company you were sailing with along with a bill. If it is Hapag, they take you back, put you on mail duty, and charge you the fees the American government charged them. Take it right out of your pay and they don't let you quit until you're done paying."

Reinhold couldn't help thinking the bosun was talking to him. Little did the bosun know that he had no real desire to live in America. It seemed like a boring country, and slightly paranoid.

"Where do we go now, Martens?" Johan asked two nights after the *Göttingen* left Norfolk.

"Albany," Martens answered, his mouth full of steak and potatoes.

"And where is that?" Reinhold asked, shoving another piece of beef into his own mouth.

Göllner had a special touch with beef and the sailors loved when he made it. Somehow, he managed not to cook it until it was tough and dry like every other ship cook.

"New York," Martens answered.

"Great," Reinhold responded. "Back to New York."

"This stop isn't the city," Martens clarified. "This is a small port a day's sail up the Hudson River. They say it is the capitol of the state, but I don't want to believe it, although, the grain elevator is pretty impressive. That is what we will be getting there, grain."

"Why don't you believe it is the capitol?" Reinhold questioned.

"You'll see."

"Did you look at a map?"

"I looked at the map and it says it's the capital. After that, we sail back down the Hudson to Brooklyn to pick up more grain. I wish they would just dredge the damn river so we only had to make one stop at Albany before heading home."

Martens wandered away, grumbling about the shortcomings of local governments, leaving Reinhold and Johan staring after him.

"He knows way too much about this route. Maybe he should switch ships and go somewhere new, like Australia." Johan said, grinning, pulling two cigarettes out of his breast pocket, handing one to Reinhold.

Chapter 90: The Dirtiest Port

Several days later, the *Göttingen* moored in the Port of Albany. After making the journey up the Hudson, Reinhold understood Martens complaints. Even the pilot had some difficulty navigating the narrow shipping channel. Reinhold stood Quartermaster for the last four hours of the trip and was happy when they finally docked.

"These aren't Erie Canal days anymore," was Martens response when Reinhold mentioned the trip to him. "They have to get with the times. Ships are bigger now."

"You've been with this ship for too long, Martens."

"You're probably right about that," the man agreed.

Reinhold stood at the rail surveying this new port in what was, probably, the capital of New York State. It was small. There were only a couple of other ships docked on their side of the river while a few more were docked on the other side. The grain elevator was huge, probably one of the largest Reinhold had seen. Looking around at the landscape, he figured that there was a lot of farmland outside the city. This place had a very European feel to it but he wasn't sure why. It was probably the tight packed, old looking downtown area across the street from the port. It reminded him somewhat of Amsterdam or Rotterdam, just smaller, less cared for.

Reinhold noted that it was filthy. There was grain everywhere, scattered around like chicken feed and piled like snow fallen off a roof but with no evidence left of the vehicle or piece of machinery that it fell from. He expected to see the ever present vagrants, but none were visible. He was pondering this when Kladetzke approached with Otto and the other Scholz, Edgar.

"Scholz, go with these two and start getting the rat guards on the aft lines and be quick about it. No doubt the critters already know we're here."

"Rat guards, sir?"

"You heard me. Get going."

Reinhold headed aft with the other two. He had never put rat guards on the lines before. He had heard about ships taking this preventative measure in the West Indies, but was surprised they were necessary here.

"Look around," Otto told him. "There is food everywhere for the vermin."

The farm boy in him remembered Herr Muuss being very particular about where and how the grain was stored. Back then, Reinhold thought he was just being a cheap bastard when he made the boys go out into the yard and clean up all the grain that had fallen off the stalks on the drive to the silo. Now, he realized it was to keep the rats from following the trail to the mother lode. It would have been disastrous to have rats get into the grain.

"Why don't they clean this place up?" Reinhold asked. He meant it to be a rhetorical question but Edgar answered him.

"Why don't you ask Martens? He seems to know everything."

"You sound jealous, Edgar." Reinhold stated before ignoring the man for the rest of their job together. He had no use for someone who was jealous of someone smarter than them.

Makes so much more sense to learn from the person, he thought.

Once the rat guards were in place, the whole crew was on rat patrol. Any rat seen scampering around the ship was killed immediately. It was in the Port of Albany that Reinhold first experienced a raised gangplank. By order of the Captain, the end of the gangplank was to remain one meter off the ground. It was the belief that rats couldn't jump that high.

"We're going to take a walk, Scholz," Johan called from mid deck. "You coming?"

"Sure." Reinhold called back. "Why not?"

They hadn't been off the ship since Norfolk. Reinhold showered, dressed in clean gear, filled his flask from a bottle in his sea chest, and meet the guys on deck. They left the ship, jumped down from the end of the raised gangplank, and headed across the port. Reinhold was surprised the see Martens with them.

"Martens," he called. "What is it about this place that gets you off the ship?"

Martens grinned at him. "Ladies, Scholz. You're not the only one that likes them."

Reinhold was surprised. "There's girls here?" He questioned. "Real girls? That we can have?"

Martens nodded, the cigarette in his teeth bobbing up and down, leaving burning trails in the gathering gloom.

"Where are they?" Reinhold questioned.

"Just ahead," Martens gestured his chin toward a row of buildings across the street from the port. "At the Port Bar."

The sailors hopped across the rail tracks, found the gate in the perimeter fence, and crossed the street. Martens led them a block to a row of brick storefronts. Reinhold could hear music coming from one of the buildings and suspected it was the place. He took a couple of quick swigs from his flask before following his friends into the darkened interior of the Port Bar.

It took a second for his eyes to adjust. It was a long, thin room with a bar to the left and tables to the right. The music was coming from a jukebox at the end of the bar. There were plenty of people there, including girls. They settled themselves at a table in the middle of the room while Martens bought the first round. Reinhold scanned the room and quickly found that all the girls were darker in color than he preferred. One of the ladies approached the table, running her hand across Johan's shoulders as she walked by, a sly smile playing around her full lips. She didn't stop but kept going, glancing back at the sailors before turning the corner around the bar and disappearing into an unseen back room. A girl standing at the bar barked something at them.

"She wants us to come talk to her," Johan translated.

Another girl got up off the lap of a scruffy looking dock worker, judging by how he was dressed, to make her way to the newcomers. She purred something under her breath as she took a position next to the girl at the bar. The two whispered together briefly before breaking out into an unattractive cackle.

"I would say there are available girls here," Johan said cheerfully. "These girls are obviously interested in a little one on one. I wonder how much they charge."

"Twenty *mark*," Martens answered as he put four mugs of beer on the table. "Well, the equivalent of, anyway."

"Twenty *mark*!" Reinhold exclaimed. "That's double what they get in the Reeperbahn."

"This is America, my friend, things are more expensive here," Martens said, taking a pull from his cigarette before adding, "Especially when you were on the losing side. I thought you guys figured this out already."

"Relax, Scholz," Otto drawled, eyeing an attractive girl at the next table. "These girls are providing an important community service. They deserve the money for their efforts."

The night wore on. They took turns buying rounds. The girls circled like sharks, looking for a nibble on the lines they were throwing out. A sailor from another ship, a freighter out of Rotterdam, bought them a round of schnapps before leaving with a dark girl.

"That guy has the right idea," Otto said, watching the door close. He squeezed the girl sitting on his lap. "How about we get out of here?"

She didn't understand his German but she understood his intentions by the nod of his head in the direction of the door. Johan and Martens followed Otto's example and got ready to go with their girls. They picked a good time to leave. Twenty feet from where they were sitting a fight broke out between two guys over a girl. It struck Reinhold as odd because she was a hooker. Why fight over a hooker?

"The one guy thinks she is his girlfriend" Johan explained. They watched the fight play itself out for a few minutes, sidestepping when it got to close. The bartender broke it up after a few minutes by hitting one guy with a baseball bat.

"What about you, Reinhold?" Johan questioned. "Are you getting a girl?"

"I am going back to the ship to get some sleep. I hope anyway. Where are you guys going?"

"They take us to their rooms," Martens explained.

"Sounds good. But what about you, Reinhold?" Johan asked again. "Are you going back alone?"

"I'll be fine," Reinhold said, understanding Johan's meaning. "The ship is only a few hundred yards from here."

Reinhold parted ways with his friends and headed back to the *Göttingen*. As he walked alone, he could hear the squeaks and scurries of rats in the darkness. Standing on the deck of the *Brandenburg*, Reinhold shuddered. He was thousands of miles and almost a year away from that night, but still gave him the creeps. He hated rats. To make matters worse, when he got back to the ship that night, there was a huge example of a river rat hanging by its claws from the end of the gangplank. The creature had obviously jumped and, miraculously, managed to grab the grooved metal. Reinhold vividly remembered watching it hanging, desperately pedaling its short back legs, trying to gain traction before it finally fell. Screwing itself up, it jumped again, missing its target and trying again, undeterred by Reinhold's approaching footsteps.

Bold things they are, he thought to himself. *Albany really knows how to breed determined rats. And a good quantity of them, too.*

After missing its third attempt and collecting itself for a fourth, Reinhold decided it was time to get rid of it. Positioning himself just so, he kicked the preoccupied rat, sending it toward the gap between the ship and the dock. He made contact with the soft body of the animal, but failed to get it into the river, sending it further to the left then he wanted. The stunned animal took off into the darkness. Shuddering, Reinhold jumped up on to the gangplank and headed to the galley to get a slice of bread and some anchovies.

They spent two days in the Port of Albany. Johan, Otto, and Martens told Reinhold about their experiences with the girls. They had a good time but they grumbled a bit at the amount of time their twenty *mark* bought. They spent most of their time in Albany drinking on the ship and walking around the port. The more Reinhold saw of it, the less he liked it. He just didn't understand why the capital of a place he had heard about his whole life was so badly cared for. Not only was there grain everywhere, but there was a good amount of discarded scrap metal and wood as well as trash in the form of newspapers, bottles, and food wrappers. Even the buoys in the river were beyond rusty and their warning sounds came out in a distorted moan.

"One guy just last year bought a newspaper here because he thought the same thing as you, Reinhold." Martens told them their last night in Albany.

They were sitting on the pier enjoying a beautiful late spring night with a couple of beers when Reinhold voiced his opinions.

"He didn't learn anything from it but a tugboat operator told him that the mayor here isn't interested in the port."

"Not interested in the port? What kind of mayor isn't interested in a port?" Otto asked.

Martens shrugged. "This kind, I guess."

The *Göttingen* made one more stop in Brooklyn to pick up the rest of the grain it was carrying to Europe. They moored early in the morning and left late that night. The Atlantic crossing was rough. Reinhold remarked to Johan as they secured loose lines in heavy seas that he was done sailing. Johan agreed, confessing that he had been thinking about getting a job with his cousin at Blohm and Voss. That was the best alternative to sailing that Reinhold had ever heard.

In Rotterdam, they unloaded two hatches, including the bales of tobacco. They were back to sea in less than twenty-four hours, headed for Bremen. Kristal was there waiting, looking as beautiful as ever. Johan and Otto covered for him so he could run away with her for a few hours. As soon as the cargo was done unloading, the *Göttingen* was on its way to Hamburg. They spent three days in the port unloading grain and loading goods bound for the United States, mostly small machinery this trip.

Reinhold paid a visit to the agent's office in the port to see if he could get a ship going to the Pacific but there were none available. He went back to the *Göttingen* like a man that returns home to a marriage that is happy and restrictive at the same time, like a plush and gilded cage. They sailed out of Hamburg for another cycle through America.

They left on a Saturday in late May and arrived in New York on June 12, 1956. There was no excitement for Reinhold about visiting New York this time. He ventured out with his friends and paid more attention to the architecture than the people or the sights. They stopped in to the Heidelberg for a couple of beers and maybe to pick up a girl but there were no girls around this night. All in all it was a disappointing time. They left the city with higher hopes for Philadelphia.

Philadelphia disappointed also. Reinhold wandered the port, sipping from his flask, and taking in scenes of the American waterfront. He wished he was an artist so he could draw what he saw; modern, expensive equipment surrounded by squalor. He took pictures instead, knowing that if he was to tell the old timers in Ratekau that the America ports were filthy they wouldn't believe him unless he had a picture.

"Baltimore next, boys," Martens reminded everyone when they left Philadelphia.

There was a collective groan. The whole ship was scheduled to have two days off in Baltimore again, a situation that drew another collective groan when the bosun announced it. Everyone agreed that the tight schedule kept by the *Göttingen* was one of the only saving graces of working on the ship. The more they worked, the less it bothered them to be traveling in this dreary country. Once they were moored in the port, Reinhold resigned himself to spending the rest of the time until they shoved off for Norfolk drinking and reading. The weather was supposed to be nice, at least.

The morning of their first day in the no-man's-land port outside Baltimore dawned with a promise of beautiful weather. After doing chores: laundry, shaving, etc, Reinhold and Johan decided they were going to take a case of beer down to the pier with a couple of chairs and people watch for the afternoon. If they ran out of people, which was doubtful with all the dock activity, they would turn their attention to the birds. Thousands of them whirled around the wetlands and marshes that edged the river. Reinhold observed again, still upset by the revelation, that here, as in New York and Philadelphia, there were vagrants hanging about and expensive equipment surrounded by squalor. Reinhold commented to Johan on this and Johan agreed.

"It is surprising that there are so many homeless here," Johan said, cracking open another beer. "It is America, after all. I thought the poor and meek were supposed to come here so they didn't have a life like this."

Reinhold shrugged. His attention was drawn to a big convertible that was driving toward them. He and Johan watched it approach, the music from the radio reaching them before the car. It stopped in front of them. Two older guys looked out the driver's window at them. The driver had his arm resting on the top of the door, exposing what were obviously sailor's tattoos. The two men surveyed the ship quickly, one pointing to the flag hanging off the stern. They commented briefly on it.

"They are happy we are German," Johan told Reinhold. "And not from one of the *arschloch* countries."

"What is an *arschloch* country?" Reinhold asked. "Like Libya or Panama or Greece? The places with bad ships?"

Johan was going to answer but was cut off by the driver. He spoke a bit of German.

"Eat?" he asked, making a gesture with his hand to indicate the action. Reinhold and Johan looked at each other.

"Food?" The guy asked again.

"What do you think?" Johan asked.

"Why not?" Reinhold responded. "The guy is an ex-sailor. Maybe they are taking pity on us for being trapped here, in the middle of nowhere."

"Ok," Johan said to the driver.

The man's face broke into a huge grin. He gestured for them to get in. The sailors heaved themselves over the door into the backseat and the car took off down the pier.

The guys smiled back at them and turned the music up on the stereo. It was a man singing to a rock song that Reinhold had never heard before but liked immediately. He tapped his finger against his knee while the wind pulled at his hair. The car turned away from the river and took off down a dirt street, exiting the port. Reinhold knew a moment of apprehension but it faded away as the car speed down a black topped road, the music trailing behind them. He glanced at Johan and saw that his friend was relaxed and smiling at him. A few minutes later, the car pulled into a parking lot in front of what looked like a shack. The Americans got out of the car and gestured for the sailors to follow.

The afternoon that followed was one of the strangest Reinhold could remember. The Americans took them to a tiny restaurant overlooking one of the tributaries of the river. There was a large patio built out over the water with rectangular tables with attached benches covered in red and white checkered table clothes. They all sat down at a table, the Americans talking with the servers, gesturing to Reinhold and Johan.

A few minutes later, a bucket of steaming crabs was thrown across the table and everyone was given a small hammer. It was surprising that food was just strewn across the table but it made sense once the newbies observed their host's example. They picked up a crab, smacked it with a hammer and pulled out the meat bit by bit, discarding the shells in the bucket.

They were so good, like butter, melting in your mouth, Reinhold thought. *And the beer was good too. I wish I could remember the name. I wish I had gotten the names of those guys! It was a good afternoon, eating crabs and drinking beer. They didn't even make us pay.*

That afternoon with the Americans changed Reinhold's very critical opinion of the country. There were good people here, he saw, they just didn't hang out at the ports. When they left Baltimore, he was in better spirits.

The *Göttingen* stopped briefly in Norfolk before heading back north to Albany. He stood at the rail and watched the Statue of Liberty slip passed as they sailed to the Hudson River entrance.

Over the next twelve hours, Reinhold found himself standing often at the rail, watching the lush valley slip passed. It seemed like a nice place, with big houses on hills peering down at the passing ship while small towns and cities huddled into the slip of land between the river and the mountains to the west. It was a very green place, Reinhold remembered. The Port of Albany was, again, a disappointment. And again, they had two days off. The collective groan wasn't as bad this time because at least there were girls for hire in Albany.

"Maybe we should do what we did in Baltimore here," Johan suggested. "We'll get some beer and sit on the pier and see what happens."

Reinhold agreed and Otto joined them. He heard about their adventure in Baltimore.

They were sitting on the pier, sunbathing, drinking, and talking, for two hours before a car caught Johan's attention. It was another convertible. This one Otto recognized as a Pontiac. The car crept down the pier, the driver and his passenger looking at the ships they passed. They stopped when they reached the three sailors from the *Göttingen*. They smiled and waved in greeting, saying something that Reinhold didn't understand. Johan answered and a short conversation unfolded.

"They want to take us out," Johan translated. "The one guy feels some kind of kinship with us because his mother is German."

"How do you guys do this?" Otto asked sarcastically. "Why can't I hang out on a pier and get people to come offer to take me places? Are they gay or something?"

"I don't care if they are gay if it gets us out of here for the day. Where do they want to go?" Reinhold asked.

"They say there is a bar just over there," Johan pointed toward where the Port Bar was located in the row of brick buildings.

"The Port Bar?" Otto asked.

Johan confirmed that was the destination.

"Are they buying?" Reinhold questioned.

Johan asked the Americans and to the sailors' surprise, they said yes, in German.

Reinhold, standing on the deck of the *Brandenburg*, looked back at that moment as one of the defining of his life, he just didn't know it at the time. They got into the Pontiac and went to the Port Bar. The Americans introduced themselves as Frank Rickman and John Siloff. They hung out there all afternoon. John and Frank both spoke some German. Reinhold liked him immediately and he wasn't sure why. He didn't usually like bankers, which is what they said they were, but these guys were different.

They got bored of the Port Bar quickly. Instead of the Americans leaving and getting on with their day elsewhere in Albany, they offered to take the sailors for a drive, to see the city, and to buy them dinner. They agreed. Why eat the food on the ship, good though it was, if they could have something new and different? Dinner was postponed when, driving past the movie theater on Delaware Ave, Johan commented that they were playing a movie he had heard about called the Lone Ranger. They stopped and saw the film. Reinhold didn't understand a word of it but thought it was exciting nonetheless.

Thanks to Frank and John, Albany became Reinhold's favorite port. Three times, the pair met the sailors at the port and took them somewhere: to a movie, to the bar, or out for dinner. They always treated. It was on their third stop in Albany that Frank and John took the sailors to see a farm Frank recently bought. He had the idea of making it a working farm with livestock and crops, but mostly livestock. The big Pontiac pulled up in front of an old farmhouse situated on almost a hundred acres of rolling grassland. Everything was already there to begin raising animals, all Frank needed was the manpower.

"So, what do you guys think?" He asked the sailors as they sat under a tree eating a bagged lunch. "Is this a place where you can see yourself settling down?"

The sailors were confused, dumbfounded. They looked at each other, trying to gauge if the others heard the same comment. No one answered the question for a minute. An awkward feeling descended on the group. Finally, Reinhold broke the silence.

"Are you offering us jobs?"

"Yes," Frank answered, popping a handful of blueberries into his mouth. "Delicious, aren't they? They come from a farm just a few miles from here."

The sailors nodded absently. The blueberries were delicious, but this guy just offered them jobs. Jobs on the shore. On a farm. In America. Reinhold cleared his throat.

"But we are German."

"Yes," Frank responded quickly. He had anticipated this comment from the sailors. "That's why I would sponsor you to come here, to the United States, to work on my farm. It will be easy. My government would have no reason to turn you down since you would be coming to take jobs that are waiting for you."

Reinhold remembered that moment with painful clarity. His mind raced with thoughts of living in America. He tried to find the negatives, serious negatives, and could come up with none. It made too much sense.

"Why are you asking us?" Johan questioned, twisting the cap off a beer bottle with a bit too much enthusiasm.

"Because you are hardworking young men," Frank told them. "Don't you want more than to work on a ship until you get washed overboard or a boom lands on your head and kills you? Or, worse still, the damn ship sinks, taking you with it? How are you supposed to have a family when you sail?"

Frank's words fell on Reinhold's ears like they were spoken with his own voice. Countless times he had asked himself the same questions. He caught, out of the corner of his eye, Otto grin at him. Johan, too, glanced at him. No one spoke.

"Why don't you think about it?" John said. The sailors nodded.

Chapter 91: Going To Get A Ship

That night, Reinhold, Otto, and Johan sat on the hatch of hold three and discussed the events of the day. Johan didn't believe what he heard, thinking it was some kind of heat and alcohol induced hallucination he conjured in his mind. Otto didn't buy it and was looking for the angle.

"There has got to be plenty of men here that would take those jobs. Why go through the trouble of importing help"

Johan shrugged. "It does seem too good to be true but maybe he really does just like us. They both keep telling us that their mothers are German. Maybe it has something to do with that."

Reinhold was experiencing déjà vu.

"It was less than six months," he pointed out, "that we were talking about a job offer in Chile with a German guy at his mine. Remember?"

Otto and Johan nodded that they remembered.

"Somehow," Reinhold continued, "this job offer is more realistic than the one in Chile. This is something I could actually do. And, we would be coming to America as legal immigrants instead of jumping ship in the middle of nowhere, in a desert, where we don't speak the language or understand the customs."

But," Johan injected, "we don't speak this language or understand these customs."

Reinhold snorted. "I learned Swedish, I can learn English. There isn't much different between English and German."

"What about the customs?" Otto asked.

"The whole of America was settled by Brits and Germans," Reinhold answered. "I don't think the customs are going to be a problem."

"Sounds like you already made up your mind, Scholz." Otto observed.

"I think I am going to take Frank up on his offer. Why not? Worst comes to worst, I move back to Germany and start sailing again."

"What about Australia?" Johan asked, frowning. "I thought the goal was to get to Australia."

"We don't have to get to Australia now." Reinhold replied flatly.

Johan looked confused. "Why not?"

"Because," Otto said, a bit exasperated. "We'll have sponsors to come here. The reason for getting to Australia was to avoiding being rounded up and sent back to Germany. We would be legal here."

"Oh, right," Johan said sheepishly. He grabbed another beer and chugged half.

By the following morning, all three sailors were convinced moving to America would be good. How could it not be, they agreed. That evening, Frank and John came around and were thrilled that the sailors agreed.

"The next time you come to Albany, I'll have the papers for you to take to Germany." Frank told them. "You have to fill them out and take them to the consulate where you live."

True to his word, the next time the *Göttingen* docked in Albany, Frank gave them each a thick envelope of papers.

"My address is inside. Write me when you are done with the paperwork. I think you have to go for a physical too. What it says on the Statue of Liberty about tired and meek isn't really the way it goes. America wants to know you are fit to work." Frank winked at them as he finished.

"You guys are going to like it here," John added. "It is a lot like Germany."

Looking back, Reinhold remembered being nervously giddy about the prospect of moving to America. They were plagued by bad weather crossing the Atlantic but he didn't mind. He was thinking of it as his last crossing as a sailor. The next time he crossed this cursed ocean would be as a passenger on a luxury liner. His mind raced with all the things he had to do to prepare for moving.

"I don't know how I am going to tell my sister I am leaving," Johan said one night.

The *Göttingen* had dropped anchor in Rotterdam early that day. They were awaiting dock space to unload cargo from Baltimore. Reinhold and Johan were leaning on the rail, taking in the sights of the huge port. Reinhold was looking forward to getting off the ship when they docked and visiting the first *puff* he could find. It had been too long since he had a girl. The saltpeter was wearing off and his libido was raging. Johan mentioning his sister made him think of his own. A feeling like being punched in the stomach hit him.

How am I going to tell her I am leaving, he asked himself.

The last letter he received from Lisa arrived several months before. She wrote to say she was moving back to Ratekau. The room they were occupying in Lübeck just wasn't big enough and there were no bigger apartments in the city that they could afford. They moved into the attic, Lisa wrote, explaining that Willie had spent several months during his time off renovating the space. He fixed the roof, insulated it, and divided it into two rooms.

This means I am going to have to go home to talk to her, he thought bitterly.

The idea had crossed his mind not to tell his father or stepmother that he was leaving. That was out now. He had to go home.

"Should we bother trying to get another ship?" Johan asked. "You know, while we wait for our papers? I don't know if I can do America again, as a sailor, anyway."

Reinhold shrugged. "I guess not."

"What should we do for work while we wait?"

"We are going to go work for Blohm and Voss," Otto appeared and helped himself to a beer.

"Blohm and Voss?" Reinhold asked, intrigued.

"That's right," Otto settled himself against on the hatch. "It can't be more than a few weeks before our papers will be ready so I am going to talk to my cousin at the shipyard. They are always looking for guys for some nonsense work or other."

On the deck of the *Brandenburg*, Reinhold snorted audibly.

Nonsense work, he called it and he was so right.

He didn't think Otto would do it at first, but he managed to get them jobs at Blohm and Voss only a few days after they arrived back in Hamburg and signed off the *Göttingen*. What a disaster that was! The consulate in Hamburg told them it would be more than six months before their papers were ready. At first, they thought nothing of it and went to work at Blohm and Voss. Six weeks, six months, what is the difference, right? As long as they had jobs and a long-term plan for the future, everything was fine.

Reinhold didn't anticipate how much he was going to hate working at the shipyard. He stayed with Johan and his sister in a one-room studio in Altona. They got up every morning, took the train to the river, and crossed the bridge on foot to the shipyard. He hated the commute. People on the train in the morning were miserable and they made Reinhold miserable. The former sailors went to work to lie on their backs under old, decrepit ships in dry dock and scrap barnacles, rotten paint, and rust off the hulls. It was dirty, repetitive work and Reinhold hated it. It was October now, he didn't even want to think about what the shipyard would be like in January.

"If I wanted to scrap paint and shit off a ship, I'd still be sailing as a *Leichtmatrose*," he grumbled to Johan one night on the train.

"Stop complaining, Scholz," Johan grinned at him. "My sister is waiting for you at home. She'll fix you up."

Reinhold groaned. Johan's sister was the icing on the cake of his horrible situation. She didn't leave him alone! She was always there, fawning over him, doing annoying things such as pouting and giggling in a high-pitched way. She thought it was fun to tease and flirt with him when he was drinking even though she was told that nothing was ever going to happen. She was Johan's sister, for Christ's sake! It was driving him crazy! The thought of facing it that night was unbearable. Johan, he knew, was secretly hoping that Reinhold would fall in love with his sister and marry her so they could all go to America together. The idea made his blood race with anxiety and the desire to run was throbbing in his head. Turning to Johan, he told his friend he was done with it.

"I can't do this anymore, definitely not for another six months."

Johan was surprised. "So, what? You're quitting? We have only been there for a month."

"I am done. I am going to go visit my sister then I am going to get a ship. I'd rather spend the winter sailing than laying on my back covered in paint and rust."

"But what about America?"

"No big deal." Reinhold shrugged. "Those papers aren't going anywhere and they don't expire anytime soon. I'll get them when I get back."

Reinhold parted ways with Johan early the next morning at the train station. Johan went to work at the shipyard and Reinhold caught a train to Lübeck. Before departing Hamburg, however, he made a detour to the offices of Hapag where he told the receptionist that he was looking for a ship with a six-month schedule. An agent appeared in the waiting room to inform Reinhold that they had a ship, the *Brandenburg*, departing for the West Indies in five days on October

25. It was perfect. Reinhold signed up to report and left the office feeling optimism.

On the train to Lübeck, the bus trip to Bad Schwartau, and the bike ride to Ratekau, Reinhold thought about how he would tell Lisa he was leaving. By the time he arrived at his childhood home, he had a plan. Why should Lisa stay in Germany, living in the attic of their father's house? Once he was established and settled, he could sponsor her to come to America. There was plenty of room at the farm and Albany was close by. Lisa and Willie could work there easily. It made too much sense. He only hoped Lisa would see it also.

Lisa saw the sense, she just wasn't too keen on the idea. Willie was less so. Their stepmother, however, thought it was a brilliant idea. America, she believed, was where they would all find their fortunes. The conversation quickly turned to Isolde. She was getting worse, the tuberculosis slowly squeezing the life out of her. Reinhold agreed to visit her.

He spent the second day of his visit home at a sanitarium in Sereetz. Isolde was so happy to hear that Reinhold was going to America. Reinhold was surprised that she had a new husband, a fellow patient, and another child. She was convinced that he could get medicines in America that could cure her of the disease. He tried gently, and in vain, to explain that she should not count on that happening. He left heartbroken that she placed such hope on something that was not going to come to fruition. He promised to come see her again before he left for America.

Two days after arriving in Ratekau, Reinhold received a telegram from Hapag. They wanted him in Hamburg the following morning, two days earlier than he anticipated. He left immediately to catch the train out of Lübeck. Before he left, he reminded Lisa of the plan to bring her to America. She just smiled and said they would see.

Reinhold expected to be directed straight to the *Brandenburg* when he arrived at the Hapag offices. Instead, they told him to report to a classroom to learn the mechanics of unloading large, heavy cargo using only the ships crane and boom.

"They just loaded a locomotive and a small boat on to the *Brandenburg*. They are both headed for Veracruz, Mexico." The instructor explained. "When you get to Veracruz, you will see that there are no harbor cranes or booms. These items will have to be unloaded using only the equipment on board."

Reinhold sat through a day of classroom training barely able to keep his mind focused. There were five other sailors in the room. All of them were equally as uninterested. It was so dry and boring. At the end of the day, the instructor told the class to meet him in the morning near the Hapag pier for field training.

The field training was far more interesting. They spent the day alternating between hanging in the lines of the booms and on the deck checking weight distribution. The key was the ballasts. Every pound that moved over the side of the ship had to be compensated by filling the appropriate side of the ballast with seawater. It took all day, but the five sailors managed to set down their fifty-ton cement block on the pier and replace all the equipment to its proper place without sending their training vessel into a canter.

To celebrate their accomplishment, and to get one more night of beach fun in before setting sail the following morning, the sailors went to Reeperbahn. Johan joined them. Reinhold introduced him to Max and Heine, two of the sailors who he would be working with for the next six months.

"The West Indies?" Johan asked when Reinhold mentioned his signing on to the *Brandenburg* in the morning. "The Caribbean?"

"That's it," Reinhold confirmed.

"You lucky bastard!" Johan exclaimed. "You're going to spend your last winter as a sailor cruising around the sun drenched Caribbean. Now, if that was me, and I went to Hapag looking for a six month tour, they'd assign me to one of their short haul ships. I'd spend the winter doing laps back and forth in the accursed North Sea delivering mail or something."

Reinhold laughed at his friend's comment. He hadn't thought about it that way. He was about to comment when a grizzled old guy sitting at the table next to them interjected.

"You'd be better off in the North Sea," he said.

Johan eyed the old guy suspiciously. Reinhold knew Johan was going to tell the guy to get lost and mind his own business.

"Why would he be better off in the North Sea?" Reinhold asked quickly, cutting Johan off.

The old guy scratched his stubbly chin. Reinhold noticed he was missing both an eye and a finger on his right hand. Undeniably, this man was a beached sailor.

"Because, there's nothing to do in the West Indies." The old guy lit a cigarette before continuing. "Except go to the Tropicana."

"The Tropicana?" Reinhold questioned.

"The greatest place on Earth. It is where the rich and famous people hang out. I was there a few years ago with the last ship I sailed with. It was spectacular."

"Anyone can go there?" Johan questioned, his eyebrows raised in doubt.

"Anyone can go. It is a casino. Casinos don't turn down anyone's money."

"A casino?" Reinhold immediately lost interest.

"Not just a casino," the old guy said. "There are shows with beautiful girls wearing next to nothing. And a huge house orchestra that plays music until all hours of the night."

"That is more my speed," Reinhold said. "That is the only thing to do in the whole Caribbean?"

The old guy shrugged and took a gulp of his beer. "I think so. The cities on the islands are full of poor people and criminals. You're better off at the beach, if you have the time. When I sailed there, we did three islands a day. No time but to eat, sleep, and shit."

"Criminals?" Johan asked.

"What about Mexico?" Reinhold asked.

The *Brandenburg* was going to be at least two days in Veracruz unloading the heavy cargo.

"Mexico was fun, but don't get drunk," the old guy advised. "They'll rob you blind."

"Is there anything to look forward too?" Johan asked.

"Sunshine," the old guy said with a wink and a gravely chuckle. "Going to be cold in Germany soon."

Chapter 92: A Very Logical Decision

It was hard for Reinhold to believe that conversation with the old guy at a bar in the Reeperbahn happened only a month ago.

The son of a bitch was right, Reinhold thought to himself.

He took the pack of Lucky Strike out of his pocket, grimacing when he realized it was empty.

They did try to rob me in Mexico. I wasn't even drunk!

When the *Brandenburg* arrived in Veracruz, its first stop, the agent was late with the currency exchange. The Atlantic crossing had been particularly bad. One of the ventilators was blown over in the wind, leaving a gaping hole in the deck and allowing the heavy seas into the engine room. Max went out to cover it and was almost washed overboard. In actuality, he did get washed overboard. The rope they tied around his waist allowed the rest of the crew to haul him back on to the ship. At first, they thought he drowned because he came out of the ocean like a limp ragdoll. When they laid him on the floor of the mess, he wasn't breathing. Quick thinking on the part of the Second Mate and his knowledge of CPR brought Max back to reality, coughing, cursing, and vomiting seawater, but largely unhurt.

As soon as the ship dropped anchor and the workday was over, the sailors left for the shore. Most of them hung out on the pier taking in the sights. For Reinhold, the port was a bit strange. It was a good size, encompassing several kilometers of area, but it was ill-equipped and poor. There wasn't a single crane but there were several lines of tracks laid down, reminding him of Chile and Peru. There were chickens pecking around, reminding him of India. There were people lounging on the nearby beach, which reminded him of Venezuela. In all, it gave off a feeling of being under construction. This contrasted with what Heine told him on the trip over about the Mayan people and how they used this port for hundreds and hundreds of years before the Spanish showed up. Reinhold shrugged. He was more interested in trying the local spirit, which Heine told him was called tequila.

Reinhold, Max, and Heine went to a local port cantina where Heine arranged for Reinhold to give the owner his gold watch in exchange for drinks. The deal was the same as always. Reinhold would get his watch back when he returned the following day with really money, *pesos*, to pay. If he didn't return, the bar owner could keep the watch. It was a simple arrangement.

They had a great night. Tequila wasn't a bad drink, Reinhold decided. He liked it with the slice of fresh lime. They did shot after shot. They bought drinks for the pretty girls that clustered around them, even the one Heine caught trying to pickpocket him. He ended up taking her back to the ship later that night. Reinhold still believed that he was lucky she didn't steal everything that wasn't sea tight on her way out. Reinhold himself ended up with a girl that was cute enough but not very good in bed. She earned the money he paid her by laying there like a dead fish.

The next night, after spending thirteen hours carefully unloading the German built locomotive, the sailors returned to the bar to pay their tab and retrieve Reinhold's gold watch only to encounter a stubborn owner. He refused to return Reinhold's watch, saying he didn't know where it was, that it was probably stolen. The situation got ugly quickly. Not only were the sailors angry that the watch was not forthcoming, they were angry because they had been in such good moods when they arrived at the bar. The unloading had gone so well, that even the Captain said words of praise to the crew.

"This sounds like a bunch of lies," Max snarled, flexing a hand. "Now we have to teach this guy that no one likes a liar."

Heine translated Max's comment as best as he could. Reinhold figured the word *mentiroso* meant liar because he kept repeating it. The Mexican man kept denying he had the watch but Reinhold noted beads of sweat had broken out across his forehead. Max finally had enough of the negotiations. He reached across the bar and grabbed the bar owner by his neck, landing a punch to his chin a second later, and screaming for their property to be returned. People scattered around the bar room, who had been watching the scene, stood with the intent of coming to help their compatriot. Reinhold heard the scrapping of chairs and turned to stop them by raising his hand and shaking head his head at them warningly.

Behind him, he heard Max land three more punches while Heine demanded the watch in Spanish. Another punch to the face, a couple of body shots, and a mention of the police later, the man relented and said he had the watch and would get it if they just stopped hurting him. They walked out a few minutes later with Reinhold's property.

Standing on the deck of the *Brandenburg* in the blood red shadows of the setting sun, Reinhold shook his head at the human condition.

The old man warned us, he thought.

A noise on the gangway caught his attention and Reinhold turned to see Max approaching.

"Bosun says you can take off, Scholz. They fixed whatever problem they were having."

"Good. You have a cigarette?"

Max threw him a pack.

Reinhold headed for the galley to eat before hitting the showers. He returned to the deck with a case of beer and a book with the intention of reading. Instead of finding a quiet deck, he found an impromptu jam session. One of the old timers, Katz, was demonstrating some good skill on the button box while Oetmann was leading the tune with his harmonica. Deciding this was more entertaining than reading, Reinhold settled himself to watch the music. After a few bottles of beer, he joined in the singing, his rich baritone echoing hauntingly off the metal bulkhead.

The *Brandenburg* visited Aruba, Grenada, Martinique, Guadeloupe, Montserrat, Antigua, the British Virgin Islands, and Puerto Rico before heading back to Germany. They arrived in the dead of winter, January, 1957. Reinhold was scheduled to stay with the ship for another trip to the West Indies so when he was called to the Captain's salon the day after they docked, he wondered what was going on. He had some problems with the First Mate this trip and he figured he was being kicked off, like the *Leipzig*.

"You impressed someone, Scholz, when you went for your ballast training." The Captain said. "I received a note this morning instructing me to inform you that, if you are so inclined, Hapag would like to send you to the officer's training program. The papers are all ready. You would just have to report to pick them up and register for classes."

"Does it pay anything?"

The Captain laughed. "No. If you asked, they could probably get you a shore job while you are training. Your pay, however, would increase significantly as an officer."

"Thank you, sir, for telling me."

The Captain handed him a paper with a name and address written on it and dismissed him without further comment. Reinhold left with his head spinning. An officer? Maybe even Captain one day? This was in interesting development.

"Scholz, you have mail."

Oetmann handed him a letter as he walked passed. It was from Herbert. He mailed it from Bremerhaven three weeks ago. Reinhold ripped it open and read the letter as he left the ship. He had barely stepped on to the pier when he stopped short. The words Herbert wrote momentarily didn't make any sense. The way they read, it sounded like Herbert was headed for officers' school with Norddeutscher Lloyd. It took three readings for it to dawn on him that Herbert was indeed going to become an officer.

"Son of a bitch," he muttered to himself. "Isn't that a rare coincidence?"

With this new piece of information fueling his mind, making him question his decision to go to America, Reinhold set off on foot out of the port. It was as cold a day as it could be at the beginning of January. He retraced, as best he could in the rebuilt environment, the steps that brought him to the port of Hamburg almost ten years ago as a fourteen-year-old kid, contemplating his future.

He ended up in front of the old concrete bunker. There were still kids hanging around outside. He stared at the ugly, scarred building for a minute. When it didn't offer him any answers to his dilemma, he turned his back on the place and headed back toward the Reeperbahn in search of coffee, maybe something stronger.

Many scenarios played out in his head as he walked. He saw himself becoming an officer and spending the rest of his life on the sea, drifting from port bar to part bar looking for willing women for the night. He saw himself going to America and milking cows. He saw himself becoming an officer and settling down with Marta on Föhr. He saw himself becoming an officer and settling down in Lübeck with Lisa and Willie. He saw himself going to America and meeting a nice girl to settle down with, maybe having a family. Of all the images he conjured, the last one was the most appealing.

"I have been saying for years that I want to get out of Germany," he told himself as he walked. "This is the opportunity. Why would I blow that? Of course I have to go to America."

And if it sucks, I'll come back and go to officer school, he thought. *Maybe sail to Australia.*

Once he came to this very logical decision, he felt better, and tired. He walked back to the port and threw himself on his bunk on the *Brandenburg*. Pulling out a book, he resigned to read until dinner.

The following day, January 7, 1957, Reinhold signed off the *Brandenburg*. He returned to Kiel to his room to await notice that his papers were prepared. At the beginning of March, he received word that his green card was ready. He returned to Hamburg to find that he couldn't afford the one hundred and thirty five *mark* it cost for passage to America. Writing to Frank Rickman, he explained his situation and asked his sponsor to send him money for his fare

Three weeks later, a letter arrived from Frank Rickman containing a ticket for passage on the *Berlin*. The ship left in one week, on April 4, 1957 and Reinhold was on it.

He met a couple of very nice ladies and had a good time the two weeks and four days it took to get to New York from Hamburg. He made sure they never met each other.

When the *Berlin* docked in New York, Reinhold expected Frank Rickman to meet him. That was the plan. There was no sign of him at the port. One of the ladies he met, Elisabeth, stayed with him, waiting. She was headed for Chicago the next day on a train out of Penn Station. When Frank didn't show, Reinhold suggested he go over to the sailor's club on 42nd Street. Elisabeth went with him. He was grateful for the company, especially since she spoke perfect English.

At the sailor's club, they inquired after Frank. There was no sign or word of him. Reinhold called the number that was in the letter with the ticket. There was no answer. Panic was starting to grip him. He didn't know what to do. He ordered a drink.

It was almost ten o'clock. Reinhold and Elisabeth had been at the club for almost five hours when the door opened and in walked Frank Rickman. Reinhold gave Elisabeth a long kiss goodbye and left immediately for Albany in Frank's huge Pontiac.

It was a three hour drive. When they arrived at Frank's home on Central Avenue Reinhold was shocked to find that Frank expected them to sleep in the same bed. When he refused, Frank kicked him out of the room. Reinhold ended up sleeping in a pantry on a blanket on the floor. He wondered why it didn't dawn on him before that his sponsor was gay.

The next morning, Frank was gone. Two men in suits came looking for him around noon. They took an interest in Reinhold because he was the last person to see the missing man. One agent spoke German and asked Reinhold some questions before explaining, somewhat awkwardly, that Mr. Rickman was a wanted man. He had been embezzling from his company and clients. The suits left and so did Reinhold.

What am I supposed to do now? He wondered. *I have twenty-one mark to my name, nowhere to live, and no job. Oh, and I don't speak English. If they find me, are they going to deport me? Are they looking for me already?*

He wandered down Central Avenue, headed in the direction of the port. Two people, a girl and a guy, walked passed him. They were speaking German. He followed them, catching up, and introducing himself with his best manners. He explained his situation. They explained to him that once he was here, his sponsor didn't matter. They helped him find a place to live, a job, and got him enrolled in night school at Albany High School so he could learn English.

In the end, it was the sense of community amongst the post war German immigrants to America that saved Reinhold from running home in panic and defeat.

Epilogue:

Reinhold and Heidi, 1957/58
Photograph courtesy of Reinhold Scholz

It was at Albany High School that Reinhold met Heidi. On his first night in class, after introducing himself to the group, their eyes met as he took his seat. He fell instantly in love. It scared the crap out of him. He didn't want to get involved with girls. He had enough of girls, for the time being. He came to America to forge a life for himself and getting involved with a woman wasn't the way to accomplish his goals. Not yet anyway. He needed to get some stuff situated before he could think about dating. He had to save money to bring Lisa and Willie to America. He couldn't do that while getting involved with a girl. He purposely avoided Heidi, choosing a seat on the other side of the room from where she sat.

A couple of weeks after their eyes met, Reinhold was hanging out in the hallway outside his classroom with a few other German boys, joking and telling stories. One of them wanted to introduce Reinhold to his sister. Turning to meet the young lady, he came face to face with Heidi. Their eyes met again. She smiled at him. He smiled back.

They were married a year later.

Reinhold and Heidi with their first grandchild, Ian.
Photograph courtesy of Reinhold Scholz

www.ingramcontent.com/pod-product-compliance
Lightning Source LLC
Chambersburg PA
CBHW021129230426
43667CB00005B/71